Something Old & Something New

Louisiana Cooking With A Change Of Heart

CHEF JOHN FOLSE
& COMPANY
PUBLISHING

GONZALES, LOUISIANA

by
Chef John D. Folse, CEC, AAC
&
Craig M. Walker, MD, FACC, FACP, FCCP

Library of Congress Catalog Card Number: 96-090706

ISBN 0-9625152-1-3

First Printing: August, 1997

Copyright ©1997 by Chef John Folse & Company Publishing

Printed in Canada

If this book is not available at your local bookstore,
copies may be ordered directly from:

Chef John Folse & Company	**Cardiovascular Institute of the South**
2517 South Philippe Avenue	Marketing Department
Gonzales, LA 70737	P. O. Box 4176
(504) 644-6000	Houma, LA 70360
	(800) 425-2565

Price : $22.95 plus $4.50 shipping and handling (total $27.45)*

Also available:

Chef John Folse's, *Evolution of Cajun & Creole Cuisine*
Price: $19.95 plus $3.00 shipping and handling (total: $22.95)*

Chef John Folse's, *Plantation Celebrations*
Price: $24.95 plus $3.50 shipping and handling (total: $28.45)*

Chef John Folse's, *Louisiana Sampler*
Price: $19.95 plus $3.50 shipping and handling (total: $23.45)*

*Louisiana residents add applicable sales tax (8%)

COVER PHOTO:
Norman and Vivian Parr share a recipe with Chef Folse on the step of their barn in Lockport, Louisiana
REAR PHOTO:
Dr. Craig Walker and Chef John Folse under a oak tree at the Walker family home in Bourg, Louisiana.

ACKNOWLEDGEMENTS

It takes so many people with so much commitment to create anything good enough to share with the world. *Something Old & Something New* is one such example. Without the efforts of two very special people at Cardiovascular Institute of the South, this book would have only been a dream rather than a reality. The dynamic team of Jane Arnette and Linda Greco, LDN, RD have worked to create a book that shows their dedication to their profession and CIS. Jane and Linda have been a binding force in the growth and development at CIS, proving their leadership ability within the organization and the many communities serviced by CIS. We would also like to recognize CIS staff members; Lydia Feigler, LDN, RD, Karen Brewton,LDN, RD, Kim Elfert, and Melba Matherne for their untiring efforts toward recipe collection, modifications, nutrition analysis and the fabulous information found on many of these pages. Additionally, we wish to thank the Cardiovascular Institute of the South clinics throughout the state that hosted recipe parties, as we traveled Louisiana's backroads, soliciting traditional Cajun and Creole recipes.

A very special thanks is extended to the culinary team at Chef John Folse & Company, Nancy Bourg, Cynthia Crifasi and their assistant Brenda Johnson, along with the numerous chefs who tested the original and modified versions of the recipes. The task was a challenge to make the two recipes taste the same! To my wife, Laulie, and our other editors, Sarah Liberta and Dawn Newchurch, please accept our apologies and, at the same time, our thanks for the numerous rewrites and changes you had to live through. To Stacey Deen Griffith, our designer, Neil Alexander, Julia Sims and Martha Torres, our photographers and food stylist, thanks a million for bringing our pages to life with style and color. Your product speaks for itself! Finally, our greatest thanks to Pamela Castel for typing, retyping, formatting and fonting every word written on these pages. Your dedication to this project was immeasurable!

An additional thanks to the people who loaned items for several of the photographs in the book: Tom and Jean Braly, Hiram "Da" Dahmer, Autry Doret, Wayne Hess, Sister Rita Karam, Michael Lorenzen, Henry Richard, Paula Sautter, and Carmen Rey Torres.

— Chef John D. Folse

During the past three years, Chef John Folse and CIS have traveled around the state of Louisiana collecting recipes and stories to include in this cookbook. We have tried to keep both the recipes and stories as close to the originals as possible. However, in some cases, modifications were made. We extend our sincere appreciation to the many people who shared a part of their family culture with us.

DEDICATIONS

Father John Licari loved God, families and Louisiana food. I first met Father John in 1987 when he walked up to me at White Oak Plantation with a video camera in hand. A fellow priest had spoken to him about a benefit taking place at my plantation that day, so Father Licari drove four hours alone to view the festivities. After a brief hello, I learned of his love for Louisiana and his St. Anne's Parish in Belleview, near Pensacola. He told me about his St. Anne's Round-Up, the largest food festival held on church property in America with over 200,000 visitors attending the two day festival. By the end of the day, Father Licari had convinced me that Louisiana's Cajun and Creole cuisine was the only thing missing from his world-famous church festival. Over the next eight years, Louisiana was well represented at the Round-Up with jambalaya, etouffee, cochon de lait, fried catfish beignets, alligator sausage and red beans and rice — all dishes he loved so much.

Heart problems forced Father Licari into retirement in 1994, and ultimately took his life the first week of May, 1996. He was a wonderful friend of mine, but much more importantly he loved Louisiana, its people, its food and its music. An interesting thing about life is that often your greatest inspiration comes about from those you meet ever so briefly, and then they are gone forever. Father John Licari was indeed my brief but greatest inspiration. May God bless him!
— Chef John D. Folse

There is no greater honor for me than to dedicate this book to my patients who have placed their trust in me for their cardiovascular care. My patients from all over the world have included me in their families and have enabled me to share their lives. This makes the practice of medicine tremendously gratifying and very special.

Much of our Cajun culture revolves around our food that is clearly among the best in the world. My patients constantly bring fresh crabs, shrimp, fish, homegrown vegetables, desserts, and even complete meals to our physicians and staff members. In this book, we attempt to teach our readers how to enjoy our wonderful bounties and yet keep them heart healthy.

Our patients give to us unconditionally. This book is a tribute by word and deed, of our respectful appreciation for our patients as fellow beings who have honored us with their trust in our abilities and humanity.
— Dr. Craig M. Walker

Table of Contents

Foreword vii
Chef John D. Folse, CEC, AAC x
Dr. Craig M. Walker, MD, FACC, FACP, FCCP xi
The Photographers xii
The Heart Team & Designers xiii
Who Says Mamma's Cooking Can't Be Healthy? xiv
Become a Convert xv
The Good, The Bad and The Ugly xvi
Face the Fat xvii
Time for an Oil Change? xviii
The Rough Stuff xix
In a Pinch xx
Wake It Up — Shake It Up xxi
Are Sweets Just for the Sweet? xxii
The Perfect Balance xxiii
The Weigh to Be xxiii
Be a Good Sport xxiv

THE RECIPES
Chapter 1 / Appetizers 3
Chapter 2 / Soups 47
Chapter 3 / Salads 91
Chapter 4 / Vegetables 135
Chapter 5 / Poultry 179
Chapter 6 / Meats 223
Chapter 7 / Seafood 267
Chapter 8 / Wild Game 311
Chapter 9 / Desserts 355
Chapter 10 / Lagniappe 399

A Change of Habit 443
You Have a Choice 444
Coming to Terms 445
A Sign of the Times 446
Minding Your Peas and Q'cumbers 447
Meet Your Equal 449

Index 452

FOREWORD FROM CHEF JOHN D. FOLSE

There's an old saying here in Cajun country. "We live to eat, not eat to live!" Those simple words, although true, have double meaning today. Louisianians have always enjoyed our style of cooking, a style sought after by the rest of the world's best. It remained a well-guarded secret until the early 1980s. Once my good friend and co-conspirator in the kitchen, Chef Paul Prudhomme, threw the spotlight on this tiny region of North America with his blackened redfish, the Cajun and Creole secret was out and a craze was born. But where did it all begin?

The origin of Louisiana cooking dates back to the time of Christ. Native American Indians began experimenting with Louisiana's lush bounty here in the Mississippi River valley, present day Central and North Louisiana. They used clay ovens, fired with hot rocks, to cook catfish, ducks, rabbit and other game at Poverty Point, near the town of Delhi, Louisiana. The knowledge gained by these first Americans was shared with the first immigrants setting foot on this land in the early 1600s. They came from France, Spain, England, Africa, Germany and Italy. These settlers were taught that crawfish was a delicacy, oysters could be eaten from the half-shell, sassafras leaves were better than ground thyme and corn should not be used only as animal feed. It was here in the swamplands of Bayou country that America's best-known ethnic cuisine was born. Although the cuisine known as Cajun/Creole emerged from two quite distinct cultures, today it has become one. Even here at home, it's difficult for the locals to tell the two apart.

The Creoles were the European settlers wooed here by the Spanish to establish New Orleans in the late 1600s. The word Creole is a derivative of the old Spanish term crayola, meaning a mixture of colors. Second-born sons who could not own land or titles in their native countries were offered the opportunity to live and prosper in their family traditions here in the New World. They brought with them not only wealth and education, but a love of good food and the art of dining. With these immigrants came the knowledge of the grand European cuisines, along with the spices and the cooks needed to prepare them. After one generation in this new land, these settlers began to intermarry and the children of these multinational unions became known as the mixtures or Creoles. As their families evolved and mingled old traditions with new circumstances, so did their cuisines. It's quite easy to see the evolution of European cuisine in many popular Louisiana dishes today.

Native Indians from this region (Choctaws, Chetimatches and Houmas) befriended the early settlers and introduced them to local produce, wildlife and cooking methods. The Native Americans taught the settlers how to survive in the swamplands and helped them establish the foundation for our culinary melting pot. The French brought bouillabaisse, the great seafood soup from the Provence region near Marseilles. Making this dish with locally available ingredients gave origin to our wonderful seafood gumbo. Paella, the internationally famous Spanish rice dish made with vegetables, meat and sausage, was quickly transformed into jambalaya with many variations here in Bayou country. The Germans arrived in Louisiana with the knowledge of charcuterie and established the boucherie and fine sausage making here. They brought not only pigs, but also chicken and cattle as well. A good supply of milk and butter was seldom available prior to the arrival of the Germans. The Italians gave us our great vegetable gardens, roadside markets and produce stands.

While the English contributed their bread and butter puddings, fine casseroles and shortcakes, they established many of the grand plantations along the Mississippi River, allowing our young regional cuisine to develop and grow.

One of the most important influences in Creole cooking was that of the Africans. The "black hand in the pot," as it is lovingly referred to, helped to create the marriage of cultures, flavors and ingredients inside the cast iron pot. The Africans brought with them kingombo or okra, from their native soil. It not only gave its name to our premier soup, but also introduced a new vegetable to South Louisiana. Additionally, the Africans gave us blackeyed peas, yams, peanuts and watermelons. They became our first rice and sugarcane farmers. But much more importantly, they were the cooks in the kitchen. Although they were here against their will, they contributed more than most as they helped to define our music, our art and our food. Creole cuisine, then, is that melange of artistry and talent developed and made possible by the nations and cultures who settled in and around New Orleans. Those of us who know it and love it, keep it alive by sharing it with the rest of the world.

The cuisine of the Cajuns is a mirror image of our unique history. It is a cooking style that reflects ingenuity, creativity, adaptability and survival. The original Acadians arrived in Acadie, present day Nova Scotia, from France in the early 1600s. They were from Brittany, Vendee and Poitou. These fishermen and farmers had learned to adjust, survive and make a life for themselves on the rough shores of the Bay of Fundi.

When the English exiled the French Acadians from Nova Scotia in 1755, for failure to pledge allegiance to King George, one port of destination for the exiles was South Louisiana. As wave after wave of the Cajuns, as they were now called, arrived in New Orleans, their nation was reborn. They were free to speak their language, to believe as they pleased and to make a new life for themselves in the swamps and bayous of the French triangle in South Louisiana. Just as they had become close friends with the Micmac Indians when they were isolated in the woodlands of Canada, so they befriended the Native Americans here in Bayou country. They also quickly made friends with the Spanish and German settlements upriver from New Orleans.

Armed with their black iron pots, the Cajuns utilized what was available from the swamp floor and made no attempt to recreate the classical cuisine of Europe. Exotic spices and ingredients available to the Creoles in New Orleans were not to be found in the swamplands to the west. The Cajuns were happy to live off the land, a land abundant with fish, shellfish, wild game and bayou spices. Cajun cuisine is characterized by the use of ingredients from the Gulf of Mexico, the swamplands, the prairies and the bayous including game, salt- and fresh-water seafoods, wild greens, vegetables and herbs often combined and simmered in the cast iron pot. Truly remarkable are the variations that have resulted from similar ingredients being carefully blended in the pots of the Cajuns. Cajun cuisine is truly "a table in the wilderness," a creative adaptation of indigenous Louisiana foods. It is a cuisine forged out of a land that opened its arms to a weary traveler, the Acadian.

There can be no debate that these two cuisines have intermarried over the past two hundred years into the most sought after regional flavors in the world. But it is true in both life and food: too much of something good is often bad for you. Though the English and Italians gave us an ample supply of fresh vegetables and recipes to prepare them, the Germans, French and Spanish gave us our love of pork, sausages, spices and salt-cured, smoked meats. The result is a cuisine that can easily become excessive: too rich, too spicy, too flavorful for good health. What would a Cajun breakfast be without hog cracklin' biscuits and boudin grits? Who would sit at Sunday dinner with chicken, andouille and oyster gumbo, if it were not made with a rich, dark brown roux? Imagine a Creole brunch without smothered pork chops or grillades in rich spicy tomato sauce and a platter of deep-fried, sugar-coated beignets. Consider an outing without hog's head cheese canapés and crabmeat au gratin filled pastry made with real cream and butter.

      Yes, over the years, we have become a culture defined by too much good food. Our pioneer forefathers, because of their extremely active lifestyles, could indulge daily in such culinary feasts. But today, the new generation of Louisianians, accustomed to lives of relative ease and indulgence, find themselves in a crisis. Without the word moderation in our vocabulary and with over-indulgence a part of our tradition, it's no wonder we are the number one region in America with cardiovascular disease.

      The time has come for us to revisit our culinary traditions and to determine once and for all that it is possible to create flavor while modifying fat. This book is our attempt to achieve just that. The people of the Cajun triangle have graciously entrusted us with their old family recipes. I, along with Dr. Craig Walker and his staff at the Cardiovascular Institute of the South, have created something new with these culinary treasures. You alone must be the judge of our success in this endeavor. But remember, this is not a "low-fat" cookbook. This is a "modified-fat" cookbook. We promised the families when securing their secrets that we would not sacrifice great taste as we modified the recipes. Low-fat with no flavor was not an option. After all, here in Louisiana, we live to eat, not eat to live! We have not only modified the traditional recipes, we have

gone one step further. In order for you to test the claim that good food can be good for you, we have included the original recipe alongside the modified version, thus, *Something Old & Something New*. Give each recipe a try, and we think you'll agree that the new version is as flavorful and satisfying as the old while also being more healthful.

      Many new cookbooks include the word healthy or fat-free in the title — not ours. But if you are looking for recipes that are regional, traditional, original and healthy, this cookbook is a great investment. No matter where you live in America, the fact remains that heart disease is the #1 killer. The sections included between "Become a Convert" on page *xv* and "Be a Good Sport" on page *xxiv*, give you the basic facts you will need to lower the risks of heart disease and develop a healthier, happier lifestyle. You will quickly learn that reducing your risk factors, high blood pressure, high blood cholesterol, diabetes, obesity and lack of exercise, are all within your control through your habits. Naturally, as you peruse these pages, you may want more information on a particular subject, so please consult your physician or registered dietician.

      When creating a book of this type, it would be senseless to modify recipes and not, at the same time, give you some basics to keep you on track. On the following pages, you will find great tips on making food choices "from the label to the table." Small changes are the answer and can make a difference. With a gentle, good-humored attitude, all changes will become easier, more natural and a way of life.

      Enjoy, indulge and remember, in all things, moderation is the key! We feel that it will soon become apparent to you as it has to us . . . there's no such thing as bad food, in Louisiana there's only too much good food!

-Chef John D. Folse

CHEF JOHN D. FOLSE, CEC, AAC

Chef John Folse is the owner and executive chef of his Louisiana-based corporations. His Lafitte's Landing Restaurant in Donaldsonville, is recognized as one of the finest restaurants in and around New Orleans. White Oak Plantation, in Baton Rouge, houses his catering and events management company. Louisiana's Premier Products, his cook and chill plant in New Orleans, manufactures soups, sauces, entrees and meats for foodservice and retail establishments across the country. Chef Folse is the author of numerous books and publications available in bookstores nationally.

John is respected around the world as an authority on Cajun and Creole cuisine and culture. He hosts his own national television cooking show, "A Taste of Louisiana" on PBS. In addition, his syndicated radio show, "Stirrin' It Up!," can be heard on many stations nationwide. He has taken his famous "Taste of Louisiana" from Hollywood to the Great Wall of China, opening promotional Louisiana restaurants in Hong Kong, Japan, Beijing, London, Paris, Rome, Bogota, Taipei and Seoul. In 1987, Chef Folse was selected as "Louisiana Restaurateur of the Year" by the Louisiana Restaurant Association and in November of 1988, the Louisiana Sales and Marketing Executives named him "Louisiana's Marketing Ambassador to the World." In 1988, Chef Folse made international headlines by opening his "Lafitte's Landing East" in Moscow during the presidential summit between Ronald Reagan and Mikhail Gorbachev. This opening represented the first time an American Restaurant had operated on Soviet soil. Immediately following this venture, John hosted ten Soviet chefs for the first Soviet American Culinary Exchange. In 1989, Chef Folse was invited to create the first ever Vatican State

photo credit: Neil Alexander

Dinner in Rome, and while there had a private audience with Pope John Paul II.

In 1990, Chef Folse was named the "National Chef of the Year" by the American Culinary Federation, the highest honor bestowed upon an American chef. His Lafitte's Landing Restaurant was inducted into the "Fine Dining Hall of Fame," in 1989, and received the DiRoNA (Distinguished Restaurants of North America) award in 1996.

Chef Folse is the recipient of numerous culinary awards and recognitions, and has been honored by local, state and international governments for his continuing efforts to showcase America's regional cooking around the world. His most prestigious acknowledgement to date was Nicholls State University's decision to name their new culinary program in his honor. An Associate of Science in Culinary Arts degree program began in January of 1996, and a Bachelor of Science in Culinary Arts degree program began in January of 1997. Nicholls State, his Alma Mater, is located in Thibodaux, Louisiana. For additional information on our organization you may locate us on the Internet at: http://www.jfolse.com

DR. CRAIG M. WALKER

I love the bayou country of South Louisiana. My memories of childhood are of climbing meandering live oaks with the breeze blowing the Spanish moss against my face; of wandering through the hardwood forests amid the scent of wildflowers, muscadines and wild herbs and the sight of deer, herons and red tailed hawks.

I remember fishing with my father and catching more than 100 fish in a morning. I remember hunting bullfrogs at night in the freshwater marshes.

Most of all, though, my memories are of large, strong families, whose female elders could spin out family trees back to the Deluge. When these clans assembled, for weddings, holidays, or just for Sunday get-togethers, it was always to the accompaniment of food, in quantity and quality that would stun an outland visitor.

Food is the axis of "Cajun culture" — the center around which everything else revolves. Probably no people on earth can boast as many first-rank cooks, or a cuisine that so thoroughly embodies their character. It's no wonder that the world has fallen in love with "Cajun food." "Cajun Louisiana" has been discovered, and its food, music, haunting beauty and the joie de vivre of its inhabitants are drawing the world to its doorstep.

During my final year of cardiology fellowship at Harvard University, I was repeatedly asked why I wanted to return to South Louisiana. I, in turn, wondered to myself what could be better than coming home.

The Cardiovascular Institute of the South that I founded in 1983 has grown into one of the largest heart treatment institutions in America attempting to meet the needs of an area with one of the highest incidences of cardiovascular disease in the industrialized world. And I would be less than candid if I denied that our wonderful food plays a significant part in that grim statistic.

One of the constant battles we wage is convincing our patients that they don't have to give up the foods they love in order to eat in a heart-healthy way. They just have to change a few things, here and there. Intrinsically, the ingredients of Cajun cooking are quite healthy, with a plenitude of fresh vegetables and fruits, lean game and seafood already incorporated in the cuisine. By modifying low or no-fat ingredients in the preparation of Cajun food, you can enjoy a wonderful tasting, heart-healthy diet with low fat and sodium content and adequate dietary fiber.

photo credit: *Petersen's Studio*

Hence "Something Old & Something New."

We have assembled the best family recipes we could find from all across Acadiana, and Chef John Folse and CIS's dietitians have modified them so that they retain their marvelous taste and character without the penalty of high fat, cholesterol and sodium. And just to show how convinced we are that the new way is as good as the old, we've included the original recipe, too.

And for lagniappe (South Louisiana French for "a little something extra") we've included stories told by our recipe contributors about the origins of these dishes and about food, family, faith, hard work, a love of celebration and the other threads from which the "Cajun lifestyle" is woven.

It may not be quite as much fun as being here. But it's close.

THE PHOTOGRAPHERS

This book involved the efforts of so many people. For my part as photographer, I must thank the following for all their help: John Folse for his vision, enthusiasm and trust in having me illustrate this colorful and ambitious project; Pamela Castel for providing the organizational support while I was on the road; Martha Torres and Roz, whose food styling talents made my job easy; Glen and Michele Petri for their hospitality down on Bayou Lafourche and generous sharing of their research about Acadiana's places to see and people to meet; Phillip Gould and Judith Meriwether who offered me a home base and home cooking in the Lafayette area; the Parr and Orgeron families of Lockport for giving us everything we needed, and then some, for the cover shot; Henri Boulet and family for all the crawfish. John Broussard of KRVS for his help in showing me the world of Trail Rides; Elvis and Lena Jane Chabert for taking me in for the night and sharing their fine food and gardens; Norman and Mildred Plaisance and family of Grand Isle for having me in on their Holy Week celebrations; Ann and Frank Fitzgerald of Loyd Hall in Cheneyville who brought me into the "main house" and let me know it was home; Elmore Morgon, Jr. for his vision of the Cajun Prairie; and Alzina Toups for sharing her herb gardens, ice tea and tasty leftovers with me. Thanks also to KRVS whose music put me in touch with Acadiana and the World with my radio turned up and windows rolled down.

Finally, to all the folks I am unable to mention along the way who opened their homes and hearts to a complete stranger with a camera, and offered up some of that down home Louisiana hospitality.

Neil Alexander

photo credit: Nancy Alexander

Julia Sims' photography, well known both nationally and internationally, is testimony to her profound understanding and respect for Louisiana's marshes and bayous and the wildlife they shelter.

Seduced long ago by the dark mysteries of the swamps, Ms. Sims now spends most of her time photographing in the wetlands of South Louisiana, where she makes her home. She remains one of the few female wildlife photographers today.

Julia Sims is considered one of the premier wildlife photographers of Louisiana, and her work has been featured in such publications as National Geographic, National Wildlife and Nature Conservancy, among many others. Mrs. Sims' work is featured at Gateway Gallery in Ponchatoula, Louisiana. All original photographs are limited edition, signed and numbered, and are available framed or unframed. The gallery also offers posters and postcards.

Julia's photographs are located on pages 26/27, 70/71 and 242/243.

Julia Sims

photo credit: Scotty Sims

THE HEART TEAM & DESIGNERS

Through the years, our patients have encouraged us to provide them with recipes that would help them along the path towards a healthier lifestyle. The basic concept for Something Old & Something New began many years ago with the development of Cardiovascular Institute of the South's internationally recognized *Heart a la Carte* nutrition awareness program.

Together with the dietitians who nutritionally analyzed the recipes and provided the nutrition information, CIS's Marketing Director, Jane Arnette, coordinated and developed the contents and wrote many of the family stories. Joining CIS in 1986, Ms. Arnette is responsible for establishing the CIS marketing program. She is a published author, co-developer of *Heart a la Carte*, and extensively involved in local, state, and national organizations.

Also joining CIS in 1986, is Linda Greco, LDN, RD, Director of Nutrition Services. She has held state offices for the Louisiana Dietetic Association and American Heart Association. Mrs. Greco's active involvement in many professional organizations has earned her the honor of a Volunteer of the Year by the AHA. She is a published author and co-developed the internationally recognized Heart a la Carte program.

Lydia Feigler, LDN, RD joined the staff in 1988 as a medical nutrition therapist. She is the past president of the Bayou District Dietetic Association, is involved with the State Legislative Network for the Louisiana Dietetic Association, and has been nominated for the LDA's Outstanding Dietitian Award. A member of several professional organizations, she is also a published author.

Karen Brewton, MA, LDN, RD joined CIS in 1992 as a medical nutrition therapist. She is past executive director and president of the Louisiana Dietetic Association. In 1992, Mrs. Brewton received the LDA Outstanding Dietitian Award. She is active in several professional organizations and is a published author.

From left: Jane Arnette, Linda Greco, Lydia Feigler and Karen Brewton

photo credit: Neil Alexander

Martha C. Torres and Rosalind Richard

Martha is the owner of STYLE LIST, Inc., a New Orleans and San Antonio based company, which specializes in food styling and set design for print, commercials and television. An active member of the International Association of Culinary Professionals (IACP), Martha was a founding member of its Food Stylists and Food Photographers Committee.

Rosalind, a native New Orleanian, has been a garde manger and chef in Los Angeles and New Orleans. She has been affiliated with STYLE LIST for the past three years, specializing in food styling and recipe development.

WHO SAYS MAMMA'S COOKING CAN'T BE HEALTHY?

Cajun cooking is one of the world's most delightful cuisines — a spicy culinary reflection of a people with a blended culture. Industrious farmers, fishermen, shrimpers, oystermen, trappers, hunters, and homemakers of yesteryear bring to the world an unforgettable taste of good food. The genius of Cajun cuisine lies not in the broad range of foods that are accessible, but in the culinary flavors that please the palate.

Something Old & Something New, Louisiana Cooking With A Change of Heart, honors the old Cajun family recipes in their original form. The something new that we have crafted is a nutritionally analyzed heart-friendly version. Fear not! Cajun cuisine can be enjoyed without taking away the good taste!

Small changes are the answer and can make a difference. There are simple ways to artfully combine the natural flavors of foods to modify recipes with their own distinctive flavorful personalities.

To make our recipes heart-friendly, we have reduced the sodium, fat, cholesterol, and calories of the original recipes. Not every recipe could be reduced in all areas without compromising its quality, and that we refused to do! In some cases, the American Heart Association (AHA) nutrition guidelines do not apply. The solution is to plan your meals so those recipes can be combined with others to reach the AHA's daily goal of less than 300 mg cholesterol, fat to less than 30% and saturated fat 8-10% of your calories, and sodium less than 2400 mg. As for calories, eat sensibly to maintain a healthy weight for someone of your height, physical build, age, and activity.

Something Old & Something New is not about dieting. It's about joining lifestyles so that this cookbook can be a part of a heritage, rich in flavor and good health. Hopefully, you will share this book with your children and grandchildren to invigorate generations to come.

Many new cookbooks include the word "healthy" in the title, but if you're looking for information and recipes that are original and useful, this cookbook is a good investment. No matter where you live, the fact remains that heart disease is the number one killer. This section gives you the basic facts you will need when lowering risks of heart disease and developing a healthier lifestyle. As you will see, reducing your risk factors — high blood pressure, high cholesterol, diabetes, and obesity — are within your control through your dietary habits. The unique wealth of information of lifestyle changes makes this book more like a kitchen almanac.

We encourage you to peruse these pages with good health in mind. It isn't the answer to every lifestyle change, but rather some basic facts to help you along the way.

BECOME A CONVERT

The exercise of eating — it's one of America's favorite pastimes and, when it's done right, can help you look and feel great. Becoming a convert is really quite easy. Start one 'block' at a time — or, better yet, one serving at a time with the Food Guide Pyramid.

You won't find mummies or ancient artifacts in this Pyramid. The 'facts' that you will find are visually dramatic tools to help in planning a healthy diet. The Pyramid helps unlock the secret of a healthy diet by suggesting the number of servings to choose from each food group. Foods that should form the foundation of your diet are shown in the lower sections of the Pyramid and foods that should be eaten in smaller amounts are shown in the upper sections. No one food group is more important than another — all five are needed to be a convert.

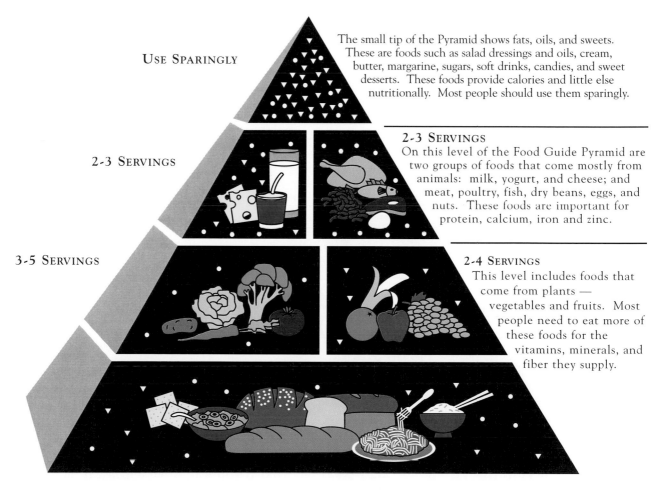

USE SPARINGLY

The small tip of the Pyramid shows fats, oils, and sweets. These are foods such as salad dressings and oils, cream, butter, margarine, sugars, soft drinks, candies, and sweet desserts. These foods provide calories and little else nutritionally. Most people should use them sparingly.

2-3 SERVINGS

2-3 SERVINGS
On this level of the Food Guide Pyramid are two groups of foods that come mostly from animals: milk, yogurt, and cheese; and meat, poultry, fish, dry beans, eggs, and nuts. These foods are important for protein, calcium, iron and zinc.

3-5 SERVINGS

2-4 SERVINGS
This level includes foods that come from plants — vegetables and fruits. Most people need to eat more of these foods for the vitamins, minerals, and fiber they supply.

6-11 SERVINGS
At the base of the Food Guide Pyramid are breads, cereals, rice and pasta — all foods from grains. You need the most servings of these foods each day.

THE GOOD, THE BAD AND THE UGLY

Y ou can't see it, hear it, or feel it. It won't make you feel sick - in fact, you may feel fine. But when your blood cholesterol level sneaks up, up and up, it does put you at risk for heart attack, heart disease, stroke and other cardiovascular diseases.

We've been hearing about the dangers of cholesterol and saturated fat for so long, they seem to go hand in hand like Bonnie and Clyde. Health conscious eaters should be wary of both, but cholesterol and saturated fat are not the same. Cholesterol is a waxy fat-like substance found only in foods that come from animals. You may be surprised to hear that cholesterol (blood cholesterol) is naturally produced by the liver and needed for normal body functioning. But excess cholesterol consumed in foods (dietary cholesterol) can raise your blood cholesterol level.

You may have read or heard that there is "good" as well as "bad" cholesterol, not found in food, but produced by your body. Cholesterol travels in the blood in "packages" of fat and protein called "lipoproteins." HDL (high density lipoprotein), made by your body, is often called "good" cholesterol because it appears to clear excess cholesterol from the arteries. LDL (low density lipoprotein), associated with sedentary lifestyle, obesity, and high fats, is often called "bad" cholesterol because too much can lead to the "ugly" or buildup of cholesterol in artery walls.

High blood cholesterol (greater than

240 mg/dL) is one of this country's most common medical conditions, affecting people from every walk of life. In addition to high cholesterol, there are other conditions that have been proven to increase risk for heart disease. These conditions are known as risk factors. The combination of high cholesterol and two or more of the following risk factors is serious:

ARE YOU:

Male, 45 years old or older?
Female, 55 years old or older or postmenopausal?
A cigarette smoker?

DO YOU HAVE:

1. *High blood pressure (greater than or equal to 140/90 or are you taking medication for high blood pressure)?*
2. *Diabetes?*
3. *Family history of heart disease or sudden death (before age 55 in a male relative or age 65 in a female relative)?*
4. *Low HDL ("good") cholesterol (less than 35 mg/dL)?*

Controlling cholesterol is a wellness way of life. It's important to keep dietary cholesterol to 300 mg a day or less, but it's more important to reduce your intake of saturated fat. Most people are not aware that it is the saturated fat more than dietary cholesterol that raises blood cholesterol levels. Look for more information to come on tips for cutting down fat in this section.

Becoming a "Convert" does not mean totally giving up your favorite foods, even if they are high in cholesterol or saturated fats. A good rule of thumb is the "80/20" rule. It says that if you watch what you eat 80% of the time, the other 20% is available to treat yourself. If you know you'll be eating a high cholesterol or high-fat meal, try to watch what you eat several meals before and after to balance your diet.

FACE THE FAT

Fat free! Low–Fat! Nonfat! Research studies show that decreasing the amount of fat you eat reduces your risk of heart disease, diabetes, obesity and some types of cancer. So whether you are trying to lose weight or simply eat healthier, low fat eating makes good sense.

YOUR FAT FACTS

The average American consumes 6-8 tablespoons of fat per day, but the body requires only one tablespoon per day. Fat is the most concentrated source of calories, providing more than twice the number of calories found in carbohydrates and protein. The easiest way to figure your fat budget is to keep in mind that the goal is to reduce your fat intake to no more than 30 percent of calories for the entire day. If you have a higher fat item during a meal, you can balance it with lower-fat choices for the rest of the day and still remain in good graces.

YOUR FAT BUDGET

To achieve a diet with 30 percent or less of total calories from fat, you first have to determine the total number of calories you eat or should eat each day based on your daily needs. To estimate your daily calorie requirements, multiply your current weight by 10 if you do not exercise and 15 if you do exercise on a regular basis. Remember that this is only a rough guide, because calorie requirements vary according to age, body size and level of activity. Add or subtract 500 calories a day to gain or

lose 1 pound a week.

Once you arrive at your personal daily caloric budget, it's easy to figure the number of fat grams you should consume each day. Divide 30% of calories by 9 to arrive at grams of fat. Use the following chart for a guide.

DAILY FAT BUDGET

Calories per Day	30% of Calories	Grams of Fat
1,200	360	40
1,500	450	50
1,800	540	60
2,000	600	67
2,200	660	73
2,500	750	83
2,800	840	93

FATS OF LIFE

There is a lot of talk about the type of fat that is the healthiest to eat. The fact is, any fat is still 100% fat, regardless of the type!

* Saturated fats are found mainly in meat and dairy products. Coconut, palm and palm kernel oils (used in cookies, crackers, and non-dairy creamers) are partially saturated. Cutting back on saturated fat can protect against heart disease, cancer and other potential health problems.

* Monounsaturated fats are found in both animal and plant fats. Olive, canola and peanut oils are especially rich sources. Where substituted for saturated, monounsaturates can help lower blood cholesterol levels.

* Polyunsaturated fats are found mainly in the fat of foods from plants: safflower, sunflower, corn, sesame and soybean oils; mayonnaise; and most margarines and salad dressings. Polyunsaturates can also help reduce blood cholesterol.

* Hydrogenated fats are vegetable oils which are processed into harder, more saturated fats like margarine or shortening. The process of hydrogenation does not make fat completely saturated, but creates trans-fatty acids which act like saturated fats.

TIME FOR AN OIL CHANGE?

Cooking oils are indispensable kitchen staples. But some are more desirable than others from a health angle - the less saturated, the better. To help you select the best oil for your cooking, as well as your arteries, here is a comparison of popular options low in saturated fatty acids.

OIL	CHARACTERISTICS / USES	MONO %	POLY %	SAT %
Avocado	Rich flavor. Salads. Works well for stir-frying due to high smoke point. (may be hard to find)	71%	21%	7%
Canola	Light, bland flavor. High smoke point. All-purpose, good for baking. Used in many processed foods.	62%	32%	6%
Corn	Tasty corn flavor. All-purpose, good for baking.	25%	32%	13%
Olive	Strong, slightly fruity flavor. Salads, stir-frying.	77%	9%	14%
Peanut	Slightly heavy, nutty flavor. Salads, stir-frying.	48%	34%	18%
Safflower	Light, bland flavor. All-purpose, good for baking.	13%	78%	9%
Sesame	Toasted varieties rich in flavor, untoasted are lighter. Salads, Asian cuisine.	42%	44%	14%
Soybean	Light, all purpose, used in many processed foods.	24%	61%	15%

To reduce your risk of heart disease, you're better off cutting back on fat of any kind to below 30% of your total calorie intake. When choosing a cooking oil or margarine spread, select one high in monounsaturated fat such as olive or canola. In the following pages you'll find a wealth of information from food purchasing to preparation to help you plan your fat strategy!

THE ROUGH STUFF

What everyone calls FIBER these days is what grandma used to call roughage. The young have joined the old in realizing that a high fiber diet just might be the thing that saves them from all kinds of illnesses - from hemorrhoids to heart disease. Dietary fiber is the portion of plant foods that the body cannot digest. Most fiber is found in the skin, roots, stems, leaves and seeds of plants.

There are two basic types of fiber (insoluble and soluble), each with different effects on body functions. Soluble fiber may lower blood cholesterol levels. Good sources of soluble fiber include oat bran, barley, dried peas and beans and many fruits and vegetables. Insoluble fiber adds bulk and helps maintain regularity. This is the type of fiber that may reduce the risk of colon cancer and may assist in preventing certain diseases such as diverticulosis. Good sources are found in whole grain products, wheat bran, vegetables and nuts.

The average daily American diet contains about 11 grams of fiber, much lower than the recommended 20-30 grams. There are many ways to get more fiber from food - gritty bread and rabbit food are not your only choices! Look over the list below and try some of the suggestions:

* Eat more fruits and vegetables.
* Choose foods that are less processed, because they have more fiber; for example, an apple has more fiber than applesauce or juice.
* Gradually increase the amount of cereal and grains that you eat. Try brown rice and whole wheat pasta.
* Look for fiber information on cereal boxes and choose cereals that have more fiber.
* Read food labels. To get bread with more fiber, look for whole wheat or whole grain flour as the first item on the ingredient list.
* Eat more cooked dry beans and peas; try these in soups, dips, salads and casseroles.
* Drink plenty of fluids (water) — at least 8 glasses a day. Eating more fiber and not drinking enough fluids can cause constipation.

IN A PINCH

ass the salt please! How often do you hear these words at your dinner table? Most people think of salt as a necessity that must be found on every dining table. Throughout history salt has played an important role. Being so plentiful, it's believed that salt was often used as money and in some places, it was nearly as precious as gold!

Everyone needs some sodium to live. However, our need for sodium can be met without using salt because sodium is found naturally in so many foods. Sodium chloride is the chemical name for common salt, which is about 40% sodium and 60% chloride.

To get down to basics, you need to be aware that Americans usually consume 4000-6000 mg of sodium a day as compared to the 3000 mg recommended by the American Heart Association. What a big difference! The health benefits can be significant for reducing sodium intake. It may aid in the reduction of blood pressure for people with high blood pressure. High blood pressure, in turn, can result in heart or kidney disease or even strokes.

Blood pressure is the force created as your heart pumps blood and moves it through your blood vessels. If anything- such as table salt - makes it difficult for blood to flow smoothly through your vessels, blood pressure rises. Rising blood pressure causes your heart to pump harder than it should to force blood through the vessels and can damage your vessels. For the person looking to cut down on salt, lower salt versions of everything from soup to nuts are available today. Take a look at these suggestions to see how you can pinch away the salt.

AT THE SUPERMARKET:
* Browse through the spices and try some of the salt substitutes. Some salt substitutes replace the sodium with potassium and in certain medical conditions this may be harmful. Savor the salty flavor and use only in small amounts. It is best to add a salt substitute to food after it is cooked since heating can sometimes make the salt substitute taste bitter.

* Be a label reader. Look at the Nutrition Facts Panel for sodium content. A product is considered low sodium if it has no more than 140 mg per serving.

* When shopping for lower sodium foods, fresh is usually best. Processed foods are usually higher in sodium.

IN THE KITCHEN:
* Adjust your recipes by reducing salt and sodium containing ingredients a little at a time. Don't be fooled by recipes that have little or no salt but call for soups, bouillon cubes or condiments that do.

* Experiment with spices and herbs as seasonings, instead of salt.

* Try a salt free herb blend.

* Cut back on salt used in cooking pasta, rice, noodles and hot cereals.

AT THE TABLE:
* Taste your food before you salt it. Try one shake instead of two!

* Watch the amount of prepared sauces and condiments you add. These can boost the sodium.

* Add zest with lemon

WAKE IT UP — SHAKE IT UP!

Many herbs and spices do not contain salt and can be used to season foods. Listed below are seasoning suggestions for various foods:

BEEF: bay leaf, dry mustard, green pepper, marjoram, fresh mushrooms, nutmeg, onion, pepper, sage, thyme

CHICKEN: green pepper, lemon juice, marjoram, fresh mushrooms, paprika, parsley, poultry seasoning, sage, thyme

FISH: bay leaf, curry powder, dry mustard, green pepper, lemon juice, marjoram, paprika

LAMB: curry powder, garlic, mint, mint jelly, pineapple, rosemary

PORK: apple, applesauce, garlic, onion, sage

VEAL: apricot, bay leaf, curry powder, ginger, marjoram, oregano

LIVER: allspice, caraway seed, garlic, marjoram, mustard seed, onion, oregano, paprika, parsley

EGGS: green pepper, onion, tarragon, oregano, paprika

MUFFINS: allspice, cinnamon, cloves, ginger

BREADS: cinnamon, cloves, dill, poppy seed

PASTA: basil, caraway seed, garlic, oregano, poppy seed

RICE: chives, green pepper, saffron, onion

ASPARAGUS: garlic, lemon juice, onion, vinegar

BROCCOLI: lemon juice, garlic

CUCUMBERS: chives, dill, garlic, onion, vinegar

GREEN BEANS: dill, lemon juice, nutmeg, marjoram

GREENS: onion, pepper, vinegar

PEAS: green pepper, mint, parsley, onion, fresh mushrooms

POTATOES: green pepper, mace, onion, paprika, parsley

SQUASH: brown sugar, cinnamon, nutmeg, mace, ginger

TOMATOES: basil, marjoram, onion, oregano

How Sweet is Sweet Enough?

If you are one of the 14 million Americans with diabetes, you can stop feeling guilty after you eat an occasional cookie or piece of heavenly hash cake. The long-held belief that sugars are more rapidly digested and absorbed than starches and therefore, more likely to cause high blood sugar levels, is not supported by scientific evidence. The message here is that the total amount of carbohydrate, not its source, is the factor affecting blood sugar levels. However, this does not mean that you can indulge in cookies and cakes every day, but allows for more flexibility when total calories and nutrients are considered.

Diabetes isn't a rare condition. It is a disease in which the body isn't able to handle food properly — because the body either doesn't produce or doesn't properly use the hormone insulin. About 10 % of people with diabetes have Type I diabetes which occurs most frequently in children and young adults. In Type I, the body's pancreas makes little or no insulin. Type II diabetes is by far the most common form. It usually occurs in overweight people after age 40. The pancreas does not make enough insulin, or the body can not use it properly. Long periods of high blood sugar levels in either type can not only increase the risk for heart disease, but can lead to vision problems, nerve damage, high blood pressure and kidney disease.

In the past, people with diabetes were given hard-and-fast rules about their diet, and those rules applied to everyone! The American Diabetes Association (ADA) emphasizes that there is no one "correct" diet for all persons with diabetes. Rather, diets need to be developed with each person's special health care needs in mind. The guidelines recommend careful selection of foods from a broad range of food groups and emphasize moderation in food consumption. Like everyone else, people with diabetes need to follow a healthy lifestyle which includes blood glucose (sugar) control and blood lipid (fat) control through diet, maintaining a healthy body weight, getting regular exercise, and taking medications if necessary.

The ADA recommends, as a first step, to encourage people with diabetes to follow the Food Guide Pyramid *(see page xv)*. Other people use the" Exchange Lists For Meal Planning." This system, established by the American Dietetic and American Diabetes Associations, separates foods into six categories based on their nutritional makeup. People following this plan choose a set amount of servings from each category daily, depending on their nutritional needs. A more sophisticated method of meal planning is "carbohydrate counting," in which grams of carbohydrate eaten are monitored and adjusted daily according to blood sugar levels.

Whatever method used, ADA recommends these general dietary guidelines:

* Fat - 30 percent or less of daily calories
* Saturated fat - 10 percent or less of daily calories
* Protein - 10 to 20 percent of daily calories.
* Cholesterol - 300 milligrams or less daily
* Fiber - about 20 to 35 grams of fiber daily

THE PERFECT BALANCE

In very simple terms, weight is controlled by a balance - or imbalance - between the number of calories you eat and the level at which you burn them off over a period of time. Keep in mind that your body counts calories even if you don't. Calories are a measure of energy you get from food. Everything you eat, yes everything, has calories and everything you do, yes everything (even sleeping), burns calories. To lose body fat, you must use more calories than you take in.

To balance the calorie dilemma, first determine how many calories you need to maintain your present weight. By eating 500 fewer calories each day, you can count on losing 1 pound of body fat a week. The best approach is to cut back 250 calories and burn another 250 calories through a regular exercise program.

Maybe the easiest way to cut calories is to eat just a little less food than usual. Rather than making dramatic changes, start by dropping one snack per day or skip the second helping. Then cut down on foods high in fat and sugar, or substitute with reduced calorie and reduced fat foods and beverages. The Food Guide Pyramid recommends eating a variety of foods and the right amount of calories to maintain a healthy weight. In general, choose more servings from the groups which are in the lower half of the pyramid. The foods in these groups are generally lower in fat and calories and higher in fiber than the foods at the top of the Pyramid.

Remember, it's time to stop "dieting" forever. That's right, no more "diets," because "diets" may change what you eat for a short time, but they don't change your eating and behavior habits. Think of it like this. When someone wants to stop smoking, he doesn't tell himself he'll stop for 6 weeks. Instead, he has to make the decision to stop smoking for the rest of his life. You must do the same for weight control. Six weeks of a "diet" won't change your life, but a change of activity level and eating patterns will.

THE WEIGH TO BE

Weight tables and formulas can help you determine how much you should weigh, but you still have to consider other factors, such as your body frame, overall health and family history. But what is most important is knowing at what weight you feel most comfortable.

ARE YOU AN APPLE OR PEAR?

For adults, body shape as well as weight is important to overall good health. Excess fat in the abdomen ("apple" shape) is thought to be of greater health risk for heart disease, diabetes and high blood pressure than fat in the hips ("pear" shape). It is actually better to be a "pear" than an "apple."

TO CHECK YOUR BODY SHAPE:

1. Measure around your waist near your navel (Example: 30 inches) without tightening abdominal muscles.

2. Measure around your hips at the fullest part. (Example: 38 inches)

3. Divide the waist measurement by the hip measurement to find your waist to hip ratio. If the ratio is less than .8 for women and .9 for men, then you are at less of a health risk (Example: 30 ÷ 38=.78)

(Source: 1995 U.S. Dietary Guidelines for Americans)

BE A GOOD SPORT!

Did you know that it takes just twenty-eight days for exercise to become a habit? Fitness does not mean you have to be a great athlete. It means feeling good! Regular physical activity is an all-around tonic for the body and mind. It helps you look, feel and perform your best and is one of the few ways in life to get something valuable for a minimal investment. By following some simple steps and making exercise part of your lifestyle, you can "add years to your life as well as life to your years!"

The simple approach for those of you who have no plans, interest or time to develop a structured exercise program is to begin by simply moving around. Try adding just one simple new activity to your daily routine. Start slowly. Do something you enjoy. Before embarking on an extensive exercise program, it is always advisable to consult your physician.

Sometimes you may wonder if exercise is worth the effort. Being more active is one of the most important ways to be healthy. Exercise strengthens your muscles, increases the endurance of your heart, lungs and circulatory system, helps control weight and blood pressure, and can increase HDL-cholesterol (good cholesterol). Exercise gives you a sense of accomplishment and makes you feel good.

Energize with exercise by following the F.I.T. principle of planning your exercise program:

FREQUENCY	4 days per week
INTENSITY	60-80% of your maximum heart rate (maximum heart rate = 220 - your age x 60-80%)
TIME	20-30 minutes

DO IT RIGHT!

While working your heart for 20 -30 minutes every other day is the centerpiece of an exercise routine, the warm-up and cool down periods are also important. Following this routine will help improve flexibility and reduce the chances of injury:

* WARM-UP — 5 minutes of gentle stretching, holding each stretch about 20 seconds. Warm-up prepares the body for activity, increases body temperature and blood flow to muscles and helps prevent injuries.

* COOL-DOWN — 5-10 minutes of easy walking and stretching. Cool-down is when you slow down aerobic activity. This helps to prevent blood pooling in the legs and allows heart rate to return to resting level.

A good fitness program is really just a way to live well. And a part of living well is living with pleasure. You're most likely to get regular exercise if you can weave it into your daily routine - and make it enjoyable. Plan to be active whenever opportunities present themselves. Soon you'll find that fitting in a little extra exercise becomes second nature, not just *one more thing you have to do!*

The Recipes

Appetizers

Chapter One

Shrimp & Okra Pie	4/5
Boiled Shrimp Mold	6/7
Marinated Shrimp & Artichokes	8/9
Shrimp Remoulade	10/11
Seafood Mousse	12/13
Lump Crabmeat Dip	14/15
Marinated Crab Claws	16/17
Crawfish-Stuffed Mushrooms	18/19
Crawfish Marinara	20/21
Oyster & Artichoke Dip	22/23
Smoked Oyster Loaf	24/25
Spicy Curry Dip	28/29
Creole Caponata	30/31
Red Bean Dip	32/33
Spinach Marguerite	34/35
Jalapeno, Cheese & Sausage Dip	36/37
Spicy Cajun Caviar	38/39
Hog's Head Cheese	40/41
Incredible Meatballs	42/43
Cheese & Cracker Casserole	44/45

The recipes for **Shrimp & Okra Pie**, *pictured at left, can be found on pages 4 and 5.*

PREP TIME: 1 Hour   SERVES: 6

☞ INGREDIENTS:

2 pounds (90–110 count) shrimp,
   peeled and deveined
3 pounds fresh okra, sliced 1/4 inch thick
1/4 cup oil
1 tbsp white vinegar
1/3 cup sliced green onions
1/3 cup chopped bell pepper
1 pie shell
1/2 cup seasoned Italian bread crumbs
salt
pepper
hot sauce

*Chef's Tips on Willpower...
at work, make it a personal policy
not to nibble at your desk.*

☞ METHOD:

Preheat oven to 375 degrees F. Place okra and oil in a 12-quart cast iron dutch oven and bake 30–45 minutes, stirring occasionally. Once okra is well sauteed and browned, add vinegar, blend well and continue to cook 10–15 minutes, stirring often. Remove pan from oven and place on burner over medium-high heat. Continue to stir while adding green onions, bell pepper and shrimp. While mixture is cooking, place pie shell in oven and bake until golden brown. Once onions and shrimp are sauteed into the mixture, sprinkle in bread crumbs. Season to taste using salt, pepper and hot sauce. Remove pie shell from oven and fill with okra mixture. Return to oven and bake 5–7 minutes.

"You just never know if a recipe is going to be a hit or not. I love shrimp and okra and decided to create a pie using these two ingredients. I tried it out on my family and they just absolutely loved it.
"In 1984, I decided to take my creation to our church fair and guess what - they sold the whole thing!"
                    Blanche O. Kugler
                    Norco, Louisiana

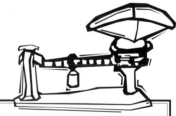

❧ Nutrition Facts...then ❧

Calories:	403
Total Fat:	18gm
Saturated Fat:	3gm
% Calories from Fat:	39
Cholesterol:	295mg
Sodium:	1003mg
Carbohydrate:	26gm
Fiber:	3gm
Protein:	37gm

PREP TIME: 1 Hour   SERVES: 6

☞ INGREDIENTS:

1 1/2 pounds (90–110) count shrimp,
        peeled and deveined
3 pounds fresh okra, sliced 1/4 inch thick
vegetable spray
1 tbsp oil
1 tbsp white vinegar
1/3 cup sliced green onions
1/3 cup chopped bell pepper
1 pie shell
1/2 cup unseasoned bread crumbs
salt substitute
pepper
hot sauce

☞ METHOD:

Preheat oven to 375 degrees F. Coat a 12-quart cast iron dutch oven with vegetable spray. Add okra and oil and bake 30–45 minutes, stirring occasionally.

Once okra is well sauteed and browned, add vinegar, blend well and continue to cook 10–15 minutes, stirring often. Remove pan from oven and place on burner over medium-high heat. Continue to stir while adding green onions, bell pepper and shrimp.

While mixture is cooking, place pie shell in oven and bake until golden brown. Once onions and shrimp are sauteed into the mixture, sprinkle in bread crumbs. Season to taste using salt substitute, pepper and hot sauce.

Remove pie shell from oven and fill with okra mixture. Return to oven and bake 5–7 minutes.

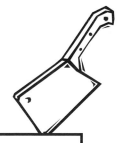

Nutrition Facts...now

Calories: 342
Total Fat: 11gm
Saturated Fat: 2gm
% Calories from Fat: 28
Cholesterol: 222mg
Sodium: 641mg
Carbohydrate: 32gm
Fiber: 3gm
Protein: 30gm

PREP TIME: 1 Hour   SERVES: 8

☞ INGREDIENTS:

1 pound boiled shrimp, chopped
vegetable spray
1/2 cup tomato sauce
1 (8-ounce) package cream cheese, cubed
1/2 cup heavy whipping cream
1 tbsp Worcestershire Sauce
1 tbsp onion juice
1 tbsp butter
2 envelopes unflavored gelatin
1/2 cup cold water
1/2 cup chopped celery
1 cup chopped green bell pepper
1/2 cup chopped green olives
1/2 cup mayonnaise
1 tsp salt
black pepper
Louisiana Gold Pepper Sauce

"I would hate to think of how many seafood recipes were developed as cold appetizers once gelatin appeared in our grocery stores. The wonderful flavor of seafood combined with fresh vegetables and spices have been long revered here in bayou country.
"This boiled shrimp mold is great for parties and holidays, but should not be reserved for such an occasion. Why not try one or two versions of this recipe when shrimp season rolls around?"
Chris Landry
Napoleonville, Louisiana

☞ METHOD:

Spray a shrimp or crab mold with non-stick vegetable spray and set aside. In a double boiler or in a cast iron pot over medium heat, add tomato sauce, cream cheese, whipping cream, Worcestershire, onion juice and butter. Stir often until cheese is melted into the tomato mixture. While cheese mixture is cooking, dissolve gelatin in water and set aside. Into pot, add celery, bell pepper and olives, blending well into cheese mixture. Remove from heat and cool slightly. Fold in shrimp and mayonnaise. Season to taste using salt, pepper and Louisiana Gold. Blend gelatin into the mixture and pour into the decorative mold. Chill a minimum of 3 hours. Serve with crackers, French bread croutons or toast points.

❊Nutrition Facts...then❊

Calories: 299
Total Fat: 24gm
Saturated Fat: 9gm
% Calories from Fat: 70
Cholesterol: 146mg
Sodium: 977mg
Carbohydrate: 6gm
Fiber: 1gm
Protein: 17gm

PREP TIME: 1 Hour   SERVES: 8

☞ **INGREDIENTS:**

1 pound boiled shrimp, chopped
vegetable spray
1/2 cup tomato sauce, no salt added
1 (8-ounce) package fat-free
        cream cheese, cubed
1/2 cup evaporated skim milk
1 tbsp low-sodium Worcestershire Sauce
1 tbsp onion juice
1 tbsp lite margarine
2 envelopes unflavored gelatin
1/2 cup cold water
1/2 cup chopped celery
1 cup chopped green bell pepper
1/4 cup chopped green olives
1/2 cup fat-free mayonnaise
salt substitute
black pepper
Louisiana Gold Pepper Sauce

One of the stations of the cross along the Catahoula Highway by the St. John-Levert Plantation in St. Martinville.

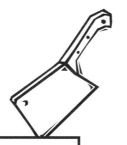

Nutrition Facts...now

Calories:	138
Total Fat:	2gm
Saturated Fat:	0gm
% Calories from Fat:	14
Cholesterol:	116mg
Sodium:	802mg
Carbohydrate:	9gm
Fiber:	1gm
Protein:	19gm

☞ **METHOD:**

Spray a shrimp or crab mold with non-stick vegetable spray and set aside.

In a double boiler or in a cast iron pot over medium heat, add tomato sauce, cream cheese, skim milk, Worcestershire, onion juice and margarine. Stir often until cheese is melted into the tomato mixture.

While cheese mixture is cooking, dissolve gelatin in water and set aside.

Into pot, add celery, bell pepper and olives, blending well into cheese mixture. Remove from heat and cool slightly. Fold in shrimp and mayonnaise. Season to taste using salt substitute, pepper and Louisiana Gold.

Blend gelatin into the mixture and pour into the decorative mold. Chill a minimum of 3 hours. Serve with crackers, French bread croutons or toast points.

PREP TIME: 1 Hour   SERVES: 8

☞ INGREDIENTS:

2 pounds (21–25 count) cooked shrimp,
      peeled and deveined
1 (14-ounce) can artichoke hearts, drained
1 cup olive oil
1/4 cup red wine vinegar
1/4 cup chopped garlic
1 tbsp Creole mustard
1/4 cup lemon juice
1 small Bermuda onion, thinly sliced
1/2 cup diced red bell pepper
1/2 cup diced yellow bell pepper
1/4 cup capers
1/4 cup sliced green onions
1 bay leaf
1 tsp fresh thyme
1 tsp chopped oregano
1 tsp salt
black pepper
Louisiana Gold Pepper Sauce

☞ METHOD:

Into a large glass mixing bowl, add olive oil, vinegar, garlic, mustard and lemon juice. Using a wire whisk, whip until ingredients are well-blended. Add onion, bell peppers, capers and green onions. Using a wooden spoon, coat all vegetables with the marinating mixture. Add herbs and season to taste using salt, pepper and Louisiana Gold. Add the shrimp and artichokes and coat well with the seasoning mixture. Cover with clear wrap and refrigerate overnight.

"It amazes me how very few people realize that artichokes flourish in many Louisiana gardens. They were used first of all as decorative plants with the by-product being a fabulous vegetable used in soups or as a stuffed entree.

"In this recipe, artichoke hearts are marinated, Louisiana-style, to produce a wonderful starter course."

John Folse
Donaldsonville, Louisiana

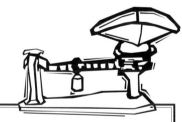

❧ Nutrition Facts...then ❧

Calories: 376
Total Fat: 27gm
Saturated Fat: 4gm
% Calories from Fat: 64
Cholesterol: 170mg
Sodium: 1292mg
Carbohydrate: 9gm
Fiber: 3gm
Protein: 25gm

PREP TIME: 1 Hour   SERVES: 8

☞ INGREDIENTS:

2 pounds (21–25 count) cooked shrimp,
    peeled and deveined
1 (14-ounce) can artichoke hearts, drained
1/2 cup olive oil
1/4 cup red wine vinegar
1/4 cup chopped garlic
1 tbsp Creole mustard
1/4 cup lemon juice
1 small Bermuda onion, thinly sliced
1/2 cup diced red bell pepper
1/2 cup diced yellow bell pepper
1 tbsp capers
1/4 cup sliced green onions
1 bay leaf
1 tsp fresh thyme
1 tsp chopped oregano
salt substitute
black pepper
Louisiana Gold Pepper Sauce

☞ METHOD:

Into a large glass mixing bowl, add olive oil, vinegar, garlic, mustard and lemon juice. Using a wire whisk, whip until ingredients are well-blended. Add onion, bell peppers, capers and green onions.

Using a wooden spoon, coat all vegetables with the marinating mixture. Add herbs and season to taste using salt substitute, pepper and Louisiana Gold.

Add the shrimp and artichokes and coat well with the seasoning mixture. Cover with clear wrap and refrigerate overnight.

Nutrition Facts...now

Calories: 257
Total Fat: 14gm
Saturated Fat: 2gm
% Calories from Fat: 47
Cholesterol: 170mg
Sodium: 909mg
Carbohydrate: 9gm
Fiber: 3gm
Protein: 25gm

PREP TIME: 30 Minutes   SERVES: 6

☞ BOILING INGREDIENTS:

3 dozen (21–25 count) shrimp, peeled and deveined
2 quarts cold water
1 diced onion
1/2 cup diced celery
3 bay leaves
1/4 cup lemon juice
1 sliced lemon
4 tbsps salt
black pepper

☞ FOR SAUCE:

1 1/2 cups mayonnaise
1/2 cup Creole mustard
1 tbsp Worcestershire sauce
Louisiana Gold Pepper Sauce
1/2 cup finely sliced green onions
1/4 cup finely diced celery
2 tbsps finely diced garlic
1/4 cup finely chopped parsley
1/2 tbsp lemon juice
1 tsp salt
black pepper

☞ METHOD FOR BOILING:

In a 4-quart stock pot, over medium-high heat, add water and all seasoning ingredients. Bring to a rolling boil, reduce to simmer and allow to cook 15 minutes for flavors to develop. Bring mixture back to a rolling boil, add shrimp and stir approximately 3–5 minutes. At this point, shrimp should be pink and curled. Test for doneness, being careful not to overcook. Once water returns to a boil, shrimp should be perfectly done. Pour off boiling water and replace with cold tap water to stop the cooking process. Drain and place shrimp in a serving bowl. Cover with clear wrap and refrigerate. This may be done the night before use.

☞ METHOD FOR SAUCE:

In a 2-quart mixing bowl, combine all of the above ingredients, whisking well to incorporate the seasonings. Once blended, cover and place in refrigerator, preferably overnight. A minimum of 4 hours will be required for flavor to develop. When ready, remove from refrigerator and adjust seasonings to taste. Place 6 shrimp on a leaf of romaine or other colored lettuce and spoon a generous serving of remoulade sauce on top of the shrimp. Sauce shrimp immediately prior to service. *They will lose their firm texture if allowed to stand in sauce.*

"I can't imagine a Louisiana cookbook without remoulade in some fashion. This is without a doubt one of the best known sauces in America. It seems we in Cajun country are always in search of flavor. Not only do we cook a dish with a tremendous amount of flavors and seasonings, but we also will then create a second sauce to dip it in.

"Just think about it for a minute - cocktail sauce, tartar sauce and remoulade sauce. Well, I guess there is a good reason for it, because I can't imagine a plate with wonderful boiled shrimp and no remoulade sauce to dip them in."

John Folse
Donaldsonvilie, Louisiana

✤Nutrition Facts...then✤

Calories:	714
Total Fat:	54gm
Saturated Fat:	9gm
% Calories from Fat:	64
Cholesterol:	370mg
Sodium:	1674mg
Carbohydrate:	16gm
Fiber:	3gm
Protein:	49gm

PREP TIME: 30 Minutes   SERVES: 6

☞ BOILING INGREDIENTS:

3 dozen (21–25 count) shrimp, peeled and deveined
2 quarts cold water
1 diced onion
1/2 cup diced celery
3 bay leaves
1/4 cup lemon juice
1 sliced lemon
salt substitute
black pepper

☞ METHOD FOR BOILING:

In a 4-quart stock pot, over medium-high heat, add water and all seasoning ingredients. Bring to a rolling boil, reduce to simmer and allow to cook 15 minutes for flavors to develop.

Bring mixture back to a rolling boil, add shrimp and stir approximately 3–5 minutes. At this point, shrimp should be pink and curled. Test for doneness, being careful not to overcook.

Once water returns to a boil, shrimp should be perfectly done. Pour off boiling water and replace with cold tap water to stop the cooking process.

Drain and place shrimp in a serving bowl. Cover with clear wrap and refrigerate. This may be done the night before use.

Nutrition Facts...now

Calories: 485
Total Fat: 22gm
Saturated Fat: 3gm
% Calories from Fat: 41
Cholesterol: 370mg
Sodium: 748mg
Carbohydrate: 23gm
Fiber: 3gm
Protein: 49gm

☞ FOR SAUCE:

1 1/2 cups reduced-fat mayonnaise
1/2 cup Creole mustard
1 tbsp low-sodium Worcestershire Sauce
1 tsp Louisiana Gold Pepper Sauce
1/2 cup finely sliced green onions
1/4 cup finely diced celery
2 tbsps finely diced garlic
1/4 cup finely chopped parsley
1/2 tbsp lemon juice
salt substitute
black pepper

Casino boats under construction outside Houma.

☞ METHOD FOR SAUCE:

In a 2-quart mixing bowl, combine all of the above ingredients, whisking well to incorporate the seasonings.

Once blended, cover and place in refrigerator, preferably overnight. A minimum of 4 hours will be required for flavor to develop.

When ready, remove from refrigerator and adjust seasonings to taste. Place 6 shrimp on a leaf of romaine or other colored lettuce and spoon a generous serving of remoulade sauce on top of the shrimp.

Sauce shrimp immediately prior to service. *They will lose their firm texture if allowed to stand in sauce.*

PREP TIME: 1 Hour   SERVES: 8

☞ INGREDIENTS:

1 pound cooked shrimp, chopped
1/2 pound claw crabmeat
1/2 cup mayonnaise
1 (8-ounce) package cream cheese, softened
juice of one lemon
2 tbsps Worcestershire sauce
1/4 cup Creole mustard
1/4 cup minced celery
1/4 cup minced red bell pepper
1/4 cup minced yellow bell pepper
1 tbsp minced garlic
1 tbsp chopped tarragon
1 tbsp chopped parsley
1/4 cup sliced green onions
1 tsp salt
black pepper
Louisiana Gold Pepper Sauce

☞ METHOD:

Normally, packaged crabmeat will contain bits and pieces of shells and cartilage. You should therefore pick through the crabmeat to remove any shells prior to using. In a large mixing bowl, combine mayonnaise and cream cheese. Using a wooden spoon, mash the cream cheese well into the mayonnaise to smooth out any lumps. Add lemon juice, Worcestershire and mustard. Using a wire whisk, blend all ingredients until creamy. Add celery, bell peppers, garlic, tarragon, parsley and green onions. Continue to whip until all ingredients are well-blended. Season to taste using salt, pepper and Louisiana Gold. Fold shrimp and crabmeat into the mayonnaise mixture. Pour seafood mousse into a decorative mold or serving bowl. Refrigerate 1–2 hours prior to use. Serve with French bread croutons or crackers.

NOTE: Gelatin (1 package) may be added to this recipe, if you wish to unmold the mixture; otherwise, use as a dip.

"Although this isn't one of those old, traditional recipes, it's a favorite in our house. This recipe doesn't call for any gelatin to hold it together, so you have to make it the night before for best results or at least refrigerate it for a few hours. It should be served more like a spread than a jelled mousse.

"I especially love this recipe because it can be made substituting chopped chicken in the place of seafood. I remember one Mother's Day when our neighbor turned this recipe into a filling for finger sandwiches...they were delicious.

"Here in Louisiana where so many recipes developed out of necessity to use up excess ingredients, often we simply combine two or three different meats or seafoods into a dish. I hope you enjoy this one!"

Dawn Newchurch
Paincourtville, Louisiana

❊Nutrition Facts...then❊

Calories: 291
Total Fat: 23gm
Saturated Fat: 9gm
% Calories from Fat: 67
Cholesterol: 136mg
Sodium: 1244mg
Carbohydrate: 4gm
Fiber: 0gm
Protein: 20gm

PREP TIME: 1 Hour   SERVES: 8

☞ INGREDIENTS:

1 pound cooked shrimp, chopped
1/2 pound claw crabmeat
1/2 cup reduced-fat mayonnaise
1 (8-ounce) package fat-free cream cheese, softened
juice of one lemon
2 tbsps low-sodium Worcestershire sauce
1/4 cup Creole mustard
1/4 cup minced celery
1/4 cup minced red bell pepper
1/4 cup minced yellow bell pepper
1 tbsp minced garlic
1 tbsp chopped tarragon
1 tbsp chopped parsley
1/4 cup sliced green onions
salt substitute
black pepper
Louisiana Gold Pepper Sauce

☞ METHOD:

Normally, packaged crabmeat will contain bits and pieces of shells and cartilage. You should therefore pick through the crabmeat to remove any shells prior to using.

In a large mixing bowl, combine mayonnaise and cream cheese. Using a wooden spoon, mash the cream cheese well into the mayonnaise to smooth out any lumps. Add lemon juice, Worcestershire and mustard. Using a wire whisk, blend all ingredients until creamy.

Add celery, bell peppers, garlic, tarragon, parsley and green onions. Continue to whip until all ingredients are well-blended. Season to taste using salt substitute, pepper and Louisiana Gold. Fold shrimp and crabmeat into the mayonnaise mixture.

Pour seafood mousse into a decorative mold or serving bowl. Refrigerate 1–2 hours prior to use. Serve with French bread croutons or crackers.

NOTE: Gelatin (1 package) may be added to this recipe if you wish to unmold the mixture; otherwise, use as a dip.

Nutrition Facts...now

Calories:	158
Total Fat:	5gm
Saturated Fat:	1gm
% Calories from Fat:	28
Cholesterol:	110mg
Sodium:	956mg
Carbohydrate:	6gm
Fiber:	0gm
Protein:	22gm

LUMP CRABMEAT DIP

PREP TIME: 1 Hour   SERVES: 6

☞ INGREDIENTS:

1 pound jumbo lump crabmeat
1/2 cup butter
1 cup diced onions
1/2 cup diced celery
1/4 cup diced red bell pepper
1/4 cup diced garlic
1/2 cup flour
3 cups heavy whipping cream
1/2 pound Swiss cheese, grated
1/2 ounce sherry
1 tsp salt
black pepper
Louisiana Gold Pepper Sauce

Hand-painted sign in Carencro.

☞ METHOD:

In a cast iron dutch oven, melt butter over medium-high heat. Add onions, celery, bell pepper and garlic. Saute 3–5 minutes or until vegetables are wilted. Sprinkle in flour and, using a wire whisk, whip until white roux is achieved. Pour in cream, bring to a rolling boil and reduce to simmer. Add cheese and sherry. Continue to cook until cheese is melted. Fold in crabmeat and season to taste using salt, pepper and Louisiana Gold. Should you wish to recreate my great-aunt's wonderful cheese and crab soup, simply add three cups of milk or chicken stock. Blend all ingredients well, heat and serve.

"My great aunt made the most wonderful crab and cheese soup in the world. One Sunday morning, she was busy in the kitchen chopping onions, celery and bell pepper in anticipation of the family coming over for lunch. Since we lived far out in the country and ingredients weren't easy to come by, we had to prepare well in advance for every dish.

"Once the soup started to come together, her old house cat, Lucy, jumped up on the kitchen counter and knocked over a pint of her half and half cream. With a blink of the eye, she looked around and said, 'Don't panic, instead of soup, we'll have my "now famous" crabmeat appetizer in its place.'"

Ruth Folse Hirsch
Donaldsonville, Louisiana

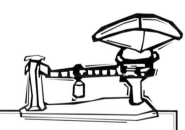

❋Nutrition Facts...then❋

Calories: 764
Total Fat: 67gm
Saturated Fat: 37gm
% Calories from Fat: 78
Cholesterol: 282mg
Sodium: 955mg
Carbohydrate: 14gm
Fiber: 1gm
Protein: 28gm

PREP TIME: 1 Hour   SERVES: 6

INGREDIENTS:

1 pound jumbo lump crabmeat
1/4 cup lite margarine
1 cup diced onions
1/2 cup diced celery
1/4 cup diced red bell pepper
1/4 cup diced garlic
1/2 cup flour
3 cups evaporated skim milk
1/2 pound lite Swiss cheese, grated
1/2 ounce sherry
salt substitute
black pepper
Louisiana Gold Pepper Sauce

METHOD:

In a cast iron dutch oven, melt margarine over medium-high heat. Add onions, celery, bell pepper and garlic. Saute 3–5 minutes or until vegetables are wilted. Sprinkle in flour and, using a wire whisk, whip until white roux is achieved.

Pour in skim milk, bring to a rolling boil and reduce to simmer. Add cheese and sherry. Continue to cook until cheese is melted.

Fold in crabmeat and season to taste using salt substitute, pepper and Louisiana Gold.

Should you wish to recreate my great-aunt's wonderful cheese and crab soup, simply add three cups of milk or chicken stock. Blend all ingredients well, heat and serve.

Chef's Tips on Dieting... don't skip meals early in the day or you may binge later.

Nutrition Facts...now

Calories:	334
Total Fat:	10gm
Saturated Fat:	1gm
% Calories from Fat:	26
Cholesterol:	82mg
Sodium:	504mg
Carbohydrate:	25gm
Fiber:	1gm
Protein:	38gm

Jimmy Ford, Jr. tries his luck on the Calcasieu River jetty in Cameron.

PREP TIME: 1 Hour   SERVES: 6

☞ INGREDIENTS:

1 pound crab claws, peeled
1 cup olive oil
1/4 cup red wine vinegar
1 tbsp lemon juice
1/4 cup chopped garlic
1 tsp horseradish
1/4 cup sliced green onions
1/4 cup chopped parsley
1/4 cup Worcestershire Sauce
1 tbsp fresh thyme
1 tbsp fresh basil
1 tsp salt
black pepper
Louisiana Gold Pepper Sauce

☞ METHOD:

In a large glass mixing bowl, add olive oil, vinegar, lemon juice, garlic, horseradish, green onions, parsley and Worcestershire Sauce. Using a wire whisk, whip until all ingredients are well-blended. Add herbs and season to taste using salt, pepper and Louisiana Gold. Add the crab claws and coat well with the seasoning mixture. Cover with clear wrap and refrigerate overnight.

"Over the past few years, we have seen less of the beautiful blue crabs from Lake Maurepas. These blue giants are sought after nationwide and have unfortunately been over-fished causing a scarcity. If you are lucky enough to get your hands on a bushel of Maurepas crabs, the recipe possibilities are endless.

"As a young boy, my family most often boiled or garlic-roasted these crabs. My favorite side dish was the marinated claws served as an appetizer, prior to sitting down to the dinner table."
Larry Folse,
Vacherie, Louisiana

Chef's Tips on Willpower... eat sensible meals and rely on a piece of fruit in between—you'll find your snack cravings go down while your energy goes up.

❋Nutrition Facts...then❋

Calories:	403
Total Fat:	37gm
Saturated Fat:	5gm
% Calories from Fat:	82
Cholesterol:	40mg
Sodium:	1274mg
Carbohydrate:	3gm
Fiber:	0gm
Protein:	15gm

PREP TIME: 1 Hour　　SERVES: 6

☞ INGREDIENTS:

1 pound crab claws, peeled
1/2 cup olive oil
1/2 cup water
1/4 cup red wine vinegar
1 tbsp lemon juice
1/4 cup chopped garlic
1 tsp horseradish
1/4 cup sliced green onions
1/4 cup chopped parsley
3 tbsps low-sodium Worcestershire Sauce
1 tbsp fresh thyme
1 tbsp fresh basil
salt substitute
black pepper
Louisiana Gold Pepper Sauce

☞ METHOD:

In a large glass mixing bowl, add olive oil, water, vinegar, lemon juice, garlic, horseradish, green onions, parsley and Worcestershire Sauce. Using a wire whisk, whip until all ingredients are well-blended.

Add herbs and season to taste using salt substitute, pepper and Louisiana Gold. Add the crab claws and coat well with the seasoning mixture. Cover with clear wrap and refrigerate overnight.

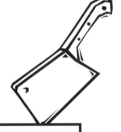

Chef's Tips on Excercise... the nice thing about a home exercise machine is that it's always there waiting for you no matter what the weather or your schedule.

Nutrition Facts...now

Calories:	272
Total Fat:	19gm
Saturated Fat:	3gm
% Calories from Fat:	73
Cholesterol:	40mg
Sodium:	992mg
Carbohydrate:	10gm
Fiber:	0gm
Protein:	15gm

PREP TIME: 1 Hour   SERVES: 6

☞ INGREDIENTS:

36 large button mushrooms, stemmed
1 pound crawfish tails, chopped
1/4 pound butter
1/4 cup minced onions
1/4 cup minced celery
1/4 cup minced red bell pepper
1/4 cup minced garlic
1/4 cup finely diced tasso
2 tbsps flour
1 cup milk
1/4 cup sliced green onions
1 tbsp chopped basil
1 tbsp chopped thyme
pinch of nutmeg
1 tsp salt
black pepper
Louisiana Gold Pepper Sauce
1 cup seasoned Italian bread crumbs
1/2 cup grated Parmesan cheese
paprika for color
6 ounces sherry

☞ METHOD:

Preheat oven to 350 degrees F. Rinse mushrooms under cold water to remove any grit or sand. In a cast iron saute pan, melt butter over medium-high heat. Add onions, celery, bell pepper, garlic and tasso. Saute 3–5 minutes or until vegetables are wilted. Sprinkle in flour and, using a wire whisk, blend well into the vegetable mixture. Slowly pour in the milk, stirring constantly. Bring to a low boil. Add crawfish, green onions, basil, thyme and nutmeg. Blend well and season to taste using salt, pepper and Louisiana Gold. Remove from heat and sprinkle in bread crumbs to absorb any remaining liquid. Once stuffing has cooled slightly, over-fill each mushroom with the stuffing. Place the mushrooms on a large baking sheet or in individual au gratin baking dishes. Top with Parmesan cheese and paprika for color. Pour sherry around the bottom of the mushrooms and bake, uncovered, 15–20 minutes. Serve 6 as an appetizer or place in a hot chafing dish.

"Cajuns love to stuff everything including themselves. When I was growing up, you couldn't find those little button mushrooms that you buy in the stores today. In my day, you had to go out into the swamps right after a rain storm and pick those large, tender and wild oyster mushrooms and bring them home to create your masterpiece.
"I remember cleaning the mushrooms while Mama made the crawfish stuffing and we would sometimes deep-fry the whole thing, but my favorite way was to bake them. Today, we just stuff the button mushroom. It's so much easier."
                    Royley Folse, Sr.
            Donaldsonville, Louisiana

❧Nutrition Facts...then❧

Calories:	426
Total Fat:	21gm
Saturated Fat:	12gm
% Calories from Fat:	44
Cholesterol:	137mg
Sodium:	1351mg
Carbohydrate:	30gm
Fiber:	1gm
Protein:	23gm

PREP TIME: 1 Hour   SERVES: 6

☞ INGREDIENTS:

36 large button mushrooms, stemmed
1 pound crawfish tails, chopped
1 tbsp olive oil
1/4 cup minced onions
1/4 cup minced celery
1/4 cup minced red bell pepper
1/4 cup minced garlic

1 tbsp finely diced tasso
2 tbsps flour
1 cup skim milk
1/4 cup sliced green onions
1 tbsp chopped basil
1 tbsp chopped thyme
pinch of nutmeg

salt substitute
black pepper
Louisiana Gold Pepper Sauce
1 cup plain bread crumbs
1/2 cup Parmesan cheese, grated
paprika for color
6 ounces sherry

☞ METHOD:

Preheat oven to 350 degrees F. Rinse mushrooms under cold water to remove any grit or sand.

In a cast iron saute pan, heat olive oil over medium-high heat. Add onions, celery, bell pepper, garlic and tasso. Saute 3–5 minutes or until vegetables are wilted. Sprinkle in flour and, using a wire whisk, blend well into the vegetable mixture. Slowly pour in the milk, stirring constantly. Bring to a low boil.

Add crawfish, green onions, basil, thyme and nutmeg. Blend well and season to taste using salt substitute, pepper and Louisiana Gold. Remove from heat and sprinkle in bread crumbs to absorb any remaining liquid.

Once stuffing has cooled slightly, over-fill each mushroom with the stuffing. Place the mushrooms on a large baking sheet or in individual au gratin baking dishes. Top with Parmesan cheese and paprika for color. Pour sherry around the bottom of the mushrooms and bake, uncovered, 15–20 minutes.

Serve 6 as an appetizer or place in a hot chafing dish.

Nutrition Facts...now

Calories:	291
Total Fat:	7gm
Saturated Fat:	2gm
% Calories from Fat:	21
Cholesterol:	89mg
Sodium:	408mg
Carbohydrate:	29gm
Fiber:	1gm
Protein:	21gm

Alaina Theriot, Queen of the 1995 Crawfish Festival, in Breaux Bridge in St. Martin Parish.

PREP TIME: 1 Hour   SERVES: 6

☞ INGREDIENTS:

1 pound crawfish tails
1/4 cup butter
1/2 cup chopped onions
1/2 cup chopped celery
1/4 cup chopped bell pepper
1/4 cup diced garlic
1/2 cup sliced mushrooms
1 (8-ounce) can tomato sauce
1 (8-ounce) can diced tomatoes, drained
2 tbsps fresh basil
1 tbsp fresh thyme
1/4 cup sliced green onions
1/4 cup chopped parsley
1 cup chicken or shellfish stock
1 tsp salt
black pepper
Louisiana Gold Pepper Sauce

☞ METHOD:

In a large saute pan, melt butter over medium-high heat. Add onions, celery, bell pepper and garlic. Saute 3–5 minutes or until vegetables are wilted. Add mushrooms, tomato sauce and tomatoes. Bring to a rolling boil, reduce to simmer and allow to cook 10–15 minutes. Add basil, thyme, green onions and parsley. Fold in crawfish tails and allow to simmer an additional 5–10 minutes. Add stock as needed to retain volume. Season to taste using salt, pepper and Louisiana Gold. Serve hot in a chafing dish with French bread croutons or over seashell pasta.

"The Marinara that I love best originated near Naples, Italy. The recipe calls for equal parts of olive and vegetable oil heated very quickly in a cast iron skillet. My mother would saute slivered garlic until the edges turned brown, while stirring that skillet constantly. We would chop a large bowl of Italian plum tomatoes...they were so sweet and bright red. This sauce was simple because the tomatoes were full of sugar and instantly turned into tomato sauce when they hit the hot olive-flavored oil.

"The only thing needed was about 1/4 cup of fresh basil and a little pepper to finish the sauce. We used this basic Marinara for pasta, over fish, under chicken and I even use it with crawfish when I'm here visiting Louisiana. However, when in Rome, do as the Romans and when in Louisiana, add the onions, celery, bell pepper, etc."

Joey Disalvo
Latrobe, Pennsylvania

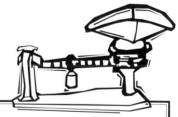

❊Nutrition Facts...then❊

Calories:	158
Total Fat:	9gm
Saturated Fat:	5gm
% Calories from Fat:	51
Cholesterol:	102mg
Sodium:	815mg
Carbohydrate:	6gm
Fiber:	2gm
Protein:	13gm

PREP TIME: 1 Hour   SERVES: 6

☞ INGREDIENTS:

1 pound crawfish tails
vegetable spray
1/2 cup chopped onions
1/2 cup chopped celery
1/4 cup chopped bell pepper
1/4 cup diced garlic
1/2 cup sliced mushrooms
1 (8-ounce) can tomato sauce,
        no salt added
1 (8-ounce) can diced tomatoes,
        no salt added, drained
2 tbsps fresh basil
1 tbsp fresh thyme
1/4 cup sliced green onions
1/4 cup chopped parsley
1 cup defatted chicken stock, unsalted
salt substitute
black pepper
Louisiana Gold Pepper Sauce

☞ METHOD:

Heat a large saute pan coated with vegetable spray. Add onions, celery, bell pepper and garlic. Saute 3–5 minutes or until vegetables are wilted. Add mushrooms, tomato sauce and tomatoes. Bring to a rolling boil, reduce to simmer and allow to cook 10–15 minutes.

Add basil, thyme, green onions and parsley. Fold in crawfish tails and allow to simmer an additional 5–10 minutes. Add stock as needed to retain volume.

Season to taste using salt substitute, pepper and Louisiana Gold. Serve hot in a chafing dish with French bread croutons or over seashell pasta.

Chef's Tips on Exercise... wash your car by hand instead of driving it through a car wash.

Nutrition Facts...now

Calories:	106
Total Fat:	1gm
Saturated Fat:	0gm
% Calories from Fat:	11
Cholesterol:	81mg
Sodium:	269mg
Carbohydrate:	9gm
Fiber:	2gm
Protein:	14gm

PREP TIME: 1 Hour   SERVES: 8

☞ INGREDIENTS:

1 pint fresh oysters, drained and chopped
1 (14-ounce) can artichoke hearts,
        drained and chopped
1/4 cup butter
1/4 cup chopped onions
1/4 cup chopped celery
1/2 cup chopped red bell pepper
1/2 cup chopped yellow bell pepper
1/4 cup diced garlic
1 tsp lemon juice
1/4 tsp chopped tarragon
1 cup heavy whipping cream
1/4 cup chopped parsley
1 tsp salt
black pepper
Louisiana Gold Pepper Sauce
1 cup seasoned Italian bread crumbs
1/2 cup grated Parmesan cheese
paprika for color

☞ METHOD:

Preheat oven to 350 degrees F. In a large cast iron skillet, melt butter over medium-high heat. Add onions, celery, bell peppers and garlic. Saute 3–5 minutes or until vegetables are wilted. Add lemon juice, tarragon, whipping cream and artichokes. Bring to a rolling boil, reduce to simmer and cook 5 minutes. Add oysters and cook to render juices. Simmer 5 additional minutes. Add parsley, remove from heat and season to taste using salt, pepper and Louisiana Gold. Sprinkle in bread crumbs and stir well to absorb all liquids. Using the bottom of your cooking spoon, smooth mixture well into the skillet. Top with Parmesan cheese and paprika. Bake 15–20 minutes, until heated thoroughly and slightly brown. Serve in the cast iron skillet with French bread croutons. You may wish to use this dip as a topping for oysters on the half shell and bake in the same manner as the casserole. This is an excellent alternative to Oysters Rockefeller or Bienville.

"Today, people are afraid to eat oysters. There have been so many news stories about polluted waters and bacteria found in oysters, that people simply walk away from this delicacy. I say, don't blame the oyster, know the supplier. Believe me, all of the large seafood markets and grocery stores are concerned about quality and would never place bad oysters in their seafood case.
"Just remember one other little tip, if any oyster is going to make you sick, in most cases, it's going to be raw, so just cook the darn thing."
Scott Cart
Rayne, Louisiana

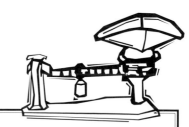

❧Nutrition Facts...then❧

Calories: 470
Total Fat: 28gm
Saturated Fat: 16gm
% Calories from Fat: 51
Cholesterol: 82mg
Sodium: 1244mg
Carbohydrate: 41gm
Fiber: 5gm
Protein: 20gm

OYSTER & ARTICHOKE DIP

PREP TIME: 1 Hour   SERVES: 8

☞ **INGREDIENTS:**

1 pint fresh oysters, drained and chopped
1 (14-ounce) can artichoke hearts,
        drained and chopped
1 tbsp lite margarine
1/4 cup chopped onions
1/4 cup chopped celery
1/2 cup chopped red bell pepper
1/2 cup chopped yellow bell pepper
1/4 cup diced garlic
1 tsp lemon juice
1/4 tsp chopped tarragon
1 cup evaporated skim milk
1/4 cup chopped parsley
salt substitute
black pepper
Louisiana Gold Pepper Sauce
1 cup plain bread crumbs
1/2 cup grated Parmesan cheese
paprika for color

☞ **METHOD:**

Preheat oven to 350 degrees F. In a large cast iron skillet, melt margarine over medium-high heat. Add onions, celery, bell peppers and garlic. Saute 3–5 minutes or until vegetables are wilted.

Add lemon juice, tarragon, skim milk and artichokes. Bring to a rolling boil, reduce to simmer

Mildred Plaisance makes her hogs head cheese at the family's annual Holy Week gathering in Grand Isle.

and cook 5 minutes. Add oysters and cook to render juices. Simmer 5 additional minutes.

Add parsley, remove from heat and season to taste using salt substitute, pepper and Louisiana Gold. Sprinkle in bread crumbs and stir well to absorb all liquids.

Using the bottom of your cooking spoon, smooth mixture well into the skillet. Top with Parmesan cheese and paprika. Bake 15–20 minutes, until heated thoroughly and slightly brown. Serve in the cast iron skillet with French bread croutons.

You may wish to use this dip as a topping for oysters on the half shell and bake in the same manner as the casserole. This is an excellent alternative to Oysters Rockefeller or Bienville.

Nutrition Facts...now

Calories:	304
Total Fat:	7gm
Saturated Fat:	2gm
% Calories from Fat:	19
Cholesterol:	8mg
Sodium:	492mg
Carbohydrate:	44gm
Fiber:	5gm
Protein:	21gm

PREP TIME: 1 Hour   SERVES: 8

☞ INGREDIENTS:

1 can smoked oysters, drained
1 (8-ounce) package cream cheese
2 tbsps mayonnaise
2 tbsps heavy whipping cream
1/2 cup finely chopped pecans
1/4 cup minced red bell pepper
1/4 cup minced yellow bell pepper
1 tsp diced garlic
1/4 cup sliced green onions
1 tsp salt
black pepper
Louisiana Gold Pepper Sauce
paprika for color
1/4 cup chopped parsley

☞ METHOD:

Once oysters are drained, pour them onto a paper towel to absorb all remaining oil. Chop oysters and place in a large mixing bowl. Add cream cheese, mayonnaise and whipping cream. Using a wooden spoon, mix ingredients well until creamy. Add pecans, peppers, garlic and green onions, blending into mixture. Season to taste using salt, pepper and Louisiana Gold. Place a 2-foot-long piece of wax paper on a flat surface. Using a pencil, mark a 7" x 9" rectangle on the sheet and dust lightly with flour. Using a spatula, spread the cheese mixture, 1/8–1/4-inch thick, over the rectangle. Lift the edge of the wax paper and roll the rectangle, jelly-roll fashion, easing it off the paper with a knife as it is rolled. When done, sprinkle with a touch of paprika and parsley for color. Chill the loaf for approximately 2 hours in the refrigerator and serve with French bread croutons or crackers.

"Every Cajun cabin up and down the bayou had its own smokehouse. It was always our job to go out and collect the hickory or pecan wood and of course, corn cobs and sugar cane, whenever it was time to fire up that smoker. It seemed that the little house was always filled with something and we could smell that great smokehouse flavor permeating the air as we came home from school.

"We smoked sausage, deer, hams, bacon, tasso, rabbit, ducks, andouille by the ton and oysters during season. I remember sitting on a sack of oysters while we reached in and grabbed one to shuck on the half shell and often we would place them in the smoker to give that great smoked flavor prior to eating them hot. Today, the canned version gives us an opportunity to remember the smokehouse when creating this loaf."

Royley Folse, Jr.
St. James, Louisiana

❊ Nutrition Facts...then ❊

Calories: 249
Total Fat: 25gm
Saturated Fat: 9gm
% Calories from Fat: 86
Cholesterol: 45mg
Sodium: 520mg
Carbohydrate: 5gm
Fiber: 1gm
Protein: 5gm

SMOKED OYSTER LOAF

PREP TIME: 1 Hour   SERVES: 8

☞ INGREDIENTS:

1 can smoked oysters, drained
1 (8-ounce) package fat-free cream cheese
2 tbsps lite mayonnaise
2 tbsps skim milk
1/4 cup finely chopped pecans
1/4 cup minced red bell pepper
1/4 cup minced yellow bell pepper
1 tsp diced garlic
1/4 cup sliced green onions
salt substitute
black pepper
Louisiana Gold Pepper Sauce
paprika for color
1/4 cup chopped parsley

☞ METHOD:

Once oysters are drained, pour them onto a paper towel to absorb all remaining oil. Chop oysters and place in a large mixing bowl.

Add cream cheese, mayonnaise and skim milk. Using a wooden spoon, mix ingredients well until creamy. Add pecans, peppers, garlic and green onions, blending into mixture. Season to taste using salt substitute, pepper and Louisiana Gold.

Place a 2-foot-long piece of wax paper on a flat surface. Using a pencil, mark a 7"x 9" rectangle on the sheet and dust lightly with flour. Using a spatula, spread the cheese mixture, 1/8–1/4-inch thick, over the rectangle. Lift the edge of the wax paper and roll the rectangle, jelly-roll fashion, easing it off the paper with a knife as it is rolled. When done, sprinkle with a touch of paprika and parsley for color.

Chill the loaf for approximately 2 hours in the refrigerator and serve with French bread croutons or crackers.

Nutrition Facts...now

Calories:	100
Total Fat:	7gm
Saturated Fat:	1gm
% Calories from Fat:	59
Cholesterol:	14mg
Sodium:	192mg
Carbohydrate:	4gm
Fiber:	1gm
Protein:	6gm

SPICY CURRY DIP

PREP TIME: 30 Minutes   MAKES: 8 Servings

INGREDIENTS:

1 tbsp curry powder
1 cup mayonnaise
2 tbsps minced onion
2 tbsps minced red bell pepper
2 tbsps minced parsley
1 tbsp lemon juice
1/4 cup chili sauce
1 tsp salt
black pepper
Louisiana Gold Pepper Sauce

METHOD:

It is important to remember that sauces and soups using numerous fresh vegetable ingredients and spices should sit in the refrigerator overnight for flavors to reach their potential. This is definitely one such recipe. In a large mixing bowl, combine all ingredients. Using a wire whip, whisk until all ingredients are well-blended. Season to taste using salt, pepper and Louisiana Gold. Cover with clear wrap and refrigerate overnight. This dip is excellent when served alongside a platter of freshly cut raw vegetables. You may wish to substitute this interesting Curry Dip in place of the usual Remoulade or cocktail sauce at your next party.

"Although curry is most often used in Middle Eastern or Indian cuisine, it has on occasion found its way onto a Louisiana table. The Port of New Orleans gave great access to international spices and with our diverse cultures, we were always in search of something.
"The curry plant was not only used as a decorative border in many plantation gardens, but the light green leaves were crushed into soups and stews for a unique flavor."

John Folse
Donaldsonville, Louisiana

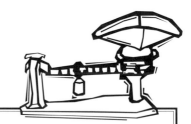

❧Nutrition Facts...then❧

Calories: 213
Total Fat: 24gm
Saturated Fat: 4gm
% Calories from Fat: 94
Cholesterol: 10mg
Sodium: 508mg
Carbohydrate: 3gm
Fiber: 0gm
Protein: 0gm

PREP TIME: 30 Minutes   MAKES: 8 Servings

☞ INGREDIENTS:

1 tbsp curry powder
1/2 cup lite mayonnaise
1/2 cup fat-free sour cream
2 tbsps minced onion
2 tbsps minced red bell pepper
2 tbsps minced parsley
1 tbsp lemon juice
1/4 cup chili sauce
salt substitute
black pepper
Louisiana Gold Pepper Sauce

☞ METHOD:

It is important to remember that sauces and soups using numerous fresh vegetable ingredients and spices should sit in the refrigerator overnight for flavors to reach their potential. This is definitely one such recipe.

In a large mixing bowl, combine all ingredients. Using a wire whip, whisk until all ingredients are well-blended. Season to taste using salt substitute, pepper and Louisiana Gold. Cover with clear wrap and refrigerate overnight.

This dip is excellent when served alongside a platter of freshly cut raw vegetables. You may wish to substitute this interesting Curry Dip in place of the usual Remoulade or cocktail sauce at your next party.

*Chef's Tips on Willpower...
if you're bored, get busy—take
a class, make vacation plans,
anything nonfoodrelated.*

Nutrition Facts...now

Calories:	62
Total Fat:	4gm
Saturated Fat:	0gm
% Calories from Fat:	58
Cholesterol:	5mg
Sodium:	260mg
Carbohydrate:	5gm
Fiber:	0gm
Protein:	1gm

PREP TIME: 2 Hours   SERVES: 15

☞ INGREDIENTS:

8 medium eggplants, peeled and cubed
1 cup olive oil
3 cups diced onions
3 cups diced celery
1 cup diced red bell pepper
1/4 cup diced garlic
2 cups tomato paste
2 cups tomato sauce
2/3 cup sugar
1 1/2 cups red wine vinegar
1 (22-ounce) jar salad olives, diced
2 tsps oregano
1 tsp salt
cayenne pepper
hot sauce

☞ METHOD:

Place eggplant in a large pot and cover by 1 inch with hot water. Bring to a rolling boil, reduce to simmer and cook 10–15 minutes. Drain and set aside. In a large cast iron saute pan, heat olive oil over medium-high heat. Add onions, celery, bell pepper and garlic. Saute 3–5 minutes or until vegetables are wilted. Add tomato paste, sauce, sugar and vinegar. Blend well into vegetable mixture and simmer 10–15 minutes. Add drained eggplant and olives. Season to taste using oregano, salt, pepper and hot sauce. Blend well into the tomato mixture and continue to cook until eggplant is extremely tender and full-flavored, approximately 30–45 minutes. You may wish to serve with crackers or French bread croutons or as a vegetable. This amount of Caponata may be packed into 10 hot sterilized Mason jars, sealed tightly and boiled for 15 minutes in a water bath.

"Despite the 'Creole' name, which suggests French or Spanish origin, this is almost certainly an Italian recipe. But it's so old and so popular around here that I don't imagine anyone could trace its origins. I've been fixing it for 50 years, but this is the first time I've ever written it down. We cook a peu pres - "a little of this, a little of that" - by taste.

"Planting, on the other hand, we did by the book. When I was young we had a big garden, and my mother always told me when to plant things. Once I planted beans without consulting her. When she learned what I'd done, she said "It won't bear fruit. You planted on the wrong moon." She was right. I had the prettiest bean bushes you ever saw. But not one bean.

"You planted above-ground crops on April 6th or 7th and again on the 14th, 29th or 30th. Root crops were planted on the 15th, 17th, 20th, 21st, 24th and 26th. Anything you planted on the 9th or 13th was a goner. What was our planting guide? The Ibert Mortuary calendar!"

Jack Thibodaux,
Franklin, Louisiana

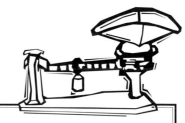

❊Nutrition Facts...then❊	
Calories:	325
Total Fat:	24gm
Saturated Fat:	3gm
% Calories from Fat:	59
Cholesterol:	0mg
Sodium:	924mg
Carbohydrate:	32gm
Fiber:	5gm
Protein:	5gm

CREOLE CAPONATA

PREP TIME: 2 Hours   SERVES: 15

INGREDIENTS:

8 medium eggplants, peeled and cubed
1/4 cup olive oil
3 cups diced onions
3 cups diced celery
1 cup diced red bell pepper
1/4 cup diced garlic
2 cups tomato paste
2 cups tomato sauce, no salt added
2/3 cup sugar
1 1/2 cups red wine vinegar
1 (10-ounce) jar salad olives, diced
2 tsps oregano
salt substitute
cayenne pepper
hot sauce

METHOD:

Place eggplant in a large pot and cover by 1 inch with hot water. Bring to a rolling boil, reduce to simmer and cook 10–15 minutes. Drain and set aside.

In a large cast iron saute pan, heat olive oil over medium-high heat. Add onions, celery, bell pepper and garlic. Saute 3–5 minutes or until vegetables are wilted.

Add tomato paste, sauce, sugar and vinegar. Blend well into vegetable mixture and simmer 10–15 minutes.

Mike Petit works his lease in Convent. The land is part of the Jesuit retreat Manressa, once Jefferson College. In the background is the Ignatius House of Prayer built as the college president's home.

Add drained eggplant and olives. Season to taste using oregano, salt substitute, pepper and hot sauce. Blend well into the tomato mixture and continue to cook until eggplant is extremely tender and full-flavored, approximately 30–45 minutes.

You may wish to serve with crackers or French bread croutons or as a vegetable. This amount of Caponata may be packed into 10 hot sterilized Mason jars, sealed tightly and boiled for 15 minutes in a water bath.

Nutrition Facts...now

Calories:	195
Total Fat:	8gm
Saturated Fat:	1gm
% Calories from Fat:	35
Cholesterol:	0mg
Sodium:	447mg
Carbohydrate:	32gm
Fiber:	4gm
Protein:	4gm

PREP TIME: 2 Hours   SERVES: 6

☞ INGREDIENTS:

1 pound dried red kidney beans
1/4 cup oil
1 cup chopped onions
1/2 cup chopped celery
1/2 cup chopped bell pepper
2 tbsps diced garlic
1 cup sliced andouille
3 quarts chicken stock
1/4 cup sliced green onions
1/4 cup chopped parsley
1 tsp salt
black pepper
Louisiana Gold Pepper Sauce

☞ METHOD:

In order to reduce the cooking time, soak beans overnight in cold water. In a 5-quart dutch oven, heat oil over medium-high heat. Add onions, celery, bell pepper, garlic and andouille. Saute 3–5 minutes or until vegetables are wilted. Add red beans and cover by 1 inch with chicken stock. Bring to a rolling boil, reduce to simmer and cook until beans are tender and mash easily with a fork. Strain chicken stock from the pot, reserving two cups for later use. Place all ingredients into the bowl of a food processor fitted with a metal blade. Process in 15 second intervals until beans are mashed thoroughly. Add green onions and parsley. Season to taste using salt, pepper and Louisiana Gold. If beans tend to be a bit too dense or stiff, add a couple of tablespoons of chicken stock to reach desired consistency. Remove the dip to a suitable mold or chafer. Serve hot or cold with fresh vegetables, tortilla chips or French bread croutons.

"I can't tell you how many times I heard the story about the Cajuns exiled from Nova Scotia in 1750 and leaving everything behind except their red beans. My grandmother also told a wonderful story about why we eat red beans, rice and sausage every Monday here in the bayous. She said that Monday was wash day and a big black pot filled with soapy boiling water was used to 'cook' the dirty clothes prior to rinsing and hanging them out in the sun to dry.

"She explained that since you had to stand over that pot anyway, why not just fire up another one alongside so that dinner could be cooked at the same time as those old blue denim jeans. I asked her once, did she remember ever putting the paddle from the soapy water into the bean pot by mistake. She just laughed and winked.

"Every now and again, the batch of clothes was larger than the batch of beans and unfortunately the beans would overcook. She said on those days, they just dipped it up with hot French bread."
                        Melissa Folse
                    Vacherie, Louisiana

❧Nutrition Facts...then❧

Calories: 336
Total Fat: 20gm
Saturated Fat: 5gm
% Calories from Fat: 52
Cholesterol: 38mg
Sodium: 1876mg
Carbohydrate: 26gm
Fiber: 8gm
Protein: 15gm

RED BEAN DIP

PREP TIME: 2 Hours   SERVES: 6

INGREDIENTS:

1 pound dried red kidney beans
1 tbsp olive oil
1 cup chopped onions
1/2 cup chopped celery
1/2 cup chopped bell pepper
2 tbsps diced garlic
1/2 cup lean ham
3 quarts defatted chicken stock, unsalted
1/4 cup sliced green onions
1/4 cup chopped parsley
salt substitute
black pepper
Louisiana Gold Pepper Sauce

METHOD:

In order to reduce the cooking time, soak beans overnight in cold water.

In a 5-quart dutch oven, heat oil over medium-high heat. Add onions, celery, bell pepper, garlic and ham. Saute 3–5 minutes or until vegetables are wilted. Add red beans and cover by 1 inch with chicken stock. Bring to a rolling boil, reduce to simmer and cook until beans are tender and mash easily with a fork.

Strain chicken stock from the pot, reserving two cups for later use. Place all ingredients into the bowl of a food processor fitted with a metal blade. Process in 15 second intervals until beans are mashed thoroughly.

Add green onions and parsley. Season to taste using salt substitute, pepper and Louisiana Gold. If beans tend to be a bit too dense or stiff, add a couple of tablespoons of chicken stock to reach desired consistency.

Remove the dip to a suitable mold or chafer. Serve hot or cold with fresh vegetables, tortilla chips or French bread croutons.

Chef's Tips on Exercise... while talking on the phone, do leg lifts or calf stretches.

Nutrition Facts...now

Calories: 235
Total Fat: 9gm
Saturated Fat: 1gm
% Calories from Fat:.................. 31
Cholesterol: 15mg
Sodium: 346mg
Carbohydrate: 26gm
Fiber: 8gm
Protein: 16gm

33

PREP TIME: 1 Hour   SERVES: 6

INGREDIENTS:

2 (10-ounce) packages frozen spinach, thawed
1/2 cup butter
1/2 cup chopped onions
1/2 cup chopped celery
1/2 cup chopped bell pepper
1/4 cup diced garlic
1 cup finely chopped ham or tasso
1/2 cup flour
2 1/2 cups heavy whipping cream
1/2 cup diced tomatoes
1/2 cup grated cheddar cheese
1/4 cup finely diced jalapeno peppers
1 tsp salt
black pepper
hot sauce

METHOD:

Preheat oven to 375 degrees F. In a 4-quart sauce pan, melt butter over medium-high heat. Add onions, celery, bell pepper, garlic and chopped ham or tasso. Saute 3–5 minutes or until vegetables are wilted. Sprinkle in flour and, using a wire whisk, stir constantly until white roux is achieved. Do not brown. Slowly add whipping cream, stirring constantly until all is incorporated. Add tomatoes, cheddar cheese and jalapeno peppers. Continue cooking for an additional 5–10 minutes, stirring constantly, as mixture will tend to stick. Add a small amount of heavy whipping cream should mixture become too thick. Season to taste using salt, pepper and hot sauce. Remove from heat and add spinach, stirring well into the seasoned white sauce. Place mixture in baking dish, cover, and bake until bubbly, approximately 20–25 minutes. Serve immediately. This spinach casserole doubles nicely as a hot hors d'oeuvre when served with garlic croutons.

"I think the dish was originally called Spinach Madeline. Chef Folse calls it Spinach Marguerite. In my family, we called it Christmas Spinach! We would serve it along with Tomato Aspic on Christmas Eve. It made a natural holiday table decoration with the red and green.
Everyone would arrive at my mother's home with presents galore, in anticipation of the festive food and the many gifts! Because the spinach and aspic were served with crackers, even the children would eat it. They thought it was a 'treat' and never realized that it was good for them! Though my parents are no longer living and we no longer have the large family holiday gatherings, my children still enjoy this special spinach dish."
Jane Arnette
Houma, Louisiana

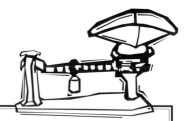

❋Nutrition Facts...then❋

Calories:	683
Total Fat:	59gm
Saturated Fat:	36gm
% Calories from Fat:	77
Cholesterol:	210mg
Sodium:	1358mg
Carbohydrate:	25gm
Fiber:	3gm
Protein:	16gm

SPINACH MARGUERITE

PREP TIME: 1 Hour   SERVES: 6

☞ INGREDIENTS:

2 (10-ounce) packages frozen spinach, thawed
1 tbsp lite margarine
1/2 cup chopped onions
1/2 cup chopped celery
1/2 cup chopped bell pepper
1/4 cup diced garlic
1 cup finely chopped lean ham
1/2 cup flour
2 1/2 cups evaporated skim milk
1/2 cup diced tomatoes
1/2 cup grated reduced-fat cheddar cheese
1/4 cup finely diced jalapeno peppers
salt substitute
black pepper
hot sauce

☞ METHOD:

Preheat oven to 375 degrees F. In a 4-quart sauce pan, melt margarine over medium-high heat. Add onions, celery, bell pepper, garlic and chopped ham. Saute 3–5 minutes or until vegetables are wilted.

Sprinkle in flour and, using a wire whisk, stir constantly until white roux is achieved. Do not brown. Slowly add skim milk, stirring constantly until all is incorporated.

Add tomatoes, cheddar cheese and jalapeno peppers. Continue cooking for an additional 5–10 minutes, stirring constantly, as mixture will tend to stick. Add a small amount of skim milk should mixture become too thick. Season to taste using salt substitute, pepper and hot sauce.

Remove from heat and add spinach, stirring well into the seasoned white sauce. Place mixture in baking dish, cover and bake until bubbly, approximately 20–25 minutes. Serve immediately.

This spinach casserole doubles nicely as a hot hors d'oeuvre when served with garlic croutons.

Nutrition Facts...now

Calories:	254
Total Fat:	4gm
Saturated Fat:	1gm
% Calories from Fat:	15
Cholesterol:	36mg
Sodium:	957mg
Carbohydrate:	32gm
Fiber:	3gm
Protein:	23gm

Kevin Hebert catching some nice crabs by Highway 27 south of Sulphur in Cameron Parish.

PREP TIME: 45 Minutes   SERVES: 20

☞ INGREDIENTS:

1 (12-ounce) can jalapenos, seeded
2 pounds Velveeta cheese, diced
1 pound heavily smoked andouille sausage
1/4 cup butter
1 cup chopped onions
1/4 cup chopped celery
1/4 cup chopped red bell pepper
2 tbsps diced garlic
4 cups mayonnaise
1 tsp salt
black pepper
Louisiana Gold Pepper Sauce
1/4 cup chopped parsley

☞ METHOD:

Dice the andouille or other smoked sausage. Allow cheese to sit at room temperature for 30 minutes. Remove seeds from jalapeno peppers and, if you are a bit squeamish, rinse the jalapenos under cold running water to remove some of the heat. In a 5-quart cast iron dutch oven, melt butter over medium-high heat. Add onions, celery, bell pepper, garlic and andouille. Saute 3–5 minutes or until vegetables are wilted. Add jalapenos and saute 2–3 additional minutes. Reduce heat to simmer, add cheese and, using a wire whisk, whip until cheese is melted and incorporated into the mixture. Fold in mayonnaise and, when well-blended, remove from heat. Season to taste using salt, pepper and Louisiana Gold. Sprinkle in parsley. Pour ingredients into a decorative serving bowl and heat to serving temperature in the microwave. Place in the center of a large serving platter surrounded by garlic croutons, toast points or tortilla chips. This dip may also be served cold and will hold well in the refrigerator for a couple of days.

"This is one of those recipes that really shows the evolution of Creole cuisine. Although the dish originated at Kent House Plantation in Alexandria, I'm sure it was developed in some Creole kitchen in New Orleans before traveling North.

"The Creoles were the children of the intermarriage between the seven different nations who settled the city. This spicy appetizer reflects three of those nations. The jalapeno peppers arrived here with the Spanish who brought them up through Mexico across the Sabine River and into South Louisiana. The cheese was a product of many nations, however, it was the Germans who started making great cheese on the Mississippi River. Most people credit the French with bringing the original andouille sausage to Louisiana even though the Germans quickly laid claim to this delicacy.

"Either way, who cares, these ingredients all went into this dip that is truly a Creole masterpiece."
Pamela Castel
Baton Rouge, Louisiana

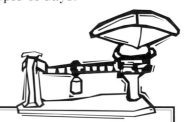

❀Nutrition Facts...then❀

Calories:	483
Total Fat:	51gm
Saturated Fat:	13gm
% Calories from Fat:	91
Cholesterol:	51mg
Sodium:	1109mg
Carbohydrate:	4gm
Fiber:	1gm
Protein:	7gm

PREP TIME: 45 Minutes   SERVES: 20

☞ INGREDIENTS:

1 (12-ounce) can jalapenos, seeded
2 pounds lite Velveeta cheese, diced
1/2 pound low-fat smoked sausage
vegetable spray
1 cup chopped onions
1/4 cup chopped celery
1/4 cup chopped red bell pepper
2 tbsps diced garlic
2 cups fat-free mayonnaise
2 cups fat-free sour cream
salt substitute
black pepper
Louisiana Gold Pepper Sauce
1/4 cup chopped parsley

☞ METHOD:

Dice the smoked sausage. Allow cheese to sit at room temperature for 30 minutes. Remove seeds from jalapeno peppers and, if you are a bit squeamish, rinse the jalapenos under cold running water to remove some of the heat.

In a 5-quart cast iron dutch oven, coated with vegetable spray, combine onions, celery, bell pepper, garlic and sausage over medium-high heat. Saute 3–5 minutes or until vegetables are wilted.

Add jalapenos and saute 2–3 minutes more. Reduce heat to simmer, add cheese and, using a wire whisk, whip until cheese is melted and incorporated into the mixture.

Fold in mayonnaise and sour cream, and when well-blended, remove from heat. Season to taste using salt substitute, pepper and Louisiana Gold. Sprinkle in parsley.

Pour ingredients into a decorative serving bowl and heat to serving temperature in the microwave. Place in the center of a large serving platter surrounded by garlic croutons, toast points or tortilla chips. This dip may also be served cold and will hold well in the refrigerator for a couple of days.

Chef's Tips on LowFat... identify sources of fat in a recipe.

Nutrition Facts...now

Calories:	176
Total Fat:	7gm
Saturated Fat:	2gm
% Calories from Fat:	35
Cholesterol:	11mg
Sodium:	806mg
Carbohydrate:	13gm
Fiber:	1gm
Protein:	14gm

PREP TIME: 30 Minutes   SERVES: 8

☞ INGREDIENTS:

3 (16-ounce) cans blackeyed peas,
     with jalapenos, drained
1 cup chopped Bermuda onions
1 cup chopped yellow bell peppers
1/4 cup diced garlic
1 cup sliced green onions
1/2 cup chopped jalapeno peppers
1/2 cup minced tasso
1 cup olive oil
1/4 cup red wine vinegar
1 tbsp chopped oregano
1 tsp chopped thyme
1 tsp chopped basil
1/2 cup diced tomatoes
1/2 cup grated Parmesan cheese
1 tsp salt
black pepper
Louisiana Gold Pepper Sauce

"If you eat blackeyed peas on New Year's Day, then you need to thank the Africans. You probably didn't realize that the African slaves brought to America some of our more popular dishes: watermelon, okra, yams and congre or blackeyed peas. Our family always smothered the peas in a light brown roux with onions, celery, bell pepper, garlic and a chunk of smoky ham.
"One day, I went over to visit a cousin who lives in Texas and ate a spicy blackeyed pea salad that they called Texas caviar. Well, I brought the recipe home, added jalapenos, tasso and a little bit of pepper sauce and it turned Cajun overnight."
Phyllis Graves
Ocean Springs, Mississippi

☞ METHOD:

In a large mixing bowl, place onions, bell pepper, garlic, green onions, jalapenos, tasso, oil and vinegar. Use a wooden spoon to blend all ingredients well. Add oregano, thyme and basil, blending well into the vegetable mixture. Add peas, tomatoes and Parmesan cheese. Season to taste using salt, pepper and Louisiana Gold. Mix all ingredients well and cover with clear wrap. Refrigerate overnight. Serve with tortilla chips or crackers. Place a generous spoonful over a mixture of greens for an interesting spicy salad.

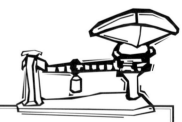

❧ Nutrition Facts...then ❧

Calories: 500
Total Fat: 31gm
Saturated Fat: 5gm
% Calories from Fat: 54
Cholesterol: 10mg
Sodium: 925mg
Carbohydrate: 39gm
Fiber: 18gm
Protein: 20gm

PREP TIME: 30 Minutes   SERVES: 8

☞ INGREDIENTS:

3 (16-ounce) cans blackeyed peas,
     with jalapenos, drained
1 cup chopped Bermuda onions
1 cup chopped yellow bell peppers
1/4 cup diced garlic
1 cup sliced green onions
1/2 cup chopped jalapeno peppers
1/4 cup minced tasso
1/4 cup olive oil
1/4 cup red wine vinegar
1 tbsp chopped oregano
1 tsp chopped thyme
1 tsp chopped basil
1/2 cup diced tomatoes, no salt added
1/2 cup grated Parmesan cheese
salt substitute
black pepper
Louisiana Gold Pepper Sauce

The Statue of Evangeline in St. Martinville, a gift of Delores Del Rio, the actress who played the roll of Evangeline in the 1920s film classic.

☞ METHOD:

In a large mixing bowl, place onions, bell pepper, garlic, green onions, jalapenos, tasso, oil and vinegar. Use a wooden spoon to blend all ingredients well. Add oregano, thyme and basil, blending well into the vegetable mixture. Add peas, tomatoes and Parmesan cheese. Season to taste using salt substitute, pepper and Louisiana Gold.

Mix all ingredients well and cover with clear wrap. Refrigerate overnight. Serve with tortilla chips or crackers. Place a generous spoonful over a mixture of greens for an interesting spicy salad.

Nutrition Facts...now

Calories:	315
Total Fat:	11gm
Saturated Fat:	3gm
% Calories from Fat:	29
Cholesterol:	7mg
Sodium:	311mg
Carbohydrate:	39gm
Fiber:	18gm
Protein:	19gm

PREP TIME: 3 Hours   MAKES: 5 loaves/10 servings per loaf

☞ INGREDIENTS FOR STOCK:

1 hog's head, halved	3 large onions, quartered	2 bay leaves
4 pounds Boston butt	4 stalks of celery, quartered	1 tsp salt
4 pig's feet	1 head of garlic, halved	black pepper

☞ METHOD FOR STOCK:

In a large stock pot, place all ingredients. Cover by 6 inches with cold water and season to taste using salt and pepper. Bring to a rolling boil, reduce heat to simmer and cook until meat is tender and falling from the bones, approximately 2–2 1/2 hours. Using a ladle, skim the foam that rises to the top of the pot during the cooking process. Once meat is tender, remove and strain and reserve poaching liquid. Debone meat and grind, using the chili blade of your meat grinder. Set aside.

☞ INGREDIENTS FOR ASSEMBLY:

reserved poaching liquid	2 cups minced celery	black pepper
4 packages unflavored gelatin	2 cups minced red bell pepper	Louisiana Gold Pepper Sauce
cooked ground pork	1/4 cup diced garlic	2 cups sliced green onions
2 cups minced onions	salt	1 cup chopped parsley

☞ METHOD FOR ASSEMBLY:

Once the poaching liquid has been strained and allowed to sit for 1 or 2 hours, oil will form on top of the stock. Using a ladle, carefully remove all of the oil from the surface of the poaching liquid and set aside. Dissolve gelatin in 1 cup of cooled poaching liquid and set aside. In a large pot, place the cooked ground pork, onions, celery, bell pepper and garlic. Cover with reserved poaching liquid by one-half inch. Bring to a rolling boil, reduce to simmer and allow ingredients to cook 25–30 minutes, adding additional stock to retain volume. Season to taste using salt, pepper and Louisiana Gold. Remove from heat and add green onions, parsley and dissolved gelatin. Allow to cool slightly. Ladle the cheese into 4"x 9" loaf pans, cover with clear wrap and refrigerate overnight.

"Hog's head cheese was one of those dishes we looked forward to once a year. On the first cold snap of fall, the pigs would be selected for fattening and the boucherie date set. This was the day that all families came together to help one another prepare the hams, sausages, roasts and of course, delicacies such as hog's head cheese.
"It really makes it a lot easier today when all we have to do is go down to the local butcher and get all of the ingredients necessary to whip up a quick batch of this bayou delicacy."
Sharon Jesowshek
French Settlement, Louisiana

❋Nutrition Facts...then❋

Calories:	197
Total Fat:	14gm
Saturated Fat:	5gm
% Calories from Fat:	64
Cholesterol:	52mg
Sodium:	293mg
Carbohydrates:	3gm
Fiber:	1gm
Protein:	15gm

PREP TIME: 3 Hours   MAKES: 5 loaves/10 servings per loaf

☞ INGREDIENTS FOR STOCK:

8 pounds lean pork loin
3 large onions, quartered
4 stalks of celery, quartered
1 head of garlic, halved
2 bay leaves
salt substitute
black pepper

☞ METHOD FOR STOCK:

In a large stock pot, place all ingredients. Cover by 6 inches with cold water and season to taste using salt substitute and pepper. Bring to a rolling boil, reduce heat to simmer and cook until meat is tender, approximately 2–2 1/2 hours.

Using a ladle, skim the foam that rises to the top of the pot during the cooking process. Once meat is tender, remove and strain and reserve poaching liquid. Grind the meat, using the chili blade of your meat grinder. Set aside.

☞ INGREDIENTS FOR ASSEMBLY:

reserved poaching liquid
4 packages unflavored gelatin
cooked lean ground pork
2 cups minced onions
2 cups minced celery
2 cups minced red bell pepper
1/4 cup diced garlic
salt substitute
black pepper
Louisiana Gold Pepper Sauce
2 cups sliced green onions
1 cup chopped parsley

☞ METHOD FOR ASSEMBLY:

Once the poaching liquid has been strained and allowed to sit for 1 or 2 hours, oil will form on top of the stock. Using a ladle, carefully remove all of the oil from the surface of the poaching liquid and set aside.

Dissolve gelatin in 1 cup of cooled poaching liquid and set aside.

In a large pot, place the cooked ground pork, onions, celery, bell pepper and garlic. Cover with reserved poaching liquid by one-half inch. Bring to a rolling boil, reduce to simmer and allow ingredients to cook 25–30 minutes, adding additional stock to retain volume. Season to taste using salt substitute, pepper and Louisiana Gold.

Remove from heat and add green onions, parsley and dissolved gelatin. Allow to cool slightly. Ladle the cheese into 4"x 9" loaf pans, cover with clear wrap and refrigerate overnight.

Nutrition Facts...now

Calories:	197
Total Fat:	9gm
Saturated Fat:	3gm
% Calories from Fat:	43
Cholesterol:	52mg
Sodium:	63mg
Carbohydrates:	2gm
Fiber:	1gm
Protein:	25gm

PREP TIME: 1 Hour   MAKES: 75

☞ INGREDIENTS:

1 pound ground beef
1/2 pound ground pork
1/2 cup minced onions
1/2 cup minced celery
1/4 cup minced red bell pepper
1/4 cup minced garlic
1/4 cup half and half cream
1 egg, slightly beaten
1/2 cup seasoned Italian bread crumbs
pinch of allspice
1 tsp salt
black pepper
Louisiana Gold Pepper Sauce
1/4 cup butter
1/4 cup flour
2 cups chicken stock
2 tsps dried dill
1 cup sour cream

☞ METHOD:

Preheat oven to 375 degrees F. In a large mixing bowl, combine meats, onions, celery, bell pepper, garlic, cream and egg. Using your hands, mix well until all ingredients are incorporated. Add bread crumbs. Season to taste using allspice, salt, pepper and Louisiana Gold. Roll into 1-inch meatballs and place in a baking pan or on a large cookie sheet with one-inch lip. Bake 20 minutes or until golden brown. Pour off oil and keep meatballs warm. In a 3-quart cast iron dutch oven, melt butter over medium-high heat. Sprinkle in flour and, using a wire whisk, whip until white roux is achieved. Slowly add chicken stock, bring to a rolling boil and whip until mixture thickens. Add dill and season to taste using salt, pepper and Louisiana Gold. Remove from heat and blend in the sour cream. Adjust seasonings if necessary. Place meatballs into a chafing dish and top with the cream sauce. Serve hot.

"Don't pass over this recipe too quickly! Many people just assume that cocktail meatballs are something thrown together in a second with no thought or character. Well, not these incredible meatballs. The combination of beef and pork along with a multitude of other flavors set these little jewels apart."

Dawn Newchurch
Paincourtville, Louisiana

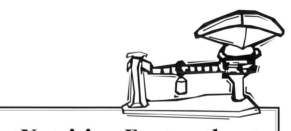

❧Nutrition Facts...then❧

Calories: 43
Total Fat: 3gm
Saturated Fat: 1gm
% Calories from Fat: 59
Cholesterol: 10mg
Sodium: 101mg
Carbohydrate: 1gm
Fiber: 0gm
Protein: 3gm

(nutrition info figured per meatball)

PREP TIME: 1 Hour   MAKES: 75

INGREDIENTS:

1 pound lean ground beef round
1/2 pound lean ground pork loin
1/2 cup minced onions
1/2 cup minced celery
1/4 cup minced red bell pepper
1/4 cup minced garlic
1/4 cup evaporated skim milk
1 egg, slightly beaten
1/2 cup seasoned Italian bread crumbs
pinch of allspice
salt substitute
black pepper
Louisiana Gold Pepper Sauce
1/4 cup lite margarine
1/4 cup flour
2 cups defatted chicken stock, unsalted
2 tsps dried dill
1 cup fat-free sour cream

Elvis Chabert mulching his garden in Golden Meadow.

METHOD:

Preheat oven to 375 degrees F. In a large mixing bowl, combine meats, onions, celery, bell pepper, garlic, milk and egg. Using your hands, mix well until all ingredients are incorporated. Add bread crumbs. Season to taste using allspice, salt substitute, pepper and Louisiana Gold.

Roll into 1-inch meatballs and place in a baking pan or on large cookie sheet with one-inch lip. Bake 20 minutes or until golden brown. Pour off oil and keep meatballs warm.

In a 3-quart cast iron dutch oven, melt margarine over medium-high heat. Sprinkle in flour and, using a wire whisk, whip until white roux is achieved. Slowly add chicken stock, bring to a rolling boil and whip until mixture thickens. Add dill and season to taste using salt substitute, pepper and Louisiana Gold.

Remove from heat and blend in the sour cream. Adjust seasonings if necessary. Place meatballs into a chafing dish and top with the cream sauce. Serve hot.

Nutrition Facts...now

Calories:	31
Total Fat:	2gm
Saturated Fat:	1gm
% Calories from Fat:	48
Cholesterol:	6mg
Sodium:	35mg
Carbohydrate:	2gm
Fiber:	0gm
Protein:	2gm

(nutrition info figured per meatball)

PREP TIME: 1 1/2 Hours   SERVES: 8

☞ **INGREDIENTS:**

1/2 pound grated cheddar cheese
1 package (1 stack) saltine crackers
1 quart milk
3 whole eggs, whipped
1/4 cup sliced green onions
1/4 cup chopped red bell pepper
cracked black pepper
hot sauce
1/2 cup jumbo lump crabmeat (optional)
vegetable spray

☞ **METHOD:**

Preheat oven to 375 degrees F. In a large mixing bowl, crumble crackers and pour in milk. Allow to stand until most of the milk is absorbed into the crackers. Add eggs, cheese, green onions and bell pepper. Blend well into the cracker mixture. Season to taste using pepper and hot sauce. No salt has been added due to the use of the saltine crackers. Add lump crabmeat at this point if used. Spray a 2-quart casserole dish with vegetable spray and fill with the cheese mixture. Cover and bake for approximately 1 hour. Serve along with toast points or French bread croutons.

"My grandmother, who invented this recipe, called it 'cheese fondue.' It was one of our Christmas and Thanksgiving favorites. She used to say it was filled with 'all the bad stuff.' But absolutely no one cared!

"One thing you aren't likely to be if you are born into or marry into a Cajun family is lonesome. My father-in-law, Durham West, had thirteen brothers and sisters.

"He said his folks used to go into town once a month and buy a pair of shoes. It didn't matter what size. They'd fit someone. My wife once started counting her first cousins. Before she was through, she'd counted 64 of them!

"Maybe that's why my father-in-law and his brother Herman founded a department store chain right after World War I. They already had a lot of experience buying in quantity!"

Ed Brandt
DeRidder, Louisiana

❋Nutrition Facts...then❋

Calories: 317
Total Fat: 18gm
Saturated Fat: 9gm
% Calories from Fat: 51
Cholesterol: 213mg
Sodium: 750mg
Carbohydrate: 22gm
Fiber: 0gm
Protein: 16gm

PREP TIME: 1 1/2 Hours   SERVES: 8

☞ INGREDIENTS:

1/2 pound reduced-fat cheddar cheese, grated
1 package (1 stack) unsalted crackers
1 quart skim milk
1 cup egg substitute
1/4 cup sliced green onions
1/4 cup chopped red bell pepper
cracked black pepper
hot sauce
1/2 cup jumbo lump crabmeat (optional)
vegetable spray

☞ METHOD:

Preheat oven to 375 degrees F. In a large mixing bowl, crumble crackers and pour in skim milk. Allow to stand until most of the milk is absorbed into the crackers.

Add egg substitute, cheese, green onions and bell pepper. Blend well into the cracker mixture. Season to taste using pepper and hot sauce. Add lump crabmeat at this point if used.

Spray a 2-quart casserole dish with vegetable spray and fill with the cheese mixture. Cover and bake for approximately 1 hour. Serve along with toast points or French bread croutons.

*Chef's Tips on Willpower...
choose an exercise that's right for you. If you don't enjoy what you're doing, you may not stick with it.*

Nutrition Facts...now

Calories:	188
Total Fat:	5gm
Saturated Fat:	0gm
% Calories from Fat:	26
Cholesterol:	38mg
Sodium:	650mg
Carbohydrate:	19gm
Fiber:	0gm
Protein:	16gm

Soups

Chapter Two

Gumbo Creole	48/49
Louisiana Seafood Gumbo	50/51
Shrimp & Okra Gumbo	52/53
Chicken, Sausage & File Gumbo	54/55
Cajun Chicken Gumbo	56/57
Madere's Shrimpboat Chowder	58/59
Shrimp & Potato Stew	60/61
Shrimp & Corn Soup	62/63
Louisiana Oyster Soup	64/65
Cabbage & Ground Beef Soup	66/67
Vegetable Beef Soup	68/69
Gizzard Soup	72/73
Cream Of Sweet Pea Soup	74/75
Grandma Breaux's Succotash Soup	76/77
Navy Bean Soup	78/79
Mirliton Soup	80/81
Gumbo Z'Herbes	82/83
Aunt "Zubee's" Corn Soup	84/85
Carmen's Black Bean Soup	86/87
Grand-Papa Porche's Potato & Ham Soup	88/89

*The recipes for **Gumbo Z'Herbes**, pictured at left, can be found on pages 82 and 83.*

PREP TIME: 1 Hour   SERVES: 8

☞ INGREDIENTS:

1 (3-pound) fryer
1 pound (21–25 count) shrimp, peeled and deveined
1 pound jumbo lump crabmeat
1/2 cup oil
1/2 cup flour
2 cups chopped onions
1 cup chopped celery
1 cup chopped bell pepper
1/4 cup diced garlic
2 cups sliced okra
1 cup diced tomatoes
3 quarts defatted chicken stock
1 bay leaf
1/2 cup sliced green onions
1/4 cup chopped parsley
1 tsp salt
black pepper
Louisiana Gold Pepper Sauce

☞ METHOD:

Cut fryer into 8–10 serving pieces. In a cast iron dutch oven, heat oil over medium-high heat. Brown chicken in oil, a few pieces at a time, until all is golden brown. Remove chicken and set aside. Add flour and, using a wire whisk, stir constantly until dark brown roux is achieved. Add onions, celery, bell pepper and garlic. Saute 3–5 minutes or until vegetables are wilted. Fold in okra and tomatoes, blending well into the roux mixture. Add chicken stock, one ladle at a time. Bring to a rolling boil and reduce to simmer. Add chicken, 1/2 of the shrimp and bay leaf. Cook 30–45 minutes or until chicken is tender. Add green onions and parsley. Season to taste using salt, pepper and Louisiana Gold. Finish the soup by adding the remaining shrimp and crabmeat. Cook 5 additional minutes or until shrimp are pink and curled. Remove bay leaf and serve over steamed white rice.

"I guess the term Creole could just as easily be defined as a mixture of everything and anything you have in the pantry. I don't think any other cuisine combines as many ingredients, especially meat and seafood, the way we Creoles do. Whenever friends come over to visit and we serve Creole gumbo, they are amazed that chicken, shrimp and crab along with many other fresh seasonings go into one cast iron pot.
"Well, I think my Grandmother answered the question best when she said, 'We have so many great things to cook with here, sometimes we just can't make up our mind, so we throw it all in the pot!'"

Debbie Martin
Port Allen, Louisiana

❧ Nutrition Facts...then ❧

Calories: 728
Total Fat: 39gm
Saturated Fat: 9gm
% Calories from Fat: 49
Cholesterol: 302mg
Sodium: 1883mg
Carbohydrate: 16gm
Fiber: 2gm
Protein: 75gm

PREP TIME: 1 Hour   SERVES: 8

☞ INGREDIENTS:

1 (3-pound) fryer, skinned
1 pound (21–25 count) shrimp, peeled and deveined
1 pound jumbo lump crabmeat
1/2 cup oil-less roux
1 cup defatted chicken stock, unsalted
2 tbsps oil
2 cups chopped onions
1 cup chopped celery
1 cup chopped bell pepper
1/4 cup diced garlic
2 cups sliced okra
1 cup diced tomatoes
3 quarts defatted chicken stock, unsalted
1 bay leaf
1/2 cup sliced green onions
1/4 cup chopped parsley
salt substitute
black pepper
Louisiana Gold Pepper Sauce

Chef's Tips on Fat... use the "loin/round" rule for beef and the "loin/leg" for pork, lamb and veal. Cuts with these words will be lean.

☞ METHOD:

Cut fryer into 8–10 serving pieces. Dissolve oil-less roux in 1 cup of chicken stock. Set aside.

In a cast iron dutch oven, heat oil over medium-high heat. Brown chicken in oil, a few pieces at a time, until all is golden brown. Remove chicken and set aside.

Add onions, celery, bell pepper and garlic. Saute 3–5 minutes or until vegetables are wilted. Fold in okra and tomatoes, blending well into the mixture. Add roux/stock mixture and additional chicken stock, one ladle at a time. Bring to a rolling boil and reduce to simmer.

Add chicken, 1/2 of the shrimp and bay leaf. Cook 30–45 minutes or until chicken is tender. Add green onions and parsley. Season to taste using salt substitute, pepper and Louisiana Gold.

Finish the soup by adding the remaining shrimp and crabmeat. Cook 5 additional minutes or until shrimp are pink and curled. Remove bay leaf and serve over steamed white rice.

Nutrition Facts...now

Calories:	364
Total Fat:	10gm
Saturated Fat:	2gm
% Calories from Fat:	25
Cholesterol:	191mg
Sodium:	891mg
Carbohydrate:	17gm
Fiber:	2gm
Protein:	51gm

PREP TIME: 1 Hour   SERVES: 12

☞ INGREDIENTS:

1 pound (35 count) shrimp, peeled and deveined
1 pound jumbo lump crabmeat
2 dozen shucked oysters, reserve liquid
1 cup vegetable oil
1 1/2 cups flour
2 cups chopped onions
1 cup chopped celery
1 cup chopped bell pepper
1/4 cup diced garlic
1/2 pound sliced andouille sausage
1 pound claw crabmeat
3 quarts shellfish stock
2 cups sliced green onions
1/2 cup chopped parsley
1 tsp salt
cayenne pepper
Louisiana Gold Pepper Sauce

"We all take so much for granted here in South Louisiana. Traveling all over the world in World War II, I soon realized that nobody else anywhere thinks of food the way we Cajuns do. I remember arriving in France and being served a bowl of shellfish soup, where the French called it bouillabaisse. They raved about the dish and there's no doubt it was good, but it simply was not Louisiana.

"In Germany, we had potato soup, cabbage soup and bean soup. You name it, we had it. Once again, the soups were incredible to the people from other states sharing the pot but after all, they had never eaten in Louisiana. In every country and over every pot, I often reminisced about our seafood gumbo.

"I often think how much I missed that special soup when I was over in Europe. Never once have I missed their soup since I have been back home."

Royley Folse, Sr.
Donaldsonville, Louisiana

☞ METHOD:

In a 2-gallon stock pot, heat oil over medium-high heat. Once oil is hot, add flour and, using a wire whisk, stir constantly until golden brown roux is achieved. Add onions, celery, bell pepper and garlic. Saute approximately 3–5 minutes or until vegetables are wilted. Add andouille, blend well into vegetable mixture and saute an additional 2–3 minutes. Add claw crabmeat and stir into roux, as this will begin to add seafood flavor to the mixture. Slowly add hot shellfish stock, one ladle at a time, stirring constantly until all is incorporated. Bring to a low boil, reduce to simmer and cook approximately 30 minutes. Add stock if necessary to retain volume. Add green onions and parsley. Season to taste using salt, pepper and Louisiana Gold. Fold shrimp, lump crabmeat, oysters and reserved liquid into soup. Return to a low boil and cook approximately 5 minutes. Adjust seasonings and serve over cooked rice.

❦ Nutrition Facts...then❦

Calories:	563
Total Fat:	30gm
Saturated Fat:	6gm
% Calories from Fat:	48
Cholesterol:	144mg
Sodium:	3240mg
Carbohydrate:	31gm
Fiber:	2gm
Protein:	40gm

PREP TIME: 1 Hour   SERVES: 12

☞ INGREDIENTS:

1 pound (35 count) shrimp, peeled and deveined
1 pound jumbo lump crabmeat
2 dozen shucked oysters, reserve liquid
1 1/2 cups oil-less roux
2 cups hot water
1/4 cup vegetable oil
2 cups chopped onions
1 cup chopped celery
1 cup chopped bell pepper
1/4 cup diced garlic
1/2 pound low-fat smoked sausage
1 pound claw crabmeat
2 1/2 quarts hot water
2 cups sliced green onions
1/2 cup chopped parsley
salt substitute
cayenne pepper
Louisiana Gold Pepper Sauce

Si Brown of Bruce Foods in front of their headquarters in New Iberia.

☞ METHOD:

Dissolve oil-less roux in 2 cups of water. Set aside.

In a 2-gallon stock pot, heat oil over medium-high heat. Add onions, celery, bell pepper and garlic. Saute 3–5 minutes or until vegetables are wilted. Add smoked sausage, blend well into vegetable mixture and saute an additional 2–3 minutes.

Add claw crabmeat, as this will begin to add seafood flavor to the mixture. Slowly add water/roux mixture and remaining water, one ladle at a time, stirring constantly until all is incorporated. Bring to a low boil, reduce to simmer and cook approximately 30 minutes. Add water if necessary to retain volume.

Add green onions and parsley. Season to taste using salt substitute, pepper and Louisiana Gold. Fold shrimp, lump crabmeat, oysters and reserved liquid into soup. Return to a low boil and cook approximately 5 minutes. Adjust seasonings and serve over cooked rice.

Nutrition Facts...now

Calories:	366
Total Fat:	13gm
Saturated Fat:	2gm
% Calories from Fat:	32
Cholesterol:	133mg
Sodium:	394mg
Carbohydrate:	23gm
Fiber:	2gm
Protein:	38gm

SHRIMP & OKRA GUMBO

PREP TIME: 2 Hours   SERVES: 8

☞ INGREDIENTS:

3 pounds (50–60 count) shrimp, peeled and deveined
3 cups sliced okra
1/2 cup vegetable oil
1/2 cup flour
2 cups diced onions
1 cup diced bell pepper
3 quarts water
1 drop liquid crab boil
1 tsp salt
black pepper
hot sauce
3 whole eggs (optional)

☞ METHOD:

You may wish to saute your okra until brown in 2–3 tablespoons of vegetable oil. This is determined by personal preference. I just add mine raw to the soup. In a cast iron dutch oven, heat oil over medium-high heat. Add flour and, using a wire whisk, stir constantly until dark brown roux is achieved. Add onions and bell pepper. Saute 3–5 minutes or until vegetables are wilted. Add water, one ladle at a time, until all is incorporated. Add crab boil, bring to a rolling boil and reduce to simmer. Cook approximately 45 minutes. Add okra and half of the shrimp. Continue cooking 30–45 minutes. Add more water as necessary to retain volume. Season to taste using salt, pepper and hot sauce. Add remaining shrimp and cook 3–5 minutes or until shrimp are pink and curled. Often, people like boiled eggs in their Shrimp and Okra Gumbo. If you do, drop the eggs into the soup. After 15 minutes, remove, peel and place whole eggs back into the pot. Serve gumbo over a bowl of steamed white rice.

"When I was a little girl, my father fell ill, and my grandmother, Enola Plaisance, came to live with us so that mom could run the family bakery. Maw Maw Plaisance not only ran the house and did the chores, but was always busy in the kitchen cooking. Of all her dishes, her shrimp and okra gumbo was my favorite.

"When I was eleven, I broke my arm and had to be hospitalized in traction. One day, as a treat, my mother brought me a thermos of Maw Maw's gumbo. Since I couldn't sit up in bed to eat it, the nurse brought me a straw. Now, eating gumbo with a straw is not easy, but I managed to get down almost every bit!

"To this day, I can think of nothing better than Maw Maw's gumbo. And though I've been cooking gumbo myself for a long time, it never seems quite the equal of hers. Maw Maw always said that the secret is long, slow cooking. But I think the love she put into the pot is what made it special."

Rachel Daigle
Gray, Louisiana

❋Nutrition Facts...then❋

Calories: 392
Total Fat: 18gm
Saturated Fat: 3gm
% Calories from Fat: 43
Cholesterol: 331mg
Sodium: 540mg
Carbohydrate: 17gm
Fiber: 1gm
Protein: 39gm

PREP TIME: 2 Hours   SERVES: 8

☞ INGREDIENTS:

2 pounds (50–60 count) shrimp, peeled and deveined
3 cups sliced okra
1/2 cup oil-less roux
1 cup hot water
2 tbsps vegetable oil
2 cups diced onions
1 cup diced bell pepper
2 1/2 quarts hot water
1 drop liquid crab boil
salt substitute
black pepper
hot sauce

☞ METHOD:

Dissolve oil-less roux in the cup of water. Set aside.

In a cast iron dutch oven, heat oil over medium-high heat. Add onions and bell pepper. Saute 3–5 minutes or until vegetables are wilted. Add water/roux mixture and remaining water, one ladle at a time, until all is incorporated. Add crab boil, bring to a rolling boil and reduce to simmer. Cook approximately 45 minutes.

Add okra and half of the shrimp. Continue cooking 30–45 minutes. Add more water as necessary to retain volume. Season to taste using salt substitute, pepper and hot sauce.

Add remaining shrimp and cook 3–5 minutes or until shrimp are pink and curled. Serve gumbo over a bowl of steamed white rice.

Nutrition Facts...now

Calories:	222
Total Fat:	6gm
Saturated Fat:	1gm
% Calories from Fat:	23
Cholesterol:	169mg
Sodium:	201mg
Carbohydrate:	16gm
Fiber:	1gm
Protein:	26gm

Chef's Tips on Fat... look for beef labeled "USDA Select" grade. It's lower in fat and calories than "Choice" or "Prime."

PREP TIME: 2 1/2 Hours   SERVES: 8

☞ **INGREDIENTS:**

1 (3-pound) baking hen	2 cups chopped onions
1 pound smoked sausage	1 cup chopped celery
1 cup oil	1 cup chopped bell pepper
1 cup flour	3 quarts chicken stock

1 cup sliced green onions	hot sauce
1/2 cup chopped parsley	2 tbsps filé
1 tsp salt	
black pepper	

☞ **METHOD:**

Cut hen into 8 or 10 serving pieces, depending on the size. Slice smoked sausage into 1/2-inch thick pieces. In a cast iron dutch oven, heat cooking oil over medium-high heat. Add flour and, using a wire whisk, stir constantly until dark brown roux is achieved. Add onions, celery and bell pepper. Saute 3–5 minutes or until vegetables are wilted. Add chicken and smoked sausage, blending well into roux mixture. Slowly add stock, one ladle at a time, until all is incorporated. Bring to a rolling boil, reduce heat to simmer and cook approximately 2 hours. Add stock as necessary to retain volume. Once chicken is tender, add green onions and parsley. Season to taste using salt, pepper and hot sauce. When done, remove from heat and stir in filé powder. A large hen usually releases a considerable amount of oil which rises to the surface during the cooking process. Remove the oil by skimming the surface with a ladle. Serve over a bowl of steamed white rice.

"This is a very old recipe, dating back at least to my grandmother, who lived to be 98. Some of my fondest childhood memories are of sitting on the front porch of my grandmother's bayou-side home in Larose, watching the tugboats while waiting for a pot of her gumbo to finish cooking.

"My maiden name was Schouest, one of those names that have undergone quite a change down here in the bayou country. It was originally the German name Schweitzer, and my 18th Century ancestors were hoodwinked into coming here by a rascal named John Law, who worked for the King of France and recruited German settlers to come to the wilderness that Louisiana then was.

"Tradition has it that the name changed from Schweitzer to Schouest because the French and Spanish-speaking priests who enrolled them in the parish records didn't understand German, and modified it to suit their own language. There are two spellings of the name - Schouest and Chouest. Some claim that if the enrolling priest was Spanish, he kept the 'S', and dropped it if he was French."

Carol LeBlanc
Raceland, Louisiana

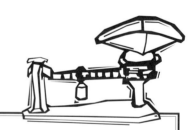

❊Nutrition Facts...then❊

Calories:	687
Total Fat:	52gm
Saturated Fat:	12gm
% Calories from Fat:	67
Cholesterol:	94mg
Sodium:	2015mg
Carbohydrate:	20gm
Fiber:	2gm
Protein:	36gm

PREP TIME: 2 1/2 Hours   SERVES: 8

☞ INGREDIENTS:

1 (3-pound) baking hen, fat and skin removed
1 pound low-fat smoked sausage
1 cup oil-less roux
2 cups defatted chicken stock, unsalted
1/4 cup oil
2 cups chopped onions
1 cup chopped celery
1 cup chopped bell pepper
3 quarts defatted chicken stock, unsalted
1 cup sliced green onions
1/2 cup chopped parsley
salt substitute
black pepper
hot sauce
2 tbsps filé

☞ METHOD:

Cut hen into 8 or 10 serving pieces, depending on the size. Slice smoked sausage into 1/2-inch thick pieces. Dissolve oil-less roux in 2 cups of chicken stock. Set aside.

In a cast iron dutch oven, heat cooking oil over medium-high heat. Add onions, celery and bell pepper. Saute 3–5 minutes or until vegetables are wilted.

Add chicken and smoked sausage. Slowly add roux/stock mixture and remaining stock, one ladle at a time, until all is incorporated. Bring to a rolling boil, reduce heat to simmer and cook approximately 2 hours. Add stock as necessary to retain volume.

Once chicken is tender, add green onions and parsley. Season to taste using salt substitute, pepper and hot sauce. When done, remove from heat and stir in filé powder.

A large hen usually releases a considerable amount of oil which rises to the surface during the cooking process. Remove the oil by skimming the surface with a ladle. Serve over a bowl of steamed white rice.

Nutrition Facts...now

Calories:	429
Total Fat:	23gm
Saturated Fat:	2gm
% Calories from Fat:	47
Cholesterol:	54mg
Sodium:	653mg
Carbohydrate:	21gm
Fiber:	2gm
Protein:	37gm

PREP TIME: 1 1/2 Hours   SERVES: 6

☞ INGREDIENTS:

1 (3-pound) chicken
1/4 cup oil
1/2 cup chopped onion
2 1/2 cups cold water
1/4 cup chopped parsley
1/2 cup chopped celery
1/4 cup sliced green onion tops
1/4 cup finely chopped bell pepper
1 gallon hot water
1/2 cup oil
1/2 cup flour
1 tsp salt
black pepper
hot sauce
1 tsp fresh filé

☞ METHOD:

Cut chicken into 8 serving pieces. In a cast iron dutch oven, heat 1/4 cup of oil over medium-high heat. Add onions and saute until lightly browned. Add 2 1/2 cups of water, parsley, celery, green onions and bell pepper. Bring to a rolling boil, reduce to simmer and cook 30 minutes. Add chicken and simmer 3–5 minutes. Add 1 gallon hot water. Bring to a rolling boil, reduce to simmer and cook 45 minutes. In an 8-inch cast iron skillet, heat 1/2 cup of oil over medium-high heat. Add flour and, using a wire whisk, stir constantly until dark brown roux is achieved. Once chicken is tender, add the roux to the boiling chicken mixture. Blend well into soup and allow to cook 5–10 additional minutes. Season to taste using salt, pepper and hot sauce. Remove gumbo from heat and allow oil to rise to the surface. Using a ladle, skim off any excess fat. Finish with gumbo filé. Serve over steamed white rice.

"This is a very well-known gumbo in the Montegut area. My mother was a school lunchroom manager for 30 years, and this was her "special occasions" recipe for the staff or whatever.

"Mother went to school in a two-room schoolhouse as a child, but had to quit after the eighth grade because there was no bus. After time out to marry, care for a husband and five kids and hold down a full-time job, she went back and got her GED - the only one of six children to do so. Now that's putting a value on education!"

Mrs. Walterine D. Brunet
Montegut, Louisiana

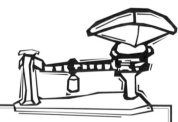

❖Nutrition Facts...then❖

Calories: 442
Total Fat: 33gm
Saturated Fat: 5gm
% Calories from Fat: 68
Cholesterol: 72mg
Sodium: 434mg
Carbohydrate: 10gm
Fiber: 1gm
Protein: 25gm

PREP TIME: 1 1/2 Hours   SERVES: 6

☞ INGREDIENTS:

1 (3-pound) chicken, skin and fat removed
2 tbsps oil
1/2 cup chopped onion
2 1/2 cups cold water
1/4 cup chopped parsley
1/2 cup chopped celery
1/4 cup sliced green onion tops
1/4 cup finely chopped bell pepper
1/2 cup oil-less roux
1 gallon hot water
1/4 tsp salt
black pepper
hot sauce
1 tsp fresh filé

☞ METHOD:

Cut chicken into 8 serving pieces. In a cast iron dutch oven, heat oil over medium-high heat. Add onions and saute until lightly browned. Add 2 1/2 cups of water, parsley celery, green onions and bell pepper. Bring to a rolling boil, reduce to simmer and cook 30 minutes.

Add chicken and simmer 3–5 minutes. Dissolve oil-less roux with 1 cup of hot water. Set aside. Add remainder of hot water to pot. Bring to a rolling boil, reduce to simmer and cook 30 minutes.

Once chicken is tender, add the roux/water mixture to the boiled chicken mixture. Blend well into soup and allow to cook 5–10 additional minutes. Season to taste using salt, pepper and hot sauce.

Remove gumbo from heat and allow oil to rise to the surface. Using a ladle, skim off any excess fat. Finish with gumbo filé. Serve over steamed white rice.

Nutrition Facts...now

Calories:	281
Total Fat:	15gm
Saturated Fat:	3gm
% Calories from Fat:	49
Cholesterol:	72mg
Sodium:	167mg
Carbohydrate:	10gm
Fiber:	1gm
Protein:	25gm

Chef's Tips on Low Fat...
when roasting or baking, roast meat on a rack to allow fat to drip.

PREP TIME: 1 Hour   SERVES: 6

☞ INGREDIENTS:

1 cup chopped clam meat with juices
1 pound jumbo lump crabmeat
2 cups water
1 cup diced potatoes
1/2 cup melted butter
2 cups chopped onions
1 cup chopped celery
1 cup chopped bell pepper
1 tbsp chopped parsley
1/4 cup sliced green onions
1 (10-ounce) can cream of mushroom soup
1 (12-ounce) can evaporated milk
1 tsp salt
black pepper
hot sauce
6 pats of butter

☞ METHOD:

In a 2-quart sauce pot over medium-high heat, place water and potatoes. Boil 15–20 minutes or until potatoes are tender but not overcooked. Drain, cool and set aside. In a cast iron dutch oven, heat butter over medium-high heat. Add onions, celery and bell pepper. Saute 3–5 minutes or until vegetables are wilted. Add clams with juice and heat 5 additional minutes. Add crabmeat, parsley, green onions, potatoes, soup and milk. Bring mixture to a low boil and reduce to simmer, stirring constantly. Season to taste using salt, pepper and hot sauce. Cook 10–15 minutes. Ladle chowder into 6 serving bowls and top each with 1 pat of cold butter. Serve immediately.

"You don't see many Cajun recipes built around clams. Clams down here tend to be small and not very good - though they're numerous enough in some areas that their shells are used for paving.

"But about 20 years ago we were trawling for shrimp in an area called California Cut on Lake Pelto. On a test throw right close to shore, our nets brought up two very large clams with grayish-black shells and meat that was bright orange - almost tangerine colored.

"Well, it was time for supper, so we added the clams to our crab and potato chowder. The result was such a hit that every time we go out shrimping in the Bayou Round area we pass by California Cut to collect enough clams for another chowder. If you don't have a shallow-draft trawler or know where California Cut is (it isn't on any map), you can use the store-bought variety of clams.

"Be careful adding salt. Clams, like oysters, can be pretty salty."
Charles E. Madere
Theriot, Louisiana

❧Nutrition Facts...then❧

Calories: 494
Total Fat: 35gm
Saturated Fat: 20gm
% Calories from Fat: 63
Cholesterol: 180mg
Sodium: 1349mg
Carbohydrate: 23gm
Fiber: 0gm
Protein: 23gm

PREP TIME: 1 Hour   SERVES: 6

☞ INGREDIENTS:

1 cup chopped clam meat with juices
1 pound jumbo lump crabmeat
2 cups water
1 cup diced potatoes
2 tbsps lite margarine
2 cups chopped onions
1 cup chopped celery
1 cup chopped bell pepper
1 tbsp chopped parsley
1/4 cup sliced green onions
1 (10-ounce) can reduced-fat cream of
        mushroom soup
1 (12-ounce) can evaporated skim milk
salt substitute
black pepper
hot sauce

☞ METHOD:

In a 2-quart sauce pot over medium-high heat, place water and potatoes. Boil 15–20 minutes or until potatoes are tender but not overcooked. Drain, cool and set aside.

In a cast iron dutch oven, heat margarine over medium-high heat. Add onions, celery and bell pepper. Saute 3–5 minutes or until vegetables are wilted.

Add clams with juice and heat 5 additional minutes. Add crabmeat, parsley, green onions, potatoes, soup and skim milk. Bring mixture to a low boil and reduce to simmer, stirring constantly. Season to taste using salt substitute, pepper and hot sauce. Cook 10–15 minutes.

Ladle chowder into 6 serving bowls. Serve immediately.

Nutrition Facts...now

Calories:	249
Total Fat:	6gm
Saturated Fat:	1gm
% Calories from Fat:	22
Cholesterol:	92mg
Sodium:	637mg
Carbohydrate:	25gm
Fiber:	0gm
Protein:	24gm

Arna Spears passes some time on Bayou Lafourche beneath Highway 90 at Raceland.

PREP TIME: 30 Minutes   SERVES: 4

☞ INGREDIENTS:

1 1/2 pounds (70–90 count) shrimp,
     peeled and deveined
6 potatoes, cubed
2 tsps oil
1 cup diced onions
1 1/2 quarts shrimp stock
1/4 cup sliced green onions
1 tbsp chopped parsley
1 tsp salt
black pepper
hot sauce

☞ METHOD:

In a large cast iron dutch oven, heat oil over medium-high heat. Add onions and saute until golden brown, stirring constantly. Add stock, potatoes and green onions. Bring to a rolling boil, reduce to simmer and cook until potatoes become so tender some are dissolved to thicken the stock. Add shrimp and parsley. Cook 5–10 additional minutes or until shrimp are pink and curled. Season to taste using salt, pepper and hot sauce.

"When I was growing up, my father had a shrimp drying platform right on the edge of the Gulf of Mexico. The shrimpers would sell him their catch because it saved them from having to come in for ice in order to keep their shrimp fresh on the trip back up the bayou.

"We would boil the shrimp, then spread them out on the platform to dry in the sun. The five of us kids had the job of turning the shrimp so they dried evenly. It took a day or two in the sun for them to dry. We covered them with tarps at night, or if it rained. Once they were dry, we'd shell them in a mechanical beater.

"We sold them to food processors from New Orleans. People bought them for gumbo and jambalaya, or omelets.

"After I married, my husband and I had our own shrimp drying business for nearly eight years. I know of at least one shrimp dryer still in operation, at the end of the bayou at Cocodrie. But now they dry them in ovens."

Elaine Lapeyrouse
Chauvin, Louisiana

❧Nutrition Facts...then❧

Calories: 640
Total Fat: 6gm
Saturated Fat: 1gm
% Calories from Fat: 9
Cholesterol: 258mg
Sodium: 815mg
Carbohydrate: 94gm
Fiber: 12gm
Protein: 49gm

PREP TIME: 30 Minutes   SERVES: 4

☞ INGREDIENTS:

1 pound (70–90 count) shrimp,
     peeled and deveined
6 potatoes, cubed
2 tsps oil
1 cup diced onions
1 1/2 quarts defatted shrimp stock, unsalted
1/4 cup sliced green onions
1 tbsp chopped parsley
1/2 tsp salt
black pepper
hot sauce

☞ METHOD:

In a large cast iron dutch oven, heat oil over medium-high heat. Add onions and saute until golden brown, stirring constantly. Add stock, potatoes and green onions. Bring to a rolling boil, reduce to simmer and cook until potatoes become so tender that some are dissolved to thicken the stock.

Add shrimp and parsley. Cook 5–10 additional minutes or until shrimp are pink and curled. Season to taste using salt, pepper and hot sauce.

*Chef's Tips on LowFat...
when boiling or steaming, use water,
defatted stock, wine or skim milk.*

Nutrition Facts...now

Calories:	580
Total Fat:	5gm
Saturated Fat:	1gm
% Calories from Fat:	8
Cholesterol:	172mg
Sodium:	465mg
Carbohydrate:	94gm
Fiber:	12gm
Protein:	38gm

SHRIMP & CORN SOUP

PREP TIME: 1 Hour   SERVES: 8

INGREDIENTS:

1 pound (70–90 count) shrimp, peeled and deveined
4 cups fresh corn
1/2 cup oil
1/2 cup flour
1 cup chopped onion
1/2 cup chopped celery
1/2 cup chopped bell pepper
1/4 cup diced garlic
1 (8-ounce) can tomato sauce
1 quart hot water
1 tsp onion salt
1 tsp salt
black pepper
hot sauce

METHOD:

In a cast iron dutch oven, heat oil over medium-high heat. Add flour and, stirring constantly, cook until flour is tan to light brown in color. Add onions, celery, bell pepper and garlic. Saute 3–5 minutes or until vegetables are wilted. Add corn, tomato sauce and half of the shrimp. Stir until all ingredients are well incorporated. Add water, bring to a rolling boil and reduce heat to simmer. Cook 15–20 minutes, stirring often. Add remaining shrimp and onion salt. Simmer 5 additional minutes or until shrimp are pink and curled. Season to taste using salt, pepper and hot sauce.

Chef's Tips on Low Fat... adapt recipes to use less fat. Consider taste and physical quality of the finished product.

"I was raised in the little community of Donner in Terrebonne Parish, on the road between Houma and Morgan City. That was in the depths of the Depression, and times were as hard there as anywhere, I suppose.

"But we had one advantage. Santa Claus lived in Donner. Actually, his name was Mr. Keller, and he was the rich man in town - rich by comparison to the rest of the town, anyway.

"Every year, Mr. Keller would have a big Christmas tree put up in the little schoolhouse, and all the children in every family in town would be invited, along with their parents, to a big party. And every child would have a present under that tree - a nice present, too.

"That was sixty years ago, and I regret to say I've forgotten Mr. Keller's full name. But I'll remember his generosity as long as I live."

Agnes Breaux (sister's recipe)
Schriever, Louisiana

❧Nutrition Facts...then❧

Calories:	318
Total Fat:	16gm
Saturated Fat:	2gm
% Calories from Fat:	43
Cholesterol:	86mg
Sodium:	862mg
Carbohydrate:	32gm
Fiber:	4gm
Protein:	16gm

SHRIMP & CORN SOUP

PREP TIME: 1 Hour   SERVES: 8

INGREDIENTS:

1 pound (70–90 count) shrimp, peeled and deveined
4 cups fresh corn
2 tbsps oil
1 cup chopped onion
1/2 cup chopped celery
1/2 cup chopped bell pepper
1/4 cup diced garlic
1/2 cup flour
1 (8-ounce) can tomato sauce, no salt added
1 quart hot water
1 tsp onion powder
salt substitute
black pepper
hot sauce

METHOD:

In a cast iron dutch oven, heat oil over medium-high heat. Add onions, celery, bell pepper and garlic. Saute 3–5 minutes or until vegetables are wilted.

Add flour and blend into the vegetable mixture. Add corn, tomato sauce and half of the shrimp. Stir until all ingredients are well incorporated. Add water, bring to a rolling boil and reduce heat to simmer. Cook 15–20 minutes, stirring often.

Add remaining shrimp and onion powder. Simmer 5 additional minutes or until shrimp are pink and curled. Season to taste using salt substitute, pepper and hot sauce.

Crab traps stacked up in Leeville on Bayou Lafourche.

Nutrition Facts...now

Calories: 230
Total Fat: 6gm
Saturated Fat: 1gm
% Calories from Fat: 20
Cholesterol: 86mg
Sodium: 219mg
Carbohydrate: 32gm
Fiber: 4gm
Protein: 16gm

PREP TIME: 1 Hour   SERVES: 8

☞ INGREDIENTS:

1 quart fresh oysters, drained
3 tbsps olive oil
2 cups chopped onions
1 cup chopped celery
1/2 cup chopped bell pepper
1/4 cup diced garlic
1 1/2 cups diced salt meat
1 (8-ounce) can tomato sauce
3 quarts water
1 cup chopped parsley
1/2 cup sliced green onions
2 tbsps Worcestershire Sauce
1/2 pound spaghetti
1 tsp salt
black pepper
hot sauce

☞ METHOD:

In a large cast iron dutch oven, heat olive oil over medium-high heat. Add onions, celery, bell pepper, garlic and salt meat. Saute 3–5 minutes or until vegetables are wilted. Continue to cook until salt meat is light brown, being careful not to scorch vegetables. Reduce heat to medium and add tomato sauce. Stir often until tomato sauce thickens and turns slightly brown, 5–10 minutes. Add oysters, blend well into the vegetable mixture, cover and allow juices to render from the oysters. Add water, parsley, green onions and Worcestershire. Bring to a rolling boil. Reduce to simmer and allow to cook, uncovered, 10–15 minutes. Add spaghetti and stir occasionally until it is tender. Season to taste using salt, pepper and hot sauce. This soup is best when served over saltine crackers.

"Cooking for a Cajun gathering is like being a chef in a restaurant full of food critics. But I've never gotten a bad review on this recipe. It comes from my wife's side of the family, and is only slightly modified from a very old recipe.

"It's our New Year's Day special - a day most folks don't consider as a time for family gatherings. So we started the tradition. We have an intimate little gathering of no more than 50 people or so, counting the kids."
Willis A. Henry
Houma, Louisiana

❖Nutrition Facts...then❖

Calories: 287
Total Fat: 6gm
Saturated Fat: 2gm
% Calories from Fat: 19
Cholesterol: 16mg
Sodium: 1023mg
Carbohydrate: 36gm
Fiber: 2gm
Protein: 22gm

PREP TIME: 1 Hour   SERVES: 8

☞ INGREDIENTS:

1 quart fresh oysters, drained
1 tbsp olive oil
2 cups chopped onions
1 cup chopped celery
1/2 cup chopped bell pepper
1/4 cup diced garlic
1 1/2 cups lean ham, diced
1 (8-ounce) can tomato sauce, no salt added
3 quarts water
1 cup chopped parsley
1/2 cup sliced green onions
2 tbsps Worcestershire Sauce
1/2 pound spaghetti
1/4 tsp salt
black pepper
hot sauce

Chef's Tips on Fat...
herbs and spices add interesting
flavors to foods and help make
fats like margarines, sauces and
gravies unnecessary.

☞ METHOD:

In a large cast iron dutch oven, heat olive oil over medium-high heat. Add onions, celery, bell pepper, garlic and ham. Saute 3–5 minutes or until vegetables are wilted.

Continue to cook until ham is light brown, being careful not to scorch vegetables. Reduce heat to medium and add tomato sauce. Stir often until tomato sauce thickens and turns slightly brown, 5–10 minutes.

Add oysters, blend well into the vegetable mixture, cover and allow juices to render from the oysters. Add water, parsley, green onions and Worcestershire. Bring to a rolling boil. Reduce to simmer and allow to cook, uncovered, 10–15 minutes.

Add spaghetti and stir occasionally until it is tender. Season to taste using salt, pepper and hot sauce. This soup is best when served over unsalted crackers.

Nutrition Facts...now

Calories:	280
Total Fat:	5gm
Saturated Fat:	1gm
% Calories from Fat:	16
Cholesterol:	14mg
Sodium:	582mg
Carbohydrate:	36gm
Fiber:	2gm
Protein:	22gm

CABBAGE & GROUND BEEF SOUP

PREP TIME: 1 1/2 Hours   SERVES: 8

☞ INGREDIENTS:

1 small cabbage, cubed
1 pound ground beef
1 cup chopped onions
1/2 cup chopped bell pepper
1/4 cup diced garlic
1 (5.5-ounce) can tomato juice
1 (10-ounce) can stewed tomatoes
1 (10-ounce) can Rotel tomatoes
3 (20-ounce) cans red kidney beans
1/4 cup white vinegar
1/4 cup sugar
2 cups water
1/2 tsp salt
black pepper
hot sauce

☞ METHOD:

In a cast iron dutch oven, brown ground beef over medium-high heat. Stir constantly to render fat, while chopping to separate the beef grain for grain. When beef is browned, add onions, bell pepper and garlic. Blend well into the meat mixture and cook 5 minutes. Add tomato juice, stewed tomatoes and Rotel tomatoes. Bring to a rolling boil and reduce to simmer. Add beans, vinegar, sugar and cabbage. Blend well into the mixture, add water and continue cooking, approximately 30 minutes. Season to taste using salt, pepper and hot sauce.

A May day on Bayou Lafourche. The St. Joseph is freshly painted while a young summer garden takes root behind a metal shed.

"Every good recipe doesn't have to be generations old. The inspiration for this one was a cabbage and ground beef soup they serve at Shoney's! I don't know where they got it. Who knows, perhaps it does go back to someone's grandmother - somewhere.
"Oh, well. Now it's going to be handed down in my family, so if it wasn't originally an old family recipe, it eventually will be!"
Brenda Brunet
Montegut, Louisiana

❋Nutrition Facts...then❋

Calories: 464
Total Fat: 14gm
Saturated Fat: 5gm
% Calories from Fat: 26
Cholesterol: 41mg
Sodium: 1314mg
Carbohydrate: 59gm
Fiber: 17gm
Protein: 29gm

CABBAGE & GROUND BEEF SOUP

PREP TIME: 1 1/2 Hours   SERVES: 8

☞ INGREDIENTS:

1 small cabbage, cubed
1 pound ground beef, extra lean
1 cup chopped onions
1/2 cup chopped bell pepper
1/4 cup diced garlic

1 (5.5-ounce) can tomato juice, no salt added
1 (10-ounce) can stewed tomatoes, no salt added
1 (10-ounce) can Rotel tomatoes
3 (20-ounce) cans red kidney beans
1/4 cup white vinegar

1/4 cup sugar
2 cups water
1/4 tsp salt
black pepper
hot sauce

☞ METHOD:

In a cast iron dutch oven, brown ground beef over medium-high heat. Stir constantly to render fat, while chopping to separate the beef grain for grain.

When beef is browned, drain fat then add onions, bell pepper and garlic. Blend well into the meat mixture and cook 5 minutes. Add tomato juice, stewed tomatoes and Rotel tomatoes. Bring to a rolling boil and reduce to simmer.

Add beans, vinegar, sugar and cabbage. Blend well into the mixture, add water and continue cooking, approximately 30 minutes. Season to taste using salt, pepper and hot sauce.

Completed in 1859, the courthouse of St. Martinville appears here in its original color.

Nutrition Facts...now

Calories:	384
Total Fat:	9gm
Saturated Fat:	3gm
% Calories from Fat:	19
Cholesterol:	35mg
Sodium:	887mg
Carbohydrate:	56gm
Fiber:	17gm
Protein:	25gm

*Chef's Tips on LowFat...
when sauteing, use stock,
vegetable or fruit juices, or wine.*

VEGETABLE BEEF SOUP

PREP TIME: 2 1/2 Hours   SERVES: 8

INGREDIENTS:

1 (4 pound) beef brisket, cubed
2 cups chopped onions
1 cup chopped celery
1 gallon water
1 cup sliced carrots
1 cup diced turnips
1 (12-ounce) can whole tomatoes, drained
1 cup diced potatoes
1 (8-ounce) can mixed vegetables
1 tsp salt
black pepper
hot sauce
2 ounces spaghetti
1/2 head cabbage, shredded

METHOD:

In a large cast iron dutch oven, place brisket, onions and celery. Add water, bring to a rolling boil and reduce to simmer. Cook until brisket is tender, approximately 1 1/2 hours. Add carrots, turnips, tomatoes, potatoes and mixed vegetables. Continue to simmer 30 additional minutes. Add water to retain volume as necessary. Season to taste using salt, pepper and hot sauce. Break spaghetti in half and add to the pot with cabbage. Continue to cook until spaghetti is tender, approximately 10–12 minutes. Adjust seasonings, if necessary.

"No, beef isn't very common in Cajun recipes, I guess because beef was a luxury for us bayou folks. We had pigs and chickens and a garden, but we didn't have cows.

"The butcher came down Big Bayou Black (where we lived) twice a week from Morgan City. He'd take our order on the first visit and bring back the meat on the second. In our case, if we ordered anything at all, it was usually a soup bone, which cost a quarter. Doesn't sound like much now. Daddy was making 90 cents a day working on a farm, so that was like prime steak prices to us. Of course, a soup bone in those days had a lot more meat on it than it does today, and a good thing it did, since there were nine of us in the family - my parents, five girls and two boys."

Marjorie Domangue
Houma, Louisiana

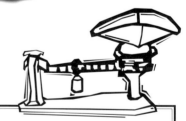

❊Nutrition Facts...then❊

Calories:	1148
Total Fat:	72gm
Saturated Fat:	29gm
% Calories from Fat:	58
Cholesterol:	301mg
Sodium:	694mg
Carbohydrate:	26gm
Fiber:	5gm
Protein:	92gm

VEGETABLE BEEF SOUP

PREP TIME: 2 1/2 Hours   SERVES: 8

☞ **INGREDIENTS:**

2 1/2 pounds lean round steak, cubed
2 cups chopped onions
1 cup chopped celery
1 gallon water
1 cup sliced carrots
1 cup diced turnips
1 (12-ounce) can whole tomatoes, drained,
        no salt added
1 cup diced potatoes
1 (8-ounce) can mixed vegetables
1/2 tsp salt
black pepper
hot sauce
2 ounces spaghetti
1/2 head cabbage, shredded

☞ **METHOD:**

In a large cast iron dutch oven, place round steak, onions and celery. Add water, bring to a rolling boil and reduce to simmer. Cook until steak is tender, approximately 1 1/2 hours.

Add carrots, turnips, tomatoes, potatoes and mixed vegetables. Continue to simmer 30 additional minutes. Add water to retain volume as necessary. Season to taste using salt, pepper and hot sauce.

Break spaghetti in half and add to the pot with cabbage. Continue to cook until spaghetti is tender, approximately 10–12 minutes. Adjust seasonings, if necessary.

Nutrition Facts...now

Calories: 392
Total Fat: 9gm
Saturated Fat: 3gm
% Calories from Fat: 22
Cholesterol: 119mg
Sodium: 334mg
Carbohydrate: 26gm
Fiber: 5gm
Protein: 49gm

Misty morning in the Manchac Swamp.

PREP TIME: 1 1/2 Hours   SERVES: 8

☞ INGREDIENTS:

3 pounds chicken gizzards	1 1/2 tsps onion powder
5 bay leaves	1 1/2 tsps dried thyme leaves
2 tsps white pepper	1 tsp dry mustard
1 tbsp salt	1 tsp black pepper
1 3/4 tsps garlic powder	1 tsp dried basil
1 3/4 tsps cayenne pepper	1/2 tsp ground cumin

1/2 cup butter	1 tbsp chopped garlic
1/2 pound chopped spinach	3 quarts beef stock
2 cups chopped onions	1 cup chopped parsley
1 cup chopped celery	1/4 cup minced lemon peel
2/3 cup flour	1/3 cup sherry
4 (8-ounce) cans tomato sauce	6 hard-boiled eggs

☞ METHOD:

Wash gizzards well and grind through the chili blade of your meat grinder. Create a seasoning mix by combining bay leaves, white pepper, salt, garlic powder, cayenne, onion powder, thyme, dry mustard, black pepper, basil and cumin. Mix thoroughly and set aside. In a cast iron dutch oven, melt butter over medium-high heat. Add ground gizzards and cook 8–10 minutes or until golden brown. Blend in the seasoning mix, spinach, onions and celery. Stir well to incorporate and cook 10–15 minutes. Sprinkle in flour, add tomato sauce and blend well. Using a wire whisk, whip until all is incorporated. Add garlic and 2–3 cups of the beef stock, blending well to dissolve any mixture that may have stuck to the bottom of the pot. Add remaining stock, bring to a rolling boil and reduce to simmer. Cook 45 minutes, stirring occasionally. Add parsley and lemon, blending well. Remove and discard the bay leaves. Add sherry. Slice eggs into 1/8–1/4 inch pieces and place in the soup prior to serving.

"This is a wonderful, low-cost alternative to turtle soup - which is just what it tastes like. Gizzards have the same texture as turtle meat, especially if they're cooked in a Cajun 'microwave' - a box made of thick wooden planks with a metal pan on top in which charcoal is burned. It cooks slowly at a temperature of about 250 degrees, and makes the meat very tender.

"We can claim something that even most folks around here can't - our house is built on oyster shells. Our lot was once part of a canal that was filled in with oyster shells - a fill 20 feet deep and 50 feet wide. That will give you some idea just how big oystering is around here - and has been for generations. When we were growing up, we would hail oyster boats coming back up the bayou around Bourg and buy an apple crate full of oysters for a quarter."
Helen and Leonard Hendricks
Houma, Louisiana

❧ Nutrition Facts...then ❧

Calories:	465
Total Fat:	20gm
Saturated Fat:	10gm
% Calories from Fat:	41
Cholesterol:	384mg
Sodium:	4819mg
Carbohydrate:	26gm
Fiber:	6gm
Protein:	37gm

PREP TIME: 1 1/2 Hours SERVES: 8

☞ INGREDIENTS:

1 pound chicken gizzards
1 pound ground turkey
5 bay leaves
2 tsps white pepper
salt substitute
1 3/4 tsps garlic powder
1 3/4 tsps cayenne pepper
1 1/2 tsps onion powder
1 1/2 tsps dried thyme leaves
1 tsp dry mustard
1 tsp black pepper
1 tsp dried basil
1/2 tsp ground cumin
1 tbsp lite margarine
1/2 pound chopped spinach
2 cups chopped onions
1 cup chopped celery
2/3 cup flour
4 (8-ounce) cans tomato sauce, no salt added
1 tbsp chopped garlic
3 quarts defatted beef stock, unsalted
1 cup chopped parsley
1/4 cup minced lemon peel
1/3 cup sherry
6 hard-boiled eggs, only 2 yolks

☞ METHOD:

Wash gizzards well and grind through the chili blade of your meat grinder.

Create a seasoning mix by combining bay leaves, white pepper, salt substitute, garlic powder, cayenne, onion powder, thyme, dry mustard, black pepper, basil and cumin. Mix thoroughly and set aside.

In a cast iron dutch oven, melt margarine over medium-high heat. Add ground gizzards and turkey. Cook 8–10 minutes or until golden brown. Blend in the seasoning mix, spinach, onions and celery. Stir well to incorporate and cook 10–15 minutes.

Sprinkle in flour, add tomato sauce and blend well. Using a wire whisk, whip until all is incorporated. Add garlic and 2–3 cups of the beef stock, blending well to dissolve any mixture that may have stuck to the bottom of the pot. Add remaining stock, bring to a rolling boil and reduce to simmer. Cook 45 minutes, stirring occasionally.

Add parsley and lemon, blending well. Remove and discard the bay leaves. Add sherry. Slice eggs and egg whites into 1/8–1/4 inch pieces and place in the soup prior to serving.

Nutrition Facts...now

Calories:	336
Total Fat:	9gm
Saturated Fat:	3gm
% Calories from Fat:	25
Cholesterol:	146mg
Sodium:	306mg
Carbohydrate:	25gm
Fiber:	6gm
Protein:	34gm

CREAM OF SWEET PEA SOUP

PREP TIME: 30 Minutes   SERVES: 6

☞ INGREDIENTS:

2 cups half and half
1 (17-ounce) can sweet peas, drained
1 tbsp flour
2 tbsps margarine
1/4 cup diced onions
1/4 tsp sugar
1/4 tsp salt
black pepper
hot sauce

A vintage neon sign advertises rooms and the king crop of Crowley.

☞ METHOD:

Place all ingredients in the bowl of a food processor fitted with a metal blade. Process on high until smooth and creamy. Pour contents into a double boiler and cook over medium-high heat, stirring occasionally for 10–15 minutes. Season to taste using salt, pepper and hot sauce. You may wish to enhance this soup by adding 1/2 cup of minced, sugar-cured ham or by garnishing the finished product with jumbo lump crabmeat.

"This soup recipe is very special because it was part of my life as I was growing up here in Raceland. I was the youngest of six children and would help my mother shell the peas from our garden. Everyone around here had gardens then, and many people still do. It's just the way we live in this part of the country.

"In my family, soups and gumbos were eaten mostly during the winter months. They were served as an extra dish at mealtime. I kept this tradition when I married and had two children of my own. I've been a widow for the past twenty-eight years but still enjoy making this soup for my son, daughter and their families.

"Some things never get outdated and this recipe is one of them. It can become a part of your family tradition just as it is for mine. Enjoy it! We do!"

Yvonne Falgout
Raceland, Louisiana

❧ Nutrition Facts...then ❧

Calories:	202
Total Fat:	13gm
Saturated Fat:	7gm
% Calories from Fat:	58
Cholesterol:	30mg
Sodium:	345mg
Carbohydrate:	16gm
Fiber:	1gm
Protein:	6gm

CREAM OF SWEET PEA SOUP

PREP TIME: 30 Minutes   SERVES: 6

Hartman LeJeune carries on his family tradition, baking French bread in Jeanerette.

☞ INGREDIENTS:

2 cups evaporated skim milk
1 (17-ounce) can sweet peas, drained
1 tbsp flour
1 tbsp lite margarine
1/4 cup diced onions
1/4 tsp sugar
salt substitute
black pepper
hot sauce

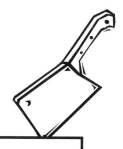

☞ METHOD:

Place all ingredients in the bowl of a food processor fitted with a metal blade. Process on high until smooth and creamy.

Pour contents into a double boiler and cook over medium-high heat, stirring occasionally for 10–15 minutes.

Season to taste using salt substitute, pepper and hot sauce.

You may wish to enhance this soup by adding 1/2 cup of minced, sugar-cured ham or by garnishing the finished product with jumbo lump crabmeat.

Nutrition Facts...now

Calories:	139
Total Fat:	1gm
Saturated Fat:	0gm
% Calories from Fat:	9
Cholesterol:	3mg
Sodium:	300mg
Carbohydrate:	22gm
Fiber:	1gm
Protein:	10gm

PREP TIME: 1 1/2 Hours   SERVES: 8

☞ INGREDIENTS:

4 cups fresh corn
1 cup fresh lima beans
2 cups chopped tomatoes
1/4 cup bacon fat
2 cups diced onions
1/2 pound ham, cubed
1 (8-ounce) can tomato sauce
2 quarts beef stock
1 tsp salt
black pepper
hot sauce

☞ METHOD:

In a cast iron dutch oven, heat bacon fat over medium-high heat. Add onions and ham. Saute 3–5 minutes or until vegetables are wilted. Add corn, beans and tomatoes, blending well into onion mixture. Add tomato sauce and beef stock, one ladle at a time. Bring to a rolling boil, reduce to simmer and cook for 1 hour. Season to taste using salt, pepper and hot sauce.

"My mother died when I was five and my brother and I were raised by our grandmother, Ernestine Breaux, who had five children of her own. My father drove a Greyhound bus, and we spent most of my growing-up years on a sugar cane farm.

"Like all rural families, our diet consisted almost entirely of what we could raise. We had a big garden, and fresh vegetables were the mainstay of our diet.

"The stock for Grandma's succotash soup was usually from a soup bone, one of the few instances in which fresh meat was part of our diet. Pickled pork and salt meat were more common, since they were cheap and kept well without refrigeration - which we didn't have, in those days.

"Every home had one room which was cooler than the others. In our house that was Grandma's bedroom, and that's where the perishable foods were kept.

"Grandma Breaux baked her bread in a wood stove that had a large reservoir on the back for heating water. I remember she tested the temperature of the oven by putting her hand inside. My job during the baking was bringing in the wood to fire the stove, on which we also heated the flatirons we used to iron clothes."

June Breaux Green
Houma, Louisiana

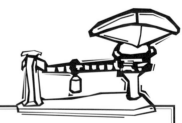

❧Nutrition Facts...then❧

Calories: 192
Total Fat: 10gm
Saturated Fat: 4gm
% Calories from Fat:................. 50
Cholesterol: 22mg
Sodium: 2830mg
Carbohydrate: 14gm
Fiber: 3gm
Protein: 8gm

PREP TIME: 1 1/2 Hours   SERVES: 8

☞ **INGREDIENTS:**

4 cups fresh corn
1 cup fresh lima beans
2 cups chopped tomatoes
2 tbsps oil
2 cups diced onions
1/2 pound lean ham, cubed
1 (8-ounce) can tomato sauce, no salt added
2 quarts defatted beef stock, unsalted
salt substitute
black pepper
hot sauce

☞ **METHOD:**

In a cast iron dutch oven, heat oil over medium-high heat. Add onions and ham. Saute 3–5 minutes or until vegetables are wilted.

Add corn, beans and tomatoes, blending well into onion mixture. Add tomato sauce and beef stock, one ladle at a time. Bring to a rolling boil, reduce to simmer and cook for 1 hour.

Season to taste using salt substitute, pepper and hot sauce.

Nutrition Facts...now

Calories: 141
Total Fat: 5gm
Saturated Fat: 1gm
% Calories from Fat: 28
Cholesterol: 14mg
Sodium: 325mg
Carbohydrate: 14gm
Fiber: 3gm
Protein: 12gm

PREP TIME: 1 1/2 Hours   SERVES: 8

☞ INGREDIENTS:

1 pound dried navy beans
1 cup chopped onions
1/2 cup chopped celery
1 cup diced tomatoes
1 cup diced potatoes
1 cup chopped cabbage
1/2 cup elbow macaroni
2 cups diced ham
1/2 cup sliced green onions
1/4 cup chopped parsley
1 tsp salt
black pepper
hot sauce

☞ METHOD:

Rinse the beans under cold running water. You may wish to soak the beans in cold water overnight to cut the cooking time by one-third. Place beans in a large cast iron dutch oven and cover by 2 inches with cold water. Bring to a rolling boil and reduce heat to simmer. Cook approximately 1 hour or until beans are tender, stirring occasionally. Add onions, celery, tomatoes, potatoes, cabbage, macaroni and ham. Blend well into the bean mixture and cook 20–30 minutes, stirring occasionally. You may need to add water to retain desired consistency. Add green onions and parsley. Season to taste using salt, pepper and hot sauce.

NOTE: When stirring beans during the cooking process, mash approximately 50% of the beans, pressing with the cooking spoon against the inside of the pot. This will give the navy bean soup a creamy consistency.

"Since my grandmother and mother were unable to read or write, recipes would have been of little use to them. So they cooked the way people before them had cooked, back to the dawn of time, I suppose. They cooked from memory.

"When you think about it, that's really quite a skill. You have to remember every ingredient of a recipe and how the end product tastes. It also means keeping a mental catalog of herbs and spices and their effects on flavor so accurate that you can add the proper amount without resorting to measuring spoons or cups.

"Of course, after a while everyone learns to cook their favorite dishes from memory - as I do this one. But imagine having to do it every time!

"This, by the way, is the 'special' version of mom's soup - the one she fixed as a treat when we had leftover ham. In the everyday version, she used salt meat."

Joyce B. Russell
Morgan City, Louisiana

❧Nutrition Facts...then❧

Calories: 189
Total Fat: 3gm
Saturated Fat: 1gm
% Calories from Fat: 12
Cholesterol: 19mg
Sodium: 747mg
Carbohydrate: 26gm
Fiber: 5gm
Protein: 16gm

PREP TIME: 1 1/2 Hours   SERVES: 8

☞ **INGREDIENTS:**

1 pound dried navy beans
1 cup chopped onions
1/2 cup chopped celery
1 cup diced tomatoes
1 cup diced potatoes
1 cup chopped cabbage
1/2 cup elbow macaroni
2 cups lean ham, diced
1/2 cup sliced green onions
1/4 cup chopped parsley
1/4 tsp salt
black pepper
hot sauce

*Chef's Tips on LowFat...
marinate less tender cuts of
meat in lite Italian dressing.*

☞ **METHOD:**

Rinse the beans under cold running water. You may wish to soak the beans in cold water overnight to cut the cooking time by one-third.

Place beans in a large cast iron dutch oven and cover by 2 inches with cold water. Bring to a rolling boil and reduce heat to simmer. Cook approximately 1 hour or until beans are tender, stirring occasionally.

Add onions, celery, tomatoes, potatoes, cabbage, macaroni and ham. Blend well into the bean mixture and cook 20–30 minutes, stirring occasionally. You may need to add water to retain desired consistency. Add green onions and parsley. Season to taste using salt, pepper and hot sauce.

NOTE: When stirring beans during the cooking process, mash approximately 50% of the beans, pressing with the cooking spoon against the inside of the pot. This will give the navy bean soup a creamy consistency.

Nutrition Facts...now

Calories:	189
Total Fat:	3gm
Saturated Fat:	1gm
% Calories from Fat:	12
Cholesterol:	19mg
Sodium:	547mg
Carbohydrate:	26gm
Fiber:	5gm
Protein:	16gm

A Second Line parade for the Zulu Social Aid and Pleasure Club passes by The Crustacean's Restaurant, Orleans Avenue, New Orleans.

MIRLITON SOUP

PREP TIME: 1 1/2 Hours   SERVES: 6

☞ INGREDIENTS:

12 mirlitons
2 pounds (70–90 count) shrimp, peeled and deveined
1/2 cup butter
2 cups diced onions
1 cup diced celery
1/2 cup sliced green onions
1/4 cup diced garlic
3/4 cup flour
3 quarts chicken stock
1 cup sliced mushrooms
1 tsp salt
black pepper
hot sauce
1 cup half and half
1/2 cup chopped parsley

☞ METHOD:

Slice mirlitons lengthwise and boil in lightly salted water until tender but not overcooked. Remove from heat and cool under tap water. Peel, remove seeds and dice into 1/4-inch cubes. Reserve approximately 1 cup of the cubes. Mash the remaining mirlitons or puree in a food processor. Set aside. In a cast iron dutch oven, heat butter over medium-high heat. Add onions, celery, green onions and garlic. Saute 3–5 minutes or until vegetables are wilted. Add the mashed mirlitons and half of the shrimp. Continue to saute until mirliton is well-blended and shrimp are pink and curled, approximately 5–10 minutes. Sprinkle in flour and incorporate well into the mirliton mixture. Slowly add chicken stock, one ladle at a time, until soup consistency is achieved. Bring to a low boil, reduce to simmer and cook 20–30 minutes, stirring often. Add remaining shrimp and mushrooms. Season to taste using salt, pepper and hot sauce. Add half and half and chopped parsley. Cook an additional 5 minutes or until shrimp are done. When serving the soup, garnish each bowl with a tablespoon of diced mirliton.

"Mirlitons are a common vegetable in South Louisiana. But finding them elsewhere might prove difficult. It's also a little hard to imagine what would substitute for them in a recipe.

"What makes mirlitons so useful is that they are very nearly tasteless themselves, but readily pick up the taste of anything they are prepared with. A mirliton dish can taste like anything from shrimp to bread pudding.

"Mirlitons are only available for about two months, and they don't hold their consistency very well when you freeze them. That's where the idea of pureeing them, freezing the puree and using them as the basis for a soup came from.

"The original recipe for this dish, which came from a neighbor of my mother, was a good deal more sinful than the present version, listing half-and-half and bacon among its ingredients."
Mildred Starnes
Morgan City, Louisiana

❀Nutrition Facts...then❀

Calories: 523
Total Fat: 25gm
Saturated Fat: 14gm
% Calories from Fat: 44
Cholesterol: 286mg
Sodium: 2288mg
Carbohydrate: 27gm
Fiber: 3gm
Protein: 45gm

PREP TIME: 1 1/2 Hours   SERVES: 6

☞ INGREDIENTS:

12 mirlitons
1 1/2 pounds (70–90 count) shrimp,
        peeled and deveined
1/4 cup lite margarine
2 cups diced onions
1 cup diced celery
1/2 cup sliced green onions
1/4 cup diced garlic
3/4 cup flour
3 quarts defatted chicken stock, unsalted
1 cup sliced mushrooms
salt substitute
black pepper
hot sauce
1 cup evaporated skim milk
1/2 cup chopped parsley

☞ METHOD:

Slice mirlitons lengthwise and boil in lightly salted water until tender but not overcooked. Remove from heat and cool under tap water.

Peel, remove seeds and dice into 1/4-inch cubes. Reserve approximately 1 cup of the cubes. Mash the remaining mirlitons or puree in a food processor. Set aside.

In a cast iron dutch oven, heat margarine over medium-high heat. Add onions, celery, green onions and garlic. Saute 3–5 minutes or until vegetables are wilted. Add the mashed mirlitons and half of the shrimp. Continue to saute until mirliton is well-blended and shrimp are pink and curled, approximately 5–10 minutes. Sprinkle in flour and incorporate well into the mirliton mixture.

Slowly add chicken stock, one ladle at a time, until soup consistency is achieved. Bring to a low boil, reduce heat to simmer and cook 20–30 minutes, stirring often. Add remaining shrimp and mushrooms. Season to taste using salt substitute, pepper and hot sauce.

Add skim milk and chopped parsley. Cook an additional 5 minutes or until shrimp are done. When serving the soup, garnish each bowl with a tablespoon of diced mirliton.

Nutrition Facts...now

Calories:	334
Total Fat:	6gm
Saturated Fat:	1gm
% Calories from Fat:	17
Cholesterol:	173mg
Sodium:	985mg
Carbohydrate:	30gm
Fiber:	3gm
Protein:	39gm

Chef's Tips on Fat...
use low roasting temperatures (about
350°) to increase the fat drip-off.

GUMBO Z'HERBES

PREP TIME: 1 1/2 Hours   SERVES: 8

☞ INGREDIENTS:

1 bunch mustard greens	1 cup diced onions
1 bunch turnip greens	1/4 cup diced garlic
1 small cabbage	2 tbsps flour
1 bunch spinach	1 tsp salt
1 bunch beet tops	black pepper
1 pound salt meat	hot sauce
2 tbsps oil	1/2 stick of butter

☞ METHOD:

Clean greens very well. Remove the stems and rinse several times under cold running water. Quarter the cabbage and slice into 1-inch pieces. In a large stock pot, place mustard, turnip and cabbage greens. Cover by 1 inch with water and boil for approximately 30 minutes. Add spinach and beet tops. Continue to boil 25–30 minutes longer. While greens are boiling, place salt meat in a separate pot with enough water to cover by 3 inches. Bring to a rolling boil, reduce to simmer and cook until tender. Drain, dice and set aside. When greens are done, strain liquid and reserve 3/4 of a gallon. Drain the greens of all liquid, allow to cool slightly and chop. In a cast iron dutch oven, heat oil over medium-high heat. Add onions and garlic. Saute 3–5 minutes or until vegetables are wilted. Sprinkle in flour and, using a wire whisk, stir constantly until well-blended. Add cubed salt meat, greens and enough of the reserved stock to cover by 2–3 inches. Bring to a rolling boil, reduce to simmer and cook 5–10 minutes or until desired consistency is achieved. Season to taste using salt, pepper and hot sauce. Immediately before serving, incorporate butter into the soup. This soup should be served over white rice or with hot corn bread.

"This recipe for vegetable gumbo - pronounced "Gumbo Zabb", by the way - is very old. Gumbo z'herbes originated with negro cooks in the Donaldsonville area more than 150 years ago. This particular version came down to us from our mother's grandmother, who lived with us when we were growing up.

"Mother was very particular about her gumbo z'herbes. Every ingredient had to be available and everything had to be fresh. Some of our neighbors used canned vegetables, but not Mama! No substitutions were allowed. If she didn't have every ingredient, she fixed something else.

"Maybe that's why she was considered the best cook in Donaldsonville."

Jeanette Jefferson,
Babbette D. Joseph
& Josephine Schomberg
Donaldsonville, Louisiana

❧ Nutrition Facts...then ❧

Calories:	287
Total Fat:	18gm
Saturated Fat:	7gm
% Calories from Fat:	52
Cholesterol:	55mg
Sodium:	786mg
Carbohydrate:	21gm
Fiber:	7gm
Protein:	17gm

PREP TIME: 1 1/2 Hours   SERVES: 8

☞ INGREDIENTS:

1 bunch mustard greens
1 bunch turnip greens
1 small cabbage
1 bunch spinach
1 bunch beet tops
1 tbsp oil
1 cup diced onions
1/4 cup diced garlic
1/2 pound lean ham, diced
2 tbsps flour
salt substitute
black pepper
hot sauce

☞ METHOD:

Clean greens very well. Remove the stems and rinse several times under cold running water. Quarter the cabbage and slice into 1-inch pieces.

In a large stock pot, place mustard, turnip and cabbage greens. Cover by 1 inch with water and boil for approximately 30 minutes. Add spinach and beet tops. Continue to boil 25–30 minutes longer.

When greens are done, strain liquid and reserve 3/4 of a gallon. Drain the greens of all liquid, allow to cool slightly and chop. In a cast iron dutch oven, heat oil over medium-high heat. Add onions, garlic and ham. Saute 3–5 minutes or until vegetables are wilted.

Sprinkle in flour and blend well into the vegetable mixture. Add greens and enough of the reserved stock to cover by 2–3 inches. Bring to a rolling boil, reduce to simmer and cook 5–10 minutes or until desired consistency is achieved. Season to taste using salt substitute, pepper and hot sauce.

This soup should be served over white rice or with hot corn bread.

Nutrition Facts...now

Calories:	145
Total Fat:	4gm
Saturated Fat:	1gm
% Calories from Fat:	23
Cholesterol:	15mg
Sodium:	563mg
Carbohydrate:	18gm
Fiber:	7gm
Protein:	13gm

Norman Plaisance shows off his prize purple garlic cultivated in his Grand Isle garden.

PREP TIME: 30 Minutes   SERVES: 6

☞ INGREDIENTS:

3 cups fresh corn cut from cob (reserve pulp)
4 tbsps oil
3 tbsps flour
1 cup diced onions
1/4 cup diced garlic
1/2 pound diced salt meat
1 quart water
1 cup diced tomatoes
2 cups diced potatoes
1 tsp salt
black pepper
hot sauce
1/4 cup sliced green onions
1/4 cup chopped parsley

☞ METHOD:

In a cast iron dutch oven, heat oil over medium-high heat. Add flour and, using a wire whisk, stir until light brown roux is achieved. Add onions, garlic and salt meat. Saute 3–5 minutes or until vegetables are wilted. Add corn and saute 5 minutes. Add reserved pulp and water. Bring to a rolling boil and reduce to simmer. Add tomatoes and potatoes and allow soup to cook 30 minutes. Season to taste using salt, pepper and hot sauce. Add green onions and parsley prior to serving.

"Not many people were lucky enough to have an Aunt Zubee, but I was. She was my father's sister, and lived in Westwego, on the West Bank of the Mississippi River, across from New Orleans.
"Although we lived on Bayou des Allemandes, two parishes (counties) away from the city, my dad drove a taxicab in New Orleans. Sometimes he would bring us to town and let us visit Aunt Zubee and her 17 children while he worked.
"Aunt Zubee's real name was Armentine, and I've never known how she came to be nicknamed Zubee. But she was a wonderful cook, and this is the corn soup she taught me to make."
                    Ruby Candies
                    Bourg, Louisiana

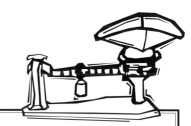

❧Nutrition Facts...then❧

Calories:	380
Total Fat:	16gm
Saturated Fat:	3gm
% Calories from Fat:	35
Cholesterol:	27mg
Sodium:	599mg
Carbohydrate:	52gm
Fiber:	4gm
Protein:	14gm

PREP TIME: 30 Minutes   SERVES: 6

☞ INGREDIENTS:

3 cups fresh corn cut from cob (reserve pulp)
1 tbsp oil
1 cup diced onions
1/4 cup diced garlic
1/2 pound lean ham
3 tbsps flour
1 quart water
1 cup diced tomatoes
2 cups diced potatoes
salt substitute
black pepper
hot sauce
1/4 cup sliced green onions
1/4 cup chopped parsley

☞ METHOD:

In a cast iron dutch oven, heat oil over medium-high heat. Add onions, garlic and ham. Saute 3–5 minutes or until vegetables are wilted.

Sprinkle in flour and blend into the vegetable mixture. Add corn and saute 5 minutes. Add reserved pulp and water. Bring to a rolling boil and reduce to simmer. Add tomatoes and potatoes and allow soup to cook 30 minutes.

Season to taste using salt substitute, pepper and hot sauce. Add green onions and parsley prior to serving.

Nutrition Facts...now

Calories:	298
Total Fat:	6gm
Saturated Fat:	1gm
% Calories from Fat:	16
Cholesterol:	20mg
Sodium:	539mg
Carbohydrate:	51gm
Fiber:	4gm
Protein:	15gm

*Chef's Tips on Fat...
when choosing hamburger, look
for the medium-to-deep color,
that means a lowfat content.*

PREP TIME: 3 Hours   SERVES: 8

☞ INGREDIENTS:

1 pound black beans
2 quarts chicken stock
1/2 cup peanut oil
1 cup chopped onions
1 cup chopped bell pepper
1/4 cup diced garlic
1 bay leaf
1 tsp cumin
1 cup Picante sauce
1 tsp salt
black pepper
hot sauce
4 tbsps lemon juice
2 1/2 tbsps olive oil

☞ METHOD:

Wash black beans well and soak them overnight in the refrigerator in cold water. Drain and rinse well. In a cast iron dutch oven, place beans and chicken stock. Bring to a rolling boil, reduce to simmer and cook approximately 45 minutes. In a 10-inch cast iron skillet, heat oil over medium-high heat. Add onions, bell pepper and garlic. Saute 3–5 minutes or until vegetables are wilted. Add to the soup along with bay leaf, cumin and Picante sauce. Bring to a rolling boil. Reduce to simmer, cover and cook 1 1/2 hours. You may need to add additional stock to retain volume. Season to taste using salt, pepper and hot sauce. Immediately prior to serving, add lemon juice and olive oil, blending well into the soup.

"Black beans aren't really Cajun. They're Latin American. My exposure to them came through a friend, whose grandmother came from Cuba, and who made the best bean soup I ever ate.

"They moved away, and I never got her recipe for black bean soup, so I had to reinvent it from remembering how the soup tasted - something any good cook can do. I think that's why people share recipes so readily around here. What one cook can invent, another can figure out from the taste.

"Everyone talks about old family recipes, but not about secret family recipes. If you can taste it, it isn't a secret in a land of good cooks."

Honorine Abel
Patterson, Louisiana

❧Nutrition Facts...then❧

Calories: 322
Total Fat: 11gm
Saturated Fat: 4gm
% Calories from Fat: 58
Cholesterol: 3mg
Sodium: 2057mg
Carbohydrate: 18gm
Fiber: 3gm
Protein: 17gm

PREP TIME: 3 Hours   SERVES: 8

☞ INGREDIENTS:

1 pound black beans
2 quarts defatted chicken stock, unsalted
2 tbsps peanut oil
1 cup chopped onions
1 cup chopped bell pepper
1/4 cup diced garlic
1 bay leaf
1 tsp cumin
1 cup Picante sauce
1/2 tsp salt
black pepper
hot sauce
4 tbsps lemon juice
2 1/2 tbsps olive oil

☞ METHOD:

Wash black beans well and soak them overnight in the refrigerator in cold water. Drain and rinse well.

In a cast iron dutch oven, place beans and chicken stock. Bring to a rolling boil, reduce to simmer and cook approximately 45 minutes.

In a 10-inch cast iron skillet, heat oil over medium-high heat. Add onions, bell pepper and garlic. Saute 3–5 minutes or until vegetables are wilted. Add to the soup along with bay leaf, cumin and Picante sauce. Bring

Hand-painted sign on Adam's Market, Bayou Lafourche.

to a rolling boil. Reduce to simmer, cover and cook 1 1/2 hours. You may need to add additional stock to retain volume.

Season to taste using salt, pepper and hot sauce. Immediately prior to serving, add lemon juice and olive oil, blending well into the soup.

Nutrition Facts...now

Calories:	195
Total Fat:	11gm
Saturated Fat:	1gm
% Calories from Fat:	49
Cholesterol:	4mg
Sodium:	446mg
Carbohydrate:	18gm
Fiber:	3gm
Protein:	8gm

PREP TIME: 45 Minutes   SERVES: 6

"My father had as strong a French heritage as anyone in Louisiana, but he was a classic American meat-and-potatoes man. This recipe was his creation. The meat and potatoes tradition isn't something you particularly associate with southern Louisiana cooking. But most Cajuns don't own meat markets, which Papa Porche did.

"His family traced its Louisiana roots back to the earliest French settlement. One of his ancestors accompanied the French-Canadian explorer Iberville in his exploration of Louisiana in the late 1600s, later settling along the Atchafalaya River. They married into a family that could trace its Louisiana heritage a lot farther back than that. They were Attakapas Indian.

"My great-grandfather moved his family to Lake Charles in the 1880s, when it was just a village at the junction of a river and a railroad.

"No one had any money, so work and food were the major means of exchange. My grandmother had 18 or 19 pecan trees, and exchanged the pecans with the Italian bakers for bread. Everybody worked with and for everyone else, like frontier settlers did everywhere in America. That's only a little more than a century ago. But in the 1880s, Lake Charles was the frontier!"

Agnes Porche Wyatt
Lake Charles, Louisiana

☞ INGREDIENTS:

3 cups diced red potatoes	1/4 cup diced garlic	1/2 tsp dill weed
2 cups lean ham, diced	1 tsp Herbs de Provence	1 finely sliced green onion
4 cups chicken stock	1 1/2 cups milk	1 tsp salt
1 cup diced onions	1 tbsp butter	black pepper
1 cup diced celery	1/4 tsp Worcestershire	hot sauce

☞ METHOD:

In a large cast iron dutch oven, heat chicken stock over medium-high heat. Add potatoes, ham, onions, celery, garlic and Herbs de Provence. Bring to a rolling boil. Reduce heat to simmer, cover and cook until vegetables are tender. Strain liquid and reserve. Separate ham, vegetables and potatoes. Using a potato masher or large spoon, mash potatoes until totally pureed. Place the ham, vegetables and potatoes back into the pot over medium-high heat. Add milk, butter, Worcestershire, dill and green onions. Add the reserved poaching liquid, one ladle at a time, and reduce to simmer. Do not boil. Season to taste using salt, pepper and hot sauce. Simmer 10–15 minutes and serve.

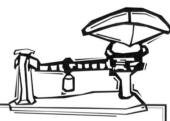

❊Nutrition Facts...then❊

Calories:	301
Total Fat:	8gm
Saturated Fat:	3gm
% Calories from Fat:	22
Cholesterol:	37mg
Sodium:	1935mg
Carbohydrate:	34gm
Fiber:	3gm
Protein:	25gm

PREP TIME: 45 Minutes   SERVES: 6

☞ INGREDIENTS:

3 cups diced red potatoes
1 cup lean ham, diced
4 cups defatted chicken stock, unsalted
1 cup diced onions
1 cup diced celery
1/4 cup diced garlic
1 tsp Herbs de Provence
1 1/2 cups skim milk
1 tbsp margarine
1/4 tsp Worcestershire
1/2 tsp dill weed
1 finely sliced green onion
1/2 tsp salt
black pepper
hot sauce

☞ METHOD:

In a large cast iron dutch oven, heat chicken stock over medium-high heat. Add potatoes, ham, onions, celery, garlic and Herbs de Provence. Bring to a rolling boil.

Reduce heat to simmer, cover and cook until vegetables are tender. Strain liquid and reserve. Separate ham, vegetables and potatoes. Using a potato masher or large spoon, mash potatoes until totally pureed.

Place ham, vegetables and potatoes back into the pot over medium-high heat. Add skim milk, margarine, Worcestershire, dill and green onions.

Add the reserved poaching liquid, one ladle at a time, and reduce to simmer. Do not boil. Season to taste using salt, pepper and hot sauce. Simmer 10–15 minutes and serve.

Nutrition Facts...now

Calories:	229
Total Fat:	5gm
Saturated Fat:	1gm
% Calories from Fat:	20
Cholesterol:	17mg
Sodium:	647mg
Carbohydrate:	34gm
Fiber:	3gm
Protein:	13gm

Salads

Chapter Three

Stuffed Creole Tomato Salad	92/93
Green Bean & Vidalia Onion Salad	94/95
Pickled Carrot Salad	96/97
Shoepeg Corn Salad	98/99
Freezer-Style Cabbage Slaw	100/101
Pasta Salad	102/103
1910 Rice Salad	104/105
Grilled Fish Salad	106/107
Grilled Chicken Salad	108/109
Grilled Sirloin & Wild Mushroom Salad	110/111
Luke Lipari's Shrimp Salad	112/113
Shrimp & Lump Crab Salad in Tomato Aspic	116/117
Hot Shrimp Salad Casserole	118/119
Layered Fruit & Shrimp Salad	120/121
Jane Arnette's Crawfish Salad	122/123
Mardi Gras Crawfish Salad	124/125
Pineapple-Carrot Congealed Salad	126/127
Warm New Potato Salad with Beer Dressing	128/129
Cottage Cheese & Fruit Souffle	130/131
Old Time Potato Salad	132/133

*The recipes for **1910 Rice Salad**, pictured at left, can be found on pages 104 and 105.*

PREP TIME: 30 Minutes   SERVES: 6

☞ INGREDIENTS:

6 Creole tomatoes, chilled
1/2 cup diced cucumber
1/2 cup diced celery
1/4 cup diced onions
1/4 cup diced bell pepper
1/2 tsp diced garlic
1/2 cup cottage cheese
1/4 cup Parmesan cheese
2 boiled eggs, diced
1/2 tsp salt
black pepper
2 tbsps Italian dressing
1/2 tsp chopped basil

☞ METHOD:

In a large mixing bowl, combine all ingredients except the tomatoes. Mix well, cover and refrigerate at least 2 hours. Cut 3/4-inch off top of each tomato and, using a teaspoon, remove the seeds and pulp. Turn the tomatoes upside down and drain well on paper towels. Dice one cup of the sliced tomato tops and mix in with the vegetable stuffing. When tomatoes are well drained, stuff them with the vegetable mixture. Serve on multi-colored lettuces as a salad or appetizer.

"We're what passes for hill-billies in Louisiana - cousins whose families both lived on farms up in North Louisiana, near Winnfield.

"Cooking in North Louisiana puts more emphasis on vegetables than is usual in South Louisiana, where we live now. Farmers' markets were everywhere, and anybody who could planted a humongous garden. There were all kinds of fruit and nut trees - Ruston peaches, especially.

"Dried beans and rice - the vegetable staples in South Louisiana - were almost unknown where we grew up. We canned everything - pickles, pears, peaches, chestnuts and every vegetable you could put up. About all we bought was white flour and salt, which required a drive to Winnfield."

Jane Bryant &
Melba Bailey Corbett
Morgan City, Louisana

❧Nutrition Facts...then❧

Calories: 113
Total Fat: 6gm
Saturated Fat: 2gm
% Calories from Fat: 50
Cholesterol: 77mg
Sodium: 404mg
Carbohydrate: 7gm
Fiber: 2gm
Protein: 7gm

PREP TIME: 30 Minutes   SERVES: 6

☞ INGREDIENTS:

6 Creole tomatoes, chilled
1/2 cup diced cucumber
1/2 cup diced celery
1/4 cup diced onions
1/4 cup diced bell pepper
1/2 tsp diced garlic
1/2 cup fat-free cottage cheese
1/4 cup fat-free Parmesan cheese
1 whole boiled egg, diced
1 boiled egg white, diced
1/4 tsp salt
black pepper
2 tbsps fat-free Italian dressing
1/2 tsp chopped basil

☞ METHOD:

In a large mixing bowl, combine all ingredients except the tomatoes. Mix well, cover and refrigerate at least 2 hours.

Cut 3/4-inch off top of each tomato and, using a teaspoon, remove the seeds and pulp. Turn the tomatoes upside down and drain well on paper towels. Dice one cup of the sliced tomato tops and mix in with the vegetable stuffing.

When tomatoes are well drained, stuff them with the vegetable mixture. Serve on multi-colored lettuces as a salad or appetizer.

Nutrition Facts...now

Calories: 65
Total Fat: 1gm
Saturated Fat: 0gm
% Calories from Fat: 16
Cholesterol: 40mg
Sodium: 272mg
Carbohydrate: 8gm
Fiber: 2gm
Protein: 6gm

PREP TIME: 30 Minutes   SERVES: 6

☞ INGREDIENTS:

2 (10-ounce) packages frozen cut green beans
1/2 cup sliced Vidalia onions
1 tbsp sugar
1/2 cup olive oil
3 tbsps white wine vinegar
1/4 tsp dried mustard
1/4 tsp salt
cayenne pepper
4 slices cooked bacon, crumbled
1 cup Swiss cheese, shredded

☞ METHOD:

Cook green beans according to package directions, drain and chill. Place the onions in a small bowl and top with sugar. Cover and chill. In a pint jar, place oil, vinegar, mustard, salt and pepper. Seal and shake vigorously to incorporate all ingredients. To serve, place beans and onions in a large bowl. Add crushed bacon and cheese. Shake salad dressing once again and pour over the bean mixture. Toss well and serve.

*Chef's Tips on Substitution...
use ground turkey or chicken
instead of ground beef for variety.*

"Vidalia Onions are certainly used in many ways, but because of their wonderful sweet taste, they add much flavor to a salad. They are often served soaked in wine vinegar and spices, mixed with fresh cucumbers. Mmmmm...what a refreshing salad, frequently served with a delicious meal of white beans and rice!

"I serve my variation mixed with green beans. It's a great dish to bring to special gatherings. The best thing about this recipe is it can be stored in the refrigerator for days. The vinegar mixture and spices are soaked into the onions and vegetables, increasing the flavor.

"Don't forget! Vidalia onions add a delightful flavor to hamburgers! They are even great all by themselves. What a wonderful source of food that can easily be considered heart healthy all by itself!"

Melba Corbett
Morgan City, Louisiana

❧Nutrition Facts...then❧

Calories:	139
Total Fat:	8gm
Saturated Fat:	4gm
% Calories from Fat:	52
Cholesterol:	21mg
Sodium:	326mg
Carbohydrate:	9gm
Fiber:	1gm
Protein:	8gm

PREP TIME: 30 Minutes   SERVES: 6

☞ INGREDIENTS:

2 (10-ounce) packages frozen cut green beans
1/2 cup sliced Vidalia onions
1 tbsp sugar
1/4 cup olive oil
3 tbsps white wine vinegar
1/4 tsp dried mustard
salt substitute
cayenne pepper
1 ounce diced ham
1 cup low-fat Swiss cheese, shredded

☞ METHOD:

Cook green beans according to package directions, drain and chill. Place the onions in a small bowl and top with sugar. Cover and chill. In a pint jar, place oil, vinegar, mustard, salt substitute and pepper. Seal and shake vigorously to incorporate all ingredients.

When ready to serve, place beans and onions in a large serving bowl. Add diced ham and cheese. Shake salad dressing once again and pour over the bean mixture. Toss well and serve.

Avie Fuselier, in his traditional bow tie, passes a Saturday morning with friends in front of his City Barber Shop next door to Fred's Lounge in Mamou.

Nutrition Facts...now

Calories:	94
Total Fat:	3gm
Saturated Fat:	2gm
% Calories from Fat:	28
Cholesterol:	13mg
Sodium:	419mg
Carbohydrate:	10gm
Fiber:	1gm
Protein:	7gm

PICKLED CARROT SALAD

PREP TIME: 1 Hour   SERVES: 6

☞ INGREDIENTS:

10 sliced carrots
1/4 cup oil
1/2 cup red wine vinegar
1/4 cup sugar
1 tbsp dried mustard
1 tbsp Worcestershire Sauce
1 can tomato soup
1/2 cup sliced Bermuda onions
1 1/2 cups julienned bell pepper

☞ METHOD:

Boil carrots in water until tender but not overcooked. Cool under running tap water. Drain and set aside. In a sauce pot, combine oil, vinegar, sugar, mustard, Worcestershire Sauce and tomato soup. Bring to a rolling boil, stirring constantly until all is incorporated. In a large serving bowl, arrange carrots, onions and bell pepper in layers. Pour boiling soup mixture over carrots. Allow to cool slightly and refrigerate a minimum of 12 hours prior to serving.

"When I was about ten years old, my friend Ola and I collected Spanish moss as a way of making a little money. You took a pushpole and hammered a nail into each fork, and used that to pull the moss down from the limbs of the oak trees.

"It's gray when you gather it, but after it's cured by being hung over a fence, it turns black.

"Just about everybody back then used Spanish moss to stuff their summer mattresses because feather beds were too hot for summer use. The moss wasn't very durable, though. You had to restuff the mattresses every year or so. You also had to sew a rosette through the mattress every 18 inches or so to keep the moss from clumping up. I remember we used an umbrella spine as a needle for sewing the rosettes.

"Most of the family's feather beds in those days were stuffed with wild duck feathers my grandmother saved in flour sacks during duck season. I remember her fluffing up the feather beds by beating them with a broomhandle."

Gloria Cannatella
Golden Meadow, Louisiana

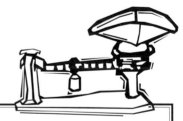

❧ Nutrition Facts...then❧

Calories:	175
Total Fat:	10gm
Saturated Fat:	1gm
% Calories from Fat:	49
Cholesterol:	0mg
Sodium:	385mg
Carbohydrate:	22gm
Fiber:	2gm
Protein:	2gm

PREP TIME: 1 Hour   SERVES: 6

☞ INGREDIENTS:

10 sliced carrots
2 tbsps oil
1/2 cup red wine vinegar
1/4 cup sugar
1 tbsp dried mustard
1 tbsp Worcestershire Sauce
1 can tomato soup
1/2 cup sliced Bermuda onions
1 1/2 cups julienned bell pepper

☞ METHOD:

Boil carrots in water until tender but not overcooked. Cool under running tap water. Drain and set aside.

In a sauce pot, combine oil, vinegar, sugar, mustard, Worcestershire Sauce and tomato soup. Bring to a rolling boil, stirring constantly until all is incorporated.

In a large serving bowl, arrange carrots, onions and bell pepper in layers. Pour boiling soup mixture over carrots. Allow to cool slightly and refrigerate a minimum of 12 hours prior to serving.

Nutrition Facts...now

Calories:	134
Total Fat:	5gm
Saturated Fat:	1gm
% Calories from Fat:	34
Cholesterol:	0mg
Sodium:	385mg
Carbohydrate:	22gm
Fiber:	2gm
Protein:	2gm

SHOEPEG CORN SALAD

PREP TIME: 1 Hour   SERVES: 6

☞ INGREDIENTS:

3 (11-ounce) cans white
      shoepeg corn, drained
1 cup mayonnaise
1/4 cup Canola oil
2 tbsps red wine vinegar
1 tsp dried mustard
1 tsp sugar
1/2 tsp salt
black pepper
Louisiana Gold Pepper Sauce
1 cup chopped celery
1/2 cup chopped red bell pepper
1/2 cup finely sliced green onions
2 diced tomatoes

Turtle eggs at June's Seafood in Ville Platte.

☞ METHOD:

In a large mixing bowl, combine mayonnaise, salad oil, vinegar, mustard and sugar. Using a wire whisk, whip until well-blended. Season to taste using salt, pepper and Louisiana Gold. You may wish to slightly over-season with the pepper to enhance the corn. Fold in corn, celery, bell pepper and green onions. Stir well to coat the ingredients thoroughly. Once blended, add tomatoes, taking care not to break the tomatoes in the process. Cover with clear wrap and place in refrigerator a minimum of 6 hours prior to use. You may serve as a buffet-type salad or mix with fresh spinach leaves as a starter course.

"I'm sure many 'old timers' will fondly remember shoepeg corn. Now that we have all of these 'designer' varieties, this older, white and tiny corn isn't used very often.
"You will still see it in the grocery store, canned, and in roadside vegetable markets. When you do, pick some up and try this recipe."

John Folse
Donaldsonville, Louisiana

❧Nutrition Facts...then❧

Calories:	546
Total Fat:	43gm
Saturated Fat:	6gm
% Calories from Fat:	65
Cholesterol:	13mg
Sodium:	556mg
Carbohydrate:	46gm
Fiber:	7gm
Protein:	6gm

SHOEPEG CORN SALAD

PREP TIME: 1 Hour   SERVES: 6

☞ **INGREDIENTS:**

3 (11-ounce) cans white shoepeg corn, drained
2/3 cup lite mayonnaise
2 tbsps red wine vinegar
1 tsp dried mustard
1 tsp sugar
salt substitute
black pepper
Louisiana Gold Pepper Sauce
1 cup chopped celery
1/2 cup chopped red bell pepper
1/2 cup finely sliced green onions
2 diced tomatoes

☞ **METHOD:**

In a large mixing bowl, combine mayonnaise, vinegar, mustard and sugar. Using a wire whisk, whip until well-blended. Season to taste using salt substitute, pepper and Louisiana Gold. You may wish to slightly over-season with the pepper to enhance the corn.

Fold in corn, celery, bell pepper and green onions. Stir well to coat the ingredients thoroughly.

Once blended, add tomatoes, taking care not to break the tomatoes in the process. Cover with clear wrap and place in refrigerator a minimum of 6 hours prior to use.

You may serve as a buffet-type salad or mix with fresh spinach leaves as a starter course.

Nutrition Facts...now

Calories:	270
Total Fat:	9gm
Saturated Fat:	1gm
% Calories from Fat:	27
Cholesterol:	9mg
Sodium:	219mg
Carbohydrate:	48gm
Fiber:	7gm
Protein:	6gm

Chef's Tips on Substitution...
use margarine instead of
butter when cooking or baking.

PREP TIME: 1 Hour   SERVES: 16

☞ INGREDIENTS:

2 pounds shredded cabbage
1 cup chopped onions
1 cup julienned red bell pepper
1 cup honey
1/2 cup sugar
1/2 cup vegetable oil
1 tsp celery seed
1/2 tsp salt
black pepper
Louisiana Gold Pepper Sauce

"The Germans were the first to plant cabbage here in South Louisiana. They created many dishes using the vegetable but their favorite was the home-made sauerkraut.

"Often after shredding the cabbage and filling the crock jars with kraut, the leftover cabbage would be blended with seasonings and honey for the chilled slaw. The flavor is great and it can be made well in advance and frozen until ready to use."

Debbie Martin
Port Allen, Louisiana

☞ METHOD:

In a large mixing bowl, combine cabbage, onions and bell pepper. Set aside. In a cast iron sauce pot, combine honey, sugar, oil and celery seed. Using a wire whisk, blend until well incorporated. Bring to a low boil, stirring constantly, and cook until sugar is totally dissolved. Pour boiling mixture over the cabbage mixture, stirring occasionally until mixture cools. Season to taste using salt, pepper and Louisiana Gold. Place in refrigerator until chilled. Place slaw into containers and freeze until ready to use.

Chef's Tips on Low-fat... omit the oil from your favorite sauce recipes— they will still taste great.

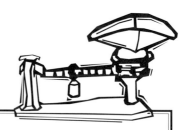

❧ Nutrition Facts...then❧

Calories: 211
Total Fat: 7gm
Saturated Fat: 1gm
% Calories from Fat: 29
Cholesterol: 0mg
Sodium: 98mg
Carbohydrate: 37gm
Fiber: 3gm
Protein: 3gm

PREP TIME: 1 Hour   SERVES: 16

☞ INGREDIENTS:

2 pounds shredded cabbage
1 cup chopped onions
1 cup julienned red bell pepper
1 cup honey
1/2 cup sugar
1/4 cup vegetable oil
1 tsp celery seed
salt substitute
black pepper
Louisiana Gold Pepper Sauce

☞ METHOD:

In a large mixing bowl, combine cabbage, onions and bell pepper. Set aside.

In a sauce pot, combine honey, sugar, oil and celery seed. Using a wire whisk, blend until well incorporated. Bring to a low boil, stirring constantly, and cook until sugar is totally dissolved.

Pour boiling mixture over the cabbage mixture, stirring constantly until mixture cools. Season to taste using salt substitute, pepper and Louisiana Gold.

Place in refrigerator until chilled. Place slaw into containers and freeze until ready to use.

*Chef's Tips on Substitution...
if a recipe calls for buttered
bread crumbs, try crushed
cereal instead.*

Nutrition Facts...now

Calories: 181
Total Fat: 4gm
Saturated Fat: 1gm
% Calories from Fat: 18
Cholesterol: 0mg
Sodium: 32mg
Carbohydrate: 37gm
Fiber: 3gm
Protein: 3gm

PASTA SALAD

PREP TIME: 1 Hour   SERVES: 6

☞ INGREDIENTS:

12 ounces elbow macaroni, cooked
2 cups diced tomatoes
1/2 cup diced red bell pepper
1/2 cup diced green bell pepper
1 cup diced Bermuda onions
8 ounces cheddar cheese, diced
6 boiled eggs
1 cup mayonnaise
1/3 cup mustard
2 tbsps Worcestershire Sauce
garlic powder
1 tsp salt
cayenne pepper
1/4 cup sliced green onions

☞ METHOD:

In a large mixing bowl, combine macaroni, tomatoes, bell peppers, onions and cheese. Using a wooden spoon, mix well. Cover and set aside. Using a sharp paring knife, separate boiled yolks from egg whites. Dice egg whites and set aside. Place the yolks in a separate bowl and add mayonnaise, mustard and Worcestershire Sauce. Using a fork, mash yolks into the mayonnaise mixture until smooth and blended. Fold in egg whites and add to the pasta mixture. Using a wooden spoon, blend the mayonnaise dressing into the pasta until all is incorporated. Season to taste using garlic powder, salt and pepper. Place in a decorative serving bowl and garnish with green onions. Cover and chill 2–3 hours prior to serving. Diced ham may be added to this dish when serving it as an entree.

"This recipe came from a family friend named Charlie Boudreaux, who invented it in his camp up on Three-Mile Lake. Its contents may not be what most folks think of as Cajun, but it is just the sort of recipe that goes with a family gathering down here - which means it's easy to fix in big quantities.
"A typical family get-together for us is 50 people. A wedding can easily draw 100.
"It's also just the thing to take to someone who's sick."
Elaine Guillory
Opelousas, Louisiana

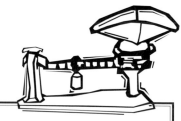

❖Nutrition Facts...then❖

Calories: 620
Total Fat: 51gm
Saturated Fat: 15gm
% Calories from Fat: 71
Cholesterol: 266mg
Sodium: 1190mg
Carbohydrate: 26gm
Fiber: 3gm
Protein: 21gm

PREP TIME: 1 Hour   SERVES: 6

☞ INGREDIENTS:

12 ounces elbow macaroni, cooked
2 cups diced tomatoes
1/2 cup diced red bell pepper
1/2 cup diced green bell pepper
1 cup diced Bermuda onion

8 ounces fat-free cheddar cheese, diced
6 boiled eggs
1 cup lite mayonnaise
1/3 cup mustard
2 tbsps Worcestershire Sauce

garlic powder
salt substitute
cayenne pepper
1/4 cup sliced green onions

☞ METHOD:

In a large mixing bowl, combine macaroni, tomatoes, bell peppers, onions and cheese. Using a wooden spoon, mix well. Cover and set aside.

Using a sharp paring knife, separate boiled yolks from egg whites. Dice egg whites and set aside. Discard four yolks. Place remaining two yolks in a separate bowl. Add mayonnaise, mustard and Worcestershire Sauce. Using a fork, mash yolks into the mayonnaise mixture until smooth and blended. Fold in egg whites and add to the pasta mixture.

Using a wooden spoon, blend the mayonnaise dressing into the pasta until all is incorporated. Season to taste using garlic powder, salt substitute and pepper. Place in a decorative serving bowl and garnish with green onions.

Cover and chill 2–3 hours prior to serving. Diced ham may be added to this dish when serving it as an entree.

Chef's Tips on Low-fat... drain the extra fat when browning meat. Rinsing the meat with water removes even more fat.

Nutrition Facts...now

Calories:	323
Total Fat:	14gm
Saturated Fat:	2gm
% Calories from Fat:	38
Cholesterol:	91mg
Sodium:	720mg
Carbohydrate:	29gm
Fiber:	3gm
Protein:	21gm

Back door of a traditional Acadian cabin near Mamou.

PREP TIME: 45 Minutes   SERVES: 8

☞ INGREDIENTS:

3 cups cooked rice
4 boiled eggs, diced
1/3 cup chopped black olives
1/4 cup chopped bell pepper
1/4 cup chopped celery
2 tbsps pickle relish
1 cup cooked shrimp, chopped
1 cup smoked sausage, sliced and sauteed
1 tbsp Creole mustard
1 tbsp yellow mustard
1 tsp salt
black pepper
hot sauce

☞ METHOD:

You should determine in advance whether you wish to serve this salad hot or cold. Since the preparation is so simple, it only takes a minute to put together. When serving it as a side dish, I recommend having all of the ingredients prepped and measured prior to removing the hot steamed rice, cooked shrimp and sauteed sausage from the pots. It can be thoroughly mixed and served immediately, steaming hot. On the other hand, should you wish to serve it cold, it may be made 1–2 days in advance, allowing the flavors to enhance over time. In a large glass mixing bowl, combine all ingredients. Using a wooden spoon, toss well to incorporate the juices and flavors of the ingredients. Serve warm as a side dish or cold on a bed of lettuce.

"My grandmother, Elizabeth Clay Richard, was married on November 8, 1910 in Sacred Heart Church in Grand Coteau, Louisiana. Since her father was away racing horses in Lafayette, she was given away by her brother.

"Following the early morning nuptial Mass, there was a wedding reception at her parents' home - a big turkey breakfast that included rice salad.

"Among her most treasured wedding gifts was a handwritten cookbook, prepared by her mother and aunts. All the favorite family recipes were included - with rice salad on page three, right behind baked turkey, stewed chicken and shrimp gumbo.

"The recipes have been carefully copied and handed down ever since, thank Heaven, because, somewhere along the way, that original hand-written cookbook was lost."

Judy Greathouse
Lake Charles, Louisiana

❧Nutrition Facts...then❧

Calories: 146
Total Fat: 3gm
Saturated Fat: 1gm
% Calories from Fat: 20
Cholesterol: 148mg
Sodium: 437mg
Carbohydrate: 19gm
Fiber: 0gm
Protein: 10gm

PREP TIME: 45 Minutes   SERVES: 8

☞ **INGREDIENTS:**

3 cups cooked rice
1 boiled egg, diced
3 boiled egg whites, diced
1 tbsp chopped black olives
1/4 cup chopped bell pepper
1/4 cup chopped celery
2 tbsps pickle relish
1 cup cooked shrimp, chopped
1 cup lite smoked sausage, sliced and sauteed
1 tbsp Creole mustard
1 tbsp yellow mustard
salt substitute
black pepper
hot sauce

☞ **METHOD:**

You should determine in advance whether you wish to serve this salad hot or cold. Since the preparation is so simple, it only takes a minute to put together.

When serving it as a side dish, I recommend having all of the ingredients prepped and measured prior to removing the hot steamed rice, cooked shrimp and sauteed sausage from the pots. It can be thoroughly mixed and served immediately, steaming hot.

On the other hand, should you wish to serve it cold, it may be made 1–2 days in advance, allowing the flavors to enhance over time.

In a large glass mixing bowl, combine all ingredients. Using a wooden spoon, toss well to incorporate the juices and flavors of the ingredients. Serve warm as a side dish or cold on a bed of lettuce.

Nutrition Facts...now

Calories:	109
Total Fat:	1gm
Saturated Fat:	0gm
% Calories from Fat:	11
Cholesterol:	30mg
Sodium:	52mg
Carbohydrate:	19gm
Fiber:	0gm
Protein:	5gm

PREP TIME: 2 Hours   SERVES: 6

☞ INGREDIENTS:

2 pounds white fish fillets
1/2 cup vegetable oil
1 tbsp chopped dill
1 tsp ground sassafras
pinch of thyme
juice of 1 lemon
1 1/2 cups mayonnaise

1/2 cup sour cream
1/2 cup minced onions
1/4 cup minced celery
1/4 cup minced red bell pepper
1/4 cup minced yellow bell pepper
1 tsp chopped dill
1 tsp chopped basil

1 tsp chopped tarragon
juice of 1/2 lemon
1 tsp salt
black pepper
Louisiana Gold Pepper Sauce
1 tbsp Worcestershire Sauce

☞ METHOD:

Whenever possible, I prefer to use striped bass or flounder for this dish. However, catfish also works well. Preheat barbecue grill according to manufacturer's directions. You may wish to pre-soak some pecan wood chips to give the fish an added Louisiana flavor. In a large mixing bowl, combine fillets with oil, 1 tablespoon dill, sassafras, thyme and lemon. Season to taste using salt, pepper and Louisiana Gold. Pierce fish with a fork and allow it to marinate in the seasoning ingredients 30 minutes prior to grilling. If the fish is very delicate, you should line the grill with aluminum foil to keep fish from falling through the grill during cooking. Add the wood chips to the coals and grill fish, covered, for approximately 12–15 minutes or until done. Remove fish, place on cookie sheet and chill in the refrigerator. Once fish is chilled, chop it, including the gelatin that has collected in the pan. Place cubed fish in a large mixing bowl. Add mayonnaise, sour cream, onions, celery, bell peppers, remaining dill, basil, tarragon and lemon juice. Using a large spoon, blend all ingredients well. Season to taste using salt, pepper, Louisiana Gold and Worcestershire. Form the fish into a decorative loaf or spoon into a fish mold. Chill a minimum of 2–3 hours, allowing flavors to develop. Serve on a mixture of multi-colored lettuces or with croutons or toast points as an appetizer.

"Poached fish salads were often presented at Louisiana plantation events. Most of these homes were located on rivers and bayous, so seafoods were plentiful and had to be used.
"This is one of those dishes that survived over the years and, today, has many variations."

John Folse
Donaldsonville, Louisiana

❧Nutrition Facts...then❧

Calories: 667
Total Fat: 60gm
Saturated Fat: 11gm
% Calories from Fat: 76
Cholesterol: 29mg
Sodium: 880mg
Carbohydrate: 11gm
Fiber: 2gm
Protein: 32gm

PREP TIME: 2 Hours   SERVES: 6

☞ INGREDIENTS:

2 pounds white fish fillets
1/2 cup fat-free Italian dressing
juice of 1 lemon
1 cup fat-free mayonnaise
1/2 cup fat-free sour cream
1/2 cup minced onions
1/4 cup minced celery
1/4 cup minced red bell pepper
1/4 cup minced yellow bell pepper
1 tsp chopped dill
1 tsp chopped basil
1 tsp chopped tarragon
juice of 1/2 lemon
salt substitute
black pepper
Louisiana Gold Pepper Sauce
1 tbsp Worcestershire Sauce

☞ METHOD:

Whenever possible, I prefer to use striped bass or flounder for this dish. However, catfish also works well.

Preheat barbecue grill according to manufacturer's directions. You may wish to pre-soak some pecan wood chips to give the fish an added Louisiana flavor.

In a large mixing bowl, combine fillets with Italian dressing and lemon. Season to taste using salt substitute, pepper and Louisiana Gold. Pierce fish with a fork and allow it to marinate in the seasoning ingredients 30 minutes prior to grilling.

If the fish is very delicate, you should line the grill with aluminum foil to keep fish from falling through the grill during cooking. Add the wood chips to the coals and grill fish, covered, for approximately 12–15 minutes or until done. Remove fish, place on cookie sheet and chill in the refrigerator.

Once fish is chilled, chop it, including the gelatin that has collected in the pan. Place cubed fish in a large mixing bowl. Add mayonnaise, sour cream, onions, celery, bell peppers, dill, basil, tarragon and lemon juice.

Using a large spoon, blend all ingredients well. Season to taste using salt substitute, pepper, Louisiana Gold and Worcestershire. Form the fish into a decorative loaf or spoon into a fish mold. Chill a minimum of 2–3 hours, allowing flavors to develop.

Serve on a mixture of multi-colored lettuces or with croutons or toast points as an appetizer.

Nutrition Facts...now

Calories:	222
Total Fat:	6gm
Saturated Fat:	0gm
% Calories from Fat:	25
Cholesterol:	0mg
Sodium:	514mg
Carbohydrate:	11gm
Fiber:	2gm
Protein:	31gm

GRILLED CHICKEN SALAD

PREP TIME: 1 Hour   SERVES: 6

☞ INGREDIENTS:

8 boneless chicken breasts, skin removed
2 tbsps honey
2 tbsps olive oil
2 tbsps Worcestershire Sauce
1 tbsp diced garlic
2 tbsps Creole mustard
1 egg yolk
1 tbsp dried mustard
1 tbsp honey
1/4 cup red wine vinegar
1 cup salad oil
1/2 pound cooked bacon, crumbled,
        reserve bacon fat
1 head green leaf lettuce
1 head red leaf lettuce
1/2 cup sliced black olives
12 pickled baby corn
2 sliced carrots, cooked
1 cup chopped artichoke hearts

"Grilled chicken salad is Cajun? Sure it is! It's not generations old, but it came about the same way the traditional Cajun recipes did - as an adaptation to the world the cooks lived in. After all, the original Acadians didn't arrive from Nova Scotia with recipes for crawfish etouffee or file gumbo. They had to adapt what they knew to what was available to them.

"Today we're adapting to the opposite problem - how to stay healthy and trim amid too much food. And, in a part of the country where a good cook ministers in just about every kitchen and food is the center of social life, that's not easy!"

John and Missy Kiefe
Houma, Louisiana

☞ METHOD:

In a large mixing bowl, combine 2 tablespoons of honey, olive oil, Worcestershire sauce, garlic and 1 tablespoon of Creole mustard. Using a wire whisk, whip until all ingredients are well-blended. Add chicken breasts, coat well in the marinade and allow to sit at room temperature for 2 hours. In a separate bowl, place egg yolk, remaining mustards, honey and red wine vinegar. Using a wire whisk, whip until all ingredients are well-blended. While constantly whipping, slowly pour in oil. Add bacon and bacon fat while continuing to whip until blended. Cover and set aside. In a large salad bowl, place clean leaves of green and red lettuce. Add olives, corn, carrots and artichoke hearts. Blend well, cover and set aside. When ready to serve, remove chicken breasts from marinade and grill on outdoor pit or under the broiler in your oven. Top salad mixture with bacon/honey dressing. Toss to coat well, reserving 6 tablespoons of the dressing for the chicken. Once chicken is done, place 6 equal portions of the salad on individual serving plates. Top each with a chicken breast and a spoonful of the dressing.

❧Nutrition Facts...then❧
Calories: 968
Total Fat: 76gm
Saturated Fat:........................ 17gm
% Calories from Fat:.................. 70
Cholesterol:........................ 182mg
Sodium: 881mg
Carbohydrate: 16gm
Fiber: 2gm
Protein: 56gm

PREP TIME: 1 Hour   SERVES: 6

☞ INGREDIENTS:

8 boneless chicken breasts, skin removed
2 tbsps honey
2 tsps olive oil
2 tbsps Worcestershire Sauce
1 tbsp diced garlic
2 tbsps Creole mustard
1 tbsp dried mustard
1 tbsp honey
1/4 cup red wine vinegar
1/2 cup salad oil
1/2 pound cooked lean ham, chopped
1 head green leaf lettuce
1 head red leaf lettuce
1/4 cup sliced black olives
12 pickled baby corn
2 sliced carrots, cooked
1 cup chopped artichoke hearts

☞ METHOD:

In a large mixing bowl, combine 2 tablespoons of honey, olive oil, Worcestershire sauce, garlic and 1 tablespoon Creole mustard. Using a wire whisk, whip until all ingredients are well-blended.

Add chicken breasts, coat well in the marinade and allow to sit at room temperature for 2 hours.

In a separate bowl, place remaining mustards, honey and red wine vinegar. Using a wire whisk, whip until all ingredients are well-blended. While constantly whipping, slowly pour in oil. Add ham and stir until blended. Cover and set aside.

In a large salad bowl, place clean leaves of green and red lettuce. Add olives, corn, carrots and artichoke hearts. Blend well and set aside.

When ready to serve, remove chicken breasts from marinade and grill on outdoor pit or under the broiler in your oven.

Top salad mixture with ham/honey dressing. Toss to coat well, reserving 6 tablespoons of the dressing for the chicken.

Once chicken is done, place 6 equal portions of the salad on individual serving plates. Top each with a chicken breast and a spoonful of the dressing.

Nutrition Facts...now

Calories:	498
Total Fat:	25gm
Saturated Fat:	3gm
% Calories from Fat:	45
Cholesterol:	134mg
Sodium:	605mg
Carbohydrate:	17gm
Fiber:	2gm
Protein:	51gm

Chef's Tips on Substitution... use a non-stick cooking spray when the recipe calls for a "greased" pan.

PREP TIME: 1 Hour   SERVES: 6

☞ INGREDIENTS:

2 pounds boneless beef sirloin steak
1 cup wild oyster or whole button mushrooms
1 small red bell pepper, halved
3/4 cup salad oil
1/2 cup orange juice
1 tbsp Louisiana cane syrup
1 tbsp Creole mustard
1 tsp chopped thyme
1 tsp chopped basil
1/2 tsp chopped tarragon
1 tsp diced garlic
1 tsp salt
black pepper
Louisiana Gold Pepper Sauce

Country store outside Opelousas.

☞ METHOD:

Have your butcher cut a 2 pound sirloin approximately 2-inches thick. Preheat barbecue grill or oven broiler according to manufacturer's directions. Season steak well on both sides using salt, pepper and Louisiana Gold. Allow steak to sit at room temperature while salad dressing is being made. In a large mixing bowl, combine oil, juice, cane syrup, mustard, thyme, basil, tarragon and garlic. Using a wire whisk, whip until all ingredients are well-blended. Season to taste using salt, pepper and Louisiana Gold. Remove 1/4 cup of the dressing and brush as a marinade over the sirloin, mushrooms and bell pepper. Once grill is ready, cook steak 12–15 minutes on each side, turning occasionally, for medium-rare to medium. While steak is cooking, grill the mushrooms and bell pepper to impart a char-broiled flavor. Remove and julienne or slice the vegetables. Remove steak from pit or oven and allow to cool slightly. Using a sharp knife, slice the steak into 1/4-inch strips. Place steak, mushrooms and peppers in dressing bowl and toss to coat well. You may serve this salad warm over colorful mixed greens and tiny pear tomatoes or refrigerate and allow the meat to marinate to serve as a cold meat salad.

"It isn't often that we see a quality cut of meat like sirloin used in a salad.
"With a lack of refrigeration in plantation days, the cooks often used leftovers to prepare interesting dishes. This one was a favorite of the Randolph family at Nottoway Plantation."
                                    John Folse
                        Donaldsonville, Louisiana

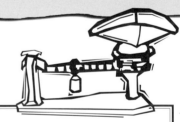

❧ Nutrition Facts...then ❧

Calories: 486
Total Fat: 38gm
Saturated Fat: 8gm
% Calories from Fat: 70
Cholesterol: 91mg
Sodium: 460mg
Carbohydrate: 6gm
Fiber: 0gm
Protein: 31gm

GRILLED SIRLOIN & WILD MUSHROOM SALAD   ...Something New

PREP TIME: 1 Hour   SERVES: 6

☞ INGREDIENTS:

2 pounds boneless, lean beef sirloin steak
1 cup wild oyster or whole button mushrooms
1 small red bell pepper, halved
1/4 cup salad oil
1/2 cup orange juice
1 tbsp Louisiana cane syrup
1 tbsp Creole mustard
1 tsp chopped thyme
1 tsp chopped basil
1/2 tsp chopped tarragon
1 tsp diced garlic
salt substitute
black pepper
Louisiana Gold Pepper Sauce

The Orgeron and Parr families care for their Texas Longhorn Okra before the heat of the day in Lockport.

☞ METHOD:

Have your butcher cut a 2 pound sirloin approximately 2-inches thick. Preheat barbecue grill or oven broiler according to manufacturer's directions. Season steak well on both sides using salt substitute, pepper and Louisiana Gold. Allow steak to sit at room temperature while salad dressing is being made.

In a large mixing bowl, combine oil, juice, cane syrup, mustard, thyme, basil, tarragon and garlic. Using a wire whisk, whip until all ingredients are well-blended. Season to taste using salt substitute, pepper and Louisiana Gold.

Remove 1/4 cup of the dressing and brush as a marinade over the sirloin, mushrooms and bell pepper. Once grill is ready, cook steak 12–15 minutes on each side, turning occasionally, for medium-rare to medium.

While steak is cooking, grill the mushrooms and bell pepper to impart a charbroiled flavor. Remove and julienne or slice the vegetables.

Remove steak from pit or oven and allow to cool slightly. Using a sharp knife, slice the steak into 1/4-inch strips. Place steak, mushrooms and peppers in dressing bowl and toss to coat well.

You may serve this salad warm over colorful mixed greens and tiny pear tomatoes or refrigerate and allow the meat to marinate to serve as a cold meat salad.

Nutrition Facts...now

Calories: 293
Total Fat: 16gm
Saturated Fat: 4gm
% Calories from Fat: 50
Cholesterol: 87mg
Sodium: 104mg
Carbohydrate: 6gm
Fiber: 0gm
Protein: 31gm

111

PREP TIME: 1 Hour SERVES: 8

☞ INGREDIENTS:

3 pounds (50–60 count) shrimp, peeled and deveined
1 onion, quartered
1 lemon, sliced
1 bay leaf
2 pods of garlic
1/2 tsp salt
1 1/2 cups mayonnaise
1 cup ketchup
2 tbsps horseradish
hot sauce
1 head of lettuce
2 tomatoes, diced
1 cup diced celery
1/2 cup diced onion

☞ METHOD:

In a 5-quart sauce pan, add quartered onion, lemon, bay leaf, garlic and salt to 2 quarts of water. Bring to a rolling boil and allow to cook for 15 minutes in order for flavors to develop. Add shrimp. When water returns to a boil, cook 2–3 minutes or until shrimp are pink and curled. Do not overcook. Chill under cold tap water. Remove shrimp and set aside. In a large mixing bowl, combine mayonnaise, ketchup and horseradish. Season to taste using hot sauce. (NOTE: Luke used 1/4 of a small bottle.) Using a wire whisk, blend well until all is incorporated. Fold in shrimp, coat well with the sauce and refrigerate. When ready to serve, wash lettuce and tear into bite-size salad pieces. Drain and place in a large salad bowl, along with tomatoes, celery, diced onion and shrimp/dressing mixture. Using a wooden spoon, blend well until all ingredients are incorporated. Serve on 8 individual salad plates. NOTE: You may wish to boil the shrimp in crab boil.

"This is my father-in-law's recipe, which dates back at least 35 years. Mr. Lipari, like many South Louisiana men, likes to cook. And his taste runs to rather exuberant spicing - horseradish and hot sauce being two notable elements.

"A goodly portion of the population in this area is of Italian extraction. Both sides of my wife's family, for instance, trace their origins to Sicily, and I'm half Italian and half French. So when people start ticking off the influences in Cajun cooking - Acadian French, African, American Indian - they should be careful to include Italian, too."

Frank Russo, Jr.
Berwick, Louisiana

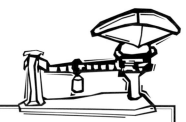

❧Nutrition Facts...then❧

Calories: 494
Total Fat: 38gm
Saturated Fat: 6gm
% Calories from Fat: 66
Cholesterol: 277mg
Sodium: 1060mg
Carbohydrate: 14gm
Fiber: 3gm
Protein: 30gm

PREP TIME: 1 Hour   SERVES: 8

☞ INGREDIENTS:

3 pounds (50–60 count) shrimp, peeled and deveined
1 onion, quartered
1 lemon, sliced
1 bay leaf
2 pods of garlic
salt substitute
1 cup lite mayonnaise
1 cup ketchup
2 tbsps horseradish
hot sauce
1 head of lettuce
2 tomatoes, diced
1 cup diced celery
1/2 cup diced onion

☞ METHOD:

In a 5-quart sauce pan, add quartered onion, lemon, bay leaf, garlic and salt substitute to 2 quarts of water. Bring to a rolling boil and allow to cook for 15 minutes in order for flavors to develop. Add shrimp. When water returns to a boil, cook 2–3 minutes or until shrimp are pink and curled. Do not overcook. Chill under cold tap water. Remove shrimp and set aside.

In a large mixing bowl, combine mayonnaise, ketchup and horseradish. Season to taste using hot sauce. (NOTE: Luke used 1/4 of a small bottle.) Using a wire whisk, blend well until all is incorporated. Fold in shrimp, coat well with the sauce and refrigerate.

When ready to serve, wash lettuce and tear into bite-size salad pieces. Drain and place in a large salad bowl, along with tomatoes, celery, diced onion and shrimp/dressing mixture. Using a wooden spoon, blend well until all ingredients are incorporated. Serve on 8 individual salad plates.

NOTE: You may wish to boil the shrimp in crab boil.

Nutrition Facts...now

Calories:	274
Total Fat:	10gm
Saturated Fat:	1gm
% Calories from Fat:	32
Cholesterol:	272mg
Sodium:	748mg
Carbohydrate:	16gm
Fiber:	3gm
Protein:	30gm

Marshland with blooming water lilies just north of Creole in Cameron Parish.

PREP TIME: 1 Hour   SERVES: 6

☞ INGREDIENTS:

1 cup (150–200 count) shrimp, cooked and peeled
1 cup jumbo lump crabmeat
11 ounces V-8 juice
11 ounces tomato juice
2 packages unflavored gelatin,
      (dissolved in 1/2 cup cold water)
1/4 cup chopped parsley
1/4 cup sliced green onions
1/4 cup finely diced onions
1/4 cup finely diced celery
1/2 cup finely diced stuffed olives
1 peeled avocado, finely diced
2 tbsps lemon juice
2 tsps Worcestershire Sauce
1 tsp salt
black pepper
Louisiana Gold Pepper Sauce
1 tsp sugar

☞ METHOD:

In a 2-quart sauce pot, heat V-8 juice and tomato juice over medium-high heat. Add dissolved gelatin and blend well into the juice. Remove from heat and add parsley, green onions, onions, celery and olives. Allow mixture to cool slightly before adding avocado, lemon juice and Worcestershire. Season to taste using salt, pepper, Louisiana Gold and sugar. Fold in shrimp and crabmeat. Adjust seasonings, if necessary, and pour into your favorite seafood mold. Chill in refrigerator until firm, at least several hours. This full-flavored aspic salad is wonderful as an accompaniment to roasted leg of lamb or any wild game dish. However, you may wish to use it as a luncheon entree by serving it over a mixture of salad greens.

> "It is no wonder, with the Creole influence in and around the city of Natchitoches, that a tomato aspic salad would emerge.
> "This simple salad has an added twist with the addition of shrimp and crabmeat. You may try adding a bit of leftover grilled chicken or roast beef to this recipe in place of the seafood."
>
> John Folse
> Donaldsonville, Louisiana

❧ Nutrition Facts...then ❧

Calories:	126
Total Fat:	6gm
Saturated Fat:	0gm
% Calories from Fat:	42
Cholesterol:	41mg
Sodium:	1037mg
Carbohydrate:	7gm
Fiber:	5gm
Protein:	12gm

PREP TIME: 1 Hour   SERVES: 6

☞ INGREDIENTS:

1 cup (150–200 count) shrimp, cooked and peeled
1 cup jumbo lump crabmeat
11 ounces V-8 juice, no salt added
11 ounces tomato juice, no salt added
2 packages unflavored gelatin,
         (dissolved in 1/2 cup cold water)
1/4 cup chopped parsley
1/4 cup sliced green onions
1/4 cup finely diced onions
1/4 cup finely diced celery
1/4 cup finely diced stuffed olives
1/2 peeled avocado, finely diced
2 tbsps lemon juice
2 tsps Worcestershire Sauce
black pepper
Louisiana Gold Pepper Sauce
1 tsp sugar

☞ METHOD:

In a 2-quart sauce pot, heat V-8 juice and tomato juice over medium-high heat. Add dissolved gelatin and blend well into the juice. Remove from heat and add parsley, green onions, onions, celery and olives.

Allow mixture to cool slightly before adding avocado, lemon juice and Worcestershire. Season to taste using pepper, Louisiana Gold and sugar. Fold in shrimp and crabmeat. Adjust seasonings, if necessary, and pour into your favorite seafood mold. Chill in refrigerator until firm, at least several hours.

This full-flavored aspic salad is wonderful as an accompaniment to roasted leg of lamb or any wild game dish. However, you may wish to use it as a luncheon entree by serving it over a mixture of salad greens.

Nutrition Facts...now

Calories:	109
Total Fat:	4gm
Saturated Fat:	0gm
% Calories from Fat:	31
Cholesterol:	41mg
Sodium:	369mg
Carbohydrate:	7gm
Fiber:	4gm
Protein:	11gm

HOT SHRIMP SALAD CASSEROLE

PREP TIME: 30 Minutes   SERVES: 6

☞ INGREDIENTS:

1 pound (50–60 count) shrimp, peeled
2 cups chopped celery
1/4 cup grated onion
1/2 cup sliced water chestnuts or pecans
2 hard boiled eggs, diced
2 tbsps lemon juice
3/4 cup mayonnaise
1 tsp salt
black pepper
1/2 cup shredded American cheese
1 cup crushed potato chips

A summer squall line sweeps across farmland near Arnaudville just west of the Atchafalaya Basin.

☞ METHOD:

Devein the shrimp and boil in lightly salted water 2–3 minutes or until shrimp are pink and curled. Do not overcook. In a large mixing bowl, combine shrimp, celery, onions, water chestnuts, eggs, lemon juice and mayonnaise. Season to taste using salt and pepper. Using a wooden spoon, spread the mixture evenly into an 8-inch round Pyrex baking dish. When ready to serve, cover with wax paper and microwave on high for 4 minutes, stirring at 2-minute intervals. Sprinkle with American cheese and microwave 1 minute longer. Top the melted cheese with potato chips and microwave 1 additional minute.

"It really is amazing how many dishes in South Louisiana use shrimp as a main ingredient. Since my grandfather had a shrimp boat, we created recipes that used shrimp in a million different ways.

"This particular recipe was created at the camp after the shrimp boats were in and somehow made it home to our table. It is still a family favorite today!"
Pamela Castel
Baton Rouge, Louisiana

❧ Nutrition Facts...then❧

Calories: 347
Total Fat: 29gm
Saturated Fat: 5gm
% Calories from Fat: 72
Cholesterol: 198mg
Sodium: 715mg
Carbohydrate: 6gm
Fiber: 1gm
Protein: 19gm

(nutrition info figured on chestnuts)

PREP TIME: 30 Minutes   SERVES: 6

☞ INGREDIENTS:

1 pound (50–60 count) shrimp, peeled
2 cups chopped celery
1/4 cup grated onion
1/2 cup sliced water chestnuts
2 boiled egg whites, diced
2 tbsps lemon juice
1/2 cup fat-free mayonnaise
black pepper
1/2 cup low-fat American cheese, shredded
1 cup crushed cracker crumbs, unsalted

☞ METHOD:

Devein the shrimp and boil in water 2–3 minutes or until shrimp are pink and curled. Do not overcook.

In a large mixing bowl, combine shrimp, celery, onions, chestnuts, egg whites, lemon juice and mayonnaise. Discard egg yolks. Season to taste using pepper. Using a wooden spoon, spread the mixture evenly into an 8-inch round Pyrex baking dish.

When ready to serve, cover with wax paper and microwave on high for 4 minutes, stirring at 2-minute intervals. Sprinkle with American cheese and microwave 1 minute longer. Top the melted cheese with cracker crumbs and microwave 1 additional minute.

Nutrition Facts...now

Calories: 179
Total Fat: 4gm
Saturated Fat: 0gm
% Calories from Fat: 19
Cholesterol: 115mg
Sodium: 506mg
Carbohydrate: 19gm
Fiber: 1gm
Protein: 17gm

PREP TIME: 1 Hour   SERVES: 10

☞ INGREDIENTS:

2 cups watermelon balls
2 cups cantaloupe balls
2 cups honeydew balls
2 cups sliced peaches
2 cups sliced pears
2 cups quartered orange sections
2 cups sliced plums
1 cup fresh blueberries
1 cup fresh strawberries
1 cup cubed pineapple
2 dozen (21–25 count) boiled shrimp
2 cups crawfish tails
1 cup jumbo lump crabmeat
6 chopped apple mint leaves
6 chopped lemon balm leaves
1 cup orange juice
8 ounces strawberry yogurt
1/2 cup chopped pecans

☞ METHOD:

In a large glass serving bowl, layer fruit by alternating stratas of color. Once all the fruit has been layered, line shrimp, crawfish and crabmeat in a decorative pattern around the edge of the bowl. In a separate bowl, combine apple mint, lemon balm, orange juice and yogurt. Using a wire whisk, whip until ingredients are well-blended. When ready to serve, sprinkle in pecans and pour the yogurt dressing over the salad ingredients. Toss the mixture to blend the dressing into the fruit. Serve immediately.

"Fruit is not just for dessert anymore! With its wide range of colors and textures, nothing makes a more beautiful entree salad than layers of fresh or canned fruit.

"Why not create an interesting and unique summer salad by combining colorful, healthful fruit with fresh shrimp or other seafoods?"

John Folse
Donaldsonville, Louisiana

❧Nutrition Facts...then❧

Calories:	540
Total Fat:	9gm
Saturated Fat:	1gm
% Calories from Fat:	15
Cholesterol:	623mg
Sodium:	755mg
Carbohydrate:	44gm
Fiber:	5gm
Protein:	72gm

PREP TIME: 1 Hour   SERVES: 10

☞ **INGREDIENTS:**

2 cups watermelon balls
2 cups cantaloupe balls
2 cups honeydew balls
2 cups sliced peaches
2 cups sliced pears
2 cups quartered orange sections
2 cups sliced plums
1 cup fresh blueberries
1 cup fresh strawberries
1 cup cubed pineapple
1 dozen (21–25 count) boiled shrimp
1/2 cup crawfish tails
1 cup jumbo lump crabmeat
6 chopped apple mint leaves
6 chopped lemon balm leaves
1 cup orange juice
8 ounces low-fat strawberry yogurt
1/2 cup chopped pecans

☞ **METHOD:**

In a large glass serving bowl, layer fruit by alternating stratas of color. Once all the fruit has been layered, line shrimp, crawfish and crabmeat in a decorative pattern around the edge of the bowl.

In a separate bowl, combine apple mint, lemon balm, orange juice and yogurt. Using a wire whisk, whip until ingredients are well-blended.

When ready to serve, sprinkle in pecans and pour the yogurt dressing over the salad ingredients. Toss the mixture to blend the dressing into the fruit. Serve immediately.

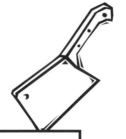

Nutrition Facts...now

Calories: 368
Total Fat: 7gm
Saturated Fat: 1gm
% Calories from Fat: 16
Cholesterol: 316mg
Sodium: 402mg
Carbohydrate: 41gm
Fiber: 5gm
Protein: 39gm

JANE ARNETTE'S CRAWFISH SALAD

PREP TIME: 1 Hour   SERVES: 6

☞ INGREDIENTS:

2 cups boiled crawfish tails
6 large tomatoes
2 boiled eggs, chopped
1 tbsp mustard
3/4 cup mayonnaise
1/2 cup minced onions

1/2 cup minced celery
1 cup whole kernel corn
2 tbsps pickled relish
1/2 tsp salt
black pepper

☞ METHOD:

Hollow and core tomatoes, reserving 1 cup of
tomato pulp. Drain the tomatoes well by turning
them upside down on layers of paper towels.
Remove most of the seeds when selecting the
1 cup of the tomato pulp for the recipe. In a
ceramic bowl, combine the boiled eggs with the
mustard and mayonnaise. Using a fork, blend
well to create a dressing. Add crawfish, onions,
celery, corn, pickled relish and tomato pulp.
Season to taste using salt and pepper. Stuff the
mixture into the drained tomatoes and chill
2–3 hours. Serve as a light luncheon salad
or as an appetizer.

*Window sill at the home of J. D. Soileau in
Ville Platte.*

"Seafood boils are part of the culture
of South Louisiana where seafood is abundant. I remember gathering with the entire family under the old oak tree at my
grandparents' home in Houma, Louisiana.
My mother was one of ten children, so
there were plenty of relatives to share
in the occasion. Leftover seafood was
peeled and cleaned to use in gumbos,
stews, or salads for another meal.

"So many things are different now, but
I remember my grandfather, Ernest
Bonvillain, would walk up the bayou to
Houma to get hot French bread from the
old Excelsior bakery, along with the
wonderful sweet rolls they made called
chic du vielle femme. "Old lady style"
rolls were named for their shape, which
resembled the chignon or bun which older
women wore in those days

"The bakery is gone now, but you can
still get hot French bread in many of
the grocery stores and there are still a
couple of bakeries where you can get the
chic du vielle femme roll. Everytime I
taste one of these special treats, I
think of those large family gatherings
and the fun we used to have just being
together."

Jane Arnette
Houma, Louisiana

❊Nutrition Facts...then❊

Calories: 343
Total Fat: 28gm
Saturated Fat: 6gm
% Calories from Fat: 73
Cholesterol: 215mg
Sodium: 563mg
Carbohydrate: 15gm
Fiber: 3gm
Protein: 9gm

PREP TIME: 1 Hour   SERVES: 6

INGREDIENTS:

2 cups boiled crawfish tails
6 large tomatoes
1 boiled egg, chopped
1 boiled egg white, chopped
1 tbsp mustard
1/2 cup lite mayonnaise
1/2 cup minced onions
1/2 cup minced celery
1 cup whole kernel corn
2 tbsps pickled relish
1/4 tsp salt
black pepper

METHOD:

Hollow and core tomatoes, reserving 1 cup of tomato pulp. Drain the tomatoes well by turning them upside down on layers of paper towels. Remove most of the seeds when selecting the 1 cup of the tomato pulp for the recipe.

In a ceramic bowl, combine the boiled egg and whites with the mustard and mayonnaise. Using a fork, blend well to create a dressing. Add crawfish, onions, celery, corn, pickled relish and tomato pulp. Season to taste using salt and pepper.

Stuff the mixture into the drained tomatoes and chill 2–3 hours. Serve as a light luncheon salad or as an appetizer.

Chef's Tips on Substitution... use two egg whites in place of an egg yolk in scrambled eggs and baked goods.

In from the country: garlic and watermelon at the French Market in New Orleans.

Nutrition Facts...now

Calories:	164
Total Fat:	9gm
Saturated Fat:	1gm
% Calories from Fat:	45
Cholesterol:	114mg
Sodium:	336mg
Carbohydrate:	16gm
Fiber:	3gm
Protein:	7gm

PREP TIME: 30 Minutes   SERVES: 6

☞ INGREDIENTS:

2 cups cooked crawfish tails
1 head red leaf lettuce
1 (10-ounce) package fresh spinach leaves
1/2 cup cooked bacon, crumbled
1/2 cup chopped Bermuda onions
2 cups mandarin orange sections, canned
1 cup sliced mushrooms
3/4 cup salad oil
1/2 cup cider vinegar
1/4 cup sugar
1/4 cup orange juice
1 tsp dried mustard
1 tbsp chopped sage
1 tbsp chopped basil
1 tsp salt
black pepper

☞ METHOD:

Wash lettuce and spinach leaves well under cold water. Remove large stems and tear into 1-inch pieces. Drain and place in a large mixing bowl. Add crawfish, bacon, onions, oranges and mushrooms. Toss well to blend ingredients. Allow to sit for 30 minutes. In a separate bowl, combine oil, vinegar, sugar and juice. Using a wire whisk, whip until all ingredients are well-blended. Add mustard, sage and basil. Season to taste using salt and pepper. Pour dressing over salad mixture. Toss to coat all ingredients well. Serve equal portions on 6 cold salad plates. NOTE: You may wish to drain juice from orange sections and reserve for use in place of orange juice.

"Though Mardi Gras or Fat Tuesday is celebrated the day before Ash Wednesday, dishes named after the holiday are served all year long.
  "This particular salad can be made with or without the sea-food, however, you may wish to substitute smoked chicken or cottage cheese in its place."
                    John Folse
        Donaldsonville, Louisiana

❧Nutrition Facts...then❧

Calories: 351
Total Fat: 28gm
Saturated Fat: 4gm
% Calories from Fat: 69
Cholesterol: 13mg
Sodium: 424mg
Carbohydrate: 24gm
Fiber: 3gm
Protein: 5gm

PREP TIME: 30 Minutes   SERVES: 6

☞ INGREDIENTS:

2 cups cooked crawfish tails
1 head red leaf lettuce
1 (10-ounce) package fresh spinach leaves
1/4 cup imitation bacon bits
1/2 cup chopped Bermuda onions
2 cups mandarin orange sections, canned
1 cup sliced mushrooms
1/4 cup oil
1/2 cup cider vinegar
1/4 cup sugar
1/4 cup orange juice
1 tsp dried mustard
1 tbsp chopped sage
1 tbsp chopped basil
salt substitute
black pepper

☞ METHOD:

Wash lettuce and spinach leaves well under cold water. Remove large stems and tear into 1-inch pieces. Drain and place in a large mixing bowl.

Add crawfish, bacon bits, onions, oranges and mushrooms. Toss well to blend ingredients. Allow to sit for 30 minutes.

In a separate bowl, combine oil, vinegar, sugar and juice. Using a wire whisk, whip until all ingredients are well-blended. Add mustard, sage and basil. Season to taste using salt substitute and pepper. Pour dressing over salad mixture. Toss to coat all ingredients well.

Serve equal portions on 6 cold salad plates. NOTE: You may wish to drain juice from orange sections and reserve for use in place of orange juice.

Nutrition Facts...now

Calories:	209
Total Fat:	11gm
Saturated Fat:	1gm
% Calories from Fat:	44
Cholesterol:	13mg
Sodium:	179mg
Carbohydrate:	25gm
Fiber:	3gm
Protein:	6gm

PREP TIME: 1 Hour   SERVES: 6

☞ INGREDIENTS:

1 (20-ounce) can crushed pineapple
3/4 cup grated carrots
1 (4-ounce) envelope lime gelatin
1 3/4 cup cold water
1/3 cup sugar
1/4 cup lemon juice
1/4 tsp salt
3/4 cup chopped celery
2 tbsps mayonnaise
lettuce leaves for garnish

☞ METHOD:

In a 2-quart sauce pot, combine gelatin and water, stirring until dissolved. Add sugar, lemon juice and salt. Bring mixture to a rolling boil, reduce to simmer and stir constantly until gelatin is thoroughly dissolved and clear, approximately 3–5 minutes. Remove from heat and add pineapple with its juice, carrots and celery. Blend well into mixture and allow to cool to room temperature. Using a wire whisk, blend in mayonnaise until completely incorporated. Pour mixture into a decorative mold, cover with clear wrap and refrigerate until firm. To serve, unmold the congealed salad onto a platter garnished with colored lettuces.

"This is a very refreshing dish on one of South Louisiana's long, hot summer days. As kids, we thought it was a dessert, and were forever pestering our mother or great-grandmother to make it for us. Pineapple was something of a novelty to kids growing up on a farm in Louisiana more than a half-century ago.

"This dish was also a staple of social events and family gatherings."

Roderick Lafargue
Lafayette, Louisiana

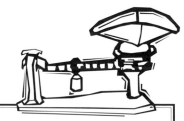

❧Nutrition Facts...then❧

Calories: 196
Total Fat: 4gm
Saturated Fat: 1gm
% Calories from Fat: 18
Cholesterol: 2mg
Sodium: 178mg
Carbohydrate: 40gm
Fiber: 2gm
Protein: 2gm

PREP TIME: 1 Hour   SERVES: 6

☞ INGREDIENTS:

1 (20-ounce) can crushed pineapple
3/4 cup grated carrots
1 (4-ounce) envelope lime gelatin
1 3/4 cup cold water
1/3 cup sugar
1/4 cup lemon juice
3/4 cup chopped celery
2 tbsps fat-free mayonnaise
lettuce leaves for garnish

☞ METHOD:

In a 2-quart sauce pot, combine gelatin and water, stirring until dissolved. Add sugar and lemon juice. Bring mixture to a rolling boil, reduce to simmer and stir constantly until gelatin is thoroughly dissolved and clear, approximately 3–5 minutes.

Remove from heat and add pineapple with its juice, carrots and celery. Blend well into mixture and allow to cool to room temperature.

Using a wire whisk, blend in mayonnaise until completely incorporated. Pour mixture into a decorative mold, cover with clear wrap and refrigerate until firm.

To serve, unmold the congealed salad onto a platter garnished with colored lettuces.

Norman and Vivian Parr in from the gardens with some of their bounty near Lockport.

Nutrition Facts...now

Calories:	163
Total Fat:	0gm
Saturated Fat:	0gm
% Calories from Fat:	1
Cholesterol:	0mg
Sodium:	127mg
Carbohydrate:	40gm
Fiber:	2gm
Protein:	2gm

Chef's Tips on Low fat... make soups low in fat by skimming off the fat layer that floats to the top.

127

PREP TIME: 1 Hour   SERVES: 6

INGREDIENTS:

3 pounds red new potatoes
1 cup Heineken beer
1/4 cup olive oil
1/4 cup sliced green onions
1/4 cup chopped parsley
2 tbsps Louisiana cane syrup
1 tbsp diced garlic
1 tbsp Creole mustard
1/2 tsp sugar
1/4 cup salad oil
1 tsp salt
black pepper
Louisiana Gold Pepper Sauce
2 small Bermuda onions, sliced
1/4 cup julienned green bell pepper
1/4 cup julienned yellow bell pepper

"No two ingredients are more German than potatoes and beer. Both of these staples were in great supply in and around St. James and St. John the Baptist Parishes from the time the Germans arrived in the early 1700s.

"This dish is exceptional for a patio party or backyard barbecue."

John Folse
Donaldsonville, Louisiana

METHOD:

In a 1-gallon stock pot, boil potatoes in lightly salted water until tender, approximately 20–25 minutes. Do not overcook. When tender, drain, spread on cutting board and allow to cool slightly. In a 10-inch cast iron skillet, heat olive oil over medium-high heat. Add green onions, parsley, beer, cane syrup and garlic. Bring to a low boil and cook for approximately 2–3 minutes. Place the hot ingredients in a blender or food processor fitted with a metal blade. Add mustard and sugar and blend ingredients well. While blending, slowly pour in salad oil. Remove from blender and season to taste using salt, pepper and Louisiana Gold. When potatoes are cool enough to handle but still warm, slice 1/4-inch thick. Place in a large mixing bowl and add onions and bell peppers. Coat with dressing and serve immediately.

❧ Nutrition Facts...then ❧

Calories: 328
Total Fat: 10gm
Saturated Fat: 1gm
% Calories from Fat: 27
Cholesterol: 0mg
Sodium: 407mg
Carbohydrate: 54gm
Fiber: 4gm
Protein: 5gm

PREP TIME: 1 Hour   SERVES: 6

☞ INGREDIENTS:

3 pounds red new potatoes
1 cup Heineken beer
1/4 cup sliced green onions
1/4 cup chopped parsley
2 tbsps Louisiana cane syrup
1 tbsp diced garlic
1 tbsp Creole mustard
1/2 tsp sugar
2 tbsps olive oil
1/2 tsp salt
black pepper
Louisiana Gold Pepper Sauce
2 small Bermuda onions, sliced
1/4 cup julienned green bell pepper
1/4 cup julienned yellow bell pepper

☞ METHOD:

In a 1-gallon stock pot, boil potatoes in lightly salted water until tender, approximately 20–25 minutes. Do not overcook. When tender, drain, spread on cutting board and allow to cool slightly.

In a 10-inch cast iron skillet, heat green onions, parsley, beer, cane syrup and garlic over medium-high heat. Bring to a low boil and cook for approximately 2–3 minutes.

Place the hot ingredients in a blender or food processor fitted with a metal blade. Add mustard and sugar and blend ingredients well. While blending, slowly pour in olive oil. Remove from blender and season to taste using salt, pepper and Louisiana Gold.

When potatoes are cool enough to handle but still warm, slice 1/4-inch thick. Place in a large mixing bowl and add onions and bell peppers. Coat with dressing and serve immediately.

Nutrition Facts...now	
Calories:	245
Total Fat:	1gm
Saturated Fat:	0gm
% Calories from Fat:	3
Cholesterol:	0mg
Sodium:	229mg
Carbohydrate:	54gm
Fiber:	4gm
Protein:	5gm

Chef's Tips on Substitution... steam or poach onions and other vegetables in a very small amount of water or broth instead of oil.

PREP TIME: 1 Hour   SERVES: 6

☞ INGREDIENTS:

3/4 cup cottage cheese
1 cup crushed pineapple
1 apple, diced
1 cup water
1 1/2 tbsps vinegar
3/4 cup Coca-Cola
1 (4-ounce) package lemon gelatin
1/2 cup shredded carrots
1/3 cup chopped celery
1/2 cup mayonnaise

"Often a recipe becomes family tradition without anyone ever knowing the source. I remember sitting on the front porch of our home in Morgan City and mixing fruits and vegetables with cottage cheese as sort of an afternoon treat.
"This simple recipe was a mini-version of the fruit souffle that we often served on holidays. Until today, we still don't quite know who gave us this little gem, but it sure is tasty."

Gia Stephens
Morgan City, Louisiana

☞ METHOD:

In a large sauce pan, heat water, vinegar and Coca-Cola over medium-high heat. Bring to a low boil, remove from heat and blend in gelatin. Once mixture is thoroughly dissolved, pour it into a large bowl and chill in refrigerator until firm around the edges but soft in the center. Remove from refrigerator. Using a rotary mixer, whip the gelatin, souffle-style. Add cheese, pineapple, apple, carrots, celery and mayonnaise. Using a rubber spatula, fold the ingredients into the whipped gelatin. Pour into a decorative mold and chill until firm. Serve as a light luncheon salad over multi-colored lettuces or as a summer dessert.

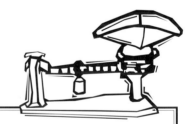

❦Nutrition Facts...then❦

Calories: 274
Total Fat: 17gm
Saturated Fat: 3gm
% Calories from Fat: 55
Cholesterol: 11mg
Sodium: 254mg
Carbohydrate: 28gm
Fiber: 1gm
Protein: 4gm

PREP TIME: 1 Hour   SERVES: 6

☞ INGREDIENTS:

3/4 cup fat-free cottage cheese
1 cup crushed pineapple
1 apple diced
1 cup water
1 1/2 tbsps vinegar
3/4 cup Coca-Cola
1 (4-ounce) package lemon gelatin
1/2 cup shredded carrots
1/3 cup chopped celery
1/2 cup fat-free mayonnaise

☞ METHOD:

In a large sauce pan, heat water, vinegar and Coca-Cola over medium-high heat. Bring to a low boil, remove from heat and blend in gelatin.

Once mixture is thoroughly dissolved, pour it into a large bowl and chill in refrigerator until firm around the edges but soft in the center. Remove from refrigerator.

Using a rotary mixer, whip the gelatin, souffle-style. Add cheese, pineapple, apple, carrots, celery and mayonnaise. Using a rubber spatula, fold the ingredients into the whipped gelatin.

Pour into a decorative mold and chill until firm. Serve as a light luncheon salad over multi-colored lettuces or as a summer dessert.

Alzina Toups with some of her prized canned vegetables in Galliano.

Nutrition Facts...now

Calories:	147
Total Fat:	0gm
Saturated Fat:	0gm
% Calories from Fat:	1
Cholesterol:	1mg
Sodium:	383mg
Carbohydrate:	32gm
Fiber:	1gm
Protein:	5gm

OLD TIME POTATO SALAD

PREP TIME: 1 Hour   SERVES: 6

☞ INGREDIENTS:

6 medium potatoes
2 boiled eggs
1 raw egg yolk
2 tsps oil
1 cup mayonnaise
2 tsps vinegar
1 tsp salt
cracked pepper
1/4 tsp granulated garlic

☞ METHOD:

Peel and wash potatoes well. In a large cast iron dutch oven, place potatoes in lightly salted water to cover by 1 inch. Boil until tender but not overcooked and mushy. Drain and set aside. Using a paring knife, remove the yolks from the boiled eggs, dice the whites and set aside. In a large mixing bowl, mash the two boiled egg yolks. Add the raw yolk and oil. Using a wire whisk, blend until well incorporated. Add mayonnaise, diced egg whites and vinegar. Continue to mix until well-blended. When potatoes are slightly cooled, slice into rounds and layer on a serving platter or bowl. Alternate potato layers with sauce, seasoning each layer with salt, pepper and granulated garlic. Retain enough of the sauce to spread over the top. You may wish to garnish with paprika and parsley for color.

Chef's Tips on Low-fat... when using the meat juices for gravy, skim or pour off the fat first.

"How often I think of the time when there simply weren't any sandwich spreads, pickles, relish or any of those 'good things' to put into potato salad. In those days, you just 'made do.'
"I remember how easy it was to throw together a potato salad that tasted so much better than the one filled with all those 'foreign' ingredients. Every now and then, we still make Old Timey Potato Salad and the grandkids seem to like it better."
Elaine Lapeyrouse
Chauvin, Louisiana

❧Nutrition Facts...then❧

Calories:	438
Total Fat:	37gm
Saturated Fat:	6gm
% Calories from Fat:	72
Cholesterol:	119mg
Sodium:	573mg
Carbohydrate:	27gm
Fiber:	2gm
Protein:	5gm

PREP TIME: 1 Hour   SERVES: 6

☞ INGREDIENTS:

6 medium potatoes
2 boiled eggs
1 tsp oil
3/4 cup lite mayonnaise
1 tbsp water
2 tsps vinegar
cracked pepper
1/4 tsp granulated garlic

☞ METHOD:

Peel and wash potatoes well. In a large cast iron dutch oven, place potatoes in water to cover by 1 inch. Boil until tender but not overcooked and mushy. Drain and set aside.

Using a paring knife, remove the yolks from the boiled eggs, dice the whites and set aside. Discard one egg yolk.

In a large mixing bowl, mash the boiled egg yolk. Add oil and using a wire whisk, blend until well incorporated. Add mayonnaise, water, diced egg whites and vinegar. Continue to mix until well-blended.

When potatoes are slightly cooled, slice into rounds and layer on a serving platter or bowl. Alternate potato layers with sauce, seasoning each layer with pepper and granulated garlic. Retain enough of the sauce to spread over the top. You may wish to garnish with paprika and parsley for color.

Nutrition Facts...now

Calories:	219
Total Fat:	10gm
Saturated Fat:	1gm
% Calories from Fat:	40
Cholesterol:	46mg
Sodium:	57mg
Carbohydrate:	29gm
Fiber:	2gm
Protein:	4gm

Vegetables

Chapter Four

Mama's Eggplant Casserole Supreme	136/137
Eggplant Casserole Bilello	138/139
Shrimp-Sauced Cauliflower	140/141
Maw Rhodes' Eggplant Beignets	142/143
Macaroni & Cheese Casserole	144/145
Smothered Okra & Tomatoes	146/147
Old Fashioned Smothered Potatoes	148/149
Sweet Potato Delight	150/151
Louisiana White or Red Beans with Ham	152/153
Eggplant-Stuffed Bell Peppers	156/157
Green Bean & Artichoke Casserole	158/159
Roberta's Baked Artichokes	160/161
Quick Spinach Casserole	162/163
Baked Corn Casserole	164/165
Bacon-Wrapped Green Beans	166/167
Vegetable Jambalaya	168/169
Broccoli with Dijon Vinaigrette	170/171
Cous Cous Cajun-Style	172/173
Uncle Bro's Cajun-Style Stuffed Mirliton	174/175
Maque Choux Acadian	176/177

*The recipes for **Roberta's Baked Artichokes**,
pictured at left, can be found on pages 160 and 161*

PREP TIME: 2 Hours   SERVES: 10

☞ INGREDIENTS:

2 large eggplants, diced
1/4 cup butter
1 pound chicken livers
1 pound chicken gizzards
1 cup diced onions
1 cup diced celery
1/2 cup diced yellow bell peppers
1/2 cup diced red bell peppers
2 tbsps diced garlic
1 pound hot pork sausage
1 tsp minced parsley
1 tsp minced tarragon
1 tsp minced thyme
1 tsp minced oregano
cayenne pepper
1 (12–inch) skillet–cooked cornbread
1/4 cup minced chives

☞ METHOD:

Preheat oven to 300 degrees F. In a 12-inch cast iron skillet, melt butter over medium-high heat. Saute chicken livers and gizzards until golden brown. Remove, chop and return to skillet. Add onions, celery, bell peppers and garlic. Saute 3–5 minutes or until vegetables are wilted. Add sausage and cook until it is well browned. While sausage is cooking, place eggplant in a microwavable bowl and cook on high 3–5 minutes or until eggplant is soft. Do not add water, as eggplant will make its own liquid. Add eggplant to sausage mixture and continue to saute. Add parsley, tarragon, thyme and oregano. Season to taste using cayenne pepper. This mixture should be moist but not too juicy. In a large mixing bowl, break the cooked cornbread into small pieces. Add the meat mixture and blend well into the cornbread. Adjust seasonings if necessary. Place eggplant in a large casserole dish and bake for approximately 1 hour. Garnish with fresh chives.

"This basic recipe has been handed down in my family for three generations. My great, great grandmother, Marie Stephanie Decuir, was part Attakapus Indian, born in New Iberia, Louisiana. Her Indian name was Tinkletwan. She was a fabulous cook and, although she died in 1845, we still know a great deal about her life.

"I am the oldest daughter in my family, born in 1938. Like her mother and grandmother, my mother was a great cook. From her, I learned to love cooking and to improve upon the recipes."

Agnes Wyatt
Lake Charles, Louisiana

❊Nutrition Facts...then❊

Calories: 520
Total Fat: 27gm
Saturated Fat: 10gm
% Calories from Fat:................. 47
Cholesterol: 415mg
Sodium: 1123mg
Carbohydrate: 36gm
Fiber: 1gm
Protein: 33gm

PREP TIME: 2 Hours   SERVES: 10

☞ INGREDIENTS:

2 large eggplants, diced
1/4 cup lite margarine
1/2 pound chicken livers
1 pound chicken gizzards
1 cup diced onions
1 cup diced celery
1/2 cup diced yellow bell peppers
1/2 cup diced red bell peppers
2 tbsps diced garlic
1 pound lean ground pork loin
1 tsp minced parsley
1 tsp minced tarragon
1 tsp minced thyme
1 tsp minced oregano
cayenne pepper
1 (12–inch) skillet–cooked cornbread
1/4 cup minced chives

*Chef's Tips on Low Fat...
use egg whites and skim milk
to make cornbread.*

☞ METHOD:

Preheat oven to 300 degrees F. In a 12-inch cast iron skillet, melt margarine over medium-high heat. Saute chicken livers and gizzards until golden brown. Remove, chop and return to pan.

Add onions, celery, bell peppers and garlic. Saute 3–5 minutes or until vegetables are wilted. Add pork loin and cook until it is well browned.

While pork is cooking, place eggplant in a microwavable bowl and cook on high 3–5 minutes or until eggplant is soft. Do not add water, as eggplant will make its own liquid.

Add eggplant to pork mixture and continue to saute. Add parsley, tarragon, thyme and oregano. Season to taste using cayenne pepper. This mixture should be moist but not too juicy.

In a large mixing bowl, break the cooked cornbread into small pieces. Add the meat mixture and blend well into the cornbread. Adjust seasonings if necessary.

Place eggplant in a large casserole dish and bake for approximately 1 hour. Garnish with fresh chives.

Nutrition Facts...now

Calories:	361
Total Fat:	12gm
Saturated Fat:	3gm
% Calories from Fat:	30
Cholesterol:	246mg
Sodium:	527mg
Carbohydrate:	35gm
Fiber:	1gm
Protein:	28gm

PREP TIME: 2 Hours   SERVES: 8

INGREDIENTS:

4 large eggplants, peeled and sliced 1/4-inch thick
1 tbsp peanut oil
1 cup chopped onions
1 cup chopped bell pepper
2 tbsps diced garlic
2 cups water
3 cups tomato sauce
1 tsp salt
black pepper
1 1/2 tsps garlic powder
1/2 cup Parmesan cheese
4 hard boiled eggs, sliced

METHOD:

Preheat oven to 400 degrees F. Sprinkle salt over the eggplant and place in a large bowl or colander, with a heavy weight on top, to help squeeze the water from the eggplant. Set aside for approximately 1 hour. In a 5-quart cast iron dutch oven, heat oil over medium-high heat. Add onions, bell pepper and garlic. Saute 3–5 minutes or until vegetables are wilted. Add water and tomato sauce. Bring to a rolling boil and reduce to simmer. Season to taste using salt and pepper. Cook for approximately 45 minutes, stirring occasionally. Place the drained eggplant slices on a pre-greased cookie sheet and bake for 30 minutes. Divide the eggplant into 3 equal parts and place the first 1/3 in the bottom of a 9" x 13" casserole dish. Sprinkle with a small amount of garlic powder and cheese. Spoon 1/3 of the gravy on top of the eggplant and finish with 3–4 slices of eggs. Continue the process in layers until all is used up. Pour any excess sauce over the top of the eggplant and sprinkle with remaining Parmesan cheese. Bake, uncovered, for 30 minutes. NOTE: Fresh basil and oregano may be added to the seasoning mixture.

"Salvatore Mancuso arrived in New Orleans with his young wife in 1870. After working for many years on White Plantation, he saved enough money to buy his own farm and had a family of his own. One of his daughters, Vita, married Antonio Bilello and they started a family eventually consisting of seven sons.

"Since there were no girls in the family, the second oldest boy, Salvatore, was responsible for helping with the children and cooking, while the oldest son worked on the farm. Salvatore soon became an accomplished cook and, when he grew up, opened his own restaurant in Thibodaux.

"Today, Bilello's Restaurant is a landmark on Bayou Lafourche. It all started with a young Sicilian arriving here in the late 1800s."

Sam Bilello
Lafayette, Louisiana

❋Nutrition Facts...then❋

Calories: 147
Total Fat: 7gm
Saturated Fat: 2gm
% Calories from Fat: 38
Cholesterol: 111mg
Sodium: 976mg
Carbohydrate: 16gm
Fiber: 2gm
Protein: 8gm

PREP TIME: 2 Hours   SERVES: 8

☞ INGREDIENTS:

4 large eggplants, peeled and sliced 1/4-inch thick
1 tbsp peanut oil
1 cup chopped onions
1 cup chopped bell pepper
2 tbsps diced garlic
2 cups water

3 cups tomato sauce, no salt added
1/4 tsp salt
black pepper
1 1/2 tsps garlic powder
1/2 cup fat–free Parmesan cheese
2 hard boiled eggs, sliced

☞ METHOD:

Preheat oven to 400 degrees F. Sprinkle salt over the eggplant and place in a large bowl or colander, with a heavy weight on top, to help squeeze the water from the eggplant. Set aside for approximately 1 hour.

In a 5-quart cast iron dutch oven, heat oil over medium-high heat. Add onions, bell pepper and garlic. Saute 3–5 minutes or until vegetables are wilted. Add water and tomato sauce. Bring to a rolling boil and reduce to simmer. Season to taste using salt and pepper. Cook for approximately 45 minutes, stirring occasionally.

Place the drained eggplant slices on a non-stick cookie sheet and bake for 30 minutes. Divide the eggplant into 3 equal parts and

Handpainted sign in Sulphur.

place the first 1/3 in the bottom of a 9" x 13" casserole dish. Sprinkle with a small amount of garlic powder and cheese. Spoon 1/3 of the gravy on top of the eggplant and finish with 2–3 slices of eggs. Continue the process in layers until all is used up. Pour any excess sauce over the top of the eggplant and sprinkle with remaining Parmesan cheese. Bake, uncovered, for 30 minutes.

NOTE: Fresh basil and oregano may be added to the seasoning mixture.

Nutrition Facts...now

Calories:	107
Total Fat:	2gm
Saturated Fat:	0gm
% Calories from Fat:	12
Cholesterol:	58mg
Sodium:	158mg
Carbohydrate:	18gm
Fiber:	2gm
Protein:	6gm

PREP TIME: 1 Hour   SERVES: 6

☞ INGREDIENTS:

1/2 pound (70–90 count) shrimp, cooked
2 pounds cauliflower
3 tbsps butter
3 tbsps flour
2 cups milk
1/2 cup grated American cheese
2 tsps prepared horseradish
garlic powder
1 tsp salt
white pepper

☞ METHOD:

Preheat oven to 350 degrees F. Trim stems from cauliflower and cut into serving pieces. In a 5-quart sauce pot, place cauliflower with enough lightly salted water to cover by 2 inches. Bring to a rolling boil and cook 10–12 minutes or until cauliflower is tender. Drain and keep warm. In a 3-quart cast iron dutch oven, melt butter over medium-high heat. Add flour and, using a wire whisk, whip constantly until white roux is achieved. Add milk and continue to blend until sauce is smooth and thickened. Stir in cheese and continue cooking until it is melted. Stirring constantly, add horseradish and garlic powder. Season to taste using salt and pepper. Fold in shrimp and stir until heated thoroughly. Place cauliflower in a casserole dish and top with the shrimp sauce. You may wish to dust with paprika and parsley for color. Cover and bake 10–15 minutes or until sauce is bubbly.

"My maternal grandfather's name was Xavier Eschete, but everyone called him 'Bee.' Like most Cajuns of his day, he had to do many things to make a living. One was shucking oysters - for a nickel a gallon, in those days! He was still shucking oysters when I was growing up.

"Another of his jobs was delivering French bread to the countryside for the old Excelsior Bakery here in Houma. He had mounted a tire rim on his old car and I used to ride with him when I was a little girl and pound on that tire rim with a ball peen hammer to let people know we were coming. He made his bread rounds every other day. And his customers depended on him. There weren't any grocery stores to run to in those days. There weren't even any paved roads!

"The old Excelsior Bakery also made hardtack, which the shrimpers, fishermen and trappers carried. And gingerbread - they made the most wonderful gingerbread!"

Bobbie Lee Belanger
Houma, Louisiana

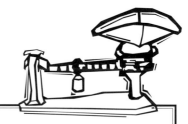

❋Nutrition Facts...then❋

Calories: 211
Total Fat: 12gm
Saturated Fat: 7gm
% Calories from Fat: 48
Cholesterol: 105mg
Sodium: 673mg
Carbohydrate: 13gm
Fiber: 0gm
Protein: 15gm

SHRIMP-SAUCED CAULIFLOWER

PREP TIME: 1 Hour   SERVES: 6

☞ INGREDIENTS:

1/2 pound (70–90 count) shrimp, cooked
2 pounds cauliflower
1 tbsp oil
3 tbsps flour
2 cups skim milk
1/2 cup low–fat American cheese, grated
2 tsps prepared horseradish
garlic powder
salt substitute
white pepper

☞ METHOD:

Preheat oven to 350 degrees F. Trim stems from cauliflower and cut into serving pieces.

In a 5-quart sauce pot, place cauliflower with enough lightly salted water to cover by 2 inches. Bring to a rolling boil and cook 10–12 minutes or until cauliflower is tender. Drain and keep warm.

In a 3-quart cast iron dutch oven, heat oil over medium-high heat. Add flour and, using a wire whisk, whip constantly until white roux is achieved. Add skim milk and continue to blend until sauce is smooth and thickened. Stir in cheese and continue cooking until it is melted.

Stirring constantly, add horseradish and garlic powder. Season to taste using salt substitute and pepper. Fold in shrimp and stir until heated thoroughly.

Place cauliflower in a casserole dish and top with the shrimp sauce. You may wish to dust with paprika and parsley for color. Cover and bake 10–15 minutes or until sauce is bubbly.

Nutrition Facts...now

Calories: 156
Total Fat: 5gm
Saturated Fat: 2gm
% Calories from Fat: 27
Cholesterol: 79mg
Sodium: 302mg
Carbohydrate: 14gm
Fiber: 0gm
Protein: 16gm

MAW RHODES' EGGPLANT BEIGNETS

PREP TIME: 1 Hour   SERVES: 6

☞ INGREDIENTS:

2 large eggplants, peeled and diced
3/4 cup sugar
2 large eggs, beaten
2 cups all purpose flour
2 tbsps vanilla extract
2 tsps baking powder
1/4 tsp salt
oil for deep frying
powdered sugar (optional)

☞ METHOD:

Maw Rhodes prefers the long firm eggplants over the larger ones. The larger ones tend to have more seeds and are not quite so firm. In a 5-quart cast iron dutch oven, boil eggplant in water over medium-high heat until very tender. Drain in colander and set aside to cool. Chop cooled eggplant until it appears to be almost mashed. Place the chopped eggplant in a large mixing bowl. Add sugar and eggs, blending well into the eggplant mixture. Add flour, vanilla and baking powder, continuing to stir after each addition. Add salt and blend well into the mixture. In a homestyle deep fryer, such as Fry Daddy, heat oil to 350 degrees F. Using a teaspoon, drop the batter into the hot oil, 4–6 fritters at a time. Fry until golden brown and beignets float to the surface. Drain well on paper towels. If serving as a breakfast item, you may wish to sprinkle the beignets with powdered sugar. However, they are wonderful served simply as a vegetable fritter.

> "My mother-in-law, Vivian Rhodes, is well known here in Montegut. She managed the school cafeteria for nineteen years, catered for parties and weddings, and cooked countless meals for friends and families. Although she is probably best known for her chicken gumbo, no one can ever resist her eggplant beignets."
>
> Dana Rhodes
> Montegut, Louisiana

Clark Charpentier, Sr. works his early summer crop of beans south of Houma.

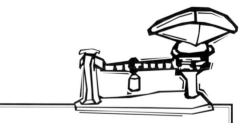

❦Nutrition Facts...then❦

Calories:	383
Total Fat:	11gm
Saturated Fat:	2gm
% Calories from Fat:	27
Cholesterol:	71mg
Sodium:	233mg
Carbohydrate:	62gm
Fiber:	1gm
Protein:	7gm

PREP TIME: 1 Hour   SERVES: 6

☞ INGREDIENTS:

2 large eggplants, peeled and diced
3/4 cup sugar
4 egg whites
2 cups all purpose flour
2 tbsps vanilla extract
2 tsps baking powder
1/4 tsp salt
vegetable spray
powdered sugar (optional)

*Chef's Tips on Substitution...
use cholesterol-free egg substitutes
or egg whites instead of whole eggs
to coat chicken, fish or other meats
before breading.*

☞ METHOD:

Maw Rhodes prefers the long firm eggplants over the larger ones. The larger ones tend to have more seeds and are not quite so firm.

In a 5-quart cast iron dutch oven, boil eggplant in water over medium-high heat until very tender. Drain in colander and set aside to cool.

Chop the cooled eggplant until it appears to be almost mashed. Place the chopped eggplant in a large mixing bowl. Add sugar and egg whites, blending well into the eggplant mixture. Add flour, vanilla and baking powder, continuing to stir after each addition. Add salt and blend well into the mixture.

Coat a griddle with vegetable spray. On hot griddle, using a teaspoon, drop the batter, 4–6 fritters at a time. Grill until beignets are puffy and golden brown.

As an alternative, preheat oven to 375 degrees F. Coat a cookie sheet with vegetable spray. Dip batter by spoonfuls, place on cookie sheet and bake until golden brown.

If serving as a breakfast item, you may wish to sprinkle the beignets with powdered sugar. However, they are wonderful served simply as a vegetable fritter.

Nutrition Facts...now

Calories:	289
Total Fat:	1gm
Saturated Fat:	0gm
% Calories from Fat:	2
Cholesterol:	0mg
Sodium:	249mg
Carbohydrate:	62gm
Fiber:	1gm
Protein:	7gm

PREP TIME: 1 1/2 Hours   **SERVES: 8**

☞ INGREDIENTS:

16 ounces spaghetti
8 ounces grated cheddar cheese
4 slices American cheese
1 (22–ounce) can evaporated milk
22 ounces whole milk
3 eggs, beaten
1/3 cup sugar
1 tsp salt
1/2 stick butter
1/2 stick butter

☞ METHOD:

Preheat oven to 375 degrees F. In a large mixing bowl, combine evaporated milk, milk, eggs, sugar and salt. Using a wire whisk, whip until all ingredients are well-blended. Slice 1/2 stick of butter into pats and add to the mixture. Fold in the cheddar cheese and blend well. Cook spaghetti according to package directions. When tender, drain and add to mixture. The hot spaghetti will melt the butter and cheese, creating a wonderful sauce. Pour spaghetti into 5 quart casserole dish and top with American cheese. Cut the remaining butter into pats and place on top of the cheese. Using your hands, press the spaghetti down tightly into the casserole dish allowing milk to cover the spaghetti. Bake for 45 minutes.

"Macaroni and cheese isn't Cajun, of course. It's sort of all-American. Now that I think about it, there just aren't many Cajun recipes that use cheese. It was a kind of treat for the seven of us kids, growing up on a farm worker's wages on Big Bayou Black.

"Those were hard days, but they were good days. We never lacked for food. We had our garden, our chickens and our pigs. My mother baked bread in the oven of a wood cookstove. There was no way to regulate the heat, not even a thermometer to tell you what the temperature was. She just knew when it was right.

"We didn't have electricity, a car, or even indoor plumbing - this was 60 years ago, or more. But you don't miss what you never had, so we didn't think much about it. On the other hand, Christmas meant one present per child. One Christmas, my present was a doll with a china head, and I accidentally broke the head. I can smile about it now, but then-oh!-I was devastated!"
Marjorie Domangue
Gibson, Louisiana

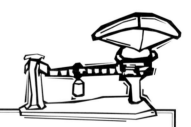

❋Nutrition Facts...then❋

Calories: 648
Total Fat: 35gm
Saturated Fat: 16gm
% Calories from Fat: 48
Cholesterol: 208mg
Sodium: 1136mg
Carbohydrate: 52gm
Fiber: 1gm
Protein: 31gm

PREP TIME: 1 1/2 Hours   SERVES: 8

INGREDIENTS:

16 ounces spaghetti
4 ounces reduced fat cheddar cheese, grated
4 slices reduced fat American cheese
1 (22-ounce) can evaporated skim milk
22 ounces skim milk
3/4 cup egg substitute
1/3 cup sugar
salt substitute
1/4 cup lite margarine

METHOD:

Preheat oven to 375 degrees F. In a large mixing bowl, combine evaporated skim milk, skim milk, egg substitute, sugar and salt substitute. Using a wire whisk, whip until all ingredients are well-blended. Fold margarine into the cheddar cheese and blend well.

Cook spaghetti according to package directions. When tender, drain and add to mixture. The hot spaghetti will melt the margarine and cheese, creating a wonderful sauce.

Pour spaghetti into 5-quart casserole dish and top with American cheese. Using your hands, press the spaghetti down tightly into the casserole dish allowing milk to cover the spaghetti. Bake for 45 minutes.

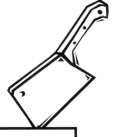

Chef's Tips on Lowfat... make "mock" sour cream. Blend one cup low-fat or fat-free cottage cheese, two teaspoons nonfat milk and one teaspoon lemon juice.

Nutrition Facts...now

Calories:	349
Total Fat:	8gm
Saturated Fat:	2gm
% Calories from Fat:	22
Cholesterol:	42mg
Sodium:	908mg
Carbohydrate:	42gm
Fiber:	1gm
Protein:	25gm

PREP TIME: 1 1/2 Hours   SERVES: 6

☞ INGREDIENTS:

2 quarts fresh okra, sliced
1 1/2 cups diced tomatoes
3 tbsps vegetable oil
1 cup chopped onions
1 cup chopped yellow bell pepper
1 tsp salt
cayenne pepper

☞ METHOD:

In a 5-quart cast iron dutch oven, heat oil over medium-high heat. Add onions and bell pepper. Saute 3–5 minutes or until vegetables are wilted. Add okra and tomatoes. Saute, stirring occasionally, for approximately 1 hour. The okra will take on a slimey look during the early stages of cooking. This look will disappear when the okra is thoroughly cooked. Season to taste using salt and pepper. Smothered okra may be eaten as a vegetable or side dish, but it is best used in gumbo such as shrimp and okra.

Mark Ortega tends the levees in rice fields just outside Ville Platte.

"This is a recipe right out of a Cajun garden. You look at the vegetables in our food, and you'll find them in our gardens - okra, tomatoes, corn, potatoes, beans, yams, onions, garlic.
"I'm 72 and an old cook - old-style cook - from 'way back...Why, I've got a whole slew of iron cookware 100 years old if it's a day! It just gets better with age. I've still got an old garde manger. You know what that is? It's a screened cabinet where you kept food after it was prepared."
                    Marjorie Domangue
                    Gibson, Louisiana

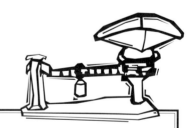

❊Nutrition Facts...then❊

Calories: 126
Total Fat: 7gm
Saturated Fat: 1gm
% Calories from Fat: 47
Cholesterol: 0mg
Sodium: 460mg
Carbohydrate: 15gm
Fiber: 3gm
Protein: 3gm

SMOTHERED OKRA & TOMATOES

PREP TIME: 1 1/2 Hours   SERVES: 6

INGREDIENTS:

2 quarts fresh okra, sliced
1 1/2 cups diced tomatoes
vegetable spray
1 tbsp vegetable oil
1 cup chopped onions
1 cup chopped yellow bell pepper
1/2 tsp salt
cayenne pepper

The Texas Longhorn Okra of the Orgeron and Parr families.

METHOD:

In a 5-quart cast iron dutch oven, coated with vegetable spray, heat oil over medium-high heat. Add onions and bell pepper. Saute 3–5 minutes or until vegetables are wilted.

Add okra and tomatoes. Saute, stirring occasionally, for approximately 1 hour. The okra will take on a slimey look during the early stages of cooking. This look will disappear when the okra is thoroughly cooked. Season to taste using salt and pepper.

Smothered okra may be eaten as a vegetable or side dish, but it is best used in gumbo such as shrimp and okra.

Nutrition Facts...now

Calories:	86
Total Fat:	3gm
Saturated Fat:	0gm
% Calories from Fat:	25
Cholesterol:	0mg
Sodium:	283mg
Carbohydrate:	15gm
Fiber:	3gm
Protein:	3gm

OLD FASHIONED SMOTHERED POTATOES

PREP TIME: 30 Minutes   SERVES: 6

☞ INGREDIENTS:

6 medium red potatoes,
      peeled and sliced 1/4–inch thick
1/2 cup vegetable oil
1 tsp salt
black pepper
garlic powder
1 tbsp diced garlic
1/4 cup sliced green onions

☞ METHOD:

In a 12-inch cast iron skillet, heat oil over medium-high heat. Season potatoes with salt, pepper and garlic powder. When oil is hot, add potatoes and cook, uncovered, stirring occasionally. After 10 minutes, add garlic and green onions. Continue to cook, stirring often, until potatoes are tender and resemble home fries. This dish is excellent when served as a breakfast accompaniment with eggs and sausage, but it should be considered as a potato side dish for any meal. You may wish to further flavor by using 1/2 teaspoon of chopped parsley at the end of cooking.

"I'll tell you something about sweet potatoes and yams. When I was a little girl on Big Bayou Black, we raised sweet potatoes in our garden. But we didn't have any place to store them where they'd keep well, like the root cellars they have in other parts of the country. So we made a mound in the yard - a layer of straw, a layer of dirt, a layer of potatoes, another layer of straw, and so on. They'd keep that way through the winter. We'd bake them in the oven of the wood cookstove or in the ashes of the fireplace.

"That was a fireplace for you! You could bake yams in the ashes, but it wouldn't keep you warm five feet away. People who think fireplaces are cozy, never depended on one for their only winter heat! But, then, our houses down here are built for long, long summers. We don't get a lot of winter."
                    Marjorie Domangue
                    Gibson, Louisiana

❧Nutrition Facts...then❧

Calories: 291
Total Fat: 18gm
Saturated Fat: 2gm
% Calories from Fat: 55
Cholesterol: 0mg
Sodium: 364mg
Carbohydrate: 30gm
Fiber: 2gm
Protein: 3gm

PREP TIME: 30 Minutes   SERVES: 6

☞ INGREDIENTS:

6 medium red potatoes,
        peeled and sliced 1/4–inch thick
vegetable spray
2 tbsps vegetable oil
1/2 tsp salt
black pepper
garlic powder
1 tbsp diced garlic
1/4 cup sliced green onions

*Chef's Tips on Substitution...
substitute buttermilk for
whole milk in biscuits, cakes
and pancakes.*

☞ METHOD:

In a 12-inch cast iron skillet, coated with vegetable spray, heat oil over medium-high heat. Season potatoes with salt, pepper and garlic powder.

When oil is hot, add potatoes and cook, uncovered, stirring occasionally. After 10 minutes, add garlic and green onions. Continue to cook, stirring often, until potatoes are tender and resemble home fries.

This dish is excellent when served at breakfast but it should be considered as a potato side dish for any meal. You may wish to further flavor by using 1/2 teaspoon of chopped parsley at the end of cooking.

Nutrition Facts...now

Calories:	170
Total Fat:	5gm
Saturated Fat:	0gm
% Calories from Fat:	24
Cholesterol:	0mg
Sodium:	187mg
Carbohydrate:	30gm
Fiber:	2gm
Protein:	3gm

SWEET POTATO DELIGHT

PREP TIME: 1 Hour   SERVES: 6

☞ INGREDIENTS:

1 (4-pound) can Louisiana yams
1/2 stick softened butter
4 tbsps brown sugar
1/2 tsp salt
1 tsp cinnamon
1/2 tsp nutmeg
1 tsp almond extract
1/2 cup raisins
1 cup miniature marshmallows

Norman and Mildred Plaisance in their garden near Grand Isle.

☞ METHOD:

Preheat oven to 375 degrees F. Drain yams and reserve liquid. Pour potatoes into a large mixing bowl and mash until creamy. Add butter, sugar, salt, cinnamon, nutmeg, almond extract and raisins. Blend spices well into the potato mixture. If potatoes tend to be a little stiff, you may wish to add some of the reserved juices until consistency is similar to mashed potatoes. Pour mixture into a well-greased casserole dish and bake, uncovered, 30–40 minutes. Remove, top with marshmallows and brown under the broiler.

"This recipe is indeed a delight to share. It was given to me back in 1940 by my Home Economics teacher.
"Today, this recipe is a family favorite, part of our traditional holiday dinners. If you are looking for a compliment, just serve this Sweet Potato Delight and I'm sure you'll get one."
Mrs. L.R. Stagg
Lafayette, Louisiana

❧Nutrition Facts...then❧

Calories: 552
Total Fat: 8gm
Saturated Fat: 5gm
% Calories from Fat: 13
Cholesterol: 21mg
Sodium: 293mg
Carbohydrate: 118gm
Fiber: 8gm
Protein: 6gm

PREP TIME: 1 Hour   SERVES: 6

INGREDIENTS:

1 (4-pound) can Louisiana yams
1/4 cup lite margarine
4 tbsps brown sugar
1/4 tsp salt
1 tsp cinnamon
1/2 tsp nutmeg
1 tsp almond extract
1/2 cup raisins
1 cup miniature marshmallows

METHOD:

Preheat oven to 375 degrees F. Drain yams and reserve liquid.

Pour potatoes into a large mixing bowl and mash until creamy. Add margarine, sugar, salt, cinnamon, nutmeg, almond extract and raisins. Blend spices well into the potato mixture.

If potatoes tend to be a little stiff, you may wish to add some of the reserved juices until consistency is similar to mashed potatoes.

Pour mixture into a well-greased casserole dish and bake, uncovered, 30–40 minutes. Remove, top with marshmallows and brown under the broiler.

Nutrition Facts...now

Calories: 484
Total Fat: 1gm
Saturated Fat: 0gm
% Calories from Fat: 1
Cholesterol: 0mg
Sodium: 126mg
Carbohydrate: 118gm
Fiber: 8gm
Protein: 6gm

PREP TIME: 1 1/2 Hours   SERVES: 8

☞ INGREDIENTS:

1 pound dried white or kidney beans
1/2 cup vegetable shortening
1 cup chopped onions
1 cup chopped celery
1/2 cup chopped bell pepper
1/4 cup diced garlic
1 cup sliced green onions
2 cups diced smoked ham
6 (3–inch) links andouille sausage
1/2 cup chopped parsley
1 cup sliced green onions
1/2 tsp salt
black pepper
Louisiana Gold Pepper Sauce

☞ METHOD:

The cooking time of beans will be cut about 1/3 if the beans are soaked overnight in cold water. This will help soften the outer shell. In a 4-quart sauce pot, melt shortening over medium-high heat. Add onions, celery, bell peppers, garlic, green onions and smoked ham. Saute 3–5 minutes or until vegetables are wilted. Add andouille sausage and beans. Blend well with vegetables and cook 2–3 minutes. Add enough cold water to cover beans by approximately 2 inches. Bring to a rolling boil and allow to cook 30 minutes, stirring occasionally to avoid scorching. Reduce heat to simmer and cook approximately 1 hour or until beans are tender. Stir from time to time, as beans will settle to the bottom of the pot as they cook. Add chopped parsley and additional green onions. Season to taste using salt, pepper and Louisiana Gold. Using a metal spoon, mash approximately 1/3 of the beans against the side of the pot to make the dish creamy. Once beans are tender and creamy, they are ready to be served. In order for the maximum flavor to develop, this dish should be cooked one day before it is to be served.

"White beans have often been referred to as poor man's meat. For a long time, I wondered why red and white beans were always found on the Monday dinner table here in Louisiana. I finally found out when reading an old cookbook.

"Since Monday was wash day, a cast iron pot of beans and ham hocks was always found simmering next to the cast iron pot of soapy water and clothes. The lady of the house could boil the dirty clothes and stir the bean pot at the same time. I can never think of a Monday that we didn't have beans on the table."

Royley Folse, Sr.
Donaldsonville, Louisiana

❋Nutrition Facts...then❋

Calories: 341
Total Fat: 21gm
Saturated Fat: 6gm
% Calories from Fat: 54
Cholesterol: 45mg
Sodium: 942mg
Carbohydrate: 20gm
Fiber: 4gm
Protein: 21gm

PREP TIME: 1 1/2 Hours   SERVES: 8

INGREDIENTS:

1 pound dried white or kidney beans
1/4 cup oil
1 cup chopped onions
1 cup chopped celery
1/2 cup chopped bell pepper
1/4 cup diced garlic
1 cup sliced green onions
2 cups low-fat smoked ham
6 (3-inch) links low-fat smoked sausage
1/2 cup chopped parsley
1 cup sliced green onions
salt substitute
black pepper
Louisiana Gold Pepper Sauce

METHOD:

The cooking time of white and red beans will be cut about 1/3 if the beans are soaked overnight in cold water. This will help soften the outer shell.

In a 4-quart sauce pot, heat oil over medium-high heat. Add onions, celery, bell peppers, garlic, green onions and smoked ham. Saute 3–5 minutes or until vegetables are wilted.

Add sausage and beans. Blend well with vegetables and cook 2–3 minutes. Add enough cold water to cover beans by approximately 2 inches. Bring to a rolling boil and allow to cook 30 minutes, stirring occasionally to avoid scorching.

Reduce heat to simmer and cook approximately 1 hour or until beans are tender. Stir from time to time, as beans will settle to the bottom of the pot as they cook. Add chopped parsley and additional green onions. Season to taste using salt substitute, pepper and Louisiana Gold.

Using a metal spoon, mash approximately 1/3 of the beans against the side of the pot to make the dish creamy. Once beans are tender and creamy, they are ready to be served.

In order for the maximum flavor to develop, this dish should be cooked one day before it is to be served.

Nutrition Facts...now

Calories:	260
Total Fat:	12gm
Saturated Fat:	1gm
% Calories from Fat:	42
Cholesterol:	28mg
Sodium:	561mg
Carbohydrate:	19gm
Fiber:	4gm
Protein:	19gm

*Chef's Tips on Low-fat...
make "cream" soups with nonfat,
1% milk or evaporated skim milk.*

PREP TIME: 1 1/2 Hours   SERVES: 6

INGREDIENTS:

2 eggplants, diced
2 whole green bell peppers
2 whole yellow bell peppers
2 whole red bell peppers
1 pound ground beef
1/2 cup chopped onions
1/2 cup chopped celery
1/2 cup chopped bell pepper
2 tbsps diced garlic
2 cups beef stock
1 tsp salt
black pepper
1/2 cup sliced green onions
1 cup seasoned Italian bread crumbs

METHOD:

Preheat oven to 350 degrees F. Cut the tops from the bell peppers and clean the pulp from inside. In a large pot, place bell peppers and top by 2 inches with lightly salted water. Bring to a low boil and cook 5–8 minutes. Remove peppers from pot and cool under cold tap water. In the same pot, boil eggplants until tender, approximately 10–15 minutes. Strain and reserve until later. In a 5-quart cast iron dutch oven, cook ground beef over medium-high heat. Continue to stir and chop until meat begins to brown and render juices. Once meat is golden brown and separated grain for grain, add onions, celery, bell pepper and garlic. Saute 3–5 minutes or until vegetables are wilted. Add stock to retain moisture. Add boiled eggplant, blend well into the meat mixture and cook 15–20 additional minutes. Season to taste using salt and pepper. Add green onions and sprinkle in just enough bread crumbs to absorb the excess moisture. Stuff the mixture into the bell peppers, place on a large baking sheet and top with additional bread crumbs. Bake 15–20 minutes or until bread crumbs are well browned and peppers are heated thoroughly. You may wish to cook the stuffed peppers in a casserole dish, topped with your favorite tomato or marinara sauce.

"One thing about growing up on a sugar planation in South Louisiana, vegetables are everywhere. In our plantation garden, the rows were about a half mile long and produced enough food to feed a small army. We ate as much as we could, sold some, but more often than not, we just gave the excess away to friends.

"Often, our cook, Mary, would combine one or two vegetables into an interesting entree. Her bell peppers stuffed with eggplant is one such creation."
Philip Folse
Gloucester, Massachusetts

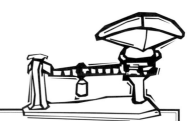

❧ Nutrition Facts...then ❧

Calories:	283
Total Fat:	12gm
Saturated Fat:	5gm
% Calories from Fat:	38
Cholesterol:	46mg
Sodium:	1186mg
Carbohydrate:	26gm
Fiber:	4gm
Protein:	18 gm

PREP TIME: 1 1/2 Hours   SERVES: 6

INGREDIENTS:

2 eggplants, diced
2 whole green bell peppers
2 whole yellow bell peppers
2 whole red bell peppers
1 pound extra lean ground beef
1/2 cup chopped onions
1/2 cup chopped celery
1/2 cup chopped bell pepper
2 tbsps diced garlic
2 cups defatted beef stock, unsalted
salt substitute
black pepper
1/2 cup sliced green onions
1 cup seasoned Italian bread crumbs

METHOD:

Preheat oven to 350 degrees F. Cut the tops from the bell peppers and clean the pulp from inside.

In a large pot, place bell peppers and top by 2 inches with lightly salted water. Bring to a low boil and cook 5–8 minutes. Remove peppers from pot and cool under cold tap water.

In the same pot, boil eggplant until tender, approximately 10–15 minutes. Strain and reserve until later.

In a 5-quart cast iron dutch oven, cook ground beef over medium-high heat. Continue to stir and chop until meat begins to brown and render juices. Once meat is golden brown and separated grain for grain, drain fat and add onions, celery, bell pepper and garlic. Sautc 3–5 minutes or until vegetables are wilted. Add stock to retain moisture.

Add boiled eggplant, blend well into the meat mixture and cook 15–20 additional minutes. Season to taste using salt substitute and pepper. Add green onions and sprinkle in just enough bread crumbs to absorb the excess moisture.

Stuff the mixture into the bell peppers, place on a large baking sheet and top with additional bread crumbs. Bake 15–20 minutes or until bread crumbs are well browned and peppers are heated thoroughly.

You may wish to cook the stuffed peppers in a casserole dish, topped with your favorite low-fat sauce.

Nutrition Facts...now

Calories: 275
Total Fat: 10gm
Saturated Fat: 4gm
% Calories from Fat: 32
Cholesterol: 46mg
Sodium: 605mg
Carbohydrate: 26gm
Fiber: 4gm
Protein: 21gm

PREP TIME: 30 Minutes   SERVES: 6

☞ INGREDIENTS:

2 cans green beans, drained
1 can water-packed artichoke hearts, drained
1 tsp salt
black pepper
1 cup seasoned Italian bread crumbs
1/2 cup olive oil
1/2 cup Parmesan cheese

☞ METHOD:

Preheat oven to 350 degrees F. Place green beans and artichoke hearts in a 2-quart casserole dish. Blend well and season to taste using salt and pepper. Fold in bread crumbs and drizzle with olive oil. Sprinkle evenly with Parmesan cheese and bake, uncovered, 20–30 minutes.

Adam Claybert LeBas with a sample from his garden outside Ville Platte on Highway 167.

"If there are two vegetables I constantly yearn for, they are green beans and artichokes. Often, I just open the can or jar and sit on the patio and eat directly from the container.

"With my hectic schedule, I am always searching for a means of creating a great casserole in just a few minutes. I figure since I love these vegetables cold and from the can, a quick blending of the two makes sense. Why not give it a try, as I did. The results are perfect!"

Pamela Castel
Baton Rouge, Louisiana

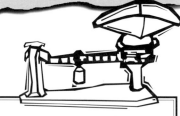

❊Nutrition Facts...then❊

Calories:	304
Total Fat:	21gm
Saturated Fat:	4gm
% Calories from Fat:	61
Cholesterol:	7mg
Sodium:	1266mg
Carbohydrate:	22gm
Fiber:	3gm
Protein:	9gm

PREP TIME: 30 Minutes SERVES: 6

☞ INGREDIENTS:

2 cans green beans, drained
1 can water-packed artichoke hearts, drained
salt substitute
black pepper
1 cup seasoned Italian bread crumbs
1/4 cup olive oil
1/2 cup fat-free Parmesan cheese

☞ METHOD:

Preheat oven to 350 degrees F. Place green beans and artichoke hearts in a 2-quart casserole dish. Blend well and season to taste using salt substitute and pepper.

Fold in bread crumbs and drizzle with olive oil. Sprinkle evenly with Parmesan cheese and bake, uncovered, 20–30 minutes.

Chef's Tips on Low-Fat...
mix equal amounts of reduced-fat or nonfat mayonnaise and low-fat or nonfat yogurt for use as a dressing with chicken or tuna salad.

Nutrition Facts...now

Calories:	133
Total Fat:	1gm
Saturated Fat:	0gm
% Calories from Fat:	8
Cholesterol:	7mg
Sodium:	816mg
Carbohydrate:	24gm
Fiber:	3gm
Protein:	8gm

PREP TIME: 1 Hour   SERVES: 6

☞ INGREDIENTS:

3 (15-ounce) cans artichoke bottoms
1/2 cup reserved artichoke juice
1/2 cup olive oil
1/2 cup melted butter
1/4 cup chopped water-packed black olives
1/4 cup chopped pimento-stuffed olives
1 tbsp diced garlic
1 tbsp olive juice
1 1/2 cups seasoned Italian bread crumbs
1/2 cup Mozzarella cheese

☞ METHOD:

Preheat oven to 350 degrees F. Drain artichoke bottoms, reserving 1/2 cup of the liquid, and cut into fours. In a 10-inch cast iron skillet, heat olive oil and butter over medium-high heat. Add artichoke bottoms and saute 3–5 minutes. Add olives and garlic. Saute until heated thoroughly. Add olive juice and reserved artichoke liquid. Pour contents of skillet into a 2-quart casserole dish. Fold in 1 cup of bread crumbs, blending well to absorb liquids. Top the casserole with cheese and enough bread crumbs to absorb excess liquid. Be careful not to allow the mixture to become too dry. Bake, uncovered, 30 minutes.

"Most people from other parts of the country think this area and its cooking is all French. But it isn't - no, indeed! There are many Italian families in the Houma-Franklin area, and so there is a great deal of Italian cooking.

"Being an Olivier married to a Porretto, I guess it isn't surprising that I cook both French and Italian. I think all our friends like the Italian dishes best.

"Families are so important here. I grew up among many, many relatives - a lot of family gatherings. Those gatherings were usually at my grandmother's house when I was very young, then they moved to my mother's house, and now to mine. I'm not sure how those family focal points come about. I suspect it has something to do with cooking, though.

"I have friends who complain that their children never visit. I tell them 'You want your children to come? Just say you're going to cook. They'll be there!'"

Roberta Claire Porretto
Houma, Louisiana

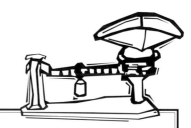

❧Nutrition Facts...then❧

Calories: 534
Total Fat: 42gm
Saturated Fat: 15gm
% Calories from Fat: 68
Cholesterol: 59mg
Sodium: 1445mg
Carbohydrate: 32gm
Fiber: 4gm
Protein: 12gm

PREP TIME: 1 Hour   SERVES: 6

☞ INGREDIENTS:

3 (15-ounce) cans artichoke bottoms
1/2 cup reserved artichoke juice
1/4 cup olive oil
1/4 cup lite margarine
1/4 cup chopped water-packed black olives
1/4 cup chopped pimento-stuffed olives
1 tbsp diced garlic
1 tbsp olive juice
1 1/2 cups plain bread crumbs
1/2 cup low-fat Mozzarella cheese

☞ METHOD:

Preheat oven to 350 degrees F. Drain artichoke bottoms, reserving 1/2 cup of the liquid, and cut into fours.

In a 10-inch cast iron skillet, heat olive oil and margarine over medium-high heat. Add artichoke bottoms and saute 3–5 minutes. Add olives and garlic. Saute until heated thoroughly. Add olive juice and reserved artichoke liquid.

Pour contents of skillet into a 2-quart casserole dish. Fold in 1 cup of bread crumbs, blending well to absorb liquids. Top the casserole with cheese and enough bread crumbs to absorb excess liquid. Be careful not to allow the mixture to become too dry. Bake, uncovered, 30 minutes.

Chef's Tips on Spices...
use a dash of Worcestershire sauce
instead of fat to add flavor to meat
and vegetable recipes.

Nutrition Facts...now

Calories:	234
Total Fat:	10gm
Saturated Fat:	1gm
% Calories from Fat:	36
Cholesterol:	3mg
Sodium:	781mg
Carbohydrate:	30gm
Fiber:	4gm
Protein:	9gm

QUICK SPINACH CASSEROLE

PREP TIME: 1 1/2 Hours   SERVES: 6

☞ INGREDIENTS:

2 (10-ounce) packages frozen spinach, chopped
1 cup water
1/4 cup chopped onions
1/4 cup diced red bell pepper
1/4 cup diced garlic
1/2 stick butter
8 ounces cottage cheese
3 tbsps flour
3 eggs, beaten
1/2 tsp salt
black pepper
1/2 cup grated cheddar cheese
paprika for color

"Greens are a staple here on Bayou Lafourche. Spinach, mustard, collards and even poke salad are a common site. The great thing about greens is that they can be eaten raw or cooked, in everything from salads to casseroles.

"This quick spinach dish was given to me by a friend, and I've since twisted and turned it a little so it's become one of my family's favorites."
                    Brenda Johnson
                    Klotzville, Louisiana

☞ METHOD:

Preheat oven to 350 degrees F. In a 12-inch cast iron skillet, poach spinach in water 5–10 minutes. Drain well and return to skillet. Add onions, bell pepper and garlic. Saute 3 additional minutes or until vegetables are wilted. Add butter and stir until well-blended. Add cottage cheese and flour. Continue to blend until thoroughly incorporated. Fold in eggs and pour into a 2-quart casserole dish. Season to taste using salt and pepper. Cover with cheddar cheese and bake for approximately 1 hour. Garnish with paprika.

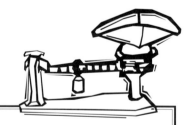

❧Nutrition Facts...then❧

Calories: 226
Total Fat: 15gm
Saturated Fat: 9gm
% Calories from Fat: 59
Cholesterol: 143mg
Sodium: 581mg
Carbohydrate: 10gm
Fiber: 2gm
Protein: 14gm

QUICK SPINACH CASSEROLE

PREP TIME: 1 1/2 Hours   SERVES: 6

☞ INGREDIENTS:

2 (10-ounce) packages frozen spinach, chopped
1 cup water
1/4 cup chopped onions
1/4 cup diced red bell pepper
1/4 cup diced garlic
2 tbsps lite margarine
8 ounces fat-free cottage cheese
3 tbsps flour
3/4 cup egg substitute
salt substitute
black pepper
1/2 cup low-fat grated cheddar cheese
paprika for color

☞ METHOD:

Preheat oven to 350 degrees F. In a 12-inch cast iron skillet, poach spinach in water 5–10 minutes. Drain well and return to skillet.

Add onions, bell pepper and garlic. Saute 3 additional minutes or until vegetables are wilted. Add margarine and stir until well-blended. Add cottage cheese and flour. Continue to blend until thoroughly incorporated.

Fold in egg substitute and pour into a 2-quart casserole dish. Season to taste using salt substitute and pepper. Cover with cheddar cheese and bake for approximately 1 hour. Garnish with paprika.

Mr. Comeaux and a neighbor with a load of new potatoes for market in Sunset.

Nutrition Facts...now

Calories:	120
Total Fat:	4gm
Saturated Fat:	1gm
% Calories from Fat:	25
Cholesterol:	4mg
Sodium:	294mg
Carbohydrate:	11gm
Fiber:	2gm
Protein:	13gm

PREP TIME: 1 1/2 Hours   SERVES: 6

☞ INGREDIENTS:

1 (15-ounce) can cream-style corn
2 (15-ounce) cans whole kernel corn, drained
3 eggs, beaten
1/2 cup grated Swiss cheese
1/4 cup corn meal
1/4 cup chopped parsley
1 cup sliced green onions
1/4 cup melted butter
1/2 tsp salt
black pepper
1/4 cup Parmesan cheese

☞ METHOD:

Preheat oven to 325 degrees F. In a large mixing bowl, combine cream-style corn, whole corn and eggs. Using a wooden spoon, blend well to incorporate all ingredients. Add Swiss cheese and corn meal, mixing well after each addition. Fold in parsley, green onions and butter. Season to taste using salt and pepper. Pour contents into a buttered 2-quart casserole dish. Sprinkle with Parmesan cheese and bake, covered, 40–45 minutes. Remove cover and brown slightly.

"I was first introduced to Silver Queen corn by my good friend, Fred Miller. Fred lived on Lake Bruin in Tensas Parish, Louisiana. Knowing that I loved boiled corn, he delivered a sack of his fresh-picked Silver Queen to my doorstep. I'll never forget his words, 'John, now you'll find out what real corn tastes like!'

"Well, Fred was right. I have never had better corn and although Fred passed away in the early summer of 1996, I'll always remember him for introducing me to the best corn in the world."

John Folse
Donaldsonville, Louisiana

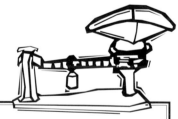

❧Nutrition Facts...then❧

Calories:	305
Total Fat:	12gm
Saturated Fat:	6gm
% Calories from Fat:	33
Cholesterol:	84mg
Sodium:	1012mg
Carbohydrate:	46gm
Fiber:	4gm
Protein:	9gm

BAKED CORN CASSEROLE

PREP TIME: 1 1/2 Hours   SERVES: 6

☞ **INGREDIENTS:**

1 (15-ounce) can cream-style corn
2 (15-ounce) cans whole kernel corn, drained
3/4 cup egg substitute
1/2 cup low-fat grated Swiss cheese
1/4 cup corn meal
1/4 cup chopped parsley
1 cup sliced green onions
1 tbsp lite margarine, melted
salt substitute
cayenne pepper
vegetable spray
1/4 cup fat-free Parmesan cheese

☞ **METHOD:**

Preheat oven to 325 degrees F. In a large mixing bowl, combine cream-style corn, whole corn and egg substitute. Using a wooden spoon, blend well to incorporate all ingredients. Add Swiss cheese and corn meal, mixing well after each addition. Fold in parsley, green onions and margarine. Season to taste using salt substitute and pepper.

Pour contents into a 2-quart casserole dish coated with vegetable spray. Sprinkle with Parmesan cheese and bake, covered, 40–45 minutes. Remove cover and brown slightly.

Nutrition Facts...now

Calories:	302
Total Fat:	7gm
Saturated Fat:	3gm
% Calories from Fat:	19
Cholesterol:	15mg
Sodium:	809mg
Carbohydrate:	48gm
Fiber:	4gm
Protein:	18gm

PREP TIME: 1 1/2 Hours   SERVES: 6

☞ INGREDIENTS:

1 pound bacon
2 pounds frozen green beans
1/4 cup margarine
1/2 cup chopped onions
1/4 cup chopped red bell pepper
1/4 cup chopped yellow bell pepper
1 (8-ounce) can tomato sauce
1 tsp mustard
1 tbsp Worcestershire Sauce
1 tsp brown sugar
1 tbsp white sugar
1/2 tsp salt
cayenne pepper

☞ METHOD:

Preheat oven to 400 degrees F. In a 12-inch cast iron skillet, partially cook bacon, a few slices at a time, to melt some of the fat. Do not cook crispy. Drain on paper towels and set aside. Discard bacon fat and, in the same skillet, melt margarine over medium-high heat. Add onions and bell peppers. Saute 3–5 minutes or until vegetables are wilted. Add tomato sauce, mustard and Worcestershire Sauce. Bring to a rolling boil and reduce to simmer. Add sugars and simmer approximately 15 minutes, stirring occasionally. You may need to add a small amount of water should tomato sauce become too thick. Season to taste using salt and pepper. Roll 3 green beans in 1 strip of bacon and secure with a toothpick. Line the rolled green beans in a 9" x 13" casserole dish. When all of the beans are wrapped, pour the tomato sauce over the rolls and adjust seasonings if necessary. Bake 35–45 minutes or until bacon is crispy.

"Food is sort of the centerpiece of life around here - food and family. No matter what the occasion or purpose of the gathering, food always seems to figure in it. People are more relaxed with food and drink.

"This is an old recipe I revised just a little. I got it from my sister, who got it from a friend of hers. Most people don't think of a vegetable dish when they think of Cajun food. But we've always had gardens.

"Most people who aren't from around here also think Cajun food is defined by cayenne pepper and hot sauce. That's not so. Cajun food is not hot - spicy, yes, but not make-your-eyes-water hot. Well, maybe further west, around Lafayette, it's a little hotter but certainly not enough to impair the taste of the food.

"The cuisine is changing for health reasons now that we're having to watch our cholesterol and such. But leave us our spices and our seafood and chicken and we'll make it good, even if it's got to be good for us!"

Keith Waguespack
Thibodaux, Louisiana

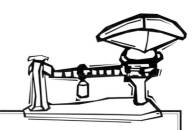

❧Nutrition Facts...then❧

Calories: 570
Total Fat: 45gm
Saturated Fat: 15gm
% Calories from Fat: 71
Cholesterol: 64mg
Sodium: 1778mg
Carbohydrate: 16gm
Fiber: 1gm
Protein: 26gm

PREP TIME: 1 1/2 Hours   SERVES: 6

☞ INGREDIENTS:

1 pound lean ham, cut into 1-inch strips
2 pounds frozen green beans
2 tbsps lite margarine
1/2 cup chopped onions
1/4 cup chopped red bell pepper
1/4 cup chopped yellow bell pepper
1 (8-ounce) can tomato sauce, no salt added
1 tsp mustard
1 tbsp Worcestershire Sauce
1 tsp brown sugar
1 tbsp white sugar
salt substitute
cayenne pepper

Bounty from the kitchen of Alzina Toups on Bayou Lafourche in Galliano.

*Chef's Tips on Spices...
lemon, dill, chives, parsley, tarragon and basil are all favorite fish flavor enhancers.*

Nutrition Facts...now

Calories:	176
Total Fat:	5gm
Saturated Fat:	2gm
% Calories from Fat:	22
Cholesterol:	38mg
Sodium:	775mg
Carbohydrate:	19gm
Fiber:	1gm
Protein:	17gm

☞ METHOD:

Preheat oven to 400 degrees F. In a 12-inch cast iron skillet, melt margarine over medium-high heat. Add onions and bell peppers. Saute 3–5 minutes or until vegetables are wilted. Add tomato sauce, mustard and Worcestershire Sauce. Bring to a rolling boil and reduce to simmer. Add sugars and simmer approximately 15 minutes, stirring occasionally.

You may need to add a small amount of water should tomato sauce become too thick. Season to taste using salt substitute and pepper.

Roll 3 green beans in 1 strip of ham and secure with a toothpick. Line the rolled green beans in a 9" x 13" casserole dish.

When all of the beans are wrapped, pour the tomato sauce over the rolls and adjust seasonings if necessary. Bake 35–45 minutes.

PREP TIME: 1 1/2 Hours   SERVES: 8

☞ INGREDIENTS:

1/4 cup diced yellow squash
1/4 cup diced zucchini
1/4 cup blackeyed peas
1/4 cup whole kernel corn
1/4 cup lima beans
1/2 cup diced onion
1/2 cup diced red bell pepper
1/4 cup diced celery
1 tbsp diced garlic
1/2 cup sliced mushrooms
2 tbsps extra virgin olive oil
2 cups long grain converted rice, uncooked
4 cups chicken stock
1/2 cup tomato sauce
1/2 tsp salt
black pepper

☞ METHOD:

Preheat oven to 350 degrees F. The interesting thing about this dish is that any substitutions are acceptable. Should you wish to add chicken, fish or sausage, it's okay. The important thing is that you assemble all of your ingredients together. It is best to place the dish in the oven exactly 1 1/2 hours prior to serving. In a 5-quart cast iron dutch oven, combine all ingredients. Using a wooden spoon, stir well to incorporate all flavors. Adjust seasonings if necessary and feel free to add a touch of your own spices. Cover tightly and bake for 1 hour or until rice is fluffy and dry. Remove from the oven and allow to sit, covered, 15–20 minutes prior to serving. Serve with a great salad.

"People are gonna' say 'Nora, what are you doing in this book? You're from Mississippi!' We did cook differently in Natchez, where I'm from - lots more lima beans and peas and corn dishes. When I moved to New Orleans, it did take me a while to get used to having rice with everything! And I had to learn about seafood, too.

"But I've been involved with cooking all my life, and I'm open to new ideas - and so are Louisiana cooks. They're also very fair. If you come up with a good idea, they'll adopt it and give you credit for it. Vegetable jambalaya isn't traditional, but it's an honest variation on the jambalaya theme, and it's good, so it's gotten to be real popular.

"Like most of the folks in this book, I've got versions of this recipe to feed the multitudes, even though my own family is small. I have to - I'm a caterer. Besides, I've got a long list of single friends with standing invitations to Christmas dinner!"

Nora Dejoie
New Orleans, Louisiana

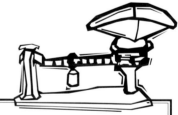

❊Nutrition Facts...then❊

Calories:	238
Total Fat:	2gm
Saturated Fat:	1gm
% Calories from Fat:	7
Cholesterol:	9mg
Sodium:	732mg
Carbohydrate:	49gm
Fiber:	3gm
Protein:	6gm

PREP TIME: 1 1/2 Hours   SERVES: 8

☞ INGREDIENTS:

1/4 cup diced yellow squash
1/4 cup diced zucchini
1/4 cup blackeyed peas
1/4 cup whole kernel corn
1/4 cup lima beans
1/2 cup diced onion
1/2 cup diced red bell pepper
1/4 cup diced celery
1 tbsp diced garlic
1/2 cup sliced mushrooms
2 tbsps extra virgin olive oil
2 cups long grain converted rice, uncooked
4 cups defatted chicken stock, unsalted
1/2 cup tomato sauce, no salt added
1/4 tsp salt
black pepper

☞ METHOD:

Preheat oven to 350 degrees F. The interesting thing about this dish is that any substitutions are acceptable. Should you wish to add chicken, fish or sausage, it's okay. The important thing is that you assemble all of your ingredients together. It is best to place the dish in the oven exactly 1 1/2 hours prior to serving.

In a 5-quart cast iron dutch oven, combine all ingredients. Using a wooden spoon, stir well to incorporate all flavors. Adjust seasonings if necessary and feel free to add a touch of your own spices. Cover tightly and bake for 1 hour or until rice is fluffy and dry. Remove from the oven and allow to sit, covered, 15–20 minutes prior to serving.

Serve with a great salad.

Nutrition Facts...now

Calories:	233
Total Fat:	1gm
Saturated Fat:	0gm
% Calories from Fat:	3
Cholesterol:	0mg
Sodium:	338mg
Carbohydrate:	48gm
Fiber:	3gm
Protein:	8gm

BROCCOLI WITH DIJON VINAIGRETTE

PREP TIME: 30 Minutes   SERVES: 6

☞ INGREDIENTS:

2 pounds fresh broccoli spears
4 tsps olive oil
1/4 cup sliced green onions
1/4 tsp dried tarragon
1/2 tsp dry mustard
1 tbsp minced garlic
2 tbsps red wine vinegar
4 tbsps water
1 tbsp Dijon mustard
1/2 tsp salt
black pepper

☞ METHOD:

Cut broccoli into serving size pieces. Place broccoli in a 5-quart sauce pan and cover with water by 2 inches. Bring to a rolling boil and cook 4–5 minutes. Do not overcook. Drain broccoli, place in a serving bowl and keep warm. In an 8-inch cast iron skillet, heat olive oil over medium–high heat. Add green onions, tarragon, mustard and garlic. Using a wooden spoon, blend all ingredients and saute 2–3 minutes. Remove from heat and add vinegar, water and Dijon mustard. Season to taste using salt and pepper. Drizzle the hot vinaigrette over the steamed broccoli and serve immediately as a salad or vegetable.

"I guess most people think Cajuns are very insular people who live on the bayous and never see the rest of the world. But we're really some of the world's most widely-traveled people. We've followed the oil industry all over the world...and taken our love of food with us. If we find something we like, it gets assimilated.

"My father worked for an oil company. I started school in Franklin, but I graduated high school in the Hague, and I've traveled widely on my own since then.

"Speaking of traveling, my grandfather had a great tall tale he told us while we grandkids sat around watching him mend fish nets - a story he said was very old. When the Acadians were forced to leave Nova Scotia, the story goes, they were mourning the fact that they would never again be able to eat lobster. The lobsters heard this and were touched. And they promised the Acadians that, if they traveled by sea, the lobsters would follow them. But they traveled so far in coming to Louisiana that the lobsters were worn down to little bitty crawfish by the time they got here! Of course crawfish aren't really worn-down lobsters, but I love the story!"

Judy Guidry
Houma, Louisiana

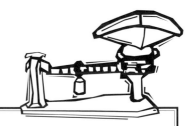

❧Nutrition Facts...then❧

Calories: 43
Total Fat: 1gm
Saturated Fat: 0gm
% Calories from Fat: 14
Cholesterol: 0mg
Sodium: 270mg
Carbohydrate: 7gm
Fiber: 2gm
Protein: 4gm

PREP TIME: 30 Minutes   SERVES: 6

☞ INGREDIENTS:

2 pounds fresh broccoli spears
2 tsps olive oil
1/4 cup sliced green onions
1/4 tsp dried tarragon
1/2 tsp dry mustard
1 tbsp minced garlic
2 tbsps red wine vinegar
4 tbsps water
1 tbsp Dijon mustard
1/4 tsp salt
black pepper

☞ METHOD:

Cut broccoli into serving size pieces. Place broccoli in a 5-quart sauce pan and cover with water by 2 inches. Bring to a rolling boil and cook 4–5 minutes. Do not overcook. Drain broccoli, place in a serving bowl and keep warm.

In an 8-inch cast iron skillet, heat olive oil over medium-high heat. Add green onions, tarragon, mustard and garlic. Using a wooden spoon, blend all ingredients and saute 2–3 minutes. Remove from heat and add vinegar, water and Dijon mustard. Season to taste using salt and pepper.

Drizzle the hot vinaigrette over the steamed broccoli and serve immediately as a salad or vegetable.

What is fat?
It is a source of energy found in many foods and oils. It supplies calories that your body uses for energy.

A rice elevator off Highway 90 near Crowley.

Nutrition Facts...now

Calories:	43
Total Fat:	1gm
Saturated Fat:	0gm
% Calories from Fat:	14
Cholesterol:	0mg
Sodium:	182mg
Carbohydrate:	7gm
Fiber:	2gm
Protein:	4gm

COUS COUS CAJUN-STYLE

PREP TIME: 30 Minutes   SERVES: 6

INGREDIENTS:

2 cups yellow corn meal
1/2 cup vegetable oil
1 1/2 tsps salt
1 tsp baking powder
1 1/2 cups milk

METHOD:

In a 12-inch cast iron skillet, heat oil over medium-high heat. In a large mixing bowl, combine corn meal, salt, baking powder and milk. Using a wire whisk, blend ingredients until well incorporated. Pour the cous cous into the hot skillet. Do not stir. Allow a crust to form. Once formed, stir well and lower heat to simmer. Cover and cook approximately 15 minutes, stirring often. Serve with milk and sugar or with hot coffee milk as a cereal.

"My mother was a real Cajun from Jeanerette. Like all good Cajuns, we ate pretty well. I especially remember Lent as one of my favorite times for good eating. Since we were strict Catholics, we had to fast and abstain from meat many times during the Lenten season. This meant many creative meatless meals.

"Often at night we enjoyed breakfast foods such as cous cous. Mom and I always ate ours with sweet coffee milk, while my dad and brother ate theirs with a glass of cold milk. I've come to learn that the secret to making good cous cous is a very old, well seasoned cast iron skillet."

Brenda Martin
Morgan City, Louisiana

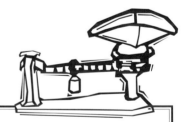

❧Nutrition Facts...then❧

Calories:	492
Total Fat:	22gm
Saturated Fat:	4gm
% Calories from Fat:	40
Cholesterol:	8mg
Sodium:	609mg
Carbohydrate:	65gm
Fiber:	1gm
Protein:	9gm

COUS COUS CAJUN-STYLE

PREP TIME: 30 Minutes   SERVES: 6

☞ INGREDIENTS:

2 cups yellow corn meal
2 tbsps vegetable oil
1/4 tsp salt
1 tsp baking powder
1 1/2 cups skim milk

☞ METHOD:

In a 12-inch cast iron skillet, heat oil over medium-high heat.

In a large mixing bowl, combine corn meal, salt, baking powder and skim milk. Using a wire whisk, blend ingredients until well incorporated.

Pour the cous cous into the hot skillet. Do not stir. Allow a crust to form. Once formed, stir well and lower heat to simmer. Cover and cook approximately 15 minutes, stirring often.

Serve with skim milk and sugar or with hot coffee milk as a cereal.

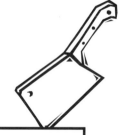

Nutrition Facts...now

Calories:	355
Total Fat:	6gm
Saturated Fat:	1gm
% Calories from Fat:	15
Cholesterol:	1mg
Sodium:	166mg
Carbohydrate:	65gm
Fiber:	1gm
Protein:	9gm

PREP TIME: 1 1/2 Hours   SERVES: 8

INGREDIENTS:

12 medium-size mirlitons
1/2 cup vegetable oil
1/2 pound tasso ham, diced
1/2 pound loose breakfast sausage
2 cups chopped onions
1 cup chopped celery

1 cup chopped bell pepper
1/4 cup diced garlic
1 (10-ounce) can Rotel tomatoes, chopped
1 pound crawfish tails
1/2 cup sliced green onions
1/4 cup chopped parsley

1 cup chicken stock
1/2 tsp salt
black pepper
4 whole eggs
2 cups seasoned Italian bread crumbs
1/2 cup Romano cheese

METHOD:

Preheat oven to 350 degrees F. Place mirlitons in a large pot and cover by 2 inches with lightly salted water. Bring to a rolling boil and cook until tender. Do not overcook. Remove from pot, drain and cool under cold tap water. Slice mirlitons in half and remove flat seed. Using a metal spoon, gently scoop all of the pulp out of the shells. Reserve pulp and save shells for stuffing later. In a 7-quart cast iron dutch oven, heat oil over medium-high heat. Add tasso and sausage. Cook until golden brown and separated grain for grain. Tilt the pot and remove all but approximately 2 tablespoons of the oil. Add onions, celery, bell pepper, garlic and Rotel tomatoes. Saute 3–5 minutes or until vegetables are wilted. Add crawfish, reserved mirliton pulp, green onions and parsley. Continue to cook 15–20 additional minutes. Should mixture become too dry, add chicken stock to retain moistness. Season to taste using salt and pepper. Remove from heat and quickly stir in eggs. Be careful not to scramble eggs. Sprinkle in 1 cup of bread crumbs to absorb any remaining moisture in the stuffing. Fill hollowed shells with stuffing and place on a flat baking sheet. Top shells with bread crumbs and cheese. Bake 15–20 minutes or until golden brown and cheese has melted.

"Uncle Bro - that's pronounced like 'Bruh', not 'Broh' - was the youngest son, and frequently around here, the youngest son gets nicknamed 'Brother.' That gets shortened to 'Bro' like 'sister' becomes 'sis', and the nephews and nieces added 'Uncle.'

"Anyway, this is a recipe from the male side of the family, which isn't at all unusual. Men down here are often as good cooks as their wives - sometimes better. But the smart ones don't say that out loud too often. I belong to a country club, and if a bunch of us go out on Saturday to play golf, and it rains, we'll just go back to the club and cook."

Doug Gulrin
Morgan City, Louisiana

❄Nutrition Facts...then❄

Calories: 664
Total Fat: 34gm
Saturated Fat: 8gm
% Calories from Fat: 45
Cholesterol: 287mg
Sodium: 3391mg
Carbohydrate: 46gm
Fiber: 4gm
Protein: 44gm

PREP TIME: 1 1/2 Hours   SERVES: 8

☞ INGREDIENTS:

12 medium-size mirlitons
2 tbsps oil
1/4 pound lean ham, diced
1/2 pound lean turkey sausage
2 cups chopped onions
1 cup chopped celery

1 cup chopped bell pepper
1/4 cup diced garlic
1 (10-ounce) can Rotel tomatoes, chopped
1 pound crawfish tails
1/2 cup sliced green onions
1/4 cup chopped parsley

1 cup defatted chicken stock, unsalted
salt substitute
black pepper
1 cup egg substitute
2 cups plain bread crumbs
1/4 cup fat-free Parmesan cheese

Agatha Badeaux prepares a pot of white beans at her home in Larose.

☞ METHOD:

Preheat oven to 350 degrees F. Place mirlitons in a large pot and cover by 2 inches with lightly salted water. Bring to a rolling boil and cook until tender. Do not overcook. Remove from pot, drain and cool under cold tap water.

Slice mirlitons in half and remove flat seed. Using a metal spoon, gently scoop all of the pulp out of the shells. Reserve pulp and save shells for stuffing later.

In a 7-quart cast iron dutch oven, heat oil over medium-high heat. Add ham and sausage. Cook until golden brown and separated grain for grain. Tilt the pot and remove all fat.

Add onions, celery, bell pepper, garlic and Rotel tomatoes. Saute 3–5 minutes or until vegetables are wilted. Add crawfish, reserved mirliton pulp, green onions and parsley. Cook 15–20 additional minutes. Should mixture become too dry, add chicken stock to retain moistness. Season to taste using salt substitute and pepper.

Remove from heat and quickly stir in egg substitute. Be careful not to scramble eggs. Sprinkle in 1 cup of bread crumbs to absorb any remaining moisture in the stuffing.

Fill hollowed shells with stuffing and place on a flat baking sheet. Top shells with bread crumbs and cheese. Bake 15–20 minutes or until golden brown and cheese has melted.

Nutrition Facts...now

Calories:	464
Total Fat:	16gm
Saturated Fat:	3gm
% Calories from Fat:	30
Cholesterol:	152mg
Sodium:	1301mg
Carbohydrate:	42gm
Fiber:	3gm
Protein:	40gm

PREP TIME: 1 1/2 Hours   SERVES: 6

INGREDIENTS:

1 (3-pound) chicken
6 ears fresh corn
1/4 cup vegetable oil
flour for dusting
1 cup chopped onions
1 cup chopped celery
1/2 cup chopped bell pepper
1 tbsp diced garlic
1 cup chopped tomatoes
2 cups chicken stock
1/2 tsp salt
black pepper
cayenne pepper
1/4 cup sliced green onions
1/4 cup chopped parsley

METHOD:

Using a sharp paring knife, cut kernels of corn from the cob. Scrape the cobs with the back of the knife to remove the rich corn juices attached to the cob. Set aside. In a 7-quart cast iron dutch oven, heat oil over medium-high heat. Cut chicken into 8 serving pieces and season to taste using salt and peppers. Dust lightly in flour and saute on both sides until golden brown. Remove and set aside. Add corn and juices from pulp to the dutch oven. Saute 2–3 minutes. Add onions, celery, bell pepper and garlic. Saute 3–5 minutes or until vegetables are wilted. Add tomatoes and chicken stock. Season to taste using salt and peppers. Return the chicken to the corn mixture and add green onions and parsley. Cover, reduce heat to simmer and cook until chicken is tender, approximately 45 minutes. Serve over steamed white rice.

"Although Maque Choux is normally thought of as a vegetable dish or corn and shrimp soup, my mother-in-law had a different use for the recipe. Her name was Julie Green Brown and she was raised near Iota, Louisiana. After she married, she moved to the heart of Cajun country, the town of Eunice, Louisiana. She was a wonderful cook, and I first tasted this interesting version of an old Cajun dish at her home. I liked it so much that she decided to teach me how to cook it. I'd like to share it with you."
Florence Brown
Lake Charles, Louisiana

*Chef's Tips on Weight Loss...
did you know that a gram of fat
has more than double the calories
of a gram of carbohydrate or a
gram of protein?*

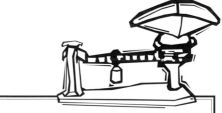

❧Nutrition Facts...then❧

Calories:	603
Total Fat:	36gm
Saturated Fat:	9gm
% Calories from Fat:	52
Cholesterol:	128mg
Sodium:	556mg
Carbohydrates:	38gm
Fiber:	4gm
Protein:	37gm

PREP TIME: 1 1/2 Hours   SERVES: 6

☞ INGREDIENTS:

1 (3-pound) chicken, skinned
6 ears fresh corn
1/4 cup vegetable oil
flour for dusting
1 cup chopped onions
1 cup chopped celery
1/2 cup chopped bell pepper
1 tbsp diced garlic
1 cup chopped tomatoes
2 cups defatted chicken stock, unsalted
1/4 tsp salt
black pepper
cayenne pepper
1/4 cup sliced green onions
1/4 cup chopped parsley

☞ METHOD:

Using a sharp paring knife, cut kernels of corn from the cob. Scrape the cobs with the back of the knife to remove the rich corn juices attached to the cob. Set aside.

In a 7-quart cast iron dutch oven, heat oil over medium-high heat. Cut chicken into 8 serving pieces and season to taste using salt and peppers. Dust lightly in flour and saute on both sides until golden brown. Remove and set aside.

Add corn and juices from pulp to the dutch oven. Saute 2–3 minutes. Add onions, celery, bell pepper and garlic. Saute 3–5 minutes or until vegetables are wilted. Add tomatoes and chicken stock. Season to taste using salt and peppers.

Return the chicken to the corn mixture and add green onions and parsley. Cover, reduce heat to simmer and cook until chicken is tender, approximately 45 minutes. Serve over steamed white rice.

Nutrition Facts...now

Calories: 395
Total Fat: 16gm
Saturated Fat: 3gm
% Calories from Fat: 35
Cholesterol: 72mg
Sodium: 290mg
Carbohydrates: 36gm
Fiber: 4gm
Protein: 31gm

Poultry

Chapter Five

Chicken Sauce Piquante	180/181
Smothered Chicken with Butter Beans	182/183
Me Me's Ol' Time Chicken & Dumplin's	184/185
Chicken Stew	186/187
Chicken & Artichoke Hearts	188/189
Southern Fried Chicken	190/191
Aunt Florence's Baked Chicken & Spaghetti	192/193
Chicken Parmigiano	194/195
Cajun-Style Chicken & Eggplant Casserole	196/197
Chicken Drummette Jambalaya	198/199
Howard's Chicken & Rice Casserole	200/201
Sunday Morning Chicken Fricassee	204/205
Chicken & Creole Tomato Pomodori	206/207
Chicken Loaf Graham	208/209
Skillet Chicken & Gravy	210/211
Chicken Bonne Femme	212/213
Chicken Beignets	214/215
Braised Chicken Creole	216/217
Coq Au Vin	218/219
Barbecued Chicken Italian-Style	220/221

The recipes for **Me Me's Ol' Time Chicken & Dumplin's**, *pictured at left, can be found on pages 184 and 185.*

PREP TIME: 1 1/2 Hours   SERVES: 6

☞ INGREDIENTS:

6 chicken breasts
1 1/2 cups oil
1 cup flour
1 (6-ounce) can tomato paste
1 cup chopped onions
1/2 cup chopped celery
1/2 cup chopped bell pepper
2 tbsps diced garlic
1 (10-ounce) can Rotel tomatoes
1 (16-ounce) can whole tomatoes
1 quart chicken stock
2 tbsps sugar
1 tsp salt
black pepper
cayenne pepper
1/2 tsp oregano
2 tbsps Worcestershire sauce
1/2 cup sliced green onions
1/4 cup chopped parsley

☞ METHOD:

In a 12-quart cast iron dutch oven, heat oil over medium-high heat. Season chicken breasts using salt and pepper, and saute until golden brown. Remove from oil and keep warm. Add flour to pot and, using a wire whisk, stir until dark brown roux is achieved. Add tomato paste and continue to stir 5–6 minutes or until the sauce is a nice brown color. Add onions, celery, bell pepper and garlic. Saute 3–5 minutes or until vegetables are wilted. Add tomatoes and chicken stock. Blend well into the roux mixture, bring to a rolling boil and reduce to simmer. Add chicken, sugar, salt and peppers. Blend well. Add oregano and Worcestershire. Allow to simmer 45 minutes or until chicken is tender. Finish with green onions and parsley. Serve over a plate of steamed white rice.

"When I was growing up, back during the Great Depression, food was something we had a lot more of than money. In fact, that's how I paid my tuition at Mt. Carmel School in New Iberia - with vegetables and chickens.

"I was the oldest of 15 children, and had to leave school in the eighth grade so the younger children could go. In those days you went to school as much to learn the catechism as reading and writing. I always valued education, though. I went back to school and got my high school diploma at 55.

"I've cooked forever. When most of the family was out in the fields, I'd be left home to cook and mind the babies. I started cooking when I was ten, and had to stand on a wooden box to reach the wood stove."

Thelma Lemaire
Lafayette, Louisiana

❊Nutrition Facts...then❊

Calories:	1066
Total Fat:	71gm
Saturated Fat:	12gm
% Calories from Fat:	61
Cholesterol:	165mg
Sodium:	1533mg
Carbohydrates:	37gm
Fiber:	4gm
Protein:	67gm

PREP TIME: 1 1/2 Hours   SERVES: 6

INGREDIENTS:

6 skinless chicken breasts
1 cup oil-less roux
1 quart defatted chicken stock, unsalted
1/4 cup oil
1 cup chopped onions
1/2 cup chopped celery
1/2 cup chopped bell pepper
2 tbsps diced garlic
1 (6-ounce) can tomato paste, no salt added
1 (10-ounce) can Rotel tomatoes
1 (16-ounce) can whole tomatoes, no salt added
2 tbsps sugar
salt substitute
black pepper
cayenne pepper
1/2 tsp oregano
2 tbsps Worcestershire sauce
1/2 cup sliced green onions
1/4 cup chopped parsley

METHOD:

Dissolve oil-less roux in stock and set aside. In a 12-quart cast iron dutch oven, heat oil over medium-high heat. Season chicken breasts using salt substitute and pepper and saute until golden brown. Remove from oil and keep warm.

Add onions, celery, bell pepper and garlic. Saute 3–5 minutes or until vegetables are wilted. Add tomato paste, tomatoes and chicken stock/roux mixture. Blend well into the vegetable mixture, bring to a rolling boil and reduce to simmer.

Add chicken, sugar, salt substitute and peppers. Blend well. Add oregano and Worcestershire. Allow to simmer 45 minutes or until chicken is tender. Finish with green onions and parsley. Serve over a plate of steamed white rice.

Nutrition Facts...now

Calories:	551
Total Fat:	16gm
Saturated Fat:	3gm
% Calories from Fat:	26
Cholesterol:	146mg
Sodium:	515mg
Carbohydrates:	38gm
Fiber:	3gm
Protein:	62gm

SMOTHERED CHICKEN WITH BUTTER BEANS

PREP TIME: 1 1/2 Hours   SERVES: 6

☞ INGREDIENTS:

1 (3-pound) fryer
4 cups fresh butter beans
1/4 cup oil
1/4 cup flour
1 cup chopped onions
1 cup chopped red bell pepper
1/4 cup diced garlic
3 cups chicken stock
1 tsp salt
black pepper
1/2 cup sliced green onions

☞ METHOD:

Cut fryer into 8 serving pieces. Rinse, drain, and set aside. In a 7-quart cast iron dutch oven, heat oil over medium-high heat. Add flour and, using a wire whisk, whip until golden brown roux is achieved. Add onions, bell pepper and garlic. Saute 3–5 minutes or until vegetables are wilted. Add chicken, blend well into the roux mixture and cook 5–10 minutes or until chicken is seared. Add chicken stock, blending well into the roux mixture. Additional stock or water may be necessary to achieve a stew-like consistency. Add butter beans and season to taste using salt and pepper. Bring to a rolling boil, reduce to simmer and cook 30–45 minutes. Add green onions and adjust seasonings if necessary. Serve over steamed white rice.

A patch of Blackeyed Susans with the setting sun outside Cheneyville in Evangeline Parish.

"This is a 'Grandma's Sunday dinner recipe' literally. I grew up spending Sundays with my grandmother, Zelda Blanchard, and she would often fix this, using vegetables from her own garden and a chicken from her own coop.

"It's unique to my family, as far as I know. My son fixes it now, so it's being carried into at least the fourth generation.

"Knowing how to cook for a big family can come in handy. We're in the Cruisin' Cajuns motor home club. We've been to six-state rallies in Arkansas and Oklahoma where we cooked for 100 people."
Elaine Lapeyrouse
Chauvin, Louisiana

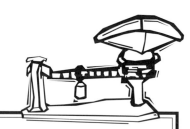

❧ Nutrition Facts...then❧

Calories: 770
Total Fat: 39gm
Saturated Fat: 9gm
% Calories from Fat: 46
Cholesterol: 220mg
Sodium: 897mg
Carbohydrates: 34gm
Fiber: 9gm
Protein: 69gm

SMOTHERED CHICKEN WITH BUTTER BEANS

PREP TIME: 1 1/2 Hours   SERVES: 6

☞ INGREDIENTS:

1 (3-pound) fryer, skinned
4 cups fresh butter beans
1/4 cup oil-less roux
3 cups defatted chicken stock, unsalted
1 tbsp oil
1 cup chopped onions
1 cup chopped red bell pepper
1/4 cup diced garlic
1/4 tsp salt
black pepper
1/2 cup sliced green onions

The Romero brothers, Lennis and Ophe, play their traditional songs in the shadow of the Evangeline Oak on the banks of Bayou Teche in St. Martinville.

☞ METHOD:

Dissolve oil-less roux in stock and set aside. Cut fryer into 8 serving pieces. Rinse, drain, and set aside.

In a 7-quart cast iron dutch oven, heat oil over medium heat. Add onions, bell pepper and garlic. Saute 3–5 minutes or until vegetables are wilted.

Add chicken, blend well into the vegetable mixture and cook 5–10 minutes or until chicken is seared. Add chicken stock/roux mixture, blending well into the vegetable mixture. Additional stock or water may be necessary to achieve a stew-like consistency.

Add butter beans and season to taste using salt and pepper. Bring to a rolling boil, reduce to simmer and cook 30–45 minutes. Add green onions and adjust seasonings if necessary. Serve over steamed white rice.

Nutrition Facts...now

Calories: 366
Total Fat: 9gm
Saturated Fat: 2gm
% Calories from Fat: 21
Cholesterol: 72mg
Sodium: 322mg
Carbohydrates: 34gm
Fiber: 9gm
Protein: 37gm

PREP TIME: 2 1/2 Hours   SERVES: 6

"Times sure have changed since the days when Me Me cooked dinner for us. Many Louisiana families called the noon meal "dinner" back then. When she knew we were coming for lunch, she would go out into the chicken yard and pick a hen. She would wring its neck and clean, scald and pluck it until the meat was white as pearls. As a child, I don't remember being upset at this inhumane sight, because, back then, it was simply a way of life. However, I do remember the wonderful old time Chicken and Dumplings that we could attribute to Me Me and that hen."
Wendy Walton Sibilie
Opelousas, Louisiana

INGREDIENTS:

1 (5-pound) baking hen
2 cups chopped onions
1 cup chopped celery
1/2 cup chopped bell pepper
1/4 cup diced garlic
3 quarts water
3 cups flour
1 cup milk
1 tsp oil
1 tsp baking powder
1 tsp salt
black pepper
1/2 cup sliced green onions

METHOD:

Cut hen into 8 serving pieces. Rinse well under cold water and season to taste using salt and pepper. In a 7-quart cast iron dutch oven, place hen, onions, celery, bell pepper, garlic and water. Bring to a rolling boil, reduce to simmer and allow chicken to cook for approximately 1 1/2 hours or until tender. During the cooking process, foam will rise to the surface of the stock. Using a ladle, skim as much of the impurities as possible from the surface. This will guarantee a nice, clear stock. Add water if necessary to retain volume. In a large mixing bowl, combine flour, milk, oil and baking powder. Season to taste using salt and pepper. Keep an extra cup of flour handy, should the mixture become too sticky. Using your hands, mix the dumpling batter well, being careful not to knead too long, which will cause the dumplings to become tough. Sprinkle a small amount of flour onto a flat surface and roll the dumpling dough out very thin, approximately 1/4-inch. Allow dough to rest for 10 minutes and cut into 1-inch squares. When chicken stock is full-flavored and chicken is tender, adjust seasonings if necessary. Add green onions and dumplings, one at a time, until all is incorporated. Allow each dumpling to cook 30 seconds prior to adding the next. Bring stock back to a boil and cook 5 additional minutes. Serve in a large soup bowl with a generous amount of the dumplings.

Nutrition Facts...then
Calories: 1106
Total Fat: 50gm
Saturated Fat: 14gm
% Calories from Fat: 41
Cholesterol: 371mg
Sodium: 661mg
Carbohydrates: 57gm
Fiber: 3gm
Protein: 101gm

PREP TIME: 2 1/2 Hours   SERVES: 6

☞ INGREDIENTS:

1 (5-pound) baking hen, skinned
2 cups chopped onions
1 cup chopped celery
1/2 cup chopped bell pepper
1/4 cup diced garlic
3 quarts water
3 cups flour
1 cup skim milk
1 tsp oil
1 tsp baking powder
1/2 tsp salt
black pepper
1/2 cup sliced green onions

Chef's Tips on Low-Fat...
use lowfat or nonfat Ricotta and
Mozzarella cheese in recipes like
lasagna.

☞ METHOD:

Cut hen into 8 serving pieces. Rinse well under cold water and season to taste using salt and pepper.

In a 7-quart cast iron dutch oven, place chicken, onions, celery, bell pepper, garlic and water. Bring to a rolling boil, reduce to simmer and allow chicken to cook for approximately 1 1/2 hours or until tender.

During the cooking process, foam will rise to the surface of the stock. Using a ladle, skim as much of the impurities as possible from the surface. This will guarantee a nice, clear stock. Add water if necessary to retain volume.

In a large mixing bowl, combine flour, skim milk, oil and baking powder. Season to taste using salt and pepper. Keep an extra cup of flour handy, should the mixture become too sticky. Using your hands, mix the dumpling batter well, being careful not to knead too long, which will cause the dumplings to become tough. Sprinkle a small amount of flour onto a flat surface and roll the dumpling dough out very thin, approximately 1/4-inch. Allow dough to rest for 10 minutes and cut into 1-inch squares.

When chicken stock is full-flavored and chicken is tender, adjust seasonings if necessary. Add green onions and dumplings, one at a time, until all is incorporated. Allow each dumpling to cook 30 seconds prior to adding the next.

Bring stock back to a boil and cook 5 additional minutes. Serve in a large soup bowl with a generous amount of the dumplings.

Nutrition Facts...now

Calories:	536
Total Fat:	11gm
Saturated Fat:	3gm
% Calories from Fat:	20
Cholesterol:	121mg
Sodium:	338mg
Carbohydrates:	57gm
Fiber:	3gm
Protein:	49gm

PREP TIME: 1 1/2 Hours   SERVES: 6

"This recipe was handed down from my grandmother, Agnes Marie Guerin, whose family came to Louisiana directly from France. Grandfather Guerin had a butcher shop, but they lived on a farm, where, as a little girl, I would visit.

"My grandmother, like most farm women, kept chickens for eggs and meat, and I was strictly forbidden to enter the chicken yard. The idea that chickens were rather ornery critters no doubt muted any squeamishness I might have felt watching Grandmother Guerin efficiently wring the neck of the one selected to be the evening's meal.

"While grandmother wasn't Cajun in the strictest sense, her chicken stew definitely is, with its roux base.

"A roux isn't particularly difficult to make, but it is a little time-consuming, which calls to mind an interesting trend I've noted among some younger couples of my acquaintance - couples who both work. The men, increasingly, are the ones who are doing the traditional cooking, while the women tend to the house and children.

"I wonder if, three generations hence, restaurants will be boasting of serving Cajun food 'just like Grandpa used to make'."

Honorine Abel
Patterson, Louisiana

☞ INGREDIENTS:

1 (4-pound) fryer, cut into pieces	1 1/2 cups chopped celery	3 medium red potatoes, peeled and cubed
1 cup oil	1 cup chopped bell pepper	1 pound sliced fresh mushrooms
3/4 cup flour	1/4 cup diced garlic	1/4 cup chopped parsley
2 cups chopped onions	1 (8-ounce) can tomato sauce	1 tsp salt
1/2 cup sliced green onions, bottoms only	1 1/2 quarts chicken stock	black pepper
	1 bay leaf	

☞ METHOD:

In a 7-quart cast iron dutch oven, heat oil over medium-high heat. Add flour and, using a wire whisk, whip constantly until dark brown roux is achieved. Add onions, green onions, celery, bell pepper and garlic. Saute 3–5 minutes or until vegetables are wilted. Add tomato sauce and blend well into the roux mixture. Add chicken stock, one ladle at a time, until all is incorporated. Bring to a rolling boil, stirring constantly until sauce-like consistency is achieved. Reduce heat to simmer. Add chicken and bay leaf. Cook 30 minutes. Season to taste using salt and pepper. Add potatoes and mushrooms. Simmer an additional 30 minutes and add parsley. Adjust seasonings if necessary. Serve over steamed white rice.

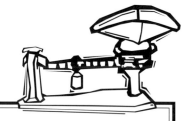

❋Nutrition Facts...then❋
Calories:	746
Total Fat:	43gm
Saturated Fat:	9gm
% Calories from Fat:	51
Cholesterol:	160mg
Sodium:	1547mg
Carbohydrates:	39gm
Fiber:	3gm
Protein:	52gm

CHICKEN STEW

PREP TIME: 1 1/2 Hours   SERVES: 6

Rooster for sale at the Vietnamese market in New Orleans East.

☞ INGREDIENTS:

1 (4-pound) fryer, skinned and cut into pieces
3/4 cup oil-less roux
1 1/2 quarts defatted chicken stock, unsalted
1/4 cup oil
2 cups chopped onions
1/2 cup sliced green onions, bottoms only
1 1/2 cups chopped celery
1 cup chopped bell pepper
1/4 cup diced garlic
1 (8-ounce) can tomato sauce, no salt added
1 bay leaf
3 medium red potatoes, peeled and cubed
1 pound sliced fresh mushrooms
1/4 cup chopped parsley
1/2 tsp salt
black pepper

☞ METHOD:

Dissolve oil-less roux in stock and set aside. In a 7-quart cast iron dutch oven, heat oil over medium heat. Add onions, green onions, celery, bell pepper and garlic. Saute 3–5 minutes or until vegetables are wilted.

Add tomato sauce and blend well into the vegetable mixture. Add chicken stock/roux mixture, one ladle at a time, until all is incorporated.

Bring to a rolling boil, stirring constantly until sauce-like consistency is achieved. Reduce heat to simmer. Add chicken and bay leaf. Cook 30 minutes. Season to taste using salt and pepper.

Add potatoes and mushrooms. Simmer an additional 30 minutes and add parsley. Adjust seasonings if necessary. Serve over steamed white rice.

Nutrition Facts...now

Calories:	452
Total Fat:	19gm
Saturated Fat:	3gm
% Calories from Fat:	37
Cholesterol:	96mg
Sodium:	651mg
Carbohydrates:	30gm
Fiber:	3gm
Protein:	43gm

PREP TIME: 1 1/2 Hours   SERVES: 6

"I grew up in New Orleans, and we often visited my grandmother in Mandeville, on the north shore of Lake Pontchartrain. That was long before the Causeway across the lake was built, so you crossed it by one of two ferryboats.

"My grandmother had a Dodge touring car - a big old truck of a vehicle with what was called a Universal transmission - stick shift, but with a reversed gear pattern - which my uncle taught me to drive - at the ripe old age of eleven!

"Many's the time I drove my grandmother to Slidell - nearly a hundred miles round trip, along the narrow, twisting road following the north shore of the lake. She never seemed to have any concern that the driver of her car was still in grade school.

"That was 60 years ago. My grandmother obviously had a good deal of faith in me. Being the first grandchild - and her namesake - probably counted for as much as my driving skills."

"My first encounter with this recipe dates from about that same time. My mother learned it from a friend whose family brought it over from Italy. She fixed it almost weekly thereafter, and I have done the same. Now it's a favorite with my children."

Catherine O. Bouis
Lake Charles, Louisiana

INGREDIENTS:

6 chicken breasts, skinned
2 cans artichoke hearts, drained
1/4 cup olive oil
1/4 cup vegetable oil
1/4 cup flour

1 cup chopped onions
2 tbsps diced garlic
1 cup sliced green onions
4 cups chicken stock
1 (8-ounce) can green peas

1/2 cup chopped parsley
1/2 tsp salt
black pepper

METHOD:

In a 5-quart cast iron dutch oven, heat olive oil over medium-high heat. Season chicken breasts using salt and pepper. Saute chicken until golden brown on both sides. Remove and set aside. Remove olive oil and add vegetable oil. Add flour and, using a wire whisk, whip constantly until golden brown roux is achieved. Add onions, garlic and green onions. Saute 3–5 minutes or until vegetables are wilted. Add chicken stock, blending well into the roux mixture. Bring to a rolling boil and reduce to simmer. Add chicken, artichokes and peas. Cover and cook 45 minutes. Season to taste using salt and pepper. Finish with chopped parsley. Serve over steamed white rice or pasta.

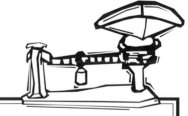

❧Nutrition Facts...then❧

Calories: 521
Total Fat: 17gm
Saturated Fat: 3gm
% Calories from Fat: 30
Cholesterol: 147mg
Sodium: 1033mg
Carbohydrates: 27gm
Fiber: 9gm
Protein: 64gm

PREP TIME: 1 1/2 Hours   SERVES: 6

INGREDIENTS:

6 chicken breasts, skinned
2 cans artichoke hearts, drained
1/4 cup oil-less roux
4 cups defatted chicken stock, unsalted
1 tbsp olive oil
1 tbsp vegetable oil
1 cup chopped onions
2 tbsps diced garlic
1 cup sliced green onions
1 (8-ounce) can green peas
1/2 cup chopped parsley
salt substitute
black pepper

METHOD:

Dissolve oil-less roux in stock and set aside. In a 5-quart cast iron dutch oven, heat oils over medium heat.

Season chicken breasts using salt substitute and pepper. Saute chicken until golden brown on both sides. Remove and set aside.

Add onions, garlic and green onions. Saute 3–5 minutes or until vegetables are wilted.

Add chicken stock/roux mixture, blending well into the vegetables. Bring to a rolling boil and reduce to simmer. Add chicken, artichokes and peas. Cover and cook 45 minutes.

Season to taste using salt substitute and pepper. Finish with chopped parsley. Serve over steamed white rice or pasta.

Nutrition Facts...now

Calories:	446
Total Fat:	9gm
Saturated Fat:	2gm
% Calories from Fat:	18
Cholesterol:	146mg
Sodium:	562mg
Carbohydrates:	28gm
Fiber:	9gm
Protein:	64gm

PREP TIME: 1 Hour   SERVES: 6

☞ INGREDIENTS:

1 (3-pound) fryer
1 quart buttermilk
2 cups flour
1 cup vegetable oil
2 tbsps flour
3/4 cup chicken broth
1/2 cup cream
1/4 tsp salt
1/2 tsp black pepper
2 tsps garlic powder

Chef's Tips on Weight Loss... top five fat foods...salad dressing, margarine, cheese, ground beef, luncheon meats and sausages.

☞ METHOD:

Cut chicken into 8 serving pieces and soak in buttermilk 2 hours, preferably overnight. Remove and drain excess liquid. Season flour to taste using salt, pepper and garlic powder. In a 12-inch cast iron skillet, heat approximately 1/4 inch of cooking oil over medium-high heat to 325 degrees F. Dredge chicken in seasoned flour and pan fry 10–12 minutes on each side, turning occasionally. Chicken will be done when golden brown and juices run clear when pricked with a fork. Remove and keep warm. When done, remove all but 2 teaspoons of oil from the skillet. Sprinkle in 2 tablespoons of flour and, using a wire whisk, blend well. Add chicken broth and cream, stirring constantly. Bring to a rolling boil and reduce to simmer. Season to taste using salt, pepper and garlic powder. Cook approximately 5–10 minutes and serve the country gravy with fried chicken.

"No, southern fried chicken didn't originate with the Cajuns but you can't get much further south than here, can you? There were Cajuns in the Confederate army, you know. My great-grandfather was a member of what they called the Louisiana Tigers in General Lee's army.

"Angel biscuits? They're yeast biscuits, so light they'll float right up to heaven! They were my grandmother's recipe. It was at her house where the family all congregated for holidays and things.

"There'd be so many of us we couldn't all eat at once. We ate in three sittings - the men, first, then the women, then the children. That's the way people stayed. The men would be in one room talking, the women in another room talking and the kids outside playing.

"There was a big sugar cane field out behind their house in Cade, near New Iberia. After the harvest, there was always some cane left in the field for us kids to suck the juice from."

Theresa Fruge
Lake Charles, Louisiana

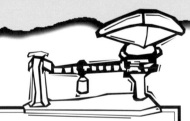

❦ Nutrition Facts...then ❦

Calories:	1115
Total Fat:	71gm
Saturated Fat:	16gm
% Calories from Fat:	58
Cholesterol:	257mg
Sodium:	545mg
Carbohydrates:	44gm
Fiber:	1gm
Protein:	72gm

SOUTHERN OVEN-FRIED CHICKEN

PREP TIME: 1 Hour   SERVES: 6

☞ INGREDIENTS:

1 (3-pound) fryer, skinned
1 quart low-fat buttermilk
2 cups yellow corn flour
vegetable spray
2 tbsps vegetable oil
2 tbsps flour
3/4 cup defattted chicken stock, unsalted
1/2 cup evaporated skim milk
1/4 tsp salt
black pepper
2 tsps garlic powder

☞ METHOD:

Preheat oven to 350 degrees F. Cut chicken into 8 serving pieces and soak in buttermilk 2 hours, preferably overnight.

Season yellow corn flour to taste using salt, pepper and garlic powder. Remove the chicken and drain excess liquid. Dredge chicken in seasoned corn flour. Spray a 12-inch cast iron skillet generously with vegetable spray. Place chicken in skillet and spray lightly with additional vegetable spray. Bake chicken 1 1/2 hours. Chicken will be done when golden brown and juices run clear when pricked with a fork. Remove chicken and keep warm.

Place 2 tablespoons of oil in the skillet. Sprinkle in 2 tablespoons of flour and, using a wire whisk, blend well. Add chicken stock and skim milk, stirring constantly. Bring to a rolling boil and reduce to simmer. Season to taste using salt, pepper and garlic powder. Cook approximately 5–10 minutes and serve the country gravy with oven-fried chicken.

NOTE: This simple country gravy really brings out the flavor in this oven-fried recipe.

Kitchen window with a basket of fresh eggs and a sweet potato taking root in Mamou, Evangeline Parish.

Nutrition Facts...now

Calories:	434
Total Fat:	13gm
Saturated Fat:	3gm
% Calories from Fat:	28
Cholesterol:	79mg
Sodium:	390mg
Carbohydrates:	43gm
Fiber:	6gm
Protein:	35gm

PREP TIME: 1 Hour 45 Minutes   SERVES: 6

☞ INGREDIENTS:

1 (3-pound) fryer
1 (12-ounce) package spaghetti
2 cups chopped onions
2 cups chopped celery
1 bay leaf
1/4 pound butter
2 tbsps flour
1 (14-ounce) can crushed tomatoes
1 cup sliced mushrooms
3 cups reserved chicken stock
1 cup grated cheddar cheese
1/4 tsp salt
cayenne pepper

☞ METHOD:

Preheat oven to 350 degrees F. Cut fryer into 8 serving pieces. In a large pot, place chicken with enough water to cover by 2 inches. Add 1 cup onions, 1 cup celery and bay leaf. Season the water to taste using salt and pepper. Bring to a rolling boil, reduce to simmer and cook until chicken is tender, approximately 45 minutes. Strain and reserve the chicken stock. Cool and debone chicken. In a 5-quart cast iron dutch oven, melt butter over medium-high heat. Add flour and, using a wire whisk, stir until white roux is achieved. Add remaining onions and celery. Saute 3–5 minutes or until vegetables are wilted. Add tomatoes, mushrooms and reserved chicken stock. Bring to a rolling boil, reduce to simmer and cook an additional 5–10 minutes. Prepare spaghetti according to package directions. Drain and set aside. In an oven-proof casserole dish, layer the spaghetti, chicken, sauce and cheese. Continue with a second layer until all ingredients are used. Add a couple cooking spoons of chicken stock and bake 20–30 minutes. Additional chicken stock may be added, should sauce become too thick in the cooking process.

"Aunt Florence was Florence Schanz, who taught third grade in Sulphur, Louisiana for 35 years. When she started teaching, it was during the Depression. She taught in a one-room school in Edgerly. She lived with a family in the area during the week, and went home to Vinton on weekends.

"Aunt Florence also cooked for the kids in her school making soup for their lunch. It probably wasn't a formal part of her job, but if she hadn't, many of the kids would have had nothing to eat.

"Everybody in this area knew Aunt Florence. She was a red-haired lady, and I'll always remember her bustling around the kitchen, saying how hot she was and fanning with her petticoats. But she did love to cook, and the heat must not have hurt her. She lived to be 87!"

Nina LaFleur Vincent
Sulphur, Louisiana

❧Nutrition Facts...then❧

Calories: 1023
Total Fat: 53gm
Saturated Fat: 22gm
% Calories from Fat: 47
Cholesterol: 301mg
Sodium: 1120mg
Carbohydrates: 56gm
Fiber: 2gm
Protein: 77gm

AUNT FLORENCE'S BAKED CHICKEN & SPAGHETTI   ...Something New

PREP TIME: 1 Hour 45 Minutes   SERVES: 6

☞ INGREDIENTS:

1 (3-pound) fryer, skinned
1 (12-ounce) package spaghetti
2 cups chopped onions
2 cups chopped celery
1 bay leaf
1 tbsp lite margarine
2 tbsps flour
1 (14-ounce) can crushed tomatoes, no salt added
1 cup sliced mushrooms
3 cups defatted reserved chicken stock, unsalted
1 cup low-fat cheddar cheese, grated
1/4 tsp salt
cayenne pepper

☞ METHOD:

Preheat oven to 350 degrees F. Cut fryer into 8 serving pieces. In a large pot, place chicken with enough water to cover by 2 inches. Add 1 cup onions, 1 cup celery and bay leaf. Season the water to taste using salt and pepper. Bring to a rolling boil, reduce to simmer and cook until chicken is tender, approximately 45 minutes. Strain and reserve the chicken stock.

Cool and debone chicken. In a 5-quart cast iron dutch oven, melt margarine over medium-high heat. Add flour and, using a wire whisk, stir until white roux is achieved. Add remaining onions and celery. Saute 3–5 minutes or until vegetables are wilted.

Add tomatoes, mushrooms and reserved chicken stock. Bring to a rolling boil, reduce to simmer and cook an additional 5–10 minutes.

Prepare spaghetti according to package directions. Drain and set aside.

In an oven-proof casserole dish, layer spaghetti, chicken, sauce and cheese. Continue with a second layer until all ingredients are used.

Add a couple cooking spoons of chicken stock and bake 20–30 minutes. Additional chicken stock may be added, should sauce become too thick in the cooking process.

Nutrition Facts...now

Calories:	446
Total Fat:	9gm
Saturated Fat:	2gm
% Calories from Fat:	18
Cholesterol:	75mg
Sodium:	408mg
Carbohydrates:	54gm
Fiber:	2gm
Protein:	36gm

193

PREP TIME: 1 1/2 Hours   SERVES: 6

INGREDIENTS:

6 boneless chicken breasts
1/4 cup olive oil
2 cups chopped onions
1/4 cup chopped garlic
1 (16-ounce) can chopped tomatoes
1 (6-ounce) can tomato paste
2 cups hot water
1/2 tsp oregano
1 tsp dried basil
1 tsp sugar
4 eggs
2 tbsps water
1/2 cup olive oil
2 cups Italian bread crumbs
1/2 cup grated Parmesan cheese
6 slices Mozzarella cheese
1/4 tsp salt
black pepper

METHOD:

Preheat oven to 400 degrees F. In a 12-inch cast iron skillet, heat 1/4 cup olive oil over medium-high heat. Add onions and garlic. Saute 3–5 minutes or until vegetables are wilted. Add tomatoes and paste and blend well into the onion mixture, stirring constantly. Simmer mixture for 20 minutes. Add water, oregano, basil and sugar. Season to taste using salt and pepper and simmer approximately 20 additional minutes. Remove and keep warm. Using a meat mallet, lightly flatten the chicken breasts. Season to taste using salt and pepper. In a small mixing bowl, whip eggs and water. In another 12-inch cast iron skillet, heat 1/2 cup olive oil over medium-high heat. Dip chicken breasts into egg mixture and into bread crumbs. Saute 3–5 minutes on each side until golden brown. Remove chicken and keep warm. Pour tomato sauce into the bottom of an 11" x 7" baking dish. Place sauteed chicken breasts in sauce. Top each with Parmesan cheese and 1 slice of Mozzarella. Bake 15–20 minutes or until cheese is melted and chicken is heated thoroughly. This dish is excellent when served over angel hair pasta or spaghetti.

"When I was growing up my family had a Spanish moss gin. People collected Spanish moss from the trees and brought it to the gin, where we cleaned it, dried it and shipped it up north by rail, where they used it to upholster automobile seats. I think it's still used some in upholstering.

"Times do change. When I was growing up, the men would get together and have a boucherie several times a year, where they would slaughter and dress out pigs or a cow. Preserving fresh meat was a real problem. I remember we used to cook grillades (thin strips of meat) and store them in crocks of lard to preserve them.

"I guess there isn't any meat I haven't eaten - liver, brains, hearts, kidneys. My father had a grocery store when I was growing up. Whatever fresh meat didn't sell was brought home for the family!

"The Italian influence in my cooking comes from my husband's family. He was raised on it, and I had learned Cajun cooking from my mother. So I had to learn a second style of cooking when we got married."

Honorine Russo
Morgan City, Louisiana

❧ Nutrition Facts...then ❧

Calories: 626
Total Fat: 29gm
Saturated Fat: 7gm
% Calories from Fat: 41
Cholesterol: 168mg
Sodium: 1923mg
Carbohydrates: 46gm
Fiber: 2gm
Protein: 46gm

PREP TIME: 1 1/2 Hours   SERVES: 6

☞ INGREDIENTS:

6 boneless chicken breasts, skinned
1 tbsp olive oil
2 cups chopped onions
1/4 cup chopped garlic
1 (16-ounce) can chopped tomatoes, no salt added
1 (6-ounce) can tomato paste, no salt added

2 cups hot water
1/2 tsp oregano
1 tsp dried basil
1 tsp sugar
1 cup egg substitute
2 tbsps water

1/4 cup olive oil
2 cups plain bread crumbs
1/2 cup grated nonfat Parmesan cheese
6 slices low-fat Mozzarella cheese
salt substitute
black pepper

☞ METHOD:

Preheat oven to 400 degrees F. In a 12-inch cast iron skillet, heat 1 tablespoon olive oil over medium heat. Add onions and garlic. Saute 3–5 minutes or until vegetables are wilted.

Add tomatoes and paste and blend well into the onion mixture, stirring constantly. Simmer mixture for 20 minutes. Add water, oregano, basil and sugar. Season to taste using salt substitute and pepper and simmer approximately 20 additional minutes. Remove and keep warm.

Using a meat mallet, lightly flatten the chicken breasts and season to taste using salt substitute and pepper.

In a small mixing bowl, whip egg substitute and water. In another 12-inch cast iron skillet, heat 1/4 cup olive oil over medium heat. Dip chicken breasts into egg mixture and

into bread crumbs. Saute 3–5 minutes on each side until golden brown. Remove chicken and keep warm.

Pour tomato sauce into the bottom of an 11" x 7" baking dish. Place sauteed chicken breasts in sauce. Top each with Parmesan cheese and 1 slice of Mozzarella. Bake 15–20 minutes or until cheese is melted and chicken is heated thoroughly.

This dish is excellent when served over angel hair pasta or spaghetti.

Nutrition Facts...now

Calories:	492
Total Fat:	13gm
Saturated Fat:	2gm
% Calories from Fat:	24
Cholesterol:	86mg
Sodium:	688mg
Carbohydrates:	45gm
Fiber:	1gm
Protein:	48gm

A traditional hen house in Mamou keeps the hen in and the chicks free to come and go.

PREP TIME: 1 Hour   SERVES: 6

☞ INGREDIENTS:

6 chicken breasts
3 eggplants, diced
1/2 cup flour
1/4 cup melted butter
1 cup chopped onions
1 cup chopped celery
1/2 cup chopped bell pepper
1/4 cup diced garlic
1 cup sliced black olives
1 (8-ounce) package shredded cheddar cheese
1/4 tsp salt
cayenne pepper

☞ METHOD:

Preheat oven to 350 degrees F. Lightly season the flour to taste using salt and pepper. Rub a small amount of the butter on each chicken breast and dust lightly in the seasoned flour. Place breasts on a cookie sheet and bake 10–15 minutes. Remove and keep warm. Poach eggplant in lightly salted water until tender. Using a fork, mash eggplant and set aside. In a 10-inch cast iron skillet, heat remaining butter over medium-high heat. Add onions, celery, bell pepper and garlic. Saute 3–5 minutes or until vegetables are wilted. Add eggplant, blend well into the vegetable mixture and simmer 10–15 minutes longer. Season to taste using salt and pepper. Place chicken breasts in a 2-quart casserole dish. Cover with the eggplant mixture, black olives and 1/2 of the shredded cheese. Using a fork, blend the ingredients well over the chicken. Top with the remaining cheese. Bake, uncovered, 15–20 minutes.

> "This is a Greek-Cajun-Mexican recipe. How many of those have you encountered before? It started with an eggplant and black olive dish a Greek friend brought over for us to try some years ago. I thought it was good, but could use some Cajun-style pepping up. The Mexican part is the longhorn cheese - something I adapted from a recipe I learned when we lived in Arizona some years ago. Cheese isn't something you often find in Cajun cooking.
>
> "You know how to choose a good eggplant? Choose the ones with the lighter purple skin. The female ones are best. Look at the bottom of the eggplant. If the center is circular, it's a male eggplant. A female eggplant has a more elongated center - and fewer seeds."
>
> Martha Butler
> Houma, Louisiana

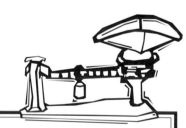

❋Nutrition Facts...then❋

Calories:	652
Total Fat:	30gm
Saturated Fat:	9gm
% Calories from Fat:	43
Cholesterol:	207mg
Sodium:	569mg
Carbohydrates:	21gm
Fiber:	1gm
Protein:	70gm

PREP TIME: 1 Hour   SERVES: 6

☞ INGREDIENTS:

6 chicken breasts, skinned
3 eggplants, diced
1/2 cup flour
vegetable spray
2 tbsps lite margarine
1 cup chopped onions
1 cup chopped celery
1/2 cup chopped bell pepper
1/4 cup diced garlic
1/2 cup sliced black olives
1 (8-ounce) package shredded,
        low-fat cheddar cheese
salt substitute
cayenne pepper

☞ METHOD:

Preheat oven to 350 degrees F. Lightly season the flour to taste using salt substitute and pepper. Dust chicken lightly in the seasoned flour. Place breasts on a cookie sheet, coated with vegetable spray, and bake 10–15 minutes. Remove and keep warm.

Poach eggplant in water until tender. Using a fork, mash eggplant and set aside.

In a 10-inch cast iron skillet, heat margarine over medium heat. Add onions, celery, bell pepper and garlic. Saute 3–5 minutes or until vegetables are wilted.

Add eggplant, blend well into the vegetable mixture, and simmer 10–15 minutes longer. Season to taste using salt substitute and pepper.

Place chicken breasts in a 2-quart casserole dish. Cover with the eggplant mixture, black olives and 1/2 of the shredded cheese. Using a fork, blend the ingredients well over the chicken. Top with the remaining cheese. Bake, uncovered, 15–20 minutes.

*Chef's Tips on Weight Loss...
high fat foods...whole milk,
french fries, shortening, eggs,
bacon and butter.*

Nutrition Facts...now

Calories:	485
Total Fat:	15gm
Saturated Fat:	6gm
% Calories from Fat:	29
Cholesterol:	173mg
Sodium:	378mg
Carbohydrates:	18gm
Fiber:	1gm
Protein:	67gm

PREP TIME: 1 Hour   SERVES: 6

☞ INGREDIENTS:

1 pound chicken drummettes
1/2 pound smoked sausage
1/2 cup vegetable oil
1 cup diced onions
1/2 cup diced red bell pepper
1/4 cup diced garlic
3 cups chicken stock
2 cups long grain rice, uncooked
1/4 cup sliced green onions
1/4 cup chopped parsley
1 tsp salt
black pepper
hot sauce

☞ METHOD:

In a 5-quart cast iron dutch oven, heat oil over medium-high heat. Season the drummettes well using salt, pepper and hot sauce. Saute drummettes until golden brown and well caramelized in the bottom of the pot. This is very important because the color of the jambalaya depends on this caramelizing. Add smoked sausage and continue to cook 10–15 minutes longer. Add onions, bell pepper and garlic. Saute 3–5 minutes or until vegetables are wilted. Add stock, bring to a rolling boil and reduce to simmer. Add rice and season to taste using salt and pepper. Reduce the heat to the lowest setting, cover and cook 30 minutes. Remove the lid, stir in green onions and parsley. Cover and cook 5 additional minutes. Check to make sure rice is thoroughly cooked. Serve hot.

In Galliano, on Bayou Lafourche, an enterprising chicken business takes to the road.

"We Cajuns are famous for being able to come up with a recipe for almost anything we can raise or hunt. Nowadays, like everyone else, we do a lot of hunting around for food ideas in the supermarket. That's where the idea for this "last minute" jambalaya came from.

"Chicken wings or legs are usually available on sale or at an inexpensive price. I prefer the drumettes, myself."

Joe E. Thibodaux
Lafayette, Louisiana

❧ Nutrition Facts...then ❧

Calories: 623
Total Fat: 36gm
Saturated Fat: 9gm
% Calories from Fat: 52
Cholesterol: 48mg
Sodium: 1102mg
Carbohydrates: 55gm
Fiber: 1gm
Protein: 20gm

PREP TIME: 1 Hour   SERVES: 6

☞ INGREDIENTS:

1 pound chicken drummettes, skinned
1/2 pound low-fat smoked sausage
1/4 cup vegetable oil
1 cup diced onions
1/2 cup diced red bell pepper
1/4 cup diced garlic
3 cups defatted chicken stock, unsalted
2 cups long grain rice, uncooked
1/4 cup sliced green onions
1/4 cup chopped parsley
salt substitute
black pepper
hot sauce

Chef's Tips on Weight Loss... did you know that in an average individual, 40% of all the calories eaten are fat?

☞ METHOD:

In a 5-quart cast iron dutch oven, heat oil over medium-high heat. Season the drummettes well using salt substitute, pepper and hot sauce. Saute drummettes until golden brown and well caramelized in the bottom of the pot. This is very important because the color of the jambalaya depends on this caramelizing.

Add smoked sausage and continue to cook 10–15 minutes longer. Add onions, bell pepper and garlic. Saute 3–5 minutes or until vegetables are wilted.

Add stock, bring to a rolling boil and reduce to simmer. Add rice and season to taste using salt substitute and pepper. Reduce the heat to the lowest setting, cover and cook 30 minutes.

Remove the lid, stir in green onions and parsley. Cover and cook 5 additional minutes. Check to make sure rice is thoroughly cooked. Serve hot.

Nutrition Facts...now

Calories:	450
Total Fat:	18gm
Saturated Fat:	2gm
% Calories from Fat:	37
Cholesterol:	13mg
Sodium:	190mg
Carbohydrates:	54gm
Fiber:	1gm
Protein:	16gm

PREP TIME: 1 Hour   SERVES: 6

☞ INGREDIENTS:

1 (1 1/2-pound) fryer
3 cups converted rice, uncooked
1/4 cup butter
5 cups water
1 (8-ounce) can whole kernel corn
1 (8-ounce) can green peas
1/2 cup sliced red bell pepper
1/4 cup diced garlic
1 cup sliced mushrooms
1/2 cup diced pimentos
1/4 cup diced tasso
1/4 cup beer (optional)
2 eggs, whipped
1 cup grated cheddar cheese
1/4 tsp salt
black pepper
Louisiana Gold Pepper Sauce

☞ METHOD:

Preheat oven to 300 degrees F. Cut chicken into 8 serving pieces and place in a 1-gallon stock pot. Cover chicken by 3 inches with cold water. Bring to a rolling boil, reduce to simmer and cook until meat is tender and falling from the bones. Remove chicken, cool and debone. Discard bones and reserve stock for later use. In a 2-quart sauce pot, combine rice, butter and water. Bring to a rolling boil, reduce to simmer, cover and cook 30 minutes. Set aside. In a 12-inch cast iron skillet, combine corn, peas, bell pepper, garlic, mushrooms, pimentos and tasso. Bring to a low simmer and heat thoroughly. Strain ingredients through a colander. Keep warm. In a large casserole dish, place cooked rice and sprinkle with beer. Add eggs and, using a fork, disperse evenly through the rice. Once the vegetables are thoroughly drained, add to casserole dish and blend well into the rice. Place deboned chicken meat on rice and season to taste using salt, pepper and Louisiana Gold. Sprinkle with grated cheese and bake, uncovered, 25–30 minutes.

"This recipe came about because I won a sales contest back around 1950 for selling Chambers ranges - a prestige brand of cookstove. The prize was a four or five day holiday in Cuba - a popular vacation destination in those pre-Castro days.

"My boss was so pleased that I'd qualified for the trip that he bought a ticket for my wife, so she could accompany me.

"Among our souvenirs from the trip was the memory of this traditional Cuban main course. From that memory I developed this version - sort of a Cuban dish with a Cajun accent. But I wouldn't be at all surprised to find that there was a very similar original Cajun dish. There's nothing in it that couldn't have been combined as readily in Lafayette as Havana.

"It's not only good, it's inexpensive - and that was to prove a boon as our family grew. With six kids, a nourishing dish that feeds a lot of people for a little money is assured of becoming a family tradition."

Howard Cornay
Lafayette, Louisiana

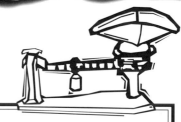

❧Nutrition Facts...then❧

Calories: 746
Total Fat: 21gm
Saturated Fat: 6gm
% Calories from Fat:................. 26
Cholesterol: 165mg
Sodium: 1581mg
Carbohydrates: 92gm
Fiber: 5gm
Protein: 43gm

PREP TIME: 1 Hour   SERVES: 6

☞ INGREDIENTS:

1 (1 1/2-pound) fryer, skinned
3 cups converted rice, uncooked
1 tbsp lite margarine
5 cups water
1 (8-ounce) can whole kernel corn
1 (8-ounce) can green peas
1/2 cup sliced red bell pepper
1/4 cup diced garlic
1 cup sliced mushrooms
1/2 cup diced pimentos
1/4 cup diced tasso
1/4 cup beer (optional)
1/2 cup egg substitute
1 cup low-fat cheddar cheese, grated
salt substitute
black pepper
Louisiana Gold Pepper Sauce

☞ METHOD:

Preheat oven to 300 degrees F. Cut chicken into 8 serving pieces and place in a 1-gallon stock pot. Cover chicken by 3 inches with cold water. Bring to a rolling boil, reduce to simmer and cook until meat is tender and falling from the bones. Remove chicken, cool and debone. Discard bones and reserve stock for later use.

In a 2-quart sauce pot, combine rice, margarine and water. Bring to a rolling boil, reduce to simmer, cover and cook 30 minutes. Set aside.

In a 12-inch cast iron skillet, combine corn, peas, bell pepper, garlic, mushrooms, pimentos and tasso. Bring to a low simmer and heat thoroughly. Strain ingredients through a colander. Keep warm.

In a large casserole dish, place cooked rice and sprinkle with beer. Add egg substitute and, using a fork, disperse evenly through the rice. Once the vegetables are thoroughly drained, add to casserole dish and blend well into the rice.

Place deboned chicken meat on rice and season to taste using salt substitute, pepper and Louisiana Gold. Sprinkle with grated cheese and bake, uncovered, 25–30 minutes.

Nutrition Facts...now

Calories:	510
Total Fat:	6gm
Saturated Fat:	2gm
% Calories from Fat:	10
Cholesterol:	39mg
Sodium:	279mg
Carbohydrates:	90gm
Fiber:	5gm
Protein:	23gm

PREP TIME: 1 1/2 Hours   SERVES: 8

☞ INGREDIENTS:

1 (2-pound) fryer
1/2 cup vegetable oil
3/4 cup flour
2 cups chopped onions
1 cup chopped celery
1/2 cup chopped red bell pepper
1/4 cup chopped garlic
1 1/2 quarts chicken stock
1/2 cup sliced green onions
1/2 cup chopped parsley
1/4 tsp salt
black pepper
hot sauce

Chef's Tips on Weight Loss... did you know that a moderately active woman who eats 1,800 calories a day should consume about 60 grams of fat?

☞ METHOD:

Cut chicken into 8 serving pieces and rinse under cold water. Drain and set aside. In a 5-quart cast iron dutch oven, heat oil over medium-high heat. Add flour and, using a wire whisk, stir until light brown roux is achieved. Add onions, celery, bell pepper and garlic. Saute 3–5 minutes or until vegetables are wilted. Add chicken and blend well into the roux mixture. Saute 5–6 minutes, stirring occasionally to render juices. Add chicken stock, one cup at a time, stirring until all is incorporated. Bring to a rolling boil, reduce to simmer and cook 1 hour until chicken is tender. Season to taste using salt, pepper and hot sauce. Add green onions and parsley. Serve over steamed white rice.

"The smell of good old-fashioned chicken stew brings to mind Sunday mornings when I was growing up. I was the youngest of eight children, and stew was an excellent meal stretcher.

"My mother would catch a chicken from the yard on Saturday, wring its neck, put it across an old tree stump in the back yard and chop its neck off. I can still see her small patch of parsley and onion tops she grew right by the back porch. They were some of the last ingredients she used when cooking, so I knew it wouldn't be long before it would be cooked when she asked me to get them for her.

"She always used these ingredients in her stews, gumbos and beans. It seemed to take forever for that stew to cook, but it was well worth waiting for. I could never make chicken stew to taste like hers without adding extra ingredients."

Melba Matherne
Houma, Louisiana

❧Nutrition Facts...then❧

Calories: 461
Total Fat: 29gm
Saturated Fat: 6gm
% Calories from Fat: 57
Cholesterol: 110mg
Sodium: 743mg
Carbohydrates: 15gm
Fiber: 1gm
Protein: 34gm

PREP TIME: 1 1/2 Hours   SERVES: 8

☞ INGREDIENTS:

1 (2-pound) fryer, skinned
3/4 cup oil-less roux
6 cups defatted chicken stock, unsalted
1/4 cup vegetable oil
2 cups chopped onions
1 cup chopped celery
1/2 cup chopped red bell pepper
1/4 cup chopped garlic
1/2 cup sliced green onions
1/2 cup chopped parsley
salt substitute
black pepper
hot sauce

☞ METHOD:

Dissolve oil-less roux in stock and set aside. Cut chicken into 8 serving pieces and rinse under cold water. Drain and set aside.

In a 5-quart cast iron dutch oven, heat oil over medium heat. Add onions, celery, bell pepper and garlic. Saute 3–5 minutes or until vegetables are wilted.

Add chicken and blend well into the vegetable mixture. Saute 5–6 minutes, stirring occasionally to render juices. Add chicken stock/roux mixture, one cup at a time, stirring until all is incorporated. Bring to a rolling boil, reduce to simmer and cook 1 hour until chicken is tender.

Season to taste using salt substitute, pepper and hot sauce. Add green onions and parsley. Serve over steamed white rice.

Nutrition Facts...now

Calories: 221
Total Fat: 10gm
Saturated Fat: 2gm
% Calories from Fat: 41
Cholesterol: 36mg
Sodium: 302mg
Carbohydrates: 15gm
Fiber: 1gm
Protein: 18gm

PREP TIME: 1 Hour   SERVES: 6

INGREDIENTS:

4 boneless chicken breasts
2 1/2 cups diced Creole tomatoes
3 tbsps poultry seasoning
1/2 cup extra virgin olive oil
1/2 cup grated Parmesan cheese
1 cup diced onions
1/4 cup diced garlic
1 cup dry white wine
2 bay leaves
pinch of oregano
pinch of rosemary
pinch of basil
pinch of thyme
1/2 tsp salt
black pepper
hot sauce

"Here, in a Cajun cookbook, is an Italian dish created by this Mississippi-born cook for a culinary demonstration at the Creole Tomato Festival in the French Quarter of New Orleans! How's that for a litany of influences?

"One thing that makes Italian tomato sauces so good is the Roma tomato, for which the Louisiana Creole tomato is a worthy alternative. It's a firm, tasty, acidic tomato that is wonderful for cooking. Most important of all, it's vine-ripened.

"If you are preparing this dish at a time or place where Creole tomatoes aren't available, a good brand of canned tomatoes will work far better than the green-picked, tasteless, hydroponic "fresh" tomatoes you're likely to be offered in supermarkets.

"You can't say it too often: the key to good cooking is good ingredients."
Nora Dejoie
New Orleans, Louisiana

METHOD:

Slice chicken breasts into 1/2-inch strips and season to taste using poultry seasoning, salt, pepper and hot sauce. In a 12-inch cast iron skillet, heat 1/4 cup olive oil over medium-high heat. Saute chicken until golden brown, remove and sprinkle with Parmesan cheese. Set aside and keep warm. Pour remaining olive oil into the skillet. Add onions and garlic. Saute 3–5 minutes or until vegetables are wilted. Add tomatoes, blending well into the onion mixture. Saute until tomatoes are tender and juices flow from them. Add wine, bay leaves, oregano, rosemary, basil and thyme. Bring to a rolling boil, reduce to simmer and cook 10 minutes. Transfer chicken to the tomato sauce and distribute evenly with a cooking spoon. Cover and cook 10 additional minutes. Season to taste using salt and pepper. This chicken dish is excellent when served over rice, pasta or with a toasted loaf of garlic bread.

❧Nutrition Facts...then❧

Calories:	384
Total Fat:	15gm
Saturated Fat:	5gm
% Calories from Fat:	36
Cholesterol:	117mg
Sodium:	593mg
Carbohydrates:	9gm
Fiber:	1gm
Protein:	45gm

CHICKEN & CREOLE TOMATO POMODORI

PREP TIME: 1 Hour SERVES: 6

☞ INGREDIENTS:

4 boneless chicken breasts, skinned
2 1/2 cups diced Creole tomatoes
3 tbsps poultry seasoning
1/4 cup extra virgin olive oil
1/2 cup fat-free Parmesan cheese,
    grated
1 cup diced onions
1/4 cup diced garlic
1 cup dry white wine
2 bay leaves
pinch of oregano
pinch of rosemary
pinch of basil
pinch of thyme
salt substitute
black pepper
hot sauce

*A bird's eye view of a neighborhood in Cut Off.
The Intercoastal Waterway is in the background.*

☞ METHOD:

Slice chicken breasts into 1/2-inch strips and season to taste using poultry seasoning, salt substitute, pepper and hot sauce.

In a 12-inch cast iron skillet, heat 1/4 cup olive oil over medium-high heat. Saute chicken until golden brown, remove and sprinkle with Parmesan cheese. Set aside and keep warm.

Add onions and garlic. Saute 3–5 minutes or until vegetables are wilted. Add tomatoes, blending well into the onion mixture. Saute until tomatoes are tender and juices flow from them.

Add wine, bay leaves, oregano, rosemary, basil and thyme. Bring to a rolling boil, reduce to simmer and cook 10 minutes. Transfer chicken to the tomato sauce and distribute evenly with a cooking spoon. Cover and cook 10 additional minutes. Season to taste using salt substitute and pepper.

This chicken dish is excellent when served over rice, pasta or with a toasted loaf of garlic bread.

Nutrition Facts...now

Calories:	281
Total Fat:	5gm
Saturated Fat:	1gm
% Calories from Fat:	17
Cholesterol:	104mg
Sodium:	314mg
Carbohydrates:	12gm
Fiber:	1gm
Protein:	40gm

CHICKEN LOAF GRAHAM

PREP TIME: 1 1/2 Hours   SERVES: 6

INGREDIENTS:

1 (1 1/2-pound) fryer
3 cups cooked spaghetti
2 cups seasoned Italian bread crumbs
3 cups hot milk
4 tbsps melted butter
2 cups grated American cheese
2 eggs, beaten
1/2 tsp salt
black pepper
hot sauce

*Chef's Tips on Weight Loss...
did you know that a moderately
active man who eats 2,400 calories a
day should consume about 80 grams
of fat?*

METHOD:

Preheat oven to 300 degrees F. Cut chicken into 8 serving pieces. Place chicken in a large stock pot and cover by 3 inches with cold water. Bring to a rolling boil, reduce to simmer, and cook until chicken is tender and falling from the bones. Remove and allow to cool. Reserve stock and freeze for later use. When chicken is cool, debone and dice it into 1/2-inch pieces. Discard bones. Cut the cooked spaghetti into 3- to 4-inch links. Place chicken and spaghetti in large mixing bowl and combine with all remaining ingredients. Blend well and season to taste using salt, pepper and hot sauce. Spoon mixture into a buttered 3-quart casserole dish. Create a water bath by placing casserole dish in a larger pan filled half way with hot water. Bake, uncovered, for approximately 1 hour or until casserole is set. This dish is great served either hot or cold.

"With the possible exception of an Army chow hall, I doubt that you could find a more improbable source for a family favorite than a hospital kitchen. But that's exactly where this one came from!

"I was in the Houston Veterans Administration hospital briefly for an ulcer in 1955, and, when I left, I was given a typed collection of recipes that were supposed to be suitable for someone with an ulcer which makes finding something as tasty as this all the more surprising.

"I've never known who created this recipe, but this is just the way it was given to me. We haven't altered a thing about it in more than 40 years."

Browning Graham
Morgan City, Louisiana

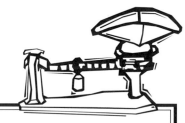

❀Nutrition Facts...then❀

Calories: 835
Total Fat: 43gm
Saturated Fat: 21gm
% Calories from Fat: 47
Cholesterol: 328mg
Sodium: 1729mg
Carbohydrates: 55gm
Fiber: 1gm
Protein: 55gm

PREP TIME: 1 1/2 Hours   SERVES: 6

INGREDIENTS:

1 (1 1/2-pound) fryer, skinned
3 cups cooked spaghetti
2 cups unseasoned bread crumbs
3 cups hot skim milk
2 tbsps lite margarine, melted
2 cups low-fat American cheese, grated
1/2 cup egg substitute
salt substitute
black pepper
hot sauce

METHOD:

Preheat oven to 300 degrees F. Cut chicken into 8 serving pieces. Place chicken in a large stock pot and cover by 3 inches with cold water. Bring to a rolling boil, reduce to simmer, and cook until chicken is tender and falling from the bones. Remove and allow to cool. Reserve stock and freeze for later use.

When chicken is cool, debone and dice it into 1/2-inch pieces. Discard bones.

Cut the cooked spaghetti into 3- to 4-inch links. Place chicken and spaghetti in large mixing bowl and combine with all remaining ingredients. Blend well and season to taste using salt substitute, pepper and hot sauce. Spoon mixture into a buttered 3-quart casserole dish.

Create a water bath by placing casserole dish in a larger pan filled half way with hot water. Bake, uncovered, for approximately 1 hour or until casserole is set.

This dish is great served either hot or cold.

Nutrition Facts...now

Calories:	422
Total Fat:	10gm
Saturated Fat:	3gm
% of Calories from Fat:	21
Cholesterol:	45mg
Sodium:	535mg
Carbohydrates:	53gm
Fiber:	1gm
Protein:	29gm

SKILLET CHICKEN & GRAVY

PREP TIME: 1 1/2 Hours   SERVES: 6

☞ INGREDIENTS:

1 (2-pound) fryer
1/2 cup vegetable oil
2 large onions, sliced
1 cup sliced celery
1 cup sliced bell pepper
1/4 cup diced garlic
4 cups chicken stock
1/4 cup chopped parsley
1/2 tsp salt
black pepper
1 tsp garlic powder
hot sauce

☞ METHOD:

Cut fryer into 8 serving pieces. Rinse under cold water and drain. Season chicken thoroughly with salt, pepper, garlic powder and hot sauce. In a 15-inch cast iron skillet, heat oil over medium-high heat. Brown chicken well on all sides, remove and keep warm. It is important to brown the chicken thoroughly since the color of the finished product depends on the caramelized color on the bottom of the skillet. Add onions, celery, bell pepper and garlic. Saute until vegetables are tender and sliced onions are transparent. Return the chicken to the skillet and add chicken stock. Bring to a rolling boil, reduce to simmer, cover and cook approximately 1 hour, stirring occasionally. Add water as needed to prevent chicken from sticking. Once chicken is tender, adjust seasonings using salt and pepper and sprinkle in chopped parsley. Turn off heat and allow chicken to sit 5–10 minutes. Skim off any excess fat that rises to the surface. The onion gravy may be served over rice, pasta or whipped potatoes.

"Our home in Port Sulphur, Louisiana, was a place where friends and family always came to visit. Everyone felt right at home and joined in the constant celebration that took place. Even our parish priests would join us regularly. We would often have marathon card games of bridge and pedro going on all night long. If someone got tired, they would go to bed and another would take their place.

"Being a country community, the grocery store was not that close by so we would cook many meals and have them ready so people could just eat when they felt like it. Many of the card games were interrupted by the delicious aroma of skillet chicken, simmering in a pan smothered in onions.

"I remember those days not so long ago, especially when I cook up a pan of my skillet chicken."
                    Dale Gabriel
              Ponchatoula, Louisiana

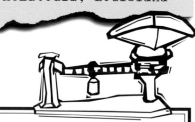

❧Nutrition Facts...then❧

Calories:	539
Total Fat:	38gm
Saturated Fat:	8gm
% Calories from Fat:	64
Cholesterol:	147mg
Sodium:	802mg
Carbohydrates:	6gm
Fiber:	1gm
Protein:	41gm

PREP TIME: 1 1/2 Hours   SERVES: 6

☞ INGREDIENTS:

1 (2-pound) fryer, skinned
1/4 cup vegetable oil
2 large onions, sliced
1 cup sliced celery
1 cup sliced bell pepper
1/4 cup diced garlic
4 cups defatted chicken stock, unsalted
1/4 cup chopped parsley
salt substitute
black pepper
1 tsp garlic powder
hot sauce

☞ METHOD:

Cut fryer into 8 serving pieces. Rinse under cold water and drain. Season chicken thoroughly with salt substitute, pepper, garlic powder and hot sauce.

In a 15-inch cast iron skillet, heat oil over medium-high heat. Brown chicken well on all sides, remove and keep warm. It is important to brown the chicken thoroughly since the color of the finished product depends on the caramelized color on the bottom of the skillet.

Add onions, celery, bell pepper and garlic. Saute until vegetables are tender and sliced onions are transparent. Return the chicken to the skillet and add chicken stock. Bring to a rolling boil, reduce to simmer, cover and cook approximately 1 hour, stirring occasionally. Add water as needed to prevent chicken from sticking.

Once chicken is tender, adjust seasonings using salt substitute and pepper and sprinkle in chopped parsley. Turn off heat and allow chicken to sit 5–10 minutes. Skim off any excess fat that rises to the surface.

The onion gravy may be served over rice, pasta or whipped potatoes.

Cajun Pickled Quail Eggs produced by Paul Hulin and his family near New Iberia.

Nutrition Facts...now

Calories:	224
Total Fat:	13gm
Saturated Fat:	2gm
% Calories from Fat:	53
Cholesterol:	48mg
Sodium:	272mg
Carbohydrates:	6gm
Fiber:	1gm
Protein:	20gm

CHICKEN BONNE FEMME

PREP TIME: 2 Hours   SERVES: 6

☞ INGREDIENTS:

2 (1 1/2-pound) fryers
10 large baking potatoes
1/2 cup vegetable oil
juice of 1 lemon
1 pound sliced bacon
2 cups diced onions
1 (8-ounce) can sliced mushrooms, drained
1/4 cup chopped parsley
1/4 tsp salt
black pepper
hot sauce

☞ METHOD:

Place oven on broil setting to preheat. Cut chicken into 8 quarters, rinse and drain. Peel potatoes and cube into 1-inch pieces. Place potatoes in a bowl of ice water to keep from turning brown and set aside. In a 3-inch deep baking pan large enough to hold the quarters, season chicken using salt, pepper and hot sauce. Lay chicken skin-side down and brush with vegetable oil and lemon juice. Lay 2–3 strips of bacon over each quarter and broil in the oven until chicken is golden brown and bacon is crispy. You should move the bacon strips from time to time to allow the chicken to brown evenly. Remove bacon and set aside. Turn chicken skin-side up, brush with oil and lemon juice, cover with additional strips of fresh bacon and continue to broil until golden brown. Remove from oven and set aside. Reduce oven setting to 250 degrees F. When bacon is cool, crush or chop it and reserve for later use. In each of two large cast iron skillets, heat 1/4 cup of oil over medium-high heat. Drain potatoes well and divide between the two skillets. Brown the potatoes on all sides and add equal parts of onions into each skillet. When onions and potatoes are brown, add mushrooms and crumbled bacon. Season to taste using salt and pepper. Spoon potato mixture over the chicken quarters in the baking pan. Place the pan on the lower shelf of the oven. Bake 1 1/2 hours, basting occasionally, using the pan drippings to keep the potatoes from scorching. When chicken and potatoes are tender, remove from the oven, place on a large serving platter and garnish with parsley.

"Newcomers and visitors often get Cajuns and Creoles confused. Cajuns are descendants of the Acadian French, who came to South Louisiana after being exiled by the British from Nova Scotia. The Creoles are descendants of the early Spanish or French settlers of New Orleans.

"In terms of their equally famous cuisines, Creole cooking is a modification of the classic Parisian French cuisine, while Cajun harks back to the heartier provincial styles. This recipe has its origins in the Creole style, but has taken on a Cajun accent.

"When my brother-in-law got married in the mid-1940s, he and his bride spent their honeymoon in New Orleans, enjoying the nightlife and cuisine of the French Quarter. One evening, they were so taken with this delightful specialty of one Quarter restaurant, that my sister-in-law paid an uninvited visit to the kitchen from which she emerged with the recipe.

"It has been a family staple ever since."
Carol Canerday
Singer, Louisiana

❦ Nutrition Facts...then ❦

Calories:	1268
Total Fat:	84gm
Saturated Fat:	23gm
% Calories from Fat:	60
Cholesterol:	283mg
Sodium:	1628mg
Carbohydrates:	42gm
Fiber:	2gm
Protein:	84gm

PREP TIME: 2 Hours   SERVES: 6

INGREDIENTS:

2 (1 1/2-pound) fryers, skinned
10 large baking potatoes
1/4 cup vegetable oil
juice of 1 lemon
1/2 pound lean ham, sliced
vegetable spray
2 cups diced onions
1 (8-ounce) can sliced mushrooms, drained
1/4 cup chopped parsley
salt substitute
black pepper
hot sauce

Chef's Tips on Weight Loss... did you know that most people should cut 15 to 20 grams of fat a day from their diet?

Nutrition Facts...now

Calories: 476
Total Fat: 17gm
Saturated Fat: 4gm
% Calories from Fat: 33
Cholesterol: 93mg
Sodium: 742mg
Carbohydrates: 41gm
Fiber: 2gm
Protein: 39gm

METHOD:

Place oven on broil setting to preheat. Cut chicken into 8 quarters, rinse and drain. Peel potatoes and cube into 1-inch pieces. Place potatoes in a bowl of ice water to keep from turning brown and set aside.

In a 3-inch deep baking pan large enough to hold the quarters, season chicken using salt substitute, pepper and hot sauce. Lay chicken down and brush with vegetable oil and lemon juice. Lay 2–3 strips of ham over each quarter and spray generously with vegetable spray. Broil in the oven until chicken is golden brown. Remove ham and set aside.

Turn chicken over, brush with oil and lemon juice, cover with additional strips of fresh ham, and continue to broil until golden brown. When done, remove and set aside.

Reduce oven setting to 250 degrees F. In each of two large cast iron skillets, heat remaining oil over medium heat. Drain potatoes well and divide between the two skillets. Brown the potatoes on all sides and add equal parts of onions into each skillet. When onions and potatoes are brown, add mushrooms and season to taste using salt substitute and pepper.

Spoon potato mixture over the chicken quarters in the baking pan, and coat lightly with vegetable spray. Place the pan on the lower shelf of the oven. Bake 1 1/2 hours, basting occasionally, using the pan drippings to keep the potatoes from scorching.

When chicken and potatoes are tender, remove from the oven, place on a large serving platter and garnish with parsley.

PREP TIME: 1 1/2 Hours   SERVES: 6

☞ INGREDIENTS:

1 (2-pound) fryer
1/2 cup melted butter
1/2 cup minced onions
1/2 cup minced celery
1/4 cup diced pimentos
1 tbsp minced garlic
2/3 cup flour
2 cups reserved chicken stock
2 eggs, beaten
2 tbsps minced parsley
4 cups seasoned Italian bread crumbs
3 eggs, beaten
1/2 cup milk
6 tbsps oil
1/2 tsp salt
black pepper

☞ METHOD:

Cut chicken into 8 serving pieces and place in a large stock pot. Cover chicken by 3 inches with cold water and boil until chicken is tender and falling from the bones. Remove chicken. Cool, debone and chop the meat. Reserve stock. In a 5-quart cast iron dutch oven, heat butter over medium-high heat. Add onions, celery, pimentos and garlic. Saute 3–5 minutes or until vegetables are wilted. Sprinkle in flour and, using a wire whisk, whip until white roux is achieved. Pour in chicken stock, one cup at a time, whisking constantly. Season to taste using salt and pepper. Add chopped chicken. Blend well, remove from heat and adjust seasonings. Pour chicken into a mixing bowl and allow to cool slightly. Add 2 eggs and parsley, blending quickly into the chicken mixture. Sprinkle in approximately 1/2 cup of bread crumbs and blend well. Shape into croquettes or beignets. Combine 3 eggs and milk, whisking well into an eggwash. Season lightly with salt and pepper. Heat oil in a 12-inch cast iron skillet to approximately 325 degrees F. Dip beignets into eggwash and into seasoned bread crumbs. Pan fry 2 minutes on each side or until golden brown. Drain and serve warm.

"There are many different types of beignets in cooking. Most often when people think of beignets, they think of the sweet doughnut type served with cafe au lait on Sunday mornings throughout Louisiana.
"When I think of beignets, however, I think of the special treat created by my grandmother with her leftover chicken from Sunday lunch. Sometimes she would even cook one chicken extra just to have enough meat to create her chicken beignets. She served them as an entree, however, we have often used them as an appetizer or a sandwich."
Jerry Folse
Laplace, Louisiana

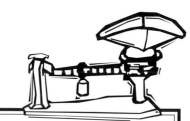

❊Nutrition Facts...then❊
Calories: 1015
Total Fat: 55gm
Saturated Fat: 19gm
% Calories from Fat: 49
Cholesterol: 303mg
Sodium: 2851mg
Carbohydrates: 70gm
Fiber: 1gm
Protein: 59gm

PREP TIME: 1 Hour   SERVES: 6

☞ INGREDIENTS:

1 (2-pound) fryer, skinned	2/3 cup flour	1/2 cup skim milk
1/4 cup melted lite margarine	2 cups reserved chicken stock, defatted and unsalted	vegetable spray
1/2 cup minced onions	1/2 cup egg substitute	salt substitute
1/2 cup minced celery	2 tbsps minced parsley	black pepper
1/4 cup diced pimentos	4 cups plain bread crumbs	
1 tbsp minced garlic	3/4 cup egg substitute	

☞ METHOD:

Cut chicken into 8 serving pieces and place in a large stock pot. Cover chicken by 3 inches with cold water and boil until chicken is tender and falling from the bones. Remove chicken. Cool, debone and chop the meat. Reserve stock.

In a 5-quart cast iron dutch oven, heat margarine over medium heat. Add onions, celery, pimentos and garlic. Saute 3–5 minutes or until vegetables are wilted. Sprinkle in flour and, using a wire whisk, stir until white roux is achieved.

Pour in chicken stock, one cup at a time, whisking constantly. Season to taste using salt substitute and pepper. Add chopped chicken. Blend well, remove from heat and adjust seasonings.

Pour chicken into a mixing bowl and allow to cool slightly. Add 1/2 cup egg substitute and parsley, blending quickly into

Crepe Myrtles in full bloom in June are a common sight throughout Louisiana.

the chicken mixture. Sprinkle in approximately 1/2 cup of bread crumbs and blend well. Shape into croquettes or beignets.

Combine 3/4 cup egg substitute and milk, whisking well into an eggwash. Season lightly with salt substitute and pepper. Heat a 12-inch cast iron skillet, coated with vegetable spray, over medium heat. Dip beignets into eggwash and into bread crumbs. Pan fry 2 minutes on each side or until golden brown. Continue to spray skillet as beignets are added. Serve warm.

Nutrition Facts...now

Calories:	533
Total Fat:	13gm
Saturated Fat:	3gm
% Calories from Fat:	23
Cholesterol:	49mg
Sodium:	963mg
Carbohydrates:	66gm
Fiber:	1gm
Protein:	35gm

PREP TIME: 1 1/2 Hours   SERVES: 6

☞ INGREDIENTS:

2 (1-pound) fryers
1/2 cup olive oil
2 cups seasoned flour
2 cups diced onions
1/2 cup diced celery
1/2 cup diced green bell pepper
1/4 cup diced garlic
1/2 cup sliced black olives
1/2 cup sliced pimento olives
1 cup sliced mushrooms
2 (8-ounce) cans tomato sauce
1 (6-ounce) can V-8 juice
1/2 cup hot water
2 tbsps sherry
1/2 cup sliced green onions
1/2 cup chopped parsley
1/2 tsp salt
black pepper
Louisiana Gold Pepper Sauce

☞ METHOD:

Cut each fryer into 8 serving pieces. Rinse well under cold water and drain. In a 7-quart cast iron dutch oven, heat olive oil over medium-high heat. Dust chicken lightly in seasoned flour, shaking off all excess, and brown well on all sides. Remove chicken and keep warm. Add onions, celery, bell pepper and garlic to the same oil. Saute 3–5 minutes or until vegetables are wilted. Add olives and continue to saute for an additional minute. Add mushrooms, tomato sauce, V-8 juice and water. Blend well into the vegetable mixture. Add sherry, green onions and parsley. Bring to a low boil and reduce heat to simmer. Season with salt, pepper and Louisiana Gold. Place chicken in sauce, cover and braise approximately 45 minutes. Additional water may be needed in order to maintain sauce consistency. Stir occasionally during the cooking process. When chicken is tender, adjust seasonings if necessary and serve over steamed white rice or pasta.

Since many of the Creoles came from the Mediterranean area, especially the South of France, many dishes typical of that area are seen here in Louisiana. Most of the typical red sauces called Creole today are actually of that Provencal region.

"This dish is definitely New Orleans Creole but could fit just as perfectly in any home on the Mediterranean.

John Folse
Donaldsonville, Louisiana

❧ Nutrition Facts...then❧

Calories:	547
Total Fat:	20gm
Saturated Fat:	5gm
% Calories from Fat:	34
Cholesterol:	145mg
Sodium:	851mg
Carbohydrates:	45gm
Fiber:	4gm
Protein:	43gm

BRAISED CHICKEN CREOLE

PREP TIME: 1 1/2 Hours SERVES: 6

INGREDIENTS:

2 (1-pound) fryers, skinned
1/4 cup olive oil
2 cups seasoned flour
2 cups diced onions
1/2 cup diced celery
1/2 cup diced green bell pepper
1/4 cup diced garlic
1/4 cup sliced black olives
1/2 cup sliced pimento olives
1 cup sliced mushrooms
2 (8-ounce) cans tomato sauce, no salt added
1 (6-ounce) can V-8 juice, no salt added
1/2 cup hot water
2 tbsps sherry
1/2 cup sliced green onions
1/2 cup chopped parsley
salt substitute
black pepper
Louisiana Gold Pepper Sauce

Chef's Tips on Weight Loss... did you know that your daily fat intake should be no more than 30% of your total calories?

METHOD:

Cut each fryer into 8 serving pieces. Rinse well under cold water and drain.

In a 7-quart cast iron dutch oven, heat olive oil over medium-high heat. Dust chicken lightly in seasoned flour, shaking off all excess, and brown well on all sides. Remove chicken and keep warm.

Add onions, celery, bell pepper and garlic to the same oil. Saute 3–5 minutes or until vegetables are wilted. Add olives and continue to saute for an additional minute. Add mushrooms, tomato sauce, V-8 juice and water. Blend well into the vegetable mixture. Add sherry, green onions and parsley. Bring to a low boil and reduce heat to simmer. Season with salt substitute, pepper and Louisiana Gold.

Place chicken in sauce, cover and braise approximately 45 minutes. Additional water may be needed in order to maintain sauce consistency. Stir occasionally during the cooking process.

When chicken is tender, adjust seasonings if necessary and serve over steamed white rice or pasta.

Nutrition Facts...now

Calories:	331
Total Fat:	5gm
Saturated Fat:	1gm
% Calories from Fat:	14
Cholesterol:	48mg
Sodium:	92mg
Carbohydrates:	46gm
Fiber:	4gm
Protein:	23gm

PREP TIME: 1 1/2 Hours   SERVES: 6

☞ INGREDIENTS:

2 (1 1/2-pound) fryers
1/4 cup olive oil
1/2 pound bacon
1 cup chopped onions
1/2 cup chopped celery
1/2 cup chopped red bell pepper
1/4 cup diced garlic
3 cups chicken stock
1 1/2 cups dry white wine
2 carrots, sliced
12 pearl onions, peeled
12 small button mushrooms
1/2 tsp fresh thyme
1 tsp fresh basil
1 bay leaf
1/2 cup sliced green onions
1/2 cup chopped parsley
1/2 tsp salt
black pepper
Louisiana Gold Pepper Sauce

☞ METHOD:

Cut chicken into 8 serving pieces. Rinse under cold water and drain. Season chicken well using salt, pepper and Louisiana Gold. In a 12- or 15-inch cast iron skillet, heat olive oil over medium-high heat. Dice bacon and saute in olive oil until bacon fat is rendered and bacon is crispy. Using a slotted spoon, remove bacon and keep warm. Brown chicken well in reserved oil, turning occasionally until golden brown on both sides. As chicken browns, remove and keep warm. Using the same skillet, add onions, celery, bell pepper and garlic. Saute 3–5 minutes or until vegetables are wilted. Add chicken stock and wine. Bring to a rolling boil and reduce to simmer. Return chicken to skillet and add bacon, carrots, onions, mushrooms, thyme, basil and bay leaf. Cover and braise chicken approximately 45 minutes. Add green onions and parsley. Once chicken is tender, remove it to a serving platter and reduce the sauce to a slightly thickened consistency. Adjust seasonings, if necessary, using salt, pepper and Louisiana Gold. Pour vegetables and liquid over chicken and serve with rice or pasta.

Braised chicken with wine sauce has been a Louisiana favorite since the early plantation days. The recipe for this famous dish varied, depending on the availability of wine from house to house. My grandfather always had his five-gallon crock of wild plum wine fermenting in the corn shed. When the wine reached its peak after about six to eight weeks, he would bottle the wine and reserve one or two quarts for his famous Coq Au Vin
                Celeste Bouchereau
        Donaldsonville, Louisiana

❧Nutrition Facts...then❧

Calories: 817
Total Fat: 48gm
Saturated Fat: 15gm
% Calories from Fat: 54
Cholesterol: 252mg
Sodium: 1455mg
Carbohydrates: 11gm
Fiber: 3gm
Protein: 72gm

COQ AU VIN

PREP TIME: 1 1/2 Hours   SERVES: 6

☞ INGREDIENTS:

2 (1 1/2-pound) fryers, skinned
1/4 cup olive oil
1/2 pound lean ham, cubed
1 cup chopped onions
1/2 cup chopped celery
1/2 cup chopped red bell pepper
1/4 cup diced garlic
3 cups defatted chicken stock, unsalted
1 1/2 cups dry white wine
2 carrots, sliced
12 pearl onions, peeled
12 small button mushrooms
1/2 tsp fresh thyme
1 tsp fresh basil
1 bay leaf
1/2 cup sliced green onions
1/2 cup chopped parsley
salt substitute
black pepper
Louisiana Gold Pepper Sauce

Gone to pasture — an old plow and new cotton at Loyd Hall Plantation near Cheneyville, Evangeline Parish.

☞ METHOD:

Cut chicken into 8 serving pieces. Rinse under cold water and drain. Season chicken well using salt substitute, pepper and Louisiana Gold.

In a 12- or 15-inch cast iron skillet, heat olive oil over medium-high heat. Brown chicken well in oil, turning occasionally until golden brown on both sides. As chicken browns, remove and keep warm.

Using the same skillet, add ham, onions, celery, bell pepper and garlic. Saute 3–5 minutes or until vegetables are wilted. Add chicken stock and wine. Bring to a rolling boil and reduce to simmer.

Return chicken to skillet and add carrots, onions, mushrooms, thyme, basil and bay leaf. Cover and braise chicken approximately 45 minutes. Add green onions and parsley.

Once chicken is tender, remove it to a serving platter and reduce the sauce to a slightly thickened consistency. Adjust seasonings if necessary using salt substitute, pepper and Louisiana Gold. Pour vegetables and liquid over chicken and serve with rice or pasta.

Nutrition Facts...now

Calories:	314
Total Fat:	9gm
Saturated Fat:	2gm
% Calories from Fat:	25
Cholesterol:	93mg
Sodium:	865mg
Carbohydrates:	11gm
Fiber:	3gm
Protein:	37gm

PREP TIME: 1 1/2 Hours   SERVES: 6

INGREDIENTS:

2 (2-pound) fryers
1/4 cup olive oil
1/4 cup vegetable oil
1/2 cup red wine vinegar
1/2 cup water
1/4 tsp basil
1/4 tsp thyme
1/4 tsp oregano
1/4 tsp rosemary
1/4 cup chopped garlic
1/2 cup chopped parsley
1 cup sliced Bermuda onions
1/2 cup Parmesan cheese
1/4 tsp salt
black pepper
Louisiana Gold Pepper Sauce

METHOD:

Cut chicken into 8 serving pieces. Rinse under cold water and drain well. In a large mixing bowl, combine all of the remaining ingredients to create an Italian-flavored marinade. Place the chicken pieces in the marinade and toss to coat pieces thoroughly with the flavors. The chicken must sit in the marinade at room temperature a minimum of 3 hours and should be turned frequently. While chicken is marinating, preheat barbecue grill according to manufacturer's directions. A small amount of smoke wood may be soaked in wine or water for use on the grill if desired. Once the chicken is marinated, move the hot coals to one side of the pit and place the chicken over indirect heat on the other. Add the smoke wood if desired and cook, covered, for 1 hour or until chicken is cooked thoroughly. Keep the bowl of marinade on the side of the pit and, every 15–20 minutes, dip the chicken in the marinade and return to the pit. Once chicken is totally done, pour the remaining marinade and vegetable seasonings over the chicken, close the lid and allow to steam 10–15 minutes longer. This recipe is excellent for an oven version, should the weather not permit barbecuing. Simply preheat oven to 325 degrees F, place chicken in a baking dish and bake approximately 1 hour.

"The Bouchereau family was well known in and around the Donaldsonville area. Many people knew Mr. Clarence from the Assumption Bank; Bud, the printer; Lloyd the postmaster; Donald, the engineer; Paul, the chemist; Linden, the newspaper man; Laulie, the nurse; and Helen, the oldest sister.
"On any Sunday morning, the family could be seen gathering at Bittersweet Plantation for their Sunday lunch. This was one family recipe that often found its way to the grill."
Bouchereau Family
Metairie, Louisiana

Nutrition Facts...then

Calories: 798
Total Fat: 50gm
Saturated Fat: 13gm
% Calories from fat: 57
Cholesterol: 299mg
Sodium: 452mg
Carbohydrates: 5gm
Fiber: 0gm
Protein: 78gm

BARBECUED CHICKEN ITALIAN-STYLE

PREP TIME: 1 1/2 Hours   SERVES: 6

☞ INGREDIENTS:

2 (2-pound) fryers, skinned
1 tbsp olive oil
1 tbsp vegetable oil
1/2 cup red wine vinegar
1/2 cup water
1/4 tsp basil
1/4 tsp thyme
1/4 tsp oregano
1/4 tsp rosemary
1/4 cup chopped garlic
1/2 cup chopped parsley
1 cup sliced Bermuda onions
1/2 cup fat-free Parmesan cheese
salt substitute
black pepper
Louisiana Gold Pepper Sauce

☞ METHOD:

Cut chicken into 8 serving pieces. Rinse under cold water and drain well. In a large mixing bowl, combine all of the remaining ingredients to create an Italian-flavored marinade.

Place the chicken pieces in the marinade and toss to coat pieces thoroughly with the flavors. The chicken must sit in the marinade at room temperature a minimum of 3 hours and should be turned frequently.

While chicken is marinating, preheat barbecue grill according to manufacturer's directions. A small amount of smoke wood may be soaked in wine or water for use on the grill if desired.

Once the chicken is marinated, move the hot coals to one side of the pit and place the chicken over indirect heat on the other. Add the smoke wood if desired and cook, covered, for 1 hour or until chicken is cooked thoroughly. Keep the bowl of marinade on the side of the pit and every 15–20 minutes, dip the chicken in the marinade and return to the pit.

Once chicken is totally done, pour the remaining marinade and vegetable seasonings over the chicken, close the lid and allow to steam 10–15 minutes longer.

This recipe is excellent for an oven version, should the weather not permit barbecuing. Simply preheat oven to 325 degrees F, place chicken in a baking dish and bake approximately 1 hour.

Nutrition Facts...now

Calories:	268
Total Fat:	11gm
Saturated Fat:	2gm
% Calories from Fat:	36
Cholesterol:	103mg
Sodium:	151mg
Carbohydrates:	7gm
Fiber:	0gm
Protein:	35gm

Chef's Tips on Fat Cutters... drinking one glass of 1% milk instead of whole milk cuts 5 grams of fat from your diet.

Meats

Chapter Six

A Duo of Pot Roasts	224/225
Ventress Island Rump Roast	226/227
Daube Glace Dixie	228/229
Bayouland Beef Stew with Vegetables	230/231
Beef Bourguignonne	232/233
Sauce Picante Oberlin	234/235
Tillie's Round Steak & Gravy	236/237
Braised Veal Shanks Bayou Lafourche	238/239
Cajun Stuffed Ponce	240/241
Braised Beef Heart with Savory Oyster Stuffing	244/245
Creole Pork & Rice Casserole	246/247
Pork Chops St. Dizier	248/249
Pork Ribs in Sherry Sauce	250/251
Mama Fresina's Lasagna	252/253
Stuffed Eggplant in Italian Gravy	254/255
Meatballs & Tomato Gravy Caro	256/257
Grandma Thibodaux's Breakfast Hash	258/259
Breazeale Meat Pies	260/261
The Bayou Two Step	262/263
Doc's Primo Chili	264/265

*The recipes for **The Bayou Two Step**,*
pictured at left, can be found on pages 262 and 263.

PREP TIME: 3 Hours   SERVES: 8

☞ INGREDIENTS:

4-pound beef rump roast
4-pound Boston butt
1/2 cup diced garlic
1/2 cup sliced green onions
1/4 cup salt
black pepper
1 cup seasoned flour
1/2 cup vegetable oil
3 cups diced onions
1 cup diced celery
1/2 cup diced bell pepper
4 cups beef bouillon

☞ METHOD:

In a large mixing bowl, combine garlic, green onions and half of the salt and pepper. Using a paring knife, cut 8–10 one-inch slits in each of the roasts. Divide the garlic and seasoning mixture and stuff each roast. Season the outside of each roast with remaining salt and pepper and dust each in seasoned flour. In a large cast iron dutch oven, heat oil over medium-high heat. Brown roasts evenly on all sides to sear in the juices. Once browned, remove roasts to a holding platter. In the same dutch oven, add onions, celery and bell pepper. Saute 3–5 minutes or until vegetables are wilted. Return the roasts to the dutch oven and add beef bouillon. Bring to a rolling boil and reduce to simmer. Cover and cook 2–3 hours or until roasts are fork-tender. Remove meat and reduce the sauce until the gravy is slightly thickened. Slice the roasts and top with the hot natural juices. This is excellent when served with a fresh lettuce and tomato salad and baked sweet potatoes. Try the leftovers on a hot French bread sandwich.

"In all large families, it is often difficult to please everyone at the dinner table. It was certainly no different in our family, especially at Sunday dinner get-togethers.

"My husband's family seemed to come up with the perfect solution for pot roast. Since some people loved pork roast and others craved beef, my mother-in-law solved the problem by cooking both in the same pot. The results were magnificent, with the pork roast adding excellent flavor to the beef in the process."

Evelyn Belanger
Houma, Louisiana

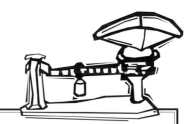

❧Nutrition Facts...then❧

Calories: 1247
Total Fat: 92gm
Saturated Fat: 32gm
% Calories from Fat: 67
Cholesterol: 248mg
Sodium: 4011mg
Carbohydrate: 21gm
Fiber: 3gm
Protein: 81gm

PREP TIME: 3 Hours   SERVES: 8

☞ INGREDIENTS:

3-pound lean beef rump roast
3-pound lean Boston butt, trimmed
1/2 cup diced garlic
1/2 cup sliced green onions
salt substitute
1/4 cup black pepper
1 cup flour
1/4 cup vegetable oil
3 cups diced onions
1 cup diced celery
1/2 cup diced bell pepper
4 cups defatted beef bouillon, unsalted

☞ METHOD:

In a large mixing bowl, combine garlic, green onions, salt substitute and pepper. Using a paring knife, cut 8–10 one-inch slits in each of the roasts. Divide the garlic and seasoning mixture and stuff each of the roasts. Season the outside of each roast with remaining salt substitute and pepper and dust each in flour.

In a large cast iron dutch oven, heat oil over medium-high heat. Brown roasts evenly on all sides to sear in the juices. Once roasts are browned, remove them to a holding platter.

In the same dutch oven, add onions, celery and bell pepper. Saute 3–5 minutes or until vegetables are wilted. Return the roasts to the dutch oven and add beef bouillon. Bring to a rolling boil and reduce to simmer. Cover and cook 2–3 hours or until roasts are fork-tender.

Remove the meat and reduce the sauce until the gravy is slightly thickened. Slice the roasts and top with the hot natural juices. This is excellent when served with a fresh lettuce and tomato salad and baked sweet potatoes. Try the leftovers on a hot French bread sandwich.

Nutrition Facts...now

Calories:	793
Total Fat:	39gm
Saturated Fat:	12gm
% Calories from Fat:	45
Cholesterol:	201mg
Sodium:	704mg
Carbohydrate:	21gm
Fiber:	3gm
Protein:	86gm

PREP TIME: 4 Hours   SERVES: 8

☞ INGREDIENTS:

4-pound boneless rump roast
4 large potatoes
8 carrots
1 large onion, minced
1/4 cup diced red bell pepper
1/4 cup diced yellow bell pepper
1/4 cup diced green bell pepper
1/4 cup minced garlic
1 medium jalapeno, diced

1/4 cup Worcestershire Sauce
1/4 cup Liquid Smoke
1/4 cup peanut oil
1/2 cup seasoned flour
2 cups beef consomme
1 cup sliced mushrooms
1 1/2 tbsps salt
black pepper

☞ METHOD:

Preheat oven to 350 degrees F. Peel potatoes and cut into 1-inch cubes. Slice carrots into 1-inch slices. Set aside. In a large mixing bowl, combine onions, bell peppers, garlic, jalapenos, salt and pepper. Blend well and set aside. In a separate bowl, combine Worcestershire and Liquid Smoke and set aside. Using a paring knife, cut 10–12 two-inch slits around the rump roast. Stuff each slit with equal parts of the seasoning mixture. Add 1/4 teaspoon of the combined Worcestershire/Liquid Smoke mixture. Take remainder of Worcestershire and Liquid Smoke and apply to the outside of the roast. Season to taste using salt and pepper. It is best to allow the roast to sit overnight or a minimum of 1 hour prior to cooking. In a 7-quart cast iron dutch oven, heat oil over medium-high heat. Dust roast in seasoned flour to coat well. Brown the roast on all sides to seal in the juices. Drain off excess oil and pour in consomme. Bring to a rolling boil, cover and bake for approximately 2 hours. Remove the lid and add potatoes, carrots and mushrooms. Cover and cook until tender, approximately 1–1 1/2 hours. You may wish to baste the roast from time to time. Once the roast is tender, slice and arrange it with vegetables on a serving platter. Top with the natural juices and serve over steamed white rice.

"My father is from New Roads, Louisiana, and my mother hails from across False River at Ventress, also known as the 'Island Side'. You see a great mixture of cultures in this area, and it is from here that I learned to love cooking.

"Sunday dinner at my grandfather's home in Ventress was always special. We would drive up from Baton Rouge to spend weekends with him and Sunday was our feast day. It all started after 6:00 Mass, when we joined in the kitchen to put everything together. Naturally, I was right in the middle of it, even at a young age, watching everything.

"This rump roast is a family favorite. I named it in honor of my grandfather, Felix Hebert, who lived to age 95. Every time I cook it, my mind wanders back to Sunday on the 'Island Side'."

Gaylord Boyd
Opelousas, Louisiana

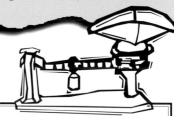

❀Nutrition Facts...then❀

Calories:	565
Total Fat:	17gm
Saturated Fat:	5gm
% Calories from Fat:	28
Cholesterol:	120mg
Sodium:	1774mg
Carbohydrate:	44gm
Fiber:	7gm
Protein:	57gm

PREP TIME: 4 Hours   SERVES: 8

☞ INGREDIENTS:

3-pound lean boneless rump roast, trimmed
4 large potatoes
8 carrots
1 large onion, minced
1/4 cup diced red bell pepper
1/4 cup diced yellow bell pepper
1/4 cup diced green bell pepper
1/4 cup minced garlic
1 medium jalapeno, diced
1/4 cup Worcestershire Sauce
1/4 cup Liquid Smoke
2 tbsps peanut oil
1/2 cup flour

2 cups defatted beef consomme, unsalted
1 cup sliced mushrooms
salt substitute
black pepper

Ronnie Andrus, near St. Landry, feeds his Waddle Hogs, a breed brought to this country from Australia.

☞ METHOD:

Preheat oven to 350 degrees F. Peel potatoes and cut into 1-inch cubes. Slice carrots into 1-inch slices. Set aside.

In a large mixing bowl, combine onions, bell peppers, garlic, jalapenos, salt substitute and pepper. Blend well and set aside.

In a separate bowl, combine Worcestershire and Liquid Smoke and set aside. Using a paring knife, cut 10–12 two-inch slits around the rump roast. Stuff each slit with equal parts of the seasoning mixture. Add 1/4 teaspoon of the combined Worcestershire/Liquid Smoke mixture. Take remainder of Worcestershire and Liquid Smoke and apply to the outside of the roast. Season to taste using salt substitute and pepper. It is best to allow the roast to sit overnight or a minimum of 1 hour prior to cooking.

In a 7-quart cast iron dutch oven, heat oil over medium-high heat. Dust roast in flour to coat well. Brown the roast on all sides to seal in the juices.

Drain off the excess oil and pour in consomme. Bring to a rolling boil, cover and bake for approximately 2 hours.

Remove the lid and add potatoes, carrots and mushrooms. Cover and cook until tender, approximately 1–1 1/2 hours. You may wish to baste the roast from time to time.

Once the roast is tender, slice and arrange it with vegetables on a serving platter. Top with the natural juices and serve over steamed white rice.

Nutrition Facts...now

Calories:	457
Total Fat:	11gm
Saturated Fat:	3gm
% Calories from Fat:	22
Cholesterol:	90mg
Sodium:	349mg
Carbohydrate:	44gm
Fiber:	7gm
Protein:	45gm

PREP TIME: 5 Hours   SERVES: 8

☞ INGREDIENTS:

1/4 pound salt meat	pinch of ground allspice	2 quarts water	1 tsp dried thyme	1 tsp salt
2 tbsps thyme	5-pound beef rump roast	2 pig's feet	ground cloves	black pepper
2 tbsps parsley	1/4 cup vegetable oil	2 pounds veal shank	4 quarts water	
1 tbsp ground bay leaves	3 cups diced onions	1 whole bay leaf	1/4 cup chopped parsley	
pinch of ground cloves	1/4 cup chopped garlic	1 cup minced onions	1/4 cup diced red pimento	

☞ METHOD:

Cut salt meat into thin ribbon strips. Place a generous amount of thyme, parsley, bay leaf powder, cloves, allspice, salt and pepper on each strip and roll in a circle. Using a sharp paring knife, cut 3-inch slits, 1 inch deep, around the rump roast. Season the inside of the slits well with salt and pepper and force one of the seasoned salt meat strips into each hole. This will not only flavor but also keep the rump roast moist during cooking. Season the entire roast well with salt and pepper. In a 7-quart cast iron dutch oven, heat vegetable oil over medium-high heat. Brown the rump roast on all sides. Add diced onions and garlic with enough water to measure 1–2 inches on the side of the pot. Season with salt and pepper. Slightly overseason, because dish will be eaten cold.

Bring to a rolling boil, reduce to simmer and cover. Cook 4 hours, turning occasionally. While the roast is cooking, place pig's feet, veal shanks, bay leaf, minced onions, thyme and cloves in a pot with 4 quarts of water. Season to taste using salt and pepper. Bring to a rolling boil, reduce to simmer and cook 3–4 hours or until meat is falling from the bone. Strain the stock and add chopped parsley and pimento for color. Reserve and cool the meat. Mince the meat from the pig's feet and veal shank. Discard bones and tendons. Return meats to the stock and pour into a large oblong pan. When the rump roast is tender, remove and place it in the oblong pan over the stock and minced meat. Allow to cool. Cover and refrigerate overnight. The next day, slice the daube glace and serve it with a tablespoon of the gelee.

"This fabulous recipe was found in a 1934 cookbook authored by Florence and Sam Robert of DeRidder. Mrs. Robert was a member of a famous pioneer family in Beauregard Parish. Her husband, Dr. Sam, was a prominent physician, well respected in Northwest Louisiana. Their book was well ahead of its time for 1934.
"Dixie Meals included table setting and service ideas, special menus for holidays and menus featuring European cuisine. There was a whole section on 'invalid diets' and tables of nutritional value. The book included a section on the best time to harvest Louisiana products as well as how to can and preserve them. This little-known book has given me many hours of enjoyment in my own kitchen. It is a peek into the past of Louisiana cooking."
Mackie T. Bienvenu
DeRidder, Louisiana

❧Nutrition Facts...then❧

Calories:	1109
Total Fat:	60gm
Saturated Fat:	20gm
% Calories from Fat:	50
Cholesterol:	408mg
Sodium:	760mg
Carbohydrate:	9gm
Fiber:	1gm
Protein:	127gm

DAUBE GLACE DIXIE

PREP TIME: 5 Hours   SERVES: 8

☞ INGREDIENTS:

1/8 pound lean salt meat, trimmed
2 tbsps thyme
2 tbsps parsley
1 tbsp ground bay leaves
pinch of ground cloves
pinch of ground allspice
5-pound beef rump roast
vegetable spray
3 cups diced onions
1/4 cup chopped garlic
2 quarts water
1 pig's foot
2 pounds veal shank
1 whole bay leaf
1 cup minced onion
1 tsp dried thyme
ground cloves
4 quarts water
1/4 cup chopped parsley
1/4 cup diced red pimento
salt substitute
black pepper

☞ METHOD:

Cut salt meat into thin ribbon strips. Place a generous amount of thyme, parsley, bay leaf powder, cloves, allspice, salt substitute and pepper on each strip and roll in a circle.

Using a sharp paring knife, cut 3-inch slits, 1 inch deep, around the rump roast. Season the inside of the slits well with salt substitute and pepper and force one of the seasoned salt meat strips into each hole. This will not only flavor but also keep the rump roast moist during cooking.

Season the entire roast well with salt substitute and pepper. Spray a 7-quart cast iron dutch oven with vegetable spray. Brown the rump roast on all sides. Add diced onions and garlic with enough water to measure 1–2 inches on the sides of the pot. Season with salt substitute and pepper. Slightly overseason, because dish will be eaten cold. Bring to a rolling boil, reduce to simmer and cover. Cook 4 hours, turning occasionally.

While the roast is cooking, place pig's foot, veal shanks, bay leaf, minced onions, thyme and cloves in a pot with 4 quarts of water. Season to taste using salt substitute and pepper. Bring to a rolling boil, reduce to simmer and cook 3–4 hours or until meat is falling from the bone. Strain the stock and add chopped parsley and pimento for color. Reserve and cool the meat.

Mince the meat from the pig's foot and veal shank. Discard bones and tendons. Return meats to the stock and pour into a large oblong pan.

When the rump roast is tender, remove and place it in the oblong pan over the stock and minced meat. Allow to cool. Cover and refrigerate overnight. The next day, slice the daube glace and serve it with a tablespoon of the gelee.

Nutrition Facts...now

Calories:	926
Total Fat:	45gm
Saturated Fat:	16gm
% Calories from Fat:	45
Cholesterol:	347mg
Sodium:	370mg
Carbohydrate:	9gm
Fiber:	1gm
Protein:	114gm

PREP TIME: 2 Hours   SERVES: 6

☞ INGREDIENTS:

3 pounds beef chuck, cubed
1/3 cup all purpose flour
1/4 cup vegetable oil
1 cup diced onions
1 cup diced celery
1/2 cup celery leaves
1/4 cup chopped garlic
1 bay leaf
2 tbsps Worcestershire Sauce
1 quart hot water
1 pound sliced carrots
2 pounds small red potatoes, quartered
1 pound sliced mushrooms
1 cup sliced green onions
1/2 cup chopped parsley
1 tsp salt
black pepper
hot sauce

☞ METHOD:

Place cubed chuck in a large mixing bowl and season well using salt, pepper and hot sauce. Sprinkle in flour to coat the meat well on all sides. In a 7-quart cast iron dutch oven, heat oil over medium-high heat. Add seasoned meat and brown on all sides. Once meat is golden brown and caramelized on the bottom of the dutch oven, remove and keep warm. Add onions, celery, celery leaves and garlic. Saute 3–5 minutes or until vegetables are wilted. Return the meat to the pot, blend well into the vegetable seasonings and add bay leaf and Worcestershire sauce. Add hot water, scraping the bottom of the pot to remove any of the drippings. Add carrots and potatoes, bring to a rolling boil and reduce to simmer. Cover and cook for approximately 1–1 1/2 hours, until meat is tender. Add mushrooms, green onions and parsley and adjust seasonings, if necessary. Cook 5–10 minutes longer. Serve over steamed white rice.

"Actually, there's no particular story that goes with this recipe. It's just my own recipe for beef stew, and one of my family's favorites.

"But isn't the great thing about food the associations it has in your own life? Let's say you tried this recipe, and your family liked it, and it became something you cooked for years and years. Why, then it would become your beef stew, and your children would adopt it because it was 'Mama's beef stew' and, maybe someday, 'Grandma's beef stew.'

"Of course by then three generations of cooks would have added a little dab of this and a pinch of that, and it wouldn't even be the same recipe. It's not so much the recipe that matters; it's the memories."

Millie Broussard
Lafayette, Louisiana

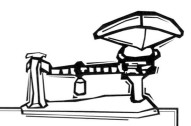

❧Nutrition Facts...then❧

Calories: 854
Total Fat: 37gm
Saturated Fat: 12gm
% Calories from Fat: 39
Cholesterol: 197mg
Sodium: 629mg
Carbohydrate: 50gm
Fiber: 3gm
Protein: 79gm

PREP TIME: 2 Hours   SERVES: 6

☞ INGREDIENTS:

3 pounds lean bottom round, trimmed and cubed
1/3 cup all purpose flour
1 tbsp vegetable oil
1 cup diced onions
1 cup diced celery
1/2 cup celery leaves
1/4 cup chopped garlic
1 bay leaf
2 tbsps Worcestershire Sauce

1 quart hot water
1 pound sliced carrots
2 pounds small red potatoes, quartered
1 pound sliced mushrooms
1 cup sliced green onions
1/2 cup chopped parsley
salt substitute
black pepper
hot sauce

☞ METHOD:

Place cubed beef in a large mixing bowl. Season well using salt substitute, pepper and hot sauce. Sprinkle in the flour to coat the meat well on all sides.

In a 7-quart cast iron dutch oven, heat oil over medium-high heat. Add seasoned meat and brown on all sides. Once meat is golden brown and caramelized in the bottom of the dutch oven, remove and keep warm.

Add onions, celery, celery leaves and garlic. Saute 3–5 minutes or until vegetables are wilted. Return the meat to the pot and blend well into the vegetable seasonings. Add bay leaf and Worcestershire sauce. Add hot water, scraping the bottom of the pot to remove any of the

drippings. Add carrots and potatoes, bring to a rolling boil and reduce to simmer. Cover and cook for approximately 1–1 1/2 hours, until meat is tender.

Add mushrooms, green onions and parsley and adjust seasonings, if necessary. Cook 5–10 minutes longer. Serve over steamed white rice.

Ray's Boudin on Highway 190 just east of Opelousas.

Nutrition Facts...now

Calories:	793
Total Fat:	30gm
Saturated Fat:	11gm
% Calories from Fat:	34
Cholesterol:	197mg
Sodium:	274mg
Carbohydrate:	49gm
Fiber:	3gm
Protein:	79gm

PREP TIME: 1 Hour   SERVES: 6

☞ INGREDIENTS:

2 1/2-pound beef chuck, cubed
1/3 cup all purpose flour
1/4 cup vegetable oil
4 slices of bacon
2 cups diced onions
1/2 cup grated carrots
1/4 cup diced garlic
1 cup sliced mushrooms
2 cups dry red wine
2 cups beef broth
1 tbsp tomato paste
1/2 tsp dried thyme
1 1/2 cups sliced green onions
1/4 cup chopped parsley
1 tsp salt
black pepper

Chef's Tips on Snacks...
50 calories or less: one cup of onion soup, one cup of strawberries, one cup of watermelon, one kiwi fruit, six ounces of instant chicken noodle soup.

☞ METHOD:

In a large mixing bowl, season meat to taste using salt and pepper. Sprinkle in flour to coat well. In a 5-quart cast iron dutch oven, heat oil over medium-high heat. Saute sliced bacon until golden brown. Remove, crush and keep warm. Add meat, in three separate batches, in order to brown it totally on all sides. The meat should be allowed to caramelize well in the bottom of the dutch oven. As the meat browns, remove and keep warm. Into the dutch oven, add onions, carrots and garlic. Saute 3–5 minutes or until vegetables are wilted. Add mushrooms, red wine, beef broth and tomato paste. Blend well into the sauteed vegetables, scraping the bottom of the pot to release the caramelized flavor. Return the meat to the dutch oven and add bacon and thyme. Cover and simmer 1 1/2 hours or until meat is tender. Add green onions and parsley. Adjust seasonings, if necessary and serve over hot pasta.

"Here is a recipe that's closer to the Cordon Bleu than the bayou. It is a traditional French recipe which I got from a teacher friend, Rita Duhon, as a reward for helping her put together an authentic Parisian dinner for her French language students at St. Thomas More High School here in Lafayette.
"Once you try it, you'll see why I consider myself very well-paid indeed for the favor. I've resisted the Cajun cook's inclination to improve upon a recipe with a little of this and a soupçon of that. I wanted to keep it authentic, and it certainly didn't need any improvement!"
                    Dotsie Butcher
                    Lafayette, Louisiana

❧ Nutrition Facts...then ❧

Calories: 826
Total Fat: 53gm
Saturated Fat: 18gm
% Calories from Fat: 51
Cholesterol: 193mg
Sodium: 884mg
Carbohydrate: 15gm
Fiber: 2gm
Protein: 57gm

PREP TIME: 1 Hour   SERVES: 6

☞ INGREDIENTS:

2 1/2-pound lean beef chuck, cubed and trimmed
1/3 cup all purpose flour
1 tbsp vegetable oil
4 slices turkey bacon
2 cups diced onions
1/2 cup grated carrots
1/4 cup diced garlic
1 cup sliced mushrooms
2 cups dry red wine
2 cups defatted beef broth, unsalted
1 tbsp tomato paste
1/2 tsp dried thyme
1 1/2 cups sliced green onions
1/4 cup chopped parsley
salt substitute
black pepper

☞ METHOD:

In a large mixing bowl, season meat to taste using salt substitute and pepper. Sprinkle in flour to coat well.

In a 5-quart cast iron dutch oven, heat oil over medium-high heat. Saute sliced turkey bacon until golden brown. Remove, crush and keep warm.

Add meat, in three separate batches, in order to brown it totally on all sides. The meat should be allowed to caramelize well in the bottom of the dutch oven. As the meat browns, remove and keep warm.

Into the dutch oven, add onions, carrots and garlic. Saute 3–5 minutes or until vegetables are wilted. Add mushrooms, red wine, beef broth and tomato paste. Blend well into the sauteed vegetables, scraping the bottom of the pot to release the caramelized flavor.

Return the meat to the dutch oven and add bacon and thyme. Cover and simmer 1 1/2 hours or until meat is tender. Add green onions and parsley. Adjust seasonings, if necessary and serve over hot pasta.

Nutrition Facts...now

Calories:	632
Total Fat:	27gm
Saturated Fat:	10gm
% Calories from Fat:	39
Cholesterol:	170mg
Sodium:	355mg
Carbohydrate:	15gm
Fiber:	2gm
Protein:	67gm

PREP TIME: 1 Hour   SERVES: 8

☞ INGREDIENTS:

3 pounds lean stew meat, cubed
1 pound smoked tasso, cubed
1/2 cup water
2 cups chopped Bermuda onions

1 cup chopped celery
1 cup chopped bell pepper
1/4 cup diced garlic
2 (10-ounce) cans Rotel tomatoes

1 (4-ounce) can sliced mushrooms
1/2 cup sliced green onions
1 tsp salt
cayenne pepper

Kermit and Jonathan Lejeune hold a stick of smoked sausage. They cut and split their own wood to smoke the homemade sausage sold in the family store in Eunice.

☞ METHOD:

Season stew meat with salt and cayenne pepper. In a 7-quart cast iron dutch oven, bring water to a low simmer. Add stew meat and tasso, stirring constantly to render the fat from the meats. Many people use oil to saute stew meat and tasso, but a little water will render the natural fat and extra oil can be eliminated. After meat has browned evenly, add onions, celery, bell pepper and garlic. Saute 3–5 minutes or until vegetables are wilted. Add tomatoes and mushrooms, including the liquids. Bring to a rolling boil, reduce to simmer and cook approximately 1 hour or until meat is tender. Add green onions and adjust seasonings, if necessary. Often, my family adds a cup of beer to this recipe during the simmering for an interesting taste variation. This dish is great served over white rice.

"This is one of those recipes that goes back many years in my family. The recipe changed quite often, depending on what we had to put in the pot, but we definitely ate a variation of this dish weekly.

"My favorite memory of this particular dish is how Dad spent all morning cooking it in a black iron pot while we worked the cattle. He would cook it outside over a wooden fire and slow-simmer it for hours at a time. Looking back over the years, it just never did get any better than this!"

Don Duplechian
Oberlin, Louisiana

❊Nutrition Facts...then❊

Calories:	541
Total Fat:	24gm
Saturated Fat:	7gm
% Calories from Fat:	40
Cholesterol:	152mg
Sodium:	1613mg
Carbohydrate:	16gm
Fiber:	2gm
Protein:	64gm

PREP TIME: 1 Hour SERVES: 8

☞ INGREDIENTS:

3 pounds lean stew meat, cubed
1/2 pound smoked tasso, cubed
1/2 cup water
2 cups chopped Bermuda onions

1 cup chopped celery
1 cup chopped bell pepper
1/4 cup diced garlic
2 (10-ounce) cans Rotel tomatoes

1 cup fresh mushrooms, sliced
1/2 cup sliced green onions
salt substitute
cayenne pepper

☞ METHOD:

Season stew meat with salt substitute and cayenne pepper. In a 7-quart cast iron dutch oven, bring water to a low simmer. Add stew meat and tasso, stirring constantly to render the fat from the meats. Many people use oil to saute stew meat and tasso, but a little water will render the natural fat and extra oil can be eliminated.

After meat has browned evenly, add onions, celery, bell pepper and garlic. Saute 3–5 minutes or until vegetables are wilted. Add tomatoes and mushrooms, including the liquid. Bring to a rolling boil, reduce to simmer and cook approximately 1 hour or until meat is tender.

Add green onions and adjust seasonings, if necessary. Often, my family adds a cup of beer to this recipe during the simmering for an interesting taste variation. This dish is great served over white rice.

At a Zydeco festival in New Roads, Emanuel Butler, the World's Finest Pigtail Daddy, takes a break from stirring his frying pigtails.

Nutrition Facts...now

Calories:	475
Total Fat:	21gm
Saturated Fat:	7gm
% Calories from Fat:	40
Cholesterol:	152mg
Sodium:	810mg
Carbohydrate:	12gm
Fiber:	2gm
Protein:	58gm

PREP TIME: 2 Hours   SERVES: 6

☞ INGREDIENTS:

2-pound round steak, bone-in
1/4 cup vegetable oil
2 cups diced onions
1/2 cup diced celery
1/4 cup diced bell pepper
1/4 cup diced garlic
3 cups water
1/4 cup sliced green onions
1/4 cup chopped parsley
1 tsp salt
black pepper

☞ METHOD:

Cut steak into 2- or 3-inch serving pieces and season lightly with salt and pepper. In a 12-inch cast iron skillet, heat oil over medium-high heat. When oil reaches 375 degrees F, place the steak pieces into the skillet and brown well on both sides. The oil should be very hot prior to sauteing, in order to seal in the juices and caramelize the meat on the bottom of the skillet. This brown caramelization will give the gravy its final color. When meat is done, remove it from the skillet and keep warm. Add onions, celery, bell pepper and garlic. Saute 3–5 minutes or until vegetables are wilted and caramelized residue has dissolved in the bottom of the pan. Pour in water and stir into the seasoning mixture. Return the meat to the skillet, bring liquid to a rolling boil and reduce heat to simmer. Cover and cook approximately 1 1/2 hours or until meat is tender. Additional water may be needed to keep meat moist. When meat is tender, add green onions and parsley and adjust seasonings, if necessary. Cook an additional 3–5 minutes. Serve with steamed white rice and a side dish of smothered green peas.

"Mama was a good cook and always had time to prepare a hot meal for the table. She came from a long line of good cooks, growing up on St. James Estate Plantation in St. James Parish. Her mother lived to be 100. Many of my grandmother's conversations late in life revolved around their dinner table.

"Every Sunday, Mama smothered round steak in gravy. It was always served with tiny green peas also smothered in a roux. I still consider this dish to be my first choice, especially on my birthday."
Laulie Bouchereau Folse
Donaldsonville, Louisiana

❧Nutrition Facts...then❧

Calories:	382
Total Fat:	16gm
Saturated Fat:	4gm
% Calories from Fat:	38
Cholesterol:	75mg
Sodium:	692mg
Carbohydrate:	22gm
Fiber:	4gm
Protein:	37gm

PREP TIME: 2 Hours   SERVES: 6

☞ INGREDIENTS:

2-pound round steak, bone-in
2 tbsps vegetable oil
2 cups diced onions
1/2 cup diced celery
1/4 cup diced bell pepper
1/4 cup diced garlic
3 cups water
1/4 cup sliced green onions
1/4 cup chopped parsley
1/4 tsp salt
black pepper

*Chef's Tips on Fat Cutters...
eat a fig bar or a slice of angel
food cake instead of a piece of
pie — cut at least 10 grams.*

☞ METHOD:

Cut steak into 2- or 3-inch serving pieces and season lightly with salt and pepper. In a 12-inch cast iron skillet, heat oil over medium-high heat.

When oil reaches 375 degrees F, place the steak pieces into the skillet and brown well on both sides. The oil should be very hot prior to sauteing, in order to seal in the juices and caramelize the meat on the bottom of the skillet. This brown caramelization will give the gravy its final color. When meat is done, remove it from the skillet and keep warm.

Add onions, celery, bell pepper and garlic. Saute 3–5 minutes or until vegetables are wilted and caramelized residue has dissolved in the bottom of the pan. Pour in water and stir into the seasoning mixture.

Return the meat to the skillet, bring liquid to a rolling boil and reduce heat to simmer. Cover and cook approximately 1 1/2 hours or until meat is tender. Additional water may be needed to keep meat moist.

When meat is tender, add green onions and parsley and adjust seasonings, if necessary. Cook an additional 3–5 minutes. Serve with steamed white rice and a side dish of smothered green peas.

Nutrition Facts...now

Calories:	342
Total Fat:	11gm
Saturated Fat:	3gm
% Calories from Fat:	30
Cholesterol:	75mg
Sodium:	425mg
Carbohydrate:	22gm
Fiber:	4gm
Protein:	37gm

PREP TIME: 3 Hours   SERVES: 6

☞ INGREDIENTS:

12 (2-inch thick) veal shanks
1/2 cup seasoned flour
1/2 cup vegetable oil
2 cups diced onions
1 cup diced celery
1 cup diced red bell pepper
1/4 cup chopped garlic
1 cup diced carrots
6 cups beef bouillon
2 cups diced tomatoes in juice
1 cup red wine
1 tsp basil
1/2 tsp thyme
1/2 tsp oregano
1 tsp salt
black pepper
Louisiana Gold Pepper Sauce

☞ METHOD:

Preheat oven to 350 degrees F. Season meat well using salt, pepper and Louisiana Gold. Dust meat lightly with seasoned flour, shaking off all of the excess. In a 12-quart cast iron dutch oven, heat oil over medium-high heat. Brown veal shanks slowly, a few at a time, until shanks are golden brown and well caramelized in the bottom of pot. As shanks brown, remove and set them aside. In the same pot, add onions, celery, bell pepper and garlic. Saute 3–5 minutes or until vegetables are wilted. Add carrots, bouillon, tomatoes and red wine. Blend well into the vegetable mixture. Season with basil, thyme and oregano. Return the shanks to the pot, bring to a rolling boil, cover and place the pot in the oven. Bake 2 hours, until veal is tender. Adjust seasonings, if necessary. Remove shanks to a large platter and keep warm. Strain solids from the sauce, reduce it slightly and ladle it over shanks. Shanks may be served with rice or pasta.

"Although Clarence Bouchereau, Uncle Bud, was a printer most of his life, he turned out to be a fabulous cook at the same time. I remember the many mornings we sat and had coffee and talked about the dish that he was going to cook later that evening. He was as meticulous about his preparation as he was about his printing.

"Although I think his barbecued dishes were some of the best I've ever eaten, I'll never forget his braised veal shanks."

John Folse
Donaldsonville, Louisiana

Chef's Tips on Fat Cutters... make rich gravies by boiling vegetables in chicken broth to 1/3 the original amount.

❦Nutrition Facts...then❦

Calories:	431
Total Fat:	24gm
Saturated Fat:	5gm
% Calories from Fat:	49
Cholesterol:	74mg
Sodium:	1599mg
Carbohydrate:	26gm
Fiber:	5gm
Protein:	23gm

PREP TIME: 3 Hours   SERVES: 6

INGREDIENTS:

12 (2-inch thick) veal shanks
1/2 cup seasoned flour
2 tbsps vegetable oil
2 cups diced onions
1 cup diced celery
1 cup diced red bell pepper
1/4 cup chopped garlic
1 cup diced carrots
6 cups defatted beef bouillon,
        unsalted
2 cups fresh tomatoes, diced
1 cup red wine
1 tsp basil
1/2 tsp thyme
1/2 tsp oregano
salt substitute
black pepper
Louisiana Gold Pepper Sauce

Big Rob Collins and Little Rob tend the pork chops served up at the King Ranch trail ride in Carencro.

METHOD:

Preheat oven to 350 degrees F. Season meat well using salt substitute, pepper and Louisiana Gold. Dust meat lightly with seasoned flour, shaking off all of the excess.

In a 12-quart cast iron dutch oven, heat oil over medium-high heat. Brown veal shanks slowly, a few at a time, until shanks are golden brown and well caramelized in the bottom of pot. As shanks brown, remove and set aside.

In the same pot, add onions, celery, bell pepper and garlic. Saute 3–5 minutes or until vegetables are wilted. Add carrots, bouillon, tomatoes and red wine. Blend well into the vegetable mixture. Season with basil, thyme and oregano.

Return the shanks to the pot, bring to a rolling boil, cover and place the pot in the oven. Bake 2 hours until veal is tender.

Adjust seasonings, if necessary. Remove shanks to a large platter and keep warm. Strain solids from sauce, reduce it slightly and ladle over shanks. Shanks may be served with rice or pasta.

Nutrition Facts...now

Calories: 297
Total Fat: 10gm
Saturated Fat: 2gm
% Calories from Fat: 29
Cholesterol: 74mg
Sodium: 272mg
Carbohydrate: 25gm
Fiber: 5gm
Protein: 21gm

PREP TIME: 2 1/2 Hours   SERVES: 6

☞ INGREDIENTS:

1 hog ponce, cleaned	1 cup diced red bell pepper
2 pounds ground pork	1/4 cup diced garlic
2 cups diced onions	1/2 cup sweet potato, cubed
2 cups diced celery	2 slices dried bread

3/4 cup milk	black pepper
1 cup sliced green onions	cayenne pepper
1 cup chopped parsley	1/4 cup vegetable oil
1 tsp salt	1 quart beef stock

☞ METHOD:

Have your butcher clean the ponce inside and out. In a large mixing bowl, place pork and half of the onions, celery, bell pepper and garlic. Blend the seasonings well into the ground pork and add the sweet potato. Soak the sliced bread in milk and chop into the ground pork mixture. Add half of the green onions and parsley. Season generously using salt and peppers. Stuff the ponce with the ground meat stuffing and sew it closed with butcher's twine. Season the outside well using salt and peppers. In a 7-quart cast iron dutch oven, heat vegetable oil over medium-high heat. Brown the ponce well on all sides, turning often to keep it from sticking. NOTE: It is imperative to take time to brown the ponce well because this will affect not only the finished color of the meat but also the gravy. Once the ponce is browned, remove it from the dutch oven and add remaining onions, celery, bell pepper and garlic. Saute 3–5 minutes or until vegetables are wilted. Return the ponce to the pot, adding beef stock. Bring to a rolling boil and reduce to simmer. Cover and cook approximately 2 hours, adding water if necessary to keep from scorching. When done, sprinkle in remaining green onions and parsley. Cook 5 minutes longer. Slice the ponce and serve with natural drippings over steamed white rice.

"As we all know, pork and pork products are the main ingredients for most of Louisiana's Cajun recipes. More so than game or chicken, pork is revered here in Cajun and Creole country.

"This recipe for stuffed ponce (pig's stomach) is very traditional in Louisiana. Just about every culture in the world has a dish similar to ours. This particular version is from the late Mrs. L.G. Seale, Sr., one of the greatest prairie cooks in Eunice, Louisiana."

Charles Seale
Eunice, Louisiana

❀Nutrition Facts...then❀

Calories:	759
Total Fat:	52gm
Saturated Fat:	17gm
% Calories from Fat:	62
Cholesterol:	171mg
Sodium:	1717mg
Carbohydrate:	11gm
Fiber:	2gm
Protein:	60gm

PREP TIME: 2 1/2 Hours   SERVES: 6

☞ INGREDIENTS:

1 hog ponce, cleaned
1/2 pound lean ground pork
1 pound lean ground beef
2 cups diced onions
2 cups diced celery
1 cup diced red bell pepper
1/4 cup diced garlic
1/2 cup sweet potato, cubed
2 slices dried bread
3/4 cup skim milk
1 cup sliced green onions
1 cup chopped parsley
salt substitute
black pepper
cayenne pepper
vegetable spray
1 quart water

☞ METHOD:

Have your butcher clean the ponce inside and out. In a large mixing bowl, place pork, beef and half of the onions, celery, bell pepper and garlic. Blend the seasonings well into the ground meat and add the sweet potato.

Soak the sliced bread in milk and chop into the ground pork and beef mixture. Add half of the green onions and parsley. Season generously using salt substitute and peppers.

Stuff the ponce with the ground meat stuffing and sew it closed with butcher's twine. Season the outside well using salt substitute and peppers.

Spray a 7-quart cast iron dutch oven with vegetable spray and brown the ponce well on all sides. Turn the ponce often to keep it from sticking. NOTE: It is imperative to take time to brown the ponce well because this will affect not only the finished color of the meat but also the gravy.

Once the ponce is browned, remove it from the dutch oven and add remaining onions, celery, bell pepper and garlic. Saute 3–5 minutes or until vegetables are wilted. Return the ponce to the pot, adding water. Bring to a rolling boil and reduce to simmer. Cover and cook approximately 2 hours, adding water if necessary to keep from scorching.

When done, sprinkle in remaining green onions and parsley. Cook 5 minutes longer. Slice the ponce and serve with natural drippings over steamed white rice.

Nutrition Facts...now

Calories: 567
Total Fat: 34gm
Saturated Fat: 13gm
% Calories from Fat: 55
Cholesterol: 157mg
Sodium: 484mg
Carbohydrate: 10gm
Fiber: 2gm
Protein: 53gm

BRAISED BEEF HEART WITH SAVORY OYSTER STUFFING *Something Old...*

PREP TIME: 3 Hours SERVES: 8

INGREDIENTS:

3 1/2-pound beef heart, cleaned
1 cup chopped oysters
1/4 cup butter
1 cup diced onions
1/2 cup diced celery
1 tbsp chopped garlic
1/4 tsp rubbed sage
1/4 tsp thyme leaves
1 1/2 cups seasoned Italian bread crumbs
1 tsp salt
black pepper
hot sauce
1/4 cup vegetable oil
4 cups beef consomme
1/4 cup water
4 large skewers
4 (10-inch) pieces butcher's twine

METHOD:

Preheat oven to 350 degrees F. Cut the heart lengthwise and wash it thoroughly inside and out. In a 10-inch cast iron skillet, melt butter over medium-high heat. Add onions, celery and garlic. Saute 3–5 minutes or until vegetables are wilted. Add sage, thyme and oysters. Cook 5 minutes or until oyster juice has been rendered. Sprinkle in bread crumbs to absorb the liquid and create a savory stuffing. Season to taste using salt, pepper and hot sauce. Cool the stuffing slightly and place in a generous layer on one side of the heart. Cover with the second side and, using the four skewers, skewer the heart on both sides, top and bottom. Using the four pieces of string, tie the two sides tightly around the skewers to hold in place. Season well using salt, pepper and hot sauce. In a 5-quart cast iron dutch oven, heat oil over medium-high heat. Saute the stuffed heart well on all sides until golden brown. Add beef consomme and water. Bring to a rolling boil, cover and place the pot in the oven. Bake for 3 hours or until meat is tender. When it is done, remove skewers, slice and serve the meat with a generous portion of the stuffing. NOTE: The amount of consomme should be increased for moisture, if stuffing is too dry.

"I suppose this is a small challenge from a Midwestern chef to the chefs and cooks of South Louisiana. As a retired professional chef, I spend about half of each year visiting my daughter and Cajun son-in-law in Erath, Louisiana, so I'm very familiar with - and very fond of - South Louisiana cuisine.

"In all my travels and dining around Louisiana, however, I've never encountered beef heart on a menu. The original recipe came from my grandmother, Anna Myrtle Barcus, who used a sausage stuffing, since oysters were not exactly easy to come by in Graham, Missouri.

"The challenge? It's the same one you always use on me when you present me with something I haven't tasted before: 'Try it. You'll like it!'"

Juanita Decker
Erath, Louisiana

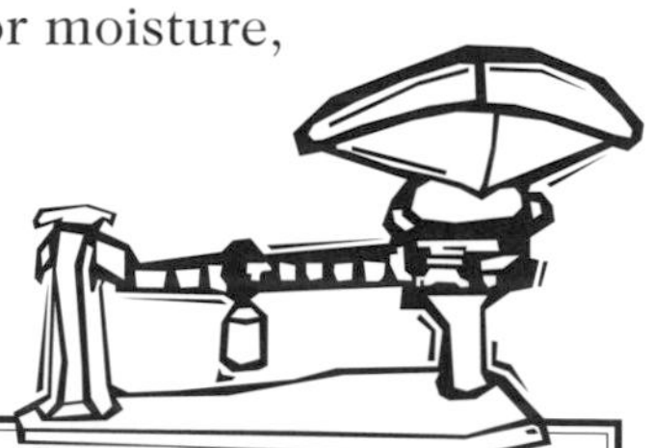

Nutrition Facts...then

Calories:	454
Total Fat:	22gm
Saturated Fat:	7gm
% Calories from Fat:	43
Cholesterol:	302mg
Sodium:	2027mg
Carbohydrate:	24gm
Fiber:	0gm
Protein:	43gm

PREP TIME: 3 Hours   SERVES: 8

INGREDIENTS:

3 1/2-pound beef heart, cleaned
1 cup chopped oysters
1 tbsp vegetable oil
1 cup diced onions
1/2 cup diced celery
1 tbsp chopped garlic
1/4 tsp rubbed sage
1/4 tsp thyme leaves
1 1/2 cups plain bread crumbs
salt substitute
black pepper
hot sauce
vegetable spray
4 cups defatted beef consomme, unsalted
1/4 cup water
4 large skewers
4 (10-inch) pieces butcher's twine

METHOD:

Preheat oven to 350 degrees F. Cut the heart lengthwise and wash it thoroughly inside and out.

In a 10-inch cast iron skillet, heat vegetable oil over medium-high heat. Add onions, celery and garlic. Saute 3 5 minutes or until vegetables are wilted. Add sage, thyme and oysters. Cook 5 minutes or until oyster juice has been rendered.

Sprinkle in bread crumbs to absorb the liquid and create a savory stuffing. Season to taste using salt substitute, pepper and hot sauce. Cool the stuffing slightly and place in a generous layer on one side of the heart. Cover with the second side and, using the four skewers, skewer the heart on both sides, top and bottom. Using the four pieces of string, tie the two sides tightly around the skewers to hold in place.

Season well using salt substitute, pepper and hot sauce. In a 5-quart cast iron dutch oven, coated with vegetable spray, saute the stuffed heart well on all sides until golden brown. Add beef consomme and water. Bring to a rolling boil, cover and place the pot in the oven. Bake for 3 hours or until meat is tender.

When it is done, remove skewers, slice and serve the meat with a generous portion of the stuffing. NOTE: The amount of consomme should be increased for moisture, if stuffing is too dry.

Nutrition Facts...now

Calories: 384
Total Fat: 14gm
Saturated Fat: 3gm
% Calories from Fat: 34
Cholesterol: 287mg
Sodium: 502mg
Carbohydrate: 24gm
Fiber: 0gm
Protein: 38gm

*Chef's Tips on Snacks...
100 calories or less: one frozen fruit bar, 40 pretzel sticks, two squares graham crackers, 1/2 cup of fruit gelatin, ten bite-size cheese crackers.*

PREP TIME: 1 1/2 Hours   SERVES: 6

☞ INGREDIENTS:

6 (1/2-inch thick) center-cut pork chops
1 cup converted rice, uncooked
1/2 cup olive oil
1 cup chopped onions
1/2 cup chopped celery
1/2 cup chopped green bell pepper
1/2 cup chopped yellow bell pepper
1/2 cup diced garlic
1 (8-ounce) can tomato sauce
1 cup beef consomme
1/2 cup water
1 bay leaf
1 tsp chopped basil
1/2 cup sliced green onions
1/4 cup chopped parsley
1 tsp salt
black pepper
Louisiana Gold Pepper Sauce

☞ METHOD:

Preheat oven to 325 degrees F. In a 12-inch cast iron skillet, heat oil over medium-high heat. Season chops well using salt, pepper and Louisiana Gold. Brown chops well on both sides, allowing them to caramelize in the bottom of the skillet. Once they are golden brown, remove and keep them warm. In the same skillet, add onions, celery, bell peppers and garlic. Saute 3–5 minutes or until vegetables are wilted. Add tomato sauce, consomme and water. Bring to a low boil and reduce to simmer. Add bay leaf and basil. Season to taste using salt and pepper. Remember to slightly over-season since the rice will absorb most of the flavor. Blend in rice, stirring well into the mixture. Layer pork chops over sauce and top with green onions. Cover and bake 1 hour or until rice is totally cooked. When done, sprinkle with chopped parsley and serve hot.

"I love to cook Italian food. Coming from a family who often cooked casserole-type dishes, it just seemed natural to blend the two combinations.

"This wonderful pork dish can be served either with or without the rice. However, when the rice is added it becomes another one of those famous one pot meals. This dish is also great because the meat and sauce can be prepared in advance and even frozen, then the rice can be added prior to finishing the dish."

Pamela Castel
Baton Rouge, Louisiana

❋Nutrition Facts...then❋

Calories: 890
Total Fat: 61gm
Saturated Fat: 18gm
% Calories from Fat:................. 62
Cholesterol: 126mg
Sodium: 836mg
Carbohydrate: 30gm
Fiber: 2gm
Protein: 53gm

PREP TIME: 1 1/2 Hours   SERVES: 6

☞ INGREDIENTS:

6 (1/2-inch thick) lean center-cut pork chops
1 cup converted rice, uncooked
1 tbsp olive oil
1 cup chopped onions
1/2 cup chopped celery
1/2 cup chopped green bell pepper
1/2 cup chopped yellow bell pepper
1/2 cup diced garlic
1 (8-ounce) can tomato sauce, no salt added
1 cup defatted beef consomme, unsalted
1/2 cup water
1 bay leaf
1 tsp chopped basil
1/2 cup sliced green onions
1/4 cup chopped parsley
salt substitute
black pepper
Louisiana Gold Pepper Sauce

Grazing cattle off Highway 24 between Cut Off and Bourg.

*Chef's Tips on Snacks...
50 calories or less: four
vanilla wafers, 1/2 cup of
plain yogurt, one medium
peach, 1/2 cup of blueberries,
two cups of raw veggies.*

Nutrition Facts...now

Calories:	385
Total Fat:	14gm
Saturated Fat:	4gm
% Calories from Fat:	32
Cholesterol:	56mg
Sodium:	76mg
Carbohydrate:	31gm
Fiber:	2gm
Protein:	33gm

☞ METHOD:

Preheat oven to 325 degrees F. In a 12-inch cast iron skillet, heat oil over medium-high heat. Season chops well using salt substitute, pepper and Louisiana Gold.

Brown chops well on both sides, allowing them to caramelize in the bottom of the skillet. Once they are golden brown, remove and keep them warm.

In the same skillet, add onions, celery, bell peppers and garlic. Saute 3–5 minutes or until vegetables are wilted. Add tomato sauce, consomme and water. Bring to a low boil and reduce to simmer.

Add bay leaf and basil. Season to taste using salt substitute and pepper. Remember to slightly over-season, since the rice will absorb most of the flavor. Blend in rice, stirring well into the mixture.

Layer pork chops over sauce and top with green onions. Cover and bake 1 hour or until rice is totally cooked. When done, sprinkle with chopped parsley and serve hot.

PREP TIME: 1 1/2 Hours SERVES: 6

☞ INGREDIENTS:

6 (1-inch) pork chops, butterflied
1/2 cup soy sauce
3/4 cup orange juice
1/2 cup water
2 cups mixed dried fruit, diced
1 tsp salt
black pepper

☞ METHOD:

Season pork chops well using salt and pepper. Place chops in a large casserole dish and top with soy sauce, orange juice, water and dried fruit. Cover and marinate overnight. Preheat oven to 350 degrees F. Lightly cover the casserole dish with aluminum foil and bake for 1 hour or until pork chops are tender. Naturally, the length of cooking time will depend on the size of the chops. The orange juice and dried fruit make a great sauce that we like to serve over noodles.

"This was a recipe I inherited from my mother - one she could almost never prepare on weekends. My father, you see, was a "boataholic," so we rarely had a weekend on dry land.

"He was a Ford dealer in New Iberia, but his great enthusiasm in life was boats. He started with a small, wooden Chris Craft runabout (this was back in the 1940s), and every couple of years traded up to something bigger. Barring just about any inconvenience this side of a hurricane, he would bundle my mother and me (and, as the boats grew in size, perhaps another family or two) on board his boat de jour and off we'd go out on Vermilion Bay, fishing, crabbing, shrimping or whatever combination of the three was appropriate to whim and season.

"Once we'd landed the day's catch, we'd go ashore for a cook-out at the water's edge. My mother always brought along sandwich makings, 'just in case.' But they were rarely needed. In those days, you could catch 50 pounds of shrimp in 30 minutes in Vermilion Bay.

"Many people might find that such early exposure to the water made a lifetime outdoorsperson of them. But, to tell you the truth, I had enough of the great outdoors by the time I was grown to last me a lifetime!"

Betty St. Dizier
Lafayette, Louisiana

Chef's Tips on Fat Cutters... tomato-based sauces are naturally lower in fat.

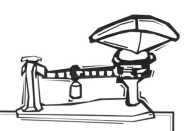

❊Nutrition Facts...then❊

Calories: 522
Total Fat: 31gm
Saturated Fat: 11gm
% Calories from Fat: 53
Cholesterol: 107mg
Sodium: 1661mg
Carbohydrate: 31gm
Fiber: 3gm
Protein: 30gm

PORK CHOPS ST. DIZIER

PREP TIME: 1 1/2 Hours   SERVES: 6

☞ INGREDIENTS:

6 (4-ounce) lean center-cut loin chops
1/4 cup lite soy sauce
1 cup orange juice
1/2 cup water
2 cups mixed dried fruit, diced
salt substitute
black pepper

☞ METHOD:

Season pork chops well using salt substitute and pepper. Place chops in a large casserole dish and top with soy sauce, orange juice, water and dried fruit. Cover and marinate overnight.

Preheat oven to 350 degrees F. Lightly cover the casserole dish with aluminum foil and bake for 1 hour or until pork chops are tender. Naturally, the length of cooking time will depend on the size of the chops.

The orange juice and dried fruit make a great sauce that we like to serve over noodles.

Nutrition Facts...now

Calories: 419
Total Fat: 15gm
Saturated Fat: 5gm
% Calories from Fat: 29
Cholesterol: 86mg
Sodium: 498mg
Carbohydrate: 31gm
Fiber: 3gm
Protein: 51gm

PREP TIME: 1 1/2 Hours   SERVES: 6

☞ INGREDIENTS:

2 (2-pound) slabs of baby back ribs
1/2 cup sherry
6 (6-inch) links smoked sausage
1 (8-ounce) can tomato sauce
2 tbsps red wine vinegar
2 tbsps minced onions
1/2 cup honey
1/4 cup diced garlic
1 tbsp celery seed
1/4 cup Worcestershire Sauce
1 tsp salt
black pepper
hot sauce
2 cups hot water

☞ METHOD:

Preheat oven to 350 degrees F. You may wish to cut the ribs in half for a better fit in the baking pan. Season the ribs well, using salt and pepper. Place the ribs in a baking pan with a 1-inch lip, along with the smoked sausage, and set aside. In a 1-quart sauce pot, combine all remaining ingredients except water. Bring to a rolling boil and reduce to simmer. Cook for approximately 30 minutes, stirring occasionally while flavors develop. If you like spicy sauce, you may wish to add more hot sauce or cayenne pepper to the sauce. Using a pastry brush, paint the ribs and sausages generously with the sauce mixture. Pour the water into the baking pan and cover the pan loosely with aluminum foil. Bake for approximately 1 hour, basting with the sauce occasionally. Once the ribs are tender, remove the foil and brown them evenly. These ribs may also be cooked on your barbecue pit with a touch of your favorite smoked wood or cooked in a dutch oven on the stove, with the sauce poured on top and simmered for approximately 1 1/2 hours. Add water as necessary, to retain volume.

"When I was a little girl living on a rice farm south of Lake Charles, Louisiana, Daddy always had lots of hogs in the pen. On cold winter days, when he would butcher one, we would create lots of different dishes with the meat.

"One of my favorites at that time of year was the pork ribs - the ones with lots of meat on 'em! After I got married, I asked Mom how to cook those famous ribs. She told me how, but naturally I had to figure out the amounts of seasonings to use. As we have all come to learn in life, mamas never measure anything."
Eva Prudhomme-Hollard
Irving, Texas

❧Nutrition Facts...then❧

Calories: 1210
Total Fat: 65gm
Saturated Fat: 23gm
% Calories from Fat: 49
Cholesterol: 270mg
Sodium: 1626mg
Carbohydrate: 32gm
Fiber: 1gm
Protein: 116gm

PORK RIBS IN SHERRY SAUCE

PREP TIME: 1 1/2 Hours   SERVES: 6

☞ INGREDIENTS:

2 (2-pound) slabs of lean baby back ribs
1/2 cup sherry
6 ounces low-fat smoked sausage
1 (8-ounce) can tomato sauce, no salt added
2 tbsps red wine vinegar
2 tbsps minced onions
1/2 cup honey
1/4 cup diced garlic
1 tbsp celery seed
1/4 cup Worcestershire Sauce
salt substitute
black pepper
hot sauce
2 cups hot water

The cracklins of Raymond Plaisance, Sr. almost ready for eating.

☞ METHOD:

Preheat oven to 350 degrees F. You may wish to cut the ribs in half for a better fit in the baking pan. Season the ribs well using salt substitute and pepper. Place the ribs in a baking pan with a 1-inch lip, along with the smoked sausage, and set aside.

In a 1-quart sauce pot, combine all remaining ingredients except water. Bring to a rolling boil and reduce to simmer. Cook for approximately 30 minutes, stirring occasionally while flavors develop. If you like spicy sauce, you may wish to add more hot sauce or cayenne pepper to the sauce.

Using a pastry brush, paint the ribs and sausages generously with the sauce mixture. Pour the water into the baking pan and cover the pan loosely with aluminum foil. Bake for approximately 1 hour, basting with the sauce occasionally.

Once the ribs are tender, remove the foil and brown them evenly. These ribs may also be cooked on your barbecue pit with a touch of your favorite smoked wood or cooked in a dutch oven on the stove, with the sauce poured on top and simmered for approximately 1 1/2 hours. Add water as necessary, to retain volume.

Nutrition Facts...now

Calories:	1039
Total Fat:	49gm
Saturated Fat:	15gm
% Calories from Fat:	43
Cholesterol:	216mg
Sodium:	295mg
Carbohydrate:	30gm
Fiber:	1gm
Protein:	110gm

PREP TIME: 1 1/2 Hours   SERVES: 6

☞ INGREDIENTS:

2 pounds ground beef
1 (8-ounce) package lasagna noodles
1/4 cup olive oil
2 cups diced onions
1/4 cup minced garlic
1 tsp oregano
2 tsps parsley
2 tsps sweet basil
1/2 tsp garlic salt
1 tsp salt
black pepper
3 (8-ounce) cans tomato sauce
2 (6-ounce) cans tomato paste
1 cup fresh mushrooms, sliced
1 cup cottage cheese
1 cup Ricotta cheese
2 cups frozen spinach, drained
2 cups shredded Mozzarella cheese

Chef's Tips on Fat Cutters...
by leaving one ounce of cream
out of your coffee five times a
day, you can lose 2 3/4 pounds in
one month.

"With a name like Lena Fresina, there's no debate what culture my family represents! Italians are known for their great cooking and so many famous Louisiana dishes can be traced back to humble Italian beginnings in bayou country.

"Whenever I get a craving for my favorite dish, I jump in my car and head home to Mama's. She and I can whip up a pan of lasagna in about an hour."
                                    Lena Fresina
                                    Louisiana

☞ METHOD:

Preheat oven to 350 degrees F. In lightly salted water, boil lasagna noodles according to package directions. Drain, toss with a little olive oil to prevent sticking, and set aside. In a 5-quart cast iron dutch oven, brown ground meat over medium-high heat. Continue to chop and cook ground beef until it separates, grain for grain. After meat is well browned, approximately 20–30 minutes, add onions and garlic. Saute 3–5 minutes or until vegetables are wilted. Drain the excess fat. Season with oregano, parsley, basil, garlic salt, salt and pepper. Add tomato sauce and tomato paste. Blend well into the meat mixture and bring to a low simmer. Add mushrooms and cook, stirring occasionally, 15–20 minutes. Remove from heat and adjust seasonings, if necessary. Add cottage cheese, Ricotta and spinach to the mixture. Once all is well-blended, place a layer of sauce in the bottom of a 9" x 13" baking dish. Add one layer of noodles, top with sauce and shredded Mozzarella. Repeat 3 times, leaving approximately 1/2 inch at the top of the dish for overflow. Sprinkle the top layer evenly with Mozzarella cheese. Bake, uncovered, for 30 minutes.

❧ Nutrition Facts...then❧

Calories:	760
Total Fat:	42gm
Saturated Fat:	17gm
% Calories from Fat:	45
Cholesterol:	151mg
Sodium:	1692mg
Carbohydrate:	40gm
Fiber:	6gm
Protein:	55gm

MAMA FRESINA'S LASAGNA

PREP TIME: 1 1/2 Hours   SERVES: 6

☞ INGREDIENTS:

1 pound extra lean ground beef
1 pound extra lean ground turkey
1 (8-ounce) package lasagna noodles
2 cups diced onions
1/4 cup minced garlic
1 tsp oregano
2 tsps parsley
2 tsps sweet basil
1/2 tsp garlic powder
salt substitute
black pepper
3 (8-ounce) cans tomato sauce, no salt added
2 (6-ounce) cans tomato paste, no salt added
1 cup fresh mushrooms, sliced
1 cup fat-free cottage cheese
1 cup fat-free Ricotta cheese
2 cups frozen spinach, drained
2 cups low-fat Mozzarella cheese, shredded

☞ METHOD:

Preheat oven to 350 degrees F. In lightly salted water, boil lasagna noodles according to package directions. Drain, rinse well to prevent sticking, and set aside.

In a 5-quart cast iron dutch oven, brown ground beef and turkey over medium-high heat. Continue to chop and cook meats until they separate, grain for grain.

After meats are well browned, approximately 20–30 minutes, add onions and garlic. Saute 3–5 minutes or until vegetables are wilted. Drain the excess fat. Season with oregano, parsley, basil, garlic powder, salt substitute and pepper.

Add tomato sauce and tomato paste. Blend well into the meat mixture and bring to a low simmer. Add mushrooms and cook, stirring occasionally, 15–20 minutes. Remove from heat and adjust seasonings, if necessary.

Add cottage cheese, Ricotta and spinach to the mixture. Once all is well-blended, place a layer of sauce in the bottom of a 9" x 13" baking dish. Add one layer of noodles and top with sauce and shredded Mozzarella. Repeat three times, leaving approximately 1/2 inch at the top of the dish for overflow. Sprinkle the top layer evenly with Mozzarella cheese. Bake, uncovered, for 30 minutes.

Nutrition Facts...now

Calories:	712
Total Fat:	25gm
Saturated Fat:	10gm
% Calories from Fat:	31
Cholesterol:	149mg
Sodium:	544mg
Carbohydrate:	45gm
Fiber:	6gm
Protein:	79gm

PREP TIME: 3 Hours   SERVES: 8

☞ INGREDIENTS:

4 large eggplants
2 gallons ice water
1 (8-ounce) block Mozzarella, grated
1 pound ground beef
1 cup chopped onions
1/2 cup chopped celery
1/2 cup chopped bell pepper
1/4 cup chopped parsley
1 tbsp Worcestershire Sauce
1/4 cup evaporated milk

2 eggs, beaten
3/4 cup seasoned Italian bread crumbs
3/4 cup olive oil
2 cups diced onions
1 cup diced celery
1/2 cup diced bell pepper
1/4 cup chopped garlic
2 (16-ounce) cans whole tomatoes
4 (8-ounce) cans tomato sauce

2 (6-ounce) cans tomato paste
3 cups water
1 tbsp dried basil
1 tbsp dried oregano
2 tsps sugar
1 tsp salt
black pepper
3/4 cup grated Romano cheese
3/4 cup grated Parmesan cheese

☞ METHOD:

Peel eggplant completely, split down the center and cut three 1-inch deep vertical slits down the center of each half. Soak eggplant in ice water for about 15–20 minutes. Remove, drain and completely dry eggplant. Divide the Mozzarella into 8 equal portions and sprinkle it inside the slits of each eggplant. Cover and set aside. In a large mixing bowl, combine beef, onions, celery, bell pepper and parsley. Mix the ingredients well. Add Worcestershire, milk, eggs and bread crumbs. Using your hands, blend well to form the stuffing. Season to taste using salt and pepper. Stuff the slits of the eggplant by pushing a generous amount of the ground meat stuffing into each slit over the Mozzarella. Any leftover stuffing may be formed into meatballs and added to the dish. In a large oval dutch oven, heat 1/2 cup of the olive oil over medium-high heat. Gently sear each eggplant in the hot olive oil by slowly rolling the eggplant over and over until the meat is well seared. Once all have been seared, drain and keep warm. In the same dutch oven, add remaining 1/4 cup olive oil. Add remaining onions, celery, bell pepper and garlic. Saute 3–5 minutes or until vegetables are wilted. Add whole tomatoes, crushing through your fingers. Add tomato sauce, paste and water, blending well into the sauteed vegetables. Season with basil, oregano, sugar, salt and pepper. Allow the tomato sauce to simmer 1 hour. Add stuffed eggplants to tomato sauce, baste well, and cook

"Although I love to cook Cajun, my fondest memories in the kitchen are of the times I spent cooking with my Italian grandmother, Mary. This recipe is one that she loved to cook using fresh eggplants and tomatoes from her garden. My grandfather butchered his own cattle and made homemade cheese. Like all Italian recipes, this one must be cooked with ample time and lots of love."
Diana Politz
Napoleonville, Louisiana

until eggplants are extremely tender to the fork, approximately 1–1 1/2 hours. When done, serve eggplant over a side dish of pasta, garnishing with grated Romano and Parmesan cheese.

❦Nutrition Facts...then❦

Calories:	628
Total Fat:	32gm
Saturated Fat:	13gm
% Calories from Fat:	46
Cholesterol:	166mg
Sodium:	1843mg
Carbohydrate:	42gm
Fiber:	6gm
Protein:	42gm

PREP TIME: 3 Hours   SERVES: 8

☞ INGREDIENTS:

4 large eggplants
2 gallons ice water
1 (8-ounce) block low-fat Mozzarella, grated
1/2 pound extra lean ground beef
1/2 pound extra lean ground turkey
1 cup chopped onions
1/2 cup chopped celery
1/2 cup chopped bell pepper
1/4 cup chopped parsley
1 tbsp Worcestershire Sauce
1/4 cup evaporated skim milk
1/2 cup egg substitute
3/4 cup plain bread crumbs
1/4 cup olive oil
2 cups diced onions
1 cup diced celery
1/2 cup diced bell pepper
1/4 cup chopped garlic
2 (16-ounce) cans whole tomatoes, no salt added
4 (8-ounce) cans tomato sauce, no salt added
2 (6-ounce) cans tomato paste, no salt added
3 cups water
1 tbsp dried basil
1 tbsp dried oregano
2 tsps sugar
salt substitute
black pepper
1/4 cup Romano cheese, grated
3/4 cup fat-free Parmesan cheese, grated

☞ METHOD:

Peel eggplant completely, split down the center and cut three 1-inch deep vertical slits down the center of each half. Soak eggplant in ice water for about 15–20 minutes. Remove, drain and completely dry eggplant.

Divide the Mozzarella into 8 equal portions and sprinkle it inside the slits of the eggplant. Cover and set aside.

In a large mixing bowl, combine ground beef, turkey, onions, celery, bell pepper and parsley. Mix the ingredients well. Add Worcestershire, skim milk, egg substitute and bread crumbs. Using your hands, blend well to form the stuffing. Season to taste using salt substitute and pepper.

Stuff the slits of the eggplant by pushing a generous amount of the stuffing into each slit over the Mozzarella. Any leftover stuffing may be formed into meatballs and added to the dish.

In a large oval dutch oven, heat 1/8 cup of the olive oil over medium-high heat. Gently sear each eggplant in the hot olive oil by slowly rolling the eggplant over and over until the meat is well seared. Once all have been seared, drain and keep warm.

In the same dutch oven, add remaining olive oil. Add remaining onions, celery, bell pepper and garlic. Saute 3–5 minutes or until vegetables are wilted. Add whole tomatoes, crushing through your fingers. Add tomato sauce, paste and water, blending well into the sauteed vegetables. Season with basil, oregano, sugar, salt substitute and pepper. Allow the tomato sauce to simmer 1 hour.

Add stuffed eggplant to tomato sauce, baste well and cook until eggplants are extremely tender to the fork, approximately 1–1 1/2 hours. When done, serve eggplant over a side dish of pasta, garnishing with grated Romano and Parmesan cheeses.

Nutrition Facts...now

Calories:	505
Total Fat:	15gm
Saturated Fat:	7gm
% Calories from Fat:	27
Cholesterol:	85mg
Sodium:	979mg
Carbohydrate:	56gm
Fiber:	6gm
Protein:	37gm

MEATBALLS & TOMATO GRAVY CARO

PREP TIME: 2 Hours   SERVES: 8

☞ INGREDIENTS:

4 pounds ground beef
1 cup minced onions
1 cup minced celery
1/2 cup minced bell pepper
1/4 cup minced garlic
4 eggs, beaten
1 cup milk
3 cups seasoned Italian bread crumbs
1/4 cup olive oil
4 (6-ounce) cans tomato paste
1 cup diced onions
1 cup diced celery
1 cup diced bell pepper
1/4 cup diced garlic
6 cups water
1 tsp salt
black pepper
hot sauce

☞ METHOD:

In a large mixing bowl, combine ground beef, minced onions, celery, bell pepper, garlic, eggs and milk. Season with salt and pepper. Using your hands, mix the ingredients well. Add the bread crumbs and blend until they are totally incorporated into the meat mixture. Form the ground meat into medium-size balls and set aside. In a 7-quart cast iron dutch oven, heat oil over medium-high heat. Lower temperature to simmer and brown meatballs on all sides. Remove from oil and keep warm. In the same dutch oven, saute tomato paste in reserved olive oil over low heat, stirring constantly until a rusty-brown color is achieved. Add diced onions, celery, bell pepper and garlic. Saute 3–5 minutes or until vegetables are wilted. Add water and blend well into the tomato paste. Season lightly with salt, pepper and hot sauce. Add meatballs and cook for approximately 1 hour. Correct seasonings, if necessary, and serve over boiled pasta.

"Grandma and Grandpa Caro lived in a big house on Caffrey Street in Franklin, Louisiana. Every Sunday and certainly every holiday was spent over at Grandpa's house enjoying another of his many feasts. The dishes he created were too numerous to recall; however, every dinner started out in the same fashion. The children, their spouses and the grandchildren all sat around a huge dining room table and began every meal with Grandpa Caro's famous spaghetti.

"Every child had a portion identical to his or her size, and under each plate was a coin. This coin was a gift from our grandparents but, naturally, before we could touch the coin, we had to eat all of the pasta on the plate. In fact, the plate had to be clean enough to turn upside down in order to retrieve the coin.

"I will never forget that ritual or the anticipation of that coin. This dish is still a favorite of mine."
                              Shirley Breaux
                          Franklin, Louisiana

❧Nutrition Facts...then❧

Calories:	1078
Total Fat:	72gm
Saturated Fat:	27gm
% Calories from Fat:	60
Cholesterol:	302mg
Sodium:	2382mg
Carbohydrate:	55gm
Fiber:	5gm
Protein:	52gm

MEATBALLS & TOMATO GRAVY CARO

PREP TIME: 2 Hours   SERVES: 8

INGREDIENTS:

2 pounds extra lean ground beef
2 pounds extra lean ground turkey
1 cup minced onions
1 cup minced celery
1/2 cup minced bell pepper
1/4 cup minced garlic
1 cup egg substitute
1 cup skim milk
3 cups plain bread crumbs
vegetable spray
4 (6-ounce) cans tomato paste, no salt added
1 cup diced onions
1 cup diced celery
1 cup diced bell pepper
1/4 cup diced garlic
6 cups water
salt substitute
black pepper
hot sauce

METHOD:

In a large mixing bowl, combine ground beef, turkey, minced onions, celery, bell pepper, garlic, egg substitute and skim milk. Season with salt substitute and pepper. Using your hands, mix the ingredients well.

Add the bread crumbs and blend until they are totally incorporated into the meat mixture. Form the ground meat into medium-size balls and set aside.

In a 7-quart cast iron dutch oven, coated with vegetable spray, brown meatballs on all sides. Remove and keep warm.

In the same dutch oven, saute tomato paste over low heat, stirring constantly until a rusty-brown color is achieved. Add diced onions, celery, bell pepper and garlic. Saute 3–5 minutes or until vegetables are wilted. Add water and blend well into the tomato paste. Season lightly with salt substitute, pepper and hot sauce.

Add meatballs and cook for approximately 1 hour. Correct seasonings, if necessary, and serve over boiled pasta.

Nutrition Facts...now

Calories: 878
Total Fat: 50gm
Saturated Fat: 17gm
% Calories from Fat: 50
Cholesterol: 153mg
Sodium: 681mg
Carbohydrate: 52gm
Fiber: 5gm
Protein: 56gm

PREP TIME: 1 Hour   SERVES: 6

☞ INGREDIENTS:

2 cups cooked roast beef, diced
1/2 cup vegetable oil
1/2 cup flour
1 cup diced onions
1 cup diced celery
1 tbsp chopped garlic
1 quart beef stock
2 cups diced potatoes
1 cup sliced green onions
1/2 cup chopped parsley
1 tsp salt
black pepper

Mildred Plaisance follows a family tradition making hog's head cheese during her family's Holy Week gathering.

☞ METHOD:

In a 7-quart cast iron dutch oven, heat oil over medium-high heat. Add flour and, using a wire whisk, stir constantly until golden brown roux is achieved. Add onions, celery and garlic. Saute 3–5 minutes or until vegetables are wilted. Add 1 cup cooked roast beef and blend it well into the vegetable mixture. Add beef stock, one ladle at a time, stirring constantly until stew consistency is achieved. Bring to a rolling boil, reduce to simmer and cook 30 minutes, stirring occasionally. Add the remaining roast beef, potatoes, green onions and parsley. Season to taste using salt and pepper. Cook hash until potatoes are tender, adding more stock as necessary to retain volume. Adjust seasonings and serve over rice or grits.

Grandma Thibodaux celebrated her 90th birthday in November, 1994. She graduated from Charity Hospital School of Nursing back in 1930. Although she worked as a registered nurse at Our Lady of the Lake in Baton Rouge, she always enjoyed her time at the stove.

"We often tease her because everything she cooks begins with the roux. She has a golden rule in her kitchen, 'Don't try to cook anything without parsley and green onions.'

"This is an original recipe from Grandma's kitchen. She often makes it with corned beef. She says she only uses roast beef when there is some leftover from Sunday dinner."

Anita Thibodaux
DeRidder, Louisiana

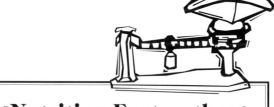

✾Nutrition Facts...then✾

Calories: 380
Total Fat: 25gm
Saturated Fat: 4gm
% Calories from Fat: 60
Cholesterol: 48mg
Sodium: 445mg
Carbohydrate: 13gm
Fiber: 1gm
Protein: 25gm

PREP TIME: 1 Hour   SERVES: 6

☞ INGREDIENTS:

2 cups lean cooked roast beef, diced
1/2 cup oil-less roux
1 quart water
vegetable spray
1 cup diced onions
1 cup diced celery
1 tbsp chopped garlic
2 cups diced potatoes
1 cup sliced green onions
1/2 cup chopped parsley
salt substitute
black pepper

Chef's Tips on Fat Cutters... give up one teaspoon of sugar in five cups of coffee a day and lose one pound in a month.

Nutrition Facts...now

Calories:	241
Total Fat:	11gm
Saturated Fat:	3gm
% Calories from Fat:	42
Cholesterol:	48mg
Sodium:	92mg
Carbohydrate:	10gm
Fiber:	1gm
Protein:	24gm

☞ METHOD:

Dissolve oil-less roux in water. Set aside. Place a 7-quart cast iron dutch oven, coated with vegetable spray, over medium-high heat. Add onions, celery and garlic. Saute 3–5 minutes or until vegetables are wilted.

Add 1 cup cooked roast beef and blend well into the vegetable mixture. Add roux/water mixture, stirring constantly, until stew consistency is achieved. Bring to a rolling boil, reduce to simmer and cook 30 minutes, stirring occasionally.

Add the remaining roast beef, potatoes, green onions and parsley. Season to taste using salt substitute and pepper. Cook hash until potatoes are tender, adding more water as necessary to retain volume. Adjust seasonings and serve over rice or grits.

Eunice Superette Inc., a slaughter house in the heart of the Cajun Prairie outside of Eunice.

BREAZEALE MEAT PIES

PREP TIME: 1 1/2 Hours   MAKES: 12 (5-inch) pies

☞ INGREDIENTS:

1 pound ground pork	1 cup sliced green onions	black pepper	3/4 cup milk
1 pound ground beef	1/2 cup water	hot sauce	1/4 cup flour (dusting)
1 cup diced onions	1/2 cup flour	3 cups self rising flour	1 egg
1/4 cup diced celery	1/4 cup chopped parsley	1/2 cup shortening	1/4 cup milk
1/4 cup chopped garlic	1 tsp salt	2 eggs, beaten	

☞ METHOD:

Preheat oven to 325 degrees F. In a 12-inch cast iron skillet, combine ground pork and beef. Using a large cooking spoon, blend well. Press evenly into the skillet, cover and bake approximately 1/2 hour until browned. Remove from the oven and place skillet over medium-high heat. Raise oven temperature to 350 degrees F. Stir in onions, celery, garlic and half of the green onions. Chop meat to separate well while vegetables are cooking. You may need to add approximately 1/2 cup of water to the mixture, should it become dry during the cooking process. Continue to cook until meat is separated grain for grain and juicy in the skillet, approximately 20 minutes. Sprinkle in 1/2 cup flour and blend well into the mixture. Cook 3–5 minutes, remove from heat and add remaining green onions and parsley. Season to taste using salt, pepper and hot sauce. Blend well into the mixture and set aside to cool. In a large mixing bowl, combine self-rising flour and shortening. Using a pastry cutter, blend until mixture resembles a coarse corn meal. Make a well in the center of the bowl. Add two of the eggs and 3/4 cup of the milk. Combine the ingredients until soft dough is formed. Do not overwork, as this will toughen the pie crust. Once dough ball is formed, cover it with a damp cloth and refrigerate for 1 hour. Dust your table surface with the 1/4 cup flour. Roll dough into a large rectangle, approximately 1/8-inch thick. Using a saucer as measurement, cut 5-inch circles from the dough. In a small mixing bowl, combine remaining egg and 1/4 cup of milk. Whip and set aside. Once the meat is cool, spoon a generous serving into the center of each circle. Using the eggwash and a pastry brush, paint the inner edge of the dough and fold it over into a 1/2-moon shape. Press down the edges of the dough with a fork to seal. Cut a small hole, approximately 1/4-inch, at the center of each, to allow steam to escape during baking. Place on cookie sheet and paint the top side of the pie crust lightly with eggwash. Bake approximately 20 minutes or until golden brown.

> "This recipe goes back at least four generations, possibly originating from the English side of my family. It's a bit of a stretch to talk about a 'recipe' for these pies until now. My grandmother learned it by watching over her mother-in-law's shoulder as she prepared them. And that's how she taught me."
> Judy Breazeale Prejean
> Lafayette, Louisiana

❈Nutrition Facts...then❈

Calories:	460
Total Fat:	29gm
Saturated Fat:	10gm
% Calories from Fat:	58
Cholesterol:	118mg
Sodium:	653mg
Carbohydrate:	29gm
Fiber:	4gm
Protein:	19gm

PREP TIME: 1 1/2 Hours   MAKES: 12 (5-inch) pies

☞ INGREDIENTS:

1/2 pound lean ground pork	1 cup sliced green onions	black pepper	3/4 cup skim milk
1 pound lean ground beef	1/2 cup water	hot sauce	1/4 cup flour (dusting)
1 cup diced onions	1/2 cup flour	3 cups self rising flour	1 egg white
1/4 cup diced celery	1/4 cup chopped parsley	1/3 cup oil	1/4 cup skim milk
1/4 cup chopped garlic	salt substitute	1/2 cup egg substitute	

☞ METHOD:

Preheat oven to 325 degrees F. In a 12-inch cast iron skillet, combine ground pork and beef. Using a large cooking spoon, blend well. Press evenly into the skillet, cover and bake approximately 1/2 hour until browned.

Remove the pan from the oven and place the skillet over medium-high heat. Raise oven temperature to 350 degrees F. Stir in onions, celery, garlic and half of the green onions. Chop meat to separate it well while vegetables are cooking. You may need to add approximately 1/2 cup of water to the mixture should it become dry during the cooking process. Continue to cook until meat is separated grain for grain and juicy in the skillet, approximately 20 minutes.

Sprinkle in the 1/2 cup of flour and blend well into the mixture. Cook 3–5 minutes, remove from heat and add remaining green onions and parsley. Season to taste using salt substitute, pepper and hot sauce. Blend well into the mixture and set aside to cool.

In a large mixing bowl, combine self-rising flour and oil. Using a pastry cutter, blend until mixture resembles a coarse corn meal. Make a well in the center of the bowl. Add egg substitute and 3/4 cup of skim milk. Combine the ingredients until soft dough is formed. Do not overwork, as this will toughen the pie crust. Once dough ball is formed, cover it with a damp cloth and refrigerate for 1 hour.

Dust your table surface with the remaining 1/4 cup flour. Roll dough into a large rectangle, approximately 1/8-inch thick. Using a saucer as measurement, cut 5-inch circles from the dough.

In a small mixing bowl, combine egg white and 1/4 cup of skim milk. Whip and set aside. Once the meat is cool, spoon a generous serving into the center of each circle. Using the eggwash and a pastry brush, paint the inner edge of the dough and fold over into a 1/2-moon shape. Press down the edges of the dough with a fork to seal. Cut a small hole, approximately 1/4-inch, at the center of each pie, to allow steam to escape during baking. Place pies on a cookie sheet and paint the top side of the crust lightly with eggwash. Bake approximately 20 minutes or until golden brown.

Nutrition Facts...now

Calories:	274
Total Fat:	10gm
Saturated Fat:	2gm
% Calories from Fat:	33
Cholesterol:	28mg
Sodium:	458mg
Carbohydrate:	28gm
Fiber:	4gm
Protein:	18gm

Chef's Tips on Snacks...
100 calories or less: eight animal crackers, six gum drops, two fig bar cookies, one ounce of cereal.

PREP TIME: 1 Hour   SERVES: 8

☞ INGREDIENTS:

1 1/2 pounds fresh seasoned
     pork sausage
1 1/2 pounds Italian sausage
1/4 cup vegetable oil
2 cups sliced Bermuda onions
1/2 cup diced celery
1 red bell pepper, sliced

1 yellow bell pepper, sliced
1 green bell pepper, sliced
1/4 cup diced garlic
1 cup sliced green onions
1 (15-ounce) can diced tomatoes,
     drained
1 tsp basil

1 tsp thyme
1 cup beef bouillon
1 tsp salt
black pepper
Louisiana Gold Pepper Sauce
1/4 cup chopped parsley

☞ METHOD:

Preheat oven to 375 degrees F. Leaving the sausage in its original length, place the 2 sausages side by side and roll into a circle, jelly-role fashion. The finished product should be a complete spiral with alternating lengths of Italian and pork sausage, from the center to outside. Using a small paring knife or toothpick, pierce the sausage casings at 1-inch intervals to allow the juices to flow from the sausages during the cooking process. Using your hands, pick up the spiral sausage and place it into a 14-inch cast iron skillet. Pour in the vegetable oil and place the skillet over medium-high heat. Cook until the sausage is well browned on the bottom. Using a large spatula, flip the sausage spiral over to brown the other side. Once the sausage is browned, use the same spatula to remove it from the skillet and hold it on a large platter. Drain all but 1/4 cup of the oil from the skillet. Add onions, celery, bell peppers and garlic. Saute 3–5 minutes or until vegetables are wilted. Add green onions, tomatoes, basil and thyme. Blend well into the sauteed vegetables. Return the sausage spiral to the skillet, placing it directly on top of the sauteed vegetables. Season to taste using salt, pepper and Louisiana Gold. Add bouillon, bring to a rolling boil, cover and place the pan in the oven. Cook 30–45 minutes or until sausage is thoroughly cooked. When done, garnish with chopped parsley and adjust seasonings, if necessary. Cut spirals into 6-inch links and serve over steamed white rice.

"Sausage making has always been a very important part of Cajun and Creole cooking. Not only did it make use of the trimmings and pieces left over from the butchering of animals, but it also made excellent use of tougher cuts of meat.

"With the ample supply of wild game, seafood and pork here in Cajun country, we often find either a combination of meats going into the sausage or two different sausages cooked together for added appeal and flavor.

"I can remember serving this Bayou Two Step at many of our hunting camp dinners using Italian sausage in the skillet until, of course, we had killed our first deer!"

Royley Folse, Sr.
Donaldsonville, Louisiana

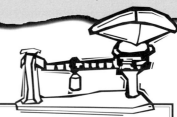

❧ Nutrition Facts...then ❧

Calories: 729
Total Fat: 55gm
Saturated Fat: 18gm
% Calories from Fat: 69
Cholesterol: 138mg
Sodium: 2626mg
Carbohydrate: 20gm
Fiber: 3gm
Protein: 37gm

PREP TIME: 1 Hour   SERVES: 8

☞ INGREDIENTS:

1 1/2 pounds low-fat smoked sausage
1 pound Italian sausage
2 cups sliced Bermuda onions
1/2 cup diced celery
1 red bell pepper, sliced
1 yellow bell pepper, sliced

1 green bell pepper, sliced
1/4 cup diced garlic
1 cup sliced green onions
1 (15-ounce) can diced tomatoes,
        no salt added, drained
1 tsp basil

1 tsp thyme
1 cup low-sodium beef bouillon
salt substitute
black pepper
Louisiana Gold Pepper Sauce
1/4 cup chopped parsley

☞ METHOD:

Preheat oven to 375 degrees F. Leaving the sausage in its original length, place the 2 sausages side by side and roll into a circle, jelly-role fashion. The finished product should be a complete spiral with alternating lengths of Italian and pork sausage, from the center to outside.

Using a small paring knife or toothpick, pierce the sausage casings at 1-inch intervals to allow the juices to flow from the sausages during the cooking process. Using your hands, pick up the spiral sausage and place it into a 14-inch cast iron skillet. Place the skillet over medium-high heat. Cook until the sausage is well browned on the bottom.

Using a large spatula, flip the sausage spiral over to brown the other side. Once the sausage is browned, use the same spatula to remove it

Tim Punch (left) gets a little help carving a 200 lb. pig at the Lockport Volunteer Fire Department.

from the skillet and hold it on a large platter.

Add onions, celery, bell peppers and garlic. Saute 3–5 minutes or until vegetables are wilted. Add green onions, tomatoes, basil and thyme. Blend well into the sauteed vegetables.

Return the sausage spiral to the skillet, placing it directly on top of the sauteed vegetables. Season to taste using salt substitute, pepper and Louisiana Gold. Add bouillon, bring to a rolling boil, cover and place the pan in the oven. Cook 30–45 minutes or until sausage is thoroughly cooked.

When done, garnish with chopped parsley and adjust seasonings, if necessary. Cut spirals into 6-inch links and serve over steamed white rice.

Nutrition Facts...now

Calories:	346
Total Fat:	26gm
Saturated Fat:	5gm
% Calories from Fat:	66
Cholesterol:	44mg
Sodium:	546mg
Carbohydrate:	9gm
Fiber:	2gm
Protein:	21gm

PREP TIME: 3 1/2 Hours   SERVES: 15

☞ INGREDIENTS:

6 pounds ground chicken gizzards
1/2 cup vegetable oil
3 large onions, diced
1 cup diced celery
1 cup diced bell pepper
1/4 cup diced garlic
1 (28-ounce) can tomatoes
1 (28-ounce) can V-8 juice
3 ounces beef bouillon
3 tbsps Liquid Smoke
1/2 cup beer
3 tsps cumin
6 ounces chili powder
2 tsps paprika
2 tbsps apple spice
6 tbsps ground fennel seed
1 tsp cocoa powder
1 tsp salt
black pepper
hot sauce
3 jalapeno peppers, seeded and diced

☞ METHOD:

In a 12-quart cast iron dutch oven, heat oil over medium-high heat. Add ground gizzards and cook until golden brown, stirring occasionally. While meat is browning, place onions, celery, bell pepper and garlic into the bowl of a food processor. Chop until vegetables are almost to the liquid state. When meat is golden brown, add contents of food processor to the pot. Continue to saute until all vegetables are incorporated and wilted. Add tomatoes, V-8, beef bouillon, Liquid Smoke and beer. Blend well into the vegetable mixture, bring to a rolling boil and reduce to simmer. Add cumin, chili powder, paprika, apple spice, fennel and cocoa. Stir well into the tomato liquid. Season lightly using salt, pepper, hot sauce and jalapenos. Reduce heat to simmer and cook 4 hours, stirring often. Naturally, the longer chili cooks, the better it tastes. If you like your chili with beans, feel free to add one can of cooked kidney beans, 10 minutes prior to serving. Adjust seasonings, if necessary.

"Now chili isn't something you necessarily associate with the Louisiana bayou country. But a hearty, spicy dish like this just naturally appeals to our palates. What's more, it's one of the few things you can cook competitively. I make a pretty good crawfish egg roll, too. But no one ever has crawfish egg roll cook-offs.

"Like most serious chili recipes, mine has bits and pieces borrowed from other chili cooks and some innovations of my own - like using chicken gizzards as the meat, and apple pie spice and cocoa powder among the seasonings.

"There's one other secret to good chili - the longer you cook it, the better it tastes."
Dr. Leonard Hendricks
Houma, Louisiana

❧Nutrition Facts...then❧

Calories: 339
Total Fat: 15gm
Saturated Fat: 1gm
% Calories from Fat: 38
Cholesterol: 206mg
Sodium: 738mg
Carbohydrate: 34gm
Fiber: 6gm
Protein: 34gm

DOC'S PRIMO CHILI

PREP TIME: 3 1/2 Hours   SERVES: 15

☞ INGREDIENTS:

3 pounds ground chicken gizzards
3 pounds ground chicken
3 large onions, diced
1 cup diced celery
1 cup diced bell pepper
1/4 cup diced garlic
1 (28-ounce) can tomatoes, no salt added
1 (28-ounce) can V-8 juice, low-sodium
3 ounces defatted beef bouillon, unsalted
3 tbsps Liquid Smoke
1/2 cup beer
3 tsps cumin
6 ounces chili powder
2 tsps paprika
2 tbsps apple spice
6 tbsps ground fennel seed
1 tsp cocoa powder
salt substitute
black pepper
hot sauce
3 jalapeno peppers, seeded and diced

☞ METHOD:

In a 12-quart cast iron dutch oven, heat gizzards and chicken over medium-high heat. Cook until golden brown, stirring occasionally.

While meat is browning, place onions, celery, bell pepper and garlic into the bowl of a food processor. Chop until vegetables are almost to the liquid state.

When meat is golden brown, add contents of food processor to the pot. Continue to saute until all vegetables are incorporated and wilted. Add tomatoes, V-8, beef bouillon, Liquid Smoke and beer. Blend well into the vegetable mixture, bring to a rolling boil and reduce to simmer.

Add cumin, chili powder, paprika, apple spice, fennel and cocoa. Stir well into the tomato liquid. Season lightly using salt substitute, pepper, hot sauce and jalapenos. Reduce heat to simmer and cook 4 hours, stirring often.

Naturally, the longer chili cooks, the better it tastes. If you like your chili with beans, feel free to add one can of cooked kidney beans 10 minutes prior to serving. Adjust seasonings, if necessary.

*Chef's Tips on Fat Cutters...
substitute canned tuna packed
in water for tuna in oil —
cut 15 grams.*

Nutrition Facts...now

Calories:	344
Total Fat:	8gm
Saturated Fat:	1gm
% Calories from Fat:	22
Cholesterol:	77mg
Sodium:	302mg
Carbohydrate:	21gm
Fiber:	7gm
Protein:	47gm

Seafood

Chapter Seven

Crabmeat Boudreaux	268/269
Creole Style Crab Stew	270/271
Crabmeat Pasta Etouffee	272/273
Stuffed Crabs	274/275
Crabmeat Au Gratin	276/277
Grandpa Joe's Crawfish Pie	278/279
Memaw Hoffman's Crawfish Bisque	280/281
Mr. Royley's Crawfish Stew	282/283
Aunt Dora's Crawfish Etouffee	284/285
Boiled Crawfish	286/287
Barbecued Shrimp Longman	288/289
Shrimp Treats Streva	292/293
Mama's Shrimp Spaghetti	294/295
Mina Pitre's Dried Shrimp Stew	296/297
Baked Shrimp	298/299
Dugas' Oyster Pie	300/301
Oyster Fritters	302/303
George's Stuffed Flounder	304/305
Redfish Courtbouillon	306/307
Fillet of Speckled Trout Albert	308/309

*The recipes for **Barbecued Shrimp Longman**, pictured at left, can be found on pages 288 and 289.*

PREP TIME: 1 Hour   SERVES: 6

☞ **INGREDIENTS:**

1 1/2 pounds lump crabmeat
1/4 cup butter
1/2 cup diced onions
1/4 cup diced celery
1 tbsp chopped garlic
1/4 cup chopped parsley
1/4 cup diced pimento
1/4 cup heavy whipping cream
2 eggs, beaten
1/2 cup mayonnaise
1 tsp salt
black pepper
hot sauce
1/2 cup seasoned Italian bread crumbs

☞ **METHOD:**

Whenever using crabmeat, it is important to spread the meat over a cookie sheet and pick all remaining cartilage and shells from the meat. When using lump crabmeat, make sure to handle it gently in order not to break the lumps into smaller pieces. Preheat oven to 350 degrees F. In a 12-inch cast iron skillet, melt butter over medium-high heat. Add onions, celery, garlic, parsley and pimento. Saute 3–5 minutes or until vegetables are wilted. Remove from heat and fold in the crabmeat, blending well with the seasonings. Combine cream, eggs and mayonnaise. Pour into the crabmeat mixture and gently stir until all is incorporated. Season to taste using salt, pepper and hot sauce. You may stuff the mixture lightly into crab shells, roll into crab cakes or place in au gratin style dishes. Top with bread crumbs and bake until slightly brown and bubbly, approximately 20–30 minutes, depending on method of service.

"This recipe was invented by my step-grandfather, Darryl Boudreaux, who was for many years the supervisor of the East St. Mary Parish school system.

"Like many Cajun men, he was probably the best cook in that generation of his family. His great delight was to go to restaurants in New Orleans or Lafayette, or anywhere else he happened to be in search of interesting dishes. He never asked for recipes, though. He would just remember the dish and go home to develop his own version. So there is no way of knowing what culinary experience inspired this dish - but inspired it certainly is! Grandpa Boudreaux must have thought so, too. It was frequently one of his contributions to the Thanksgiving and Christmas family feasts.

"My mother was also a superb cook, and I have a brother who is a chef. So the interest in cooking certainly has come down through the generations. For me, it's stress management."

Beth Boulet
Morgan City, Louisiana

❋Nutrition Facts...then❋

Calories: 491
Total Fat: 39gm
Saturated Fat: 15gm
% Calories from Fat: 67
Cholesterol: 246mg
Sodium: 1221mg
Carbohydrate: 10gm
Fiber: 0gm
Protein: 27gm

PREP TIME: 1 Hour   SERVES: 6

☞ INGREDIENTS:

1 1/2 pounds lump crabmeat
1 tbsp margarine
1/2 cup diced onions
1/4 cup diced celery
1 tbsp chopped garlic
1/4 cup chopped parsley
1/4 cup diced pimento
1/4 cup evaporated skim milk
4 egg whites, beaten
1/2 cup lite mayonnaise
1/4 tsp salt
black pepper
hot sauce
1/2 cup seasoned Italian bread crumbs

☞ METHOD:

Whenever using crabmeat, it is important to spread the meat over a cookie sheet and pick all remaining cartilage and shells from the meat. When using lump crabmeat, make sure to handle it gently in order not to break the lumps into smaller pieces.

Preheat oven to 350 degrees F. In a 12-inch cast iron skillet, melt margarine over medium-high heat. Add onions, celery, garlic, parsley and pimento. Saute 3–5 minutes or until vegetables are wilted. Remove from heat and fold in the crabmeat, blending well with the seasonings.

Combine skim milk, egg whites and mayonnaise. Pour into the crabmeat mixture and gently stir until all is incorporated. Season to taste using salt, pepper and hot sauce.

You may stuff the mixture lightly into crab shells, roll into crab cakes or place in au gratin-style dishes. Top with bread crumbs and bake until slightly brown and bubbly, approximately 20–30 minutes, depending on method of service.

Chef's Tips on Weight loss... forfeit two Scotch and sodas a day and drop two pounds in a month.

Nutrition Facts...now

Calories:	220
Total Fat:	7gm
Saturated Fat:	1gm
% Calories from Fat:	25
Cholesterol:	114mg
Sodium:	782mg
Carbohydrate:	11gm
Fiber:	0gm
Protein:	28gm

PREP TIME: 1 Hour   SERVES: 6

☞ INGREDIENTS:

1 1/2 pounds lump crabmeat	2 (8-ounce) cans tomato sauce	1/2 cup diced bell pepper	1 bay leaf
1 dozen small crabs, cleaned and halved	2 cups hot water	1 tbsp chopped garlic	1 tsp salt
1 (6-ounce) can tomato paste	2 cups diced onions	1 tbsp Worcestershire sauce	black pepper
1/4 pound melted butter	1 cup diced celery	2 tbsps sugar	hot sauce

Seventy-five pounds of catfish are skillfully prepared by members of the Lockport Volunteer Fire Department.

☞ METHOD:

Have your seafood supplier clean the crabs well and cut in half, reserving the large claws. Rinse well and set aside. It is important to spread the lump crabmeat on a cookie sheet and pick all remaining cartilage and shells from the meat. In a 5-quart cast iron dutch oven, brown tomato paste over medium-high heat. Add melted butter, tomato sauce and water. Blend well into the tomato paste and cook 5–10 minutes or until mixture is simmering. Add onions, celery, bell pepper and garlic. Simmer 10 additional minutes and add Worcestershire, sugar and bay leaf. Add the shelled crabs and claws into the sauce and simmer for approximately 1 hour. You may need to add additional water should the mixture become too thick. Season to taste using salt, pepper and hot sauce. When flavor is fully developed in the sauce, add the lump crabmeat and gently fold it into the mixture. Adjust seasonings if necessary and cook 10 additional minutes. Serve over rice or pasta. Eat the shelled crabs and claws exactly as you would boiled crabs.

"Leftovers here in Cajun country are more likely to be seafood than red meat. So it takes a more inventive cook to find a tasty way to use them.

"This recipe came about because we had some crabs left over from a weekend crab boil at our camp on the bayou near Stephensville. My husband, who was the chef in the family, conjured up this recipe to make use of the crabs and crabmeat. It was so good it became our "company" recipe - the one we prepared for visitors.

Donald & Bobbie Kreider
Morgan City, Louisiana

❧Nutrition Facts...then❧

Calories:	343
Total Fat:	18gm
Saturated Fat:	10gm
% Calories from Fat:	45
Cholesterol:	155mg
Sodium:	1558mg
Carbohydrate:	22gm
Fiber:	4gm
Protein:	26gm

CREOLE STYLE CRAB STEW

PREP TIME: 1 Hour   SERVES: 6

☞ INGREDIENTS:

1 1/2 pounds lump crabmeat
1 dozen small crabs, cleaned
        and halved
1 (6-ounce) can tomato paste,
        no salt added
2 tbsps margarine
2 (8-ounce) cans tomato sauce,
        no salt added
2 cups hot water
2 cups diced onions
1 cup diced celery
1/2 cup diced bell pepper
1 tbsp chopped garlic
1 tbsp Worcestershire sauce
2 tbsps sugar
1 bay leaf
1/4 tsp salt
black pepper
hot sauce

Old and new shrimp boats tied up in Grand Isle at the opening of the shrimping season in May.

☞ METHOD:

Have your seafood supplier clean the crabs well and cut in half, reserving the large claws. Rinse well and set aside. It is important to spread the lump crabmeat on a cookie sheet and pick all remaining cartilage and shells from the meat.

In a 5-quart cast iron dutch oven, brown tomato paste over medium-high heat. Add margarine, tomato sauce and water. Blend well into the tomato paste and cook 5–10 minutes or until mixture is simmering.

Add onions, celery, bell pepper and garlic. Simmer 10 additional minutes and add Worcestershire, sugar and bay leaf. Add the shelled crabs and claws into the sauce and simmer for approximately 1 hour. You may need to add additional water should the mixture become too thick.

Season to taste using salt, pepper and hot sauce. When flavor is fully developed in the sauce, add the lump crabmeat and gently fold it into the mixture. Adjust seasonings if necessary and cook 10 additional minutes. Serve over rice or pasta.

Eat the shelled crabs and claws exactly as you would boiled crabs.

Nutrition Facts...now

Calories:	248
Total Fat:	6gm
Saturated Fat:	1gm
% Calories from Fat:	22
Cholesterol:	113mg
Sodium:	544mg
Carbohydrate:	22gm
Fiber:	4gm
Protein:	26gm

CRABMEAT PASTA ETOUFFEE

PREP TIME: 1 1/2 Hours   SERVES: 6

☞ INGREDIENTS:

1 dozen fresh crabs, cleaned and halved	1 tsp dried oregano
1 pound jumbo lump crabmeat	1 tsp dried sage
1/4 cup vegetable oil	1 tsp dried dill
2 cups diced onions	1 tsp dried Italian seasoning
1 cup diced celery	2 tsps salt
1 cup diced bell pepper	black pepper
1/4 cup chopped garlic	hot sauce
1 (8-ounce) can tomato sauce	1 (12-ounce) package large shell macaroni
1 (16-ounce) can whole tomatoes	1/2 cup chopped parsley
1 tsp dried basil	

☞ METHOD:

Have your seafood supplier clean the crabs well and cut in half, reserving the large claws. Rinse well and set aside. It is important to spread the lump crabmeat on a cookie sheet and pick all remaining cartilage and shells from the meat. In a 7-quart cast iron dutch oven, heat oil over medium-high heat. Add onions, celery, bell pepper and garlic. Saute 3–5 minutes or until vegetables are wilted. Add tomato sauce, blending well into the vegetable seasonings. Once tomato sauce is simmering, add the whole tomatoes and chop them into smaller pieces with the side of your cooking spoon. Bring the mixture to a low boil and reduce to simmer. Add the raw shelled crabs and claws, making sure that the orange fat and natural juices are combined with the crabs into the tomato sauce. Simmer for 20–25 minutes to allow flavors to develop. Add all dry seasonings and hot sauce to taste, blending well into the tomato sauce. Add pasta and enough water to cover the pasta by 1 inch. Fold in the lump crabmeat, stirring once. Be careful not to break the pasta shells. Reduce heat to low, cover and cook 30 minutes. Do not remove the lid during this cooking time. Cook until pasta is tender and some sauce remains to moisten the pasta. Sprinkle with parsley and serve hot.

"Many years ago, someone gave my grandfather a dozen crabs. Normally, with live crabs, he'd either boil them or make a stew. But he didn't have enough to boil, and he was a little bored with crabmeat stew. So he decided to experiment with cooking macaroni in the pot with a crab jambalaya instead of using the traditional rice.

"It was a huge success, and became a family tradition whenever fresh crabs were available."
                    Delores Cheramie
                    Morgan City, Louisiana

❧ Nutrition Facts...then❧

Calories:	491
Total Fat:	13gm
Saturated Fat:	2gm
% Calories from Fat:	24
Cholesterol:	132mg
Sodium:	1497mg
Carbohydrate:	56gm
Fiber:	3gm
Protein:	37gm

CRABMEAT PASTA ETOUFFEE

PREP TIME: 1 1/2 Hours   SERVES: 6

☞ INGREDIENTS:

1 dozen fresh crabs, cleaned and halved,
    fat removed
1 pound jumbo lump crabmeat
2 tbsps vegetable oil
2 cups diced onions
1 cup diced celery
1 cup diced bell pepper
1/4 cup chopped garlic
1 (8-ounce) can tomato sauce, no salt added
1 (16-ounce) can whole tomatoes, no salt added
1 tsp dried basil
1 tsp dried oregano
1 tsp dried sage
1 tsp dried dill
1 tsp dried Italian seasoning
1/2 tsp salt
black pepper
hot sauce
1 (12-ounce) package large shell macaroni
1/2 cup chopped parsley

☞ METHOD:

Have your seafood supplier clean the crabs well and cut in half, reserving the large claws. Rinse well and set aside. It is important to spread the lump crabmeat on a cookie sheet and pick all remaining cartilage and shells from the meat.

In a 7-quart cast iron dutch oven, heat oil over medium-high heat. Add onions, celery, bell pepper and garlic. Saute 3–5 minutes or until vegetables are wilted. Add tomato sauce, blending well into the vegetable seasonings.

Once tomato sauce is simmering, add the whole tomatoes and chop them into smaller pieces with the side of your cooking spoon. Bring the mixture to a low boil and reduce to simmer.

Add the raw shelled crabs and claws into the tomato sauce. Simmer for 20–25 minutes to allow flavors to develop.

Add all dry seasonings and hot sauce to taste, blending well into the tomato sauce. Add pasta and enough water to cover the pasta by 1 inch. Fold in the lump crabmeat, stirring once. Be careful not to break the pasta shells. Reduce heat to low, cover and cook 30 minutes. Do not remove the lid during this cooking time.

Cook until pasta is tender and some sauce remains to moisten the pasta. Sprinkle with parsley and serve hot.

Chef's Tips on Weight loss... leave out two 12-ounce beers a day and drop two pounds in a month.

Nutrition Facts...now

Calories:	452
Total Fat:	8gm
Saturated Fat:	1gm
% Calories from Fat:	16
Cholesterol:	132mg
Sodium:	595mg
Carbohydrate:	57gm
Fiber:	3gm
Protein:	37gm

STUFFED CRABS

PREP TIME: 1 Hour   SERVES: 8

INGREDIENTS:

2 pounds jumbo lump crabmeat	1 tsp chopped thyme	black pepper
1/2 pound butter	1 tsp chopped basil	Louisiana Gold Pepper Sauce
1/2 cup diced onions	1/4 cup chopped parsley	2 cups seasoned Italian bread crumbs
1/2 cup diced celery	1/4 cup sliced green onions	8–10 cleaned crab shells
1/2 cup diced red bell pepper	2 eggs, beaten	
1/4 cup diced garlic	1 tsp salt	

METHOD:

Preheat oven to 350 degrees F. Should you be lucky enough to have approximately 2 pounds of picked crabmeat from leftover boiled crabs, use it in place of the jumbo lump in this recipe. You must remember, however, that the crabmeat is previously seasoned and may affect the finished flavor. It is important to spread the crabmeat over a cookie sheet and pick all remaining cartilage and shells from the meat. When using lump crabmeat, make sure to handle it gently in order not to break the lumps into smaller pieces. In a 12-inch cast iron skillet, melt butter over medium-high heat. Add onions, celery, bell pepper and garlic. Saute 3–5 minutes or until vegetables are wilted. Add thyme, basil, parsley and green onions, and saute 3–5 minutes longer. Remove from heat and place sauteed ingredients into a large mixing bowl. Fold in lump crabmeat and blend well into the sauteed seasonings. Blend in eggs and season to taste using salt, pepper and Louisiana Gold. Sprinkle in enough of the bread crumbs to hold the mixture together. Be careful not to dry out the stuffing. Divide the stuffing equally into 8–10 servings and fill each of the crab shells. If shells are not available, you may wish to use au gratin dishes or ramekins. Place stuffed crabs on a cookie sheet and top with bread crumbs. Bake 15–20 minutes or until crabs are thoroughly heated and golden brown.

"Crabs are another of the versatile ingredients available to the Louisiana cook. I clearly remember the huge tables of boiled crabs on Fourth of July and everyone sharing in the task of picking the crabmeat from the leftovers after everyone was through eating. This meat was destined for the stuffed crabs, since it was already full-flavored from the crab boil.

"Even today, crabs are my favorite seafood, but the stuffed crabs made from yesterday's crab boil are what I love most."

John Folse
Donaldsonville, Louisiana

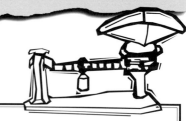

❀Nutrition Facts...then❀

Calories:	457
Total Fat:	27gm
Saturated Fat:	15gm
% Calories from Fat:	53
Cholesterol:	229mg
Sodium:	1638mg
Carbohydrate:	24gm
Fiber:	1gm
Protein:	30gm

PREP TIME: 1 Hour   SERVES: 8

INGREDIENTS:

2 pounds jumbo lump crabmeat
2 tbsps margarine
1/2 cup diced onions
1/2 cup diced celery
1/2 cup diced red bell pepper
1/4 cup diced garlic
1 tsp chopped thyme
1 tsp chopped basil
1/4 cup chopped parsley
1/4 cup sliced green onions
1 whole egg
2 egg whites
salt substitute
black pepper
Louisiana Gold Pepper Sauce
2 cups plain bread crumbs
8–10 cleaned crab shells

Jack Benjamin downs a dozen oysters at Uglesich's Restaurant in New Orleans.

METHOD:

Preheat oven to 350 degrees F. Should you be lucky enough to have approximately 2 pounds of picked crabmeat from leftover boiled crabs, use it in place of the jumbo lump in this recipe. You must remember, however, that the crabmeat is previously seasoned and may affect the finished flavor.

It is important to spread the crabmeat over a cookie sheet and pick all remaining cartilage and shells from the meat. When using lump crabmeat, make sure to handle it gently in order not to break the lumps into smaller pieces.

In a 12-inch cast iron skillet, melt margarine over medium-high heat. Add onions, celery, bell pepper and garlic. Saute 3–5 minutes or until vegetables are wilted. Add thyme, basil, parsley and green onions, and saute 3–5 minutes longer.

Remove from heat and place sauteed ingredients into a large mixing bowl. Fold in lump crabmeat and blend well into the sauteed seasonings. Blend in egg and whites. Season to taste using salt substitute, pepper and Louisiana Gold. Sprinkle in enough of the bread crumbs to hold the mixture together. Be careful not to dry out the stuffing.

Divide the stuffing equally into 8–10 servings and fill each of the crab shells. If shells are not available, you may wish to use au gratin dishes or ramekins. Place stuffed crabs on a cookie sheet and top with bread crumbs. Bake 15–20 minutes or until crabs are thoroughly heated and golden brown.

Nutrition Facts...now

Calories:	272
Total Fat:	7gm
Saturated Fat:	1gm
% Calories from Fat:	23
Cholesterol:	140mg
Sodium:	618mg
Carbohydrate:	22gm
Fiber:	1gm
Protein:	28gm

PREP TIME: 30 Minutes   SERVES: 6

☞ INGREDIENTS:

1 pound jumbo lump crabmeat	1/2 cup flour	hot sauce
1/4 pound butter	1 (12-ounce can) evaporated milk	1/4 cup chopped parsley
1 cup diced onions	2 egg yolks, beaten	1/4 cup sliced green onions
1 cup diced celery	pinch of nutmeg	1/4 cup diced pimento
1/2 cup diced bell pepper	1 1/2 tsps salt	1 cup grated cheddar cheese
1 tbsp chopped garlic	black pepper	paprika for color

☞ METHOD:

Preheat oven to 375 degrees F. It is important to spread the crabmeat over a cookie sheet and pick all remaining cartilage and shells from the meat. When using lump crabmeat, make sure to handle it gently in order not to break the lumps into smaller pieces. In a 5-quart cast iron dutch oven, melt butter over medium-high heat. Add onions, celery, bell pepper and garlic. Saute 3–5 minutes or until vegetables are wilted. Sprinkle in flour and, using a wire whisk, whip until blonde roux is achieved. Cook 2–3 minutes, stirring occasionally, allowing flavor to develop in the roux. Whip together the evaporated milk and egg yolks and slowly pour into the roux mixture, stirring constantly. Blend well and season to taste using nutmeg, salt, pepper and hot sauce. Bring the mixture to a low simmer while stirring occasionally. Be careful not to scorch the white sauce or curdle the eggs. Should the sauce become too thick during the cooking process, you may wish to add a little hot water or milk to thin it to a sauce consistency. Once the sauce has simmered for 5–10 minutes, remove it from heat and blend in parsley, green onions and pimentos. Adjust seasonings if necessary. Place the lump crabmeat in 6 individual au gratin dishes and top with equal portions of the au gratin sauce. Sprinkle with grated cheese and paprika. Place the au gratin dishes on a cookie sheet and bake 15–20 minutes or until cheese is lightly browned.

"It is hard to say when crabmeat au gratin first became so important in Louisiana cooking. It is amazing how a dish so delicate and classical could find its way onto seafood platters and on every back road diner menu in bayou country. Everybody has his favorite recipe for this dish.

"It is often flavored with many different herbs and spices, depending on family heritage. During crab season, this dish was always found on our dinner table once or twice a week."

Louanne Matherne
Manchac, Louisiana

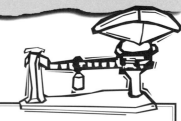

❧Nutrition Facts...then❧

Calories:	450
Total Fat:	30gm
Saturated Fat:	17gm
% Calories from Fat:	56
Cholesterol:	226mg
Sodium:	1108mg
Carbohydrate:	19gm
Fiber:	1gm
Protein:	27gm

PREP TIME: 30 Minutes   SERVES: 6

☞ INGREDIENTS:

1 pound jumbo lump crabmeat
2 tbsps margarine
1 cup diced onions
1 cup diced celery
1/2 cup diced bell pepper
1 tbsp chopped garlic
1/2 cup flour
1 (12-ounce) can evaporated skim milk
1/2 cup egg substitute
pinch of nutmeg
1/4 tsp salt
black pepper
hot sauce
1/4 cup chopped parsley
1/4 cup sliced green onions
1/4 cup diced pimento
1 cup low-fat cheddar cheese, grated
paprika for color

*Chef's Tips on Weight loss...
giving up two cans of soft drink
a day will cause you to lose 2 1/2
pounds in a month.*

☞ METHOD:

Preheat oven to 375 degrees F. It is important to spread the crabmeat over a cookie sheet and pick all remaining cartilage and shells from the meat. When using lump crabmeat, make sure to handle it gently in order not to break the lumps into smaller pieces.

In a 5-quart cast iron dutch oven, heat margarine over medium-high heat. Add onions, celery, bell pepper and garlic. Saute 3–5 minutes or until vegetables are wilted. Sprinkle in flour and, using a wire whisk, whip until blonde roux is achieved. Cook 2–3 minutes, stirring occasionally, allowing flavor to develop in the roux.

Whip together the evaporated skim milk and egg substitute. Slowly pour into the roux mixture, stirring constantly. Blend well and season to taste using nutmeg, salt, pepper and hot sauce.

Bring the mixture to a low simmer, stirring occasionally. Be careful not to scorch the white sauce or curdle the eggs. Should the sauce become too thick during the cooking process, you may wish to add a little hot water or skim milk to thin it to a sauce consistency. Once the sauce has simmered for 5–10 minutes, remove it from heat and blend in parsley, green onions and pimentos. Adjust seasonings, if necessary.

Place the lump crabmeat in 6 individual au gratin dishes and top with equal portions of the au gratin sauce. Sprinkle with grated cheese and paprika. Place the au gratin dishes on a cookie sheet and bake 15–20 minutes or until cheese is lightly browned.

Nutrition Facts...now

Calories:	276
Total Fat:	9gm
Saturated Fat:	2gm
% Calories from Fat:	26
Cholesterol:	88mg
Sodium:	733mg
Carbohydrate:	21gm
Fiber:	1gm
Protein:	28gm

GRANDPA JOE'S CRAWFISH PIE

Something Old...

PREP TIME: 1 Hour   SERVES: 6

☞ INGREDIENTS:

1 pound chopped crawfish tails
1/2 cup melted butter
1 cup diced onions
1 cup diced celery
1 cup diced red bell pepper
1/4 cup chopped garlic
1 cup heavy whipping cream
1/2 cup seasoned Italian bread crumbs
1 egg, beaten
1/2 cup sliced green onions
1/2 cup chopped parsley
1/4 tsp salt
black pepper
Louisiana Gold Pepper Sauce
2 (9-inch) deep-dish pie crusts

☞ METHOD:

Preheat oven to 450 degrees F. Press 1 of the unbaked pie crusts into a pie pan and set aside. In a 10-inch cast iron skillet, melt butter over medium-high heat. Add onions, celery, bell pepper and garlic. Saute 3–5 minutes or until vegetables are wilted. Add crawfish, blend well into the vegetable mixture and saute 3–5 minutes. Add heavy whipping cream, simmer for 10 minutes and remove from heat. Add seasoned bread crumbs and egg, blending well into the crawfish. Add green onions and parsley. Season to taste using salt, pepper and Louisiana Gold. Place the mixture in the pie crust and cover with the second crust. Make four 1-inch knife slits in the top crust for ventilation. Place the pie on a cookie sheet and bake for 10 minutes. Reduce heat to 350 degrees F and bake 20 additional minutes, or until crust is golden brown. Serve hot.

"Every summer when I was young, I would spend a couple of weeks at my Grandpa Joe's house. I loved to go there because there was always plenty of good food and because he lived on a farm with crawfish and catfish ponds and other animals.

"One thing that stands out in my mind is the dish that everybody raved over - Grandpa's Crawfish Pie. Often, Grandpa would give the dish an extra twist by using leftover boiled crawfish tails with extra spice and flavor.

"Every time I eat crawfish pies today, I think of those summers at Grandpa's house. It brings a smile to my face as memories of summers spent on the farm come rushing back to mind. Life seemed so much simpler back then."

Amy Brumfield
Gross Tete, Louisiana

Chef's Tips on Weight loss... cut out three ice cream cones a week and in a month shed one pound.

❋Nutrition Facts...then❋

Calories: 628
Total Fat: 46gm
Saturated Fat: 24gm
% Calories from Fat:.................. 66
Cholesterol: 232mg
Sodium: 903mg
Carbohydrate: 34gm
Fiber: 1gm
Protein: 19gm

278

PREP TIME: 1 Hour   SERVES: 6

☞ INGREDIENTS:

1 pound chopped crawfish tails
2 tbsps margarine
1 cup diced onions
1 cup diced celery
1 cup diced red bell pepper
1/4 cup chopped garlic
1 cup evaporated skim milk
1/2 cup seasoned Italian bread crumbs
2 egg whites
1/2 cup sliced green onions
1/2 cup chopped parsley
1/8 tsp salt
black pepper
Louisiana Gold Pepper Sauce
2 (9-inch) deep-dish pie crusts

Push poling his pirogue around his crawfish farm, Henri Boulet harvests crawfish that will end up on restaurant tables in Europe.

Chef's Tips on Weight loss... give up three fast food hamburgers a week and you can give up two pounds in a month.

Nutrition Facts...now

Calories:	415
Total Fat:	19gm
Saturated Fat:	6gm
% Calories from Fat:	42
Cholesterol:	102mg
Sodium:	794mg
Carbohydrate:	38gm
Fiber:	1gm
Protein:	21gm

☞ METHOD:

Preheat oven to 450 degrees F. Press 1 of the unbaked pie crusts into a pie pan and set aside.

In a 10-inch cast iron skillet, melt margarine over medium-high heat. Add onions, celery, bell pepper and garlic. Saute 3–5 minutes or until vegetables are wilted.

Add chopped crawfish, blend well into the vegetable mixture and saute 3–5 minutes. Add skim milk and simmer for 10 minutes. Remove from heat, add seasoned bread crumbs and egg whites, and blend well into the crawfish. Add green onions and parsley. Season to taste using salt, pepper and Louisiana Gold.

Place the mixture in the pie crust and cover with the second crust. Make four 1-inch knife slits in the top crust for ventilation. Place the pie on a cookie sheet and bake for 10 minutes at 450 degrees F. Reduce heat to 350 degrees F and bake 20 additional minutes or until crust is golden brown. Serve hot.

PREP TIME: 2 Hours   SERVES 10

☞ INGREDIENTS FOR STUFFING:

7 pounds crawfish tails	2 cups diced celery	1 cup sliced green onions	5 eggs, beaten	hot sauce
1 cup vegetable oil	1 cup diced bell pepper	1 cup chopped parsley	1 tsp salt	175 cleaned
5 cups diced onions	1/4 cup chopped garlic	5 slices toasted bread, diced	black pepper	crawfish heads

☞ METHOD FOR STUFFING:

Preheat oven to 350 degrees F. In a 7-quart cast iron dutch oven, heat oil over medium-high heat. Add onions, celery, bell pepper and garlic. Saute 3–5 minutes or until vegetables are wilted. Add crawfish tails, blend well into the vegetable seasonings and cook 10–15 minutes. Remove the sauteed crawfish and chop in a food processor or grind using a homestyle meat grinder. Return ground tails to the pot and add green onions and parsley. Blend well into the vegetable mixture. Add the diced bread and beaten eggs. Continue to cook until mixture reaches the consistency of a seafood stuffing. Season to taste using salt, pepper and hot sauce. Stuff the crawfish heads with the mixture, place on a cookie sheet and bake for approximately 30 minutes. Remove and set aside.

☞ INGREDIENTS FOR STEW:

4 pounds crawfish tails	2 cups diced onions	1/4 cup chopped garlic	2 bay leaves	hot sauce
1 1/4 cups cooking oil	2 cups diced celery	1/2 cup tomato sauce	1 tsp salt	1 cup sliced green onions
1 1/2 cups flour	1 cup diced bell pepper	3 quarts water	black pepper	1/2 cup chopped parsley

☞ METHOD FOR STEW:

In a 7-quart cast iron dutch oven, heat oil over medium-high heat. Add flour and, using a wire whisk, stir constantly until dark brown roux is achieved. Add onions, celery, bell pepper and garlic. Saute 5–10 minutes or until vegetables are wilted. Add tomato sauce, blending well into the roux mixture. Stir in the crawfish tails and simmer 3–5 minutes. Slowly add water, 1 quart at a time, until stew consistency is achieved. Add bay leaves, bring to a rolling boil and reduce to simmer. Allow to cook 1 hour, stirring occasionally. Additional water may be added as necessary to retain volume. Season to taste using salt, pepper and hot sauce. Add the stuffed heads to the stew and simmer approximately 20 minutes. Add green onions and parsley. Adjust seasonings, if necessary. Serve over steamed white rice.

"Crawfish bisque,the dish that defines the serious Cajun cook, is a big undertaking in its traditional form

"Of course the simplest way of dealing with the complexity of crawfish bisque was the one my Uncle Herman perfected - crawfish bisque radar. It seemed every time we cooked it, he managed to show up for a visit. I never knew how he could tell we were fixing crawfish bisque 50 miles away. But he could."

Gwen Bouterie
Thibodaux, Louisiana

❧Nutrition Facts...then❧

Calories:	1079
Total Fat:	59gm
Saturated Fat:	8gm
% Calories from Fat:	50
Cholesterol:	771mg
Sodium:	1125mg
Carbohydrate:	36gm
Fiber:	4gm
Protein:	93gm

PREP TIME: 2 Hours   SERVES 10

☞ INGREDIENTS FOR STUFFING:

7 pounds crawfish tails
1/4 cup vegetable oil
5 cups diced onions
2 cups diced celery
1 cup diced bell pepper
1/4 cup chopped garlic
1 cup sliced green onions
1 cup chopped parsley
5 slices toasted bread, diced
1 1/4 cups egg substitute
1/4 tsp salt
black pepper
hot sauce
175 cleaned crawfish heads

☞ METHOD:

Preheat oven to 350 degrees F. In a 7-quart cast iron dutch oven, heat oil over medium-high heat. Add onions, celery, bell pepper and garlic. Saute 3–5 minutes or until vegetables are wilted.

Add crawfish tails, blend well into the vegetable seasonings and cook 10–15 minutes. Remove the sauteed crawfish and chop in a food processor or grind using a homestyle meat grinder.

Return ground tails to the pot and add green onions and parsley. Blend well into the vegetable mixture. Add the diced bread and egg substitute. Continue to cook until mixture

reaches the consistency of a seafood stuffing. Season to taste using salt, pepper and hot sauce.

Stuff the crawfish heads with the mixture, place on a cookie sheet and bake for approximately 30 minutes. Remove and set aside.

☞ INGREDIENTS FOR STEW:

4 pounds crawfish tails
2 tbsps vegetable oil
1 cup oil-less roux
2 cups diced onions
2 cups diced celery
1 cup diced bell pepper
1/4 cup chopped garlic
1/2 cup tomato sauce, no salt added
2 1/2 quarts water
2 bay leaves
1/4 tsp salt
black pepper
hot sauce
1 cup sliced green onions
1/2 cup chopped parsley

☞ METHOD:

Dissolve oil-less roux in 1 quart water. Set aside.

In a 7-quart cast iron dutch oven, heat oil over medium-high heat. Add onions, celery, bell pepper and garlic. Saute 5–10 minutes or until vegetables are wilted. Add tomato sauce, blending well into the vegetable mixture.

Stir in the crawfish tails and simmer 3–5 minutes. Slowly add roux/water mixture. Add water, a little at a time, until stew consistency is achieved. Add bay leaves, bring to a rolling boil and reduce to simmer. Allow to cook 1 hour, stirring occasionally. Additional water may be added as necessary to retain volume.

Season to taste using salt, pepper and hot sauce. Add the stuffed heads to the stew and simmer approximately 20 minutes. Add green onions and parsley. Adjust seasonings, if necessary. Serve over steamed white rice.

Nutrition Facts...now

Calories:	686
Total Fat:	16gm
Saturated Fat:	2gm
% Calories from Fat:	23
Cholesterol:	665mg
Sodium:	751mg
Carbohydrate:	31gm
Fiber:	4gm
Protein:	93gm

MR. ROYLEY'S CRAWFISH STEW

PREP TIME: 1 Hour   SERVES: 10

☞ INGREDIENTS:

5 pounds crawfish tails
1 cup crawfish fat, optional
2 cups crawfish claws, optional
1/4 cup vegetable oil
1 1/2 cups oil
1 1/2 cups flour

2 cups diced onions
1 cup diced celery
1 cup diced bell pepper
1/4 cup chopped garlic
1 cup tomato sauce
3 quarts water

2 bay leaves
1 tsp salt
black pepper
Louisiana Gold Pepper Sauce
1 cup sliced green onions
1 cup chopped parsley

☞ METHOD:

In a 12-inch cast iron skillet, heat 1/4 cup vegetable oil over medium-high heat. Drain the crawfish tails well in a colander, reserving the fat and natural juices. Saute tails in 1/4 cup vegetable oil 5–10 minutes, until the tails are curled and heated thoroughly but not overcooked. Season to taste using salt and pepper. Set aside. In a 12-quart cast iron dutch oven, heat 1 1/2 cups oil over medium-high heat. Add flour and, using a wire whisk, stir constantly until dark brown roux is achieved. Add onions, celery, bell pepper and garlic. Saute 3–5 minutes or until vegetables are well caramelized in the roux. Stir occasionally to keep the vegetables from scorching in the hot roux. Add the tomato sauce and continue to cook 3 minutes longer. Slowly add the water, 1 quart at a time, until thick stew consistency is achieved. Add the crawfish fat, reserved drippings and bay leaves. Season the liquid lightly using salt and pepper. Bring the stock to a rolling boil, reduce to simmer and add the sauteed crawfish, including pan drippings. Allow the stew to simmer, stirring occasionally, for approximately 45 minutes. Do not allow the stew to boil. Additional liquid may be needed during the cooking process to retain volume and consistency. Once the stew is full-flavored, adjust seasonings with salt, pepper and Louisiana Gold. Add green onions, parsley and optional crawfish claws. Continue to cook until desired richness is achieved, 15–20 minutes longer. Adjust seasonings, if necessary. Serve over steamed white rice.

"I don't think anybody makes a better crawfish stew than Daddy. There is only one person who made one as good and that's the man who gave him the recipe, Uncle Paul Zeringue.

"They would spend hours at Zeringue's camp on Cabanocey Plantation preparing every imaginable dish associated with Cajun cooking. They often got us involved with the chopping of onions, celery, bell pepper, etc. and even though we would have preferred to be doing something else at the time, boy, am I thankful for those moments now!"

Jerry Folse
Laplace, Louisiana

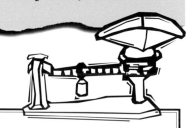

❀Nutrition Facts...then❀

Calories: 818
Total Fat: 62gm
Saturated Fat: 16gm
% Calories from Fat: 69
Cholesterol: 324mg
Sodium: 591mg
Carbohydrate: 20gm
Fiber: 2gm
Protein: 41gm

MR. ROYLEY'S CRAWFISH STEW

PREP TIME: 1 Hour   SERVES: 10

☞ INGREDIENTS:

5 pounds crawfish tails
1 cup oil-less roux
2 quarts defatted chicken stock, unsalted
2 tbsps vegetable oil
vegetable spray
2 cups diced onions
1 cup diced celery
1 cup diced bell pepper
1/4 cup chopped garlic
1 cup tomato sauce, no salt added
2 bay leaves
1/4 tsp salt
black pepper
Louisiana Gold Pepper Sauce
1 cup sliced green onions
1 cup chopped parsley

Hand-painted mural on a store front window celebrates the Etouffee Festival.

☞ METHOD:

Dissolve oil-less roux in stock. Set aside. In a 12-inch cast iron skillet, heat 2 tablespoons of vegetable oil over medium-high heat. Drain the crawfish tails well in a colander and discard the fat and natural juices. Saute tails 5–10 minutes until the tails are curled and heated thoroughly but not overcooked. Season to taste using salt and pepper. Set aside.

Coat the bottom of a 12-quart cast iron dutch oven generously with vegetable spray. Over low heat, saute onions, celery, bell pepper and garlic. Since no oil has been added, the vegetables should be turned often over the low heat until translucent and natural juices are rendered. Stir often to keep the vegetables from scorching. Add the tomato sauce and continue to cook 3 minutes longer.

Slowly add the roux/stock mixture, 1 quart at a time, until thick stew consistency is achieved. Add bay leaves and season the liquid lightly using salt and pepper. Bring the stock to a rolling boil, reduce to simmer and add crawfish. Allow the stew to simmer, stirring occasionally, for approximately 45 minutes. Do not allow the stew to boil. Additional liquid may be needed during the cooking process to retain volume and consistency.

Once the stew is full-flavored, adjust seasonings with salt, pepper and Louisiana Gold. Add green onions and parsley. Continue to cook until desired richness is achieved, 15–20 minutes longer. Adjust seasonings, if necessary. Serve over steamed white rice.

Nutrition Facts...now

Calories:	321
Total Fat:	6gm
Saturated Fat:	1gm
% Calories from Fat:	17
Cholesterol:	302mg
Sodium:	290mg
Carbohydrate:	21gm
Fiber:	2gm
Protein:	41gm

PREP TIME: 30 Minutes   SERVES: 6

INGREDIENTS:

2 pounds crawfish tails
1/2 pound butter
1 cup chopped onions
1 cup chopped celery
1/2 cup chopped red bell pepper
1/4 cup diced garlic
1/2 cup tomato sauce
1 cup heavy whipping cream
pinch of basil
pinch of thyme
1 bay leaf
1/2 cup sliced green onions
1/4 cup chopped parsley
1 tsp salt
black pepper
Louisiana Gold Pepper Sauce

METHOD:

In a 12-inch cast iron skillet, melt butter over medium-high heat. Add onions, celery, bell pepper and garlic. Saute 3–5 minutes or until vegetables are wilted. Add tomato sauce and half of the crawfish tails. Continue to saute 5–10 minutes longer or until crawfish are heated thoroughly. Add heavy whipping cream, basil, thyme and bay leaf. Bring to a rolling boil, reduce to simmer, and allow crawfish to simmer 15–20 minutes. Add green onions and parsley. Season to taste using salt, pepper and Louisiana Gold. Once the sauce is thickened and full-flavored, add the remaining crawfish tails and season to taste. The etouffee is best served over rice or pasta.

"Doralice Fontaine was a true character in Louisiana history. Not only did she teach music at LSU, but she wrote the state song, 'Give Me Louisiana.' Later on in life, she turned her beautiful home, The Fontaine House in Baton Rouge, into a catering house for weddings and receptions.
"One of her most sought-after dishes was Crawfish Etouffee, served in crepes, patty shells or over a mound of steamed white rice."

Chris Landry
Napoleonville, Louisiana

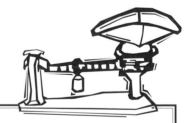

❧Nutrition Facts...then❧

Calories: 568
Total Fat: 47gm
Saturated Fat: 29gm
% Calories from Fat:................. 75
Cholesterol: 339mg
Sodium: 972mg
Carbohydrate: 7gm
Fiber: 1gm
Protein: 28gm

PREP TIME: 30 Minutes   SERVES: 6

☞ INGREDIENTS:

2 pounds crawfish tails
1 tbsp margarine
1 cup chopped onions
1 cup chopped celery
1/2 cup chopped red bell pepper
1/4 cup diced garlic
1/2 cup tomato sauce, no salt added
1 cup evaporated skim milk
pinch of basil
pinch of thyme
1 bay leaf
1/2 cup sliced green onions
1/4 cup chopped parsley
1/2 tsp salt
black pepper
Louisiana Gold Pepper Sauce

☞ METHOD:

In a 12-inch cast iron skillet, melt margarine over medium-high heat. Add onions, celery, bell pepper and garlic. Saute 3–5 minutes or until vegetables are wilted. Add tomato sauce and half of the crawfish tails. Continue to saute 5–10 minutes longer or until crawfish are heated thoroughly.

Add skim milk, basil, thyme and bay leaf. Bring to a rolling boil, reduce to simmer, and allow crawfish to simmer 15–20 minutes. Add green onions and parsley. Season to taste using salt, pepper and Louisiana Gold.

Once the sauce is thickened and full-flavored, add the remaining crawfish tails and season to taste. The etouffee is best served over rice or pasta.

Nutrition Facts...now

Calories:	212
Total Fat:	4gm
Saturated Fat:	1gm
% Calories from Fat:	18
Cholesterol:	203mg
Sodium:	424mg
Carbohydrate:	11gm
Fiber:	1gm
Protein:	30gm

BOILED CRAWFISH

PREP TIME: 2 Hours   SERVES: 12

☞ INGREDIENTS:

50 pounds cleaned crawfish
30 quarts cold water
12 medium onions, quartered
6 heads of garlic, split in half, exposing pods
1 dozen lemons, quartered
1 quart vegetable oil
4 pounds salt
1/2 pound cayenne pepper
4 (3-ounce) bags crab boil
24 medium red potatoes
12 ears of corn

☞ METHOD:

Live crawfish may be purchased already washed from your seafood supplier. However, a second rinsing in cold water would not hurt. The purging of crawfish, that is, washing the crawfish in cold salted water, has been found to be useless other than to place the animal under unnecessary stress. So forget the purging, rinsing in cold water will suffice. In a 60-quart stock pot, bring water to a rolling boil. Add onions, garlic, lemons, cooking oil, salt, pepper and crab boil and continue to boil for 30 minutes. This boiling of the vegetables will ensure a good flavor in the boiling liquid. Add red potatoes and cook approximately 10–12 minutes. Add corn and cook 10 minutes before adding the crawfish. Once the water returns to a boil, cook crawfish 7–10 minutes, turn off heat and allow the crawfish to sit in boiling liquid 12 additional minutes. Crawfish should be served hot with potatoes and corn and pitchers of iced cold beer.

"There is no place in this entire world other than south Louisiana where you can get the very best boiled crawfish. These little creatures have become a major commodity for our state with crawfish farms abundant. There is actually an art to peeling boiled crawfish, scooping out the fat, and sucking the heads. By the way, we pronounce it CRAWfish...not CRAYfish!

"A standard crawfish boil includes potatoes boiled with the crawfish, and sometimes corn on the cob and sausage. It's quite common to have a side dish of a spicy dip to use with this enjoyable meal. And...what a meal enjoyed by thousands of people! In fact, crawfish boils are an excuse to have a party!

"If you are ever in the area, look for a seafood restaurant that offers this succulent delicacy or try this wonderful recipe. Experience the pleasure of this tasty cuisine. Become a part of a Louisiana way of life and enjoy it!"
                                    Jane Arnette
                                    Houma, Louisiana

❊Nutrition Facts...then❊

Calories: 1224
Total Fat: 80gm
Saturated Fat: 11gm
% Calories from Fat: 56
Cholesterol: 302mg
Sodium: 3971mg
Carbohydrate: 89gm
Fiber: 9gm
Protein: 51gm

BOILED CRAWFISH

PREP TIME: 2 Hours   SERVES: 12

☞ INGREDIENTS:

50 pounds cleaned crawfish
30 quarts cold water
12 medium onions, quartered
6 heads of garlic, split in half, exposing pods
1 dozen lemons, quartered
1/2 cup cooking oil
1/2 pound salt
1/2 pound cayenne pepper
4 (3-ounce) bags crab boil
24 medium red potatoes
12 ears of corn

☞ METHOD:

Live crawfish may be purchased already washed from your seafood supplier. However, a second rinsing in cold water would not hurt. The purging of crawfish, that is, washing the crawfish in cold salted water, has been found to be useless other than to place the animal under unnecessary stress. So forget the purging, rinsing in cold water will suffice.

In a 60-quart stock pot, bring water to a rolling boil. Add onions, garlic, lemons, cooking oil, salt, pepper and crab boil and continue to boil for 30 minutes. This boiling of the vegetables will ensure a good flavor in the boiling liquid.

Brandon Martinez shows off one of his dad's catch at Guidry's Bait Shop in Golden Meadow.

Add red potatoes and cook approximately 10–12 minutes. Add corn and cook 10 minutes before adding the crawfish. Once the water returns to a boil, cook crawfish 7–10 minutes, turn off heat and allow the crawfish to sit in boiling liquid 12 additional minutes. Crawfish should be served hot with potatoes and corn and pitchers of iced cold beer.

Nutrition Facts...now

Calories:	663
Total Fat:	17gm
Saturated Fat:	2gm
% Calories from Fat:	21
Cholesterol:	302mg
Sodium:	842mg
Carbohydrate:	89gm
Fiber:	9gm
Protein:	51gm

Chef's Tips on Weight loss... do not skip meals. You are less likely to overeat if you are not too hungry.

287

BARBECUED SHRIMP LONGMAN

PREP TIME: 30 Minutes   SERVES: 6

☞ INGREDIENTS:

4 dozen (21-25 count) shrimp, head-on
1/2 pound butter
1/4 cup olive oil
4 cloves minced garlic
1/3 cup Worcestershire Sauce
hot sauce
1 tsp paprika
2 tsps salt
black pepper
1/4 cup chopped parsley

☞ METHOD:

Preheat oven to 350 degrees F. Place the shrimp in a large baking pan with 1-inch lip. In a 15-inch cast iron skillet, melt butter over medium-high heat. Add olive oil and, when thoroughly heated, add garlic, Worcestershire, hot sauce, paprika, salt and pepper. Blend well into the butter mixture and saute 1–2 minutes. Sprinkle in parsley and saute 1 additional minute. Pour garlic sauce over the shrimp and bake 10–12 minutes, turning shrimp occasionally. Pour shrimp and sauce into a large ceramic serving bowl and serve warm with French bread.

Chef's Tips on Weight loss... by deleting one ounce of salad dressing each day, you can lose 1 1/2 pounds each month.

"This recipe came from my mother-in-law, Ruth Levy Longman. It was one of a cookbook's worth of handwritten recipes that were part of her legacy to me.

"She was a good cook, but since she was a school teacher for 40 years in western St. Mary Parish, she didn't spend as much time in the kitchen as many do in this part of the country.

"Still, she was insistent that her husband and children had a hot lunch, so over the years, she had a succession of cooks, mostly drawn from the families of the men who worked on the Longman sugar cane farm, to come in and cook lunch for my father-in-law, Ralph Longman, Sr. and their four children. How many of her recipes were influenced by or taught to her by that parade of Cajun country cooks I can't even guess.

"My theory about this recipe, however, is that it might have been inspired by the barbecued shrimp at Pascal's Manale, the old New Orleans restaurant that's famous for them. It was one of their favorite eating places when they went to the city."

Martha Longman
Franklin, Louisiana

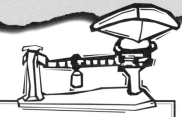

❊Nutrition Facts...then❊

Calories:	491
Total Fat:	35gm
Saturated Fat:	20gm
% Calories from Fat:	64
Cholesterol:	370mg
Sodium:	1457mg
Carbohydrate:	5gm
Fiber:	0gm
Protein:	39gm

BARBECUED SHRIMP LONGMAN

PREP TIME: 30 Minutes   SERVES: 6

☞ INGREDIENTS:

4 dozen (21–25 count) shrimp, head-on
1 tbsp lite margarine
1 tbsp olive oil
4 cloves minced garlic
1/3 cup Worcestershire Sauce
hot sauce
1 tsp paprika
1/2 tsp salt
black pepper
1/4 cup chopped parsley

☞ METHOD:

Preheat oven to 350 degrees F. Place the shrimp in a large baking pan with 1-inch lip.

In a 15-inch cast iron skillet, melt margarine over medium-high heat. Add olive oil and, when thoroughly heated, add garlic, Worcestershire, hot sauce, paprika, salt and pepper. Blend well into the margarine mixture and saute 1–2 minutes. Sprinkle in parsley and saute 1 additional minute.

Pour garlic sauce over the shrimp and bake 10–12 minutes, turning shrimp occasionally. Pour shrimp and sauce into a large ceramic serving bowl and serve warm with French bread.

Nutrition Facts...now

Calories:	233
Total Fat:	5gm
Saturated Fat:	1gm
% Calories from Fat:	22
Cholesterol:	287mg
Sodium:	637mg
Carbohydrate:	5gm
Fiber:	0gm
Protein:	39gm

PREP TIME: 2 1/2 Hours   MAKES: 80 portions

☞ INGREDIENTS:

2 1/2 pounds (70-90 count) shrimp,
    peeled and deveined
2 1/2 pounds catfish fillets
2 quarts water
1 cup butter
2 cups minced onions
1 1/2 cups minced celery
1 cup minced red bell pepper
1/4 cup diced garlic
1 cup sliced green onions
1 cup chopped parsley
2 (12-ounce) boxes corn flakes
1 cup cracker meal
1 quart mayonnaise
2 tsps salt
black pepper
80 aluminum crab shells (optional)

☞ METHOD:

In a large stock pot, bring water to a rolling boil and reduce to simmer. Place shrimp and fish in unseasoned water and cook until fish is tender, approximately 3–5 minutes. Using a slotted spoon or strainer, remove fish and shrimp. Set aside. Reserve the stock for later use. In a 3-quart cast iron dutch oven, melt butter over medium-high heat. Add onions, celery, bell pepper and garlic. Saute 3–5 minutes or until vegetables are wilted. Add green onions and parsley. Saute an additional 2–3 minutes. In the bowl of a food processor, place the shrimp, fish and sauteed vegetables. Pulse 2–3 minutes or until finely chopped. Place the chopped mixture in the hot stock. Add corn flakes and cracker meal. Mix the seasonings and seafood well into the stock. The mixture should resemble a breaded seafood stuffing. Add mayonnaise, salt and pepper. Continue to blend until all is incorporated and adjust seasonings, if necessary. If mixture tends to be a little loose, more cracker meal may be added. Stuff the filling into the crab shells or roll into seafood patties. Place in ziplock bags and freeze for later use or bake at 350 degrees F 10–15 minutes or until thoroughly heated.

"Mr. Leo Streva created this recipe in the late 1950s. He had a wonderful little grocery store and meat market where he developed this recipe and sold the product. Samples of the dish were submitted to a large seafood distributor who was so impressed with the taste that they wanted to take the recipe national.

"They shocked Mr. Leo by wanting 12,000-30,000 pieces per week for the initial roll out. Since Mr. Streva was not geared to producing such large quantities, he abandoned the idea but continued to sell his famous seafood dish in the grocery store for many years.

"I remember creating this dish in 1961 for a large American Legion banquet and everyone raved over the wonderful 'stuffed crab' dish! I never admitted that the recipe had no crab in it at all. This recipe should be made in quantity for the freezer or divided up among your friends."

Leo Streva
Morgan City, Louisiana

❊Nutrition Facts...then❊

Calories: 161
Total Fat: 12gm
Saturated Fat: 3gm
% Calories from Fat: 65
Cholesterol: 43mg
Sodium: 246mg
Carbohydrate: 9gm
Fiber: 1gm
Protein: 5gm

PREP TIME: 2 1/2 Hours   MAKES: 80 portions

☞ INGREDIENTS:

2 1/2 pounds (70–90 count) shrimp,
        peeled and deveined
2 1/2 pounds catfish fillets
2 quarts water
1/4 cup margarine
2 cups minced onions
1 1/2 cups minced celery
1 cup minced red bell pepper
1/4 cup diced garlic
1 cup sliced green onions
1 cup chopped parsley
2 (12-ounce) boxes corn flakes
1 cup cracker meal
1 quart lite mayonnaise
salt substitute
black pepper
80 aluminum crab shells (optional)

☞ METHOD:

In a large stock pot, bring water to a rolling boil and reduce to simmer. Place shrimp and fish in unseasoned water and cook until fish is tender, approximately 3–5 minutes. Using a slotted spoon or strainer, remove fish and shrimp. Set aside. Reserve the stock for later use.

In a 3-quart cast iron dutch oven, heat margarine over medium-high heat. Add onions, celery, bell pepper and garlic. Saute 3–5 minutes or until vegetables are wilted. Add green onions and parsley. Saute an additional 2–3 minutes.

In the bowl of a food processor, place the shrimp, fish and sauteed vegetables. Pulse 2–3 minutes or until finely chopped. Place the chopped mixture in the hot stock. Add corn flakes and cracker meal. Mix the seasonings and seafood well into the stock. The mixture should resemble a breaded seafood stuffing.

Add mayonnaise, salt substitute and pepper. Continue to blend until all is incorporated and adjust seasonings, if necessary. If mixture tends to be a little loose, more cracker meal may be added. Stuff the filling into the crab shells or roll into seafood patties. Place in ziplock bags for later use and freeze, or bake at 350 degrees F 10–15 minutes or until thoroughly heated.

Nutrition Facts...now

Calories:	97
Total Fat:	4gm
Saturated Fat:	1gm
% Calories from Fat:	37
Cholesterol:	36mg
Sodium:	133mg
Carbohydrate:	10gm
Fiber:	1gm
Protein:	5gm

PREP TIME: 1 Hour   SERVES: 8

☞ INGREDIENTS:

5 pounds (50–60 count) shrimp, peeled and deveined
1 (16-ounce) package spaghetti, cooked
1/2 cup vegetable oil
1/2 cup pancake mix
2 cups chopped onions
1/4 cup chopped bell pepper
1 tbsp minced garlic
1 (10-ounce) can Rotel tomatoes
2 (6-ounce) cans tomato paste
2 tbsps Worcestershire sauce
5 cups water
1 tsp celery salt
1 tsp salt
black pepper
1 cup sliced green onions
1/4 cup chopped parsley

☞ METHOD:

In a 2-gallon stock pot, heat oil over medium-high heat. Add pancake mix and, using a wire whisk, stir until dark brown roux is achieved. Add onions, bell pepper and garlic. Saute 3–5 minutes or until vegetables are wilted. Add Rotel and tomato paste, blending well into the roux mixture. Cook 2–3 minutes, stirring occasionally. Add Worcestershire sauce and water. Blend well to create a slightly thickened tomato sauce. Bring to a rolling boil, reduce to simmer and add half of the shrimp. Bring back to simmer and stirring occasionally, cook 30–45 minutes. Season the sauce to taste using celery salt, salt and pepper. Add green onions, parsley and the remaining shrimp. Cook 5–10 minutes longer and serve over hot spaghetti.

Raymond Perilloux cleans the morning catch in Lake Des Allemands.

"From my earliest memories of growing up, this was a dish Mama fixed for us. It was the only spaghetti sauce she made that was based on a roux, but that's what made this one special.
"Using pancake mix in the roux, rather than flour was unusual, but you certainly can't fault the results. Mama is no longer with us, but I think of her every time I fix this recipe."

Carol Benoit
Morgan City, Louisiana

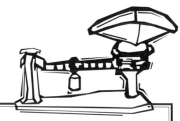

❧Nutrition Facts...then❧

Calories: 640
Total Fat: 18gm
Saturated Fat: 3gm
% Calories from Fat: 25
Cholesterol: 437mg
Sodium: 1634mg
Carbohydrate: 62gm
Fiber: 4gm
Protein: 57gm

MAMA'S SHRIMP SPAGHETTI

PREP TIME: 1 Hour   SERVES: 8

☞ INGREDIENTS:

5 pounds (50–60 count) shrimp, peeled and deveined
1 (16-ounce) package spaghetti, cooked
2 tbsps vegetable oil
1/2 cup pancake mix
2 cups chopped onions
1/4 cup chopped bell pepper
1 tbsp minced garlic
1 (10-ounce) can Rotel tomatoes
2 (6-ounce) cans tomato paste, no salt added
2 tbsps Worcestershire sauce
5 cups water
1/2 tsp celery salt
salt substitute
black pepper
1 cup sliced green onions
1/4 cup chopped parsley

☞ METHOD:

In a 2-gallon stock pot, heat oil over medium-high heat. Add 1/4 cup pancake mix and, using a wire whisk, stir until dark brown roux is achieved. Add remaining mix to roux and continue to stir until well-blended.

Add onions, bell pepper and garlic. Saute 3–5 minutes or until vegetables are wilted. Add Rotel and tomato paste, blending well into the roux mixture. Cook 2–3 minutes,

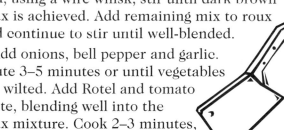

A Vietnamese fisherman puts the final touches on a shrimp boat before the season begins.

stirring occasionally.

Add Worcestershire sauce and water. Blend well to create a slightly thickened tomato sauce. Bring to a rolling boil, reduce to simmer and add half of the shrimp. Bring back to simmer and, stirring occasionally, cook 30–45 minutes.

Season the sauce to taste using celery salt, salt substitute and pepper. Add green onions, parsley and the remaining shrimp. Cook 5–10 minutes longer and serve over hot spaghetti.

Nutrition Facts...now

Calories:	551
Total Fat:	7gm
Saturated Fat:	1gm
% Calories from Fat:	12
Cholesterol:	437mg
Sodium:	929mg
Carbohydrate:	61gm
Fiber:	4gm
Protein:	58gm

PREP TIME: 1 Hour   SERVES: 6

☞ INGREDIENTS:

1 cup dried shrimp
5 medium size potatoes
1 cup vegetable oil
1 cup flour
2 cups diced onions
1/2 cup diced celery
1 cup diced bell pepper
1/4 cup chopped garlic
2 quarts water
8 boiled eggs, halved
1 cup sliced green onions
1/2 cup chopped parsley
3 tsps salt
cayenne pepper

☞ METHOD:

Peel and dice potatoes into 1-inch cubes. Set aside. In a 7-quart cast iron dutch oven, heat oil over medium-high heat. Sprinkle in flour and, using a wire whisk, stir constantly until dark brown roux is achieved. Add onions, celery, bell pepper and garlic. Saute 3–5 minutes or until vegetables are wilted. Soak shrimp in 1 cup water for 30 minutes and then discard water. After sauteing vegetables, add water until stew-like consistency is achieved. Blend well with a whisk until smooth. Add shrimp and cook for 30 minutes. Add potatoes and cook an additional 15 minutes. Add eggs, green onions and parsley and allow to cook an additional 10 minutes. Season to taste using salt and pepper.

"Prior to refrigeration, the best way to preserve shrimp was to dry them in the sun - a skill the early Cajun settlers learned from the Indians. Dried shrimp, packed in little cellophane bags, were sold in every grocery store in the bayou country when I was growing up, and are still widely available today.

"The distinctive flavor of these dried shrimp was enjoyed in everything from spaghetti sauce to this favorite dish of my mother. They have a more concentrated, stronger shrimp taste than fresh shrimp. So, for flavor, a cup of dried shrimp is about like a pound of fresh shrimp.

"Knowing that might come in handy if you live in some other part of the country. In our travels, and talking to relatives who have moved out of South Louisiana, we've learned that dried shrimp simply aren't to be found elsewhere."

Elaine Guillory
Opelousas, Louisiana

❧ Nutrition Facts...then ☙

Calories: 862
Total Fat: 57gm
Saturated Fat: 11gm
% Calories from Fat: 62
Cholesterol: 781mg
Sodium: 1322mg
Carbohydrate: 48gm
Fiber: 4gm
Protein: 39gm

PREP TIME: 1 Hour   SERVES: 6

☞ INGREDIENTS:

1 cup dried shrimp
1 cup oil-less roux
1 quart water
5 medium size potatoes
1 tbsp vegetable oil
2 cups diced onions
1/2 cup diced celery
1 cup diced bell pepper
1/4 cup chopped garlic
1 quart water
3 boiled eggs, halved
1 cup sliced green onions
1/2 cup chopped parsley
1 tsp salt
cayenne pepper

☞ METHOD:

Dissolve roux in 1 quart of water. Set aside. Peel and dice potatoes into 1-inch cubes. Set aside.

In a 7-quart cast iron dutch oven, heat oil over medium-high heat. Add onions, celery, bell pepper and garlic. Saute 3–5 minutes or until vegetables are wilted.

Soak shrimp in 1 cup water for 30 minutes and then discard water. After sauteing vegetables, add roux/stock mixture and 1 quart of water until stew-like consistency is achieved. Blend well with a whisk until smooth.

Add shrimp and cook for 30 minutes. Add potatoes and cook an additional 15 minutes. Add eggs, green onions and parsley and allow to cook an additional 10 minutes. Season to taste using salt and pepper.

Chef's Tips on Weight loss... forfeit three chocolate bars a week and in a month be one pound lighter.

Nutrition Facts...now

Calories: 385
Total Fat: 11gm
Saturated Fat: 3gm
% Calories from Fat: 27
Cholesterol: 293mg
Sodium: 471mg
Carbohydrate: 47gm
Fiber: 4gm
Protein: 25gm

BAKED SHRIMP

PREP TIME: 1 Hour   SERVES: 6

☞ INGREDIENTS:

5 pounds (50 count) shrimp, unpeeled
1 pound butter
4 medium onions
2 stalks of celery
2 bell peppers
10 cloves of garlic
8 carrots, cleaned
6 medium potatoes, skin-on
1 bunch green onions
1 lemon, sliced
2 tsps salt
black pepper
cayenne pepper

☞ METHOD:

Preheat oven to 450 degrees F. Cut all vegetables into 1-inch cubes. Set aside. In a 7-quart cast iron dutch oven, melt butter over medium-high heat. Add onions, celery, bell pepper and garlic. Saute 3–5 minutes or until vegetables are wilted. Add carrots and potatoes, blending well into the vegetable mixture. Saute 3–5 additional minutes. Remove from heat and set aside. In a baking container large enough to hold the shrimp, add approximately 1/4 of the vegetable/butter mixture. Top with 1/4 of the shrimp, green onions and lemons. Season to taste using salt and peppers. Continue the process with equal layers of shrimp, vegetables and seasonings until all is used up. Pour any excess butter or juices over the shrimp and place the pan on the center oven rack. Bake 25–30 minutes, stirring every 15 minutes to blend the seasonings and shrimp. Serve equal portions of the shrimp and vegetables in soup bowls with hot French bread.

"This may not be the oldest Cajun recipe in the world (I created it about 15 years ago as an alternative to the traditional boiled shrimp). But it is definitely Cajun in concept, as well as content and taste.

"Food, down here in the Louisiana bayou country, comes close to being a state religion - as much ceremony as sustenance - and it's generally a social occasion.

"Since the shrimp are baked in their shells, the family shrimp boil tradition of sitting around the table peeling shrimp as you eat them is preserved. And it takes about an hour to prepare, so there's ample time for hanging around the kitchen visiting with the cook!"

Kay Walker Mabile
Bourg, Louisiana

❧Nutrition Facts...then❧

Calories: 1121
Total Fat: 65gm
Saturated Fat: 39gm
% Calories from Fat: 51
Cholesterol: 749mg
Sodium: 2063mg
Carbohydrate: 67gm
Fiber: 9gm
Protein: 69gm

BAKED SHRIMP

PREP TIME: 1 Hour   SERVES: 6

☞ INGREDIENTS:

5 pounds (50 count) shrimp, unpeeled
1/2 cup lite margarine
4 medium onions
2 stalks of celery
2 bell peppers
10 cloves of garlic
8 carrots, cleaned
6 medium potatoes, skin-on
1 bunch green onions
1 lemon, sliced
salt substitute
black pepper
cayenne pepper

☞ METHOD:

Preheat oven to 450 degrees F. Cut all vegetables into 1-inch cubes. Set aside.

In a 7-quart cast iron dutch oven, melt margarine over medium-high heat. Add onions, celery, bell pepper and garlic. Saute 3–5 minutes or until vegetables are wilted. Add carrots and potatoes, blending well into the vegetable mixture. Saute 3–5 additional minutes. Remove from heat and set aside.

In a baking container large enough to hold the shrimp, add approximately 1/4 of the vegetable/margarine mixture. Top with 1/4 of the shrimp, green onions and lemons. Season to taste using salt substitute and peppers. Continue the process with equal layers of shrimp, vegetables and seasonings until all is used up. Pour any excess margarine or juices over the shrimp and place the pan on the center oven rack. Bake 25–30 minutes, stirring every 15 minutes to blend the seasonings and shrimp.

Serve equal portions of the shrimp and vegetables in soup bowls with hot French bread.

Nutrition Facts...now

Calories:	647
Total Fat:	11gm
Saturated Fat:	2gm
% Calories from Fat:	16
Cholesterol:	583mg
Sodium:	904mg
Carbohydrate:	67gm
Fiber:	9gm
Protein:	69gm

PREP TIME: 1 Hour   SERVES: 6

☞ INGREDIENTS:

3 dozen oysters	1/4 cup diced garlic
2 cups oyster liquid	1 tsp salt
4 tbsps vegetable oil	black pepper
4 tbsps flour	1/4 cup sliced green onions
1 cup diced onions	1/4 cup chopped parsley
1/2 cup diced celery	2 (9-inch) prepared pie crusts

☞ METHOD:

Preheat oven to 375 degrees F. In a 3-quart cast iron dutch oven, heat oil over medium-high heat. Add flour and, using a wire whisk, stir until golden brown roux is achieved. Add onions, celery and garlic. Blend well into the roux mixture and slowly add the oyster liquid, 1 cup at a time, until thick sauce consistency is achieved. As liquid comes to a boil, the sauce will continue to thicken. Dilute with remaining oyster liquid as necessary to retain consistency. Bring to a rolling boil, reduce heat to simmer and cook 15–20 minutes. While sauce is cooking, line the bottom of a pie pan with one of the pastry crusts. Press it well into the pan, reserving the second sheet. Season the sauce with salt and pepper. Add the oysters, blending well into the sauce mixture, until oysters begin to curl slightly. Add green onions and parsley. Once oysters have cooked 5–10 minutes, remove from heat and allow to cool slightly. Ladle the oyster stew into the pie crust and top with the second layer. Seal the edges of the top and bottom crusts. Prick with a fork to create steam holes and bake until golden brown, approximately 20 minutes.

"As far as I know this recipe is unique. I've never seen another recipe for oyster pie, nor have I ever seen it on a restaurant menu. I got it from my Aunt Minnie - Bernadette Hymel Dugas - but whether she invented it or had it handed down to her from an older relative, I don't know. And since she and all of her contemporaries are gone now, I suppose we'll never know. It did appear in print once before - in the Ladies Altar Society Cookbook in Donaldsonville many years ago. Oh, well. A little mystery just adds its own spice to a recipe, I suppose.

"I associate it with my growing-up years in the little fishing village of Delcambre back in the '40s and '50s. That was classic small-town America - if you overlook the fact that a lot of people still spoke Cajun French as a first language, and did their harvesting in the Gulf of Mexico rather than a Midwestern wheat or corn field.

"But no one locked their doors and people sat out on screened porches in the evening and visited with neighbors, going in and out of each other's houses as casually as they entered rooms of their own.

"I suppose today's youngsters would consider us deprived, since the one movie house in town was only open on Thursday and Sunday evening and Saturday afternoon, and the only place for teenagers to go was Doris' Place - a classic '50s short order restaurant with a jukebox as its big attraction. They just don't know what they missed."

Peggy Vice
New Iberia, Louisiana

❧Nutrition Facts...then❧

Calories:	389
Total Fat:	25gm
Saturated Fat:	6gm
% Calories from Fat:	57
Cholesterol:	20mg
Sodium:	1032mg
Carbohydrate:	33gm
Fiber:	1gm
Protein:	8gm

PREP TIME: 1 Hour   SERVES: 6

☞ INGREDIENTS:

3 dozen oysters
2 cups oyster liquid
5 tbsps oil-less roux
1 tbsp vegetable oil
1 cup diced onions
1/2 cup diced celery
1/4 cup diced garlic
1/4 tsp salt
black pepper
1/4 cup sliced green onions
1/4 cup chopped parsley
2 (9-inch) prepared pie crusts

☞ METHOD:

Preheat oven to 375 degrees F. Dissolve oil-less roux in 2 cups oyster liquid. Set aside. In a 3-quart cast iron dutch oven, heat oil over medium-high heat. Add onions, celery and garlic. Saute 3–5 minutes or until vegetables are wilted.

Pour in roux/liquid mixture. Bring to a rolling boil, stirring constantly, and cook 3–5 minutes.

While sauce is cooking, line the bottom of a pie pan with one of the pastry crusts. Press it well into the pan, reserving the second sheet. Season the sauce with salt and pepper. Add the oysters, blending well into the sauce mixture, until oysters begin to curl slightly. Add green onions and parsley.

Once oysters have cooked 5–10 minutes, remove from heat and allow to cool slightly. Ladle the oyster stew into the pie crust and top with the second layer. Seal the edges of the top and bottom crusts. Prick with a fork to create steam holes. Bake until golden brown, approximately 20 minutes.

Nutrition Facts...now

Calories:	329
Total Fat:	18gm
Saturated Fat:	5gm
% Calories from Fat:	49
Cholesterol:	20mg
Sodium:	766mg
Carbohydrate:	33gm
Fiber:	1gm
Protein:	9gm

PREP TIME: 1 Hour   SERVES: 6

☞ INGREDIENTS:

2 dozen raw oysters
1 cup all purpose flour
3 tbsps baking powder
1/3 cup milk
2 eggs, beaten
1/4 cup minced onions
1 tbsp minced garlic
1 tbsp chopped parsley
1/2 tsp salt
cayenne pepper
oil for deep frying

☞ METHOD:

Place vegetable oil into a deep fryer and preheat according to manufacturer's directions. If using a cast iron dutch oven, add approximately 2 inches of oil to the pot and heat to 350 degrees F. In a large mixing bowl, sift flour and baking powder together. In a separate bowl, whip the milk and eggs. Add to flour and stir well to incorporate. Coarsely chop the oysters and add them to the flour mixture, along with the onions, garlic, parsley, salt and pepper. Continue to stir the batter until ingredients are well-blended. Once oil is hot, drop the batter into the oil in tablespoon-size fritters. Fry until golden brown and fritters float. When done, drain on a paper towel and serve with tartar or remoulade sauce.

Chef's Tips on Weight loss... cutting out six strips of bacon a week will help you lose an additional 1 1/4 pound in a month.

"When I was a little girl, right after World War I, we made our living harvesting oysters. During oyster season, we lived in a camp on an island across Lake Pelto from Whiskey Bay. You might say the living conditions were a little crowded. We had two bedrooms for my parents and nine kids, at that time.

"Of course, we never lacked for plenty of fresh oysters, but the trick was to keep coming up with new ways to fix them. The oyster fritters were my favorite.

"We had three or four chickens for eggs and a washtub in which we planted parsley and green onions for seasoning.

"It doesn't sound like a lot, but we were very self-sufficient. We only went to "make groceries" once a month. And you'd better not forget anything because the grocery run took three days - a day to get to town, a day for shopping and a day to get back!"

Leontine Callais
Cut Off, Louisiana

❈Nutrition Facts...then❈

Calories:	318
Total Fat:	21gm
Saturated Fat:	3gm
% Calories from Fat:	60
Cholesterol:	61mg
Sodium:	356mg
Carbohydrate:	24gm
Fiber:	1gm
Protein:	8gm

PREP TIME: 1 Hour   SERVES: 6

Arma Spears tells stories that go way back while passing time fishing Bayou Lafourche.

☞ INGREDIENTS:

2 dozen raw oysters
1 cup all purpose flour
3 tbsps baking powder
1/3 cup skim milk
1/2 cup egg substitute
1/4 cup minced onions
1 tbsp minced garlic
1 tbsp chopped parsley
1/4 tsp salt
cayenne pepper
1/4 cup oil for deep frying
vegetable spray

☞ METHOD:

In a large mixing bowl, sift flour and baking powder together. In a separate bowl, whip the skim milk and egg substitute. Add to flour and stir well to incorporate.

Coarsely chop the oysters and add them to the flour mixture, along with the onions, garlic, parsley, salt and pepper. Continue to stir the batter until ingredients are well-blended. Place oil in 12-inch cast iron skillet over medium heat. Drop batter in tablespoon-size portions into skillet.

Spray top of fritter with vegetable spray and cook 3 minutes. Turn fritter and fry until golden brown on all sides. When done, drain on a paper towel and serve with lite tartar or remoulade sauce.

Nutrition Facts...now

Calories:	236
Total Fat:	11gm
Saturated Fat:	2gm
% Calories from Fat:	43
Cholesterol:	20mg
Sodium:	292mg
Carbohydrate:	24gm
Fiber:	1gm
Protein:	9gm

GEORGE'S STUFFED FLOUNDER

PREP TIME: 1 Hour   SERVES: 6

☞ INGREDIENTS:

6 (1-pound) flounders, cleaned
1 pound jumbo lump crabmeat
1 1/2 cups (90–110 count) shrimp,
     peeled and deveined
1/4 pound butter
1/2 cup minced onions
1/2 cup minced celery
1/4 cup minced bell pepper
1/4 cup minced garlic
1/4 cup sliced green onions
1 tsp salt
black pepper
1/8 tsp chopped thyme
1/4 cup chopped parsley
1 egg
1 cup seasoned Italian
     bread crumbs
3/4 cup white wine
1/4 cup melted butter
6 lemon slices
paprika for color

☞ METHOD:

Preheat oven to 375 degrees F. Scale the flounders completely, clean the stomach cavity and rinse under cold water. The head and eyes may be removed or left intact, depending on preference. Using a sharp paring knife, cut a pocket in the center of the dark side of the flounder from head to tail. Following the rib cage, continue with the paring knife to create a cavity for the stuffing. In a 12-inch cast iron skillet, melt butter over medium-high heat. Add onions, celery, bell pepper, garlic and green onions. Saute 3–5 minutes or until vegetables are wilted. Add crabmeat and shrimp, blend well into the vegetable mixture and cook until shrimp are pink and curled. Do not overcook. Season with salt, pepper and thyme. Once the shrimp are done, remove the stuffing mixture to a large bowl and allow it to cool slightly. Add parsley, egg and enough bread crumbs to absorb the moisture and hold the stuffing together. Adjust seasonings if necessary. Stuff the pocket on each flounder with an equal amount of the mixture. You may wish to over-stuff in order to use all of the stuffing. Place the stuffed flounders in a large baking pan with 1-inch lip. Pour in wine and top each flounder with melted butter, a lemon slice and paprika for color. Bake for approximately 30 minutes or until stuffing is thoroughly heated. The flounders may be stuffed well in advance and frozen for later use.

"The flounder is a flat, bottom-dwelling fish, and the way we catch them comes as quite a surprise to folks from other parts of the country who think of fishing as purely a rod-and-reel affair.

"When we want fresh flounder, my wife and I go out to the Isles Dernieres, the "Last Islands," the little barrier islands between the tip of Terrebonne Parish and the Gulf of Mexico. After sundown, we walk out into the shallows on the ocean side with barbed spears and lanterns and move along parallel to the beach, looking for flounders on the bottom.

"I don't know why they come into the shallows at night like that. Maybe it's to feed. Maybe it's to avoid predators. Whatever it is, they obviously don't take into account the existence of Cajuns with fishing spears, Coleman lanterns and a recipe for stuffed flounder!

"If necessary, you can also buy fresh flounder at the supermarket. But it's not nearly as much fun."
     George Bourgeois
     Houma, Louisiana

❋Nutrition Facts...then❋

Calories: 803
Total Fat: 31gm
Saturated Fat: 16gm
% Calories from Fat: 35
Cholesterol: 366mg
Sodium: 2321mg
Carbohydrate: 17gm
Fiber: 1gm
Protein: 104gm

PREP TIME: 1 Hour   SERVES: 6

☞ INGREDIENTS:

6 (1/2-pound) flounders, cleaned
1 pound jumbo lump crabmeat
1 cup (90–110 count) shrimp, peeled and deveined
2 tbsps lite margarine
1/2 cup minced onions
1/2 cup minced celery
1/4 cup minced bell pepper
1/4 cup minced garlic
1/4 cup sliced green onions
salt substitute
black pepper
1/8 tsp chopped thyme
1/4 cup chopped parsley
1/2 cup egg substitute
1 cup plain bread crumbs
3/4 cup white wine
2 tbsps lite margarine
6 lemon slices
paprika for color

☞ METHOD:

Preheat oven to 375 degrees F. Scale the flounders completely, clean the stomach cavity and rinse under cold water. The head and eyes may be removed or left intact, depending on preference. Using a sharp paring knife, cut a pocket in the center of the dark side of the flounder from head to tail. Following the rib cage, continue with the paring knife to create a cavity for the stuffing.

In a 12-inch cast iron skillet, melt margarine over medium-high heat. Add onions, celery, bell pepper, garlic and green onions. Saute 3–5 minutes or until vegetables are wilted. Add crabmeat and shrimp, blend well into the vegetable mixture and cook until shrimp are pink and curled. Do not overcook. Season with salt substitute, pepper and thyme.

Once the shrimp are done, remove the stuffing mixture to a large bowl and allow it to cool slightly. When cool, add parsley, egg substitute and enough bread crumbs to absorb the moisture and hold the stuffing together. Adjust seasonings, if necessary.

Stuff the pocket on each flounder with an equal amount of the mixture. You may wish to overstuff in order to use all of the stuffing. Place the stuffed flounders in a large baking pan with 1-inch lip. Pour in wine and top each flounder with melted margarine, a lemon slice and paprika for color.

Bake for approximately 30 minutes or until stuffing is thoroughly heated. The flounders may be stuffed well in advance and frozen for later use.

Nutrition Facts...now

Calories:	398
Total Fat:	9gm
Saturated Fat:	2gm
% Calories from Fat:	21
Cholesterol:	143mg
Sodium:	884mg
Carbohydrate:	16gm
Fiber:	1gm
Protein:	55gm

PREP TIME: 1 Hour   SERVES: 6

☞ INGREDIENTS:

2 pounds redfish fillets
1/2 cup vegetable oil
1/2 cup flour
1 cup diced onions
1 cup diced celery
1 cup diced bell pepper
1/4 cup diced garlic
1 (16-ounce) can diced tomatoes, in liquid
3 quarts water
1/4 cup Worcestershire sauce
1/2 cup sliced green onions
1/4 cup chopped parsley
1 tsp salt
black pepper
3 lemon slices

☞ METHOD:

If you are lucky enough to have the bones of the fish, you should make a stock by boiling the fish bones with 1–2 quarts of water, 1 diced onion, 1 bay leaf and 1 tablespoon of black peppercorns. Simmer the fish stock for 30 minutes, strain and use it in place of water in this recipe. Fish bouillon cubes, available at your local grocery store, are also a good substitute. Slice the fish fillets into 1 1/2-inch thick pieces. In a 7-quart cast iron dutch oven, heat oil over medium-high heat. Add flour and, using a wire whisk, stir until dark brown roux is achieved. Add onions, celery, bell pepper and garlic. Saute 3–5 minutes or until vegetables are wilted. Add tomatoes and blend well into the roux mixture. Add water or fish stock and Worcestershire. Bring to a rolling boil, reduce to simmer and cook for 30 minutes, adding water or stock as necessary to retain volume and consistency. Add green onions and parsley. Season to taste using salt and pepper. Add the fish fillets and lemon slices, being careful not to break the fish as they simmer in the stock. Cook 5–10 minutes. When fish is done, adjust seasonings if necessary. Serve the rich sauce over bowls of steamed white rice.

"This recipe comes from one of my more colorful relatives, Aunt Lydia Escudier. Aunt Lydia was an avid sports fisherman and hunter at a time - the 1930s and 1940s - when that sort of thing was pretty rare for a city girl, even in Cajun country. (Okay, so Lafayette wasn't exactly a huge metropolis back then - or now, for that matter. But it was - and is - the biggest town in Acadiana.)

"As a result of her enthusiasm, she had a lot of recipes for fish and game. And this was one of my favorites. So I asked her for the recipe. Like a lot of good cooks, Aunt Lydia's recipes were "a pinch of this, a bit of that". Getting the recipe meant watching her prepare the dish and making notes as we went along. But it was certainly worth it!"

L.R. Stagg
Lafayette, Louisiana

❋ Nutrition Facts...then ❋

Calories:	404
Total Fat:	20gm
Saturated Fat:	3gm
% Calories from Fat:	46
Cholesterol:	56mg
Sodium:	817mg
Carbohydrate:	19gm
Fiber:	3gm
Protein:	35gm

PREP TIME: 1 Hour   SERVES: 6

INGREDIENTS:

2 pounds redfish fillets
1 cup oil-less roux
1 quart water
1 tbsp vegetable oil
1 cup diced onions
1 cup diced celery
1 cup diced bell pepper
1/4 cup diced garlic
1 (16-ounce) can diced tomatoes,
        in liquid, no salt added
2 quarts water
1/4 cup Worcestershire sauce
1/2 cup sliced green onions
1/4 cup chopped parsley
1/2 tsp salt
black pepper
3 lemon slices

METHOD:

Dissolve oil-less roux in 1 quart of the water. Set aside. If you are lucky enough to have the bones of the fish, you should make a stock by boiling the fish bones with 1–2 quarts of water, 1 diced onion, 1 bay leaf and 1 tablespoon of black peppercorns. Simmer the fish stock for 30 minutes, strain and use it in place of water in this recipe.

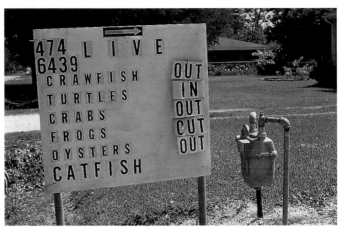

Louisiana's seafood bounty is temporarily out at this roadside market, except for turtles; they're in.

Slice the fish fillets into 1 1/2-inch thick pieces. In a 7-quart cast iron dutch oven, heat oil over medium-high heat. Add onions, celery, bell pepper and garlic. Saute 3–5 minutes or until vegetables are wilted. Add tomatoes and blend well into the vegetable mixture. Add roux/water mixture and Worcestershire. Bring to a rolling boil, reduce to simmer and cook for 30 minutes. Add remaining water, a little at a time, to maintain a soup-like consistency.

Add green onions and parsley. Season to taste using salt and pepper. Add the fish fillets and lemon slices, being careful not to break the fish as they simmer in the stock. Cook 5–10 minutes. When fish is done, adjust seasonings if necessary. Serve the rich sauce over bowls of steamed white rice.

Chef's Tips on Weight loss... you can cut out a lot of calories and just a little food by avoiding fats, sugars, sweets and alcohol.

Nutrition Facts...now

Calories:	290
Total Fat:	5gm
Saturated Fat:	1gm
% Calories from Fat:	15
Cholesterol:	56mg
Sodium:	397mg
Carbohydrate:	25gm
Fiber:	2gm
Protein:	36gm

PREP TIME: 1 Hour   SERVES: 6

☞ INGREDIENTS:

6 (6-ounce) trout fillets
1/4 pound butter
1/4 cup sliced green onions
1/4 cup chopped parsley
1 tbsp minced garlic
1/2 pound crawfish tails
4 tbsps flour
2 cups water
1/4 cup red wine
1 tsp salt
cayenne pepper
Louisiana Gold Pepper Sauce
juice of one lemon

☞ METHOD:

Preheat oven to 350 degrees F. In a 5-quart cast iron dutch oven, melt butter over medium-high heat. Add green onions, parsley and garlic. Saute 3–5 minutes or until vegetables are wilted. Add crawfish tails, blend well into the vegetable mixture and saute until crawfish are thoroughly heated. Sprinkle in flour and blend well to form a blonde roux. Slowly add the water and red wine until etouffee-type sauce is achieved. Bring to a rolling boil, reduce to simmer and cook 5–10 minutes. Add salt, pepper, Louisiana Gold and lemon juice. Remove from heat and adjust seasonings if necessary. In the bottom of a Pyrex-type baking dish, place the fillets of trout. Top with the Albert Sauce, cover and bake 20–25 minutes or until trout is perfectly done. Remove to a serving plate and garnish with fresh parsley.

"Growing up in Donaldsonville, we became accustomed to eating catfish and perch more often than any other seafood. Somewhere along the way, speckled trout from the Gulf of Mexico became available even as far inland as Ascension Parish.

"This recipe is excellent using any species of firm white-flesh fish. You may wish to try the Albert sauce over grilled chicken or veal."
Paul Bouchereau
Metairie, Louisiana

❧Nutrition Facts...then❧

Calories: 392
Total Fat: 22gm
Saturated Fat: 11gm
% Calories from Fat: 51
Cholesterol: 178mg
Sodium: 595mg
Carbohydrate: 5gm
Fiber: 0gm
Protein: 41gm

PREP TIME: 1 Hour   SERVES: 6

☞ INGREDIENTS:

6 (6-ounce) trout fillets
1 tbsp lite margarine
1/4 cup sliced green onions
1/4 cup chopped parsley
1 tbsp minced garlic
1/2 pound crawfish tails
4 tbsps flour
2 cups water
1/4 cup red wine
1/2 tsp salt
cayenne pepper
Louisiana Gold Pepper Sauce
juice of one lemon

☞ METHOD:

Preheat oven to 350 degrees F. In a 5-quart cast iron dutch oven, melt margarine over medium-high heat. Add green onions, parsley and garlic. Saute 3–5 minutes or until vegetables are wilted. Add crawfish tails, blend well into the vegetable mixture and saute until crawfish are thoroughly heated.

Sprinkle in flour and blend well to form a blonde roux. Slowly add water and red wine until etouffee-type sauce is achieved. Bring to a rolling boil, reduce to simmer and cook 5–10 minutes.

Add salt, pepper, Louisiana Gold and lemon juice. Remove from heat and adjust seasonings, if necessary.

In the bottom of a Pyrex-type baking dish, place the fillets of trout. Top with the Albert Sauce, cover and bake 20–25 minutes or until trout is perfectly done. Remove to a serving plate and garnish with fresh parsley.

Nutrition Facts...now

Calories:	236
Total Fat:	6gm
Saturated Fat:	1gm
% Calories from Fat:	26
Cholesterol:	121mg
Sodium:	252mg
Carbohydrate:	4gm
Fiber:	0gm
Protein:	36gm

Wild Game

Chapter Eight

Baked Stuffed Rabbit	312/313
Baked Rabbit in Burgundy Sauce	314/315
Fricassee of Wild Rabbit	316/317
Venison Sauce Piquante	318/319
Venison Roast	320/321
Venison Pie	322/323
Rack of Venison with Muscadine Glaze	324/325
Venison Mince Meat	326/327
Squirrel Jambalaya	328/329
Smothered Squirrel in Pan Gravy	330/331
Sauteed Quail Crosby	332/333
Dove & Wild Rice Casserole	336/337
Sherried Doves	338/339
Louisiana Mallards in Mandarin Glaze	340/341
Glenda's Apple-Roasted Duck	342/343
Uncle Paul's Woodcock	344/345
Baked Goose Holly Beach	346/347
Baked Wild Turkey with Muscadine Jus	348/349
Stewed Turtle Creole	350/351
Alligator Patties	352/353

BAKED STUFFED RABBIT

PREP TIME: 2 1/2 Hours   SERVES: 8

☞ INGREDIENTS:

4 pounds cleaned wild rabbit
1 1/2 pounds ground chuck
1 pint raw oysters
3 cups diced onions
2 cups diced celery
1 1/2 cups diced red bell pepper
1/4 cup chopped garlic
3/4 cup oil
1/2 cup flour
2 cups sliced green onions
1 cup chopped parsley
4 carrots, diced
6 cups beef or chicken stock
1/2 tsp salt
black pepper
hot sauce

"Growing up in Southwest Louisiana, I soon learned that beagle dogs and rabbit hunting were simply a way of life. Many rainy days were spent around the dinner table hearing stories of the hunt, told by my father. Soon my job was to help load the dogs from their kennel when it was time to hunt. I can also remember vividly the lonesome howls of those beagles as the night train whistle sounded in the darkness.

"When I married - you guessed it - it was to a hunter. He wanted me to participate in the rabbit hunts and naturally being adventuresome, I went along. I soon became a pretty good shot and killed my share of rabbits. I remember once, my husband lost his job for about six months and we would go rabbit hunting to put food on the table. We cooked so many rabbit dishes during this time that the term "hop to bed" had a whole new meaning for our children. I was always looking for new rabbit recipes. This one was given to me by my veterinarian's wife, who told me it came from her grandmother."
Linda Neal
Welsh, Louisiana

☞ METHOD:

Preheat oven to 350 degrees F. Wash rabbits well inside and out under cold running water and set aside to drain. In a large mixing bowl, combine ground chuck and raw oysters. Place half of the onions, celery, bell pepper and garlic into the meat mixture and blend well to create a stuffing. Season to taste using salt, pepper and hot sauce. Once rabbits have drained well, season inside and out with salt, pepper and hot sauce. Stuff the inside of the rabbits with the stuffing mixture until all is used. In the bottom of a large roaster, heat oil over medium-high heat. Add flour and, using a wire whisk, stir constantly until dark brown roux is achieved. Add all of the remaining seasonings and carrots. Saute 2–3 minutes until vegetables are wilted. Add stock and blend well into the roux mixture to create the braising liquid. Place the stuffed rabbits in the vegetable mixture, cover and bake 2 hours or until rabbits are tender and stuffing is thoroughly cooked. You may need to add a little additional stock during the cooking process should sauce become too thick. Once rabbits are tender, remove cover and allow rabbits to brown thoroughly in oven an additional 10–15 minutes, if necessary.

❦Nutrition Facts...then❦

Calories: 756
Total Fat: 40gm
Saturated Fat: 9gm
% Calories from Fat: 48
Cholesterol: 249mg
Sodium: 1143mg
Carbohydrate: 22gm
Fiber: 4gm
Protein: 74gm

PREP TIME: 2 1/2 Hours   SERVES: 8

☞ INGREDIENTS:

4 pounds cleaned wild rabbit
1 1/2 pounds extra lean ground meat
1 pint raw oysters
3 cups diced onions
2 cups diced celery
1 1/2 cups diced red bell pepper
1/4 cup chopped garlic
1 tbsp oil
1/2 cup flour
2 cups sliced green onions
1 cup chopped parsley
4 carrots, diced
6 cups defatted beef or chicken stock, unsalted
1/4 tsp salt
black pepper
hot sauce

☞ METHOD:

Preheat oven to 350 degrees F. Wash rabbits well inside and out under cold running water and set aside to drain.

In a large mixing bowl, combine ground meat and raw oysters. Place half of the onions, celery, bell pepper and garlic into the meat mixture and blend well to create a stuffing. Season to taste using salt, pepper and hot sauce.

Once rabbits have drained well, season inside and out with salt, pepper and hot sauce. Stuff the inside of the rabbits with the stuffing mixture until all is used.

In the bottom of a large roaster, heat oil over medium-high heat. Add flour and, using a wire whisk, stir constantly until dark brown roux is achieved. Add all of the remaining seasonings and carrots. Saute 2–3 minutes until vegetables are wilted. Add stock and blend well into the roux mixture to create the braising liquid.

Place the stuffed rabbits in the vegetable mixture, cover and bake 2 hours or until rabbits are tender and stuffing is thoroughly cooked. You may need to add a little additional stock during the cooking process should sauce become too thick.

Once rabbits are tender, remove cover and allow rabbits to brown thoroughly in oven an additional 10–15 minutes, if necessary.

*Chef's Tips on Weight Loss...
drink plenty of water to
eliminate that hungry feeling.*

Nutrition Facts...now

Calories: 580
Total Fat: 19gm
Saturated Fat: 6gm
% Calories from Fat: 30
Cholesterol: 236mg
Sodium: 583mg
Carbohydrate: 22gm
Fiber: 3gm
Protein: 77gm

PREP TIME: 5 Hours   SERVES: 6

☞ INGREDIENTS:

2 (1 1/2-pound) young
      rabbits, quartered
4 cups Burgundy wine
2 cups diced apples
4 cloves
2 bay leaves
8 peppercorns
1 large onion, diced

1 tbsp tarragon
1 tbsp thyme
1/4 pound butter
1 cup diced onions
1/2 cup diced celery
4 diced shallots
1/4 cup diced garlic
1 cup sliced mushrooms

1 cup chicken stock
4 cups reserved marinade
1 cup sliced green onions

2 tsps salt
black pepper
cayenne pepper

"Burgundy and Zinfandel seem to have been the preferred wines of the antebellum plantation owners. Although over the years we got away from using wine in much of our cooking, Burgundy survived in many of our wild game dishes.
"Like Coq Au Vin (chicken with wine), rabbit with wine is often seen on our table during hunting season. I guess this is one of those hold overs from the old French culture in bayou country. I love to cook this simple country dish."
      Dr. Michel Hirsch
      Donaldsonville, Louisiana

Dale Bihm presents a tray of his rabbit fryers.

☞ METHOD:

In a large ceramic bowl, marinate rabbits in wine, apples, cloves, bay leaves, peppercorns, large onion, tarragon and thyme. Blend well with the rabbit and allow to sit at room temperature for 2–3 hours. Preheat oven to 375 degrees F. Once rabbits are marinated, remove and pat dry. Strain and reserve the marinade for later use. In a 12-quart cast iron dutch oven, heat butter over medium-high heat. Add rabbit and brown lightly on all sides. Remove and keep warm. In the same pot, add remaining onions, celery, shallots, garlic and mushrooms. Saute 3–5 minutes or until vegetables are wilted. Add chicken stock and reserved marinade. Bring to a rolling boil and reduce to simmer. Add rabbit and green onions. Season to taste using salt and peppers. Cover, place in oven and cook 1–1 1/2 hours or until rabbit is tender.

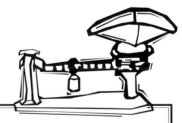

❋Nutrition Facts...then❋

Calories: 638
Total Fat: 29gm
Saturated Fat: 14gm
% Calories from Fat: 40
Cholesterol: 173mg
Sodium: 1238mg
Carbohydrate: 22gm
Fiber: 3gm
Protein: 48gm

BAKED RABBIT IN BURGUNDY SAUCE

PREP TIME: 5 Hours   SERVES: 6

☞ INGREDIENTS:

2 (1 1/2-pound) young rabbits, quartered
4 cups Burgundy wine
2 cups diced apples
4 cloves
2 bay leaves
8 peppercorns
1 large onion, diced
1 tbsp tarragon
1 tbsp thyme
2 tbsps margarine
1 cup diced onions
1/2 cup diced celery
4 diced shallots
1/4 cup diced garlic
1 cup sliced mushrooms
1 cup defatted chicken stock, unsalted
4 cups reserved marinade
1 cup sliced green onions
1/2 tsp salt
black pepper
cayenne pepper

Visitors to the Crawfish Festival in Breaux Bridge are treated to a tantalizing selection of Louisiana specialties in St. Martin Parish.

☞ METHOD:

In a large ceramic bowl, marinate rabbits in wine, apples, cloves, bay leaves, peppercorns, large onion, tarragon and thyme. Blend well with the rabbit and allow to sit at room temperature for 2–3 hours. Preheat oven to 375 degrees F.

Once rabbits are marinated, remove and pat dry. Strain and reserve the marinade for later use.

In a 12-quart cast iron dutch oven, heat margarine over medium-high heat. Add rabbit and brown lightly on all sides. Remove and keep warm.

In the same pot, add remaining onions, celery, shallots, garlic and mushrooms. Saute 3–5 minutes or until vegetables are wilted. Add chicken stock and reserved marinade. Bring to a rolling boil and reduce to simmer.

Add rabbit and green onions. Season to taste using salt and peppers. Cover, place in oven and cook 1–1 1/2 hours or until rabbit is tender.

Nutrition Facts...now

Calories: 535
Total Fat: 17gm
Saturated Fat: 5gm
% Calories from Fat: 29
Cholesterol: 128mg
Sodium: 490mg
Carbohydrate: 22gm
Fiber: 3gm
Protein: 48gm

PREP TIME: 2 Hours   SERVES: 6

☞ INGREDIENTS:

2 (2-pound) wild rabbits
3/4 cup oil
2 cups flour
2 cups chopped onions
1 cup chopped celery
1 cup chopped bell pepper
2 tbsps diced garlic
1 cup diced tomatoes
2 cups sliced oyster mushrooms
6 cups beef or chicken stock
1 cup sliced green onions
1/4 cup chopped parsley
1 tsp salt
black pepper

☞ METHOD:

Cut each rabbit into 6 serving-size pieces. In a 3-gallon cast iron pot, heat oil over medium-high heat. Season rabbits well with salt and pepper. Dredge in flour and brown well on all sides in hot oil. Once rabbit is browned, remove and set aside. In the same oil, add onions, celery, bell pepper, garlic and tomatoes. Saute 3–5 minutes or until vegetables are wilted. Return rabbit to pot and stir well into seasonings. Add mushrooms and beef stock. Adjust seasonings if necessary. Bring the stock to a low boil and reduce heat to simmer. Cover pot and allow to braise for 1 1/2 hours. Rabbit will be done when tender to the touch. Add stock if necessary during the cooking process, should mixture become too dry. Add green onions and parsley and adjust seasonings if necessary. Cook 5 additional minutes. This dish should be served over hot white rice that's been covered with good ole' white beans.

"One good thing about growing up on a sugar plantation in South Louisiana was that there was always lots of good food. Most of it came to us in the form of produce from the garden and wild game from the surrounding bayou country.

"I raised eight children on Cabanocey Plantation, and just about everything in the refrigerator either had wings or webbed feet. Whenever things got a little lean in the pantry, I could always walk out the back door and count on finding a dozen or so rabbits feeding at the edge of the field. Naturally, we had many good recipes, but this fricassee was one of our favorites."
                    Royley Folse, Jr.
                    St. James, Louisiana

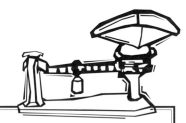

❦Nutrition Facts...then❦

Calories: 779
Total Fat: 35gm
Saturated Fat: 6gm
% Calories from Fat: 41
Cholesterol: 245mg
Sodium: 529mg
Carbohydrate: 41gm
Fiber: 3gm
Protein: 72gm

PREP TIME: 2 Hours   SERVES: 6

INGREDIENTS:

2 (2-pound) wild rabbits
2 tbsps oil
2 cups flour
2 cups chopped onions
1 cup chopped celery
1 cup chopped bell pepper
2 tbsps diced garlic
1 cup diced tomatoes
2 cups sliced oyster mushrooms
6 cups defatted beef or chicken stock, unsalted
1 cup sliced green onions
1/4 cup chopped parsley
1/4 tsp salt
black pepper

METHOD:

Cut each rabbit into 6 serving-size pieces. In a 3-gallon cast iron pot, heat oil over medium-high heat. Season rabbits well with salt and pepper. Dredge in flour and brown well on all sides in hot oil. Once rabbit is browned, remove and set aside.

In the same oil, add onions, celery, bell pepper, garlic and tomatoes. Saute 3–5 minutes or until vegetables are wilted.

Return rabbit to pot and stir well into seasonings. Add mushrooms and beef stock. Adjust seasonings if necessary. Bring the stock to a low boil and reduce heat to simmer. Cover pot and allow to braise for 1 1/2 hours.

Rabbit will be done when tender to the touch. Add stock, if necessary during the cooking process, should mixture become too dry. Add green onions and parsley and adjust seasonings if necessary. Cook 5 additional minutes.

This dish should be served over hot white rice that's been covered with good ole' white beans.

Nutrition Facts...now

Calories:	595
Total Fat:	12gm
Saturated Fat:	3gm
% Calories from Fat:	19
Cholesterol:	245mg
Sodium:	327mg
Carbohydrate:	41gm
Fiber:	3gm
Protein:	76gm

PREP TIME: 3 Hours   SERVES: 8

☞ INGREDIENTS:

5 pounds cubed venison roast
1 1/2 cups vegetable oil
2 cups flour
3 cups diced onions
1/2 cup diced celery
1 cup diced bell pepper
1/4 cup chopped garlic
1 (15-ounce) can tomato sauce
1 (10-ounce) can Rotel tomatoes
1 cup sliced mushrooms
4 quarts water
3 lemon slices
1/2 cup sliced green onions
1/4 cup chopped parsley
3 tsps salt
cayenne pepper
black pepper
Louisiana Gold Pepper Sauce

☞ METHOD:

In a large mixing bowl, combine cubed venison with salt, peppers and Louisiana Gold. Toss to blend seasonings completely. In a 12-quart cast iron dutch oven, heat oil over medium-high heat. Add flour and, using a wire whisk, stir constantly until dark brown roux is achieved. Add onions, celery, bell pepper and garlic. Saute 3–5 minutes or until vegetables are wilted. Add venison, blending well into the roux mixture. Cook 5–10 minutes, stirring occasionally. Add tomato sauce, Rotel tomatoes and mushrooms. Add approximately 2 quarts of water, blending well into the roux mixture. Bring to a rolling boil and reduce to simmer. Add additional hunter stock as necessary to achieve a sauce-like consistency. Add lemon slices, cover, and cook for approximately 2 hours or until venison is tender. You should stir the pot well at 15–20 minute intervals to avoid sticking. More stock may be needed as the venison cooks. Once meat is tender, add green onions and parsley. Cook 5 additional minutes and serve over steamed white rice or pasta.

"'Piquante' comes from the French and the Spanish cultures and refers to the spiciness of a dish. Naturally in Louisiana, many of our wild game dishes tend to be a little spicy since most were created by the hunters in their swampland camps.

"I have come to realize the importance of a good hunter stock when cooking my wild game dishes. Often, we tend to throw away the bones and trimmings when butchering wild game. These are really the most important ingredients to the great finish of a dish.

"Brown the bones and trimmings in the oven for 20-30 minutes to get that great color, and then place the browned ingredients in a stock pot. Add about 2-3 quartered onions, 1 stick of celery, 1 carrot and season lightly with salt, pepper and bay leaf. Bring to a boil, reduce to low simmer and cook for about 3-4 hours, skimming occasionally. Use this wonderful stock in the place of water in your wild game recipes."

Jerry Folse
Laplace, Louisiana

❧Nutrition Facts...then❧

Calories: 867
Total Fat: 48gm
Saturated Fat: 8gm
% Calories from Fat: 50
Cholesterol: 237mg
Sodium: 1410mg
Carbohydrate: 38gm
Fiber: 4gm
Protein: 70gm

PREP TIME: 3 Hours   SERVES: 8

INGREDIENTS:

5 pounds cubed venison roast
2 tbsps vegetable oil
1 1/2 cups oil-less roux
1 quart water
3 cups diced onions
1/2 cup diced celery
1 cup diced bell pepper
1/4 cup chopped garlic
1 (15-ounce) can tomato sauce, no salt added
1 (10-ounce) can Rotel tomatoes
1 cup sliced mushrooms
2 quarts water
3 lemon slices
1/2 cup sliced green onions
1/4 cup chopped parsley
1/2 tsp salt
cayenne pepper
black pepper
Louisiana Gold Pepper Sauce

Chef's Tips on Weight Loss... try eating slowly and putting your fork down between mouthfuls. Chew each mouthful 20 times before swallowing.

METHOD:

Dissolve oil-less roux in 1 quart of water and set aside.

In a large mixing bowl, combine cubed venison with salt, peppers and Louisiana Gold. Toss to blend seasonings completely.

In a 12-quart cast iron dutch oven, heat oil over medium-high heat. Add onions, celery, bell pepper and garlic. Saute 3–5 minutes or until vegetables are wilted.

Add venison and blend well into the vegetable mixture. Cook 5–10 minutes, stirring occasionally. Add tomato sauce, Rotel tomatoes and mushrooms. Add roux/water mixture, one ladle at a time, until all is incorporated. Add approximately 2 quarts water, blending well. Bring to a rolling boil and reduce to simmer. Add additional water as necessary to achieve a sauce-like consistency.

Add lemon slices, cover, and cook for approximately 2 hours or until venison is tender. You should stir the pot well at 15–20 minute intervals to avoid sticking. More stock may be needed as the venison cooks.

Once meat is tender, add green onions and parsley. Cook 5 additional minutes and serve over steamed white rice or pasta.

Nutrition Facts...now

Calories:	512
Total Fat:	11gm
Saturated Fat:	3gm
% Calories from Fat:	19
Cholesterol:	237mg
Sodium:	425mg
Carbohydrate:	32gm
Fiber:	3gm
Protein:	69gm

PREP TIME: 3 Hours   SERVES: 8

☞ INGREDIENTS:

1 (3-pound) venison roast
20 garlic cloves
1/2 cup finely sliced green onions
6 strips of bacon
1 cup Worcestershire sauce
1/4 cup vegetable oil

2 cups diced onions
1/2 cup diced celery
1/4 cup diced red bell pepper
1/4 cup chopped garlic
1 cup dry red wine
6 cups beef stock

2 cups sliced mushrooms
4 red potatoes, quartered
6 carrots, sliced
3 tsps salt
black pepper
Louisiana Gold Pepper Sauce

☞ METHOD:

Preheat oven to 350 degrees F. Using a paring knife, slice garlic into slivers and place in a mixing bowl with green onions. Cut the bacon strips into 1/4-inch pieces and mix with the green onions and garlic. Place 1 teaspoon each of salt and pepper into the mixture and blend well. Using a paring knife, cut approximately 15 one-inch slits in the roast for stuffing. Divide the garlic/bacon mixture equally and press firmly into the 15 slits. Place the stuffed roast in a large Ziploc bag and pour in the Worcestershire sauce. Marinate in the refrigerator overnight, turning the bag from time to time. In a 3-gallon cast iron dutch oven, heat oil over medium-high heat. Remove roast from bag and season with remaining salt, pepper and Louisiana Gold. Brown roast well on all sides. Remove from pot and set aside. Add onions, celery, bell pepper and garlic to the pot. Saute 3–5 minutes or until vegetables are wilted. Return roast to the pot and add red wine, beef stock and mushrooms. Cover and bake roast for 2 hours, checking every 30 minutes and adding stock if necessary. Add potatoes and carrots, cover and cook until vegetables are tender. Remove roast from the pot and, when cool enough, slice into serving pieces. Return the slices to the pot and allow to marinate in gravy 20–30 minutes before serving.

"My mother and father were great cooks, but game wasn't served often in our home. Coming from the Alsace region of France, they moved here to South Louisiana after World War II. Before long, game found its place on our new American table.

"After marrying into the Folse family, I became a true lover of wild game dishes. Today, many of my best moments are spent in the kitchen cooking up another test batch of a new game delicacy similar to my venison roast."

Dr. Michel Hirsch
Donaldsonville, Louisiana

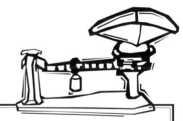

❧ Nutrition Facts...then ❧

Calories: 449
Total Fat: 14gm
Saturated Fat: 4gm
% Calories from Fat: 29
Cholesterol: 146mg
Sodium: 1983mg
Carbohydrate: 28gm
Fiber: 4gm
Protein: 48gm

(calculations on 3 pound roast)

PREP TIME: 3 Hours   SERVES: 8

☞ INGREDIENTS:

1 (3-pound) venison roast
20 garlic cloves
1/2 cup finely sliced green onions
6 strips of turkey bacon
1 cup low-sodium Worcestershire sauce
2 tbsps vegetable oil
2 cups diced onions
1/2 cup diced celery
1/4 cup diced red bell pepper
1/4 cup chopped garlic
1 cup dry red wine
6 cups defatted beef stock, unsalted
2 cups sliced mushrooms
4 red potatoes, quartered
6 carrots, sliced
1/2 tsp salt
black pepper
Louisiana Gold Pepper Sauce

☞ METHOD:

Preheat oven to 350 degrees F. Using a paring knife, slice garlic into slivers and place in a mixing bowl with green onions.

Cut the turkey bacon strips into 1/4-inch pieces and mix with the green onions and garlic. Place 1/4 teaspoon of salt and pepper into the mixture and blend well.

Using a paring knife, cut approximately 15 one-inch slits in the roast for stuffing. Divide the garlic/bacon mixture equally and press firmly into the 15 slits. Place the stuffed roast in a large Ziploc bag and pour in the Worcestershire sauce. Marinate in the refrigerator overnight, turning the bag from time to time.

In a 3-gallon cast iron dutch oven, heat oil over medium-high heat. Remove roast from bag and season with remaining salt, pepper and Louisiana Gold. Place roast in bottom of dutch oven and brown well on all sides. Remove and set aside.

Add onions, celery, bell pepper and garlic. Saute 3–5 minutes or until vegetables are wilted. Return roast to the pot and add red wine, beef stock and mushrooms. Cover and bake roast for 2 hours, checking every 30 minutes and adding stock if necessary. Add potatoes and carrots, cover and cook until vegetables are tender.

Remove roast from the pot and, when cool enough, slice into serving pieces. Return the slices to the pot and allow to marinate in gravy 20–30 minutes before serving.

Nutrition Facts...now	
Calories:	419
Total Fat:	10gm
Saturated Fat:	3gm
% Calories from Fat:	23
Cholesterol:	149mg
Sodium:	579mg
Carbohydrate:	30gm
Fiber:	4gm
Protein:	48gm

(calculations on 3 pound roast)

PREP TIME: 2 1/2 Hours   SERVES: 6

☞ INGREDIENTS:

1 1/2 pounds lean cubed venison	1 tsp chopped thyme	2 tsps sugar
2 tbsps bacon fat	3 cups rich chicken or beef stock	1 tbsp baking powder
1 tsp salt	4 carrots, diced	1/2 tsp salt
cayenne pepper	1/4 cup diced celery	3/4 cup milk
2 cups diced onions	2 cups tiny English peas	3 tbsps vegetable oil
1/4 cup diced garlic	1 cup flour	1 whole egg, beaten
2 cups diced tomatoes	3/4 cup yellow corn meal	

☞ METHOD:

Preheat oven to 425 degrees F. In a 12-inch cast iron skillet, heat bacon fat over medium-high heat. Season meat thoroughly using salt and cayenne pepper. Brown venison in bacon fat. Add onions and garlic. Saute 3–5 minutes or until vegetables are wilted. Add tomatoes, thyme and chicken stock. Bring to a rolling boil, reduce to simmer and cover. Cook 1–1 1/2 hours or until venison is tender. Add carrots, celery and peas, blending well into the sauce. Cook 5–10 minutes longer. In a large mixing bowl, combine flour, corn meal, sugar, baking powder and salt. When blended, add milk, oil and egg into the mixing bowl. Mix thoroughly and spoon over the venison stew. Bake 25–30 minutes or until topping has cooked thoroughly and browned evenly. The topping should resemble that of a homemade cobbler.

The old bell of St. James Catholic Church has called parishioners to one of Acadiana's oldest parishes; it was founded in 1757.

"I am a transplanted Cajun, having been born and reared in the Great Lakes Country of Wisconsin. I came to South Louisiana after accepting a chef's position at the Fairmont Hotel in New Orleans.

"You cannot exist here in Bayou country without a freezer full of wild game, especially if you plan to exist here with a Cajun girl from French Settlement. My wife's family, the Mathernes, were not only great deer hunters, but they sure knew how to prepare the meat. From sausage making to venison pies, I think they create some of the best dishes in Cajun country."

Louis Jesowshek
French Settlement, Louisiana

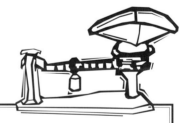

❧ Nutrition Facts...then❧

Calories:	524
Total Fat:	18gm
Saturated Fat:	5gm
% Calories from Fat:	30
Cholesterol:	148mg
Sodium:	1351mg
Carbohydrate:	56gm
Fiber:	7gm
Protein:	37gm

VENISON PIE

PREP TIME: 2 1/2 Hours   SERVES: 6

☞ INGREDIENTS:

1 1/2 pounds lean cubed venison
vegetable spray
1/4 tsp salt
cayenne pepper
2 cups diced onions
1/4 cup diced garlic
2 cups diced tomatoes
1 tsp chopped thyme
3 cups defatted chicken or beef stock, unsalted
4 carrots, diced
1/4 cup diced celery
2 cups tiny English peas
1 cup flour
3/4 cup yellow corn meal
2 tsps sugar
1 tbsp baking powder
salt substitute
3/4 cup skim milk
1 tbsp vegetable oil
2 egg whites, beaten

☞ METHOD:

Preheat oven to 425 degrees F. Spray a 12-inch cast iron skillet with vegetable spray and place over medium-high heat. Season meat thoroughly using salt and cayenne pepper. Brown venison in skillet. Add onions and garlic. Saute 3–5 minutes or until vegetables are wilted.

Add tomatoes, thyme and chicken stock. Bring to a rolling boil, reduce to simmer and cover. Cook 1–1 1/2 hours or until venison is tender. Add carrots, celery and peas, blending well into the sauce. Cook 5–10 minutes longer.

In a large mixing bowl, combine flour, corn meal, sugar, baking powder and salt substitute. When blended, add skim milk, oil and egg whites into the mixing bowl. Mix thoroughly and spoon over the venison stew. Bake 25–30 minutes or until topping has cooked thoroughly and browned evenly.

The topping should resemble that of a homemade cobbler.

Eric Soileau makes his boudin at the Country Store in Vidrine in Evangeline Parish.

Nutrition Facts...now

Calories:	433
Total Fat:	7gm
Saturated Fat:	2gm
% Calories from Fat:	14
Cholesterol:	99mg
Sodium:	588mg
Carbohydrate:	56gm
Fiber:	6gm
Protein:	39gm

PREP TIME: 2 Hours   SERVES: 8

☞ INGREDIENTS:

6 (4-bone) racks of venison
1 cup fresh muscadines
1/2 cup melted butter
1/2 tsp dried thyme
1/2 tsp dried basil
1/2 tsp dried rosemary
2 tbsps dried tarragon
3 tbsps minced garlic
3 tsps salt
black pepper
1/4 cup vegetable oil
2 (10 1/2-ounce) cans beef consomme

☞ METHOD:

Preheat oven to 400 degrees F. In a large baking pan, spread venison racks evenly. Top each rack with an equal amount of the butter and rub to coat evenly. Sprinkle each rack with a generous amount of the dried seasonings, garlic, salt and pepper. Once again, using your hands, rub the seasonings into the racks. Allow to sit at room temperature for 1 hour. In a 12-inch cast iron skillet, heat vegetable oil over medium-high heat. Brown the racks, 1 or 2 at a time, until golden brown on all sides. As the racks are cooked, return them to the baking pan. In the same skillet, place the muscadines and beef consomme. Bring to a low boil and cook until volume has reduced by 1/2 and consistency is slightly thickened. While the sauce is simmering, bake the venison racks approximately 15 minutes for medium rare or 20 minutes for medium. When meat is cooked to your liking and the sauce is properly thickened, strain it to remove the muscadine pulp. Keep warm. Slice 3–4 venison chops onto each plate and top with the muscadine glaze.

"As a young man, I loved hunting in Pointe Coupee Parish with my grandfather, Paul Frank Caciabauda. I'll never forget the day he taught me how to select the ripest wild muscadines off the vines. While hunting, we would eat these for a little treat, but mostly we would bring them home to cook with the venison.

"Most hunters would remove the tenderloin or backstrap from the rib cage and take this home as a prize cut. My grandfather would leave the rib bones and loin intact and cook the chops as his masterpiece in the kitchen. This is still my favorite today."

Paul Bailey
Port Allen, Louisiana

Chef's Tips on Weight Loss... learn to stop eating before you are full.

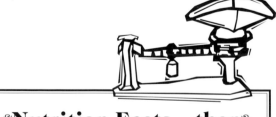

❧ Nutrition Facts...then ❧

Calories: 372
Total Fat: 22gm
Saturated Fat: 9gm
% Calories from Fat: 54
Cholesterol: 149mg
Sodium: 1314mg
Carbohydrate: 8gm
Fiber: 1gm
Protein: 34gm

RACK OF VENISON WITH MUSCADINE GLAZE

PREP TIME: 2 Hours   SERVES: 8

☞ INGREDIENTS:

6 (4-bone) racks of venison
1 cup fresh muscadines
1/2 cup lite margarine
1/4 cup dried thyme
1/4 cup dried basil
1/4 cup dried rosemary
2 tbsps dried tarragon
3 tbsps minced garlic
1 tsp salt
black pepper
vegetable spray
2 (10 1/2-ounce) cans defatted beef consomme,
          unsalted

☞ METHOD:

Preheat oven to 400 degrees F. In a large baking pan, spread venison racks evenly. Top each rack with an equal amount of margarine and rub to coat evenly. Sprinkle each rack with a generous amount of the dried seasonings, garlic, salt and pepper. Once again, using your hands, rub the seasonings into the racks. Allow to sit at room temperature for 1 hour.

Spray a 12-inch cast iron skillet with vegetable spray and place over medium-high heat. Brown the racks, 1 or 2 at a time, until golden brown on all sides. As the racks are cooked, return them to the baking pan.

In the same skillet, place the muscadines and beef consomme. Bring to a low boil and cook until volume has reduced by 1/2 and consistency is slightly thickened.

While the sauce is simmering, bake the venison racks approximately 15 minutes for medium rare or 20 minutes for medium. When meat is cooked to your liking and the sauce is properly thickened, strain it to remove the muscadine pulp. Keep warm. Slice 3–4 venison chops onto each plate and top with the muscadine glaze.

Nutrition Facts...now

Calories:	259
Total Fat:	10gm
Saturated Fat:	2gm
% Calories from Fat:	34
Cholesterol:	118mg
Sodium:	478mg
Carbohydrate:	8gm
Fiber:	1gm
Protein:	35gm

PREP TIME: 6 Hours   MAKES: 6 pounds – 48 (2-ounce) servings

☞ INGREDIENTS:

6 pounds cubed venison
1 bay leaf
8 whole cloves
8 peppercorns
1 small cinnamon stick
3 cups apple cider
1 cup cider vinegar
2 gallons water
8 pounds chopped apples

2 pounds currants
2 pounds raisins
1 pound citron
1 lemon chopped
2 pounds chopped suet
6 pounds brown sugar
1 tsp cinnamon
1 tbsp allspice
1 tsp cloves

1/2 ounce mace
2 tsps salt
4 cups dry sherry
1 cup Cognac
3 quarts reserved venison stock

Route 27 south of Sulphur, along the Creole Nature Trail on the way to Holly Beach.

☞ METHOD:

In a large stock pot, combine venison, bay leaf, cloves, peppercorns, cinnamon stick, apple cider, cider vinegar and enough water to cover by 4 inches. Bring to a rolling boil, reduce to simmer and cook 1 1/2–2 hours or until meat is very tender. Strain and reserve 3 quarts of the liquid. When meat is cooled, shred it and set aside. In a large double boiler or stock pot, add all remaining ingredients with venison, except reserved stock. Ladle in enough of the stock to cover the ingredients by 1/8-inch. Cook over the double boiler for 4 hours or until mixture is quite thick and resembles a pie filling. You may pack the mince meat in sterile jars, following approved canning procedures, or place in the refrigerator 7–10 days. This venison mince meat is excellent in pies or cookies.

> "My husband, Bob, is an architect and I am a special education teacher. Often Bob likes to get away from his drawing board and head into the woods near San Angelo, Texas, for a deer hunt. His Thanksgiving season hunt with a group of his friends has become a tradition over the years.
> "Whenever their outings are successfull, which is often, they split the bounty evenly. Many will make roast or sausage out of their share, but I like to experiment a little. One of my favorite creations is venison mince meat which I later turn into pies or cookies."
>
> Nell Hardy
> Rayne, Louisiana

❉ Nutrition Facts...then ❉

Calories:	683
Total Fat:	21gm
Saturated Fat:	10gm
% Calories from Fat:	28
Cholesterol:	68mg
Sodium:	174mg
Carbohydrate:	106gm
Fiber:	4gm
Protein:	15gm

VENISON MINCE MEAT

PREP TIME: 6 Hours   MAKES: 6 pounds – 48 (2-ounce) servings

☞ INGREDIENTS:

6 pounds cubed venison
1 bay leaf
8 whole cloves
8 peppercorns
1 small cinnamon stick
3 cups apple cider
1 cup cider vinegar
2 gallons water
8 pounds chopped apples
2 pounds currants
2 pounds raisins
1 pound citron
1 lemon chopped
1 cup vegetable oil
3 pounds brown sugar
1 tsp cinnamon
1 tbsp allspice
1 tsp cloves
1/2 ounce mace
2 tsps salt
4 cups dry sherry
1 cup Cognac
3 quarts reserved venison stock

Paul Hulin and his stepson, John Vicknair, show off their tasty Nite Owl brand of pickled quail eggs.

Nutrition Facts...now

Calories:	447
Total Fat:	6gm
Saturated Fat:	1gm
% Calories from Fat:	13
Cholesterol:	47mg
Sodium:	162mg
Carbohydrate:	79gm
Fiber:	4gm
Protein:	15gm

☞ METHOD:

In a large stock pot, combine venison, bay leaf, cloves, peppercorns, cinnamon stick, apple cider, cider vinegar and enough water to cover by 4 inches. Bring to a rolling boil, reduce to simmer and cook 1 1/2–2 hours or until meat is very tender. Strain and reserve 3 quarts of the liquid. When meat is cooled, shred it and set aside.

In a large double boiler or stock pot, add all remaining ingredients with venison, except reserved stock. Ladle in enough of the stock to cover the ingredients by 1/8-inch. Cook over the double boiler for 4 hours or until mixture is quite thick and resembles a pie filling.

You may then pack the mince meat in sterile jars, following approved canning procedures, or place in the refrigerator 7–10 days. This venison mince meat is excellent in pies or cookies.

SQUIRREL JAMBALAYA

PREP TIME: 1 Hour   SERVES: 8

☞ INGREDIENTS:

5 (1/2-pound) squirrels, cleaned
2 tbsps Cajun seasoning
Louisiana Gold Pepper Sauce
1 tbsp Worcestershire sauce
3 tsps salt
cayenne pepper
1/4 cup white vinegar
1/4 cup cooking oil
2 cups diced onions
1/2 cup diced celery
1/4 cup chopped garlic
6 cups water
3 cups long grain rice, uncooked
1/2 cup sliced green onions
1/2 cup chopped parsley

☞ METHOD:

Cut each squirrel into 8 serving pieces and rinse thoroughly under cold running water. Once squirrels are well drained, place in a large mixing bowl and season with Cajun seasoning, Louisiana Gold, Worcestershire, salt, pepper and vinegar. Blend well to distribute seasonings. In a 3-gallon cast iron pot, heat oil over medium-high heat. Add seasoned squirrel and cook until golden brown on all sides and there is good color in the bottom of the pot. The squirrels should be cooked approximately 25 minutes so that they will be brown enough to color the finished jambalaya. Add onions, celery and garlic. Saute 3–5 minutes or until vegetables are wilted. Add water and bring to a rolling boil. Cover and allow the squirrel to simmer until tender, approximately 30 minutes. Stir in rice and adjust seasonings if necessary. NOTE: Remember that the rice will absorb all of the flavoring, so you should make sure that there is enough salt and pepper for the finished taste. Reduce heat to simmer, cover and cook 15 minutes. Remove lid, add green onions and parsley. Do not stir. Cover and cook 15 additional minutes. Prior to serving, stir well to incorporate the green seasonings.

"When I was a young boy growing up on Cabanocey Plantation in St. James Parish, one of my greatest loves was hunting. We lived right on the edge of the swamp, and there were many varieties of game available back in the 1950s and 1960s.

"Squirrel hunting was probably the most difficult for a young boy because anybody who ever hunted squirrels knows that you have to sit very quietly under a tree without moving for hours at a time.

"How I remember walking home with a rope tied around my waist and a dozen or more squirrels hanging down like a skirt. As I walked down the railroad track, everybody would yell to find out about my secret hunting place...of course, I'd never tell."
                    Royley Folse, Jr.
                    St. James, Louisiana

❧Nutrition Facts...then❧

Calories: 509
Total Fat: 12gm
Saturated Fat: 2gm
% Calories from Fat: 22
Cholesterol: 118mg
Sodium: 2016mg
Carbohydrate: 61gm
Fiber: 2gm
Protein: 36gm

PREP TIME: 1 Hour   SERVES: 8

☞ INGREDIENTS:

5 (1/2-pound) squirrels, cleaned
2 tbsps salt-free Cajun seasoning
Louisiana Gold Pepper Sauce
1 tbsp Worcestershire sauce
1 tsp salt
cayenne pepper
1/4 cup white vinegar
2 tbsps cooking oil
2 cups diced onions
1/2 cup diced celery
1/4 cup chopped garlic
6 cups water
3 cups long grain rice, uncooked
1/2 cup sliced green onions
1/2 cup chopped parsley

*Chef's Tips on Weight Loss...
a gradual weight loss of one or
two pounds a week is best. Fast
weight loss can be harmful.*

☞ METHOD:

Cut each squirrel into 8 serving pieces and rinse thoroughly under cold running water. Once squirrels are well drained, place in a large mixing bowl and season with Cajun seasoning, Louisiana Gold, Worcestershire, salt, pepper and vinegar. Blend well to distribute seasonings.

In a 3-gallon cast iron pot, heat oil over medium-high heat. Add seasoned squirrel and cook until golden brown on all sides and there is good color in the bottom of the pot. The squirrels should be cooked approximately 25 minutes so that they will be brown enough to color the finished jambalaya.

Add onions, celery and garlic. Saute 3–5 minutes or until vegetables are wilted. Add water and bring to a rolling boil.

Cover and allow the squirrel to simmer until tender, approximately 30 minutes. Stir in rice and adjust seasonings if necessary.

Cover and cook 15 minutes. Remove lid and add green onions and parsley. Do not stir. Cover and cook 15 additional minutes. Prior to serving, stir well to incorporate the green seasonings.

Nutrition Facts...now

Calories:	478
Total Fat:	9gm
Saturated Fat:	1gm
% Calories from Fat:	16
Cholesterol:	118mg
Sodium:	463mg
Carbohydrate:	61gm
Fiber:	2gm
Protein:	36gm

PREP TIME: 2 Hours   SERVES: 6

☞ INGREDIENTS:

3 (1/2-pound) squirrels, quartered
3 tsps salt
black pepper
cayenne pepper
Louisiana Gold Pepper Sauce
1 cup plain flour
1/2 cup vegetable oil
2 cups diced onions
1 cup diced bell pepper
1/4 cup chopped garlic
3 cups water
1 cup sliced green onions

☞ METHOD:

Rinse the squirrel well under cold running water. In a large ceramic bowl, place squirrel and season with salt, peppers and Louisiana Gold. Dust the squirrel in flour, shaking off all of the excess, to avoid a heavy coating. In a 12- or 15-inch cast iron skillet, heat oil over medium-high heat. Brown squirrel well on all sides by turning often in the hot oil. When browned, remove and keep warm. Into the skillet, add onions, bell pepper and garlic. Saute 3–5 minutes or until vegetables are wilted. Return the squirrel to the sauteed vegetables and add water, one cup at a time. Bring to a rolling boil, reduce to simmer, cover, and cook approximately 1–1 1/2 hours, until squirrels are tender. Continue to add water as necessary during the cooking process to simmer the squirrels and develop the gravy. When squirrels are tender, add green onions and serve over steamed white rice.

"Many people talk about the good old days, but the good old days never ended at our house. Today, as in the past, most of our meals come from the swamps, from either fishing or hunting.

"Our family always raised a big vegetable garden, so naturally there was plenty to feed the family. It's amazing how fabulous the meals are when cooked simply with fresh ingredients from the land. We always said, 'You don't need a lot of fancy spices and seasonings, when you have a little bit of all the right things in the pot.'

"This recipe is usually cooked using rabbit because we have so many back in the field, but often we substitute squirrel, as in this version."
Robert and Bea Newchurch
Paincourtville, Louisiana

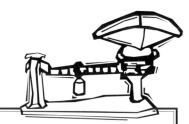

❧Nutrition Facts...then❧

Calories: 402
Total Fat: 22gm
Saturated Fat: 3gm
% Calories from Fat: 50
Cholesterol: 94mg
Sodium: 1200mg
Carbohydrate: 23gm
Fiber: 2gm
Protein: 27gm

SMOTHERED SQUIRREL IN PAN GRAVY

PREP TIME: 2 Hours   SERVES: 6

INGREDIENTS:

3 (1/2-pound) squirrels, quartered
1 tsp salt
black pepper
cayenne pepper
Louisiana Gold Pepper Sauce
1 cup plain flour
2 tbsps vegetable oil
2 cups diced onions
1 cup diced bell pepper
1/4 cup chopped garlic
3 cups water
1 cup sliced green onions

Saturday morning at Fred's, in Mamou, finds Emmet Francois taking a break from the dancing inside. With him, the horse he rode in on.

Chef's Tips on Weight Loss... fizzle your fries—cutting back from four times a week to two times.

Nutrition Facts...now

Calories: 282
Total Fat: 9gm
Saturated Fat: 1gm
% Calories from Fat: 28
Cholesterol: 94mg
Sodium: 490mg
Carbohydrate: 23gm
Fiber: 2gm
Protein: 27gm

METHOD:

Rinse the squirrel well under cold running water. In a large ceramic bowl, place squirrel and season with salt, peppers and Louisiana Gold. Dust the squirrel in flour, shaking off all of the excess, to avoid a heavy coating.

In a 12- or 15-inch cast iron skillet, heat oil over medium-high heat. Brown squirrel well on all sides by turning often in the hot oil. When browned, remove and keep warm.

Into the skillet, add onions, bell pepper and garlic. Saute 3–5 minutes or until vegetables are wilted. Return the squirrel to the sauteed vegetables and add water, one cup at a time. Bring to a rolling boil, reduce to simmer, cover, and cook approximately 1–1 1/2 hours, until squirrels are tender. Continue to add water as necessary during the cooking process to simmer the squirrels and develop the gravy.

When squirrels are tender, add green onions and serve over steamed white rice.

PREP TIME: 30 Minutes   SERVES: 6

☞ INGREDIENTS:

12 whole quail
1/8 pound butter
1/4 cup olive oil
2 tsps salt
black pepper
cayenne pepper
1 tsp rosemary
1 tsp tarragon
1 tsp thyme
1 shallot, diced
1 tsp chopped garlic
1 cup dry white wine
1/4 cup Port Wine
1 tbsp corn starch
2 cups beef consomme

☞ METHOD:

In a 12-inch cast iron skillet, heat butter and olive oil over medium-high heat. Rinse quail and season to taste using salt, peppers, rosemary, tarragon, thyme, shallots and garlic. Rub the seasoning well into the quail. Brown evenly in the hot oil, turning often, every 5–10 minutes. Once quail are golden brown, add white wine. Bring to a rolling boil, reduce heat to medium and cook until wine has evaporated to approximately 3–4 tablespoons. Add Port and continue to simmer. Dissolve corn starch in consomme and add to the skillet. Simmer until sauce is reduced and thickened, approximately 10–15 minutes. You may wish to serve the quail over toast points or English muffins with a generous portion of the Port sauce.

"Back in 1985, I was asked to prepare a special dinner for a group of ambassadors at the Watergate Hotel in Washington, D.C. At that event, I had the pleasure of meeting Katherine Crosby, widow of the famous movie star, Bing Crosby.

"She is an extraordinary woman who took time to come into the kitchen and talk about cooking and one of her famous dishes. She went on to say that she and Bing were avid hunters and she particularly loved quail.

"A year later, at her request, I accepted the position of Executive Chef of the Crosby Golf Tournament and prepared this dish in her honor."

John Folse
Donaldsonville, Louisiana

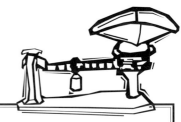

❊Nutrition Facts...then❊

Calories:	536
Total Fat:	35gm
Saturated Fat:	12gm
% Calories from Fat:	59
Cholesterol	21mg
Sodium	957mg
Carbohydrate:	2gm
Fiber	0gm
Protein:	42gm

PREP TIME: 30 Minutes   SERVES: 6

☞ INGREDIENTS:

12 whole quail, skinned
1/4 cup lite margarine
1 tbsp olive oil
1 tsp salt
black pepper
cayenne pepper
1 tsp rosemary
1 tsp tarragon
1 tsp thyme
1 shallot, diced
1 tsp chopped garlic
1 cup dry white wine
1/4 cup Port Wine
1 tbsp corn starch
2 cups defatted beef consomme, unsalted

☞ METHOD:

In a 12-inch cast iron skillet, heat margarine and olive oil over medium-high heat. Rinse quail and season to taste using salt, peppers, rosemary, tarragon, thyme shallots and garlic. Rub the seasoning well into the quail.

Brown evenly in the hot oil, turning often, every 5–10 minutes. Once quail are golden brown, add white wine. Bring to a rolling boil, reduce heat to medium and cook until wine has evaporated to approximately 3–4 tablespoons.

Add Port and continue to simmer. Dissolve corn starch in consomme and add to the skillet. Simmer until sauce is reduced and thickened, approximately 10–15 minutes.

You may wish to serve the quail over toast points or English muffins with a generous portion of the Port sauce.

Nutrition Facts...now	
Calories:	329
Total Fat:	13gm
Saturated Fat:	3gm
% Calories from Fat:	35
Cholesterol:	0mg
Sodium:	517mg
Carbohydrate:	2gm
Fiber:	0gm
Protein:	42gm

DOVE & WILD RICE CASSEROLE

PREP TIME: 1 1/2 Hours   SERVES: 6

☞ INGREDIENTS:

18 (2-ounce) dove breasts, cleaned
3 cups wild rice mix
4 tsps salt
black pepper
cayenne pepper
1 tbsp granulated garlic
1/2 cup vegetable oil
1 cup diced onions
1 cup diced celery
1 cup diced red bell pepper
1/4 cup diced garlic
1 cup canned tomatoes, diced
1 cup sliced mushrooms
1 tbsp chopped basil
1 tbsp chopped thyme
5 cups chicken stock
1 cup sliced green onions

☞ METHOD:

Clean doves by removing legs, wings and back bones. Rinse under cold running water. Season the breasts well using salt, peppers and granulated garlic. In a 12-quart cast iron dutch oven, heat vegetable oil over medium-high heat. Brown the dove breasts well by turning often in the hot oil. When the breasts are golden brown, remove and keep warm. Into the same pot, add onions, celery, bell pepper and garlic. Saute 3–5 minutes or until vegetables are wilted. Add tomatoes, mushrooms, basil and thyme and saute 2 additional minutes. Add chicken stock, stirring well to incorporate into the sauteed seasonings. Place dove breasts back into the pot. Bring to a rolling boil, reduce heat to simmer and cook 30 minutes to tenderize breasts. Add rice and green onions, stirring gently into the stock. Cover and cook 30 additional minutes. Do not stir during the cooking process, because tender doves will break apart into the rice. Check to make sure that the heat is on the lowest setting, in order to keep rice from scorching. Serve 3 dove breasts with a generous portion of the wild rice.

"Dove hunting was always considered great sport in St. James Parish, Louisiana, but we preferred to eat quail and duck because they were meatier. Another problem with dove is that the small bones that break off from the legs, thighs and backs during the cooking process. This makes dove dishes less appealing to eat.

"Once at a camp dinner, the cook solved the problem by cutting away the wings, legs and backs and preparing the dish with only the breasts. Ever since that experience, I've always made my dove casserole in this manner."
          Henry Schexnayder III
          Donaldsonville, Louisiana

❊Nutrition Facts...then❊

Calories: 944
Total Fat: 47gm
Saturated Fat: 12gm
% Calories from Fat: 45
Cholesterol: 151mg
Sodium: 2510mg
Carbohydrate: 85gm
Fiber: 4gm
Protein: 46gm

PREP TIME: 1 1/2 Hours   SERVES: 6

☞ INGREDIENTS:

18 (2-ounce) dove breasts, cleaned and skinned
3 cups wild rice mix
1 tsp salt
black pepper
cayenne pepper
1 tbsp granulated garlic
2 tbsps vegetable oil
1 cup diced onions
1 cup diced celery
1 cup diced red bell pepper
1/4 cup diced garlic
1 cup diced canned tomatoes, no salt added
1 cup sliced mushrooms
1 tbsp chopped basil
1 tbsp chopped thyme
5 cups defatted chicken stock, unsalted
1 cup sliced green onions

☞ METHOD:

Clean doves by removing legs, wings and back bones. Rinse under cold running water. Season the breasts well using salt, peppers and granulated garlic.

In a 12-quart cast iron dutch oven, heat vegetable oil over medium-high heat. Brown the dove breasts well by turning often in the hot oil. When the breasts are golden brown, remove and keep warm.

Into the same pot, add onions, celery, bell pepper and garlic. Saute 3–5 minutes or until vegetables are wilted. Add tomatoes, mushrooms, basil and thyme and saute 2 additional minutes. Add chicken stock, stirring well to incorporate into the sauteed seasonings.

Place dove breasts back into the pot. Bring to a rolling boil, reduce heat to simmer and cook 30 minutes to tenderize breasts. Add rice and green onions, stirring gently into the stock. Cover and cook 30 additional minutes.

Do not stir during the cooking process, because tender doves will break apart into the rice. Check to make sure that the heat is on the lowest setting, in order to keep rice from scorching. Serve 3 dove breasts with a generous portion of the wild rice.

Nutrition Facts...now

Calories: 660
Total Fat: 13gm
Saturated Fat: 3gm
% Calories from Fat: 17
Cholesterol: 0mg
Sodium: 805mg
Carbohydrate: 83gm
Fiber: 3gm
Protein: 52gm

SHERRIED DOVES

PREP TIME: 3 Hours   SERVES: 8

☞ INGREDIENTS:

1/2 cup sherry
20 (5-ounce) doves, cleaned
2 cups Italian salad dressing
1/2 cup vegetable oil
1/2 cup flour
1 cup diced onions
1 cup diced celery
1/2 cup diced bell pepper
1/4 cup chopped garlic
1 quart chicken stock
1 can Rotel tomatoes
1/2 tsp thyme
1/2 tsp sweet basil
2 cups sliced mushrooms
1 1/2 tsps salt
cayenne pepper
1/2 cup sliced green onions
1/4 cup chopped parsley

☞ METHOD:

Rinse doves well under cold running water. In a large bowl, marinate doves in Italian dressing overnight. When ready to prepare, remove doves from marinade and drain. In a 12-quart cast iron dutch oven, heat oil over medium-high heat. Add flour and, using a wire whisk, stir constantly until dark brown roux is achieved. Add onions, celery, bell pepper and garlic. Saute 3–5 minutes or until vegetables are wilted. Add chicken stock, Rotel tomatoes, sherry, thyme and basil. Bring to a rolling boil, reduce to simmer and add mushrooms. Season the doves using salt and pepper. Place doves, breast side up, in the simmering stock. Cover and cook approximately 2 1/2 hours or until doves are tender. When done, add green onions and parsley. Serve over wild or saffron rice.

"I first experienced this recipe, or a version of it, on a trip to Rosedown Plantation in St. Francisville. This area, referred to as the rolling Felicianas, is typical of English countryside. Large flocks of dove, quail and woodcock come to feed here in the corn and cane fields of this parish.

"In fact, John James Audubon, the great naturalist, painted many of his 'Birds of America' here in the St. Francisville area. It was probably an old English family who decided to tip the sherry bottle into a pot of simmering doves. Boy, I wish I knew who they were, so I could thank them."

John Folse
Donaldsonville, Louisiana

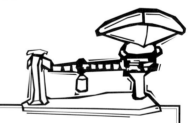

❧ Nutrition Facts...then❧

Calories:	1229
Total Fat:	97gm
Saturated Fat:	24gm
% Calories from Fat:	71
Cholesterol:	290mg
Sodium:	1716mg
Carbohydrate:	20gm
Fiber:	2gm
Protein:	65gm

PREP TIME: 3 Hours   SERVES: 8

INGREDIENTS:

1/2 cup sherry
20 (5-ounce) doves, cleaned
        and skinned
2 cups fat-free Italian salad dressing
1 cup oil-less roux
1 quart defatted chicken stock,
        unsalted
2 tbsps vegetable oil
1 cup diced onions
1 cup diced celery
1/2 cup diced bell pepper
1/4 cup chopped garlic
1 can Rotel tomatoes
1/2 tsp thyme
1/2 tsp sweet basil
2 cups sliced mushrooms
1/2 tsp salt
cayenne pepper
1/2 cup sliced green onions
1/4 cup chopped parsley

Don Bailey, of Bailey's Seafood in Cameron, shows off some trophies in his office.

*Chef's Tips on Weight Loss...
do not eat while reading or
watching television, only eat
while sitting at a table.*

Nutrition Facts...now

Calories:	550
Total Fat:	19gm
Saturated Fat:	5gm
% Calories from Fat:	31
Cholesterol:	271mg
Sodium:	714mg
Carbohydrate:	14gm
Fiber:	1gm
Protein:	74gm

METHOD:

Rinse doves well under cold running water. In a large bowl, marinate doves in Italian dressing overnight. When ready to prepare, remove from marinade and drain.

Dissolve roux in stock and set aside. In a 12-quart cast iron dutch oven, heat oil over medium-high heat. Add onions, celery, bell pepper and garlic. Saute 3–5 minutes or until vegetables are wilted. Add roux/stock mixture, Rotel tomatoes, sherry, thyme and basil. Bring to a rolling boil, reduce to simmer and add mushrooms.

Season the doves using salt and pepper. Place doves, breast side up, in the simmering stock. Cover and cook approximately 2 1/2 hours or until doves are tender. When done, add green onions and parsley. Serve over wild or saffron rice.

PREP TIME: 3 Hours   SERVES: 6

☞ INGREDIENTS:

3 (1-pound) Mallard ducks
6 mandarins, peeled and sectioned
3 cups chopped onions
2 cups chopped celery
2 cups chopped bell pepper
2 cups diced carrots
1/2 cup diced garlic
1 cup flour
1/2 cup vegetable oil
1/4 cup orange juice concentrate
1 1/2 quarts chicken stock
12 strips bacon
4 tsps salt
black pepper
cayenne pepper
Louisiana Gold Pepper Sauce

☞ METHOD:

Preheat oven to 375 degrees F. Make sure ducks are well cleaned and all visible shot removed. Place ducks in a large ceramic mixing bowl and season them well inside and out using salt, peppers and Louisiana Gold. Place 1/2 of the vegetable seasonings into the cavities of the ducks and dust lightly in flour. In a 12-quart cast iron dutch oven, heat oil over medium-high heat. Brown ducks well on all sides by turning occasionally in the hot oil. When ducks are browned, surround them with remaining onions, celery, bell pepper, carrots and garlic. Add mandarins, orange juice and chicken stock. Bring mixture to a rolling boil, remove from heat and top each duck, breast side up, with 4 strips of bacon. Cover and bake 2 1/2 hours, checking occasionally for doneness. Ducks will be done when the legs pull apart easily from the body. Remove cover and allow ducks to brown. You may serve with the natural drippings or strain all vegetables from the stock and thicken the sauce with a light brown roux.

"I was never much of a hunter, but I loved to cook game brought in from the hunt. As a young boy, I would stand with our cook, Mary Ferchaud, and learn at her hand the secret to great game cooking.
"One Halloween Day, she sent me out to the garden to pick four ripe mandarins from a tree growing there. She then showed me how to remove the seeds and squeeze the juice into a pot of roasting mallards with fabulous results.
"Ever since that day, I have used this simple citrus-flavoring in most wild game dishes, however, I've often substituted kumquats, oranges and tangerines with the same results."
John Folse
Donaldsonville, Louisiana

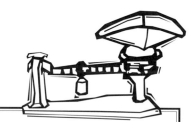

❀Nutrition Facts...then❀

Calories: 1422
Total Fat: 116gm
Saturated Fat: 35gm
% Calories from Fat: 73
Cholesterol: 201mg
Sodium: 2857mg
Carbohydrate: 58gm
Fiber: 6gm
Protein: 39gm

PREP TIME: 3 Hours   SERVES: 6

INGREDIENTS:

3 (1-pound) Mallard ducks, skinned
6 mandarins, peeled and sectioned
3 cups chopped onions
2 cups chopped celery
2 cups chopped bell pepper
2 cups diced carrots
1/2 cup diced garlic
1 cup flour
2 tbsps vegetable oil
1/4 cup orange juice concentrate
1 1/2 quarts defatted chicken stock, unsalted
6 strips turkey bacon
1/2 tsp salt
black pepper
cayenne pepper
Louisiana Gold Pepper Sauce

METHOD:

Preheat oven to 375 degrees F. Make sure ducks are well cleaned and all visible shot removed.

Place ducks in a large ceramic mixing bowl and season them well inside and out using salt, peppers and Louisiana Gold. Place 1/2 of the vegetable seasonings into the cavities of the ducks and dust lightly in flour.

In a 12-quart cast iron dutch oven, heat oil over medium-high heat. Brown ducks well on all sides by turning occasionally in the hot oil. When ducks are browned, surround them with remaining onions, celery, bell pepper, carrots and garlic. Add mandarins, orange juice and chicken stock. Bring mixture to a rolling boil, remove from heat and top each duck, breast side up, with 2 strips of bacon. Cover and bake 2 1/2 hours, checking occasionally for doneness.

Ducks will be done when the legs pull apart easily from the body. Remove cover and allow ducks to brown. You may serve with the natural drippings or strain all vegetables from the stock and thicken the sauce with a light brown roux.

Nutrition Facts...now

Calories: 636
Total Fat: 22gm
Saturated Fat: 7gm
% Calories from Fat: 30
Cholesterol: 183mg
Sodium: 987mg
Carbohydrate: 57gm
Fiber: 6gm
Protein: 56gm

GLENDA'S APPLE-ROASTED DUCK

PREP TIME: 4 Hours   SERVES: 8

INGREDIENTS:

6 (1/2-pound) pintails or teals
4 apples, quartered
2 gallons simmering water
1 cup white vinegar
3 stalks celery, quartered
3 yellow onions, quartered
2 bell peppers, quartered
1 cup flour

1/2 cup vegetable oil
4 strips bacon
3 cups diced onions
2 cups diced celery
1 cup diced bell pepper
1/4 cup diced garlic
1/4 cup chopped parsley
1 orange, sliced

1 quart chicken stock or water
1/4 cup orange juice
1/2 cup dry red wine
4 tsps salt
black pepper
cayenne pepper
1 tbsp granulated garlic
Louisiana Gold Pepper Sauce

METHOD:

Preheat oven to 350 degrees F. Clean ducks well under cold running water removing any visible shot. Place ducks in a ceramic bowl and cover with hot water and vinegar. Allow birds to soak for 1 1/2 hours. They will become very plump during this process. Drain them well and pat dry. Season the ducks inside and out, using salt, peppers, granulated garlic and Louisiana Gold. Stuff the inside cavities with the apples, quartered celery, onions and bell pepper. Dust ducks in flour, shaking off all excess. In a 12-quart cast iron dutch oven, heat oil over medium-high heat. Saute bacon until crispy brown and fat has been rendered. Remove bacon, crush and set aside. Brown the ducks, one at a time, turning often in the hot oil. Once all the ducks are golden brown, return them to the pot, breast side down. Add diced onions, celery, bell pepper, garlic and parsley. Squeeze the orange slices over the ducks and add the oranges to the pot. Add chicken stock, orange juice, red wine and crushed bacon. Bring liquids to a rolling boil, remove pan from heat, cover and bake 2–2 1/2 hours. Check for doneness by piercing breasts with fork or by pulling legs apart. When ducks are tender, remove cover and allow birds to brown evenly for 1/2 hour longer. You may wish to serve over wild rice or jambalaya.

"If you want to see variety in duck recipes, just go door-to-door here in South Louisiana and ask the question, 'What's your favorite way to cook ducks?' Every family up and down the highway has their own special technique when it comes to cooking duck. I've had it pot-roasted, baked, barbecued, stripped and deep-fried. I've even had it cooked in pie shells.
"My two favorite types of duck are teal and wood. Whenever I cook them, it's always with my grandmother's apple-roasted recipe."

Glenda Daigle
Paincourtville, Louisiana

❦Nutrition Facts...then❦

Calories: 325
Total Fat: 20gm
Saturated Fat: 4gm
% Calories from Fat: 49
Cholesterol: 823mg
Sodium: 1683mg
Carbohydrate: 38gm
Fiber: 6gm
Protein: 6gm

PREP TIME: 4 Hours   SERVES: 8

☞ INGREDIENTS:

6 (1/2-pound) pintails or teals
4 apples, quartered
2 gallons simmering water
1 cup white vinegar
3 stalks celery, quartered
3 yellow onions, quartered
2 bell peppers, quartered
1 cup flour
2 tbsps vegetable oil
4 strips turkey bacon
3 cups diced onions
2 cups diced celery
1 cup diced bell pepper
1/4 cup diced garlic
1/4 cup chopped parsley
1 orange, sliced
1 quart defatted chicken stock, unsalted
1/4 cup orange juice
1/2 cup dry red wine
1 tsp salt
black pepper
cayenne pepper
1 tbsp granulated garlic
Louisiana Gold Pepper Sauce

☞ METHOD:

Preheat oven to 350 degrees F. Clean ducks well under cold running water removing any visible shot. Place ducks in a ceramic bowl and cover with hot water and vinegar. Allow birds to soak for 1 1/2 hours. They will become very plump during this process.

Drain them well and pat dry. Season the ducks inside and out, using salt, peppers, granulated garlic and Louisiana Gold. Stuff the inside cavities with the apples, quartered celery, onions and bell pepper. Dust ducks in flour, shaking off all excess.

In a 12-quart cast iron dutch oven, heat oil over medium-high heat. Saute turkey bacon until crispy brown and fat has been rendered. Remove bacon, crush and set aside. Brown the ducks, one at a time, turning often in the hot oil.

Once all the ducks are golden brown, return them to the pot, breast side down. Add diced onions, celery, bell pepper, garlic and parsley. Squeeze the orange slices over the ducks and add the oranges to the pot. Add chicken stock, orange juice, red wine and crushed bacon. Bring liquids to a rolling boil, remove pan from heat, cover and bake 2–2 1/2 hours. Check for doneness by piercing breasts with fork or by pulling legs apart.

When ducks are tender, remove cover and allow birds to brown evenly for 1/2 hour longer. You may wish to serve over wild rice or jambalaya.

PREP TIME: 1 1/2 Hours   SERVES: 6

☞ **INGREDIENTS:**

6 (1/2-pound) woodcocks, cleaned
2 tsps salt
black pepper
cayenne pepper
5 tbsps flour
1/4 pound butter
1/4 cup vegetable oil
1 cup diced onions
1 cup diced celery
1/2 cup diced bell pepper
1/4 cup chopped garlic
1 tsp chopped tarragon
1 tbsp chopped basil
1/2 cup sliced green onions
1 cup diced carrots
2 cups sliced mushrooms
1 cup dry white wine
3 cups chicken stock
2 bay leaves
2 red apples, cored and diced

☞ **METHOD:**

Preheat oven to 350 degrees F. Season woodcocks inside and out with salt and peppers. Dust in flour. In a 12-quart cast iron dutch oven, heat butter and vegetable oil over medium-high heat. Brown the woodcocks evenly on all sides by turning occasionally, every 5–10 minutes. Add onions, celery, bell pepper and garlic. Saute 3–5 minutes or until vegetables are wilted. Add tarragon, basil, green onions, carrots, mushrooms, white wine and chicken stock. Bring to a rolling boil. Add bay leaves and apples. Cover and place in the oven for approximately 45 minutes or until woodcocks are tender. Remove cover and brown 5–10 minutes, if necessary. You may need to add additional chicken stock should the woodcocks become too dry during the cooking process. Serve over steamed white rice.

"Paul Zeringue was my mother's uncle. In addition to being an owner of Cabanocey Plantation, he was famous in the town of St. James, Louisiana, for his camp-style cooking.

"Very few great cooks in that small river village can say that their skills were not directly influenced by Uncle Paul. He spent many hours at Zeringue's camp stirring his old black pot and teaching youngsters the fine art of bayou cooking. This is one dish that I credit to Uncle Paul."
Ruth Folse Hirsch
Donaldsonville, Louisiana

Chef's Tips on Weight Loss... skim your milk—it will taste just as good to you as whole milk in two weeks.

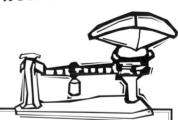

❧Nutrition Facts...then❧

Calories: 836
Total Fat: 61gm
Saturated Fat: 23gm
% Calories from Fat: 65
Cholesterol: 232mg
Sodium: 1538mg
Carbohydrate: 24gm
Fiber: 4gm
Protein: 43gm

UNCLE PAUL'S WOODCOCK

...Something New

PREP TIME: 1 1/2 Hours   SERVES: 6

☞ INGREDIENTS:

6 (1/2-pound) woodcocks, cleaned
1/2 tsp salt
black pepper
cayenne pepper
5 tbsps flour
1/2 cup margarine
1 cup diced onions
1 cup diced celery
1/2 cup diced bell pepper
1/4 cup chopped garlic
1 tsp chopped tarragon
1 tbsp chopped basil
1/2 cup sliced green onions
1 cup diced carrots
2 cups sliced mushrooms
1 cup dry white wine
3 cups defatted chicken stock, unsalted
2 bay leaves
2 red apples, cored and diced

☞ METHOD:

Preheat oven to 350 degrees F. Season woodcocks inside and out with salt and peppers. Dust in flour.

In a 12-quart cast iron dutch oven, heat margarine over medium-high heat. Brown the woodcocks evenly on all sides by turning occasionally, every 5–10 minutes.

Add onions, celery, bell pepper and garlic. Saute 3–5 minutes or until vegetables are wilted. Add tarragon, basil, green onions, carrots, mushrooms, white wine and chicken stock. Bring to a rolling boil. Add bay leaves and apples. Cover and place in the oven for approximately 45 minutes or until woodcocks are tender.

Remove cover and brown 5–10 minutes, if necessary. You may need to add additional chicken stock should the woodcocks become too dry during the cooking process. Serve over steamed white rice.

Nutrition Facts...now

Calories: 550
Total Fat: 26gm
Saturated Fat: 6gm
% Calories from Fat: 42
Cholesterol: 175mg
Sodium: 727mg
Carbohydrate: 23gm
Fiber: 4gm
Protein: 49gm

BAKED GOOSE HOLLY BEACH

PREP TIME: 3 Hours   SERVES: 8

☞ INGREDIENTS:

2 (5-pound) geese	3 cups diced carrots	1/2 cup vegetable oil	4 tsps salt
4 cups diced onions	4 apples, quartered	1 1/2 quarts chicken stock	black pepper
4 cups diced celery	2 cups red seedless grapes	1/4 cup butter	cayenne pepper
2 cups diced bell pepper	1/2 cup diced garlic	3 cups sliced mushrooms	Louisiana Gold Pepper Sauce

☞ METHOD:

Preheat oven to 375 degrees F. Rinse the geese well under cold running water and remove any visible shot. In a large baking pan, season geese well inside and out, using salt, peppers and Louisiana Gold. Stuff 1/2 of the vegetables and fruit into the cavities of the geese. Using a small pairing knife, cut slits under the breasts of each goose and stuff generously with garlic. In a cast iron dutch oven, large enough to hold the geese, heat oil over medium-high heat. Brown birds, one at a time, turning often in the hot oil. Once the geese are golden brown, surround with all remaining seasonings, fruit, and chicken stock. Bring mixture to a rolling boil, remove from heat, cover and place in oven. Bake 2 1/2 hours and check for doneness. Birds will be done when legs pull away easily from the body. Once done, remove the cover and allow geese to brown evenly. Remove the birds from the natural drippings and keep warm. Strain the cooking liquid through a sieve, discarding the solids. When the cooking juices have settled for 10–15 minutes, the oil will rise to the top. Using a ladle, skim away the oil from the juices. In a 10-inch cast iron skillet, melt butter over medium-high heat. Add mushrooms and saute 3–5 minutes or until wilted. Add the natural drippings, bring to a rolling boil and reduce to 1/2 volume. When ready to serve, slice the meat from the geese and top with the mushroom sauce.

"Most people in South Louisiana don't realize that roasted goose is the traditional Christmas or New Year's main course in France. It's only natural that the Cajuns, who left France in the early 1600s, would bring this holiday tradition to our bayou tables.

Geese are plentiful in the marshlands of Southwest Louisiana and are prized because of their size when compared to ducks. Most Cajun families had 8-10 children and two speckled-belly geese, roasted in the oven, would feed the entire family and guarantee leftovers.

"If you cannot find any wild speckled-bellies in your neighborhood, just try this recipe with a domesticated goose from your local supermarket."

Sammy Faulk - Hunting Guide
Holly Beach, Louisiana

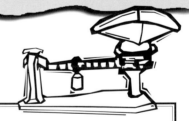

❧ Nutrition Facts...then❧

Calories:	1181
Total Fat:	98gm
Saturated Fat:	28gm
% Calories from Fat:	74
Cholesterol:	210mg
Sodium:	2134mg
Carbohydrate:	37gm
Fiber:	8gm
Protein:	41gm

BAKED GOOSE HOLLY BEACH

PREP TIME: 3 Hours   SERVES: 8

☞ INGREDIENTS:

2 (5-pound) geese, skinned
4 cups diced onions
4 cups diced celery
2 cups diced bell pepper
3 cups diced carrots
4 apples, quartered
2 cups red seedless grapes
1/2 cup diced garlic
2 tsps vegetable oil
1 1/2 quarts defatted chicken stock, unsalted
1/4 cup margarine
3 cups sliced mushrooms
1 tsp salt
black pepper
cayenne pepper
Louisiana Gold Pepper Sauce

*Chef's Tips on Weight Loss...
undress your salad—or use
a reduced calorie dressing.*

Nutrition Facts...now

Calories:	609
Total Fat:	26gm
Saturated Fat:	8gm
% Calories from Fat:	38
Cholesterol:	190mg
Sodium:	894mg
Carbohydrate:	36gm
Fiber:	7gm
Protein:	59gm

☞ METHOD:

Preheat oven to 375 degrees F. Rinse the geese well under cold running water and remove any visible shot.

In a large baking pan, season geese well inside and out, using salt, peppers and Louisiana Gold. Stuff 1/2 of the vegetables and fruit into the cavities of the geese. Using a small pairing knife, cut slits under the breasts of each goose and stuff generously with garlic.

In a cast iron dutch oven, large enough to hold the geese, heat oil over medium-high heat. Brown birds, one at a time, turning often in the hot oil.

Once the geese are golden brown, surround with all remaining seasonings, fruit, and chicken stock. Bring mixture to a rolling boil, remove from heat, cover and place in oven.

Bake 2 1/2 hours and check for doneness. Birds will be done when legs pull away easily from the body. Once done, remove the cover and allow geese to brown evenly. Remove the birds from the natural drippings and keep warm.

Strain the cooking liquid through a sieve, discarding the solids. When the cooking juices have settled for 10–15 minutes, the oil will rise to the top. Using a ladle, skim away the oil from the juices.

In a 10-inch cast iron skillet, melt margarine over medium-high heat. Add mushrooms and saute 3–5 minutes or until wilted. Add the natural drippings, bring to a rolling boil and reduce to 1/2 volume. When ready to serve, slice the meat from the geese and top with the mushroom sauce.

PREP TIME: 4 Hours   SERVES: 8

INGREDIENTS:

1 (10-pound) wild turkey
3 bunches muscadines or 4 cups seedless red grapes
4 onions, quartered
3 celery stalks, quartered
3 bell peppers, quartered
4 heads of garlic, halved
2 cups sliced mushrooms
1 1/2-quarts chicken stock
5 tsps salt
black pepper
cayenne pepper
3 tbsps granulated garlic
2 tsps celery salt
1/4 cup Worcestershire sauce
Louisiana Gold Pepper Sauce

METHOD:

Preheat oven to 400 degrees F. Rinse the bird well under cold running water. Season thoroughly with salt, peppers, granulated garlic, celery salt, Worcestershire and Louisiana Gold. Rub the seasonings well, inside and out, including under the skin of the breasts. Stuff the cavity with 1/2 of the quartered onions, celery, bell peppers and garlic. Using aluminum foil, wrap the ends of the wings to prevent overcooking during baking. Place the bird in a large cast iron roaster and surround with remaining vegetables and fruit. Add chicken stock and bring to a rolling boil on top of the stove. Remove from heat, cover tightly and place in oven. Cook 3–3 1/2 hours or until bird is tender. Remove cover and allow to brown evenly. You may wish to strain the natural cooking juices, discard solids and reduce liquid to a flavorful jus or gravy.

"Wild turkey is truly the king of all game birds. Like goose because of size, it is great for feeding a large Cajun family, but it takes skill to bring one to the table. It takes similar skill to prepare it, assuring tenderness and great taste.

"I cannot count the number of mornings I sat quietly under an oak tree and watched the turkeys feeding in a misty fog. The beauty of these magnificent wild birds is so great that often the hunter has to fight with his conscience before pulling the trigger.

"Once the decision is made to bring one home, you should definitely try cooking it with this fruity-flavorful recipe."

John Beck, Sr.
Napoleonville, Louisiana

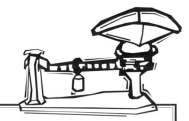

❋Nutrition Facts...then❋

Calories: 1260
Total Fat: 56gm
Saturated Fat: 16gm
% Calories from Fat: 41
Cholesterol: 555mg
Sodium: 2951mg
Carbohydrate: 19gm
Fiber: 3gm
Protein: 163gm

PREP TIME: 4 Hours   SERVES: 8

INGREDIENTS:

1 (10-pound) wild turkey, skinned
3 bunches muscadines or 4 cups seedless red grapes
4 onions, quartered
3 celery stalks, quartered
3 bell peppers, quartered
4 heads of garlic, halved
2 cups sliced mushrooms
1 1/2-quarts defatted chicken stock, unsalted
salt substitute
black pepper
cayenne pepper
3 tbsps granulated garlic
1 tsp celery salt
1/4 cup low-sodium Worcestershire sauce
Louisiana Gold Pepper Sauce

METHOD:

Preheat oven to 400 degrees F. Rinse the bird well under cold running water. Season thoroughly with salt substitute, peppers, granulated garlic, celery salt, Worcestershire and Louisiana Gold. Rub the seasonings well, inside and out.

Stuff the cavity with 1/2 of the quartered onions, celery, bell peppers and garlic. Using aluminum foil, wrap the ends of the wings to prevent overcooking during baking.

Place the bird in a large cast iron roaster and surround with remaining vegetables and fruit. Add chicken stock and bring to a rolling boil on top of the stove.

Remove from heat, cover tightly and place in oven. Cook 3–3 1/2 hours or until bird is tender. Remove cover and allow to brown evenly.

You may wish to strain the natural cooking juices, discard solids and reduce liquid to a flavorful jus or gravy.

Nutrition Facts...now

Calories:	1005
Total Fat:	23gm
Saturated Fat:	8gm
% Calories from Fat:	21
Cholesterol:	477mg
Sodium:	882mg
Carbohydrate:	19gm
Fiber:	2gm
Protein:	172gm

Chef's Tips on Weight Loss... take a walk or exercise instead of eating.

STEWED TURTLE CREOLE

PREP TIME: 3 Hours   SERVES: 8

☞ INGREDIENTS:

5 pounds snapper turtle, diced
1 3/4 cups vegetable oil
2 cups flour
3 cups diced onions
1 cup diced bell pepper
1/4 cup chopped garlic
1 (10-ounce) can Rotel tomatoes
1 (15-ounce) can tomato sauce

1 gallon water
2 cups sliced mushrooms
1 cup sliced green onions
1/4 cup chopped parsley
3 1/2 tsps salt
cayenne pepper
hot sauce

John Phillip Sylvester, of June's Seafood in Ville Platte, handles a granddaddy of a snapping turtle.

☞ METHOD:

In a 12-quart cast iron dutch oven, heat 1/4 cup vegetable oil over medium-high heat. Season turtle with salt, cayenne pepper and hot sauce. Cook turtle, stirring constantly, until all water has been rendered and the turtle has begun to fry. While turtle is frying, in a separate 5-quart cast iron dutch oven, heat 1 1/2 cups of oil over medium-high heat. Add flour and, using a wire whisk, stir constantly until dark brown roux is achieved. Remove from heat, stir to cool and set aside. Once the turtle meat is golden brown, add onions, bell pepper and garlic. Blend well into the turtle mixture and cook 5–10 minutes. Add Rotel tomatoes and tomato sauce. Cook for approximately 15 minutes. While tomatoes are simmering, add 2 quarts of water to the brown roux mixture. Using a wire whisk, blend well. Slowly add roux mixture to the simmering turtle, stirring constantly. Bring to a rolling boil, reduce to simmer and add additional water as necessary to retain a stew-like consistency. Cook, stirring occasionally, for 1 1/2–2 hours or until turtle is tender. Add mushrooms, green onions and parsley. Season to taste using salt, pepper and hot sauce. Serve over steamed white rice.

"The weekly camp dinner is one of the greatest traditions I've discovered since moving to the River Road in St. James Parish over thirty years ago. This is a custom that we enjoy in South Louisiana that very few people elsewehere ever get to experience.

"One or two nights a week, up to fifty men meet at a neighborhood hunting camp for socializing, card playing, a little bit of beer drinking and most importantly, a good Cajun camp supper. This is one of the recipes that I like to prepare when it's my turn to cook for the group."

Bruce Becnel
Vacherie, Louisiana

☆Nutrition Facts...then☆

Calories: 843
Total Fat: 50gm
Saturated Fat: 7gm
% Calories from Fat: 53
Cholesterol: 142mg
Sodium: 1631mg
Carbohydrate: 37gm
Fiber: 3gm
Protein: 62gm

STEWED TURTLE CREOLE

PREP TIME: 3 Hours   SERVES: 8

☞ INGREDIENTS:

5 pounds snapper turtle, diced
2 cups oil-less roux
2 quarts water
2 tbsps vegetable oil
3 cups diced onions

1 cup diced bell pepper
1/4 cup chopped garlic
1 (10-ounce) can Rotel tomatoes
1 (15-ounce) can tomato sauce, no salt added
2 cups sliced mushrooms

1 cup sliced green onions
1/4 cup chopped parsley
1 tsp salt
cayenne pepper
hot sauce

☞ METHOD:

Dissolve roux in water and set aside. In a 12-quart cast iron dutch oven, heat oil over medium-high heat. Season turtle with salt, cayenne pepper and hot sauce. Cook turtle, stirring constantly, until all water has been rendered and the turtle has begun to fry.

Once the turtle meat is golden brown, add onions, bell pepper and garlic. Blend well into the turtle mixture and cook 5–10 minutes.

Add Rotel tomatoes and tomato sauce. Cook for approximately 15 minutes. While tomatoes are simmering, add roux/water mixture. Blend well, bring to a rolling boil and reduce to simmer. Add additional water as necessary to retain a stew-like consistency.

Cook, stirring occasionally, for 1 1/2–2 hours or until turtle is tender. Add mushrooms, green onions and parsley. Season to taste using salt, pepper and hot sauce. Serve over steamed white rice.

Tim Hebert holds one of his young alligators in St. Martinville.

Nutrition Facts...now

Calories:	456
Total Fat:	5gm
Saturated Fat:	1gm
% Calories from Fat:	11
Cholesterol:	142mg
Sodium:	652mg
Carbohydrate:	37gm
Fiber:	3gm
Protein:	62gm

PREP TIME: 1 Hour   SERVES: 6

☞ INGREDIENTS:

3 cups ground alligator meat
9 small red potatoes
1 cup minced onions
1/2 cup minced celery
1/4 cup chopped garlic
1/2 cup finely sliced green onions
3 eggs
2 1/2 tsps salt
cayenne pepper
1/2 cup vegetable oil
2 cups seasoned flour

☞ METHOD:

Peel the potatoes and boil them in lightly salted water until tender but not overcooked. Mash them and set aside to cool. In a large mixing bowl, combine the ground alligator meat with potatoes, onions, celery, garlic and green onions. Blend well. Add eggs and season with salt and pepper. Once all the seasonings are blended, form the meat into 2- or 3-inch round, flat patties. In a 10-inch cast iron skillet, heat oil over medium-high heat. Reduce the heat to medium and coat the patties in flour. Pan fry until patties are golden brown and cooked thoroughly. You may wish to keep them warm in a 200 degree F oven until ready to serve.

"My grandparents lived in a small village on Bayou Teche in St. Mary Parish. I often went to visit them and those visits consisted mainly of going to church and cooking.

"I can still remember the wonderful aromas coming from the kitchens of those little Cajun cabins along the bayou. There was a wonderful old Indian lady who wore long skirts and a great big bonnet on her head, who always seemed to have something boiling on the stove. I would love to visit with her.

"One morning while we were talking, a couple of men brought a real big alligator they had caught in the bayou over to her home. It seems she was famous for the alligator patties or boulletes that she often made. I was lucky enough to be able to help chop the onions, measure the flour and roll the patties. Only the tail meat of the alligator was used because that seemed to be the most tender. We worked all morning and, by dinner time (that's lunch to you people), the patties were ready to serve.

I'll never forget that as the patties came out of the skillet, the whole village had shown up outside her cabin to help eat them."
Barbara Boutte
New Iberia, Louisiana

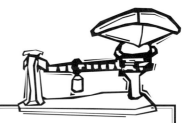

❧Nutrition Facts...then❧

Calories: 671
Total Fat: 21gm
Saturated Fat: 3gm
% Calories from Fat: 47
Cholesterol: 107mg
Sodium: 1288mg
Carbohydrate: 45gm
Fiber: 2gm
Protein: 61gm

PREP TIME: 1 Hour   SERVES: 6

☞ INGREDIENTS:

3 cups ground alligator meat
9 small red potatoes
1 cup minced onions
1/2 cup minced celery
1/4 cup chopped garlic
1/2 cup finely sliced green onions
1 egg and 3 egg whites
1/2 tsp salt
cayenne pepper
vegetable spray
2 cups flour

☞ METHOD:

Peel the potatoes and boil them in lightly salted water until tender but not overcooked. Mash them and set aside to cool.

In a large mixing bowl, combine the ground alligator meat with potatoes, onions, celery, garlic and green onions. Blend well. Add egg and whites and season with salt and pepper.

Once all the seasonings are blended, form the meat into 2- or 3-inch round, flat patties. Spray a 10-inch cast iron skillet with vegetable spray and place over medium-high heat. Reduce the heat to medium and coat the patties in flour. Pan fry until patties are golden brown and cooked thoroughly. You may wish to keep them warm in a 200 degree F oven until ready to serve.

Nutrition Facts...now

Calories:	497
Total Fat:	2gm
Saturated Fat:	0gm
% Calories from Fat:	6
Cholesterol:	36mg
Sodium:	238mg
Carbohydrate:	45gm
Fiber:	2gm
Protein:	61gm

Chef's Tips on Weight Loss... not limiting portion sizes and number of servings is one of the main reasons weight loss is unsuccessful.

Desserts

Chapter Nine

German Apple Pudding 356/357

Les Tartes Douces (Cajun Sweet Dough Pies) 358/359

Funeral Pie 360/361

Old Fashioned Lemon Pie 362/363

Petite Gateaux (Christmas Tea Cookies) 364/365

Platzchens (German Sugar Cookies) 366/367

Russian Rock Cookies 368/369

Coconut Cream Pie 370/371

Sacred Heart Chocolate Pecan Pie 372/373

Oeufs Aux Lait (Egg Custard) 376/377

Fruitcake Cookies 378/379

Cajun Ginger Cookies 380/381

Skillet Peach Cobbler 382/383

Spiced Cooking Pears 384/385

Blackberry Pinwheel Cobbler 386/387

Sweet Potato Cake 388/389

Christmas Ambrosia Roderc 390/391

Old Time Coconut Cake 392/393

Gateau De Figue (Fig Cake) 394/395

Super Moist Carrot Cake 396/397

*The recipes for **Sacred Heart Chocolate Pecan Pie**, pictured at left, can be found on pages 372 and 373.*

PREP TIME: 1 Hour   SERVES: 6

"The German tradition in this part of bayou country is almost as old as the French, so there may be other recipes for apple pudding to be found in family cookbooks. This one, however, is a more recent import. My husband's family brought it over with them when they emigrated in the late 1800s.

"I grew up outside Houma, on a small farm across Highway 90 from Big Bayou Black. My father was an insurance man, and the farm was just a small truck farm. But that was during the Depression, and it was a good thing to be on a farm back then, because, no matter how hard times got, you were never going to be without food.

"We had our chickens, pigs and cows, and the bayou itself provided us with fish and crabs - no small consideration, since Catholics were sternly forbidden, in those days, to eat meat on Friday.

"We children used to catch crabs with strings. You tied your bait on the end of the string and dangled it in the bayou. When a crab grabbed it with its claws you slowly pulled it in. As long as you didn't move too quickly, the crab would never let go, and would be dropped into the big wire mesh underwater crab cage that we kept at the bayou edge.

"There's another abiding memory of life along that bayou. When I was a very small girl, the "candy boat" would come by. We would hear the boat blow its whistle, and run across to the bayou, and the men on the boat would throw us small, wrapped candies.

"I was so young and it was so long ago that I no longer remember what the occasion was for throwing the candy, or what type of boat it was. It happened very infrequently - maybe once a year - and only one boat did it."

Rosemary Porche
Houma, Louisiana

INGREDIENTS:

3 apples, peeled and sliced
1 tbsp lemon juice
2 cups all purpose flour
2 tbsps baking powder
1/4 tsp salt
1 egg, beaten
1 cup milk
1 tbsp melted butter
1/2 cup brown sugar
1 tsp cinnamon

METHOD:

Preheat oven to 350 degrees F. Once the apples are sliced, they must be submerged in water with a tablespoon of lemon juice to keep them from turning dark. In a large mixing bowl, combine flour, baking powder and salt. Blend well. Add egg, milk and butter. Blend well to incorporate all ingredients. Butter a 9" x 13" baking pan. Pour in the batter, pressing the apples into the mixture. Top with brown sugar and cinnamon. Bake 25–30 minutes or until apples are tender. Serve with a generous dollop of whipped cream or ice cream.

❧Nutrition Facts...then❧

Calories:	314
Total Fat:	4gm
Saturated Fat:	2gm
% Calories from Fat:	13
Cholesterol:	31mg
Sodium:	159mg
Carbohydrate:	63gm
Fiber:	2gm
Protein:	6gm

GERMAN APPLE PUDDING

PREP TIME: 1 Hour   SERVES: 6

INGREDIENTS:

3 apples, peeled and sliced
1 tbsp lemon juice
2 cups all purpose flour
2 tbsps baking powder
1/4 tsp salt
1/4 cup egg substitute
1 cup evaporated skim milk
1 tbsp lite margarine
vegetable spray
1/2 cup brown sugar
1 tsp cinnamon

*Chef's Tips on Weight loss...
put spread on your bread
thinly — or check out the
reduced calorie spreads.*

METHOD:

Preheat oven to 350 degrees F. Once the apples are sliced, they must be submerged in water with a tablespoon of lemon juice to keep them from turning dark.

In a large mixing bowl, combine flour, baking powder and salt. Blend well. Add egg substitute, skim milk and margarine. Blend well to incorporate all ingredients.

Coat a 9" x 13" baking pan with vegetable spray. Pour in the batter, pressing the apples into the mixture. Top with brown sugar and cinnamon. Bake 25–30 minutes or until apples are tender.

Serve with a generous dollop of fat-free ice cream.

Nutrition Facts...now

Calories:	311
Total Fat:	2gm
Saturated Fat:	0gm
% Calories from Fat:	5
Cholesterol:	1mg
Sodium:	200mg
Carbohydrate:	66gm
Fiber:	2gm
Protein:	8gm

PREP TIME: 1 Hour   SERVES: 24

INGREDIENTS:

1/4 pound margarine
1 cup shortening
3 cups sugar
3 eggs
1 1/2 cups milk
2 tsps vanilla
10 cups all purpose flour
4 tsps baking powder
1 tsp salt
4 cups flour for kneading
3 cups fruit filling
1 egg, beaten

METHOD:

Preheat oven to 375 degrees F. In an extra large mixing bowl, cream margarine and shortening using an electric mixer. Slowly add the sugar while beating until shortening is light and fluffy. Add eggs, one at a time, beating well after each addition. Add milk and vanilla, blending well. Change the whisk blade on the mixer to a dough hook. Add 2 cups of flour at a time until the mixture is well-blended. Continue until all flour has been added. Add baking powder and salt. Continue to blend well until dough ball has formed. Flour a large work surface such as a table or counter and empty the dough mixture onto the surface. Knead well. If dough is too soft, sprinkle in a little additional flour. It should be easy to handle and should not stick to the fingers. Break the dough into 24 equal portions the size of a baseball. On the floured surface, pat each portion into a flat circle and, using a rolling pin, roll into an 8-inch circle. Place 2 tablespoons of your favorite fruit filling or preserve onto 1 side of the circle. Using a pastry brush, paint the edge of the circle with beaten egg and fold over into a half-moon shape. Pinch the edges together or crimp with a fork. Pierce 1 or 2 steam holes into the top of the pie. Repeat until all ingredients are used. Bake on a cookie sheet for approximtely 30 minutes.

"There are many traditions that have been handed down in my family. The one that stands out the most was called 'pie day.' My Grandmother Ledoux would spend all day making pies.

"She would start by making her fillings that had to be completely cooled before we could begin. My Aunt Gladys and sister, Elta, would start by mixing the flour and rolling the dough.

"This tradition was carried on for many years after my grandmother passed away. Mother simply moved the operation over to her house. After her death, pie day was moved to my home where it is still a tradition today."
Mercedes Ledoux Vidrine
Eunice, Louisiana

❦Nutrition Facts...then❦

Calories: 606
Total Fat: 14gm
Saturated Fat: 4gm
% Calories from Fat: 21
Cholesterol: 38mg
Sodium: 160mg
Carbohydrate: 110gm
Fiber: 3gm
Protein: 9gm

PREP TIME: 1 Hour   SERVES: 24

☞ INGREDIENTS:

1/2 cup lite margarine
3/4 cup vegetable oil
3 cups sugar
3/4 cup egg substitute
1 1/2 cups evaporated skim milk
2 tsps vanilla
10 cups all purpose flour
4 tsps baking powder
1/2 tsp salt
4 cups flour for kneading
3 cups fruit filling
1/2 cup egg substitute

Norris and Evon Melancon swing out at a Sunday evening dance at Marie Bourque's Club in Lewisburg.

☞ METHOD:

Preheat oven to 375 degrees F. In an extra large mixing bowl, cream margarine, oil and sugar using an electric mixer. Add egg substitute, a little at a time, beating well while adding each addition. Slowly add evaporated skim milk and vanilla.

Change the whisk blade on the mixer to a dough hook. Add 2 cups of flour at a time until the mixture is well-blended. Continue until all flour has been added. Add baking powder and salt. Continue to blend well until dough ball has formed.

Flour a large work surface such as a table or counter and empty the dough mixture onto the surface. Knead well and if dough is too soft, sprinkle in a little additional flour. It should be easy to handle and should not stick to the fingers. Break dough into 24 equal portions the size of a baseball.

On the floured surface pat each portion into a flat circle and, using a rolling pin, roll into an 8-inch circle. Place 2 tablespoons of your favorite fruit filling or preserve onto 1 side of the circle.

Using a pastry brush, paint the edge of the circle with egg substitute and fold over into a half-moon shape. Pinch the edges together or crimp with a fork. Pierce 1 or 2 steam holes into the top of the pie. Repeat until all ingredients are used. Bake on a cookie sheet for approximately 30 minutes.

Nutrition Facts...now

Calories:	575
Total Fat:	10gm
Saturated Fat:	1gm
% Calories from Fat:	16
Cholesterol:	1mg
Sodium:	138mg
Carbohydrate:	111gm
Fiber:	3gm
Protein:	10gm

PREP TIME: 1 Hour   SERVES: 8

☞ INGREDIENTS:

2 cups water
2 cups seedless raisins
1/2 cup brown sugar
1/2 cup white sugar
3 tbsps corn starch
1/2 tsp ground cinnamon
1/2 tsp allspice
1/4 tsp salt
1 tbsp cider vinegar
2 tbsps butter
1 tbsp grated orange rind
2 (9-inch) prepared pie crusts

☞ METHOD:

Preheat oven to 400 degrees F. Line a 9-inch pie pan with 1 of the crusts by pressing it firmly into the pan. In a 3-quart cast iron dutch oven, heat 2/3 cup of water, along with raisins, over medium-high heat. Simmer for 5 minutes. In a separate bowl, combine sugars, corn starch, cinnamon, allspice and salt. Whisk in remaining 1 1/3 cups of water and, when well-blended, add to the simmering raisins. Stir constantly until mixture bubbles up in the pot. Add vinegar, butter and orange rind. Continue to cook until butter melts in the mixture. Remove and allow the mixture to cool until lukewarm. Pour the cooled mixture into the unbaked pie shell. Top with the second pie crust, crimping the edges in a decorative fashion. Cut 2–3 slits in the top of the crust to allow steam to escape during cooking. Bake 25–30 minutes or until pie crust is golden brown and pie is bubbling up in the middle. Allow pie to cool completely before cutting.

"It seems that whenever there was a funeral in the neighborhood, this raisin pie was cooked and brought to the family, thus the name. I think it originally came from Ohio and was said to be of Amish descent and I am sure that is true.
"We still make the pie and around our house, it's always called funeral pie."

Mary Mistric
Arnaudville, Louisiana

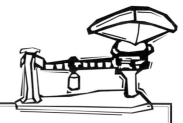

❖Nutrition Facts...then❖

Calories: 408
Total Fat: 13gm
Saturated Fat: 5gm
% Calories from Fat: 28
Cholesterol: 8mg
Sodium: 312mg
Carbohydrate: 73gm
Fiber: 2gm
Protein: 3gm

PREP TIME: 1 Hour   SERVES: 8

☞ INGREDIENTS:

2 cups water
2 cups seedless raisins
1/2 cup brown sugar
1/2 cup white sugar
3 tbsps corn starch
1/2 tsp ground cinnamon
1/2 tsp allspice
1/8 tsp salt
1 tbsp cider vinegar
2 tbsps lite margarine
1 tbsp grated orange rind
2 (9-inch) prepared pie crusts

*Chef's Tips on Weight loss...
ice cream—cut back serving by
half or use reduced calorie frozen
desserts.*

☞ METHOD:

Preheat oven to 400 degrees F. Line a 9-inch pie pan with 1 of the crusts by pressing it firmly into the pan.

In a 3-quart cast iron dutch oven, heat 2/3 cup of water, along with raisins, over medium-high heat. Simmer for 5 minutes.

In a separate bowl, combine sugars, corn starch, cinnamon, allspice and salt. Whisk in remaining 1 1/3 cups of water and, when well-blended, add to the simmering raisins. Stir constantly until mixture bubbles up in the pot. Add vinegar, margarine and orange rind. Continue to cook until margarine melts in the mixture. Remove and allow the mixture to cool until lukewarm.

Pour the cooled mixture into the unbaked pie shell. Top with the second pie crust, crimping the edges in a decorative fashion. Cut 2–3 slits in the top of the crust to allow steam to escape during cooking.

Bake 25–30 minutes or until pie crust is golden brown and pie is bubbling up in the middle. Allow pie to cool completely before cutting.

Nutrition Facts...now

Calories:	396
Total Fat:	12gm
Saturated Fat:	4gm
% Calories from Fat:	26
Cholesterol:	0mg
Sodium:	262mg
Carbohydrate:	73gm
Fiber:	2gm
Protein:	3gm

PREP TIME: 1 Hour   SERVES: 8

☞ **INGREDIENTS:**

3 tbsps lemon juice
1 tsp lemon rind
1 (9-inch) prepared pie crust
2 cups milk
3/4 cup sugar
1/4 tsp salt
4 tbsps corn starch
3 eggs, separated
1/4 tsp cream of tartar
1/2 cup sugar
1 tsp lemon juice

Strawberry season at a produce stand near Raceland.

☞ **METHOD:**

Preheat oven to 350 degrees F. Line a 9-inch pie pan with the crust, crimping the edges in a decorative fashion. Using a fork, prick 10–15 times around the bottom of the pie shell. Bake until shell is fully cooked and lightly browned. Remove and cool. In a cast iron sauce pan, heat milk to a simmer. Do not boil. In a mixing bowl, combine 3/4 cup of sugar, salt, corn starch and egg yolks. Whisk well until ingredients are thoroughly incorporated. Add approximately 1 cup of the hot milk to the egg mixture, while whisking constantly. Pour the warm egg mixture into the sauce pan with remaining milk. Continue to whisk until custard is thickened. Add 3 tablespoons of lemon juice and lemon rind. Cook 1 additional minute. Remove from heat and pour into the cooked pie shell. Once the pie has cooled slightly, make the meringue by whisking the egg whites with the cream of tartar until stiff. Slowly add the 1/2 cup of sugar while whisking constantly. Fold in the teaspoon of lemon juice and spread the whipped meringue over the cooled pie. Seal the edges to avoid shrinking. Bake 10–15 minutes or until meringue is golden brown.

"Our family goes back six generations in Louisiana. Like most families down here, we were a large group and often got together on Sundays and holidays.

"My mother was known for her famous lemon pie. Although most people use water, she always used milk and people just seemed to love the flavor."
Peggy Foreman,
Lake Charles, Louisiana

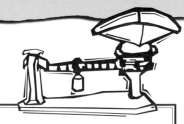

✽Nutrition Facts...then✽

Calories: 284
Total Fat: 9gm
Saturated Fat: 4gm
% Calories from Fat: 29
Cholesterol: 88mg
Sodium: 225mg
Carbohydrate: 46gm
Fiber: 0gm
Protein: 5gm

OLD FASHIONED LEMON PIE

PREP TIME: 1 Hour   SERVES: 8

INGREDIENTS:

3 tbsps lemon juice
1 tsp lemon rind
1 (9-inch) prepared pie crust
2 cups skim milk
3/4 cup sugar
1/4 tsp salt
5 tbsps corn starch
3/4 cup egg substitute
3 egg whites
1/4 tsp cream of tartar
1/2 cup sugar
1 tsp lemon juice

METHOD:

Preheat oven to 350 degrees F. Line a 9-inch pie pan with the crust, crimping the edges in a decorative fashion. Using a fork, prick 10–15 times around the bottom of the pie shell. Bake until shell is fully cooked and lightly browned. Remove and cool.

In a cast iron sauce pan, heat skim milk to a simmer. Do not boil.

In a mixing bowl, combine 3/4 cup of sugar, salt, corn starch and egg substitute. Whisk well until ingredients are thoroughly incorporated. Add approximately 1 cup of the hot milk to the egg mixture, while whisking constantly. Pour the warm egg mixture into the sauce pan with remaining milk. Continue to whisk until custard is thickened. Add 3 tablespoons of lemon juice and lemon rind. Cook 1 additional minute. Remove from heat and pour into the cooked pie shell.

Once the pie has cooled slightly, make the meringue by whisking the 3 egg whites with the cream of tartar until stiff. Slowly add in the 1/2 cup of sugar while whisking constantly. Fold in the teaspoon of lemon juice and spread the whipped meringue over the cooled pie. Seal the edges to avoid shrinking. Bake 10–15 minutes or until meringue is golden brown.

Nutrition Facts...now

Calories:	281
Total Fat:	7gm
Saturated Fat:	2gm
% Calories from Fat:	21
Cholesterol:	1mg
Sodium:	323mg
Carbohydrate:	48gm
Fiber:	1gm
Protein:	7gm

Get ready to stop, there's peaches ahead.

PREP TIME: 1 Hour   MAKES: 30 (3-inch) cookies

☞ INGREDIENTS:

1/4 pound butter
1 1/2 cups sugar
3 eggs
2 tbsps vanilla
4 cups flour
4 tsps baking powder
1/2 cup flour
1/4 pound butter
6 ounces powdered sugar
1 tsp vanilla
1/4 cup milk

☞ METHOD:

In a large mixing bowl, cream 1/4 pound butter and sugar using an electric mixer. Add eggs, one at a time, beating well after each addition. Blend in the vanilla. Gradually beat in flour and baking powder until all is well-blended. Once the dough is well mixed, roll it into a large ball, cover and place in the refrigerator overnight. When ready to bake, preheat oven to 350 degrees F. Flour a large work surface and roll the dough out to 1/4-inch thick. Cut into decorative shapes and place on a baking sheet. Bake 5–10 minutes or until cookies are lightly browned. To make the icing, place butter in a cast iron sauce pan over medium-high heat. When butter is melted, add powdered sugar and vanilla. Remove from heat and add milk to thin out the mixture. Add your favorite food coloring as desired. The consistency should be that of a soft peanut butter. Once the cookies are cool, spread with the icing and allow to dry.

"Every Christmas Eve, my grandmother, Florence Gravois, would make a batch of Petite Gateaux and divide it among her thirty-one grandchildren. Her intention was for us not to eat the cookies but to leave them out with a glass of milk for Santa Claus. Of course, mine would never make it home.

"The only way home from my grandparents' house in South Vacherie was River Road where the bonfires were lit at 7:00 pm to light the way for Santa Claus. I hope you enjoy this recipe as much as Santa does."
Melissa Folse
Vacherie, Louisiana

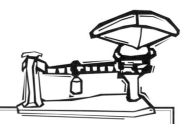

❋Nutrition Facts...then❋

Calories: 196
Total Fat: 7gm
Saturated Fat: 4gm
% Calories from Fat: 31
Cholesterol: 38mg
Sodium: 73mg
Carbohydrate: 31gm
Fiber: 1gm
Protein: 3gm

(per cookie)

PREP TIME: 1 Hour MAKES: 30 (3-inch) cookies

☞ INGREDIENTS:

1/2 cup lite margarine
1 1/2 cups sugar
3/4 cup egg substiute
2 tbsps vanilla
4 cups flour
4 tsps baking powder
1/2 cup flour
10 ounces powdered sugar
1 tsp vanilla
1/4 cup skim milk

☞ METHOD:

In a large mixing bowl, cream margarine and sugar using an electric mixer. Add egg substitute and vanilla, blending well. Combine flour and baking powder and gradually add to the creamed mixture until dough is well mixed. The dough will be sticky to the touch. Roll it into a large ball, cover and place in the refrigerator overnight.

When ready to bake, preheat oven to 350 degrees F. Flour a large work surface and roll the dough out to 1/4-inch thick. Cut into decorative shapes and place on a baking sheet. Bake 10 minutes or until cookies are lightly browned.

To make the icing, place powdered sugar, vanilla and skim milk in a cast iron sauce pan over medium-high heat. Stir until sugar is fully dissolved. Remove from heat and add your favorite food coloring as desired. The consistency should be that of a soft peanut butter.

Once the cookies are cool, spread with the icing and allow to dry.

Nutrition Facts...now

Calories:	165
Total Fat:	2gm
Saturated Fat:	0gm
% Calories from Fat:	10
Cholesterol:	0mg
Sodium:	28mg
Carbohydrate:	34gm
Fiber:	1gm
Protein:	3gm

(per cookie)

PREP TIME: 1 Hour   MAKES: 40 (3-inch) cookies

☞ INGREDIENTS:

1 cup butter
2 1/4 cups sugar
2 tbsps cream
2 eggs
1 tbsp vanilla
4 cups flour
3 tsps baking powder
1/2 tsp salt
1/2 cup flour
1/2 cup sugar
1/4 cup sugar

☞ METHOD:

Preheat oven to 350 degrees F. In a large mixing bowl, cream butter and 2 1/4 cups of sugar together with an electric mixer. When well-blended, add cream and eggs, one at a time, beating after each addition. When all is incorporated, add vanilla and blend completely. Into the mixing bowl, sift 4 cups of the flour, baking powder and salt. Continue to mix until dough is well-blended. Remove the dough ball, knead once or twice and divide it into 4 equal portions. On the top of a flat working surface, sprinkle approximately 1/2 cup flour and 1/2 cup sugar. Roll the dough really thin (the thinner the better for a crispier cookie). Sprinkle the top of the rolled pastry with about 1/4 cup of sugar. Cut the cookies with a cookie cutter and, using a spatula, place each cookie on a lightly greased baking sheet. Bake 10 minutes and, when cooled, remove from the pan. These cookies are very crisp and tender, but must be placed in an air-tight container to remain that way. Excellent when served with milk or coffee.

"We Germans of Louisiana are just like the Cajuns in that we love good food and family. I grew up in the German community of Roberts Cove, near Rayne, Louisiana.

"Although we love potatoes and sauerkraut, pastries were always my favorite. They were served mid-morning and mid-afternoon with coffee and milk. Every German family in our neighborhood kept a tin of these platzchens ready in case company dropped in.

"Both of my parents lived into their late 80s, and were the heart of a very close-knit family with a strong Catholic faith. Family, faith and food - that's what we Germans are all about."

Dot Ohlenforst Leger
Rayne, Louisiana

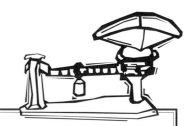

❋Nutrition Facts...then❋

Calories: 157
Total Fat: 5gm
Saturated Fat: 3gm
% Calories from Fat: 29
Cholesterol: 26mg
Sodium: 79mg
Carbohydrate: 26gm
Fiber: 0gm
Protein: 2gm

(per cookie)

PREP TIME: 1 Hour   MAKES: 40 (3-inch) cookies

☞ INGREDIENTS:

1 cup lite margarine
2 1/4 cups sugar
2 tbsps evaporated skim milk
1/2 cup egg substitute
1 tbsp vanilla
4 cups flour
3 tsps baking powder
1/4 tsp salt
1/2 cup flour
1/2 cup sugar
1/4 cup sugar

☞ METHOD:

Preheat oven to 350 degrees F. In a large mixing bowl, cream margarine and 2 1/4 cups of sugar together with an electric mixer. When well-blended, add skim milk and egg substitute. When all is incorporated, add vanilla and blend completely.

Into the mixing bowl, sift 4 cups of flour, baking powder and salt. Continue to mix until dough is well-blended. At this point, the dough will be extremely sticky and tender to the touch.

On the top of a flat working surface, sprinkle approximately 1/2 cup flour and 1/2 cup sugar. Remove the dough ball and place on the

Road sign outside Opelousas.

floured surface. Sprinkle a small amount of flour on top of the dough and knead once or twice, dividing it into 4 equal portions. Roll the dough really thin (the thinner the better for a crispier cookie). Sprinkle the top of the rolled pastry with about 1/4 cup of sugar. Cut the cookies with a cookie cutter and, using a spatula, place each cookie on a lightly greased baking sheet. Bake 10 minutes and, when cooled, remove from the pan.

These cookies are very crisp and tender, but must be placed in an air-tight container to remain that way. Excellent when served with milk or coffee.

Chef's Tips on Weight loss... treat your sweets sparingly.

Nutrition Facts...now

Calories: 89
Total Fat: 2gm
Saturated Fat: 0gm
% Calories from Fat: 16
Cholesterol: 0mg
Sodium: 49mg
Carbohydrate: 17gm
Fiber: 0gm
Protein: 1gm

(per cookie)

RUSSIAN ROCK COOKIES

PREP TIME: 1 Hour   MAKES: 5 dozen

☞ INGREDIENTS:

1/2 cup butter
1 1/2 cups sugar
3 eggs
1 tsp baking soda
1 tbsp boiling water
2 tsps ground cloves
2 tsps ground allspice
2 tsps ground nutmeg
2 1/2 cups flour
1 pound chopped pecans
1 pound raisins

☞ METHOD:

Preheat oven to 325 degrees F. In a large mixing bowl, cream butter and sugar using an electric mixer. Add eggs, one at a time, beating completely after each addition. Dissolve baking soda in boiling water and whip into the egg mixture. Add cloves, allspice and nutmeg, blending well. Add the flour, pecans and raisins. Continue to mix until well-blended. Drop the dough onto greased cookie sheets using a teaspoon. Bake the drop cookies for 20 minutes. Cool before storing in an air-tight container.

"I can remember no better smell than walking into my grandmother's kitchen when she was baking cookies. Without a doubt, Ma Mum Russo baked the best Russian Rock Cookies that I've ever eaten. Some of my fondest memories while growing up were those shared in Ma Mum's kitchen while she was baking."
Honorine Abel
Patterson, Louisiana

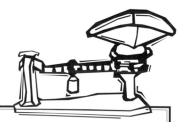

❧Nutrition Facts...then❧

Calories: 130
Total Fat: 7gm
Saturated Fat: 2gm
% Calories from Fat: 46
Cholesterol: 15mg
Sodium: 41mg
Carbohydrate: 17gm
Fiber: 1gm
Protein: 2gm

(per cookie)

PREP TIME: 1 Hour   MAKES: 5 dozen

☞ **INGREDIENTS:**

1/2 cup lite margarine
1 1/2 cups sugar
3/4 cup egg substitute
1 tsp baking soda
1 tbsp boiling water
2 tsps ground cloves
2 tsps ground allspice
2 tsps ground nutmeg
2 1/2 cups flour
1/2 pound chopped pecans
1 pound raisins
vegetable spray

☞ **METHOD:**

Preheat oven to 325 degrees F. In a large mixing bowl, cream margarine and sugar using an electric mixer. Add egg substitute, a little at a time, beating completely after each addition.

Dissolve baking soda in boiling water and whip into the egg mixture. Add cloves, allspice and nutmeg, blending well. Add the flour, pecans and raisins. Continue to mix until well-blended.

Using a teaspoon, drop the dough onto cookie sheets coated with vegetable spray. Bake the drop cookies for 20 minutes. Cool before storing in an air-tight container.

Nutrition Facts...now

Calories:	94
Total Fat:	4gm
Saturated Fat:	0gm
% Calories from Fat:	31
Cholesterol:	0mg
Sodium:	44mg
Carbohydrate:	16gm
Fiber:	1gm
Protein:	1gm

(per cookie)

PREP TIME: 1 Hour   MAKES: 2 (9-inch) pies (16 servings)

☞ INGREDIENTS:

10 ounces coconut
3 (5-ounce) cans evaporated milk
1 1/2 cups whole milk
1/2 cup sugar
3 tsps vanilla
6 tbsps corn starch
1/2 cup water
3 eggs, separated
1 tsp cream of tartar
1/2 cup sugar
2 (9-inch) baked pie shells

"Coconut pie was a two-day family undertaking when I was growing up on Big Bayou Black near Gibson.

"First we had to wait until the general store truck from Gibson came by. We would place our order one day, and our groceries (and shoes, material for clothing, medicines and just about everything else) would be delivered the next.

"Then it was my father's job to crack the coconut with a hammer and (with my help) to peel it. After that, it had to be grated on one of those slant-faced hand graters we called 'knuckle-busters,' after which the coconut was turned over to my mother.

She made the custard from fresh milk and heavy cream and the yolks of yard eggs from our own chickens and beat the whites into a meringue with a steel whisk.

Then into the wood-fired cookstove oven it went, once she had determined, by feel and timing, that the oven was the right temperature. I doubt she had ever heard the word 'thermostat.'

You had to watch carefully when something was baking, so every kitchen came equipped with a comfortable rocking chair. The kitchen table served as the 'family room' in those days."

Marjorie Domangue
Houma, Louisiana

☞ METHOD:

Preheat oven to 400 degrees F. In a cast iron sauce pan, combine evaporated milk, whole milk, 1/2 cup sugar and vanilla. Bring to a low boil, reduce to simmer and cook 10 minutes. While milk is simmering, combine corn starch and water. Add egg yolks, blending well into the corn starch mixture. Slowly pour the corn starch/egg yolk mixture into the hot milk, whisking constantly until sauce thickens. Add 8 ounces of the coconut into the cream, blend well, and remove from heat. Pour the hot mixture into the 2 baked pie shells and allow to cool slightly. Place the egg whites in a metal bowl and, with an electric mixture, beat until soft peaks begin to form. Sprinkle in cream of tartar and 1/2 cup of sugar and continue beating until egg whites are stiff. Spread mixture evenly over the 2 pie shells, making sure the edges are well sealed to keep the meringue from shrinking. Sprinkle evenly with remaining coconut and bake until meringue is golden brown.

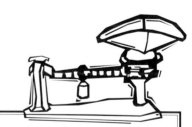

❊Nutrition Facts...then❊

Calories: 266
Total Fat: 14gm
Saturated Fat: 8gm
% Calories from Fat: 46
Cholesterol: 44mg
Sodium: 225mg
Carbohydrate: 32gm
Fiber: 1gm
Protein: 5gm

COCONUT CREAM PIE

PREP TIME: 1 Hour   MAKES: 2 (9-inch) pies (16 servings)

☞ INGREDIENTS:

10 ounces coconut
3 (5-ounce) cans evaporated skim milk
1 1/2 cups skim milk
1/2 cup sugar
3 tsps vanilla
6 tbsps corn starch
1/2 cup water
3/4 cup egg substitute
3 egg whites
1 tsp cream of tartar
1/2 cup sugar
2 (9-inch) baked pie shells

☞ METHOD:

Preheat oven to 400 degrees F. In a cast iron sauce pan, combine evaporated milk, skim milk, 1/2 cup sugar and vanilla. Bring to a low boil, reduce to simmer and cook 10 minutes.

While milk is simmering, combine corn starch and water. Add egg substitute and blend well into the corn starch mixture. Slowly pour the corn starch/egg mixture into the hot milk, whisking constantly, until sauce thickens. Add 8 ounces of the coconut into the cream, blend well, and remove from heat. Pour the hot mixture into the 2 baked pie shells and allow to cool slightly.

Early morning in the heart of Abbeville reveals the statue of The Reverend Antoine Desire Megret, the founder of the original settlement of Abbeville, next to St. Mary Magdalen Church.

Place the egg whites in a metal bowl and, with an electric mixture, beat until soft peaks begin to form. Sprinkle in cream of tartar and 1/2 cup of sugar and continue beating until egg whites are stiff.

Spread mixture evenly over the 2 pie shells, making sure the edges are well sealed to keep the meringue from shrinking. Sprinkle evenly with remaining coconut and bake until meringue is golden brown.

Nutrition Facts...now

Calories:	286
Total Fat:	13gm
Saturated Fat:	7gm
% Calories from Fat:	39
Cholesterol:	1mg
Sodium:	283mg
Carbohydrate:	37gm
Fiber:	1gm
Protein:	7gm

PREP TIME: 1 Hour   SERVES: 8

☞ INGREDIENTS:

1/2 cup semi-sweet chocolate chips
1 1/2 cups chopped pecans
1 cup sugar
1/4 tsp salt
1 cup dark corn syrup
3 eggs
1/4 pound butter, cut into small pieces
1 1/2 tsps vanilla
1 (9-inch) unbaked pie shell

☞ METHOD:

Preheat the oven to 350 degrees F. In a small sauce pan, combine sugar, salt and corn syrup. Cook over medium heat, stirring constantly, until sugar dissolves. In a separate bowl, using a wire whisk, beat the eggs until well-blended. Do not overwhip. Set aside. After sugar is completely melted, remove from heat and add butter, one piece at a time, until melted. Add eggs, vanilla and pecans, continuing to stir constantly. Fold in the chocolate. Pour the mixture into the pie shell. It is a good idea to put the pie pan on a cookie sheet to catch any spills. Bake for 40–50 minutes. Allow to cool thoroughly on a wire rack.

"The Academy of the Sacred Heart at Grand Coteau has been an important part of Acadiana since the early 1800s. Over the past 175 years, thousands of young women have walked through the halls of this institution. Since many of these young girls travelled to Grand Coteau from small towns and villages in South Louisiana, often they chose to board at the school.

"The women who cooked here were not professionally trained chefs, but people who grew up in the area, cooking indigenous foods of Cajun country. On special holidays, called Conges, the students were treated to fancier meals.

"Usually this pecan pie was the dessert served. The pecans were actually harvested from the very trees growing on and around the Academy grounds."

Marie Orgeron
Grand Coteau, Louisiana

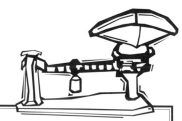

❧Nutrition Facts...then❧

Calories: 478
Total Fat: 27gm
Saturated Fat: 9gm
% Calories from Fat: 49
Cholesterol: 76mg
Sodium: 219mg
Carbohydrate: 60gm
Fiber: 1gm
Protein: 3gm

PREP TIME: 1 Hour   SERVES: 8

☞ INGREDIENTS:

1/2 cup semi-sweet reduced-fat chocolate chips
1 cup chopped pecans
1/2 cup sugar
1/4 tsp salt
1 1/4 cups dark corn syrup
1/4 cup lite margarine, cut into small pieces
3/4 cup egg substitute
1 1/2 tsps vanilla
1/2 cup Grape Nuts cereal
1 (9-inch) unbaked pie shell

☞ METHOD:

Preheat the oven to 350 degrees F. In a small sauce pan, combine sugar, salt and corn syrup. Cook over medium heat, stirring constantly, until sugar dissolves.

After sugar is completely melted, remove from heat and add margarine, one piece at a time, until melted. Add egg substitute, vanilla, pecans and Grape Nuts, while continuing to stir constantly. Fold in the chocolate.

Pour the mixture into the pie shell. It is a good idea to put the pie pan on a cookie sheet to catch any spills. Bake 45–50 minutes. Allow to cool thoroughly on a wire rack.

*Chef's Tips on Weight loss...
lighten the alcohol/dilute the drink.*

Nutrition Facts...now

Calories:	489
Total Fat:	20gm
Saturated Fat:	3gm
% Calories from Fat:	33
Cholesterol:	0mg
Sodium:	321mg
Carbohydrate:	76gm
Fiber:	2gm
Protein:	5gm

These trees are all that remain of the L'Ombrage de Chene (Shadow of the Oaks) Plantation. Today they are cared for by Ray Dufrene, the new owner of the property on Bayou Lafourche in Raceland.

PREP TIME: 1 1/2 Hours   SERVES: 10

☞ INGREDIENTS:

6 eggs
1 1/2 cups sugar
3 (5-ounce) cans evaporated milk
2 cups whole milk
2 tbsps vanilla
1/8 tsp nutmeg

☞ METHOD:

Preheat oven to 350 degrees F. In a large mixing bowl, whip eggs and sugar until pale yellow and ribbony. Add evaporated and whole milk while continuing to blend. Once eggs and milk are thoroughly incorporated, add vanilla and nutmeg. Pour the mixture into a 9" x 13" baking pan. Place on the center rack of the oven and bake for 25 minutes. Reduce oven temperature to 325 degrees F and bake an additional 30 minutes or until custard is golden brown on top. Remove from oven and allow to cool thoroughly. You may wish to cook the custard in individual custard cups or with caramel sauce for additional flavor.

Chef's Tips on Weight loss...
you're sweet enough—
cut back sugar intake by one half.

"As children, we often had Sunday dinner at Grandmother's house. It was so impressive because she never had less than seven courses. One was always her wonderful baked custard. She made it from scratch and always served it from a baking pan rather than custard cups.

"When I asked her for the recipe, she said that she had learned it from her mother, who had learned it from her mother, and so on, but that she would be happy to share it with me.

"However, it wasn't quite that simple. In fact, I had to watch my grandmother and mother prepare the dish many times to really determine the measurements. It is a simple but great recipe and I am happy to share it with you."

Cherie Zeringue
Shreiver, Louisiana

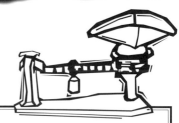

❦Nutrition Facts...then❦

Calories:	232
Total Fat:	7gm
Saturated Fat:	4gm
% Calories from Fat:	26
Cholesterol:	91mg
Sodium:	90mg
Carbohydrate:	37gm
Fiber:	0gm
Protein:	7gm

OEUFS AUX LAIT (EGG CUSTARD)

PREP TIME: 1 1/2 Hours   SERVES: 10

☞ INGREDIENTS:

1 1/2 cups egg substitute
1 1/2 cups sugar
2 tbsps corn starch
6 (5-ounce) cans evaporated skim milk
2 tbsps vanilla
1/8 tsp nutmeg

☞ METHOD:

Preheat oven to 350 degrees F. In a large mixing bowl, combine sugar and corn starch and blend well. Add egg substitute and, using a wire whisk, whip until pale yellow and ribbony. Add evaporated milk and blend into the egg mixture. Once incorporated, add vanilla and nutmeg.

Pour the mixture into a 9" x 13" baking pan. Place on the center rack of the oven and bake for 25 minutes. Reduce oven temperature to 325 degrees F and bake an additional 30 minutes or until custard is golden brown on top. Remove from oven and allow to cool thoroughly.

I find that it is best to cook the custard in 10 individual custard cups. The cups should then be placed into a baking pan with 1-inch of water surrounding the cups. This cooking process gives the custard a creamier flavor.

Nutrition Facts...now

Calories:	240
Total Fat:	1gm
Saturated Fat:	0gm
% Calories from Fat:	6
Cholesterol:	3mg
Sodium:	178mg
Carbohydrate:	43gm
Fiber:	0gm
Protein:	12gm

PREP TIME: 1 Hour   MAKES: 35 cookies

☞ INGREDIENTS:

1 cup mixed candied fruit, chopped
3/4 cup raisins
1 cup all purpose flour, sifted
1/4 cup butter
3/4 cup brown sugar
1 egg
1/4 cup evaporated milk
1 tsp lemon juice
1/4 tsp baking soda
1/4 tsp salt
1/2 tsp ground cinnamon
1/2 tsp ground cloves
1/2 tsp ground allspice
1/4 tsp ground nutmeg
1 cup chopped pecans

☞ METHOD:

Preheat oven to 375 degrees F. Coat candied fruit and raisins with 1/4 cup flour and set aside. In a large mixing bowl, cream butter and sugar until light and fluffy. Whip in the egg and incorporate totally into the mixture. Add the milk and lemon juice, while continuing to blend well. Sprinkle in the balance of the sifted flour, soda, salt and spices. Stir well to blend into the butter mixture. Add the coated fruit, raisins and pecans. When thoroughly blended, drop the dough in teaspoon-size portions onto a lightly oiled cookie sheet. Bake 12–15 minutes or until cookies are done. NOTE: The finished cookie dough will appear quite chunky with fruit and nuts and with very little dough. The dough will rise substantially in the cooking process.

"Not every dish in Cajun country comes from some ancient Acadian tradition, brought down from Nova Scotia hundreds of years ago, or from kitchens that looked out onto moss-draped oaks. If these cookies remind you a lot of the ones your grandmother made in Kentucky or Connecticut, I wouldn't be at all surprised.

"This recipe, you see, came right out of my old reliable Better Homes and Gardens Cookbook!

"But they're a part of my family's Christmas tradition. So, to me, they will always be associated with this land, my people, my friends and happy times. And that should be authentic enough for anyone."
Doris Schexnaydre
Shreiver, Louisiana

❊Nutrition Facts...then❊

Calories:	90
Total Fat:	4gm
Saturated Fat:	1gm
% Calories from Fat:	36
Cholesterol:	8mg
Sodium:	43mg
Carbohydrate:	14gm
Fiber:	1gm
Protein:	1gm

(per cookie)

FRUITCAKE COOKIES

PREP TIME: 1 Hour   MAKES: 35 cookies

☞ INGREDIENTS:

1 cup mixed candied fruit, chopped
3/4 cup raisins
1 cup all purpose flour, sifted
1/4 cup lite margarine
3/4 cup brown sugar
1/4 cup egg substitute
1/4 cup evaporated skim milk
1 tsp lemon juice
1/4 tsp baking soda
1/4 tsp salt
1/2 tsp ground cinnamon
1/2 tsp ground cloves
1/2 tsp ground allspice
1/4 tsp ground nutmeg
3/4 cup chopped pecans

Lots of kids and teachers helped create this mural on Courthouse Square in Opelousas. The project was part of the St. Landry Parish gifted student program and was completed in May of 1995.

☞ METHOD:

Preheat oven to 375 degrees F. Coat candied fruit and raisins with 1/4 cup flour and set aside.

In a large mixing bowl, cream margarine and sugar until light and fluffy. Whip in egg substitute and incorporate totally into the mixture. Add skim milk and lemon juice, while continuing to blend well. Sprinkle in the balance of sifted flour, soda, salt and spices. Stir well to blend into the margarine mixture. Add the coated fruit, raisins and pecans.

When thoroughly blended, drop the dough in teaspoon-size portions onto a lightly oiled cookie sheet. Bake 12–15 minutes or until cookies are done.

NOTE: The finished cookie dough will appear quite chunky with fruit and nuts and with very little dough. The dough will rise substantially in the cooking process.

Nutrition Facts...now

Calories:	77
Total Fat:	2gm
Saturated Fat:	0gm
% Calories from Fat:	26
Cholesterol:	0mg
Sodium:	46mg
Carbohydrate:	14gm
Fiber:	1gm
Protein:	1gm

(per cookie)

CAJUN GINGER COOKIES

PREP TIME: 1 Hour   MAKES: 45 cookies

☞ INGREDIENTS:

1 tsp ground ginger
1/2 cup plus 2 tbsps margarine
1 cup sugar
1/4 cup molasses
1 egg
2 cups all purpose flour
2 tsps baking soda
1 tsp ground cinnamon
vegetable spray

☞ METHOD:

Preheat oven to 350 degrees F. In a large mixing bowl, cream margarine and 3/4 cup of the sugar. Whip at medium speed until light and fluffy. Add molasses and egg while continuing to blend well. Combine flour, soda, ginger and cinnamon. Add to the creamed mixture, stirring constantly until well-blended. Because of the molasses and sugar, this dough will be extremely sticky. Divide the dough into 2 equal portions, cover with plastic wrap and place in the freezer for 1 hour. Coat a large cookie sheet with the vegetable spray. Tear the dough into approximately 45 one-inch balls. Roll the balls in the remaining sugar and place 2 inches apart on the cookie sheet. Bake approximately 15 minutes and cool on a wire rack.

"I can't claim this recipe goes back to antiquity - in fact, it's brand new. But it has passed the ultimate Cajun cookie test.
"My daughter is a dietitian, and she enlisted me to work with her on recipes for low-fat cookies. After we'd come up with several, I baked a batch from each recipe and invited in a group of the world's leading cookie experts - children from my neighborhood, in the little town of Sunset.
"These ginger cookies were the ones that completely disappeared. You can always trust a food critic under the age of 12!"
Alma Proffitt
Sunset, Louisiana

Chef's Tips on Weight loss... use lowfat/non fat yogurt instead of sour cream.

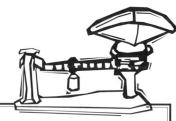

❧Nutrition Facts...then❧

Calories: 66
Total Fat: 3gm
Saturated Fat: 1gm
% Calories from Fat: 36
Cholesterol: 5mg
Sodium: 88mg
Carbohydrate: 10gm
Fiber: 0gm
Protein: 1gm

(per cookie)

PREP TIME: 1 Hour   MAKES: 45 cookies

☞ INGREDIENTS:

1 tsp ground ginger
1/2 cup plus 2 tbsps lite margarine
1 cup sugar
1/4 cup molasses
1/4 cup egg substitute
2 cups all purpose flour
2 tsps baking soda
1 tsp ground cinnamon
vegetable spray

☞ METHOD:

Preheat oven to 350 degrees F. In a large mixing bowl, cream margarine and 3/4 cup of the sugar. Whip at medium speed until light and fluffy. Add molasses and egg substitute and continue to blend well.

Combine flour, soda, ginger and cinnamon. Add to the creamed mixture, stirring constantly until well-blended. Because of the molasses and sugar, this dough will be extremely sticky.

Divide the dough into 2 equal portions, cover in plastic wrap and place in the freezer for 1 hour.

Coat a large cookie sheet with the vegetable spray. Tear the dough into approximately 45 one-inch balls. Sprinkle the balls with the remaining sugar and place 2 inches apart on the cookie sheet. Bake approximately 15 minutes and cool on a wire rack.

Nutrition Facts...now

Calories:	54
Total Fat:	1gm
Saturated Fat:	0gm
% Calories from Fat:	22
Cholesterol:	0mg
Sodium:	88mg
Carbohydrate:	10gm
Fiber:	0gm
Protein:	1mg

(per cookie)

PREP TIME: 1 Hour   SERVES: 8

☞ INGREDIENTS:

1 (29-ounce) can sliced peaches, in syrup
1 tsp corn starch
1/4 pound butter
1 cup self-rising flour
1/2 cup sugar
1 cup milk
1 tsp baking powder
1/4 tsp nutmeg

☞ METHOD:

Preheat oven to 350 degrees F. Using a wire whisk, whip approximately 1/4 cup of the peach syrup with the corn starch until well-blended. Set aside. Place the butter in an 8- or 10-inch cast iron skillet to melt over medium heat. In a large mixing bowl, combine flour and sugar. Slowly pour in milk, whisking constantly. Add baking powder and continue to whip until well-blended. Batter will appear to be slightly lumpy. Once the butter is melted, remove from heat and allow to cool slightly. Pour the batter directly into the skillet over the melted butter. Blend the dissolved corn starch with the remaining syrup, peaches and nutmeg. Pour fruit over the batter. Bake on the bottom shelf of the oven for 50–60 minutes or until cobbler is golden brown. Allow to cool slightly before serving.

"There were eleven of us in my family, growing up in the little Lafourche parish town of Lockport back in the 1920s and '30s.

"Those were very strict times, socially. I remember we had Saturday night dances as the big social event of the week, and all the parents came along to chaperone. They stayed all evening, and escorted us back home at eleven o'clock - 11:30 at the latest.

"My father was a conductor on the Southern Pacific Railroad, and, for those days, made a good living - and a steady one, which was anything but assured during the Depression.

"Still, I don't see how he and my mother managed to send all eleven of us through college. I do remember having to wait a year to start, when I graduated high school in 1933, because there were already three in college at that time. I couldn't start until someone else graduated!

"Of the eleven of us, eight became school teachers and three became doctors. I would think that very few people attached more importance to education than my parents, even though they never got to go to college themselves."
                              Lolita DeFelice
                          Raceland, Louisiana

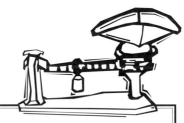

❧Nutrition Facts...then❧

Calories: 302
Total Fat: 13gm
Saturated Fat: 8gm
% Calories from Fat: 37
Cholesterol: 35mg
Sodium: 339mg
Carbohydrate: 47gm
Fiber: 3gm
Protein: 3gm

PREP TIME: 1 Hour   SERVES: 8

A New Orleans tradition, a produce vendor on Carrollton Avenue.

☞ INGREDIENTS:

1 (29-ounce) can sliced peaches, in lite syrup
1 tsp corn starch
1/2 cup lite margarine
1 cup self-rising flour
1/2 cup sugar
1 cup evaporated skim milk
1 tsp baking powder
1/4 tsp nutmeg

☞ METHOD:

Preheat oven to 350 degrees F. Using a wire whisk, whip approximately 1/4 cup of the peach syrup with the corn starch until well-blended. Set aside.

Place the margarine in an 8- or 10-inch cast iron skillet to melt over medium heat.

In a large mixing bowl, combine flour and sugar. Slowly pour in the skim milk, whisking constantly. Add baking powder and continue to whip until well-blended. Batter will appear to be slightly lumpy.

Once the margarine is melted, remove from heat and allow to cool slightly. Pour the batter directly into the skillet over the melted margarine.

Blend the dissolved corn starch with the remaining syrup, peaches and nutmeg. Pour fruit over the batter. Bake on the bottom shelf of the oven for 50–60 minutes or until cobbler is golden brown. Allow to cool slightly before serving.

Nutrition Facts...now

Calories: 237
Total Fat: 6gm
Saturated Fat: 1gm
% Calories from Fat: 23
Cholesterol: 1mg
Sodium: 294mg
Carbohydrate: 43gm
Fiber: 3gm
Protein: 4gm

PREP TIME: 1 Hour   SERVES: 12

☞ INGREDIENTS:

12 cooking pears, peeled and halved
1 cup lemon juice
1 cup brandy
2 tbsps nutmeg
3/4 cup lemon juice
4 whole cinnamon sticks
1 cup orange juice
6 lemon slices
1/4 tsp grated cinnamon
1 cup brown sugar
1 cup white sugar
1/2 cup brandy

☞ METHOD:

Once the pears are peeled and halved, soak them in cold water to retain color. In a container, combine drained pears with 1 cup lemon juice, 1 cup brandy and nutmeg. Mix well, cover and refrigerate overnight. The next day, remove the pears from the marinade, discarding the liquid. In a 5-quart cast iron dutch oven, combine 3/4 cup of lemon juice, cinnamon sticks, orange juice, lemon slices, cinnamon and brown sugar. Bring to a low simmer, stirring until sugar is dissolved. Add the marinated pears and white sugar. Remove from heat and slowly stir in the 1/2 cup of brandy. Return to heat and cook on medium, stirring occasionally, 30–40 minutes until pears are tender but not overcooked. Remove the cinnamon sticks and lemon slices. When pears are slightly cooled, they can be served with a scoop of vanilla ice cream.

Chef's Tips on Weight loss... trim fat from meat and poultry before cooking.

"Cooking pears, the large hard-core fruit found growing on trees throughout Louisiana, were often eaten raw as a snack. These pears, however, were more often canned or jarred in syrup and used as a pie or cobbler filling.

"In New Orleans, where I grew up, my mother would always cook the pears in a spicy fashion with brandy and serve them over homemade vanilla ice cream. That's where the term 'A La Mode' originated."
Captain William Eichaker, Jr.
Harahan, Louisiana

❖Nutrition Facts...then❖

Calories: 329
Total Fat: 1gm
Saturated Fat: 0gm
% Calories from Fat: 3
Cholesterol: 0mg
Sodium: 9mg
Carbohydrate: 67gm
Fiber: 5gm
Protein: 1gm

PREP TIME: 1 Hour   SERVES: 12

☞ INGREDIENTS:

12 cooking pears, peeled and halved
1 cup lemon juice
1 cup brandy
2 tbsps nutmeg
3/4 cup lemon juice
4 whole cinnamon sticks
1 cup orange juice
6 lemon slices
1/4 tsp grated cinnamon
1/2 cup brown sugar
1/2 cup white sugar
1/4 cup brandy

☞ METHOD:

Once the pears are peeled and halved, soak them in cold water to retain color.

In a container, combine drained pears with 1 cup lemon juice, 1 cup brandy and nutmeg. Mix well, cover and refrigerate overnight.

The next day, remove the pears from the marinade, discarding the liquid. In a 5-quart cast iron dutch oven, combine 3/4 cup of lemon juice, cinnamon sticks, orange juice, lemon slices, cinnamon and brown sugar. Bring to a low simmer, stirring until sugar is dissolved. Add the marinated pears and white sugar. Remove from heat and slowly stir in the 1/4 cup of brandy.

Return to heat and cook on medium, stirring occasionally, 30–40 minutes until pears are tender but not overcooked. Remove the cinnamon sticks and lemon slices. When pears are slightly cooled, they can be served with a scoop of fat-free vanilla ice cream.

Nutrition Facts...now

Calories:	251
Total Fat:	1gm
Saturated Fat:	0gm
% Calories from Fat:	4
Cholesterol:	0mg
Sodium:	5mg
Carbohydrate:	50gm
Fiber:	5gm
Protein:	1gm

PREP TIME: 1 1/2 Hours   SERVES: 10

☞ INGREDIENTS:

3 cups fresh blackberries
2 cups sugar
2 cups water
1/2 cup butter
2 1/2 cups self-rising flour
1/2 cup shortening
1/3 cup milk
1 egg
1/2 tsp ground cinnamon

☞ METHOD:

Preheat oven to 350 degrees F. In a small sauce pan, combine sugar and water. Bring to a rolling boil, stirring constantly until sugar dissolves thoroughly. Set aside and allow to cool slightly. Place butter in a 13" x 9" x 2" baking dish. Heat in the oven 2–3 minutes or until butter is melted. Remove and set aside. In a large mixing bowl, cut flour into shortening until it resembles coarse corn meal. Add milk and egg, stirring until ingredients are moistened. Turn dough out onto a floured surface and knead 4–5 times. Do not overwork. Roll dough into a 12" x 9" rectangle. Spread blackberries over the dough and sprinkle with cinnamon. Roll up in jelly-roll fashion, beginning with the 12-inch side. Cut into 1-inch slices and place, cut side down, in the buttered pan. Top with sugar syrup and bake for 1 hour or until cobbler is golden brown.

"My grandmother grew up in the country around the Red River. There she came to know how to use all of nature's gifts. Her recipe for blackberry cobbler, which she shared with my mother, only took about thirty minutes to prepare, but boy, how we grandchildren loved that dessert.

"I remember one day our city cousin came to visit. For lunch, my grandmother prepared a big meal including her famous blackberry pinwheel cobbler. Since we had no refrigerator to cool the milk, she put it down in the water well. Because it was a very hot day, the milk soured, but grandmother didn't know it and went on to serve it anyway.

"My city cousin, taking a sip of the milk discovered it to be sour. Not wanting to offend grandmother, he drank it down real fast. She served him a big wheel of cobbler and, seeing how he loved the milk, served him another big glass. We kids all laughed to ourselves. Needless to say, his next glass went down very slowly."

Bonnie Smith
DeQuincy, Louisiana

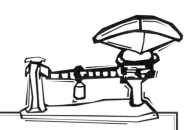

❊Nutrition Facts...then❊

Calories: 473
Total Fat: 21gm
Saturated Fat: 9gm
% Calories from Fat: 38
Cholesterol: 47mg
Sodium: 503mg
Carbohydrate: 69gm
Fiber: 7gm
Protein: 4gm

PREP TIME: 1 1/2 Hours   SERVES: 10

Rob Whitehurst tracks down another ripe blackberry along the roadside near Gramercy.

☞ INGREDIENTS:

3 cups fresh blackberries
2 cups sugar
2 cups water
vegetable spray
2 1/2 cups self-rising flour
1/2 cup lite margarine
1/3 cup evaporated skim milk
1/4 cup egg substitute
1/2 tsp ground cinnamon

☞ METHOD:

Preheat oven to 350 degrees F. In a small sauce pan, combine sugar and water. Bring to a rolling boil, stirring constantly until sugar dissolves thoroughly. Set aside and allow to cool slightly.

Spray a 13" x 9" x 2" baking dish with vegetable spray. Set aside.

In a large mixing bowl, cut flour into margarine until it resembles coarse corn meal. Add skim milk and egg substitute, stirring until ingredients are moistened. Turn dough out onto a floured surface and knead 4–5 times. Do not overwork.

Roll dough into a 12" x 9" rectangle. Spread blackberries over the dough and sprinkle with cinnamon. Roll up in jelly-roll fashion, beginning with the 12-inch side.

Cut into 1-inch slices and place, cut side down, in the sprayed baking dish. Top with sugar syrup and bake for 1 hour or until golden brown.

Nutrition Facts...now

Calories: 337
Total Fat: 5gm
Saturated Fat: 1gm
% Calories from Fat: 14
Cholesterol: 0mg
Sodium: 458mg
Carbohydrate: 70gm
Fiber: 7gm
Protein: 5gm

PREP TIME: 1 Hour   SERVES: 10

☞ INGREDIENTS:

3 cups grated raw sweet potatoes
2 cups sugar
1 cup vegetable oil
4 eggs
2 cups all purpose flour, sifted
2 tsps baking soda
2 tsps baking powder
2 tsps cinnamon
1 tsp salt
1/2 cup chopped pecans
1/2 stick margarine
1 box confectioner's sugar
1 (8-ounce) package cream cheese
2 tbsps vanilla

☞ METHOD:

NOTE: You should grate the sweet potatoes just prior to cooking; otherwise, they may turn dark. Preheat oven to 325 degrees F. Oil and flour three 9-inch cake pans. Set aside. In a large mixing bowl, combine sugar and oil. Using an electric mixer, beat until well-blended. Add eggs, one at a time, beating after each addition. In a separate bowl, combine flour, soda, baking powder, cinnamon and salt. Add, a little at a time, into the sugar mixture until all is incorporated. By hand, fold in the pecans and sweet potatoes. Evenly distribute the batter into the 3 pans. Bake 35–40 minutes or until cake tester comes out clean. While cakes are baking, create cream cheese filling by combining the softened margarine with confectioner's sugar and softened cream cheese. Using an electric mixer, whip the cream cheese mixture until smooth and fluffy. Add vanilla and continue to blend until icing is achieved. When cakes are done, remove from the oven and allow to cool. Remove cakes from pans and spread cream cheese filling between layers. Thoroughly cover cake with remaining icing.

"This recipe is a bit of culinary archeology. My grandmother, Aline Rodrigue, and my mother, Delores Robichaux, found it written on a scrap of paper tucked away in some family belongings. Since a good cook can sight-read a recipe the way a musician can sight-read a score, they knew they'd found a minor treasure.

"I'm not sure whether they made any changes, but by the time I was growing up, it was an established family favorite in this form. And we weren't the only ones who liked it. I won a prize for it in my home economics class at Raceland Junior High School, and could have gone on to the state competition, if we could have afforded the trip.

"We've never learned who wrote down that recipe, or where it originated.

"One word of caution: don't grate your sweet potatoes until just before you're ready to use them. Otherwise, they turn dark."

Darlene Foret
Raceland, Louisiana

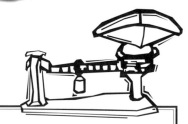

❧Nutrition Facts...then❧

Calories:	876
Total Fat:	41gm
Saturated Fat:	9gm
% Calories from Fat:	41
Cholesterol:	110mg
Sodium:	646mg
Carbohydrate:	122gm
Fiber:	1gm
Protein:	8gm

PREP TIME: 1 Hour   SERVES: 10

☞ INGREDIENTS:

3 cups grated raw sweet potatoes
2 cups sugar
3/4 cup vegetable oil
1 cup egg substitute
2 cups all purpose flour, sifted
2 tsps baking soda
2 tsps baking powder
2 tsps cinnamon
salt substitute
1/2 cup chopped pecans
1 box confectioner's sugar
1/2 tsp cream of tartar
3 egg whites
1 tbsp vanilla

☞ METHOD:

NOTE: You should grate the sweet potatoes just prior to cooking; otherwise, they may turn dark.

Preheat oven to 325 degrees F. Oil and flour three 9-inch cake pans. Set aside.

In a large mixing bowl, combine sugar and oil. Using an electric mixer, beat until well-blended. Add egg substitute a little at a time, beating after each addition.

In a separate bowl, combine flour, soda, baking powder, cinnamon and salt substitute. Add, a little at a time, into the sugar mixture until all is incorporated. By hand, fold in the pecans and sweet potatoes.

Evenly distribute the batter into the 3 pans. Bake 35–40 minutes or until cake tester comes out clean. When cakes are done, remove them from oven and allow to cool.

While cooling, create a royal icing by placing the sugar in the bowl of an electric mixer. Add cream of tartar and, while whipping on medium speed, add egg whites, one at a time. Add vanilla and blend well until stiff icing forms.

Remove cakes from pans and spread royal icing between layers. Thoroughly cover cake with remaining icing.

Nutrition Facts...now

Calories:	717
Total Fat:	21gm
Saturated Fat:	3gm
% Calories from Fat:	26
Cholesterol:	0mg
Sodium:	335mg
Carbohydrate:	121gm
Fiber:	1gm
Protein:	8gm

PREP TIME: 1 Hour   SERVES: 12

☞ INGREDIENTS:

2 red apples
2 green apples
1 tbsp lemon juice
4 peeled oranges, sectioned
4 sliced bananas
2 cups seedless red grapes
1 (20-ounce) can crushed pineapple, in juice
1 (3.5-ounce) can flaked coconut
1 (12-ounce) can evaporated milk
1 (10-ounce) jar cherries with stems, drained
1/2 cup sugar
mint leaves for garnish

☞ METHOD:

Core and dice apples. It is important that you place them in a container with water and a touch of lemon juice, to keep them from turning brown. When ready to assemble, drain the apples and place in a large mixing bowl. Cut the orange sections into bite-size pieces. Add bananas, grapes and pineapple. Toss the mixture to coat the apples with the pineapple juice to retain their color. Add the coconut, milk and cherries. Sprinkle with sugar and toss gently. Cover the bowl with clear wrap and refrigerate overnight. To serve, pour the mixture into a large cut-glass serving bowl and sprinkle with chopped mint leaves.

"I grew up in Acadia Parish, in the rural town of Ossun on Rodere Plantation. My grandfather, Constant Legere, built our Acadian-style home which consisted of two bedrooms, a living room, a dining room and the kitchen.

"There was a large garconiere upstairs where the walls were filled with mud and moss between the timbers. This was called boussillage construction. Only our living room walls were white-washed. The rest of the house, including the cypress beams, was all left unfinished.

"The dining-room table seated twelve to fourteen people. I'll never forget that, on holidays, we always had three to four seatings just to feed the family. My grandmother made a simple ambrosia that was always served on special occasions.

"Although the old home is no longer livable, it still stands on the family property. Every time I drive by to visit my son, who built a house nearby, I cannot help but remember those large family gatherings in our home. I can almost taste a plate of that great ambrosia."

Thelma Sonnier
Lafayette, Louisiana

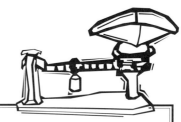

❦Nutrition Facts...then❦

Calories: 236
Total Fat: 6gm
Saturated Fat: 4gm
% Calories from Fat: 19
Cholesterol: 9mg
Sodium: 37mg
Carbohydrate: 47gm
Fiber: 3gm
Protein: 4gm

PREP TIME: 1 Hour   SERVES: 12

☞ INGREDIENTS:

2 red apples
2 green apples
1 tbsp lemon juice
4 peeled oranges, sectioned
4 sliced bananas
2 cups seedless red grapes
1 (20-ounce) can crushed pineapple in juice
1 (3.5-ounce) can flaked coconut
1 (12-ounce) can evaporated skim milk
1 (10-ounce) jar cherries with stems, drained
1/2 cup sugar
mint leaves for garnish

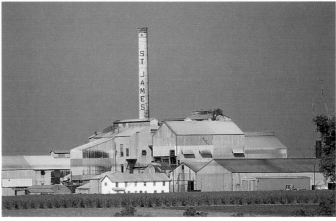

St. James Sugar Co-op in summer slumber.

*Chef's Tips on Weight loss...
when eating out, ask for dressings
and sauces on the side.*

☞ METHOD:

Core and dice apples. It is important that you place them in a container with water and a touch of lemon juice, to keep them from turning brown.

When ready to assemble, drain the apples and place in a large mixing bowl. Cut the orange sections into bite-size pieces. Add bananas, grapes and pineapple.

Toss the mixture to coat the apples with the pineapple juice to retain their color. Add the coconut, skim milk and cherries. Sprinkle with sugar and toss gently. Cover the bowl with clear wrap and refrigerate overnight.

To serve, pour the mixture into a large cut glass serving bowl and sprinkle with chopped mint leaves.

Nutrition Facts...now

Calories:	222
Total Fat:	3gm
Saturated Fat:	2gm
% Calories from Fat:	12
Cholesterol:	1mg
Sodium:	41mg
Carbohydrate:	48gm
Fiber:	3gm
Protein:	4gm

PREP TIME: 1 Hour   SERVES: 8

☞ INGREDIENTS:

FOR CAKE:
1 cup butter
2 cups sugar
3 cups cake flour, sifted
4 tsps baking powder
1 tsp salt
1 1/3 cups milk
2 tsps vanilla
6 egg whites, beaten

FOR FILLING:
1 (3 1/2-ounce) can coconut
2 cups sugar
2 tbsps flour
1 cup milk
1/2 stick butter

FOR ICING:
1 1/2 cups sugar
3 egg whites
5 tbsps water
1 tbsp corn syrup
1 tbsp vanilla
1/4 tsp cream of tartar

☞ METHOD:

Preheat oven to 350 degrees F. Butter and flour three 9-inch cake pans and set aside. In a large mixing bowl, cream together butter and sugar. In a separate bowl, combine sifted cake flour, baking powder and salt. Slowly add to the butter mixture, blending thoroughly. Should the mixture become too stiff, add some of the milk. After the flour has been well-blended, add any remaining milk and vanilla. Fold in 6 egg whites. Blend thoroughly and distribute evenly among the 9-inch baking pans. Cook for 35 minutes or until a cake tester comes out clean. Remove from oven and cool. To create the coconut filling, combine coconut, sugar and flour in a large sauce pan. Blend well. Slowly incorporate the milk, stirring constantly. Add butter. Bring to a low boil and cook, stirring occasionally, 10–15 minutes or until filling thickens. Remove, allow to cool and set aside. To create the icing, combine sugar, egg whites, water, syrup, vanilla and cream of tartar in the top of a double boiler. Blend well and cook over boiling water. Using a wire whisk, whip the mixture constantly until a smooth and creamy frosting forms, approximately 7 minutes. Remove and set aside. When cakes are cool, remove from pans and spread the coconut filling between layers. Ice with the frosting and serve. You may wish to garnish with fresh coconut over the icing.

"Every home in South Louisiana had its own favorite recipe for coconut cake. Coconut seemed to be a novelty and it was often used in dessert making.
"I can't ever think of attending a wedding in Cajun country prior to World War II where the wedding cake wasn't coconut. Yes, it was definitely a Cajun favorite."

Anita Guidry
Church Point, Louisiana

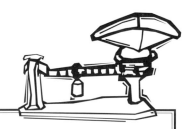

❊Nutrition Facts...then❊

Calories: 1079
Total Fat: 36gm
Saturated Fat: 23gm
% Calories from Fat: 29
Cholesterol: 87mg
Sodium: 695mg
Carbohydrate: 184gm
Fiber: 1gm
Protein: 10gm

PREP TIME: 1 Hour   SERVES: 8

☞ INGREDIENTS:

FOR CAKE:
3/4 cup lite margarine
2 cups sugar
3 cups cake flour, sifted
4 tsps baking powder
1/2 tsp salt
1 1/3 cups evaporated skim milk
2 tsps vanilla
6 egg whites, beaten

FOR FILLING:
1 (3 1/2-ounce) can coconut
1 1/2 cups sugar
2 tbsps flour
1 cup evaporated skim milk
1/4 cup lite margarine

FOR ICING:
1 box confectioner's sugar
1/2 tsp cream of tartar
3 egg whites
1 tbsp vanilla

*Chef's Tips on Exercise...
choose a plan that fits
easily into your life.*

Nutrition Facts...now

Calories:	965
Total Fat:	16gm
Saturated Fat:	6gm
% Calories from Fat:	15
Cholesterol:	2mg
Sodium:	582mg
Carbohydrate:	194gm
Fiber:	1gm
Protein:	13gm

☞ METHOD:

Preheat oven to 350 degrees F. Coat three 9-inch cake pans with vegetable spray and flour and set aside.

In a large mixing bowl, cream together margarine and sugar. In a separate bowl, combine sifted cake flour, baking powder and salt. Slowly add to the margarine mixture, blending thoroughly. Should the mixture become too stiff, add some of the skim milk.

After the flour has been well-blended, add any remaining skim milk and vanilla. Fold in egg whites. Blend thoroughly and distribute evenly among the 9-inch baking pans. Cook for 35 minutes or until a cake tester comes out clean. Remove from oven and cool.

To create the coconut filling, combine coconut, sugar and flour in a large sauce pan. Blend well. Slowly incorporate the skim milk, stirring constantly. Add margarine. Bring to a low boil and cook, stirring occasionally, 10–15 minutes or until filling thickens. Remove, allow to cool and set aside.

While cakes are cooling, create the royal icing by placing the sugar in the bowl of an electric mixer. Add cream of tartar and, while whipping on medium speed, add egg whites, one at a time. Add vanilla and blend until stiff icing forms.

When cakes are cool, remove from pans and spread the coconut filling between the layers. Ice with the frosting and serve. You may wish to garnish with fresh coconut over the icing.

GATEAU DE FIGUE (FIG CAKE)

PREP TIME: 1 1/2 Hours   SERVES: 8

☞ INGREDIENTS:

1 pint chopped fresh figs
3/4 cup butter
1 cup sugar
3 eggs
2 1/2 cups all purpose flour
1 tsp baking powder
1 tsp baking soda
1 tsp ground nutmeg
1 tsp ground cinnamon
1 tsp ground ginger
1 cup buttermilk
1 tsp vanilla
1 cup chopped pecans

☞ METHOD:

Preheat oven to 350 degrees F. Grease and flour a bundt-style pan and set aside. In a large mixing bowl, cream butter and sugar. Add the eggs, one at a time, blending after each addition. In a separate bowl, combine the flour, baking powder, soda and spices. Add these dry ingredients, alternately with the buttermilk, into the sugar mixture. Stir constantly until all ingredients are well incorporated into the batter. Add vanilla, pecans and figs. Stir well and pour into the greased pan. Bake for approximately 1 hour or until cake tester comes out clean. Allow to cool. Remove from pan. You may wish to serve with ice cream or a dollop of fresh whipped cream.

"This recipe goes back at least five generations in my family. My mother received it from my grandmother, Marie Breaux Daigle, before the turn of the century.

"My grandparents had a dozen children, and their home was the gathering place for Christmas dinner.

"Now Cajun children are no more mischief-proof than any others, and there was one standard form of mischief we got into every Christmas.

"There were so many folks at these gatherings that dinner had to be served in three shifts, with the children the last to be fed. When the grown-ups left the table at the two prior seatings - the men to go off and talk, and the women to the kitchen to prepare the next serving - we kids would dart in and help ourselves to the wine the grownups had left in their glasses. The bolder ones might even pour themselves a little more from the tall, thin bottles of Virginia Dare that were left on the table.

"I have always wondered why the adults never questioned why all the kids were so sleepy after dinner. On the other hand, they had been children in that same situation. So perhaps they knew!"

Anita Guidry
Church Point, Louisiana

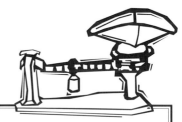

❋**Nutrition Facts...then**❋
Calories: 565
Total Fat: 31gm
Saturated Fat:...................... 13gm
% Calories from Fat:................. 48
Cholesterol: 207mg
Sodium: 416mg
Carbohydrate: 63gm
Fiber: 3gm
Protein: 11gm

GATEAU DE FIGUE (FIG CAKE)

PREP TIME: 1 1/2 Hours   SERVES: 8

☞ INGREDIENTS:

1 pint chopped fresh figs
3/4 cup lite margarine
1 cup sugar
3/4 cup egg substitute
2 1/2 cups all purpose flour
1 tsp baking powder
1 tsp baking soda
1 tsp ground nutmeg
1 tsp ground cinnamon
1 tsp ground ginger
1 cup low-fat buttermilk
1 tsp vanilla
1/2 cup chopped pecans

Ice-cold watermelon for sale near Sulphur.

Nutrition Facts...now

Calories:	406
Total Fat:	15gm
Saturated Fat:	2gm
% Calories from Fat:	32
Cholesterol:	1mg
Sodium:	430mg
Carbohydrate:	62gm
Fiber:	2gm
Protein:	9gm

☞ METHOD:

Preheat oven to 350 degrees F. Grease and flour a bundt-style pan and set aside.

In a large mixing bowl, cream margarine and sugar. Add egg substitute, a little at a time, blending after each addition. In a separate bowl, combine the flour, baking powder, soda and spices. Add these dry ingredients, alternately with the buttermilk, into the sugar mixture. Stir constantly until all ingredients are well incorporated into the batter.

Add vanilla, pecans and figs. Stir well and pour into the greased pan. Bake for approximately 1 hour and 15 minutes or until cake tester comes out clean. Allow to cool. Remove from pan. You may wish to serve with fat-free ice cream or a dollop of non-dairy topping.

PREP TIME: 1 Hour   SERVES: 8

☞ INGREDIENTS:

3 cups grated carrots
2 cups sugar
1 1/2 cups vegetable oil
4 eggs
2 cups all purpose flour
3 tsps baking powder
3 tsps baking soda
1 tsp salt
2 tsps cinnamon
1 tbsp vanilla
1 cup chopped pecans
1 (20-ounce) can crushed pineapple
1 cup sugar
2 1/2 tbsps corn starch
8-ounces cream cheese
1/2 stick butter
1 box confectioner's sugar
1 tbsp vanilla

*Chef's Tips on Exercise...
take your dog for a long walk
in the morning and evening.*

☞ METHOD:

Preheat oven to 350 degrees F. Oil and flour four 9-inch cake pans. Set aside. In a large mixing bowl, cream sugar and oil until well-blended. Add eggs, one at a time, whipping after each addition. In a separate bowl, combine flour, baking powder, soda, salt and cinnamon. Add, a little at a time, into the egg mixture, blending well until all is incorporated. Fold in the vanilla, pecans and grated carrots. Once all is well-blended, pour evenly into the 4 cake pans. Bake 30–40 minutes or until cake tester comes out clean. Remove and allow to cool. While cake is baking, make filling by combining pineapple, sugar and corn starch. Bring to a low boil over medium-high heat, stirring constantly for 5 minutes. Once mixture thickens, remove from heat and allow filling to cool. In the bowl of an electric mixer, combine cream cheese, butter, powdered sugar and vanilla. Blend on low speed until well mixed. Whip until icing is fluffy and smooth. Remove and set aside. Remove cakes from baking pans and spread pineapple filling between layers. Ice with the cream cheese frosting and serve.

"My mother, like every other mother in Cajun country, was a fabulous cook. Her dishes were always delicious, but unfortunately for us, she never used a written recipe. I learned to cook as everyone else did - just by watching and asking the right questions.

"My parents ran a grocery store and I was brought up working side by side with them. I had countless opportunities to observe Mama.

"Although she made many delicious candies and cakes, her favorite was always the gold brick fudge. I do remember her moist carrot cake, one of my favorites."

Renella Lavergne
Opelousas, Louisiana

❧Nutrition Facts...then❧

Calories:	1396
Total Fat:	71gm
Saturated Fat:	18gm
% Calories from Fat:	45
Cholesterol:	259mg
Sodium:	983mg
Carbohydrate:	181gm
Fiber:	4gm
Protein:	14gm

SUPER MOIST CARROT CAKE

PREP TIME: 1 Hour   SERVES: 8

☞ INGREDIENTS:

3 cups grated carrots
1 1/2 cups sugar
3/4 cup vegetable oil
3/4 cup applesauce, unsweetened
1 cup egg substitute
2 cups all purpose flour
3 tsps baking powder
3 tsps baking soda
1/2 tsp salt
2 tsps cinnamon
1 tbsp vanilla
3/4 cup chopped pecans
1 (20-ounce) can crushed pineapple
1/2 cup sugar
2 1/2 tbsps corn starch
1 box confectioner's sugar
1/2 tsp cream of tartar
3 egg whites
1 tbsp vanilla

☞ METHOD:

Preheat oven to 350 degrees F. Oil and flour four 9-inch cake pans. Set aside.

In a large mixing bowl, cream sugar, oil and applesauce until well-blended. Add egg substitute, a little at a time, whipping after each addition.

In a separate bowl, combine flour, baking powder, soda, salt and cinnamon. Add, a little at a time, into the egg mixture, blending well until all is incorporated. Fold in the vanilla, pecans and grated carrots.

Once all is well-blended, pour evenly into the 4 cake pans. Bake 30–40 minutes or until cake tester comes out clean. Remove and allow to cool.

While cake is baking, make filling by combining pineapple, sugar and corn starch. Bring to a low boil over medium-high heat, stirring constantly for 5–10 minutes. Once mixture thickens, remove from heat and allow filling to cool.

In the bowl of an electric mixer, place sugar. Add cream of tartar and, while whipping on medium speed, add egg whites, one at a time. Add vanilla and blend well until stiff icing forms.

Remove cakes from pans and spread pineapple filling between layers. Ice with the royal icing and serve.

Nutrition Facts...now	
Calories:	909
Total Fat:	28gm
Saturated Fat:	4gm
% Calories from Fat:	27
Cholesterol:	0mg
Sodium:	709mg
Carbohydrate:	159gm
Fiber:	4gm
Protein:	9gm

Lagniappe

Chapter Ten

Tarte à la Bouie	400/401
Lemon Nut Cake	402/403
Orange Pain Perdu	404/405
Baked Cushaw Squares	406/407
Bread Pudding Cake	408/409
Guy Disalvo's Premier Marinara Sauce	412/413
River Town Shrimp & Eggplant Jambalaya	414/415
Cajun Blackeyed Peas	416/417
Smothered Cabbage & Andouille	418/419
Zucchini Gravy	420/421
Snap Beans with New Potatoes	422/423
Corn Maque Choux	424/425
Coush Coush	426/427
Billie Landry's Coush Coush	428/429
Venison Osso Bucco	430/431
Hog's Head Cheese without the Head	432/433
Seafood Sauce Piquant, Gueydan-Style	434/435
Tad's Barbecue Sauce	436/437
Fried Oyster Dressing	438/439
Breaux's Homemade Italian Bread	440/441

*The recipes for **Venison Osso Bucco**, pictured at left, can be found on pages 430 and 431.*

TARTE à la BOUIE

PREP TIME: 1 Hour   SERVES: 8

☞ **INGREDIENTS:**

FOR CUSTARD:
2 cups milk
1 cup half and half cream
1 egg
1/2 cup sugar
4 tbsps corn starch
1 tbsp vanilla
1/2 cup butter

FOR CRUST:
2 eggs
1 cup sugar
1/4 pound butter
1 tsp vanilla
2 1/2 tsps baking powder
2 cups all purpose flour

☞ **METHOD:**

Preheat oven to 350 degrees F. You should begin the recipe by combining the milk and cream and scalding the mixture over a low fire until skin forms on the surface but milk does not boil, approximately 200 degrees F. In a large mixing bowl, combine egg, sugar and corn starch. Using a wire whisk, whip gently until corn starch and sugar are dissolved. Add approximately 1 cup of the hot milk to the egg mixture while beating constantly. This will temper the eggs, prior to adding them to the hot milk. While whipping the scalded milk, add the egg mixture and continue to whip until mixture thickens to the texture of a very heavy cream. Add vanilla and butter and continue to cook until thick custard is achieved. Remove from heat and cool thoroughly before pouring into the uncooked pie crust. In the bowl of a food processor fitted with a metal blade, combine eggs, sugar, butter and vanilla. Blend 1–2 minutes until ingredients are incorporated. Add baking powder and flour and continue to process until flour is absorbed and a dough ball forms in the process. Remove dough and refrigerate 1 hour. Roll dough into a large pie-shaped crust, approximately 1/8-inch thick. Place the dough in a pie pan, allowing the excess to rest out on the work surface. When the custard is cooled, pour it into the pie shell and fold the pie dough over to the center of the pie in an uneven fashion. It isn't necessary for the crust to be sealed on the top. Bake 30–45 minutes or until crust is golden brown.

"This is one of the oldest desserts to come out of bayou country. Since eggs and milk were so plentiful, custard-based desserts were constantly available.
"My mother made beautiful boiled custards but the best custard pie I ever ate was one cooked by Betsy Ayo, late wife of Dr. Donald Ayo, President of Nicholls State University in Thibodaux. Although she never gave me all of her secrets, she shared most of them; I, in turn, will share them with you."

John Folse
Donaldsonville, Louisiana

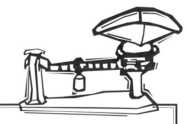

❊**Nutrition Facts...then**❊

Calories:	569
Total Fat:	29gm
Saturated Fat:	18gm
% Calories from Fat:	46
Cholesterol:	96mg
Sodium:	288mg
Carbohydrate:	70gm
Fiber:	1gm
Protein:	7gm

PREP TIME: 1 Hour   SERVES: 8

☞ INGREDIENTS:

FOR CUSTARD:
2 cups skim milk
1 cup evaporated skim milk
1/4 cup egg substitute
1/2 cup sugar
4 tbsps corn starch
1 tbsp vanilla
1/4 cup lite margarine

FOR CRUST:
1/2 cup egg substitute
1 cup sugar
1/2 cup lite margarine
1 tsp vanilla
2 1/2 tsps baking powder
2 cups all purpose flour

☞ METHOD:

Preheat oven to 350 degrees F. You should begin the recipe by combining the skim milk and evaporated skim milk and scalding the mixture over a low fire until skin forms on the surface but milk does not boil, approximately 200 degrees F.

In a large mixing bowl, combine 1/4 cup of egg substitute, sugar and corn starch. Using a wire whisk, whip gently until corn starch and sugar are dissolved. Add approximately 1 cup of the hot skim milk to the egg substitute mixture, beating constantly. This will temper the eggs, prior to adding them to the hot milk. While whipping the scalded milk, add the egg substitute mixture and continue to whip until mixture thickens to the texture of a very heavy cream. Add vanilla and 1/4 cup margarine. Continue to cook until thick custard is achieved. Remove from heat and cool thoroughly before pouring into the uncooked pie crust.

In the bowl of a food processor fitted with a metal blade, combine 1/2 cup egg substitute, sugar, 1/2 cup margarine and vanilla. Blend 1–2 minutes until ingredients are incorporated.

Add baking powder and flour and continue to process until flour is absorbed and a dough ball forms in the process. Remove dough and refrigerate 1 hour.

Roll dough in a large pie-shaped crust, approximately 1/8-inch thick. Place the dough into a pie pan, allowing the excess to rest out on the work surface.

When the custard is cooled, pour it into the pie shell and fold the pie dough over to the center of the pie in an uneven fashion. It isn't necessary for the crust to be sealed on the top. Bake 30–45 minutes or until crust is golden brown.

Nutrition Facts...now

Calories:	416
Total Fat:	10gm
Saturated Fat:	1gm
% Calories from Fat:	21
Cholesterol:	2mg
Sodium:	192mg
Carbohydrate:	73gm
Fiber:	1gm
Protein:	10gm

LEMON NUT CAKE

PREP TIME: 4 Hours   MAKES: 1 tube pan (24 slices)

☞ INGREDIENTS:

2 ounces lemon extract
4 cups chopped pecans
vegetable spray
1 tbsp flour
1 pound butter
2 cups sugar
4 cups flour
1 tsp baking powder
6 eggs
1 box golden raisins

In the heart of Lake Charles — the Old City Hall.

☞ METHOD:

Preheat oven to 225 degrees F. Spray a tube pan with vegetable spray and dust with 1 tablespoon of flour. Set aside. In a large mixing bowl, cream together butter and sugar until smooth. In a separate bowl, combine 4 cups of flour and baking powder. Alternate adding eggs, one at a time, and flour to the creamed butter mixture. Blend well after each addition. Once all is incorporated, add lemon extract, pecans and raisins. Pour batter into tube pan and bake approximately 3 hours. When the cake is done, it will pull away from the sides of the pan. *This cake should not be brown.*

"This cake has been in Ramona Avant's family for many years. It is always served at Thanksgiving and Christmas. Ramona's mother, Fleta Copeland, received this recipe from her mother, Leota Wimberly. This cake has been prepared in our family for over 80 years.

"The secret to success with this dessert is to cook it on low temperature for a long period of time and to slice it very thin. Mrs. Fleta is famous for her ability to make this cake last forever by cutting it so thin you could read a newspaper through the slices."

Tom Avant
DeRidder, Louisiana

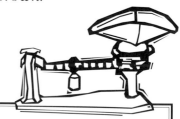

❧ Nutrition Facts...then ❧

Calories: 472
Total Fat: 29gm
Saturated Fat: 11gm
% Calories from Fat: 53
Cholesterol: 95mg
Sodium: 176mg
Carbohydrate: 51gm
Fiber: 2gm
Protein: 6gm

(per slice)

PREP TIME: 4 Hours   MAKES: 1 tube pan (24 slices)

☞ INGREDIENTS:

2 ounces lemon extract
3 cups chopped pecans
vegetable spray
1 tbsp flour
1 pound lite margarine
2 cups sugar
4 cups flour
1 tsp baking powder
1 1/2 cups egg substitute
1 cup Grape Nuts cereal
1 box golden raisins

A catfish on its way to the table.

☞ METHOD:

Preheat oven to 225 degrees F. Spray a tube pan with vegetable spray and dust with 1 tablespoon of flour. Set aside.

In a large mixing bowl, cream together margarine and sugar until smooth. In a separate bowl, combine 4 cups of flour and baking powder. Add egg substitute and flour to the creamed margarine mixture a little at a time. Blend well after each addition.

Once all is incorporated, add lemon extract, pecans, cereal and raisins. Pour batter into tube pan and bake approximately 3 hours. When the cake is done, it will pull away from the sides of the pan.

This cake should not be brown.

Nutrition Facts...now

Calories:	380
Total Fat:	18gm
Saturated Fat:	2gm
% Calories from Fat:	40
Cholesterol:	0mg
Sodium:	124mg
Carbohydrate:	54gm
Fiber:	2gm
Protein:	6gm

(per slice)

PREP TIME: 30 Minutes   SERVES: 6

☞ **INGREDIENTS:**

1/2 cup fresh squeezed orange juice
1 (8-ounce) French bread
3 eggs
1 cup sugar
1 cup whole milk
1 cup evaporated milk
1 tsp cinnamon
1/2 tsp nutmeg
1 tsp vanilla
1/3 cup butter
1/2 cup powdered sugar

Chef's Tips on Fitness... you know you're fit when...you can walk up three flights of stairs without becoming winded.

☞ **METHOD:**

Cut French bread into 1-inch slices. In a large mixing bowl, combine eggs and sugar. Using a wire whisk, blend well. Add whole milk, evaporated milk, orange juice, cinnamon, nutmeg and vanilla. Continue to whip until the custard is well-blended. In a 12-inch cast iron skillet, melt butter over medium-high heat. Dip the bread into the custard, a few slices at a time, and saute until golden brown on each side. Continue until all bread has been cooked. As the lost bread is removed from the skillet, top it with powdered sugar. If using sliced bread in this recipe, dip the bread quickly, otherwise, it will fall apart before you can place it in the skillet!

"My mother and grandmother called this 'pain perdu,' but my brother and I called it 'Lost Bread.' I don't quite understand why we differed in identifying our favorite breakfast entree, but I also know that the rest of the world calls it French Toast. The name lost bread seems to have originated from the fact that hard, crusty stale bread was preferred when making the dish. Had it not been dipped in eggs and milk, then pan fried, the bread would have certainly been lost.

"My mother always cooked lost bread to order. My brother liked his browned on both sides. I like mine soggy and mother loved hers nearly blackened on both sides.

"I can remember my brother standing at the stove eating his pieces directly from the skillet and of course, trying to take everyone else's share before it hit the platter. I guess that's why I like mine barely cooked, just so he wouldn't get to eat my portions. We always sprinkled extra powdered sugar on top of the toast before eating it."
Brenda Martin
Morgan City, Louisiana

❧Nutrition Facts...then❧

Calories: 494
Total Fat: 19gm
Saturated Fat: 10gm
% Calories from Fat: 33
Cholesterol: 152mg
Sodium: 434mg
Carbohydrate: 72gm
Fiber: 0gm
Protein: 11gm

PREP TIME: 30 Minutes   SERVES: 6

☞ INGREDIENTS:

1/2 cup fresh squeezed orange juice
1 (8-ounce) French bread
3/4 cup egg substitute
3/4 cup sugar
1 cup skim milk
1 cup evaporated skim milk
1 tsp cinnamon
1/2 tsp nutmeg
1 tsp vanilla
1/3 cup lite margarine
1/2 cup powdered sugar

☞ METHOD:

Cut French bread into 1-inch slices. In a large mixing bowl, combine egg substitute and sugar. Using a wire whisk, blend well. Add skim milk, evaporated skim milk, orange juice, cinnamon, nutmeg and vanilla. Continue to whip until the custard is well-blended.

In a 12-inch cast iron skillet, melt margarine over medium-high heat. Dip the bread into the custard, a few slices at a time, and saute until golden brown on each side. Continue until all bread has been cooked.

As the lost bread is removed from the skillet, top it with powdered sugar. If using sliced bread in this recipe, dip the bread quickly, otherwise, it will fall apart before you can place it in the skillet!

Nutrition Facts...now

Calories:	371
Total Fat:	8gm
Saturated Fat:	2gm
% Calories from Fat:	18
Cholesterol:	2mg
Sodium:	475mg
Carbohydrate:	64gm
Fiber:	0gm
Protein:	12gm

BAKED CUSHAW SQUARES

PREP TIME: 1 1/2 Hours   SERVES: 6

☞ **INGREDIENTS:**

1 medium-size cushaw
1 1/2 cups sugar
1 pound butter
1/4 cup cane syrup
1 tsp allspice
pinch of cinnamon
pinch of nutmeg
1/2 cup brown sugar

☞ **METHOD:**

Preheat oven to 400 degrees F. Using a very sharp butcher's knife, cut cushaw in half and remove the seeds and stringy pulp. Cut each half into 3-inch squares, leaving the hard shell intact. In a 1-gallon stock pot, boil the cushaw in lightly sweetened water until tender but not mushy. Using the blade of a paring knife, test for tenderness. Once tender, remove and place the squares on a large cookie sheet or pan. Set

Donald Blanchard waits for a bite while Earl Deer, Sr. shows his sons, Earl, Jr. and Corey, a few pointers off Hwy 27 near Holly Beach.

aside. In a cast iron sauce pot, place 1/2 cup of the poaching liquid along with sugar, butter and cane syrup. Bring to a low boil, stirring constantly until a bubbly syrup is achieved. Do not scorch. Add allspice, cinnamon and nutmeg. Top the cushaw pieces with the sugar mixture and sprinkle with brown sugar. Bake until thoroughly heated. When eating, scoop the sweetened meat from the shell as a snack or serve as a starch accompaniment to any entree.

"After mother died in May of 1955, the good Lord sent Mary Ferchaud into our home. If there was one thing needed then, with eight small children, it was a tireless cook. Although pickings were slim in the pantry, Mary always seemed to come up with something special to excite us at dinner time.

"She made a fabulous baked pumpkin casserole, but often with washing, ironing and getting us ready for one thing or another, there just wasn't enough time to cook in the traditional fashion. On one such day, she created her baked cushaw squares.

"Mary raised us as a mother until the last kids in our family graduated from high school. At that point, she considered her job done and she retired. I still bake her cushaw squares when the striped, long-necked pumpkins come into season."

John Folse
Donaldsonville, Louisiana

❖Nutrition Facts...then❖

Calories: 866
Total Fat: 61gm
Saturated Fat: 38gm
% Calories from Fat: 61
Cholesterol: 164mg
Sodium: 642mg
Carbohydrate: 85gm
Fiber: 0gm
Protein: 2gm

BAKED CUSHAW SQUARES

PREP TIME: 1 1/2 Hours   SERVES: 6

"I think I'll have a pound of hot boudin and a car wash!"

☞ INGREDIENTS:

1 medium-size cushaw
1 1/2 cups sugar
1/2 cup lite margarine
1/4 cup cane syrup
1 tsp allspice
pinch of cinnamon
pinch of nutmeg
1/2 cup brown sugar

☞ METHOD:

Preheat oven to 400 degrees F. Using a very sharp butcher's knife, cut cushaw in half and remove the seeds and stringy pulp. Cut each half into 3-inch squares, leaving the hard shell intact.

In a 1-gallon stock pot, boil the cushaw in lightly sweetened water until tender but not mushy. Using the blade of a paring knife, test for tenderness. Once tender, remove and place the squares on a large cookie sheet or pan. Set aside.

In a cast iron sauce pot, place 1/2 cup of the poaching liquid along with sugar, margarine and cane syrup. Bring to a low boil, stirring constantly until a bubbly syrup is achieved. Do not scorch. Add allspice, cinnamon and nutmeg.

Top the cushaw pieces with the sugar mixture and sprinkle with brown sugar. Bake until thoroughly heated.

When eating, scoop the sweetened meat from the shell as a snack or serve as a starch accompaniment to any entree.

Nutrition Facts...now

Calories:	395
Total Fat:	8gm
Saturated Fat:	1gm
% Calories from Fat:	17
Cholesterol:	0mg
Sodium:	195mg
Carbohydrate:	85gm
Fiber:	4gm
Protein:	1gm

BREAD PUDDING CAKE

Something Old...

PREP TIME: 2 hours   SERVES: 14

☞ INGREDIENTS:

5 (10-inch) loaves French bread
1 quart milk
6 whole eggs
1 1/2 cups sugar
1/4 cup vanilla
1 tbsp cinnamon
1 tbsp nutmeg
1 tbsp vegetable oil
1 cup chopped pecans
1 cup raisins

☞ METHOD:

Preheat oven to 375 degrees F. Slice French bread into 1/2-inch round croutons. In a large mixing bowl, combine milk, eggs and sugar. Using a wire whisk, blend ingredients well. Add vanilla, cinnamon and nutmeg. Continue to blend until all ingredients are well mixed. Oil a 10-inch cheesecake pan. Press 1 layer of French bread croutons into the bottom of the pan, making sure there are no void spaces. Sprinkle a small amount of pecans and raisins over this layer. Ladle in 1/3 of the custard mixture. Carefully press the custard into the croutons using the tips of your fingers. Continue this process until all croutons and custard are used up. You may find that 1–2 cups of the custard mixture will remain once the pan has been filled. This is normal and you must continue to add the custard, a little at a time, firmly pressing into the croutons until all has been used. This may take an hour or so. The bread pudding is always best if allowed to set in the refrigerator overnight before cooking. Place the bread pudding pan into a larger pan filled with water. Cook in this water bath approximately 1–1 1/2 hours. Serve warm or cold. Slice into 14 wedges.

"This recipe was given to me by the master bread pudding chef, Sharon Jesowshek. I first tasted it in French Settlement, Louisiana, and could not rest until I had secured the recipe.
"It takes patience, but is a true masterpiece."

John Folse
Donaldsonville, Louisiana

❀Nutrition Facts...then❀

Calories:	512
Total Fat:	14gm
Saturated Fat:	3gm
% Calories from Fat:	24
Cholesterol:	101mg
Sodium:	606mg
Carbohydrate:	83gm
Fiber:	1gm
Protein:	14gm

PREP TIME: 2 hours   SERVES: 14

☞ INGREDIENTS:

5 (10-inch) loaves French bread
32 ounces evaporated skim milk
1 1/2 cups egg substitute
1 1/2 cups sugar
1/4 cup vanilla
1 tbsp cinnamon
1 tbsp nutmeg
1 tbsp vegetable oil
1/2 cup chopped pecans
1 cup raisins

*Chef's Tips on Weight Loss...
fat-free does not mean
calorie-free.*

☞ METHOD:

Preheat oven to 375 degrees F. Slice French bread into 1/2-inch round croutons.

In a large mixing bowl, combine skim milk, egg substitute and sugar. Using a wire whisk, blend ingredients well. Add vanilla, cinnamon and nutmeg. Continue to blend until all ingredients are well mixed.

Oil a 10-inch cheesecake pan. Press 1 layer of French bread croutons into the bottom of the pan, making sure there are no void spaces. Sprinkle a small amount of pecans and raisins over this layer. Ladle in 1/3 of the custard mixture. Carefully press the custard into the croutons using the tips of your fingers. Continue this process until all croutons and custard are used up.

You may find that 1–2 cups of the custard mixture will remain once the pan has been filled. This is normal and you must continue to add the custard, a little at a time, firmly pressing into the croutons until all has been used. This may take an hour or so.

The bread pudding is always best if allowed to set in the refrigerator overnight before cooking. Place the bread pudding pan into a larger pan filled with water. Cook in this water bath approximately 1–1 1/2 hours. Serve warm or cold. Slice into 14 wedges.

Nutrition Facts...now

Calories:	481
Total Fat:	7gm
Saturated Fat:	1gm
% Calories from Fat:	13
Cholesterol:	2mg
Sodium:	668mg
Carbohydrate:	87gm
Fiber:	1gm
Protein:	16gm

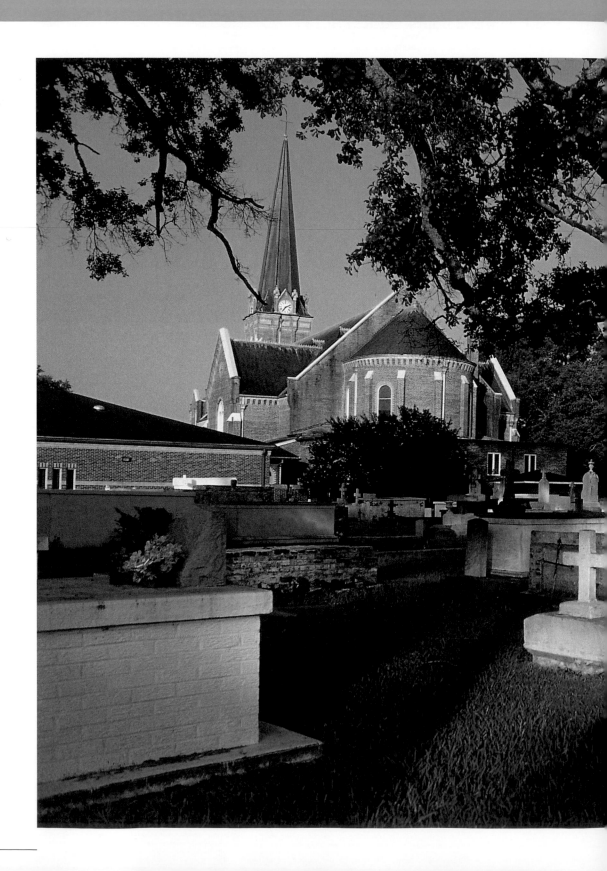

PREP TIME: 30 Minutes   MAKES: 1 Quart

☞ INGREDIENTS:

24 Roma tomatoes, peeled and seeded
1/4 cup extra virgin olive oil
1/4 cup vegetable oil
10 garlic cloves, sliced
1 cup chicken stock
12 large basil leaves, chopped
1/2 tsp cayenne pepper

☞ METHOD:

In a stainless steel sauce pot, heat oils over medium-high heat. Using a wooden spoon, saute the garlic slices until pale yellow or very light browned around the edges, approximately 3 minutes. Add the tomatoes and blend well into the garlic mixture. Bring to a low simmer and slowly add chicken stock to retain moisture and create the fresh sauce. Cook 5–7 minutes and add basil and cayenne pepper. The sauce is now ready to serve as a pasta topping or a base for fish and veal. Add additional stock as necessary to retain sauce-like consistency. When serving this sauce over pasta, drain the pasta when done and toss with a small amount of olive oil. Blend 1–2 serving spoons of the fresh marinara into the pasta along with a generous sprinkle of Parmesan cheese. Once all is well coated, place the pasta in the center of a serving platter and top with the simmering marinara.

"Guy DiSalvo, simply put, is the best of the best! I can think of no Italian chef who can create a better tastier pasta sauce with so little effort.

"Guy and his brother, Mario, came from the Old Country in search of a better life in America. They founded DiSalvo's Restaurant in Jeanette, Pennsylvania and later DiSalvo's Station in Latrobe. Guy and his wife, Rita, along with their son, Joey, continue to create magnificent Italian food in Pennsylvania while sharing it with the rest of the country.

"Often they have spent time with us here in Louisiana and honored us with a dinner and demonstration as a Visiting Chef at our Culinary Institute at Nicholls State University. His marinara is the only one served at Lafitte's Landing."
                    John Folse
            Donaldsonville, Louisiana

❧Nutrition Facts...then❧

Calories: 110
Total Fat: 8gm
Saturated Fat: 1gm
% Calories from Fat: 62
Cholesterol: 2mg
Sodium: 141mg
Carbohydrate: 9gm
Fiber: 3gm
Protein: 2gm

(per 1/2 cup serving)

PREP TIME: 30 Minutes   MAKES: 1 Quart

☞ INGREDIENTS:

24 Roma tomatoes, peeled and seeded
2 tbsps extra virgin olive oil
10 garlic cloves, sliced
1 cup defatted chicken stock, unsalted
12 large basil leaves, chopped
1/2 tsp cayenne pepper

☞ METHOD:

In a stainless steel sauce pot, heat olive oil over medium-high heat. Using a wooden spoon, saute the garlic slices until pale yellow or very light browned around the edges, approximately 3 minutes. Add the tomatoes and blend well into the garlic mixture. Bring to a low simmer and slowly add chicken stock to retain moisture and create the fresh sauce. Cook 5–7 minutes and add basil and cayenne pepper.

The sauce is now ready to serve as a pasta topping or a base for fish and veal. Add additional stock as necessary to retain sauce-like consistency.

When serving this sauce over pasta, drain the pasta when done and toss with a small amount of olive oil. Blend 1–2 serving spoons of the fresh marinara into the pasta along with a generous sprinkle of Parmesan cheese. Once all is well coated, place the pasta in the center of a serving platter and top with the simmering marinara.

Nutrition Facts...now

Calories:	48
Total Fat:	1gm
Saturated Fat:	0gm
% Calories from Fat:	19
Cholesterol:	2mg
Sodium:	141mg
Carbohydrate:	9gm
Fiber:	3gm
Protein:	2gm

(per 1/2 cup serving)

PREP TIME: 1 1/2 Hours   SERVES: 6

☞ INGREDIENTS:

1 1/2 pounds (70–90 count) shrimp,
     peeled and deveined
2 medium-sized eggplants,
     peeled and cut into 1-inch cubes
2 tbsps peanut oil
1 cup chopped onions
1/2 cup chopped celery
2 tbsps chopped bell pepper
2 tbsps diced garlic
1 bay leaf
1 tbsp chopped chives
1 tbsp chopped parsley
2 tsps chopped basil
3 1/2 cups cooked white rice
1/2 tsp salt
black pepper

☞ METHOD:

In a 1-gallon stock pot, boil eggplant in lightly salted water until tender but not overcooked. Drain well through a colander and set aside. In the same stock pot, heat oil over medium-high heat. Add onions, celery, bell pepper and garlic. Saute 3–5 minutes or until vegetables are wilted. Add shrimp and continue to cook until they are pink and curled. Add the drained eggplant, bay leaf and chives. Blend well into the vegetables and saute until liquid has reduced to approximately 1/2 cup. Once mixture is thoroughly cooked and full-flavored, remove the bay leaf and stir in parsley, basil and rice. Season to taste using salt and pepper. Remove from heat, cover and allow flavors to blend 10–15 minutes, prior to serving.

"I grew up in Plaquemine, Louisiana, a small Mississippi River town south of Baton Rouge. As a young girl, I was always excited by the arrival of Hall's horse-drawn ice wagon. Even in the 1940s, his wagon was already a novelty, a relic of days gone by. The other neighborhood kids and I would crowd around the wagon, eager to catch a few chips of cold ice flying through the hot summer air as Hall expertly chipped away the nickel or dime blocks for our mothers' ice boxes.

"Some days, Hall brought fresh fruits and vegetables from nearby fields and little sweet river-shrimp pulled from the Mississippi early that morning. On those days, Mama would purchase some tender young eggplants and a bag of river-shrimp to cook her famous jambalaya.

"Years later, after she began growing fresh herbs, virtually everything she cooked had a more complex and satisfying flavor. I hope you enjoy this updated version of her recipe."

Sarah Liberta
Baton Rouge, Louisiana

❧Nutrition Facts...then❧

Calories: 275
Total Fat: 6gm
Saturated Fat: 1gm
% Calories from Fat: 20
Cholesterol: 175mg
Sodium: 389mg
Carbohydrate: 32gm
Fiber: 1gm
Protein: 22gm

PREP TIME: 1 1/2 Hours   SERVES: 6

☞ INGREDIENTS:

1 1/2 pounds (70–90 count) shrimp,
        peeled and deveined
2 medium-sized eggplants,
        peeled and cut into 1-inch cubes
1 tbsp peanut oil
1 cup chopped onions
1/2 cup chopped celery
2 tbsps chopped bell pepper
2 tbsps diced garlic
1 bay leaf
1 tbsp chopped chives
1 tbsp chopped parsley
2 tsps chopped basil
3 1/2 cups cooked white rice
1/4 tsp salt
black pepper

*Chef's Tips on Exercise...
spend 40–60 minutes a day on
your feet and moving around.*

Nutrition Facts...now

Calories:	256
Total Fat:	4gm
Saturated Fat:	1gm
% Calories from Fat:	13
Cholesterol:	175mg
Sodium:	300mg
Carbohydrate:	32gm
Fiber:	1gm
Protein:	22gm

At a roadside stand near Houma, you'll find beautiful Gulf shrimp.

☞ METHOD:

In a 1-gallon stock pot, boil eggplant in lightly salted water until tender but not overcooked. Drain well through a colander and set aside.

In the same stock pot, heat oil over medium-high heat. Add onions, celery, bell pepper and garlic. Saute 3–5 minutes or until vegetables are wilted. Add shrimp and continue to cook until they are pink and curled. Add the drained eggplant, bay leaf and chives. Blend well into the vegetables and saute until liquid has reduced to approximately 1/2 cup.

Once mixture is thoroughly cooked and full-flavored, remove the bay leaf and stir in parsley, basil and rice. Season to taste using salt and pepper. Remove from heat, cover and allow flavors to blend 10–15 minutes, prior to serving.

PREP TIME: 1 1/2 Hours   SERVES: 6

☞ INGREDIENTS:

1 pound dried blackeyed peas
1 pound heavy-smoked pork sausage
1/2 pound smoked ham, cubed
1/2 cup shortening
1 cup chopped onions
1 cup chopped celery
1 cup chopped bell pepper
1/4 cup diced garlic
1 tsp dry basil
1 bay leaf
1/2 tsp salt
black pepper
Louisiana Gold Pepper Sauce
1 cup sliced green onions
1/2 cup chopped parsley

☞ METHOD:

It is always best to pre-soak any hard-shell bean in cold water overnight before cooking. This will cut the cooking time by 1/3. Drain peas from soaking water and rinse in cold tap water. In a 1-gallon stock pot, melt shortening over medium-high heat. Add onions, celery, bell pepper, garlic, basil, smoked sausage and ham. Saute approximately 3–5 minutes or until vegetables are wilted. Add bay leaf, peas and enough cold water to cover peas by 2 inches. Bring to a low boil and cook for 30 minutes, stirring occasionally. Reduce heat to simmer and continue cooking approximately 45 minutes or until beans are tender. Stir from time to time, as peas will settle to the bottom of the pot and tend to stick. Once they are tender, mash about 1/3 of the peas on the side of the pot using a metal cooking spoon. This will give the peas a creamy texture. Season to taste using salt, pepper and Louisiana Gold. Add green onions and parsley. Continue cooking until peas are tender and creamy.

"Blackeyed peas or congre, as the Africans call them, originated on that continent and were brought here by the slaves in the 1500s.
"Although we can thank the Africans for many of our most famous dishes, a special thanks goes to them for blackeyed peas. What would we do without this delicacy on New Year's Day? How could we make a pot of Hopping John or Texas Caviar? I don't even want to think of life without blackeyed peas. I just want to thank the Africans for this gift."

John Folse
Donaldsonville, Louisiana

Chef's Tips on Exercise... continuous movement is the key. Get moving and keep moving for 20–30 minutes at least three times a week.

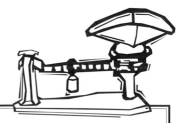

❧Nutrition Facts...then❧

Calories: 600
Total Fat: 43gm
Saturated Fat: 14gm
% Calories from Fat: 63
Cholesterol: 73mg
Sodium: 1736mg
Carbohydrate: 23gm
Fiber: 10gm
Protein: 33gm

PREP TIME: 1 1/2 Hours   SERVES: 6

☞ INGREDIENTS:

1 pound dried blackeyed peas
1 pound low-fat smoked pork sausage
1/2 pound lean smoked ham, cubed
vegetable spray
1 cup chopped onions
1 cup chopped celery
1 cup chopped bell pepper
1/4 cup diced garlic
1 tsp dry basil
1 bay leaf
1/4 tsp salt
black pepper
Louisiana Gold Pepper Sauce
1 cup sliced green onions
1/2 cup chopped parsley

☞ METHOD:

It is always best to pre-soak any hard-shell bean in cold water overnight before cooking. This will cut the cooking time by 1/3.

Drain peas from soaking water and rinse in cold tap water. Spray a 1-gallon stock pot with vegetable cooking spray and place over medium-high heat. Add onions, celery, bell pepper, garlic, basil, smoked sausage and ham. Saute approximately 3–5 minutes or until vegetables are wilted. Add bay leaf, peas and enough cold water to cover peas by 2 inches. Bring to a low boil and cook for 30 minutes, stirring occasionally. Reduce heat to simmer and continue cooking approximately 45 minutes or until beans are tender. Stir from time to time, as peas will settle to the bottom of the pot and tend to stick.

Once they are tender, mash about 1/3 of the peas on the side of the pot using a metal cooking spoon. This will give the peas a creamy texture. Season to taste using salt, pepper and Louisiana Gold. Add green onions and parsley. Continue cooking until peas are tender and creamy.

Nutrition Facts...now

Calories:	348
Total Fat:	18gm
Saturated Fat:	1gm
% Calories from Fat:	44
Cholesterol:	21mg
Sodium:	617mg
Carbohydrate:	22gm
Fiber:	10gm
Protein:	28gm

PREP TIME: 1 Hour   SERVES: 6

☞ INGREDIENTS:

1 large head of cabbage
1/2 pound andouille sausage, sliced
1/2 cup bacon drippings
1 cup chopped onions
1 cup chopped celery
1/2 cup chopped bell pepper
1/4 cup diced garlic
1 cup sliced green onions
1 1/2 cups chicken stock
1 tsp salt
black pepper
Louisiana Gold Pepper Sauce
1/2 cup chopped parsley

☞ METHOD:

Cut cabbage into quarters. Discard the center and all large exterior leaves. Chop quarters into 2 or 3 pieces and separate the leaves. In a 5-quart cast iron dutch oven, melt bacon drippings over medium heat. Add onions, celery, bell pepper, garlic, green onions and andouille. Saute 3–5 minutes or until vegetables are wilted. Add cabbage and blend well into the vegetable mixture. Continue to stir fry until cabbage leaves are wilted. Add chicken stock and reduce heat to simmer. Cover pot and allow to cook, stirring occasionally, for approximately 45 minutes. Season to taste using salt, pepper and Louisiana Gold. Add parsley and continue cooking until cabbage is well smothered. This dish will be overcooked by most standards. However, this is the method preferred by both Cajuns and Creoles.

"The Germans brought cabbage to Louisiana, but there's a major debate as to the origin of andouille - that wonderful Cajun sausage. Both the French and the German cultures lay claim to this delicacy. The great news, however, is that today we care less about who first brought andouille sausage here - we just thank them for dropping it off.

"Today, andouille is the basis of flavor in our gumbos, jambalaya and many vegetable dishes. I can think of no home in South Louisiana that would face a cold winter day without a bowl of smothered cabbage and andouille."

Henry Schexnayder III
Gonzales, Louisiana

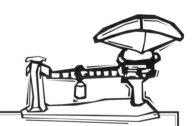

❧ Nutrition Facts...then ❧

Calories:	352
Total Fat:	29gm
Saturated Fat:	11gm
% Calories from Fat:	73
Cholesterol:	39mg
Sodium:	931mg
Carbohydrate:	15gm
Fiber:	4gm
Protein:	9gm

PREP TIME: 1 Hour   SERVES: 6

☞ INGREDIENTS:

1 large head of cabbage
1/4 pound lean andouille sausage, sliced
2 tbsps lite margarine
1 cup chopped onions
1 cup chopped celery
1/2 cup chopped bell pepper
1/4 cup diced garlic
1 cup sliced green onions
1 1/2 cups defatted chicken stock, unsalted
1/4 tsp salt
black pepper
Louisiana Gold Pepper Sauce
1/2 cup chopped parsley

Chef's Tips on Shopping... check sodium information, good buys are foods with no salt added.

☞ METHOD:

Cut cabbage into quarters. Discard the center and all large exterior leaves. Chop quarters into 2 or 3 pieces and separate the leaves.

In a 5-quart cast iron dutch oven, melt margarine over medium heat. Add onions, celery, bell pepper, garlic, green onions and andouille. Saute 3–5 minutes or until vegetables are wilted.

Add cabbage and blend well into vegetable mixture. Continue to stir fry until cabbage leaves are wilted. Add chicken stock and reduce heat to simmer.

Cover pot and allow to cook, stirring occasionally, for approximately 45 minutes. Season to taste using salt, pepper and Louisiana Gold. Add parsley and continue cooking until cabbage is well smothered.

This dish will be overcooked by most standards. However, this is the method preferred by both Cajuns and Creoles.

Henri Boulet makes up a fresh batch of crawfish for his annual Earth Day Boil in Larose.

Nutrition Facts...now

Calories:	114
Total Fat:	6gm
Saturated Fat:	0gm
% Calories from Fat:	40
Cholesterol:	8mg
Sodium:	181mg
Carbohydrate:	15gm
Fiber:	4gm
Protein:	5gm

ZUCCHINI GRAVY

PREP TIME: 1 Hour   SERVES: 6

☞ INGREDIENTS:

6 cups diced zucchini
1 pound ground chuck
1/4 cup olive oil
2 cups diced onions
1 cup diced celery
1/4 cup minced garlic
1 cup diced tomatoes
2 (8-ounce) cans tomato sauce
1 tsp salt
black pepper
Louisiana Gold Pepper Sauce
1/2 cup chopped parsley

☞ METHOD:

In a 12-inch cast iron skillet or large cast iron dutch oven, saute ground chuck until slightly browned and separated grain for grain. Add the olive oil and blend well into meat mixture. Add onions, celery and garlic. Saute 3–5 minutes or until vegetables are wilted. Add tomatoes and zucchini, blending well into the vegetable mixture. Add tomato sauce and season to taste using salt, pepper and Louisiana Gold. Cook until zucchini is tender and a rich tomato sauce has evolved. Add parsley and serve over pasta or rice.

"My husband and I are proud to grow one of the largest gardens on Bayou Lafourche. People come from miles around, regardless of season, to partake of its bounty. We grow the most beautiful beefsteak tomatoes in spring, the greatest longhorn okra in fall and our summer squash crop is second to none.

"This simple zucchini recipe was developed not only because it tasted so good but also because it made use of many garden ingredients."

Vivian Parr
Lockport, Louisiana

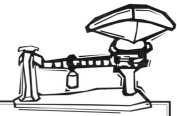

❧Nutrition Facts...then❧

Calories:	248
Total Fat:	14gm
Saturated Fat:	5gm
% Calories from Fat:	51
Cholesterol:	56mg
Sodium:	863mg
Carbohydrate:	13gm
Fiber:	3gm
Protein:	18gm

ZUCCHINI GRAVY

PREP TIME: 1 Hour   SERVES: 6

INGREDIENTS:

6 cups diced zucchini
1/2 pound ground round
2 tbsps olive oil
2 cups diced onions
1 cup diced celery
1/4 cup minced garlic
1 cup diced tomatoes
2 (8-ounce) cans tomato sauce, no salt added
salt substitute
black pepper
Louisiana Gold Pepper Sauce
1/2 cup chopped parsley

METHOD:

In a 12-inch cast iron skillet or large cast iron dutch oven, saute ground round until slightly browned and separated grain for grain. Add the olive oil and blend well into meat mixture. Add onions, celery and garlic. Saute 3–5 minutes or until vegetables are wilted.

Add tomatoes and zucchini, blending well into the vegetable mixture. Add tomato sauce and season to taste using salt substitute, pepper and Louisiana Gold.

Cook until zucchini is tender and a rich tomato sauce has evolved. Add parsley and serve over pasta or rice.

Chef's Tips on Shopping... avoid heavily processed or instant foods and packaged mixes—they contain added sodium.

Nutrition Facts...now

Calories:	131
Total Fat:	5gm
Saturated Fat:	2gm
% Calories from Fat:	34
Cholesterol:	23mg
Sodium:	66mg
Carbohydrate:	13gm
Fiber:	3gm
Protein:	9gm

SNAP BEANS WITH NEW POTATOES

PREP TIME: 1 Hour   SERVES: 6

☞ INGREDIENTS:

1 pound fresh snap beans
10 peeled new potatoes
1/2 cup shortening
1/2 cup chopped onions
1/2 cup chopped celery
1/2 cup chopped red bell pepper
1/4 cup diced garlic
1/2 pound diced smoked ham
2 cups chicken stock
1 tsp salt
black pepper
Louisiana Gold Pepper Sauce
1/2 cup sliced green onions

☞ METHOD:

In a 5-quart cast iron dutch oven, melt shortening over medium-high heat. Add onions, celery, bell pepper, garlic and smoked ham. Saute 3–5 minutes or until vegetables are wilted. Add snap beans and new potatoes. Stir fry for about 3 minutes in the vegetable mixture. Add chicken stock, cover and reduce heat to simmer. Cook approximately 30 minutes or until potatoes are tender. The snap beans will be overcooked by most standards. However, this has been the chosen method of cooking snap beans by the Cajuns. Once potatoes are tender, season to taste using salt, pepper and Louisiana Gold. Add green onions and serve over cooked white rice as a side dish or as a vegetable.

"There are certain foods that I associate with a season. I guess that is true of all of us and, after all, that's probably the way God intended it.
"When growing up on the River Road, I looked forward to chicken and sausage gumbo always being served on Sunday in the fall and winter. I remember the sugared pumpkin squares and hot baked sweet potatoes waiting on the table around Thanksgiving when we returned home from school. River shrimp and eggplant casserole was one of our favorite spring dishes.
"Whenever I see a platter of snap beans with new potatoes, I think of those great fall holidays with the family around the table in Cajun country."
                                    Melissa Folse
                                Vacherie, Louisiana

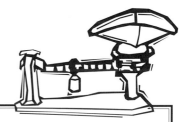

❈Nutrition Facts...then❈

Calories: 312
Total Fat: 19gm
Saturated Fat: 4gm
% Calories from Fat: 52
Cholesterol: 22mg
Sodium: 1032mg
Carbohydrate: 26gm
Fiber: 2gm
Protein: 13gm

PREP TIME: 1 Hour   SERVES: 6

☞ INGREDIENTS:

1 pound fresh snap beans
10 peeled new potatoes
2 tbsps lite margarine
1/2 cup chopped onions
1/2 cup chopped celery
1/2 cup chopped red bell pepper
1/4 cup diced garlic
1/2 pound lean smoked ham, diced
2 cups defatted chicken stock, unsalted
1/4 tsp salt
black pepper
Louisiana Gold Pepper Sauce
1/2 cup sliced green onions

*Chef's Tips on Fitness...
you know you're fit when...you
don't remember the last day
you felt sick.*

Nutrition Facts...now

Calories:	176
Total Fat:	3gm
Saturated Fat:	1gm
% Calories from Fat:	17
Cholesterol:	19mg
Sodium:	508mg
Carbohydrate:	26gm
Fiber:	2gm
Protein:	12gm

The rich alluvial soil of the Mississippi River. In the background is the Ignatius House of Prayer at Manressa, originally built as the home for the president of Jefferson College in Convent, Ascension Parish.

☞ METHOD:

In a 5-quart cast iron dutch oven, melt margarine over medium-high heat. Add onions, celery, bell pepper, garlic and smoked ham. Saute 3–5 minutes or until vegetables are wilted. Add snap beans and new potatoes. Stir fry for about 3 minutes in the vegetable mixture. Add chicken stock, cover and reduce heat to simmer.

Cook approximately 30 minutes or until potatoes are tender. The snap beans will be overcooked by most standards. However, this has been the chosen method of cooking snap beans by the Cajuns.

Once potatoes are tender, season to taste using salt, pepper and Louisiana Gold. Add green onions and serve over cooked white rice as a side dish or as a vegetable.

PREP TIME: 1 Hour SERVES: 8

☞ INGREDIENTS:

8 ears fresh corn
2 cups (150–200 count) shrimp, peeled and deveined
1/2 cup bacon drippings
1 cup chopped onions
1/2 cup chopped celery
1/2 cup chopped green bell pepper
1/2 cup chopped red bell pepper
1/4 cup diced garlic
1/4 cup finely diced andouille
2 cups coarsely chopped tomatoes
2 tbsps tomato sauce
1 cup sliced green onions
1/2 tsp salt
black pepper
Louisiana Gold Pepper Sauce

☞ METHOD:

Select tender, well-developed ears of corn. Remove shucks and silk. Using a sharp knife, cut lengthwise through the kernels to remove them from the cob. Scrape each cob using the blade of the knife to remove all milk and additional pulp from the corn. This is important since the richness of the dish will depend on how much milk and pulp can be scraped from the cobs. In a 5-quart cast iron dutch oven, melt bacon drippings over medium-high heat. Add corn, onions, celery, bell peppers, garlic and andouille. Saute approximately 15–20 minutes or until vegetables are wilted and corn begins to tenderize. Add tomatoes, tomato sauce and shrimp. Continue cooking until juices from the tomatoes and shrimp are rendered into the dish. Add green onions and season to taste using salt, pepper and Louisiana Gold. Cook an additional 15 minutes or until flavors of corn and shrimp are developed.

"No one knows for sure, but most people think that maque is a combination Indian and French word for corn, and choux for cabbage. However, this early Creole dish was never made, to my knowledge, with cabbage. I have seen maque choux served as a soup, vegetable and casserole and always made with corn, shrimp and tomatoes.

"It wasn't until visiting with some Isleno friends from St. Bernard Parish that I think the origin of the word was discovered. The Canary Islanders brought with them to South Louisiana their famous vegetable soup, caldo. One can readily see from this combination of corn and cabbage, along with meat and other vegetables, the similarity to our famous maque choux."

Â John Folse
Â Â Â Â Â Â Â Â Â Â Â Donaldsonville, Louisiana

❧ Nutrition Facts...then ❧

Calories: 274
Total Fat: 14gm
Saturated Fat: 5gm
% Calories from Fat: 44
Cholesterol: 23mg
Sodium: 283mg
Carbohydrate: 34gm
Fiber: 4gm
Protein: 7gm

CORN MAQUE CHOUX

PREP TIME: 1 Hour   SERVES: 8

☞ INGREDIENTS:

8 ears fresh corn
2 cups (150–200 count) shrimp, peeled and deveined
1/4 cup oil
1 cup chopped onions
1/2 cup chopped celery
1/2 cup chopped green bell pepper
1/2 cup chopped red bell pepper
1/4 cup diced garlic
1/4 cup low-fat smoked sausage
2 cups coarsely chopped tomatoes
2 tbsps tomato sauce
1 cup sliced green onions
salt substitute
black pepper
Louisiana Gold Pepper Sauce

☞ METHOD:

Select tender, well-developed ears of corn. Remove shucks and silk. Using a sharp knife, cut lengthwise through the kernels to remove them from the cob. Scrape each cob using the blade of the knife to remove all milk and additional pulp from the corn. This is important since the richness of the dish will depend on how much milk and pulp can be scraped from the cobs.

In a 5-quart cast iron dutch oven, heat oil over medium-high heat. Add corn, onions, celery, bell peppers, garlic and sausage. Saute approximately 15–20 minutes or until vegetables are wilted and corn begins to tenderize.

Add tomatoes, tomato sauce and shrimp. Continue cooking until juices from the tomatoes and shrimp are rendered into the dish. Add green onions and season to taste using salt substitute, pepper and Louisiana Gold. Cook an additional 15 minutes or until flavors of corn and shrimp are developed.

Nutrition Facts...now	
Calories:	220
Total Fat:	8gm
Saturated Fat:	1gm
% Calories from Fat:	31
Cholesterol:	11mg
Sodium:	149mg
Carbohydrate:	34gm
Fiber:	4gm
Protein:	7gm

PREP TIME: 30 Minutes   SERVES: 6

☞ INGREDIENTS:

2 1/2 cups white or yellow corn meal
3/4 tsp salt
1 1/4 tsps baking powder
1 3/4 cups milk
3/4 cup vegetable oil

"This is a very old Cajun recipe that was most often used as a hot cereal. I'm sure every Cajun cabin had its own method of preparation for this dish and had a different tradition for serving it. At my house, it has a very special place because whenever it's cooked, I can't help thinking of my grandparents.

"Many, many years ago, on the coldest winter nights, this dish would be cooked in a black iron pot in the fireplace. It's hard to imagine that a dish so simply prepared could taste so good, but it sure did back in that old Cajun cabin so many years ago."

Mrs. Rolan Bienvenue
Lafayette, Louisiana

☞ METHOD:

In a large mixing bowl, combine corn meal, salt, baking powder and milk. Blend well until all ingredients are incorporated. In a 12-inch cast iron skillet, heat oil over medium-high heat. When oil is hot, pour in the corn meal mixture and allow a crust to form over the edges, approximately 5 minutes. Once the crust has set, stir and lower the heat. Cook for 15 minutes, stirring occasionally to break the crust as it forms and allow yet another crust to develop. Serve with milk as a cereal or pour cane syrup over the top.

Chef's Tips on Exercise... really go to work on the lawn and in the garden.

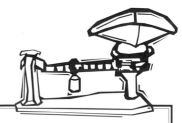

❧ Nutrition Facts...then ❧

Calories:	496
Total Fat:	31gm
Saturated Fat:	5gm
% Calories from Fat:	55
Cholesterol:	10mg
Sodium:	307mg
Carbohydrate:	48gm
Fiber:	3gm
Protein:	7gm

PREP TIME: 30 Minutes   SERVES: 6

The Palace Cafe, on courthouse square in Opelousas, has been a dining tradition for generations.

☞ INGREDIENTS:

2 1/2 cups white or yellow corn meal
1/4 tsp salt
1 1/4 tsps baking powder
1 3/4 cups skim milk
1/4 cup vegetable oil

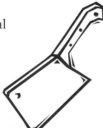

Nutrition Facts...now

Calories:	317
Total Fat:	10gm
Saturated Fat:	1gm
% Calories from Fat:	29
Cholesterol:	1mg
Sodium:	131mg
Carbohydrate:	48gm
Fiber:	3gm
Protein:	7gm

☞ METHOD:

In a large mixing bowl, combine corn meal, salt, baking powder and skim milk. Blend well until all ingredients are incorporated.

In a 12-inch cast iron skillet, heat oil over medium-high heat. When oil is hot, pour in the corn meal mixture and allow a crust to form over the edges, approximately 5 minutes. Once the crust has set, stir and lower the heat. Cook for 15 minutes, stirring occasionally to break the crust as it forms and allow yet another crust to develop.

Serve with skim milk as a cereal or pour cane syrup over the top.

PREP TIME: 45 Minutes   SERVES: 6

☞ INGREDIENTS:

2 cups white corn meal
3/4 tsp salt
1 1/2 cups water
1 tsp vegetable oil

Chef's Tips on Shopping...
when grocery shopping, beware of
products at eye level. High fat, high-
profit items are often placed there
to encourage impulse buying.

☞ METHOD:

Place an empty 12-inch cast iron skillet on high heat for 2–3 minutes or until a splash of water dances on the bottom of the pot. In a large mixing bowl, combine corn meal, salt and water. Blend thoroughly until all lumps are removed. Place the oil in the bottom of the skillet and spread corn meal mixture evenly over the bottom. Leave the flame on high until a light crust begins to form on the bottom. Lower heat to medium low or simmer. If you like coush coush lumpy, stir it only occasionally until done, approximately 25–30 minutes. If you prefer a smoother texture, stir it constantly until done. Serve in a bowl with warm milk as a cereal. You may wish to serve fig preserves or Steen's cane syrup over the coush coush.

"'Breakfast for supper' was a Sunday night tradition in the Rodrigue household as well as most Cajun homes. Although most people ate coush coush for breakfast, every now and then we substituted bacon and eggs, pancakes, crepes, beignets and of course, more coush coush.

"Not until I studied a little more about our culture did I realize that the tradition of eating fried corn meal came about because most of us were so poor. You know, it's really funny that I grew up in a home never even knowing that we were poor because of all of the great fun, family and food - especially coush coush.

"Today, my family and I normally have coush coush on Sunday night because it's one of our favorite dishes and it is certainly a tradition in our home."

Billie R. Landry
Abbeville, Louisiana

❧ Nutrition Facts...then ❧

Calories:	175
Total Fat:	2gm
Saturated Fat:	0gm
% Calories from Fat:	8
Cholesterol:	0mg
Sodium:	270mg
Carbohydrate:	36gm
Fiber:	2gm
Protein:	4gm

PREP TIME: 45 Minutes   SERVES: 6

☞ INGREDIENTS:

2 cups white corn meal
1/2 tsp salt
1 1/2 cups water
1 tsp vegetable oil

☞ METHOD:

Place an empty 12-inch cast iron skillet on high heat for 2–3 minutes or until a splash of water dances on the bottom of the pot.

In a large mixing bowl, combine corn meal, salt and water. Blend thoroughly until all lumps are removed. Place the oil in the bottom of the skillet and spread corn meal mixture evenly over the bottom. Leave the flame on high until a light crust begins to form on the bottom. Lower heat to medium low or simmer.

If you like coush coush lumpy, stir it only occasionally until done, approximately 25–30 minutes. If you prefer a smoother texture, stir it constantly until done. Serve in a bowl with warm milk as a cereal. You may wish to serve fig preserves or Steen's cane syrup over the coush coush.

Nutrition Facts...now

Calories:	175
Total Fat:	2gm
Saturated Fat:	0gm
% Calories from Fat:	8
Cholesterol:	0mg
Sodium:	181mg
Carbohydrate:	36gm
Fiber:	2gm
Protein:	4gm

PREP TIME: 3 Hours   SERVES: 6

☞ INGREDIENTS:

3 pounds venison shanks,
    including bones
1/4 pound butter
2 cups diced onions
1/2 cup diced celery
1/4 cup chopped garlic

1 cup diced carrots
3/4 cup flour
1/2 cup olive oil
1 cup dry red wine
3 cups chicken stock
1 tsp basil

1 tsp thyme
1 (14.5-ounce) can whole
    tomatoes, drained
3 bay leaves
1/2 cup chopped parsley
1/2 tsp salt

black pepper
hot sauce
1 tbsp grated lemon peel
1 tbsp minced garlic
1/4 cup chopped parsley

☞ METHOD:

Preheat oven to 350 degrees F. In a 10-inch cast iron skillet, heat butter over medium-high heat. Add onions, celery, garlic and carrots. Saute 3–5 minutes or until vegetables are wilted. Remove from heat and set aside. Season the venison shanks generously using salt, pepper and hot sauce. In order to keep the shanks from falling apart during cooking, you may wish to tie each shank across the center with a piece of butcher's twine. Coat them well in flour, shaking off all of the excess. In a 14-inch cast iron skillet, heat olive oil over medium-high heat. Brown the shanks, a few at a time, until golden brown on all sides. As the shanks brown, remove them to a large casserole dish, placing them neatly side by side. When all are done, spoon the vegetable mixture evenly over the top of the shanks. Remove all but 1 tablespoon of the olive oil from the cast iron skillet. Add red wine and bring mixture to a rolling boil. Reduce wine to approximately 1/2 cup, while scraping all of the brown drippings from the skillet into the wine. Add chicken stock, basil, thyme, tomatoes, bay leaves and 1/2 cup chopped parsley. Bring to a low boil, chopping tomatoes into the mixture. Once the liquid has come to a boil, pour the ingredients over the shanks in the casserole dish. Cover and bake 1 1/2–2 hours, basting occasionally. Test for tenderness by piercing the meat with the tip of a sharp knife or serving fork. When meat is tender, arrange the venison shanks decoratively on a heated platter and spoon the vegetable sauce from the casserole dish over the meat. Sprinkle with a garnish made by combining lemon peel, garlic and parsley. Osso Bucco should be served with pasta or risotto, or over jambalaya.

"This is a traditional Milanese dish, brought over from the Old Country by my paternal grandmother, Rosalie Russo. If there's anything better to be done with a veal shank, I can't imagine what it would be.

"But don't start it as a last-minute whim. Cooking Osso Bucco is a day-long undertaking. It's the sort of recipe you save for family get-togethers (typically, Christmas Eve at our house) or visits by special friends - the people you really like!"

Honorine Abel
Patterson, Louisiana

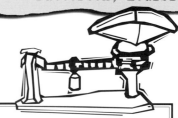

❖Nutrition Facts...then❖

Calories: 421
Total Fat: 22gm
Saturated Fat:...................... 12gm
% Calories from Fat:................. 46
Cholesterol:...................... 125mg
Sodium: 1090mg
Carbohydrate: 29gm
Fiber: 3gm
Protein: 23gm

PREP TIME: 3 Hours   SERVES: 6

INGREDIENTS:

3 pounds venison shanks, including bones
vegetable spray
2 cups diced onions
1/2 cup diced celery
1/4 cup chopped garlic
1 cup diced carrots
3/4 cup flour
1/4 cup olive oil
1 cup dry red wine
3 cups defatted chicken stock, unsalted
1 tsp basil
1 tsp thyme
1 (14.5-ounce) can whole tomatoes,
     no salt added, drained
3 bay leaves
1/2 cup chopped parsley
salt substitute
black pepper
hot sauce
1 tbsp grated lemon peel
1 tbsp minced garlic
1/4 cup chopped parsley

METHOD:

Preheat oven to 350 degrees F. Coat a 10-inch cast iron skillet with vegetable spray and place over medium-high heat. Add onions, celery, garlic and carrots. Saute 3–5 minutes or until vegetables are wilted. Remove from heat and set aside.

Season the venison shanks generously using salt substitute, pepper and hot sauce. In order to keep the shanks from falling apart during cooking, you may wish to tie each shank across the center with a piece of butcher's twine. Coat them well in flour, shaking off all of the excess.

In a 14-inch cast iron skillet, heat olive oil over medium-high heat. Brown the shanks, a few at a time, until golden brown on all sides. As the shanks brown, remove them to a large casserole dish, placing them neatly side by side. When all are done, spoon the vegetable mixture evenly over the top of the shanks.

Remove all but 1 tablespoon of the olive oil from the cast iron skillet. Add red wine and bring mixture to a rolling boil. Reduce wine to approximately 1/2 cup, while scraping all of the brown drippings from the skillet into the wine. Add chicken stock, basil, thyme, tomatoes, bay leaves and 1/2 cup chopped parsley. Bring to a low boil, chopping tomatoes into the mixture.

Once the liquid has come to a boil, pour the ingredients over the shanks in the casserole dish. Cover and bake 1 1/2–2 hours, basting occasionally. Test for tenderness by piercing the meat with the tip of a sharp knife or serving fork.

When the meat is tender, arrange the venison shanks decoratively on a heated platter and spoon the vegetable sauce from the casserole dish over the meat. Sprinkle with a garnish made by combining lemon peel, garlic and parsley. Osso Bucco should be served with pasta or risotto, or over jambalaya.

Nutrition Facts...now

Calories:	273
Total Fat:	5gm
Saturated Fat:	2gm
% Calories from Fat:	16
Cholesterol:	74mg
Sodium:	384mg
Carbohydrate:	28gm
Fiber:	3gm
Protein:	24gm

HOG'S HEAD CHEESE WITHOUT THE HEAD

PREP TIME: 3 Hours   MAKES: 3 loaf pans (36 servings)

☞ INGREDIENTS:

6 pounds pork shoulder
6 pig's feet
10 cups water
2 onions, quartered
3 cups sliced green onions
2 bay leaves
1 1/2 tsps cayenne pepper
1 1/2 tsps salt
1/2 tsp black pepper
1 cup chopped parsley

"Our mother always loved to make hog's head cheese because she knew the impact that the big hog's head would have on us children. We would always make the head cheese around the Christmas holidays because not only was it perfect for guests, but it also made excellent Christmas gifts. Mama used to always say the best gifts in the world are those that are homemade and things that people would not normally make for themselves!

"Today, we find it easier to use pork shoulder with a few pig's feet to accomplish this task rather than fighting with the hog's head."

Lillian Marks and Laura Taylor
Opelousas, Louisiana

☞ METHOD:

Cut pork shoulder into 1-inch cubes and place in a large stock pot along with pig's feet and water. Add onions, 1 1/2 cups green onions, bay leaves, cayenne, salt and pepper. Bring to a rolling boil, reduce to simmer and cook until meat falls from the bone, approximately 2 hours. Remove the meat from the liquid and strain solids from the stock. Reserve the liquid and discard vegetables. Once the meat is cooled, debone and grind or chop it finely. Return liquid to the stock pot and bring to a rolling boil. Add ground meat, remaining green onions and parsley. Cook 10 minutes, remove from heat and allow to cool slightly. Ladle the mixture into three 4" x 8" loaf pans and allow to cool. Refrigerate overnight and serve with crackers or croutons.

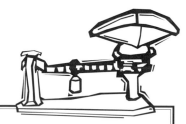

❊Nutrition Facts...then❊

Calories: 330
Total Fat: 21gm
Saturated Fat: 7gm
% Calories from Fat: 58
Cholesterol: 124mg
Sodium: 168mg
Carbohydrate: 0gm
Fiber: 0gm
Protein: 33gm

PREP TIME: 3 Hours   MAKES: 3 loaf pans (36 servings)

☞ INGREDIENTS:

6 pounds pork shoulder,
        trimmed
6 pig's feet
10 cups water
2 onions, quartered
3 cups sliced green onions
2 bay leaves
1 1/2 tsps cayenne pepper
1 tsp salt
1/2 tsp black pepper
1 cup chopped parsley

☞ METHOD:

Cut pork shoulder into 1-inch cubes and place in a large stock pot along with pig's feet and water. Add onions, 1 1/2 cups green onions, bay leaves, cayenne, salt and pepper. Bring to a rolling boil, reduce to simmer and cook until meat falls from the bone, approximately 2 hours.

Remove the meat from the liquid and strain solids from the stock. Reserve the liquid and discard vegetables. Once the meat is cooled, debone and grind or chop it finely. Return liquid to the stock pot and bring to a rolling boil. Add ground meat, remaining green onions and parsley. Cook 10 minutes, remove from heat and allow to cool slightly.

Ladle the mixture into three 4" x 8" loaf pans and allow to cool. Refrigerate overnight and serve with low-fat crackers or croutons.

Nutrition Facts...now

Calories: 287
Total Fat: 15gm
Saturated Fat: 5gm
% Calories from Fat: 47
Cholesterol: 125mg
Sodium: 159mg
Carbohydrate: 0gm
Fiber: 0gm
Protein: 36gm

PREP TIME: 3 Hours   SERVES: 6

☞ INGREDIENTS:

1/2 pound deboned turtle
1/2 pound deboned frog legs
1 pound (50–60 count) shrimp, peeled and deveined
1 pound cubed catfish fillets
3/4 cup vegetable oil
1 cup flour
2 cups diced onions
2 cups diced celery
1 cup diced bell pepper
1/4 cup diced garlic
1 (10-ounce) can Rotel tomatoes
1 (8-ounce) can tomato sauce
1 (6-ounce) can tomato paste
2 1/2 quarts hot water
1 cup sliced green onions
1/4 cup chopped parsley
1 tbsp salt
black pepper
hot sauce

☞ METHOD:

Place all seafoods in a large bowl and season with salt, pepper and hot sauce. Allow to sit in the refrigerator 4–6 hours or overnight prior to using. In a 12-quart cast iron dutch oven, heat oil over medium-high heat. Add flour and, using a wire whisk, whip constantly until dark brown roux is achieved. Add onions, celery, bell pepper and garlic. Saute 3–5 minutes or until vegetables are wilted. Add tomatoes, tomato sauce and tomato paste, blending well into the vegetable mixture. Cook 5 minutes and then add water. Bring mixture to a rolling boil and reduce to simmer. Add turtle and cook approximately 1 1/2 hours or until turtle is tender. Add frog and cook 30 additional minutes. Add shrimp and fish and cook until shrimp are pink and curled. Add green onions and parsley, blending well into the stew mixture. Season to taste using salt, pepper and hot sauce. Serve over steamed white rice or pasta.

"Growing up near Gueydan, Louisiana, our greatest hobby had to be cooking. We had large family cookouts and the pots were always filled with whatever wild game or seafood was in season. The vegetables that accompanied the main ingredients in the pot came from our garden.

"With ingredients this fresh, the final results had to be great. This seafood sauce piquant is a family favorite and today our three daughters, Kristi, Andrea and Jada, enjoy making the dish along with us."
Greg and Darlene Dupree
Gueydan, Louisiana

❧Nutrition Facts...then❧

Calories:	673
Total Fat:	32gm
Saturated Fat:	4gm
% Calories from Fat:	41
Cholesterol:	198mg
Sodium:	3719mg
Carbohydrate:	54gm
Fiber:	9gm
Protein:	48gm

SEAFOOD SAUCE PIQUANT, GUEYDAN-STYLE

PREP TIME: 3 Hours   SERVES: 6

☞ INGREDIENTS:

1/2 pound deboned turtle
1/2 pound deboned frog legs
1 pound (50–60 count) shrimp,
    peeled and deveined
1 pound cubed catfish fillets
1 cup oil-less roux
2 cups water
1/4 cup vegetable oil
2 cups diced onions
2 cups diced celery
1 cup diced bell pepper
1/4 cup diced garlic
1 (10-ounce) can Rotel tomatoes
1 (8-ounce) can tomato sauce, no salt added
1 (6-ounce) can tomato paste, no salt added
2 1/2 quarts hot water
1 cup sliced green onions
1/4 cup chopped parsley
salt substitute
black pepper
hot sauce

Henri Boulet passes a good time over some cafe au lait at the home of his Godparents, Norman and Agatha Badeaux, of Larose.

☞ METHOD:

Place all seafoods in a large bowl and season with salt substitute, pepper and hot sauce. Allow to sit in the refrigerator 4–6 hours or overnight prior to using.

Dissolve oil-less roux in 2 cups water. Set aside. In a 12-quart cast iron dutch oven, heat oil over medium-high heat. Add onions, celery, bell pepper and garlic. Saute 3–5 minutes or until vegetables are wilted. Add tomatoes, tomato sauce and tomato paste, blending well into the vegetable mixture.

Cook 5 minutes and then add roux/water mixture, blending well. Add 2 1/2 quarts of water, one ladle at a time. Bring mixture to a rolling boil and reduce to simmer. Add turtle and cook approximately 1 1/2 hours or until turtle is tender.

Add frog and cook 30 additional minutes. Add shrimp and fish and cook until shrimp are pink and curled. Add green onions and parsley, blending well into the stew mixture.

Season to taste using salt substitute, pepper and hot sauce. Serve over steamed white rice or pasta.

Nutrition Facts...now

Calories:	430
Total Fat:	13gm
Saturated Fat:	2gm
% Calories from Fat:	27
Cholesterol:	198mg
Sodium:	483mg
Carbohydrate:	34gm
Fiber:	5gm
Protein:	44gm

PREP TIME: 30 Minutes   MAKES: 8 cups

☞ INGREDIENTS:

2 (5-ounce) bottles Worcestershire sauce
1 1/2 cups lemon juice
2 (28-ounce) bottles catsup
1 (6-ounce) can tomato paste
1 cup vegetable oil
1 stick margarine
1/4 tsp celery salt
1/4 tsp garlic salt
black pepper
1/2 cup vinegar
1/2 cup soy sauce
1/4 tsp Liquid Smoke
1 tsp hot sauce
1 cup applesauce

☞ METHOD:

In a 1-gallon stock pot, place all ingredients and bring to a low boil. Reduce to simmer and cook 20–30 minutes. You may wish to jar or bottle the sauce into 1-pint containers to use as needed or to present as gifts. This volume of sauce will coat approximately 12 chickens.

"Tad was my father, James Yarbrough, for whom this sauce was as much the underpinning of his Mississippi brand of barbecuing as a favorite roux recipe would be for his Cajun counterparts.

"He'd get up at 4 a.m. to start a day's barbecuing at our home in Indianola, in the Mississippi Delta Country. But the sauce would already be prepared. He made that the previous day so it would have time to 'age.'

"From my perspective as a registered dietitian, what makes this recipe superior is the substitution of applesauce for sugar. But modern nutritional concerns weren't why my dad made it that way. He just thought it tasted better. And he was right!"

Linda Greco
Raceland, Louisiana

❧Nutrition Facts...then❧

Calories: 80
Total Fat: 5gm
Saturated Fat: 1gm
% Calories from Fat: 52
Cholesterol: 0mg
Sodium: 535mg
Carbohydrate: 9gm
Fiber: 2gm
Protein: 1gm

(2 tablespoons = one serving)

PREP TIME: 30 Minutes   MAKES: 7 1/2 cups

☞ INGREDIENTS:

2 (5-ounce) bottles Worcestershire sauce
1 1/2 cups lemon juice
2 (28-ounce) bottles catsup
1 (6-ounce) can tomato paste, no salt added
1/2 cup vegetable oil
1/2 cup soft margarine
1/4 tsp celery salt
1/4 tsp garlic powder
black pepper
1/2 cup vinegar
1/2 cup lite soy sauce
1/4 tsp Liquid Smoke
1 tsp hot sauce
1 cup applesauce

☞ METHOD:

In a 1-gallon stock pot, place all ingredients and bring to a low boil. Reduce to simmer and cook 20–30 minutes. You may wish to jar or bottle the sauce into 1 pint containers to use as needed or to present as gifts. This volume of sauce will coat approximately 12 chickens.

Nutrition Facts...now

Calories: 68
Total Fat: 3gm
Saturated Fat: 1gm
% Calories from Fat: 42
Cholesterol: 0mg
Sodium: 479mg
Carbohydrate: 10gm
Fiber: 2gm
Protein: 1gm

(2 tablespoons = one serving)

FRIED OYSTER DRESSING

PREP TIME: 1 Hour   SERVES: 8

☞ INGREDIENTS:

2 dozen select oysters	2 cups diced celery	1 bay leaf	black pepper	4 cups cooked rice
1 pint chicken livers	1 cup diced bell pepper	1 tsp thyme	hot sauce	1 egg, beaten
1 cup giblets from fowl	1/4 cup diced garlic	1 tsp basil	1 cup vegetable oil	1/2 cup sliced green onions
1/4 cup vegetable oil	1 cup chicken broth	1/2 tsp salt	1 cup corn meal	1/4 cup chopped parsley
2 cups diced onions				

☞ METHOD:

If you would prefer to substitute 1 cup of ground pork in place of the giblets, feel free to do so. Poach chicken livers in lightly salted water until firm. Strain, cool and chop the livers. Set aside. In a 10-inch cast iron skillet, heat 1/4 cup vegetable oil over medium-high heat. Add chopped chicken livers and giblets. Saute 3–5 minutes or until giblets are browned. Add onions, celery, bell pepper and garlic. Continue to saute, stirring occasionally, until vegetables are wilted, approximately 10–15 minutes. Add 1/2 cup of chicken broth to the skillet, along with bay leaf. Should mixture become too dry during the sauteing process, continue to add a small amount of broth. Blend mixture well, remove pan from heat and set aside. When ready to complete the dressing, return the giblet mixture to the heat and bring to a low simmer. Add thyme, basil, salt, pepper and hot sauce. Pour in a small amount of chicken broth to retain moisture. While mixture is simmering, heat 1 cup of vegetable oil in another 10-inch cast iron skillet over medium-high heat. Dredge the oysters in seasoned corn meal and fry, a few at a time, until golden brown and cooked. Drain on paper towels and keep warm. To the giblet mixture add rice, beaten egg, green onions and parsley, stirring quickly to coat the rice with all seasonings. Stir in fried oysters and adjust seasonings if necessary. Serve as a side dish to any roasted fowl or as a stuffing for turkeys or ducks.

"Oyster dressing is a Louisiana staple. This one is special because it includes fried oysters. To me it tastes better, because the oysters are never soggy! I got this recipe from my paternal grandmother, 'Donia' (Sarah Caldonia Vinson) Laurent. It goes back much further, but was never written down. Each generation keeps it going!

"I always associated this dish with my childhood, spending time on my grandfather's rice farm near Lake Arthur. It was during the Great Depression and everyone was as poor as church mice. There was always plenty of food, though. We used to ride horses and enjoy the nearby lake. We'd even get a nickel every 4th of July to buy an ice cream cone at the Independence Day celebration. It was a big community event. If Norman had been Cajun, he'd have painted that, for sure!"

Joy Weldon
Thibodaux, Louisiana

❧Nutrition Facts...then❧

Calories:	631
Total Fat:	39gm
Saturated Fat:	6gm
% Calories from Fat:	56
Cholesterol:	448mg
Sodium:	394mg
Carbohydrate:	45gm
Fiber:	3gm
Protein:	24gm

FRIED OYSTER DRESSING

PREP TIME: 1 Hour   SERVES: 8

☞ INGREDIENTS:

2 dozen select oysters
1/2 pint chicken livers
1 pound lean ground pork
1 tbsp vegetable oil
2 cups diced onions
2 cups diced celery
1 cup diced bell pepper
1/4 cup diced garlic
1 cup defatted chicken broth, unsalted
1 bay leaf
1 tsp thyme
1 tsp basil
1/4 tsp salt
black pepper
hot sauce
vegetable spray
1 cup corn meal
4 cups cooked rice
2 egg whites, beaten
1/2 cup sliced green onions
1/4 cup chopped parsley

☞ METHOD:

Poach chicken livers in lightly salted water until firm. Strain, cool and chop the livers. Set aside.

In a 10-inch cast iron skillet, heat vegetable oil over medium-high heat. Add chopped chicken livers and ground pork. Saute 30 minutes or until pork is browned. Add onions, celery, bell pepper and garlic. Continue to saute, stirring occasionally, until vegetables are wilted, approximately 10–15 minutes.

Add 1/2 cup of chicken broth to the skillet, along with bay leaf. Should mixture become too dry during the sauteing process, continue to add a small amount of broth. Blend mixture well, remove pan from heat and set aside.

When ready to complete the dressing, return the giblet mixture to the heat and bring to a low simmer. Add thyme, basil, salt, pepper and hot sauce. Pour in a small amount of chicken broth to retain moisture.

While mixture is simmering, spray another 10-inch cast iron skillet with vegetable spray. Dredge the oysters in seasoned corn meal and fry, a few at a time, until golden brown and cooked. Keep warm.

To the giblet mixture add rice, beaten egg whites, green onions and parsley, stirring quickly to coat the rice with all seasonings. Stir in fried oysters and adjust seasonings if necessary.

Serve as a side dish to any roasted fowl or as a stuffing for turkeys or ducks.

Sunset over a crawfish pond in Vermillion Parish.

Nutrition Facts...now

Calories:	340
Total Fat:	7gm
Saturated Fat:	2gm
% Calories from Fat:	19
Cholesterol:	210mg
Sodium:	236mg
Carbohydrate:	44gm
Fiber:	2gm
Protein:	23gm

PREP TIME: 4 Hours   MAKES: 2 Loaves (24 slices)

☞ INGREDIENTS:

1 package active dry yeast
1/4 cup warm water
2 cups warm water
2 tbsps sugar
2 tsps salt
1 tbsp shortening
6 1/2 cups enriched flour

"The highlight of my day as a small child was when Grandmother Musso said she was making her famous Italian bread. I would lean over the edge of the table and watch her collect the ingredients to make her masterpiece. Grandmother never made a small amount of bread because when the children or neighbors found out she was making it, they all seemed to stop by for a visit.

"I remember her laying a blanket on her kitchen counter and placing the pan of dough on the blanket and then covering it with a dish towel and folding the blanket over the pan. After the dough had been made into oblong loaves, they were placed on the blanket once again and covered for the final rise.

"I don't think I'll ever forget the unbelievable aroma that filled her kitchen with this wonderful yeasty smell. She would remove the cooked bread from the oven with her long wooden spatula that looked more like the paddle for grandfather's boat. The minute the breads were removed from the oven, they went back between the blankets and were wrapped in the dish towel to remain warm.

"The slowest walk grandmother ever made was the one from the table to the refrigerator to get that stick of butter to spread over that warm Italian bread."

Marie Campisi Breaux
Thibodaux, Louisiana

☞ METHOD:

Preheat oven to 400 degrees F. This will not only get the oven ready for baking, but will also help heat the kitchen to guarantee a better rise in the bread. Dissolve yeast in 1/4 cup warm water. Set aside to bloom. In a separate bowl, combine 2 cups warm water (milk may be substituted), sugar, salt and shortening. Add 2 cups of flour and the yeast mixture, blending well. Gradually add the remaining flour to make a moderately stiff dough. Turn dough on lightly floured surface and knead until smooth and satiny. Shape the dough into a ball and place in a lightly greased bowl. Turn once to grease the surface lightly. Cover the bowl with a dish towel. Allow dough to rise in a warm place until double in size, approximately 1 1/2 hours. Punch down, reshape into a ball and cover. Allow to rise again until double in size, approximately 45 minutes. Divide dough into 2 equal portions and shape each into a ball. Allow to rest for 10 minutes. You may shape the dough into loaves such as French bread or allow to remain in a round or oval shape. Place on 2 greased baking pans or French bread pans. Allow to rise until double, approximately 1 hour. Bake 45–50 minutes.

❋Nutrition Facts...then❋

Calories: 133
Total Fat: 1gm
Saturated Fat: 0gm
% Calories from Fat: 6
Cholesterol: 0mg
Sodium: 179mg
Carbohydrate: 27gm
Fiber: 1gm
Protein: 4gm

(per slice)

PREP TIME: 4 Hours   MAKES: 2 Loaves (24 slices)

☞ INGREDIENTS:

1 package active dry yeast
1/4 cup warm water
2 cups warm water
2 tbsps sugar
2 tsps salt
1 tbsp vegetable oil
6 1/2 cups enriched flour

☞ METHOD:

Preheat oven to 400 degrees F. This will not only get the oven ready for baking, but will also help heat the kitchen to guarantee a better rise in the bread. Dissolve yeast in 1/4 cup warm water. Set aside to bloom.

In a separate bowl, combine 2 cups warm water (milk may be substituted), sugar, salt and oil. Add 2 cups of flour and the yeast mixture, blending well. Gradually add the remaining flour to make a moderately stiff dough.

Turn dough on lightly floured surface and knead until smooth and satiny. Shape the dough into a ball and place in a lightly greased bowl. Turn once to grease the surface lightly. Cover the bowl with a dish towel. Allow dough to rise in a warm place until double in size, approximately 1 1/2 hours.

Punch down, reshape into a ball and cover. Allow to rise again until double in size, approximately 45 minutes.

Divide dough into 2 equal portions and shape each into a ball. Allow to rest for 10 minutes. You may shape the dough into loaves such as French bread or allow to remain in a round or oval shape. Place on 2 greased baking pans or French bread pans. Allow to rise until double, approximately 1 hour. Bake 45–50 minutes.

Nutrition Facts...now

Calories:	133
Total Fat:	1gm
Saturated Fat:	0gm
% Calories from Fat:	6
Cholesterol:	0mg
Sodium:	179mg
Carbohydrate:	27gm
Fiber:	1gm
Protein:	4gm

(per slice)

In search of
Louisiana Specialty Products?

When cooking the cuisine of South Louisiana, numerous specialty products such as cast iron pots, a 200-year old tradition, crawfish tails and andouille sausage are utilized. Most of these unique items are grown or manufactured here in our state.

At Chef John Folse & Company, we are able to make these unique items available to you anywhere in the country. If you are interested in purchasing or obtaining information on any of the products featured in this cookbook or on my PBS series, "A Taste of Louisiana with Chef John Folse & Company," please write or phone me at:

Chef John Folse & Company
2517 South Phillipe Avenue
Gonzales, LA 70737

(504) 644-6000
(504) 644-1295 Fax

Please visit us on the internet and take a walk through our Company Store at:

http://www.jfolse.com

We look forward to assisting you with any special product needs or additional information on the cuisine and culture of the Cajuns and Creoles!

442

A Change of Habit

Change of habit is hard for many people and your eating habits are no exception. Whether you want to lose weight, lower your cholesterol, or just be healthy, get ready to update your cooking habits. We have listed tips that will barely make a dent in the way your food taste, but will make a big difference in fat, calorie and sodium content.

TAKE IT OFF . . . TAKE IT ALL OFF!
Pull out your favorite recipes and adopt one or a combination of these techniques:

REDUCE an ingredient.

ELIMINATE an ingredient.

SUBSTITUTE one ingredient for another.

ADD a new ingredient.

CHANGE a preparation method.

* You can't always remove all the fat from a recipe. Use 1/3 to 1/2 the amount called for in recipes. For texture, replace it with applesauce, or low-fat or nonfat milk or yogurt.

* Use water or juice-packed canned products (fish, fruits).

* Instead of two-crust pies, serve single crust (made with oil or margarine) or use low-fat cookie crumbs.

* When sauteing vegetables for etouffees or stews, use a butter flavored vegetable spray. Saute on low heat or simmer for a longer period of time to achieve the same results.

* Make soups low in fat by skimming off the fat layer that floats on the top. After chilling, the fat layer lifts off easily.

* When roasting meat, use a rack so that the meat does not sit in the drippings while cooking.

* When using the meat juices for gravy, skim or pour off the fat first.

* Omit the oil from your favorite spaghetti sauce recipe — it'll still taste great.

* Drain the extra fat when browning meat for spaghetti or casseroles. Rinsing the meat with hot water removes even more fat.

* Baste meat with wine, fruit juice, or broth instead of the fat drippings.

* Use lean ground turkey or chicken instead of ground beef for variety. Or mix lean ground beef with lean ground turkey or chicken.

* Use a non-stick cooking spray when the recipe calls for a "greased" pan.

* Steam or poach onions and other vegetables in a very small amount of water or broth instead of oil.

* Recipe calls for buttered bread crumbs? Try crushed cereal instead.

* Mix equal amounts of reduced-fat or nonfat mayonnaise and low-fat or nonfat yogurt or sour cream for a dressing with chicken or tuna salad.

* Use a dash of Worcestershire sauce instead of fat to add flavor to meat and vegetable recipes.

* Lemon, dill, chives, parsley, tarragon and basil are all favorite fish flavor enhancers.

YOU HAVE A CHOICE

IF RECIPE CALLS FOR:	USE THIS INSTEAD:
Avocado	Asparagus or green peas pureed
Bacon	*Canadian bacon*
Bacon Bits	Soy bits
Beef	*Chicken or turkey without skin*
Bread Crumbs	Fat-free bread crumbs
Butter	*Equal amounts of applesauce*
Cheese	Low-fat or fat-free cheese
Chicken Stock	*Vegetable or chicken stock without fat*
Chocolate	Cocoa powder
Chocolate Sauce	*Cocoa & applesauce*
Potato or Corn Chips	Baked low-fat or no fat chips
Cream	*Nonfat dry milk or evaporated skim milk*
Cream Cheese	Nonfat cream cheese
Cream Sauce	*Cream sauce made with skim milk*
Evaporated Milk	Evaporated skim milk
Flour and Fat	*Pureed vegetables or corn starch*
Flour & Oil Roux	No fat browned flour roux
Fudge Sauce	*Marshmallow sauce*
Granola	Low-fat granola or puffed cereal & raisins
Gravy	*Butter flavored seasoning*
Half & Half	Evaporated skim milk
Ice Cream	*Nonfat frozen yogurt or ice cream, sherbet*
Margarine	Diet, reduced fat or fat-free (as a spread); butter flavored seasoning (in cooking)
Mayonnaise	*Nonfat or reduced fat mayonnaise*
Meat	Beans
Nuts	*Dry cereal, grapenuts*
Oils in Baking	Applesauce, pureed prunes or plums
Oils in Frying	*Non-stick cookware or non-stick spray*
Oils in Sauteing	Water or nonfat broth
Peanut Butter	*Reduced fat peanut butter or apple butter*
Salad Dressing	Nonfat salad dressing
Sour Cream	*Low-fat or nonfat sour cream or plain yogurt*
Whipped Cream	Reduced fat or fat free whipped cream substitute
Whole Egg	*2 egg whites or 1/4 cup egg substitute*
Whole Milk	Skim, 1% milk or 1/2 % milk
Wine	*Non-alcoholic wine*

COMING TO TERMS . . .

To ease your trip down the supermarket aisle, the Food and Drug Administration (FDA) has approved definitions for many nutrition labeling terms. These terms can help you choose foods that are lower in calories, fat, cholesterol and sodium, and higher in fiber, vitamins and minerals. Listed below are some of the common food labeling terms ("per serving" refers to the standard serving sizes set by the government).

SUGAR

Sugar free: Less than 0.5 grams (g) per serving
No added sugar, Without added sugar, No sugar added: No sugars added during processing or packing, including ingredients that contain sugars (for example, fruit juices, applesauce, or dried fruit).

Processing does not increase the sugar content above the amount naturally present in the ingredients. (A functionally insignificant increase in sugars is acceptable from processes used for purposes other than increasing sugar content.)

The food that it resembles and for which it substitutes normally contains added sugars.

If the food doesn't meet the requirements for a low- or reduced- calorie food, the product bears a statement that the food is not low-calorie or calorie-reduced and directs consumers' attention to the nutrition panel for further information on sugars and calorie content.
Reduced sugar: at least 25 percent less sugar per serving than referenced food

CALORIES

Calorie free: fewer than 5 calories per serving
Low calorie: 40 calories or less per serving and if the serving is 30g or less or 2 tablespoons or less, per 50g of the food
Reduced or Fewer calories: at least 25 percent fewer calories per serving than referenced food

FAT

Fat free: less than 0.5g of fat per serving
Saturated fat free: less than 0.5g per serving and the level of trans fatty acids does not exceed 1 percent of total fat
Low-fat: 3g or less per serving, and if the serving is 30g or less or 2 tablespoons or less, per 50g of the food
Low saturated fat: 1g or less per serving and not more than 15 percent of calories from saturated fatty acids
Reduced or Less fat: at least 25 percent less per serving than referenced food
Reduced or Less saturated fat: at least 25 percent less per serving than referenced food

CHOLESTEROL

Cholesterol free: less than 2mg (milligrams) of cholesterol and 2g or less of saturated fat per serving
Low cholesterol: 20mg or less and 2g or less of saturated fat per serving and, if the serving is 30g or less or 2 tablespoons or less, per 50g of the food
Reduced or Less cholesterol: at least 25 percent less and 2g or less of saturated fat per serving than referenced food

SODIUM

Sodium free: less than 5mg per serving
Low sodium: 140mg or less per serving and, if the serving is 3g or less or 2 tablespoons or less, per 50g of the food
Very low sodium: 35mg or less per serving and, if the serving is 30g or less or 2 tablespoons or less, per 50g of the food
Reduced or Less sodium: at least 25 percent less per serving than referenced food

FIBER

High fiber: 5g or more per serving (Foods making high-fiber claims must meet the definition for low-fat, or the level of total fat must appear next to the high-fiber claim.)
Good source of fiber: 2.5g to 4.9g per serving
More or Added fiber: at least 2.5g more per serving than referenced food

THE SIGN OF THE TIMES

Everybody is doing it — everywhere you look! That is, hanging out in the aisles of the supermarket staring at those food labels which are viewed as a challenge for some and stress for others. This sign of the times — the "Nutrition Facts" panel — is wrapped around 90% of all food items on the shelves and even can be found chilled out in the frozen foods section.

What are you looking for when reading the label — fat or sodium content, calories, ingredients? Probably all of the above. The idea isn't to get hung up on calculating numbers and percentages but to understand what you're eating and how it fits into your overall diet. For your shopping satisfaction, the basic format of the "Nutrition Facts" is explained below.

Serving sizes are now more consistent across product lines, are stated in both household and metric measures, and reflect the amounts people actually eat.

The **list of nutrients** covers those most important to the health of today's consumers, most of whom need to worry about getting too much of certain nutrients (fat, for example), rather than too few vitamins or minerals, as in the past.

New title signals that the label contains the newly required information.

Calories from fat are now shown on the label to help consumers meet dietary guidelines that recommend people get no more than 30 per cent of the calories in their overall diet from fat.

% Daily Value shows how a food fits into the overall daily diet.

Nutrition Facts

Serving Size: 1 Cup (227g)
Servings Per Container: 4 Servings

Amount Per Serving		% Daily Value*
Calories	162 Cal.	
Calories from Fat	81 Cal.	
Total Fat	9 Gm	**13%**
Saturated Fat	2 Gm	**10%**
Cholesterol	54 mg	**18%**
Sodium	1007 mg	**42%**
Total Carbohydrate	13 Gm	**4%**
Fiber	1 Gm	**4%**
Sugars	1 Gm	
Protein	8 Gm	

Vitamin A	13%	•	Vitamin C	30%
Calcium	6%	•	Iron	13%

* Percent Daily Values are based on a 2,000 calorie diet. Your daily values may be higher or lower depending on your calorie needs.

	Calories	2,000	2,500
Total Fat	Less than	65g	80g
Sat. Fat	Less than	20g	25g
Cholesterol	Less than	300mg	300mg
Sodium	Less than	2400mg	2400mg
Total Carbohydrate		300g	375g
Fiber		25g	30g

Calories per gram:
Fat 9 • Carbohydrates 4 • Protein 4

Daily Values are also something new. Some are maximums, as with fat (65 grams or less); others are minimums, as with carbohydrate (300 grams or more). The daily values for a 2,000- and 2,500-calorie diet must be listed on the label of larger packages.

The label of larger packages may now tell the number of calories per gram of fat, carbohydrate, and protein.

MINDING YOUR PEAS & Q'CUMBERS

Understanding food labels is one issue, putting it to use is another. With work and family, it's not always easy to find time to shop, let alone to take time to look for good, nutritious foods. But, keeping a shopping list will help; you'll buy only what you need, when you need it. Also remember to go after you've eaten. Hungry shoppers are less discriminating and tend to buy more junk food! It's also wise to shop around the outside aisles of the store first — that's where the healthiest items are found . . . breads, fresh produce, meats and dairy. Keep walking past the end-of-the-aisle displays or food samples — they're usually high in fat. Finally, use our list of shopping tips to make these healthy food choices:

MEAT DEPARTMENT
* Choose mostly lean, well-trimmed cuts of meat: round, sirloin, tenderloin, flank.
* Extra lean ground beef, or lean ground turkey.
* For less fat, choose meat that's graded "select" instead of "choice" or "prime".
* Look for lean, lower-fat deli meats: turkey, lean ham, lean roast beef, low-fat or fat free franks and sausage.
* Add fresh fish and poultry to your cart, too. They're lower in fat and saturated fats if you control the added fats used in cooking.
* If you wish, occasionally choose just a few higher-fat meats: bacon, ribs, corned beef, regular sausage.

FROZEN FOODS
* If you need to control cholesterol, look for egg substitutes (egg yolks are high in cholesterol).
* Select frozen dinners and entrees that have moderate amounts of fat, calories and sodium. Frozen meals offer "built-in" variety!
* Whether they're fresh, frozen or canned, fill your cart with enough vegetables. For frozen varieties, consider those with less fat, sodium and sauce.
* Need to control sodium and fat? Try unbreaded, frozen fish and poultry.
* Frozen juice concentrates are often the least expensive form of fruit juice.
* Portion-packed frozen desserts help curb the tendency to eat large helpings.

* Consider your frozen dessert options - frozen yogurt and low-fat and fat-free ice cream have less fat than regular ice cream. And why not try frozen fruit juice bars?

DAIRY CASE
* Include calcium-rich beverages, low-fat (1%) or skim milk and buttermilk, in your cart for kids and adults.
* For another high-calcium, low-fat treat, add low-fat or nonfat yogurt and cottage cheese to your list — each has less than 200 calories per serving.
* Trim fat, not taste — buy plain yogurt to use as a mayonnaise or sour cream substitute for vegetable toppings, dips and sandwiches.
* For less fat, look for part-skim, reduced and no-fat cheeses.

PRODUCE SELECTION
* Buy more fruits and vegetables — perhaps a greater variety, too. They add nutrients, fiber and taste to your meals. Yet, unless you add fat or sugar, they're low in calories.
* Enjoy the sweet, natural taste of exotic fruits, such as kiwi fruit, mango, papaya . . . or a new variety of pears or plums. Fruits are great vitamin C sources.
* Instead of your vegetable standbys, try new varieties, such as asparagus, beets, jicama, kohlrabi, red or yellow peppers or snow peas. Vegetables are great sources of vitamins A and C and fiber.

Tuck herbs and spices into your cart to add flavor, with less salt, to your favorite foods.

Find lower-fat versions of your favorite salad dressings and mayonnaise.

Add more legumes (beans) to your cart and to your menus. They're high in complex carbohydrates and fiber, yet low in calories.

Add soups that have little fat and low sodium for another dimension to your meals.

Canned vegetables and fruits can add variety and save time. But check nutrition labels to compare sodium and sugar.

Grains are great! Be sure to include enough whole grain bread, cereal, rice and pasta in your cart.

And grain mixes are great time savers. However, check nutrition labels — some rice and pasta mixes are high in sodium. If you buy them, try using only half the seasoning.

How about trying some pasta and low-fat prepared sauce for a quick, nutritious dinner?

For vitamin C rich beverages, look for juice, rather than fruit "drink" or "punch".

How about candies, cookies, chips, sodas, beer — include some but not too many. *(Hint: Unsalted pretzels have less fat and sodium than most dry snacks. Graham crackers, gingersnaps and fruit bars have less fat and sugar than most other cookies).*

Shop for "whole grain" and "enriched" breads, rolls and muffins. They have B vitamins and iron. Whole grains are higher in fiber, too.

You can include a few "goodies" — donuts, pastries, cake, etc. Be sure you plan to use them sparingly!

MEET YOUR EQUAL

1 pound of all-purpose flour is 4 cups (sifted)

1 pound of cake flour is 4 1/2 cups

1 pound of whole wheat flour is about 3 1/2 cups (stirred, not sifted)

1 pound of granulated sugar is 2 cups

1 pound of packed brown sugar is 2 1/4 cups

1 pound of unsifted powdered sugar is 3 1/2 to 4 cups

1 pound of cheese yields about 4 cups grated

1/4 pound of crumbled Bleu cheese is 1 cup

1 pound of butter is 2 cups or 4 sticks

1 cup unwhipped cream is 2 cups whipped

1 chicken (broiler) yields about 3 1/2 cups of cooked meat

1 chicken breast (2 halves) yields about 6 -7 ounces of cooked meat

1 pound of flaked fish is about 2 cups

1 pound ground meat is about 2 cups

1 whole egg equals about 1/4 cup

8-10 egg whites is 1 cup

12-14 egg yolks is 1 cup

1 1/2 ounces (about 7 tablespoons) of dry oat bran yields about 1 1/5 cups cooked

1 1/2 ounces (about 1/2 cup) of dry oatmeal yields about 1 1/8 cups cooked

1 1/2 ounces (3 tablespoons) of dry bulgur yields 1/2 cup plus 1 tablespoon cooked

1 cup of uncooked rice yields 3 cups cooked

1 pound (4 cups) dry macaroni yields approximately 8 cups cooked

2 ounces (about 1/2 cup) dry macaroni yields about 1 cup plus 1 tablespoon cooked

1 pound (5 cups) dry spaghetti yields approximately 10 cups cooked

3 cups dry corn flakes is 1 cup crushed

1 pound (1 1/2 cups) kidney beans yields 9 cups cooked

1 pound (2 1/3 cups) lima beans yields 6 cups cooked

1 pound (2 1/3 cups) navy beans yields 6 cups cooked

1 pound of fresh apples equals about 3 medium and yields about 3 1/2 cups peeled and sliced

1 pound of bananas is about 3 medium or 1 cup mashed bananas

1 orange equals 1/3 cup of juice

1 large lemon contains 1/4 cup (2 fluid ounces) of juice, and 1 medium lemon yields about 3 tablespoons of juice and about 1 tablespoon of grated rind

1 pound of fresh tomatoes is about 3 medium to large

1 pound of fresh potatoes is about 3 medium, and yields about 2 1/4 cups cooked

1 pound of cabbage is about 4 cups shredded

1 pound carrots is about 2 1/2 cups sliced

1 pound unshelled walnuts equals 1 1/2 to 1 3/4 cups shelled

14 square graham crackers equals 1 cup crumbs

28 saltine crackers equals 1 cup crumbs

4 slices of bread equals 1 cup crumbs

22 vanilla wafers equals 1 cup crumbs

MEASURE IT UP!

3 tsp	=	1 tbsp
2 tbsp	=	1/8 c
4 tbsp	=	1/4 c
8 tbsp	=	1/2 c
16 tbsp	=	1 c
5 tbsp + 1 tsp	=	1/3 c
12 tbsp	=	3/4 c
4 oz	=	1/2 c
8 oz	=	1 c
16 oz	=	1 lb
1 oz	=	2 tbsp
2 c	=	1 pt
2 pt	=	1 qt
1 qt	=	4 c
5/8 c	=	1/2 c + 2 tbsp
7/8 c	=	3/4 c + 2 tbsp
1 jigger	=	1 1/2 fl. oz (3 tbsp)

SIZE IT UP!

Of the different sizes of cans used by commercial canners, the most common are:

Size:	Average Contents:
8 oz	1 cup
No. 300	1 3/4 cups
No. 1 tall	2 cups
No. 303	2 cups
No. 2	2 1/2 cups
No. 2 1/2	3 1/2 cups
No. 3	4 cups
No. 10	12 to 13 cups

WHEN IT'S HOT, IT'S HOT!

General Oven Chart

Very Slow Oven	250° to 300° F
Slow Oven	300° to 325° F
Moderate Oven	325° to 375° F
Medium Hot Oven	375° to 400° F
Hot Oven	400° to 450° F
Very Hot Oven	450° to 500° F

GOT SOMETHING MISSING?

1 tbsp. cornstarch (for thickening)
    = 2 tbsp. flour
1 cup sifted all-purpose flour
    = 1 cup + 2 tbsp. sifted cake flour
1 cup sifted cake flour
    = 1 cup minus 2 tbsp. sifted all-purpose
      flour
1 tsp. baking powder
    = 1/4 tsp. baking soda + 1/2 tsp. cream
      of tartar
1 cup granulated sugar
    = 1 cup brown or 2 cups sifted powdered
      sugar
1 cup sour milk
    = 1 cup sweet milk into which 1 tbsp.
      vinegar or lemon juice has been
      stirred (let stand for 5 minutes); or
      1 cup buttermilk
1 cup sweet milk
    = 1 cup sour milk or buttermilk + 1/2
      tsp. baking soda
3/4 cup cracker crumbs
    = 1 cup bread crumbs
1 cup cream, sour, heavy
    = 1/3 cup butter and 2/3 cup milk in any
      sour milk recipe
1 tsp. dried herbs
    = 1 tbsp. fresh herbs
1 cup whole milk
    = 1/2 cup evaporated milk and 1/2 cup
      water or 1 cup reconstituted nonfat
      dry milk and 1 tbsp. butter
1 pkg. active dry yeast
    = 1 cake compressed yeast
1 tbsp. instant minced onion, rehydrated
    = 1 small fresh onion
1 tbsp. prepared mustard
    = 1 tsp. dry mustard
1/8 tsp. garlic powder
    = 1 small pressed clove of garlic
2 cups tomato sauce
    = 3/4 cup tomato paste + 1 cup water
1 lb. whole dates
    = 1 1/2 cups pitted and cut
10 miniature marshmallows
    = 1 large marshmallow

THE ROUX

In Cajun and Creole cuisine, the roux is the primary thickening agent for stocks, soups and sauces. Equal parts of butter or oil blended with flour and cooked over high heat, creates a roux. This process may not only produce roux of different colors and thickening abilities, but flavors as well. Following are three basic rouxs used in Louisiana cooking.

THE BLONDE BUTTER ROUX

1 cup butter	1 cup all purpose flour

In a 10-inch cast iron skillet, melt butter over medium-high heat. Sprinkle in flour and, using a wire whisk, stir constantly until flour is well blended into the butter. Continue to cook roux until flour is bubbly but not brown. This roux will thicken approximately 1 1/2 quarts of stock to a sauce-consistency.

8 Servings

Calories:	260
Total Fat:	23gm
Saturated Fat:	14gm
% Calories from Fat:	79%
Cholesterol:	62mg
Sodium:	235mg
Carbohydrate:	12gm
Fiber:	0
Protein:	2gm

THE DARK BROWN CAJUN ROUX

1 cup oil	1 cup all purpose flour

In a 10-inch cast iron skillet, heat oil over medium-high heat. Sprinkle in flour and, using a wire whisk, stir constantly until flour is well blended into the oil. Continue to cook, stirring constantly, until roux is caramel colored, but not quite as dark as chocolate. Remove from heat and continue stirring until cool. This roux will thicken approximately 1 1/2 quarts of stock to a proper gumbo-consistency.

8 Servings

Calories:	298
Total Fat:	27gm
Saturated Fat:	3gm
% Calories from Fat:	82%
Cholesterol:	0
Sodium:	0
Fiber:	0
Protein:	2gm

THE OIL-LESS ROUX

2 cups all purpose flour

Preheat oven to 375 degrees F. Spread flour evenly across the bottom of a 15-inch cast iron skillet. Bake, stirring occasionally, for approximately 1 hour. Make sure to stir well around the edges of the skillet so flour does not scorch. Cook flour until light or dark color is achieved, depending on use. The roux will become darker when liquid is added. When desired color is reached, cool on a large cookie sheet, stirring occasionally. Store in a sealed jar for future use. 1 cup of oil-less roux will thicken 1 1/2 quarts of stock to a proper gumbo consistency.

8 Servings

Calories:	114
Total Fat:	0
Saturated Fat:	0
% Calories from Fat:	0%
Cholesterol:	0
Sodium:	1mg
Carbohydrate:	24gm
Fiber:	1gm
Protein:	3gm

NOTE: I recommend oil-less roux manufactured and sold by Bruce Foods and Savoie's. Bruce Foods is located in New Iberia, Louisiana (318) 365-8101 and Savoie's is located in Opelousas, Louisiana (318) 942-7241.

THE INDEX

Appetizers   **Old/New**

Boiled Shrimp Mold - Chris Landry 6/7
Cheese & Cracker Casserole - Ed Brandt 44/45
Crawfish Marinara - Joey DiSalvo 20/21
Crawfish-Stuffed Mushrooms - Royley Folse, Sr. 18/19
Creole Caponata - Jack Thibodaux 30/31
Hog's Head Cheese - Sharon Jesowshek 40/41
Incredible Meatballs - Dawn Newchurch 42/43
Jalapeno, Cheese & Sausage Dip - Pamela Castel 36/37
Lump Crabmeat Dip - Ruth Folse Hirsch 14/15
Marinated Crab Claws - Larry Folse 16/17
Marinated Shrimp & Artichokes - John Folse 8/9
Oyster & Artichoke Dip - Scott Cart 22/23
Red Bean Dip - Melissa Folse 32/33
Seafood Mousse - Dawn Newchurch 12/13
Shrimp & Okra Pie - Blanche O. Kugler 4/5
Shrimp Remoulade - John Folse 10/11
Smoked Oyster Loaf - Royley Folse, Jr. 24/25
Spicy Cajun Caviar - Phyllis Graves 38/39
Spicy Curry Dip - John Folse 28/29
Spinach Marguerite - Jane Arnette 34/35

Soups   **Old/New**

Aunt "Zubee's" Corn Soup - Ruby Candies 84/85
Cabbage & Ground Beef Soup - Brenda Brunet 66/67
Cajun Chicken Gumbo - Mrs. Walterine D. Brunet 56/57
Carmen's Black Bean Soup - Honorine Abel 86/87
Chicken, Sausage & File Gumbo - Carol LeBlanc 54/55
Cream of Sweet Pea Soup - Yvonne Falgoust 74/75
Gizzard Soup - Helen and Leonard Hendricks 72/73
Grandma Breaux's Succotash Soup - June Breaux Green 76/77
Grand-Papa Porche's Potato & Ham Soup - Agnes Porche Wyatt 88/89
Gumbo Creole - Debbie Martin 48/49
Gumbo Z'Herbes - Jeanette Jefferson, Babbette O. Joseph & Josephine Schomberg 82/83
Louisiana Oyster Soup - Willis A. Henry 64/65
Louisiana Seafood Gumbo - Royley Folse, Sr. 50/51
Madere's Shrimpboat Chowder - Charles E. Madere 58/59
Mirliton Soup - Mildred Starnes 80/81
Navy Bean Soup - Joyce B. Russell 78/79
Shrimp & Corn Soup - Agnes Breaux 62/63
Shrimp & Okra Gumbo - Rachel Daigle 52/53
Shrimp & Potato Stew - Elaine Lapeyrouse 60/61
Vegetable Beef Soup - Marjorie Domangue 68/69

Salads   **Old/New**

Cottage Cheese & Fruit Souffle - Gia Stephens 130/131
Crawfish Salad - Jane Arnette 122/123

Freezer-Style Cabbage Slaw - Debbie Martin 100/101
Green Bean & Vidalia Onion Salad - Melba Corbett 94/95
Grilled Chicken Salad - John & Missy Kiefe 108/109
Grilled Fish Salad - John Folse 106/107
Grilled Sirloin & Wild Mushroom Salad - John Folse 110/111
Hot Shrimp Salad Casserole - Pamela Castel 118/119
Layered Fruit & Shrimp Salad - John Folse 120/121
Luke Lipari's Shrimp Salad - Frank Russo, Jr. 112/113
Mardi Gras Crawfish Salad - John Folse 124/125
Old Time Potato Salad - Elaine Lapeyrouse 132/133
Pasta Salad - Elaine Guillory 102/103
Pickled Carrot Salad - Gloria Cannatella 96/97
Pineapple - Carrot Congealed Salad - Roderick Lafargue 126/127
Shoepeg Corn Salad - John Folse 98/99
Shrimp & Lump Crab Salad in Tomato Aspic - John Folse 116/117
Stuffed Creole Tomato Salad - Jane Bryant & Melba Bailey Corbett 92/93
Warm New Potato Salad with Beer Dressing - John Folse 128/129
1910 Rice Salad - Judy Greathouse 104/105

Vegetables   **Old/New**
Bacon-Wrapped Green Beans - Keith Waguespack 166/167
Baked Corn Casserole - John Folse 164/165
Broccoli with Dijon Vinaigrette - Judy Guidry 170/171
Cous Cous Cajun Style   Brenda Martin 172/173
Eggplant Casserole Bilello - Sam Bilello 138/139
Eggplant-Stuffed Bell Peppers - Philip Folse 156/157
Green Bean & Artichoke Casserole - Pamela Castel 158/159
Louisiana White or Red Beans with Ham - Royley Folse, Sr. 152/153
Macaroni & Cheese Casserole - Marjorie Domangue 144/145
Mama's Eggplant Casserole Supreme - Agnes Wyatt 136/137
Maque Choux Acadian - Florence Brown 176/177
Maw Rhodes' Eggplant Beignets - Dana Rhodes 142/143
Old Fashioned Smothered Potatoes - Marjorie Domangue 148/149
Quick Spinach Casserole - Brenda Johnson 162/163
Roberta's Baked Artichokes - Roberta Claire Porretto 160/161
Shrimp-Sauced Cauliflower - Bobbie Lee Belanger 140/141
Smothered Okra & Tomatoes - Marjorie Domangue 146/147
Sweet Potato Delight - Mrs. L.R. Stagg 150/151
Uncle Bro's Cajun-Style Stuffed Mirliton - Doug Gulrin 174/175
Vegetable Jambalaya - Nora Dejoie 168/169

Poultry   **Old/New**
Aunt Florence's Baked Chicken & Spaghetti - Nina LaFleur Vincent 192/193
Barbecued Chicken Italian-Style - Bouchereau Family 220/221
Braised Chicken Creole - John Folse 216/217
Cajun-Style Chicken & Eggplant Casserole - Martha Butler 196/197
Chicken Beignets - Jerry Folse 214/215
Chicken Bonne Femme - Carol Canerday 212/213
Chicken Drummette Jambalaya - Joe E. Thibodaux 198/199
Chicken & Artichoke Hearts - Catherine O. Bouis 188/189

Chicken & Creole Tomato Pomodori - Nora Dejoie 206/207
Chicken Loaf Graham - Browning Graham 208/209
Chicken Parmigiano - Honorine Russo 194/195
Chicken Sauce Piquante - Thelma Lemaire 180/181
Chicken Stew - Honorine Abel 186/187
Coq Au Vin - Celeste Bouchereau 218/219
Howard's Chicken & Rice Casserole - Howard Cornay 200/201
Me Me's Ol' Time Chicken & Dumplin's - Wendy Walton Sibilie 184/185
Skillet Chicken & Gravy - Dale Gabriel 210/211
Smothered Chicken with Butter Beans - Elaine Lapeyrouse 182/183
Southern Fried Chicken - Theresa Frugé 190/191
Sunday Morning Chicken Fricassee - Melba Matherne 204/205

Meats   Old/New
Beef
A Duo of Pot Roasts - Evelyn Belanger 224/225
Bayouland Beef Stew with Vegetables - Millie Broussard 230/231
Beef Bourguignonne - Dotsie Butcher 232/233
Breazeale Meat Pies - Judy Breazeale Prejean 260/261
Braised Beef Heart with Savory Oyster Stuffing - Juanita Decker 244/245
Daube Glace Dixie - Mackie T. Bienvenu 228/229
Doc's Primo Chili - Dr. Leonard Hendricks 264/265
Grandma Thibodaux's Breakfast Hash - Anita Thibodaux 258/259
Mama Fresina's Lasagna - Lena Fresina 252/253
Meatballs & Tomato Gravy Caro - Shirley Breaux 256/257
Sauce Picante Oberlin - Don Duplechian 234/235
Stuffed Eggplant in Italian Gravy - Diana Politz 254/255
The Bayou Two Step - Royley Folse, Sr. 262/263
Ventress Island Rump Roast - Gaylord Boyd 226/227
Pork
A Duo of Pot Roast - Evelyn Belanger 224/225
Breazeale Meat Pies - Judy Breazeale Prejean 260/261
Cajun-Stuffed Ponce - Charles Seale 240/241
Creole Pork & Rice Casserole - Pamela Castel 246/247
Daube Glace Dixie - Mackie T. Bienvenu 228/229
Pork Chops St. Dizier - Betty St. Dizier 248/249
Pork Ribs in Sherry Sauce - Eva Prudhomme-Hollard 250/251
The Bayou Two Step - Royley Folse, Sr. 262/263
Tillie's Round Steak & Gravy - Laulie B. Folse 236/237
Veal
Braised Veal Shanks Bayou Lafourche - John Folse 238/239

Seafood   Old/New
Crab
Crabmeat Au Gratin - Louanne Matherne 276/277
Crabmeat Boudreaux - Beth Boulet 268/269
Crabmeat Pasta Etouffee - Delores Cheramie 272/273
Creole Style Crab Stew - Donald & Bobbie Kreider 270/271
Stuffed Crabs - John Folse 274/275

Crawfish
Aunt Dora's Crawfish Etouffee - Chris Landry 284/285
Boiled Crawfish - Jane Arnette 286/287
Grandpa Joe's Crawfish Pie - Amy Brumfield 278/279
Mr. Royley's Crawfish Stew - Jerry Folse 282/283
Memaw Hoffman's Crawfish Bisque - Gwen Bouterie *280/281*
Fish
Fillet of Speckled Trout Albert - Paul Bouchereau 308/309
George's Stuffed Flounder - George Bourgeois 304/305
Redfish Courtbouillon - L.R. Stagg *306/307*
Oysters
Dugas' Oyster Pie - Peggy Vice 300/301
Oyster Fritters - Leontine Callais 302/303
Shrimp
Baked Shrimp - Kay Walker Mabile 298/299
Barbecued Shrimp Longman - Martha Longman 288/289
Mama's Shrimp Spaghetti - Carol Benoit 294/295
Mina Pitre's Dried Shrimp Stew - Elaine Guillory 296/297
Shrimp Treats Streva - Leo Streva 292/293

Wild Game   **Old/New**
Alligator
Alligator Patties - Barbara Boutte 352/353
Dove
Dove & Wild Rice Casserole - Henry Schexnayder, III 336/337
Sherried Doves - John Folse 338/339
Duck
Glenda's Apple-Roasted Duck - Glenda Daigle 342/343
Louisiana Mallards in Mandarin Glaze - John Folse 340/341
Goose
Baked Goose Holly Beach - Sammy Faulk 346/347
Quail & Woodcock
Sauteed Quail Crosby - John Folse 332/333
Uncle Paul's Woodcock - Ruth Folse Hirsch 344/345
Rabbit
Baked Rabbit in Burgundy Sauce - Dr. Michel Hirsch 314/315
Baked Stuffed Rabbit - Linda Neal 312/313
Fricassee of Wild Rabbit - Royley Folse, Jr. 316/317
Squirrel
Smothered Squirrel in Pan Gravy - Robert & Bea Newchurch 330/331
Squirrel Jambalaya - Royley Folse, Jr. 328/329
Turkey
Baked Wild Turkey with Muscadine Jus - John Beck, Sr. 348/349
Turtle
Stewed Turtle Creole - Bruce Becnel 350/351
Venison
Rack of Venison with Muscadine Glaze - Paul Bailey 324/325
Venison Mince Meat - Nell Hardy 326/327
Venison Pie - Louis Jesowshek 322/323

Venison Roast - Dr. Michel Hirsch 320/321
Venison Sauce Piquante - Jerry Folse 318/319

Desserts   **Old/New**
Blackberry Pinwheel Cobbler - Bonnie Smith 386/387
Cajun Ginger Cookies - Alma Proffitt 380/381
Christmas Ambrosia Rodere - Thelma Sonnier 390/391
Coconut Cream Pie - Marjorie Domangue 370/371
Fruitcake Cookies - Doris Shexnayder 378/379
Funeral Pie - Mary Mistric 360/361
Gateau De Figue (Fig Cake) - Anita Guidry 394/395
German Apple Pudding - Rosemary Porche 356/357
Les Tartes Douces (Cajun Sweet Dough Pies) - Mercedes Ledoux Vidrine 358/359
Oeufs Aux Lait (Egg Custard) - Cherie Zeringue 376/377
Old Fashioned Lemon Pie - Peggy Foreman 362/363
Old Time Coconut Cake - Anita Guidry 392/393
Petite Gateaux (Christmas Tea Cookies) - Melissa Folse 364/365
Platzchens (German Sugar Cookies) - Dot Ohlenforst Leger 366/367
Russian Rock Cookies - Honorine Abel 368/369
Sacred Heart Chocolate Pecan Pie - Marie Orgeron 372/373
Skillet Peach Cobbler - Lolita DeFelice 382/383
Spiced Cooking Pears - Captain William Eichaker, Jr. 384/385
Sweet Potato Cake - Darlene Foret 388/389
Super Moist Carrot Cake - Renella Lavergne 396/397

Lagniappe   **Old/New**
Baked Cushaw Squares - John Folse 406/407
Billie Landry's Coush Coush - Billie R. Landry 428/429
Bread Pudding Cake - John Folse 408/409
Breaux's Homemade Italian Bread - Marie Campisi Breaux 440/441
Cajun Blackeyed Peas - John Folse 416/417
Corn Maque Choux - John Folse 424/425
Coush Coush - Mrs. Rolan Bienvenue 426/427
Fried Oyster Dressing - Joy Weldon 438/439
Guy DiSalvo's Premier Marinara Sauce - John Folse 412/413
Hog's Head Cheese without the Head - Lillian Marks and Laura Taylor 432/433
Lemon Nut Cake - Tom Avant 402/403
Orange Pain Perdu - Brenda Martin 404/405
River Town Shrimp & Eggplant Jambalaya - Sarah Liberta 414/415
Seafood Sauce Piquant, Gueydan-Style - Greg & Darlene Dupree 434/435
Smothered Cabbage & Andouille - Henry Schexnayder, III 418/419
Snap Beans with New Potatoes - Melissa Folse 422/423
Tad's Barbecue Sauce - Linda Greco 436/437
Tarte à la Bouie - John Folse 400/401
Venison Osso Bucco - Honorine Abel 430/431
Zucchini Gravy - Vivian Parr 420/421